Speech and Law in a Free Society

Franklyn S.
Haiman

Speech and Law in a Free Society

The University of Chicago Press
Chicago and London

Acknowledgments are offered for permission to reprint
excerpts from the following books:

From THE SYSTEM OF FREEDOM OF EXPRESSION by
Thomas I. Emerson. Copyright © 1970 by Thomas I.
Emerson. Reprinted by permission of Random House, Inc.

From TOP SECRET: NATIONAL SECURITY AND THE RIGHT
TO KNOW by Morton H. Halperin and Daniel N.
Hoffman. Copyright © 1977 by New Republic Books,
Washington, D.C. 20036.

From SECRECY AND PUBLICITY: DILEMMAS OF DEMOC-
RACY by Francis E. Rourke. Copyright © 1961, 1966 by
the Johns Hopkins Press, Baltimore, Md. 21218.

The University of Chicago Press, Chicago 60637
The University of Chicago Press, Ltd., London

© 1981 by The University of Chicago
All rights reserved. Published 1981

Printed in the United States of America
93 92 91 90 89 88 87 86 85   7 6 5 4 3

The author and the publisher
gratefully acknowledge the generosity of the

J. Roderick MacArthur Foundation

for its contribution toward the publication of
this book.

Contents

Foreword

The body of law which is the subject matter of this book is one that is constantly growing and changing, albeit slowly and incrementally. It is therefore likely that some of the comments I have made, especially about issues and cases pending before the courts when these pages went to press, may become outdated by virtue of later events. I am confident that the basic problems which have been discussed and the points of view which have been explored will be enduring ones, but readers should be cautioned about the transitory nature of some of the particulars and may need to make corrections here and there in the light of future developments.

I am indebted to many sources of influence on my thinking, most notably to the writings of those who have preceded me in this field and whose works are noted throughout the book. But more personally, there are the many scores of Northwestern University students whose challenging inquiries and insightful analyses in my classes over the years have enriched and sharpened my understanding of the subject.

There are also my associates, past and present, in the governing councils of the American Civil Liberties Union from whom I have drawn both inspiration and knowledge—from the example of people like the organization's founder, Roger Baldwin, who at the age of 97 is still fond of reminding us that he was "present at the creation"; from the compassion of the late Dorothy Kenyon, Edgar Bernhard, and Marvin Karpatkin; from the incisive brilliance of national executive directors Aryeh Neier and Ira Glasser; and from the incredible commitment, intelligence, and integrity of our younger generation of lawyer leaders like Bruce Ennis, David Goldberger, Ralph Temple, and John Shattuck.

Finally, I want to express appreciation to those kind colleagues who read this manuscript in one or another of its stages and offered their suggestions, some which I gratefully followed, and others which I may unwisely have spurned—Barbara O'Toole, staff counsel of the Illinois Division, ACLU; Geoffrey Stone, professor of law at the University of

Chicago; Nathaniel Nathanson, emeritus professor of law at Northwestern University; and Norman Dorsen, professor of law at New York University and national president of the ACLU. To them, my special thanks.

F.S.H.

Evanston, Illinois
March 1, 1981

Part   Introduction

1

The Contours of the Problem

Freedom of communication in America, as in any society, is encouraged and restrained by the interplay of many forces. The history and traditions of a people provide a pervasive backdrop. In America that history and those traditions have worked largely in favor of openness and against restraint. The temperaments of the individuals and subcultures that make up a society are also a significant ingredient. In our tremendously heterogeneous mix of racial, ethnic, and nationality groups there is much variety in the impulse to communicate. Some of us are highly expressive; others are exceptionally stoic. Physical environment, too, plays an important role. People who are crowded together on small islands, like the Japanese or English, tend to guard what privacy they can with more inhibitions on their interpersonal and public communication styles than has been the case, for example, in the wide-open spaces of the American West. Ultimately the law of a land, reflecting a composite of these and other forces, determines what its people will be allowed or not allowed to say. It is with the law of communication in the United States—with the restraints it imposes and the freedoms it guarantees—that this book is concerned.

The bedrock legal instrument which governs communication in America is the First Amendment to the United States Constitution. In seemingly simple and absolute terms, that amendment provides that

> Congress shall make no law . . . abridging the freedom of speech, or of the press; or the right of people peaceably to assemble and to petition the Government for a redress of grievances.

But in the nearly 200 years since those words were adopted as the law of the land, their meaning has universally been regarded as neither simple nor absolute. Neither the United States Supreme Court, which has final power to interpret the Constitution, nor leading scholars who have studied and written authoritatively about the history and status of freedom of speech in America,[1] nor the largest and most vocal civil liberties–action organization in the country, the American Civil Liberties Union,[2] have ever contended that the phrase "no law" in the First Amendment is to be understood as meaning literally and absolutely "no law." Even Supreme Court Justice Hugo Black, who often *asserted* that when the Founding Fathers said "no law" they meant literally that,[3] and who hewed as close to an absolutist line as anyone who has sat on the Supreme Court bench,[4] himself made many exceptions.[5]

The real question that has engaged and challenged the thinking of judges, scholars, and activists has not been *whether* there should be *any* legal restraints on communication but rather *where* the line should be drawn. To that question we have had a plethora of proposed answers from a variety of advocates and a multitude of decisions from the U.S. Supreme Court. To say that those decisions have left something to be desired in terms of consistency, predictability, and logical adequacy would be an understatement. Too often the opinions of Supreme Court justices on free speech issues have been superficial in their analyses, unguided by consistent principles, responsive to popular prejudices, and excessively deferential to legislative intrusions into areas that are questionably within the legitimate province of the law.

Legislative bodies, at local, state, and national levels, even less inclined than the Supreme Court to sophisticated, dispassionate, or principled First Amendment thinking, have not hesitated to take advantage of the opportunity thus left open to them. In some areas, such as the acceptance of restrictions on libel and obscenity, there has been little tension between legislatures and courts.[6] In other matters, however, such as prohibitions on the political display of red flags or on the theoretical advocacy of revolution, legislatures have clearly strayed so far outside the letter and spirit of the First Amendment that the Supreme Court has seen no choice but to call a halt to their rovings.[7]

It is easy to be critical of legislators and Supreme Court justices for their inadequacies in dealing with free speech problems. It is not so easy to suggest more sensible alternatives. The difficulty stems from the fact that, though we have a theoretical commitment—stemming from our history, traditions, temperament, and geography—to freedom of expression as a near absolute, reality forces us to recognize many competing rights and interests that tempt us, sometimes with good reason, in the direction of restraints on our systems of interpersonal and public communication. For example, unrestrained communication by one person may do serious damage to the reputation and economic well-being of another. It may constitute an unacceptable invasion of the privacy of other people. It may interfere with their right to a fair trial. Some communication is so offensive to others that it is claimed they should have a right not to see and hear it, if that is their choice. The portrayal, in words or pictures, of explicit sexual behavior or of violence is alleged to have a harmful effect on the values and predispositions of those who are exposed to it. Lies and misrepresentations, about commercial products or political candidates, may lead consumers or voters to the making of injurious choices. Intimidating communication may force people to act against their wills. Speech may be used to solicit or incite others to engage in murder, robbery, destruction of property, or other illegal acts, and it is inevitably used in the planning and execution of such acts. Certain kinds of communication may provoke hostile audiences to violent reaction. Conflicting speeches, parades, or rallies in the same place at the same time may lead to a riot. If those who own radio and television stations, or large daily newspapers, have uncontrolled discretion to air or print only what they please, others whose views they do not like may be totally excluded from any access to the mass media. A person's desire *not* to speak may impede the government's investigation or prosecution of a crime. An individual's wish to communicate anonymously or under a pseudonym, in order to protect against possible retribution, runs counter to the interest of others in being able to assess the credibility of the sources of communication to which they are exposed. The public's right to know what its government is doing, in order to vote intelligently, is in conflict with whatever legitimate interests the government may have in secrecy and confidentiality. Whenever the state acts in a supposedly neutral way to facilitate communication—by financing a postal service, library, public auditorium, or political campaign—it may, in fact, be working to the advantage of some citizens over others.

These are all knotty problems which would be hard enough to deal with even if we had clear notions of what we were trying to accomplish with their solution. The difficulty is compounded, however, by the lack of consensus in our society concerning the basic purposes and values underlying the First Amendment. Some of our deepest political and philosophical differences are implicated in these questions. Although most Americans would agree to the abstract proposition that individual liberty is a "good" and that freedom of discussion is the best means of seeking the "truth," they are parties to an uneasy alliance. That alliance splits apart when other fundamental questions are raised. For example, Are there members of our society who are not capable of handling full freedom of communication on some matters? To be more specific, Are there certain subjects (sex, violence, death) which children are not "ready" to deal with? Is it safe to share sensitive national defense or foreign policy information with people who have not had security clearances? Are some members of the public too gullible to protect themselves from misleading advertising, or too ill-informed or emotional to make intelligent political decisions? The converse of these questions, of course, is whether or not experts or the educated elite are more competent than the general public to make some kinds of decisions for the rest of society.

Another set of fundamental questions has to do with our assumptions about human free will and responsibility. To what degree can an individual, child or adult, be held accountable for his or her own behavior regardless of the communication stimuli that may have influenced that behavior? What, if any, degree of responsibility does a communicator assume for the behavior of those who may be motivated to act by the messages to which that communicator has exposed them? To what extent does any single message or campaign of messages have the power to influence the actions of others who are not already predisposed, by virtue of previous experiences, to take those actions? Each time a particular free speech conflict is adjudicated, these larger questions are always lurking in the background, affecting the decisions that we make.

It is the purpose of this book to explore some of the most troublesome problems involving freedom of speech, attempting to bring to bear upon them a more careful analysis than has commonly been applied in the past, and to evolve more consistent, predictable, and principled criteria for dealing with particular cases. Greater clarity, coherence, and service to our ultimate goals, as we confront free speech controversies, will be the aim of this endeavor. Since there is no ready agreement on what those ultimate values are, I will simply assert the ones on which this book is premised so that the reader can take or leave what he or she wants to in full knowledge of the implications of that which is proposed. I would hope that even those who do not share these premises will benefit from the analysis and be aided in crystallizing their own alternatives. My expectation is that a majority of readers will, in fact, share many of the values set forth here, since they are very much in the mainstream of this country's political-philosophical tradition. These premises are as follows:

1. Social order is a means to maximizing individual liberty and security. It is not an end in itself. The self-expression and self-fulfillment of the individuals who compose a society are ends in themselves. They also serve as the means through which a facilitative social order is developed and maintained.

2. Symbolic behavior is one of the most fundamental ways in which human beings express and fulfill themselves. Its exercise thus lies at the core of a free society. Since law is a tool designed only to prevent people from aggrandizing against one another, it is not an appropriate mechanism for the prohibition of words and deeds which do no injury to other persons.

3. The human condition is not predetermined. Individuals, within the limits of their intellectual and emotional development, their physical

environment, and the restraints which may be imposed on them by other persons, are capable of free choice and are responsible for the behavior which they choose. The philosophy of free speech presumes the existence of the freedom to accept or reject the alternatives which are offered. Communication which does not allow for this autonomous decision making violates the integrity of those to whom it is addressed and thus does injury to them.

4. Although some individuals may be more intelligent, more mature, or better educated than others, every informed person is ultimately the best judge of his or her own interests. Even if this were not the case, it is more dangerous to try to determine *who* is best equipped to make decisions for others than it is for individuals to make decisions for themselves.

5. Intellectual and emotional maturity are not exclusively, and often not even primarily, a function of chronological age. There are vast differences in these capacities across all age groups. Age-based qualifications for behaviors like voting, driving, drinking, or marrying without parental consent are arbitrary societal restrictions based on statistical probabilities of competence, and as such are deemed justifiable. Age-based limitations on access to communication are different in kind, however, because the competency in question does not involve an ability to *act* in a socially responsible way but rather to digest verbal and pictorial images. Whatever evidence there may be of a correlation between chronological age and the competence to behave responsibly with a ballot, car, drink, or spouse is lacking with respect to the capacity to deal with communicative stimuli. On the contrary, exposure to the widest possible range of communication may well be the most effective growth-producing experience.

6. Whether or not one believes, theoretically, in the existence of absolute truth, a democracy presumes that we can never be certain it has been attained by any fallible human being. Thus, reliance is placed on a free marketplace of ideas trusting that, even if the wisest decisions do not always emerge victorious, the likelihood is greater of approximating truth and avoiding the most serious errors when communication is free than when it is restricted. This principle applies to the process of self-government as well as to all other areas of human decision making.

Abstract propositions such as those just itemized inevitably contain terms that need further defining. What constitutes the kind of "aggrandizement" for which the law is an appropriate response? How "informed" must a person be in order to be the best judge of one's own best interests? These are matters that can best be dealt with later when we come to apply these principles to more concrete problems.

There are other definitions, however, which must be clarified now, for they provide the boundaries of this book. By defining each of the problematic terms that appear in the language of the First Amendment, we will be able to make a start in understanding the dimensions of the subject with which we are dealing. Four words in the amendment, italicized below, require our attention at this point:

> *Congress* shall make no law . . . abridging the freedom of *speech,* or of the *press;* or the right of the people peaceably to *assemble* and to petition the Government for a redress of grievances.

Congress

The authors of the First Amendment were concerned that the new federal government which had been established by the Constitution should not encroach upon the fundamental rights of the people. Since it was *Congress* that was empowered to make the laws which would govern the nation, it was this congressional power that most obviously needed to be fenced in. No one at that time foresaw the broad array of controls over the lives of people that would be delegated to, or captured by, the *executive* branch of government, with its present-day multitude of departments, regulatory agencies, and quasi-judicial commissions. Yet this has posed no dilemma for interpreters of the First Amendment. It has been taken for granted from the beginning that *all* branches of the federal government are subject to the restraints of the Bill of Rights. The term "Congress" in the First Amendment has thus become shorthand for the entire federal establishment, all of whose branches must live within the limits of that amendment.

Just as it has been clear from the outset that the entire federal bureaucracy is encompassed in the term "Congress," it has been equally clear that the First Amendment did *not,* as originally conceived, apply to *state* governments. For example, at the very time that the amendment was being adopted, prohibiting the establishment of any religion by Congress, there were states in the Union which, in fact, had established churches. It was not until the post–Civil War passage of the Fourteenth Amendment—"No State shall make or enforce any law which shall abridge the privileges and immunities of citizens of the United States; nor shall any State deprive any person of life, liberty, or property, without due process of law"—that the protections of the Bill of Rights were extended to encompass relationships between the individuals and the governments of the several states.

Even then, this extension was not automatic. It came about only gradually and as the result of a series of U.S. Supreme Court decisions holding, one by one, that particular provisions of the first ten amendments were applicable to the states by virtue of the Fourteenth Amendment. Indeed, it was not until 1925, in *Gitlow v. New York,* that the Supreme Court asserted that "we may and do assume that freedom of speech and of the press—which are protected by the First Amendment from abridgment by Congress—are among the fundamental personal rights and 'liberties' protected by the due process clause of the Fourteenth Amendment from impairment by the states."[8]

It was yet another dozen years until the Court made clear, in *DeJonge v. Oregon,* that "[t]he right of peaceable assembly is a right cognate to those of free speech and free press and is equally fundamental. . . . the right is one that cannot be denied without violating those fundamental principles . . . which the Fourteenth Amendment embodies in the general terms of its due process clause."[9]

Finally, in 1943, the Supreme Court could speak as though the protection of freedom of speech from state abridgment was well-settled doctrine. In striking down an effort by the West Virginia schools to require participation by all students in a daily pledge of allegiance to the U.S. flag, Justice Robert Jackson said for the Court:

> The Fourteenth Amendment, as now applied to the States, protects the citizen against the State itself and all of its creatures—Boards of Education not excepted. These have, of course, important, delicate, and highly discretionary functions, but none that they may not perform within the limits of the Bill of Rights. . . . There are village tyrants as well as village Hampdens, but none who acts under color of law is beyond the reach of the Constitution.[10]

Assemble

The right of the people peaceably to assemble is, as the Supreme Court said in *DeJonge,* a "cognate" right to speech and press and "equally fundamental." It is a recognition that in a free society the effective expression of one's views may require *collective* effort by groups of people who share common problems or who advocate common courses of action. It is not enough that a lone individual be able to get up on a soapbox to rail against government policies or to march with a picket sign in front of the White House. People must be able to meet together and to plan, organize, and execute joint campaigns to seek redress of their grievances. Thus, the broader term "freedom of association" is now often used as a substitute for the right of peaceable assembly.

Not only must people be free to gather together in meetings, rallies, and cause organizations, they must also feel assured that the government will not attempt to punish them for "guilt by association" with others who may be involved in illegal activities. One exception which has been made to this principle, and to which we will return for further analysis later, is the law of conspiracy, under which individuals can indeed be penalized for meeting, talking, and planning with others for the commission of a crime, even though they themselves may not actually participate in the final execution of that crime.

Press

What, if anything, is meant by freedom of the *press* that is not encompassed by freedom of *speech*? Did the writers of the First Amendment have essentially different phenomena in mind when they penned these two phrases, or were they being redundant?

Leonard Levy, who is regarded as the leading authority on the history of the First Amendment, has concluded that most of the writers who would have influenced the thinking of our Founding Fathers used the term freedom of speech "synonymously with freedom of the press."[11] Further evidence that the two phrases were viewed as conceptual twins is presented by Melville Nimmer when he notes the language of the constitution of Pennsylvania, adopted in 1776, which provided: "That the people have a right to freedom of speech, and of writing, and publishing their sentiments; therefore the freedom of the press ought not to be restrained."

Professor Nimmer continues:

> ...only the state constitutions of Pennsylvania and Vermont at the time of the adoption of the First Amendment purported to protect freedom of speech as such, while all but four of the states at that time expressly provided constitutional protection for freedom of the press. This fact, when combined with the prevailing rhetoric in the post-Revolutionary period recognizing freedom of speech, tends to support Professor Levy's conclusion that freedom of speech and of the press were at that time thought of as interchangeable.[12]

Why, then, the use of the two different terms? The most obvious explanation seems to be that "speech" referred to oral and "press" to written communication and that both were thought to require the same constitutional protection. The fact that the law had long recognized two kinds of punishable defamatory communication—slander if oral and libel if written—would have provided a natural basis for that kind of dichotomy.[13]

Time and technology, however, have obliterated the meaningfulness of this distinction—a change acknowledged in our legal system by the virtual demise of the notion of slander and its absorption into the law of libel. The coming of motion pictures, phonographs, loud speakers, radio, television, tape recorders, picket signs, and nonverbal protest (e.g., black armbands as symbols of opposition to the Vietnam War) have all contributed to the disintegration of a dichotomous treatment of speech and press. A movie or a taped television broadcast shares with a live public address its oral characteristics, but adds a visual dimension and a capacity for preservation and reproduction traditionally associated with the print medium. A picket sign, though "written," functions more like a soapbox speech than it does like a mass circulation daily newspaper, and a mimeographed leaflet falls somewhere in between. The display of an armband or a flag is neither oral nor written, yet no one would deny that these are forms of communication entitled to be included somewhere under the First Amendment rubrics of speech and press. It is because of these developments that the term "freedom of expression" has become so popular as a contemporary translation of the First Amendment, for it encompasses in one felicitous phrase all that is suggested, not only by speech and press but by assembly as well.[14]

In recent times a school of thought has emerged which argues for another and different kind of distinction between freedom of speech and freedom of the press. Its leading spokesman is no less influential a commentator than U.S. Supreme Court Justice Potter Stewart. In an address at Yale Law School on November 2, 1974, he described his view as follows:

> ... the Free Press guarantee is, in essence, a *structural* provision of the Constitution. Most of the other provisions in the Bill of Rights protect specific liberties or specific rights of individuals: freedom of speech, freedom of worship, the right to counsel, the privilege against compulsory self-incrimination, to name a few. In contrast, the Free Press Clause extends protection to an institution. The publishing business is, in short, the only organized private business that is given explicit constitutional protection.
>
> This basic understanding is essential, I think, to avoid an elementary error of constitutional law. It is tempting to suggest that freedom of the press means only that newspaper publishers are guaranteed freedom of expression. They *are* guaranteed that freedom, to be sure, but so are we all, because of the Free Speech Clause. If the Free Press guarantee meant no more than freedom of expression, it would be a constitutional redundancy. ...
>
> The primary purpose of the constitutional guarantee of a free press was ... to create a fourth institution outside the government as an additional check on the three official branches. ... The relevant metaphor, I think, is the metaphor of the Fourth Estate.[15]

Justice Stewart proceeded to suggest that major U.S. Supreme Court decisions in recent times involving the press—such as its libel opinions, the *Pentagon Papers* decision, and the reporters' privilege cases—were all premised on an institutional freedom of the "organized press" which would not necessarily apply to individual citizens claiming protection under the freedom-of-speech clause.

In the same issue of the law journal which reprinted Justice Stewart's remarks, Professor Nimmer agrees with him in an article which contends that freedom of speech and press not only differ as described by the Justice but may even, under some circumstances, conflict with one another. Unlike Justice Stewart, however, Nimmer does not claim that their view represents "the original understanding of the Founders"[16] or that the rest of the Supreme Court has adopted the Stewart position in the decisions to which the justice referred. Indeed, in another demurrer from the Stewart claim, Anthony Lewis describes the justice's explanation of what the Court had decided in its landmark libel opinion of 1964, *New York Times v. Sullivan,* as "breathtaking."[17] Contrary to Justice Stewart's assertion that the protections against libel suits established by that decision were designed solely for the institutionalized press, Lewis points out that Justice Brennan's opinion for the Court began by discussing "the extent to which the constitutional protections for *speech and press* limit a State's power to award damages" and concluded by reversing libel judgments against "not only the *New York Times* but also four individual defendants, Alabama clergymen."[18] Lewis also notes Justice Brennan's expressed concern in the opinion for the "citizen-critic of government" who, as Lewis sees it, "is a pole apart" from the "organized press."[19]

Adding still another voice to this debate is Chief Justice Warren Burger who asserts, "The Court has not yet squarely resolved whether the Press Clause confers upon the 'institutional press' any freedom from government restraint not enjoyed by all others."[20] It is the chief justice's own belief that the Court's precedents have "plainly intimated the contrary view"—namely, "Freedom of the press is a 'fundamental personal right' which 'is not confined to newspapers and periodicals.'"[21] The chief justice adds that "the First Amendment does not 'belong' to any definable category of persons or entities: it belongs to all who exercise its freedoms."[22] It would appear that Professor Nimmer, if not Justice Stewart, would concede Chief Justice Burger's claim that the Court has not yet embraced the view they advocate, for Nimmer closes his essay with the statement that "freedom of the press as a right recognizably distinct from that of freedom of speech is an idea whose time is past due."[23]

What advantages and disadvantages to freedom of speech and press might flow from an acceptance by a majority of the Supreme Court of Justice Stewart's position?

On the positive side, the organized press might gain some rights which, as a practical matter, cannot be extended to the entire populace as a right of freedom of speech. For example, Professor Nimmer discusses the question of interviews with prisoners, noting that prison regulations usually allow a degree of access to reporters that would not be manageable for the general public. Justice Stewart cites a reporter's privilege with respect to confidential sources of information as another example:

> . . . if freedom of the press means simply freedom of speech for reporters, this question of a reporter's asserted right to withhold information would have answered itself. None of us—as individuals—has a "free speech" right to refuse to tell a grand jury the identity of someone who has given us information relevant to the grand jury's legitimate inquiry. Only if a reporter is a representative of a protected *institution* does the question become a different one.[24]

Nimmer argues, too, that a clearer understanding of the difference in the interests served by freedom of speech and freedom of press might lead to the striking of a fairer balance between them in cases where they come into conflict. He notes, in particular, two Supreme Court decisions in which that might have been true. The first, *Columbia Broadcasting Company v. Democratic National Committee* decided in 1973, involved a clash between citizens who claimed a First Amendment right to purchase time on television for editorial advertising and broadcasters who claimed a First Amendment right to maintain a policy of refusing to sell time for that purpose. Says Nimmer: "In reaching its decision, the Court . . . recognized that it was 'balancing the various First Amendment interests involved in the broadcast media and determining what best serves the public's right to be informed.' What was *not* acknowledged was that it was the press clause which was being weighed against the speech clause."[25]

The Supreme Court, in this case, ruled in favor of the broadcasters or, in Nimmer's terms, in favor of the press. He implies that a different result might have occurred had the Court been more conscious of the competing interests of speech and press.

The other case, *Miami Herald v. Tornillo* decided in 1974, had to do with a challenge by the Miami Herald Publishing Company regarding the constitutionality of a Florida law which required newspapers to grant space for a reply to any attack they might make in their pages on a candidate for public office. Pat Tornillo was a candidate for the state legislature who had been so attacked, and he demanded his right to reply under Florida law. The Supreme Court found that law to be an unconstitutional infringement of freedom of the press, thus denying, in Nimmer's terms, Tornillo's free speech claim. Again the implication of Nimmer's commentary is that an acknowledgment by the Court that it was dealing with a "confrontation between the rights of speech and press" might have produced a different result.

It seems reasonable to conclude from these two examples that an analysis along the lines proposed by Stewart and Nimmer would have only reinforced the Court in the direction it actually took. It is clear that the Supreme Court, at least in its *CBS* opinion, was well aware that it was dealing with important First Amendment rights in conflict with each other, although it did not label one as "speech" and the other as "press." It is doubtful that an analysis which would elevate the institutionalized press to an even higher sacred-cow status than it already enjoys would strengthen competing free speech claims when they come in conflict with that institution's prerogatives.

It could conceivably happen that, if the Supreme Court were to follow Justice Stewart's lead in this matter, the result might well be a net loss for freedom of speech. The granting of special privileges to the organized press could become a rationalization for denying those rights to the ordinary citizen. For example, if journalists are permitted to visit and gather news in a country with which we have broken off diplomatic relations, might it not then be said that the rest of us have no need to go see for ourselves? Or if, as Justice Stewart claims to have been the intention of the *Gertz* decision, the institutionalized press has a broader right to make unwittingly false charges against public officials and public figures than does the individual,[26] would we not have abdicated to the journalists a fundamental responsibility of our citizenship?

Journalist and lawyer Robert M. Kaus has vigorously objected to the Stewart point of view as an elitist position, a

> claim that a distinct class of people called "the press" have rights not enjoyed by the general populace.... It is a corporate vision, in the sense that it views society as a single organism in which different citizens play different roles and have different legal needs. Academics ... would be the brains in this social corpus and reporters the "eyes and ears," leaving the rest of us to fight for the positions below the neck.[27]

Professor Steven Shiffrin echoes this criticism when he characterizes the Stewart position as "mediaocracy" rather than democracy.[28]

Distinguishing the press as an institution entitled to special rights under the freedom-of-press clause from individuals who derive their rights from the freedom-of-speech clause requires a definition as to what constitutes the press, and that can be an extremely troublesome problem. Is a high school underground newspaper "the press" and entitled to its special privileges, or is it "merely" an exercise in freedom of speech? Is an individual scholar, engaged in independent research which may or may not eventuate in the publication of a book or journal article, able to claim the same right to protection of confidential sources of information as an investigative reporter for a newspaper or television station? When cable television comes into its own, will the amateur producers of a documentary program that is broadcast over a public access cable channel not be considered members of "the press," while the paid professionals who make documentaries for CBS, NBC, ABC, and PBS are so designated?

Attorney Floyd Abrams attempts to defend the Stewart doctrine on this score by paraphrasing a famous line from one of the justice's opinions on obscenity, asserting, "In the great preponderance of cases, a court has little difficulty knowing a journalist when it sees one."[29] Abrams suggests that the "difficulty in providing a totally satisfying definition should hardly deter us from affording protection to those who are plainly entitled to it,"[30] and he offers as a sufficiently "workable, if not flawless"[31] solution the extension of press protection "not only to journalists on established newspapers, but 'to free-lance writers, radio and television stations, magazines, academicians and any other person possessing materials in connection with the dissemination to the public of a newspaper, book, broadcast or other form of communication.'"[32]

Anthony Lewis aptly responds to the Abrams position, expressed in another place as including even "the lonely pamphleteer,"[33] by noting that "if the definition is thus broadened, then any publication becomes 'the press' and Justice Stewart's thesis loses its point."[34]

It appears to me that Justice Stewart's effort to drive a wedge between freedom of speech and freedom of the press is of dubious value at best and an invitation to a vast amount of confusion at the least. A bit of "constitutional redundancy," I think, is much to be preferred. Identical twins may serve us better than sibling rivals.

Speech

This seemingly simple six-letter word, taken in the context of the First Amendment, opens so many complex questions that the entire next chapter is devoted to it.

2   What Is Speech?

Whether we regard the press as simply the written counterpart of speech, or as a separate institution which employs both voice and print to perform a "Fourth Estate" function, there is still the problem of determining the range of phenomena that are encompassed under the freedom of speech and press provision of the First Amendment. Is it only *words* that are protected? Even then, are certain kinds of verbalization excluded? Beyond language, do some forms of nonverbal communication warrant inclusion?

Clearly it has been the predominant assumption of our legal system that, unless there is good cause to treat them otherwise, words are the very thing safeguarded by the First Amendment, whether those words be spoken, sung, broadcast, or printed on a sign, button, handbill, newspaper, magazine, or even the back of a jacket. It was this latter category of message conveyance that was at issue in a 1971 landmark decision of the U.S. Supreme Court, *Cohen v. California,* involving a young man who had walked through a corridor of the Los Angeles County Courthouse wearing a jacket bearing the words "Fuck the Draft." Despite a terse, offbeat, and inexplicable dissenting view by Justices Harry Blackmun, Hugo Black, and Chief Justice Warren Burger describing "Cohen's absurd and immature antic" as being "mainly conduct and little speech," the Court majority, in an opinion written by the impeccably conservative Justice John Marshall Harlan, said, "The conviction quite clearly rests upon the asserted offensiveness of the *words* Cohen used to convey his message to the public. The only 'conduct' which the State sought to punish is the fact of communication. Thus, we deal here with a conviction resting solely upon 'speech.'"[1]

More substantial than the Blackmun-Burger-Black objection that expression such as Cohen's is "mainly conduct and little speech" is a school of thought represented by Walter Berns. He argues that our Founding Fathers were, above all, rationalists, who intended by the First Amendment to protect serious and "decent" discourse about public affairs and not the kind of "vulgar" emoting that characterized so much of the countercultural protest of the 1960s which Cohen's jacket so vividly exemplified. It is this line of thought which has led Berns and others to deplore the substitution of the phrase "freedom of expression" for "freedom of speech," because he believes that the more "commodious" word connotes greater approval of incivility in public discussion than does the more traditional term, "speech."[2]

The Supreme Court, speaking again through Justice Harlan in *Cohen v. California*, has taken a more understanding and expansive view of the communication process—a view, it is to be hoped, that will continue to command the support of a majority of the Court:

> ...we cannot overlook the fact, because it is well illustrated by the episode involved here, that much linguistic expression serves a dual communicative function: it conveys not only ideas capable of relatively precise, detached explication, but otherwise inexpressible emotions as well. In fact, words are often chosen as much for their emotive as their cognitive force. We cannot sanction the view that the Constitution, while solicitous of the cognitive content of individual speech, has little or no regard for the emotive function which, practically speaking, may often be the more important element of the overall message sought to be communicated.[3]

Or, as I have elsewhere replied to those who insist that Cohen could and should have said something more civil, like "Resist the Draft," which conveys essentially the same message, "Clearly something is lost in the translation."[4]

Somewhat akin to the rationalist view of the First Amendment is a much more sweeping doctrine expounded by Alexander Meiklejohn, which rests on the premise that a small word, "the," in the phrase, "*the* freedom of speech," is of large significance. Meiklejohn, who was this country's most recognized modern philosopher of the First Amendment, held that there are two different kinds of speech protected by two separate provisions of the Bill of Rights.[5] *The* freedom of speech, guaranteed by the First Amendment, refers only to that communication which has to do with the process of self-government. Because the citizens in a democracy are the governors, they must have the right to unrestrained freedom of discussion concerning public affairs so that the wisest societal decisions can be made. This, according to Meiklejohn, is the kind of speech, and the only kind of speech, that was contemplated by the absolute terms of the First Amendment. Private speech, on the other hand, involving individual expression unrelated to the political process, is given protection by the word "liberty" in the Fifth Amendment's provision—"No person shall...be deprived of life, liberty, or property, without due process of law." In Meiklejohn's view, this less vital kind of communication, unlike *the* freedom of speech, may be abridged so long as the restraints are imposed by due process of law.[6]

One of Meiklejohn's students, Zechariah Chafee, who himself became the nation's leading legal authority of his time on freedom of speech, took strong exception to the Meiklejohnian analysis. He charged that the bifurcation of speech which his old professor claimed to have discovered in the Bill of Rights was a figment of his imagination.[7] In the first place, argued Chafee, it is impossible to draw a defensible line between so-called private and public speech. Are the works of a poet or playwright private expression, or do they have an influence on the body politic? Furthermore, Chafee insisted, the absolute freedom accorded to political speech by the Meiklejohn thesis is far *broader* than ever has been, or can ever realistically be, accepted by our legal system, and the due process standard for curbing private speech provides far *less* shelter than that which we have properly come to expect. Chafee concluded, as have our courts, that we should not create an arbitrary hierarchy of values for various categories of speech, but that all expression must look to the First Amendment for whatever protection it may or may not obtain.

One of the motivations which apparently led Meiklejohn to seek the segregation of political from private speech was his dismay over the fact that, when the Supreme Court in 1925 made the First Amendment applicable to the states, it chose the "due process clause" rather than the "privileges and immunities clause" of the Fourteenth Amendment as the means by which to do it. The relevant sections of the Fourteenth Amendment read as follows: "No State shall make or enforce any law which shall abridge the privileges and immunities of citizens of the United States; nor shall any State deprive any person of life, liberty, or property, without due process of law."

Meiklejohn quite logically noted that the qualified nature of the rights protected from the exercise of state power by the due process clause of the Fourteenth Amendment is identical to that provided against the federal government by the Fifth Amendment. In contrast, he argued that the privileges and immunities clause of the Fourteenth Amendment is more parallel in its absolute language to that of the First Amendment and that *it* should have been the vehicle used by the Court to make *the* freedom of speech and press applicable to the states. By giving away private speech as properly within the domain of the due process clauses of the Fifth and Fourteenth Amendments, Meiklejohn hoped to rescue his more cherished political communication from being "swallowed up" in that same due process machinery.[8]

That hope appears to have been in vain, for not only has the Supreme Court declined to recognize a categorical distinction between political and private speech, it has also persistently invoked the due process clause, and not the privileges and immunities clause, of the Fourteenth Amendment as its mechanism for applying the First Amendment to the states. This pattern of decision making ultimately stirred a lone protest in 1974 from Justice William O. Douglas, but his view, like that of Meiklejohn, is likely to remain a voice in the wilderness:

> Continued recognition of the possibility of state libel suits for public discussion of public issues leaves the freedom of speech honored by the Fourteenth Amendment a diluted version of First Amendment protection. This view is only possible if one accepts the position that the First Amendment is applicable to the States only through the Due Process Clause of the Fourteenth, due process freedom of speech being only that freedom which this Court might deem to be "implicit in the concept of ordered liberty." But the Court frequently has rested state free speech and free press decisions on the Fourteenth Amendment generally rather than on the Due Process Clause alone. The Fourteenth Amendment speaks not only of due process but also of "privileges and immunities" of United States citizenship. I can conceive of no privilege or immunity with a higher claim to recognition against state abridgement than the freedoms of speech and of the press.[9]

Words That Are Like Acts

Although Zechariah Chafee opposed the notion that speech may be divided into public and private categories as suggested by Meiklejohn, he was himself an influential figure in bringing about the acceptance by our legal system of another kind of categorization—that between words which convey ideas and those which are more like *acts* and may be punished as such. Chafee described the distinction as follows:

> . . . the normal criminal law . . . is directed primarily against actual injuries. Such injuries usually are committed by acts, but the law also punishes a few classes of words like obscenity, profanity and gross libels upon individuals, because the very utterance of such words is considered to inflict a present injury upon listeners, readers, or those defamed, or else to render highly probable an immediate breach of the peace. This is a very different matter from punishing words because they express ideas which are thought to cause a future danger to the State. . . . profanity and indecent talk and pictures, which do not form an essential part of any exposition of ideas, have a very slight social value as a step toward truth, which is clearly outweighed by the social interests in order, morality, the training of the young, and the peace of mind of those who hear and see. Words of this type offer little opportunity for the usual process of counter-argument. The harm is done as soon as they are communicated, or is liable to follow

almost immediately in the form of retaliatory violence. The only sound explanation of the punishment of obscenity and profanity is that the words are criminal, not because of the ideas they communicate, but like acts because of their immediate consequences to the five senses. The man who swears in a street car is as much of a nuisance as the man who smokes there.[10]

In 1942 the U.S. Supreme Court agreed with this view. In upholding the conviction of a Jehovah's Witness who had called a police officer a "damned Fascist" and "a God damned racketeer," the Court said:

> ...it is well understood that the right of free speech is not absolute at all times and under all circumstances. There are certain well-defined and narrowly limited classes of speech, the prevention and punishment of which have never been thought to raise any constitutional problem. These include the lewd and obscene, the profane, the libelous, and the insulting or "fighting" words—those which by their very utterance inflict injury or tend to incite an immediate breach of the peace.[11]

The Supreme Court then proceeded to credit Chafee with the rationale for this position: "It has been well observed that such utterances are no essential part of any expression of ideas, and are of such slight social value as a step to truth that any benefit that may be derived from them is clearly outweighed by the social interests in order and morality."[12]

We will return later in this book to a fuller discussion of the validity of the particular restrictions on obscenity, libel, and "fighting words." At this point our concern is with the more generic question of the adequacy of the Chafee and Supreme Court definitional separation between idea-conveying words or pictures and "speech-acts."

The major difficulty with this distinction is its failure to appreciate the nature of symbols and of communication. Words and pictures which are claimed to do injury to others are *not,* as Chafee asserted, "like acts because of their immediate consequences to the five senses." "The man who swears in a street car," to continue with the Chafee example, "is as much of a nuisance as the man who smokes there," *only* if the other people on that street car understand what he says (which they would not if he spoke in an unfamiliar foreign tongue) *and if* they find what he says offensive (which they might or might not do, depending on their own attitudes and habits regarding language usage). Unlike smoke, which invades the lungs of others regardless of what goes through their minds, or the loud playing of a transistor radio, whose *noise* bombards the ears of others whether the language of the broadcast is welcome or offensive, words and pictures per se do not do injury. It is the meaning and values with which they are endowed by those who see or hear them that may cause pleasure or pain and that is a *symbolic* transaction mediated through consciousness. The childhood maxim, "Sticks and stones may break my bones, but names will never hurt me," captures this understanding.

This is not necessarily to argue that, within a given cultural context, certain symbolic behavior may not almost universally be *regarded as* undesirable, or that symbolic acts should never be restrained or punished. Those are questions we will come to later. It is only being urged that *if* we choose to restrain or punish speech we should not do so because we have confused it with injurious "acts" but because we have concluded that some kinds of symbolic, First Amendment behavior, in some circumstances justifiably may be curbed.

It is interesting to note in this connection that the Chafee passage which was quoted with such approval by the Supreme Court described the utterances in question as being "no *essential* part of any expression of ideas" and of "*slight* social value as a step to truth" (italics mine). Those qualifying adjectives would seem to suggest some recognition that even so-called speech-acts may be part of the expression of ideas, though allegedly not an "essential" part, and that they may indeed have social value, albeit "slight." To conclude, as many have done,[13] including the U.S. Supreme Court, that there can be such a thing as speech which is devoid of ideational content is therefore not only to misunderstand the consciousness-mediated nature of symbolic transactions but to ignore the qualifying phrases in the original Chafee statement. Much as one might believe that the Jehovah's Witness who called a policeman a "damned Fascist" and "a God damned racketeer" ought to have been punished, it can hardly be denied that his utterances conveyed a clear and unmistakable idea.

One other respect in which the Supreme Court ran farther with Chafee's ball than he might in retrospect have wished (although he must take responsibility for suggesting the language to them) is the notion, expressed in the 1942 *Chaplinsky* decision, that some words "*by their very utterance* inflict injury or tend to incite an immediate breach of the peace" (italics mine). We have already noted that words, *by their very utterance,* can do nothing of the sort, and that it is only as the result of a mental judgment made by others about those words in a particular context that injury may be *felt* or that *reactive* violence may occur. Even the Supreme Court, in this very same case, unconsciously admitted as much when it accepted the New Hampshire Supreme Court's definition of "fighting words": "The English language has a number of words and expressions which by general consent are 'fighting words' *when said without a disarming smile*" (italics mine).

The reason I suggest that Chafee might not have been happy about the doors that the *Chaplinsky* decision opened is the following passage he wrote shortly after the famous section quoted by the Supreme Court:

> This breach of peace theory is liable to abuse when applied against unpopular expressions and practices. It makes a man criminal simply because his neighbors have no self-control and cannot refrain from violence. The *reductio ad absurdum* of this theory was the imprisonment of Joseph Palmer . . . not because he was a communist, but because he persisted in wearing such a long beard that people kept mobbing him, until law and order were maintained by shutting him up. . . . Thus all these crimes of injurious words must be kept within very narrow limits if they are not to give excessive opportunities for outlawing heterodox ideas.[14]

It is unfortunate that Chafee's own cultural blinders did not let him see that swearing on a streetcar or displaying "indecent" pictures can be viewed as benignly as the wearing of a long beard.

Making a distinction between speech and speech-acts on the basis of whether or not an utterance conveys essential or socially valuable ideas is not the only differentiation that has been attempted. Thomas Emerson has built an entire theory of the First Amendment on a distinction between "expression" and "action" which places some "speech" on both sides of that dividing line.[15] Like Meiklejohn, Emerson looked with dismay upon the fact that much expression in our society was not being given the absolute protection of the First Amendment that it merited, and, like Meiklejohn, he set about developing a conceptual scheme whereby certain kinds of speech would be given "full protection" and others allowed to be subject to restraint or punishment. The essence of his system is the drawing of an absolute protective boundary around behavior, whether verbal or nonverbal, which he defines as "expression," as distinguished from the unprotected realm of "action," which may include some "verbal acts" as well as nonverbal behaviors.

For Emerson free expression

> includes the right to form and hold beliefs and opinions on any subject, and to communicate ideas, opinions, and information through any medium—in speech, writing, music, art, or in other ways. To some extent it involves the right to remain silent. From the obverse side it includes the right to hear the views of others and to listen to their version of the facts. It encompasses the right to inquire and, to a degree, the right of access to information. As a necessary corollary, it embraces the right to assemble and to form associations, that is, to combine with others in joint expression.[16]

Beyond this broad definition of expression, Emerson offers no generic distinction between expression and action but elaborates the difference by specific illustrations. The law of treason provides his first example. Here he notes that our Constitution excludes the possibility of conviction for the crime of treason on account of mere "expression" by the requirement of an "overt act." Says Emerson, "Under the treason provision . . . the test is not whether the expression has a tendency to aid and comfort the enemy, or presents a clear and present danger of doing so. . . . Rather, the test is whether the conduct in question constitutes expression or action. In most of the decided cases the behavior alleged to be treasonous has clearly come within the action category."[17]

He then goes on to discuss some World War II cases involving individuals who were found guilty of treason for making radio broadcasts for the enemy as part of a program of psychological warfare directed primarily to American troops. A decision of the U.S. Court of Appeals for the District of Columbia in one of those cases said of treason: "While the crime is not committed by mere expression of opinion or criticism, words spoken as part of a program of propaganda warfare, in the course of employment by the enemy in its conduct of war against the United States . . . may be an integral part of the crime. . . . The use of speech to this end . . . made acts of words."[18]

Emerson comments: "The court seems right on construing the conduct in the case as constituting 'action' rather than 'expression.' The broadcaster was part of the enemy war apparatus and in effect engaged in military activities."[19]

A second example discussed by Emerson is the category of "fighting words," with Emerson almost uncritically joining the Chafee-Supreme Court camp. Like Chafee, he believes that personal insults, delivered face to face, "can be considered the equivalent of knocking a chip off the shoulder—the traditional symbolic act that puts the parties in the role of physical combatants. It is, in short, the beginning of action."[20] He does, however, demur partially from the traditional "fighting words" rationale when he says that such utterances "fall outside the protection of the First Amendment . . . not, as the Supreme Court argued in *Chaplinsky*, because fighting words have 'slight social value,' but rather because they are 'verbal acts.'"[21]

"The same basic rules apply to heckling the speaker," Emerson continues, with a third example. "Up to a point heckling or other interruption of the speaker may be a part of the dialogue. But conduct that obstructs or seriously impedes the utterance of another, even though verbal in form, cannot be classified as expression. Rather it is the equivalent of sheer noise. It has the same effect, in preventing or disrupting communication, as acts of physical force. Consequently, it must be deemed action and is not covered by the First Amendment."[22]

A final example discussed by Emerson is the use of speech to promote a boycott. He reports a 1911 decision of the U.S. Supreme Court, in a case involving a boycott of the Bucks Stove and Range Company by the American Federation of Labor, where the union's periodical named Bucks on its "Unfair" and "We don't patronize" lists. The Court's opinion said, "In the case of an unlawful conspiracy, the agreement to act in concert when the signal is published, gives the words 'Unfair,' 'We don't patronize,' or similar expressions, a force not adhering in the words themselves, and therefore exceeding any possible right of speech which a single individual might have. Under the circumstances they become what have been called 'verbal acts.'"[23]

Although Emerson does not say explicitly whether he agrees with the categorization of this particular communication as a "verbal act," his general discussion of boycotts and picketing indicates that in these areas he *would* draw the line between "expression" and "action," as the Court seemed to do in the *Bucks Stove and Range* case, on the basis of whether the speech in question is persuasive or coercive:

> Labor picketing normally has a special kind of economic impact, derived from its institutional setting. An employer who is picketed is usually sealed off from many economic contacts by the tradition that union labor will not cross the picket line. This form of pressure is applied by closely knit, powerful organizations. . . . A labor picket line is thus not so much a rational appeal to persuasion as a signal for the application of immediate and enormous economic leverage. . . . As such it must, under ordinary circumstances, be classified as action, rather than expression.
>
> Most non-labor picketing is of a substantially different character. It is usually undertaken by relatively small groups, with relatively limited resources. . . . Such groups are not highly organized around a major economic interest, but ordinarily are more loosely put together, with a narrower claim on the loyalty of their members. They do not have at their command the apparatus for applying economic pressures that the labor organizations do. . . . Picketing under such circumstances is a call to reason, not the application of economic coercion, and as such must be classified as expression.[24]

It is perhaps evident to the reader by now, as it is to me, that Emerson's classification scheme raises more questions than it answers. If granting full protection of the First Amendment were to require that our courts define expression in every instance as Emerson might do, freedom of speech would rest on a most uncertain foundation. Let us review his examples with a critical eye.

What is it that allegedly has "made acts of words" in these four illustrations? In the first case it is because the speaker was aiding the war effort of an enemy power. In the second it is because the words spoken might provoke a fight. In the third example, of interruptive heckling, words become acts because of the noise they make. In the last instance it is the economic power that stands behind the utterances. Thus, in all but the third illustration, it is the *context* in which the speech occurs which is said to convert the words into acts. The third case is the only one in which it can be argued reasonably that the words themselves have become acts, and even then it is not really the words per se but the noise that they generate which interferes with the meeting. The same effect would occur if the hecklers screamed, moaned, whistled, or used a siren.

The point of all this is that Emerson has identified certain *contexts* within which he believes that speech may properly be punished, and he labels *that* speech "action" rather than "expression" because he does not want "expression" ever to be subject to restraints. But calling words "action" does not change their symbolic nature. Rather it confuses matters by attempting to make certain contextual considerations which may justify restrictions appear to be inherent to the speech itself. So long as someone with Emerson's deep concern for freedom of expression is making the judgments as to what kind of contexts warrant the reclassification of speech as action, no harm is likely to be done to the scope of First Amendment protections. But his system is open for anyone to call almost any symbolic event "action" because the context in which that communication occurs is viewed with disfavor. Any meaningful distinction between "expression" and "action" could thus become eroded, and categories of disliked speech that are now protected by the First Amendment because they are so simply and clearly symbolic in nature might find themselves stripped of that protection.

Freedom of expression is likely to have firmer and broader support from the First Amendment if less rubbery definitions of speech and action are employed. We should insist that the only difference between speech and action is that between symbolic and nonsymbolic behavior, *regardless* of the context in which those behaviors take place. This does not mean that symbolic behavior can never be restrained if the context in which it occurs justifies such limits. Rather, if it is to be curbed, we will be clear that it is contextual considerations that are responsible and not that words have, by the magic of redefinition, been transformed into acts.

Acts That Are Like Words

If we accept the premise that words can never justifiably be viewed as functioning like acts, does it then follow that acts can never be viewed as functioning like words? I think not. On the contrary, it is beyond question that certain kinds of nonlinguistic behavior perform precisely the same function as do words—the communication of ideas and feelings to other people.

Although it is only in recent times that nonverbal communication has become the subject of careful scholarly analysis,[25] symbolic activity other than by the use of words has been known to mankind through all of recorded history. From the cave drawings of the primitives to the rain dances of aboriginal tribes, from the march of Coxey's Army of the unemployed to Washington, D.C., in 1894 to the wearing of black armbands in protest against the Vietnam War in 1965, people have expressed some of their deepest feelings and made known many of their most urgent needs through media other than language. Indeed, it is surprising that it has taken so long for lawyers and judges to recognize the greater accuracy in substituting for the word "speech" in the First Amendment more contemporary terms like "expression" or "communication."[26]

The problem in dealing with nonverbal communication from a legal perspective lies not in the question of *whether* the First Amendment applies to such behavior, but *when*. Clearly a march or a silent vigil, either in honor of the war dead or in anger against racial discrimination, is a symbolic event entitled to First Amendment protection, but what about a lunch counter sit-in or lying down in front of a troop train? No one would question that a lone picketer, walking up and down on the sidewalk in front of the White House, is engaged in the exercise of freedom of speech, but what about a union picket line that effectively seals off entry to a store or factory? The U.S. Supreme Court has had little trouble recognizing a black armband[27] or the refusal to salute an American flag[28] as First Amendment behavior, but it has had a great deal more difficulty extending the concept of speech to protect the public burning of a draft card[29] or alleged misuses and "desecrations" of the flag.[30] Federal and state courts all over the country have been trying to figure out for several years whether wearing a beard or long hair to a public school or a public job is a constitutional right, and whether topless dancing in a night club or scenes of sexual intercourse in a movie are a part of our system of freedom of expression.

Some initial steps have been taken to establish guiding principles in this area, but the results can hardly be described as definitive. As early as 1931, in finding unconstitutional a California law prohibiting the display of red flags as a "sign, symbol or emblem of opposition to organized government," the U.S. Supreme Court implicitly acknowledged the involvement of the First Amendment in flag-display behavior.[31] By 1943, the Court was ready to be quite explicit about the matter:

> There is no doubt that, in connection with the pledges, the flag salute is a form of utterance. Symbolism is a primitive but effective way of communicating ideas. The use of an emblem or flag to symbolize some system, idea, institution, or personalization, is a short cut from

mind to mind.... Symbols of state often convey political ideas just as religious symbols come to convey theological ones.... A person gets from a symbol the meaning he puts into it, and what is one man's comfort and inspiration is another's jest and scorn.[32]

When confronted, in 1968, with a case of public draft-card burning by David Paul O'Brien, in violation of an act of Congress prohibiting such behavior, the Supreme Court felt it necessary to enunciate some constitutional principles governing nonverbal communication. Acknowledging that the conduct in question was a form of protest against the Vietnam War, the Court was also faced with the fact that a physical document had been destroyed in defiance of Congress. The decision addressed itself to both ingredients of the act:

> We cannot accept the view that an apparently limitless variety of conduct can be labelled "speech" whenever the person engaging in the conduct intends thereby to express an idea. However, even on the assumption that the alleged communicative element in O'Brien's conduct is sufficient to bring into play the First Amendment, it does not necessarily follow that the destruction of a registration certificate is constitutionally protected activity. This Court has held that when "speech" and "nonspeech" elements are combined in the same course of conduct, a sufficiently important government interest in regulating the nonspeech element can justify incidental limitations on First Amendment freedoms.... we think it is clear that a government regulation is sufficiently justified if it is within the constitutional power of government; if it furthers an important or substantial governmental interest; if the governmental interest is unrelated to the suppression of free expression; and if the incidental restriction on alleged First Amendment freedom is no greater than is essential to the furtherance of that interest.[33]

On the basis of these criteria, the Supreme Court found that the government's interest in preserving draft cards was unrelated to the suppression of free expression (despite the fact that congressional sponsors of the legislation in question were clearly motivated by their anger at this particular form of antiwar protest), and that the incidental restriction on First Amendment freedoms that might have been involved was no greater than necessary to further a legitimate state purpose.

This decision in *U.S. v. O'Brien* became the prevailing precedent governing other so-called symbolic speech (or nonverbal communication) cases that went to the courts in the ensuing years. Since the Supreme Court had conceded the possibility that there could be instances of combined "speech" and "nonspeech" conduct which, unlike O'Brien's, might be entitled to First Amendment protection, analysts and critics immediately went to work attempting to define what those might be.

A thoughtful and provocative article appearing in the *Columbia Law Review* shortly after *O'Brien,* entitled "Symbolic Conduct," argued that the O'Brien decision had failed to meet its own standards. Instead of there being a "substantial governmental interest" in the prohibition of public draft-card burning, "The Court seemed satisfied with a finding of administrative convenience," said this essay.[34] Without challenging the fundamental premise that there may indeed be substantial governmental interests that would outweigh one's right to freedom of expression, whether exercised by verbal or nonverbal means, the authors of the article proceeded to suggest their own criteria for determining when alleged symbolic conduct is entitled to First Amendment consideration. They argued, first, that the actor claiming First Amendment protection must have been "motivated only by the desire to communicate.... the intent requirement is consistent with the objectives underlying the First Amendment.... An actor who is unaware of the symbolic significance of his conduct may inadvertently contribute to the debate, but by punishing him we do not deter free media choice.... A man cannot feel his thoughts have been slighted unless he is conscious of his attempt to communicate."[35]

Second, "the conduct must be capable of being understood by others as communication."

> If there is to be a doctrine of first amendment protection for symbolic conduct, its cornerstone must be the requirement that others can recognize the conduct as communication.... If it were enough to claim that the conduct was understood as communication by one or two good friends even though the actual audience was more extensive, the result would be to invite eccentric duets. Rather, it should not be enough simply to claim that the conduct is reasonably calculated to communicate to someone. Instead the conduct must be calculated to communicate to some substantial audience.[36]

A slightly different approach was taken by lawyers for the New York Civil Liberties Union, in the immediate wake of *O'Brien,* when they were faced with writing a brief for the Supreme Court in the appeal of Sidney Street, who had been convicted of violating New York's flag desecration statute by burning his American flag in protest against the shooting of civil rights marcher James Meredith. Their method of dealing with the question as to how the First Amendment might apply to nonverbal symbolic conduct was as follows:

> Since all communication is basically symbolic, we must determine what form of symbolic traffic in ideas, that is, communication, may be suppressed in order to preserve the required degree of public order.... In attempting to answer that extraordinarily difficult question, it would be appropriate to investigate the following areas:

1. Did the Conduct in Question Have Secondary Effect Apart from the Communication of Ideas?
2. Do the Secondary Effects of the Act of Communication Impinge Upon a Substantial Government Interest?
3. Is the Governmental Regulation in Question neither Broader nor More Stringent than Necessary to Protect the Substantial Government Interest?

Concluding that the answer to all of these questions in the *Street* case was "No," the Civil Liberties Union argued that his conduct was protected by the First Amendment.[37]

Just as Thomas Emerson, in his *System of Freedom of Expression,* has classified some words as "action," he has also classified some nonverbal conduct as "expression." *His* mode of analysis for determining what kinds of conduct fall into the "expression" category appears to borrow to some extent from the *Columbia Law Review* position, in part from the Civil Liberties Union arguments, and even from the rationale of the *O'Brien* opinion, although he rejects the results of that case. What he shares with both the *O'Brien* Court majority and the ACLU brief is the concept that "when speech and nonspeech elements are combined in the same course of conduct, a sufficiently important government interest in regulating the nonspeech element can justify incidental limitations on First Amendment freedoms." Emerson puts it in only a slightly different way:

> To some extent expression and action are always mingled; most conduct includes elements of both. . . . The guiding principle must be to determine which element is predominant in the conduct under consideration. Is expression the major element and action only secondary? Or is the action the essence and the expression incidental? The answer, to a great extent, must be based on a common-sense reaction, made in the light of the functions and operations of a system of freedom of expression.[38]

Proceeding further, Emerson invokes the *Columbia Law Review* analysis: "Yet often there is something more to go on—some extrinsic points of reference which provide useful guides. The conduct must, of course, be intended as communication and capable of being understood by others as such."[39]

He then adds this further criterion to supplement one's "common-sense reaction":

> In order to determine whether the government control is directed against that element of the conduct which constitutes expression only, it is sometimes helpful to consider what comparable forms of action, divorced from expression or the particular kind of expression involved, are normally subject to government control. In the political

assassination case, for example, murder is usually the object of official sanction regardless of what is intended to be expressed by the murderer.[40]

Having established these guidelines, Emerson seems to find it quite easy to adjudicate particular cases. With respect to the burning of the draft card, for him "it seems quite clear that the predominant element in such conduct is expression (opposition to the draft) rather than action (destruction of a piece of cardboard). The registrant is not concerned with secret or inadvertent burning of his draft card, involving no communication with other persons."[41]

Likewise, for the turning in of draft cards in protest against the Vietnam War, he says, "In making this gesture the quality of expression clearly prevails over the element of action. The conduct is hardly different from writing a letter of protest."[42]

In contrast, Emerson finds:

> Certain other forms of protest against the war effort more clearly consist of conduct in which action predominates and which is therefore not protected by the First Amendment. Mass physical obstruction of draft boards . . . obstruction of troop movements by lying down in front of troop trains . . . pouring blood over Selective Service files. To attempt to bring such forms of protest within the expression category would rob the distinction between expression and action of all meaning, and would make impossible any system of freedom of expression based upon full protection of expression.[43]

One can agree with Emerson's determination that the public burning or turning in of draft cards merit First Amendment protection whereas lying down in front of troop trains or pouring blood on draft board files do not, and yet be forgiven for wondering how one gets to those conclusions as unerringly as he does using only the guidelines he has provided. In *all* of these illustrations, the actors clearly intended to communicate a message to the public, and those messages were undoubtedly well understood. Since they passed that test, how did Emerson decide which element of their behavior, expression or action, was "predominant" and which "only secondary"? Which was the "essence" and which "incidental"? The only answer he has given us is "common-sense." Unfortunately, the common sense of Supreme Court justices more conservative than Emerson is likely to lead to very different results than he has envisioned for his system.

Without denigrating any of the useful insights discussed thus far, and indeed relying on some of them, I would propose a more exhaustive analysis for determining when First Amendment consideration and possible protection is appropriate to nonverbal conduct. It seems to me that the necessary beginning point is a recognition that *all* behavior communicates, or, to put it in the apt phrase of one group of communication theorists, "one cannot not communicate."[44] Everything that one does, every action that one takes or fails to take, "speaks" to anyone who is interested in looking for the message. This is not to suggest that all behavior *consciously* communicates, is *intended* as communication, or is *perceived* by others as sending a message. But once we accept the fact that all behavior is *capable of being understood* as communication, we will have a better appreciation of the complexities we face in distinguishing among various behaviors for First Amendment purposes, and we may also find a starting point for cutting through those complexities.

If we assume that all behavior communicates, we must also assume that the First Amendment does not reach and license such an infinite range of conduct. Thomas Jefferson surely had some important distinction in mind when he said, "It is time enough for the rightful purposes of civil government for its officers to interfere when principles break out into overt acts against peace and good order."[45] But we have seen that his distinction cannot be drawn on the basis of verbal versus nonverbal conduct, for "principles" can be expressed by the latter as well as the former without "break[ing] out into overt acts against peace and good order." It is necessary to look elsewhere for the dividing line.

It will help our analysis if we recognize three broad categories of human behavior. The first category consists of conduct that is *entirely* symbolic—that is to say, it functions *only* to create meanings (ideas and feelings) inside of people.[46] Usually those meanings are communicated from one person to others, but it is also possible to use symbols to stimulate ideas and feelings in oneself—for example, the cathartic curse when one hurts oneself, or the rubbing of a rabbit's foot to bring good luck.

Behavior that is entirely symbolic is ordinarily easy to identify because of the traditional symbols it usually employs—words, gestures, pictures, sculptures, effigies, flags, emblems. All of these are inherently and only symbolic; that is, they *represent* or *stand for* something else. They are not *it;* they are *about it.*[47]

Modern technology and culture have made it more difficult than in the past to recognize the difference between a symbol and what it represents. Motion pictures and television seem so real, and indeed are so much closer to a representation of reality than words or drawings, that one sometimes forgets that they are still *pictures* of something and are not the thing itself. Live stage shows used to be clearly recognizable as *simulations* of real life. But some modern dramatic techniques which have jumped over the traditional barriers of aesthetic distance and have literally landed in the laps of the audience have sometimes fuzzed the line between the make-believe and the real. When an actor is shot with a blank bullet and bleeds ketchup we have no problem recognizing that the enactment is solely for the sake of audience reaction. But when a hero and heroine are locked in a prolonged passionate embrace we cannot be entirely sure that their performance is only for the benefit of the viewers. Just as an actual killing, in the course of a play, would cross the line from symbolism to reality, so lovemaking that is engaged in for its own sake rather than to create some effect upon its audience would cross that same divide.

The question as to whether a particular set of activities is theater (i.e., make-believe) or "real" cannot be answered by whether or not it occurs on a stage. A professional wrestling match may be the real thing or it may be, with all its grunts and groans, just a "show"—that is, a symbolic event designed only to create illusions of a real fight in the minds of the audience. A nightclub stripper "doing the bumps" is clearly engaged in symbolic activity, but when she brushes a bare breast against a customer sitting at a front table, for a brief moment she steps across the line into reality. Those antiwar protesters who burned Xerox copies of their draft cards rather than the real thing were also engaging in symbolic conduct, as was the man who aimed a toy gun at President Gerald Ford. This last illustration should serve as a reminder that we are not, at this point, discussing whether these behaviors should be protected by the freedom of speech clause of the First Amendment. That is a separate question to which we shall return. We are simply attempting here to clarify the difference between conduct that is exclusively symbolic and that which is not.

Perhaps the most difficult example of this problem is an actor who, in the course of portraying a role in a play, takes a bite of real food, sips a real alcoholic beverage, or smokes a real joint of marijuana. The actor's purpose, to create an illusion in the audience, might be achieved just as easily in the latter two instances without using real alcohol or marijuana, but it would be difficult to simulate eating without real food. Regardless of the purpose for which it is done, the ingestion of *any* substance into the body cannot be considered as *solely* a symbolic act.

A second broad category into which behavior may be classified is conduct in which people engage entirely or primarily for its own sake—that is, its function is to carry out some human need or impulse irrespective of any possible effect upon an audience or witness. This would include everything from eating, sleeping, dressing, playing, working, making love, and fighting, to serious antisocial behavior like robbery, the destruction of property, and murder. To be sure, as we indicated at the outset, all of these behaviors *also* communicate a message to anyone who chooses to view them from that perspective (like the psychiatrist who says to the companion with whom he is walking down the street, after having been greeted with a "hello" from a passerby, "I wonder what he meant by that"). But any message that is communicated by behaviors that are engaged in entirely or primarily for their own sake is only incidental. The actor does not intend the conduct as communication, and others, unless they are making a psychiatric analysis, do not evaluate it as such.

The third broad category of human behavior, and the one that is the most problematic for First Amendment purposes, consists of conduct that is not ordinarily intended or perceived as symbolic—that is, it is usually behavior that falls into our second category—but may be endowed by the actor, perceiver, or observer with meaning above and beyond the act itself. The behavior is made symbolic by the way in which it functions.

Almost any activity that is ordinarily engaged in for its own sake can be converted in this way into a "message to the world." The length or style of one's hair, or one's state of dress or undress, can be designed for personal pleasure and comfort, or they can advertise an attitude or a culture. One can sit at a lunch counter just to eat, or to make a point, or perhaps both. One can urinate, defecate, or spit in order to eliminate substances from the body, or one can perform any of those acts as a sign of anger and contempt for their target. One can refuse to pay taxes just to cheat the government, or because one does not wish to support government policies that are alien to one's point of view.

Ordinarily digging a grave is for the purpose of burying someone. But when Phillip Berrigan and two associates dug a grave in the front yard of Secretary of Defense Donald Rumsfeld's Chevy Chase home in September 1976 and mounted signs beside it reading "The Future of our Children" and "Life on Earth," they were trying to communicate a political message. Usually when a laundry line is strung across a back yard it is for the purpose of drying clothes. But when the Stover family of Rye, New York, put up a clothesline every year from 1956 to 1961 from their front porch to a tree beside the street, it was in protest against high city taxes.[48] Most arson and murder spring from some private impulse and serve some private end. However, the burning of a school that is about to be desegregated or the assassination of a Martin Luther King, Jr., may be an attempt, tragically misguided as it is, to make a statement on a public matter.

Returning now to the question of the applicability of the First Amendment to these three broad categories of human behavior, it seems self-evident that the first category requires no different treatment than that which is accorded to words. Insofar as behavior occurs that is *entirely* symbolic, although not verbal, the presumption should be that it is protected "speech." Exceptions to First Amendment protection should be allowed only where the context in which the nonverbal communication occurs justifies restraints, precisely as it might justify restraints on verbal communication under like circumstances. Thus, just as pointing a toy gun from a crowd at the president of the United States may, for many good reasons, be regarded as intolerable symbolic conduct, so verbal threats against the life of a president would be, and are in fact, similarly punishable.

It seems equally self-evident that the second category of human conduct—that which is engaged in primarily or entirely for its own sake regardless of the messages psychiatrists might read into it—is entirely outside the realm of First Amendment consideration. It is simply irrelevant to the concerns of this book.

It is the third category that presents the most difficult cases. To dismiss this category, as we do the second one, on the grounds that conduct which is not ordinarily or inherently symbolic can never be given the protection of the First Amendment is to exclude many acts that belong within the realm of freedom of expression. What we need is some basis for discriminating between a political assassination, at one extreme, and, at the other extreme, a case like that of three Pawnee Indian seventh graders who were suspended from an Oklahoma public school for insisting on the right to wear their hair in long braids in accordance with the traditions of their culture. It is astonishing that the school's authority in this matter was upheld by the U.S. Court of Appeals for the Tenth Circuit and the U.S. Supreme Court declined to review that decision.[49]

What we find in this third category of sometimes-symbolic acts are not only assassinations and hair styles but a whole range of behaviors in between. At the most violent extreme, in addition to political murders, there are ideologically motivated bombings of buildings, hijackings of airplanes, arson, and the capture and holding of hostages. Less serious because remediable, but still violative of the rights of others, are the angry breaking of windows, the splashing of paint on a home, office, or public building, digging a grave or burning a cross on someone's front lawn, and spitting or urinating on another person.

Moving another step along the continuum we find actions that are not *directly* harmful to other persons but which may interfere with the functioning of society as a whole, such as refusing to pay one's taxes, blocking a troop train, or occupying the offices of the U.S. Bureau of Indian Affairs. Behavior within this range is usually described as civil disobedience.

Still further along, and closer to the hair-style end of the line, are actions that are more of an inconvenience than they are a serious harm to others. Included here would be parades that temporarily disrupt traffic and create litter. Burning draft cards (which are replaceable), flying banners from the Statue of Liberty, or dumping piles of manure (which are removable) on the steps of city hall[50] fall in this part of the spectrum. It should be noted here that what is ordinarily a mere inconvenience could, under unusual conditions, become a greater hazard. A major traffic disruption, for example, could cost the life of someone who, in a critical emergency, was slowed down in getting to a hospital.

Finally, at the opposite extreme from assassinations are behaviors whose only impact on others is on their psyches. Here would be included nonconforming hair styles, public nudity (e.g., streaking), public sex, or a laundry line in the front yard. All of these acts function much like purely symbolic behavior—that is, they affect only the *feelings* of other people. They differ from those described in our first broad category in that the vehicle of expression is not exclusively a symbolic tool and, in most instances, is not engaged in for communicative purposes.

Having described the wide range of actions that fall into our third category of sometimes-symbolic conduct, we can now attempt to distinguish among them for First Amendment purposes. What is it intuitively that tells us that murder, for whatever motives, does not merit First Amendment protection and that the hair style of an Indian child might? The clear and essential difference lies in whether the behavior does harm to others and, if so, to how serious a degree. It does not really matter whether, in Thomas Emerson's terms, the expression or symbolic element is "predominant" or "incidental," and we can be spared the necessity of making that kind of judgment. The significant question is whether the nonsymbolic element, whether predominant or secondary in intent or in effect, is sufficiently harmful to place the total conduct beyond any possible First Amendment consideration. To put it another way, going back to the Civil Liberties Union brief in *Street v. New York,* it does not matter whether the harmful ingredient is a "secondary effect apart from the communication of ideas," or whether the communication of ideas is a secondary effect of what is primarily a harmful act. So long as the nonsymbolic or "non-meaning effect" (to incorporate Professor Melville Nimmer's language)[51] is sufficiently harmful, it does not make any difference whether that nonmeaning element is primary, secondary, the "essence," or "incidental."

By this standard it is easy to write off the assassination-bombing-kidnapping end of the third-category continuum as so obviously and seriously harmful that it would be ludicrous to think of extending First Amendment consideration to such behavior. It should be just as obvious that the behaviors at the opposite end of the continuum, where the only harm that is done may be to give offense to the moral or aesthetic sensibilities of others, are at least entitled to as much First Amendment consideration, if not protection, as purely symbolic first-category conduct which may also be perceived as offensive. It would simplify the freedom of speech problem posed by these kinds of behavior if our society were permissive enough to place all victimless conduct, such as public nudity, public sex, and neighborhood aesthetics, *whether functioning as communication or not,* outside the reach of the law. Then we would not have to worry whether it merits protection under the First Amendment when functioning symbolically. But until that day comes—if it ever does, or indeed if it ever should—we must continue to make a distinction among these acts on the basis of their symbolic or nonsymbolic uses. This, of course, creates a state of affairs in which the law is applied unequally to people with respect to certain behaviors, depending on whether or not it is decided that they are engaged in acts of communication. Such discriminatory treatment can be justified only on the grounds that when First Amendment values are implicated in a situation our society is willing to strike a different balance among competing interests than we would otherwise be inclined to do.

This can be seen more clearly when we move toward the middle ranges of our continuum, where the behavior in question may have an impact on more than the feelings of other people. Thus, for the sake of freedom of speech, we are willing to accept some disruption and re-routing of traffic to make way for a march—even at the risk of blocking someone's most direct route to a hospital—when we would not be willing to do the same if only private purposes were to be served. We will step around people who are staging a nondisruptive sit-in protest in the hallway, lobby, or reception area of an administrative office building from which mere loiterers would be ejected. A burning-in-effigy might be allowed in a public place where fires are generally prohibited; and the noise of a political rally would not evoke the negative police response that might be made to a similarly loud and boisterous neighborhood party.

We weigh the interests differently, however, when actions occur that strike physically at other people and their property—like spitting on them, breaking their windows, or digging graves in their yards. Here the presently prevailing standards of our society and legal system view the behavior, correctly I believe, as sufficiently harmful to warrant restraint, regardless of any symbolic function it may perform. Similarly, one can agree with the generally accepted view that civil disobedience directed against valid social interests, like collecting taxes, or keeping open some channels for traffic to move through the streets and people to move to their workplaces, should be punishable regardless of any message being communicated.[52] Significantly, most advocates of the philosophy of civil disobedience would acknowledge that punishment for such acts is expected and accepted and that their martyrdom may actually help them to make their point.

The closest questions arise with respect to actions that are not quite as intrusive on the rights of others or as harmful to the interests of society as those just mentioned but are more troublesome than marches, rallies, bonfires, or nondisruptive sit-ins. Illustrations would be piling manure on the steps of a city hall, blanketing an area with a massive littering of leaflets dropped from an airplane,[53] or affixing posters on public buildings. The harm may not be terribly serious and can probably be rather quickly undone, but perhaps at considerable economic cost and social inconvenience. In such instances, if First Amendment considerations are present we might be more inclined than otherwise to mitigate the punishment—for example, by limiting it to reimbursement for the cost sustained.

It is only with respect to conduct that falls toward the minimally harmful or totally harmless end of the range of behavior that is sometimes symbolic and sometimes not that the questions raised by the *Columbia Law Review* and Professor Emerson regarding communicative intentions and perceptions need even be addressed, for it is only in this area that defining the act as communication rather than as behavior engaged in for its own sake would make any difference in how it should be treated by the law. In dealing with this definitional question, Nimmer has wisely pointed out that a necessary prerequisite to such an inquiry is that the alleged communicator must make a First Amendment claim.[54] For unless the one who has acted asserts that the behavior was communicative, there is no good reason to believe that there was anything symbolic about it.

I do not believe this should mean, as the *Columbia Law Review* and Emerson have proposed, that in order for First Amendment considerations to come into play there must have been a *conscious intent* to communicate on the part of the actor at the time of the event. The Indian children in Pawnee, Oklahoma, may not have been aware that they were advertising their culture by going to school with their hair in braids. It should suffice if their parents testify on their behalf that this hairstyle was a meaningful mode of expressing their tribal values. Or, a young man who, in a fit of anger about a war he feels is unjust, impetuously burns his draft card in front of a group of friends should not have to be fully conscious at that moment that he is making a political statement. It should be enough if, after the fact, he recognizes and claims that this is what he was doing. Courts will have to have some latitude to decide in each case, on the basis of the facts available to them, whether the particular claim is a bona fide one or is simply an after-the-fact ruse to seek First Amendment protection for what was not intended, consciously or unconsciously, to be an act of communication when it occurred.

As for the *Columbia Law Review*'s suggested "requirement that others can recognize the conduct as communication" and that, furthermore, it is not sufficient for just "one or two good friends" to so recognize it, but that it "must be calculated to communicate to some substantial audience," I do not see the justification or necessity for such criteria. Quite commonly people change the styles of their hair or dress with the intention of communicating some message to others, and they go unnoticed. Such an abortive effort is still an *attempt* to communicate and deserves to be treated as such, even though it has fallen on unseeing eyes. As to the additional requirement that a "substantial audience" must perceive the act as one of communication, there seems to be no justification for that either. In the case of the dung heap on the city hall steps, for example, if only the mayor and nobody else got the message it would be as much an act of communication as if the whole world knew that something more was involved than just a pile of manure.

Sometime ago there was broadcast a televised dramatization of the autobiography of Miss Jane Pittman, an ex-slave who lived a life of dedication to the advancement of her race. The climax of her life story came when the 108-year-old Miss Pittman, closely watched by a coterie of her followers and a gathering of Southern white townspeople and policemen, slowly and leaning heavily on her cane, walked up a long sidewalk leading to the county courthouse where, just outside the building, she took a drink of water from a fountain marked "For Whites Only." In this particular instance Miss Pittman's audience had no illusion that her action occurred just because she was thirsty. But even if all of those onlookers, or all but one or two of them, had been too insensitive to comprehend what was going on, the event would have been no less symbolic because of that. It is the symbolism in the actor's behavior and not the response of the audience that should bring First Amendment considerations into play.

This is not to say that First Amendment *protection* will always follow. Just as in cases of verbal communication and of purely symbolic nonverbal conduct, the right to freedom of speech sometimes must give way to competing concerns. But it should not give way simply because acts, rather than words, were the vehicle for expression. If justifications are to be found for restraining communicative behavior they must be found in the context and in the effects of that communication upon other fundamental interests.

A Catalogue of Competing Concerns

Our real dilemma, then, in interpreting the First Amendment is not in deciding whether speech should *ever* be abridged but in determining the circumstances which may justify restrictions on communication. The history of U.S. Supreme Court decisions in the First Amendment area has been essentially a history of attempting to identify those circumstances.

In its first major effort, in 1919, the Court said, "The question in every case is whether the words used are used in such circumstances and are of such a nature as to create a clear and present danger that they will bring about the substantive evils that Congress has a right to prevent."[55]

The "substantive evil" in that particular case was resistance to wartime conscription.

In 1942, as we have seen in the last chapter, the Supreme Court ruled, "There are certain well-defined and narrowly limited classes of speech, the prevention and punishment of which have never been thought to raise any constitutional problem. These include the lewd and obscene, the profane, the libelous, and the insulting or 'fighting' words—those which by their very utterance inflict injury or tend to incite an immediate breach of the peace."[56]

To reconcile this principle with its 1919 precedent, the Court in 1952 explained, "Libellous utterances, not being within the area of constitutionally protected speech, it is unnecessary, either for us or for the State courts, to consider the issues behind the phrase 'clear and present danger.' Certainly no one would contend that obscene speech, for example, may be punished only upon a showing of such circumstances. Libel, as we have seen, is in the same class."[57]

In 1949 another kind of exception was carved from the First Amendment. In that year the Supreme Court said, "It rarely has been suggested that the constitutional freedom of speech extends its immunity to speech or writing used as an integral part of conduct in violation of a valid criminal statute. We reject the contention now."[58]

The "valid criminal statute" to which the Court was then referring was a Missouri antitrust law.

A decade later the Supreme Court was asked to decide whether an individual could, on First Amendment grounds, refuse to answer the questions of a Congressional committee investigating alleged un-American activities. Said the Court in 1959, " . . . the protections of the First Amendment . . . do not afford a witness the right to resist inquiry in all circumstances. Where First Amendment rights are asserted to bar governmental interrogation resolution of the issue always involves a balancing by the courts of the competing private and public interests at stake in the particular circumstances."[59]

On this occasion the Court struck that balance in favor of the congressional committee's interest in getting answers to its questions.

In 1965 the Supreme Court explicitly affirmed another principle which had been implicit in earlier decisions. The Court said, "The rights of free speech and assembly, while fundamental in our democratic society, still do not mean that everyone with opinions or beliefs to express may address a group at any public place and at any time. The constitutional guarantee of liberty implies the existence of an organized society maintaining public order, without which liberty itself would be lost in the excesses of anarchy."[60]

In the particular case before the Court, it was decided that, if the state wishes, it can set places like a courthouse out of bounds to demonstrators.

In its most recently enunciated general principle, the Supreme Court in 1969 decided that "the constitutional guarantees of free speech and free press do not permit a State to forbid or proscribe advocacy of the use of force or of law violation except where such advocacy is directed to inciting or producing imminent lawless action and is likely to incite or produce such action."[61] In the circumstances of the case then before it, the Court held that a speech made at a Ku Klux Klan rally in Ohio did not fall within the excepted category and was therefore protected by the First Amendment.

In all of these cases, whether the Supreme Court placed reliance on a clear-and-present-danger test, a categorization of speech into protected and unprotected classes, an integral-part-of-illegal-conduct criterion, a balancing doctrine, a time and place regulation, or an incitement-to-lawless-action formulation, the determination was made that certain kinds of competing interests can justify restrictions on communication. It shall be the purpose of the remainder of this book to examine each of the claims that are put forth as potential competitors to freedom of expression and to assess the validity of those claims in light of the long-range goals of the First Amendment and the basic values of an open society.

Part 2  Communication about Other People

3 **Defamation**

Since the First Amendment places such a high priority on the rights of the individual, it is not surprising that a most powerful and persuasive challenge to the scope of its protections comes from the claim that, in some circumstances, freedom of expression by one person about other people can do serious damage to the individual rights of another. The harms that are most often alleged are to the reputation and livelihood of the persons who may be talked about, to their rights of privacy, to their racial or ethnic integrity, and to their rights to a fair trial. Of these four categories, the first has the longest and most complex legal history. Indeed, if there is any category of expression that historians might agree upon as not intended to be protected by the authors of the First Amendment it would be that of personal defamation—in other words, libel and slander. It is to this particular problem that the present chapter will be devoted.

The Latin root for the word "defamation" is "diffamatus," meaning "ill-fame." The harms that traditionally have been thought to result from speech that sullies a person's good name are several and have been described generally by one author as injurious to a person's "relational interests."[1] A damaged reputation can cause one to lose a job, a promotion, a new employment opportunity, or income if one is self-employed. It can lead to diminished interpersonal contacts or even total social ostracism. In some cultures duels, blood feuds, and other violent self-help measures may result, particularly if the law is not viewed as providing an adequate remedy for vindication of the "honor" that has been besmirched.

To deter these "relational" injuries if possible, or to compensate and punish for them if not prevented, the common-law crime of slander was developed in the early Anglo-Saxon system of justice. In 1647 the first formal treatise on the subject, John March's *Actions for Slaunder*, was published, although the offense it described had been recognized long before that. Then, with the growth of religious and political dissent in the Renaissance and Reformation periods, and the introduction of the

43

printing press, those in power perceived a new danger in unrestrained verbal attacks upon individuals in positions of public authority—that is, upon themselves. One student of that period, W. R. Jones, has noted, "The defamation of the state and its servitors quickly came to be regarded with a degree of alarm that the slander of private persons never elicited."[2] Out of that milieu evolved the law of libel, which was far more restrictive than the common law of slander. As Jones describes it:

> The law of libel afforded the defendant none of the protections assumed by the law of slander. Words not defamatory when spoken became libelous (and criminal) when published. Truth was never admitted, as in slander, to be a valid defense.... The courts normally assumed the malicious intent of author and publisher; and until the end of the eighteenth century the mere fact of publication was considered the sole issue for the jury's consideration.[3]

With the passage of Fox's Libel Law by the British Parliament in 1792, placing greater discretion in the hands of juries in criminal libel cases, and with the growing acceptance by the courts during the nineteenth century of truth as a defense, there began to be a coalescence of the law of libel with the common law of slander. This led ultimately to the present-day situation in which oral and written defamations are for all practical purposes indistinguishable at law and are usually limited to false statements that cause injury in the eyes of others. To be entirely accurate, it should be said here that oral and written statements are not the only means of communicating defamatory messages. Nonverbal communication may serve the same purpose. Professor Jones cites one such example from English history: "One could defame with a gesture as shown by a case from an ecclesiastical court of the diocese of London in 1589, wherein the plaintiff accused a gang of rowdies of having nailed a pair of horns—the sign of the cuckold—above his doorway."[4]

Narrowing the boundaries of defamatory speech did not end with these nineteenth-century developments. The U.S. Supreme Court, in two landmark decisions a decade apart, *New York Times v. Sullivan* in 1964[5] and *Gertz v. Welch* in 1974,[6] elaborated by several lesser decisions in between,[7] substantially rewrote the law of defamation for this country. Recognizing the politically repressive nature of the English concept of seditious libel, and finding restrictions on that kind of speech to be incompatible with the "central meaning of the First Amendment," a unanimous Supreme Court in *New York Times v. Sullivan* ruled that even a false statement made about the official conduct of a public officeholder may not be punished unless proven to have been made with "actual malice"—that is, "with knowledge that it was false or with reckless disregard of whether it was false or not." The Court reasoned that, in order to preserve our "profound national commitment to the principle that debate on public issues should be uninhibited, robust, and wide open, and that it may well include vehement, caustic, and sometimes unpleasantly sharp attacks on government and public officials,"[8] it is necessary to give First Amendment protection to charges that may in fact be erroneous. Otherwise, said the Court, "would-be critics of official conduct may be deterred from voicing their criticism, even though it is believed to be true and even though it is in fact true, because of doubt whether it can be proved in court or fear of the expense of having to do so."[9]

Some of the Justices would have gone even farther than a majority of them were prepared to go. Justice Arthur Goldberg, joined by Justice Douglas, expressed the view, in a concurring opinion, that the right to criticize official conduct should not depend "upon a jury's evaluation of the speaker's state of mind."[10] They favored an absolute privilege for criticism of official conduct, making no exception for statements supposedly uttered with "actual malice," and they argued, "If individual citizens may be held liable in damages for strong words, which a jury finds false and maliciously motivated, there can be little doubt that public debate and advocacy will be constrained."[11]

The Goldberg-Douglas concurrence, however, made clear their belief that the Constitution did *not* protect "defamatory statements directed against the private conduct of a public official or a private citizen," for on that issue, they felt, "Purely private defamation has little to do with the political ends of a self-governing society."[12]

Justice Black agreed with the Goldberg-Douglas rejection of the "actual malice" test because of his belief that a "minimum guarantee of the First Amendment" is an "unconditional right to say what one pleases about public affairs."[13] But for Justice Black that was merely a minimum. Although he was content in his *New York v. Sullivan* concurrence, joined by Justice Douglas, to assert, "This nation . . . can live in peace without libel suits based on public discussions of public affairs and public officials," he made clear in other places that he found *all* restrictions on defamation to be in conflict with the First Amendment.[14] With respect to libel, Justice Black was absolute in his conviction that when the First Amendment said "no law" abridging freedom of speech it meant *no* law.

The decade following *New York Times v. Sullivan* was a period of clarification and elaboration of that decision by the Supreme Court. First, the Court made clear that its new doctrine was applicable to criminal as well as civil libel actions.[15] Then, in a case questioning whether its principle applied as far down the line of public officials as a supervisor of a state park, the Supreme Court declared that "the 'public official' designation applies at the very least to those among the hierarchy of government employees who have, or appear to the public to have, substantial responsibility for or control over the conduct of government affairs."[16]

In its next significant step, the Court decided that "public figures" as well as "public officials" should be limited by the *New York Times v. Sullivan* doctrine.[17] Four years later a plurality of the justices took the position that false statements about a *private* person's involvement in any event of public interest should be protected by the First Amendment unless made with "actual malice,"[18] but in *Gertz v. Welch* in 1974 a majority rejected that view and largely limited the application of *New York Times v. Sullivan* to the kinds of prominent individuals who voluntarily "thrust themselves to the forefront"[19] of public controversy. The *Gertz* majority believed that there is a significant difference between people who inject themselves into the arena of public debate and those who are accidentally caught up in some event that happens to attract public attention. Individuals in the former category not only must "run the risk of closer public scrutiny" because "they invite attention and comment" but, like public officials, they "usually enjoy significantly greater access to the channels of effective communication and hence have a more realistic opportunity to counteract false statements than private individuals normally enjoy."[20]

Gertz v. Welch thus brought a halt to the expansion of categories of persons limited in their ability to sue for libel by *New York Times v. Sullivan,* and in that sense it may be viewed as supporting the continued viability of the law of defamation. In two important ways, however, the *Gertz* decision furthered the longer-range trend to narrow the reach of defamation law. First, it ended the historic common-law practice of allowing recovery of damages in defamation suits on the *presumption* that certain kinds of statements were per se injurious without actual proof that any harm had been done to a particular individual (e.g., accusing a woman of unchastity, imputing the commission of a crime to someone, asserting that a person has a loathsome disease, or alleging that a person is grossly incompetent in his or her job). Under the *Gertz v. Welch* ruling, damages may no longer be awarded in defamation actions without proof of "actual injury." The injury need not be measurable in dollars and cents and may include considerations such as "personal humiliation, and mental anguish and suffering," but it cannot be presumed without evidence.[21]

A second substantial reform in the law of defamation brought about by *Gertz* was a drastic cutting back on the possibilities for recovering punitive, as opposed to compensatory, damages. To win such awards, the Supreme Court ruled that all persons, whether public officials, public figures, or private citizens, would henceforth have to prove "actual malice" as defined in *New York v. Sullivan*. The majority had this to say by way of explanation for its sharp curtailment of punitive damages:

> In most jurisdictions jury discretion over the amounts awarded is limited only by the gentle rule that they not be excessive. Consequently, juries assess punitive damages in wholly unpredictable amounts bearing no necessary relation to the actual harm done. And they remain free to use their discretion selectively to punish expressions of unpopular views. Like the doctrine of presumed damages, jury discretion to award punitive damages unnecessarily exacerbates the danger of media self-censorship.... They are not compensation for injury. Instead, they are private fines levied by civil juries to punish reprehensible conduct and to deter its future occurrence.[22]

In view of this rationale, the Court's willingness to continue allowing punitive damages for defamatory statements uttered with "actual malice" suggests that it regarded such speech as "reprehensible." That this is likely the case was made apparent in the first major libel decision following *New York Times v. Sullivan,* when a unanimous Supreme Court said:

> Although honest utterance, even if inaccurate, may further the fruitful exercise of free speech, it does not follow that the lie, knowingly and deliberately published about a public official, should enjoy a like immunity.... the use of the known lie as a tool is at odds with the premises of democratic government and with the orderly manner in which economic, social, or political change is to be effected. Calculated falsehood falls into that class of utterances which "are no essential part of any exposition of ideas."[23]

Having briefly surveyed the history and present status of the law of defamation, we now turn our attention to an evaluation of its appropriateness in a free society. Immediately we are confronted with the obvious fact that penalties for defamation constitute a significant departure from whatever wisdom there may be in the philosophy that "sticks and stones may break my bones, but names will never hurt me." The ready answer which can be given is that this children's chant is a bit of oversimplified bravado and that in the "real world" of business and social relationships the calling of names can hurt people in very substantial ways. But that response, too, is oversimplified. In order for the calling of names to hurt someone, those who are exposed to the message must believe it or think it might be true and must as a consequence change their behavior toward the target of the attack. Both of those eventualities can be avoided if there is interposed between the name-calling and the potentially injurious response additional communication sufficient to undermine the credibility of the name-caller. As Justice Louis Brandeis said so well of freedom of speech in general: "If there be time to expose through discussion the falsehood and fallacies, to avert the evil by the processes of education, the remedy to be applied is more speech, not enforced silence. Only an emergency can justify repression."[24]

The principle enunciated by Justice Brandeis that, where time permits, the proper remedy for false speech is more speech has gained only partial acceptance in contemporary judicial doctrine concerning defamation. The Supreme Court, in noting that public officials and public figures have greater access to the media of communication to answer false accusations than do private persons, has indicated that, at least in the realm of public affairs, it views replies as preferable to lawsuits. However, with respect to private defamations, as well as to all other libels uttered with "actual malice," our society has continued looking to litigation as the remedy rather than to providing greater access to the media for "more speech." This is not because we are unaware of any mechanism to accomplish the latter end, for the idea of a right of reply as an alternative to actions for defamation has been known and advocated for a long time.[25] Many foreign nations have had right-to-reply laws on their books, and our own states of Florida, Mississippi, and Nevada have had such legislation as well.

These laws come in several varieties. German law has limited one's right to reply to a correction of allegations of fact, whereas French law has allowed also for an answer to expressions of opinion.[26] While Mississippi's law provided for a limited right of reply only to alleged defamations, the law of Florida required that any newspaper which attacked either the personal character or official record of any candidate for public office, irrespective of the truth of the charges, was obligated, upon the candidate's request, to provide equivalent space for an answer to the attack.

It was this Florida law which provided the basis, in 1974, for the U.S. Supreme Court's only confrontation to date with the right-to-reply issue. The Miami Herald Publishing Company claimed that the state law requiring it to print material it did not wish to publish was in violation of its freedom of the press, and the Supreme Court unanimously agreed.[27] The language of the Court's opinion was so sweeping in its condemnation of the idea of the government telling a newspaper to print something it might not want to that Justices William Brennan and William Rehnquist felt moved to report, in a one-sentence concurrence, their understanding that the decision did not invalidate statutes which compel publication of a retraction as a remedy in cases where a plaintiff has proven defamation in court.[28]

Laws which might establish a right to reply to alleged defamations, as a *substitute* for libel actions in court, would be neither as narrow as those noted with apparent approval by Justices Brennan and Rehnquist nor need they be as broad as the condemned Florida statute, which went beyond defamation to include any political attack. Thus it is an open question whether or not they would pass constitutional muster in the eyes of the present justices. Our concern here, however, should not be with what the Court might think but with what we should think about such laws.

The arguments which have been made against the concept of a right to reply to alleged defamations as an alternative to litigation are readily answered. The major objection, of course, is the one voiced by the Supreme Court in the *Miami Herald* case—that of compelling communicators to utter words or publish material they may not wish to. This problem can be met, in part at least, by framing the law in such a way as to provide those accused of defamation with the threefold choice of either retracting their statements, disseminating a reply, or contesting a potential libel or slander lawsuit. Thus, persons who feel so righteous or confident about what they have communicated that they are unwilling to participate in the distribution of a reply would have the option of refusing to do so and facing, as they already do under present law, the risk of having to defend themselves in court. If, on the other hand, they agreed to a retraction or to disseminate a reply, at their own expense of course, through the same medium and with an equivalent degree of prominence and length, the law would immunize them from any further liability.

Another argument offered against the right to reply as a remedy for defamation is that an answer never completely catches up with the original charges and, even if it does, may not succeed entirely in wiping out the doubts that have been planted in people's minds. The same thing can be said, of course, about the verdict in a lawsuit for defamation. There is no assurance that the court's finding that a plaintiff has been defamed will receive any greater publicity than would a reply. To be sure, the plaintiff may be compensated financially for the harm that has been done, and there also may be a deterrent effect on future would-be defamers. But as far as public opinion about the reputation of that particular defamed person is concerned, a successful lawsuit many months or even years after the original charges have been circulated may actually be less effective than a more immediate reply that is guaranteed distribution through the same medium of communication.[29]

Furthermore, there is a glaring inconsistency between our dependence on the courts to set the public's thinking straight about a person's reputation and our sharply contrasting reliance on the competition of the marketplace of ideas to counteract fallacious political or religious propositions. If the public could be educated to respond to personal

attacks upon individuals with the same degree of skepticism and suspended judgment with which they ideally should react to the advocacy of
social doctrines, replies to alleged defamations could be a sufficiently
effective way to deal with that problem. Because we know that many
people do not listen as critically as they should to the false political and
religious prophets to whom they are exposed, we do not therefore assign
to our courts the task of cleansing their minds. We trust that in the long
run the truth will somehow emerge. Perhaps that same trust is in order
with respect to personal defamations.

Implicit in the foregoing line of thought is the answer to another of
the criticisms that have been made of right-to-reply laws as a remedy for
defamatory speech. That criticism is that a reply from an individual who
has been defamed, because it is obviously an expression springing from
self-interest, will not have as much credibility as a pronouncement by an
impartial court that the charges which were made are false. It may very
well be that the public, *if* they hear about it, might be more inclined to
believe a court verdict that a statement about an individual is untrue
than a response from that individual. But that again is a more authoritar-
ian than democratic way of dealing with the problem. We do not look to
our courts to tell us what is true or false in the realm of public affairs, but
have to figure it out for ourselves on the basis of the competing messages
available to us. As a part of that process we must learn to assess the
relative credibility of the various messengers. There is no reason that we
should not be expected to make the same kinds of judgments in the
realm of personal attacks and counterattacks, without the assistance of
an "impartial tribunal." We do it all the time in the intimate circles of our
families, friendships, and work groups, and are thus not without experience in figuring out who is lying and who is telling the truth.

A final argument that has been made against a statutory right-to-reply
scheme is that such laws will have a chilling effect on the willingness of
the media of communication to report personal charges which the public
ought to hear.[30] The reasoning offered in support of this contention is
that publishers or broadcasters, in order to avoid the possibility of having to give free space or time to people who demand their right to reply
to allegedly defamatory statements, will simply refrain from communicating any material that is the least bit risky. This criticism assumes
the kind of right-to-reply which requires granting a reply request without the option of refusing that request and taking the risk of a lawsuit.
Even if that were the case, however, it is difficult to conceive how a right
to reply would be any greater a deterrent to potentially defamatory
statements than the danger of a libel suit. At least with a right-to-reply
law, publishers and broadcasters would know precisely what the limits of
their liability could be—that is, the provision of space or time equivalent

to that involved in the original charges. Given the probable infrequency of reporting allegedly defamatory statements, that could hardly be a prohibitively costly matter for any medium of communication other than one that specializes in personal attacks. Libel suits, on the other hand, are much more unpredictable, both with respect to when they may occur and the kinds of damages that might be awarded. Only one thing about them is certain and that is the lawyers' fees that the media have to pay in defending themselves.

Although one becomes convinced that the right-to-reply remedy proposed here is neither unconstitutional, ineffective, nor unacceptably inhibitory, further persuasion may be needed to win agreement to the limitation on defamation actions which the reply option would create. For that purpose we must explore the advantages and disadvantages of defamation law itself.

Perhaps the most frequently voiced argument on behalf of prohibitions against slander and libel is that, in the absence of such restrictions, people who are defamed will take the law into their own hands and strike out violently against their defamers. It is a philosophy of frontier justice which suggests that no red-blooded man is going to take defamation lying down and that, if the law does not provide retribution, fists, swords, or guns will. We will encounter this same rationale, incidentally, when we come to examine some of the justifications for laws against obscenity and "fighting words."

The problem with this argument, of course, is that it presumes a kind of primitive society in which self-restraint in response to offensive symbolic conduct is considered to be either impossible or unlikely. The validity of that premise in contemporary America is open to serious question. Indeed, the sexist nature of the proposition about "red-blooded men" suggests something of its outdatedness, or at least of its parochialism. Not all persons, male or female, are unable to control themselves in the face of symbolic provocations by others, and it ought to be a goal of a democratic society to help people learn to handle their disputes in nonviolent ways. By that standard it must be admitted that defamation litigation was an advance over duels, but perhaps we are now ready to graduate to an even less revengeful substitute.

A second argument that has been offered in support of defamation laws is that without them the credibility of the press would suffer so seriously that it could no longer effectively serve its vital watchdog function.[31] The theory here is that the public, knowing that the press is free to indulge in irresponsible journalism without fear of punishment, would feel no assurance that what is communicated is true and would therefore become distrustful of everything that is said. Since, according to this line of thought, the press has a hard enough time even now in maintaining the confidence of the public, its problem of credibility would be multiplied if everyone knew that it was not legally accountable for any defamatory statements it might circulate.

If the press is having problems in maintaining its credibility in the minds of the public, the existence of the defamation remedy is a thin reed on which to lean as even a partial solution. The reasoning seems analogous to a proposition that the only way people can trust other human beings not to cheat, rob, or murder them is in the knowledge that any potential assailant is taking the risk of being caught, convicted, and punished. If that were the only basis, or even the primary basis, for interpersonal trust in our society, we would either have to have far more policemen, courts, and jails than can be imagined, or we would all have to be on our guard every moment of our lives.

Newspapers and broadcasters win or lose the confidence of their readers or listeners on the basis of many variables, only one of which may be the awareness that they can be sued for making libelous statements. It is hard to believe that a restriction on that possibility would have anything more than a minimal negative impact on the credibility of the press. On the other hand, it might have the salutary effect of placing greater responsibility on the consumer of communication to become a more careful and critical listener or reader.

A third and bottom-line justification for the law of defamation is that even if the news about a vindication in court does not reach all who heard and may have believed the original charges, at least the victim may be provided with some monetary compensation for the injuries suffered, and the punishment meted out to the defamer may serve as an example and deterrent to other potential offenders. These are irrefutable benefits of our present system and must simply be weighed against the disadvantages which also inhere in that system. We turn to those considerations now.

To say that defamation law is a deviation from First Amendment principles, which along with Justice Black I think it is, is to make a conclusory judgment that is not likely to persuade the unconvinced. Nor will many converts be won with the guilt-by-association argument that the defamation remedy seems to have its strongest appeal to those who are not noted for their liberal political philosophies.[32] There are more substantial reasons for concern about the law of defamation than its reactionary friends in the United States Senate.

If it is acknowledged that the law of defamation serves as a deterrent to some willfully irresponsible communication, it follows that it must also have a chilling effect on the expression of those who are not sure whether charges they feel impelled to voice could be proven to the satisfaction of a court if suit were brought. Although it can be argued that such comments, unless verifiable, are best kept to oneself, the rationale of the *New York Times v. Sullivan* decision was that, in the realm of public affairs, it is better if suspicions of wrongdoing are expressed rather than inhibited, even if eventually they are shown to be untrue and then, presumably, rejected. The Supreme Court's reluctance to extend that same permissiveness beyond the realm of public affairs appears to draw its inspiration from the old Meiklejohnian concept that discussion of matters related to the process of self-government warrants a higher degree of First Amendment protection than "mere" private discourse—a concept which the Court has never admitted to embracing, although some justices have occasionally flirted with the idea.[33]

If Zechariah Chafee was right, as I believe he was for reasons discussed earlier, in rejecting as invalid and unworkable Meiklejohn's distinction between "public" and "private" speech, then the Supreme Court has mistakenly deviated from its general adherence to the Chafee view in its not-altogether-predictable efforts with respect to libel to draw a line between private and public affairs. If it is important for a citizen who suspects the city treasurer of stealing the taxpayers' money to speak up and say so, it would seem just as important that similar suspicions be aired about a merchant who may be fleecing customers, an auto mechanic making unsafe car repairs, a doctor giving harmful advice to patients, or a father sexually molesting his daughter.

As if the mere existence of defamation law were not sufficient to cast a chilling effect on potentially valuable communication, the use of the law as a tool of harassment by plaintiffs with dubious cases seriously compounds the problem. Publishers and broadcasters with large corporate assets are tempting targets for the adventurer who sees the possibility, at best, of winning a sizable judgment for a libel that a jury can be convinced has been committed or, at worst, of getting paid off in the out-of-court settlement which may be far less costly to the defendant than fighting the case through to even a victorious conclusion. At the other end of the harassment spectrum is the wealthy plaintiff who can well afford the costs of litigation, and a defendant of modest means (such as the leader of a protest movement or the publisher of a cause journal) who is dragged into court and put to the expense of a legal defense for having dared to criticize the plaintiff. Examples of both kinds of lawsuits abound.[34]

Just as there are many libel actions in which the plaintiff may have no real justification for suing, so there are countless situations in which a genuinely defamed individual does not sue. It is costly to engage attorneys for a lawsuit, and the possibility of success is so unpredictable as to make it an uncertain investment. Also, there is the discouraging example of people like John Henry Faulk, a McCarthy-era radio personality who was blacklisted from employment as a result of being labeled a "subversive" in a publication called *Red Channels*. Faulk won a handsome damage award in a libel suit against the publication's author but was never able to collect a cent from the defendant who had become impoverished.

Furthermore, there is the emotional turmoil that going through a trial entails, for plaintiff as much as defendant, as well as the possibility that news coverage of that event may give the alleged defamation even wider circulation than the original charges received. Thus, as a practical matter, for many people legal action as a remedy for defamation is not an attractive course of action.

Another serious disadvantage of defamation law is the hole it opens in the already difficult line of defense the press has been trying to maintain to protect the confidentiality of its sources of information and of its editorial processes. Just as the Supreme Court has ruled that the First Amendment does not give a journalist the right to refuse to divulge to a grand jury confidentially obtained information about a possible criminal act,[35] so our courts have held that the plaintiff in a libel suit is entitled to discover not only the confidential source of allegedly defamatory remarks reported by the press but even to explore the thought processes of those making the editorial decisions.[36]

A final and seemingly boundless danger to freedom of expression posed by the law of libel is exemplified by a 1979 decision of a California appellate court, refused review by the Supreme Courts of both California and the United States.[37] The case involved a novel entitled *Touching* written by author Gwen Davis Mitchell, based on her experiences in a nude marathon encounter group conducted by psychologist Paul Bindrim. The book relates, in highly critical fashion, the story of a nude encounter group, with events and dialogue remarkably similar to episodes that actually occurred in Bindrim's sessions (as documented in court by tape recordings the psychologist had made). The novel, however, had as its group therapist a psychiatrist named Simon Herford who was a "fat Santa Claus type with long white hair, white sideburns, a cherubic rosy face and rosy forearms," whereas the real psychologist, Paul Bindrim, was nearly bald, clean-shaven, and a much younger person. Also Herford, unlike Bindrim, used vulgar and abusive language toward group participants.

Bindrim's counsel offered as witnesses in his suit for libel three persons who had observed or participated in his group sessions and who testified that they recognized Herford as Bindrim. The court accepted this testimony, and the fact that "the only difference between plaintiff and the Herford character in 'Touching' were physical appearance and that Herford was a psychiatrist rather than psychologist,"[38] as bases for determining that Mitchell's "substantially inaccurate descriptions of what happened" were "false statements of fact,"[39] punishable as libel.

To the author's argument that a work of fiction by its very nature contains material which is false-to-fact and "inaccurate" in its "descriptions of what happened," the court responded that merely labeling a book a "novel" does not immunize it from the contention of its real-life subjects that the story is really intended as a factual representation designed to defame them.[40] The question, said the court,

> is whether a reasonable person, reading the book, would understand that the fictional character therein pictured was, in actual fact, the plaintiff acting as described.
> Whether a reader, identifying the plaintiff ... would regard the passages ... as mere fictional embroidering or as reporting actual language and conduct, was for the jury. Its verdict adverse to the defendants cannot be overturned by this court.[41]

To argue for limiting defamation lawsuits to those circumstances in which the opportunity to reply has been denied is not to suggest that calculated falsehoods are a valuable part of the public dialogue. They may, indeed, be "reprehensible," as the Supreme Court has said. But the question we must face is how best to deal with them in the context of a free society. That question was dramatically posed in a Pennsylvania case where a state appellate court even went so far as to give approval to a *prior* restraint on defamatory speech—a generally more frowned-upon restriction on communication than post facto punishment. It was a combination of unusual circumstances that led this Pennsylvania court to the extreme remedy of granting an injunction against a woman who was picketing a law office carrying a sign which accused the attorneys within of stealing money from her. The picketed lawyers had already sued for defamation and had won a judgment that the charge was false and defamatory. However, since the woman was indigent, they were not only unable to collect the damages that were awarded, but any threat of further damages could have no deterrent effect on her since she could not afford to pay those either. If ever there was a situation in which speech seemed totally without justification, and no remedy other than an injunction apparently available, this was surely it. The court's majority said of the woman's remarks that "the evidence of their untruth is so overwhelming that one can only infer that the defendant's intent is purely malicious ... the suggestion is that the Constitution requires the plaintiffs to endure a continuing and utterly false attack upon their reputations without affording any relief whatsoever..... We cannot agree that the Constitution permits any such inverse condemnation of these valuable personal rights."[42]

The three dissenters from this decision argued that courts of equity lack the power to issue an injunction against defamatory matter, and it was this view that was later upheld by the supreme court of Pennsylvania.[43] That judgment seems more in line with the U.S. Supreme Court's only pronouncement on this subject in its landmark decision of 1931 in *Near v. Minnesota,* when the rule was laid down that prior restraints on communication are permissible only in the most exceptional cases and that the appropriate remedy for the defamation that was alleged in that instance was a libel action following publication, not a previous restraint upon publication.[44]

If the Pennsylvania Supreme Court was right in holding that even demonstrated falsehoods should not be enjoined, the only practical recourse these lawyers would have had would be to arrange for some kind of communication of their own designed to counteract the woman's charges or to undermine her credibility. Is that such a bad alternative? Since this was a continuing problem, there was ample opportunity to plan and implement a corrective campaign, thus conforming to Justice Brandeis's principle that if there is time to expose falsehood by further discussion "the remedy to be applied is more speech, not enforced silence." Granted, such a course of action would entail time, energy, and possibly some expense for the aggrieved parties. But that is also the case in countless other situations where individuals find themselves having to expend their resources dealing with the sick, malicious, or otherwise bizarre behavior of people they encounter in their everyday relationships—behavior for which the legal system provides no recourse. What about the teacher who is frequently diverted from his or her teaching responsibilities by the "problem student"? What about the co-workers of an individual who is an alcoholic or who has some other personal difficulty, temporary or permanent, that puts an unfair burden of work on everyone else in the group? What of the trouble we often have to go to in getting repairs made to our cars, homes, or personal belongings because someone else has carelessly or accidentally caused some damage? Why should we not view the picketing of the woman in the Pennsylvania case as a similar kind of nuisance, perhaps prompted by some sickness of mind, that must be dealt with through nonlitigative methods?

A reliance on countercommunication as the preferred remedy for defamation fails to deal adequately with those few situations in which there is not time for a reply, where the harm that is done by the defamatory remarks is immediate and irreparable. An example of such a circumstance would be the distribution of a leaflet on the eve of a local election falsely accusing one of the candidates of engaging in some kind of personal behavior that is unacceptable to most of the voters in that community. Before the libel can be exposed, the votes will have been cast and the defamed candidate defeated. One possible way of dealing with that kind of problem, in the spirit of "more speech" as the best answer to defamation, would be to invalidate the election and schedule a rerun. However, since one could never know for sure that the defamatory leaflets did, in fact, influence any voters and account for the results, it would be difficult to justify such a radical remedy, either as an expenditure of the taxpayers' money or in terms of its possible unfairness to the winner, who may have had nothing to do with the leaflet and may not have benefited at all from its circulation.

For cases of this unusual sort there would seem to be a need to continue to have available the possible deterrence and compensation that an unqualified right to sue for defamation might provide. This is not to suggest that the risk of being sued would necessarily deter the kind of defamation described in the election example, or that money damages could be adequate compensation for the loss of an election. But in this context, something would appear to be better than nothing.

I would want to draw exceedingly narrow limits on the possibilities for this kind of defamation action. A heavy burden should be placed upon the plaintiff to demonstrate that the injury done was indeed immediate and irreparable and left no possibility of correcting the situation by exposing with more speech the falsehood that was communicated.

Furthermore, with respect to this context as well as to situations where a request to reply has been denied and a defamation suit therefore allowable, I would propose, for reasons suggested earlier concerning the dubiousness of the dichotomy between public and private speech, that all persons, whether public officials, public figures, or private persons, should have to prove actual malice in order to win a judgment. This would eliminate the problem our courts have faced in the past several years of having to decide in each case whether the plaintiff is or is not a public figure, or whether the person did or did not voluntarily thrust himself or herself into the public eye. It would not matter, since everyone who sought damages for defamation would have to establish "actual malice."

Finally, I would redefine actual malice to mean only "knowing" or "calculated" falsehood, thus dropping the second half of the *New York Times v. Sullivan* formulation which included "reckless disregard" of whether a statement is false or not. This would substantially reduce the amount of mind reading that needs to be done by the trial judge or jury in defamation suits and would impose upon the plaintiff the burden of presenting hard evidence that the defendant knew the remarks to be false, not simply that he or she acted in reckless disregard of their truth or falsity. The latter standard allows far too much latitude of interpretation and seems to differ only in degree from the more traditional libel requirement of "negligence." How negligent or careless must one be to become reckless?

I believe that a careful reading of Justice Brennan's opinion for the Supreme Court in *Garrison v. Louisiana,* in which he elaborates on the rationale for the Court's *New York Times v. Sullivan* determination that statements made with actual malice are beyond First Amendment protection, lends support to my view that a distinction should be made between statements that are knowingly false and those that may have been made in reckless disregard of their possible falsity. The entire line of argument presented by the Court seems to be directed only to *deliberate* falsehoods, with the notion of recklessness merely slipped in without explanation:

> Although honest utterance, even if inaccurate, may further the fruitful exercise of the right of free speech, it does not follow that the lie, knowingly and deliberately published about a public official, should enjoy a like immunity. At the time the First Amendment was adopted, as today, there were those unscrupulous enough and skillful enough to use deliberate or reckless falsehood as an effective political tool to unseat the public servant or even topple an administration. That speech is used as a tool for political ends does not automatically bring it under the protective mantle of the Constitution. For the use of the known lie as a tool is at odds with the premises of democratic government and with the orderly manner in which economic, social, or political change is to be effected. Calculated falsehood falls into that class of utterances which "are no essential part of any exposition of ideas."[45]

Under the standard being proposed here, admittedly it would be extremely difficult to win a defamation suit. The paranoid-type personality, who believes the falsehoods uttered to be true, would be protected, as would the person for whom no evidence could be uncovered proving that individual's knowledge of the falsity of the remarks made. But that is how it should be. The dangers of a different course were well illustrated in a libel suit won by William Buckley, Jr., against Franklin H. Littell, a professor of religion at Temple University and the author of a book, *Wild Tongues,* published in 1969. In the course of the book's discussion of spokesmen of the "radical right," Littell was charged with having described Buckley as a "fellow traveler" of "fascism," and a journalist who used his writings to spread material from "openly fascist journals."

Littell also wrote, "Like Westbrook Pegler, who lied day after day in his column about Quentin Reynolds and goaded him into a lawsuit, Buckley could be taken to court by any one of several people who had money to hire competent legal counsel and nothing else to do."

A federal district court judge found these statements to be defamatory and to have been made with "actual malice," and he awarded Buckley one dollar in compensatory damages and $7,500 in punitive damages.[46] The U.S. Court of Appeals for the Second Circuit reversed this judgment with respect to the comments concerning fascism, finding them to be debatable matters of opinion rather than factually false statements. On the last matter, however, the appellate court upheld the finding that this was, indeed, a factually false statement and that it had been written with "actual malice." The evidence of "actual malice" relied upon by the courts was Littell's own testimony at the trial. The court of appeals opinion describes that testimony, and its own conclusions from it, as follows:

> While Littell suggested that he intended in the passage only to criticize Buckley's "goading, hounding, and excessive pursuit" of many people, particularly of certain church men and church women Littell had in mind, as well as of Martin Luther King and Robert Kennedy, he also testified that he equated Buckley's frequent literary attacks as "falling within the general category of lying." Although he testified that he did not remember the specifics of the Pegler libels and did not mean to make a direct analogy between Pegler's libels and Buckley, what is critical is that Littell knew, as is evident from the passage itself, that Pegler's lies had been proved (by Reynolds) to be libels. Littell must have known that when he directly compared Buckley's statements with those of a proven libeler, the clear meaning to be inferred was that he considered Buckley to be a libeler like Pegler.
> In response to Buckley's proof of the falsity of this accusation of libelous journalism, appellant's only rebutting proof of the truth of his charge was that Buckley had been sued in the past for libel; only one suit, however, had been successful, and that only by way of settlement. As we read Judge Griesa's findings, he found that Littell's statement that Buckley engaged in libelous journalism was made with knowledge of its falsity or in reckless disregard of its truth or falsity, and this is a finding based in part upon credibility and demeanor which we cannot go behind. In this connection we emphasize that Littell's testimony clearly indicated that he could recall no instances of Buckley's lies about people as matters of fact, and that the lies he had in mind were not really "precise detailed lies" but rather lies on "a theoretical level" involving, as the record makes clear, Buckley's political opinions.[47]

Because it had overturned the lower court on two of the three alleged libels in question, and because Littell was a man of modest means, the appellate court reduced the amount of damages from $7,500 to $1,000. The Supreme Court refused to review the case.[48]

Had actual malice been limited to deliberate, knowing, calculated falsehood, rather than including the rubbery "reckless disregard" phrase, it would have been much more difficult, if not impossible, to find Littell in violation of that standard. The grammatical structure of the sentence, "Like Westbrook Pegler, who lied day after day . . ." is certainly such as to leave open the possibility that Littell was not knowingly and literally accusing Buckley of being a proven libeler. Furthermore, his testimony as well as his entire career are more suggestive of a sincere, if perhaps careless, crusader than of a deliberate liar. For such persons to be subjected to the tribulations of a trial and a damage judgment vividly demonstrates what is wrong, not only with the "actual malice" test as it now stands but with the law of defamation itself as a departure from the principles of a free society. Let us limit its use, narrowed as has been suggested above, to emergency situations where the democratic process does not have time to function or where those accused of defamation would rather take their chances in a lawsuit than assume responsibility for providing the channel for a reply. In that way we will place greater trust in the ultimate good sense of the public to distinguish the true from the false rather than relying so heavily on our courts to make that determination for us.

4

Invasion of Privacy

The idea that the law should provide remedies for defamatory speech originated very early in the history of our legal system. In contrast, the belief that there should be restraints on communications that invade the privacy of others is of far more recent vintage. Although similar in the concern that talking about other people can do them damage, a suit for defamation seeks to remedy an injury to the reputation of an individual *in the eyes of others,* whereas an action for invasion of privacy asks redress for an injury only to the *feelings or the peace of mind of the one who is talked about.*[1] To be sure, the two are closely related, for the disturbance to one's peace of mind that may follow from the public exposure of private information must, in fact, be due to that individual's concern about the reaction of others.[2] The difference is that defamatory remarks do the kind of damage to one's image which leads to tangible harms, whereas communication that invades one's privacy may have no consequence beyond its being felt to be presumptuous, intrusive, or embarrassing by the target individual.

What will be considered presumptuous, intrusive, or embarrassing by an individual depends in large measure on the value which the person's culture places on privacy, and that is a highly variable phenomenon. Not only do primitive cultures tend to have far less concern than modern industrialized societies about individual privacy in general but the specific kinds of behavior that are thought to require seclusion differ widely from culture to culture. Alan Westin has noted that

> the openness with which people in most nonliterate societies engage in evacuation makes this a "public" affair in contrast to modern norms in a society like the United States. Similarly, the individual's moments of birth, illness, and death are considered taboo and are secluded from general view in many societies, but as some people conduct these affairs in casual view, they cannot be considered universal matters of privacy.
>
> Needs for privacy do appear in the intimacy of sexual relations. . . : Only in a few cultures, such as the Formosan and among Yap natives of the Pacific, is the sexual act performed openly in public.[3]

Although Francis Beytagh was certainly correct in asserting that privacy is far more than a "trivial, middle class value,"[4] it is surely far less than a universal constant.

Given the fact that the desire for privacy seems to intensify as a society becomes more advanced technologically, it is understandable that the movement to secure protection against unwanted publicity would be relatively late in arriving on the legal scene. It was not until 1890 that the publication in the United States of two significant essays gave impetus to that movement. An article in *Scribner's* magazine written by the editor of the *New York Evening Post* described a growing tension between the urge for privacy and the increased tendency of the press to cater to the public's curiosity about other people's affairs.[5] In December of that same year the *Harvard Law Review* published an article by Samuel D. Warren and Louis D. Brandeis,[6] that, in the words of John H. F. Shattuck, "launched a new legal concept which eventually broadened into a principle of information privacy."[7] Westin has summarized that development:

> Over the next sixty years a majority of the states (including four by legislation) adopted the common-law principle of an individual right of privacy. Nearly 300 right-to-privacy cases were decided between 1890 and 1950 (and these were only the cases that produced appellate rulings). In addition, there was a remarkable outpouring of law-review articles, text discussions, and press coverage of the common-law right-of-privacy issue in these decades.[8]

The most authoritative law review article on the subject was written by the dean of the University of California Law School, William Prosser, and appeared in 1960.[9] Dean Prosser's review of the cases led him to conclude that the common-law wrong of invasion of privacy "is not one tort, but a complex of four."[10] By following the Prosser analysis we can better understand and assess the weight of the privacy interests that sometimes come in conflict with unrestrained speech and press.

The first of Prosser's four categories consists of what he called "Intrusion" cases, where material that may later be published is gathered by peeping or taking pictures through a window, bugging a room, wiretapping a telephone, or other surreptitious techniques that are akin to trespass but do not necessarily involve actual physical entry into a person's private domains. As Prosser describes it, "[T]his branch of the tort . . . has been used chiefly to fill in the gaps left by trespass, nuisance, the intentional infliction of emotional distress."[11] Just as the Fourth Amendment provides a constitutional safeguard against unreasonable searches and seizures by *government* authorities of "persons, houses, papers, and effects," this common-law tort offers a remedy for unwelcome intrusions on privacy *by our fellow citizens* that seems indisputably fair and reasonable.

A second category is labeled "Appropriation," and includes cases in which a person's name or likeness is "appropriated" by someone else for monetary gain. The most common instances are those in which the name or picture of a prominent or photogenic individual is used, without that person's consent, in the advertising of a commercial product. As early as 1903 the New York legislature, reacting against a decision the previous year by that state's highest court which had denied common-law relief to an individual whose picture had been appropriated to advertise a product,[12] passed a law providing protection against such communication. Two years later the supreme court of Georgia ruled in favor of the plaintiff in a common-law action against appropriation,[13] and thereafter many courts across the country followed the Georgia precedent. Today, either in common law or by virtue of state statute, it is generally accepted that one has a legal remedy if another presumes to use one's name or picture, without consent, for personal gain.

Although the unwanted association of one's image with a commercial product may cause psychological distress, the primary interest protected in these kinds of cases, as Prosser well states it, "is not so much a mental as a proprietary one."[14] What is really involved here is a theft of symbolic property, not unlike the reproduction and sale, without permission or payment of royalties, of a book, play, or film covered by a copyright.[15] To use another's name or picture without consent to promote the sale of a product or service is essentially no different. We have said earlier that the context in which purely symbolic activity takes place may provide justification for restrictions on that activity. Surely stealing for personal profit, albeit only of images, is such a justification.

Accepting the general proposition that "appropriation" can be restrained without violating the First Amendment does not answer a number of closely related questions that are somewhat more complex. What if the name "appropriated" is John Smith and thus not clearly a referent to any single individual (unless in a small community where there is only one John Smith)? Since that particular name belongs to so many, no one can claim an exclusive proprietary interest in it, and an invasion of privacy suit for its use would make no sense.

What if the name *is* unique, and clearly identified with a prominent individual, but a devoted admirer decides to adopt it as his or her own? Is that legally actionable? In the absence of any evidence that such a change of name is undertaken with a profit motive, courts would not and should not treat such behavior as an invasion of privacy. If monetary gain were involved it would pose a much closer question and one that might, with sufficient proof, be legitimately answered in the same way as a simpler case of appropriation. The key would be whether or not we were dealing with what was essentially a matter of theft.[16]

That same key can and should provide the answer to several other kinds of problems. Prominent persons who take public positions on political or social issues are not having anything stolen from them if supporters of those positions use their names or pictures, even without their consent, to help promote their causes. By the same token, opponents should be free, if they wish, to use those same names and pictures in an unfavorable context. Thus a Rhode Island law allowing damage actions for the use of a person's name in a newspaper advertisement without consent, as interpreted to require the *Providence Journal* to refuse to print an ad critical of Jimmy Carter without his consent, was clearly incompatible with the First Amendment.[17]

What about the publication of an unauthorized biography of an individual of public interest? Here there may indeed be a profit motive on the part of the author and publisher that makes it look like a simple case of appropriation, but now a new element enters the picture. Where there is a public interest in the subject of the book, can that book be restrained because the person about whom it has been written does not want it circulated? Such a case was that of a prominent baseball player, Warren Spahn, who sought injunctive relief and damages in the New York courts against an unauthorized and partly fictionalized biography.[18] It was only the fact that the book contained false statements about him that saved Spahn's case from total failure, and we will come to that issue when we discuss Prosser's third category, the so-called false light invasion-of-privacy cases. But insofar as a publication contains true statements about a newsworthy public figure, the courts in this and similar cases have been unwilling to allow limitations to be imposed.[19] Thus, the weight that has been assigned to the First Amendment right of the public to be informed about newsworthy people (even if the communicator makes a profit in the process), as against the competing interests of the public figure whose privacy has been "appropriated," seems to be correct.

Finally, there is the circumstance in which public communication about a newsworthy event comes seriously into conflict with substantial economic interests of the individuals involved in that event. When an Ohio television station, in 1972, broadcast as part of its news coverage a fifteen-second film showing the entire performance of Hugo Zacchini's "human cannonball" act at the Geauga County Fair, Zacchini sued for damages, alleging an unlawful appropriation of his "right of publicity." The supreme court of Ohio rejected his claim, holding that under the First and Fourteenth Amendments a "TV station has a privilege to report in its newscasts matters of legitimate public interest which would otherwise be protected by an individual's right of publicity, unless the actual intent of the TV station was to appropriate the benefit of the publicity for some nonprivileged private use, or unless the actual intent was to injure that individual."[20]

In June of 1977 the U.S. Supreme Court, by a 5–4 vote, reversed that decision. Said the majority:

> Wherever the line in particular situations is to be drawn between media reports that are protected and those that are not, we are quite sure that the First and Fourteenth Amendments do not immunize the media when they broadcast a performer's entire act without his consent. The Constitution no more prevents a State from requiring respondent to compensate petitioner for broadcasting his act on television than it would privilege respondent to film and broadcast a copyrighted dramatic work without liability to the copyright owner.... The broadcast of a film of petitioner's entire act poses a substantial threat to the economic value of that performance.... Much of its economic value lies in the "right of exclusive control over the publicity given to his performance"; if the public can see the act for free on television, they will be less willing to pay to see it at the fair.[21]

Justice Lewis Powell, speaking for three of the dissenters, argued:

> I do not view respondent's actions as comparable to unauthorized commercial broadcasts of sporting events, theatrical performances, and the like where the broadcaster keeps the profits. There is no suggestion here that respondent made any such use of the film. Instead, it simply reported on what petitioner concedes to be a newsworthy event, in a way hardly surprising for a television station—by means of film coverage. The report was part of an ordinary daily news program, consuming a total of 15 seconds. It is a routine example of the press fulfilling the informing function so vital to our system.... In my view the First Amendment commands a different analytical starting point from the one selected by the Court. Rather than begin with a quantitative analysis of the performer's behavior—is this or is this not his entire act?—we should direct initial attention to the actions of the news media: what use did the station make of the film footage? When a film is used, as here, for a routine portion of a regular news program, I would hold that the First Amendment protects the station from a "right of publicity" or "appropriation" suit, absent a strong showing by the plaintiff that the news broadcast was a subterfuge or cover for private or commercial exploitation.[22]

Admittedly this is a difficult case. Ordinarily there would be no question that a fifteen-second film would constitute legitimate coverage of any news event. But the fact that such coverage in this particular instance exposed Zacchini's entire performance to free public view did give him grounds to feel aggrieved. Yet if we keep the concept of *theft* at the center of our attention, it would appear that the Ohio Supreme Court and the U.S. Supreme Court dissenters were right in holding that the television station was not engaged here in an unlawful appropriation of another's property. It was not the broadcaster's purpose to make a profit at Zacchini's expense by "stealing his act." Indeed, it is conceivable, as the U.S. Supreme Court majority conceded in a footnote to its opinion, that the news broadcast could have had the effect of increasing "the value of the petitioner's performance by stimulating the public's interest in seeing the act live,"[23] in which case the Court said that damages would not be justified. Where such contradictory results are possible, and where the communicator is fulfilling the function of informing the public on matters in which it has an interest, the privacy claims of the person who has been publicized must simply be subordinated to freedom of expression. What we have in the Zacchini case, as in many other such instances, is an unfortunate victim of unwanted publicity who must pay a perhaps unfair share of the price of preserving the First Amendment for all of us.

We have already alluded to the third of Prosser's invasion-of-privacy categories, in which a plaintiff claims to have been disturbed by public communication that has placed that person in a "false light." Such cases are similar to defamation actions in that they hinge on the communication's being false. The difference, if there is one, is that for a defamation suit to be viable there must be clear damage to one's reputation in the eyes of others, whereas it may suffice for the purposes of false-light invasion of privacy that the individual has experienced mental distress.[24] Despite this possible distinction, the U.S. Supreme Court has decided that the same First Amendment principles which govern libel cases shall also be applied to false-light privacy actions, at least where newsworthy persons or events are concerned. In two such false-light cases that have been decided by the Supreme Court, the ruling has been that in order to succeed a false light invasion-of-privacy suit involving communication about newsworthy subjects must establish "actual malice" on the part of the communicator, just as in cases of alleged libel of public officials and public figures.[25]

Melville Nimmer has been sharply critical of the first of these two decisions, *Time v. Hill*.[26] The second case, *Cantrell v. Forest City Publishing Company*, was not decided until six years after the publication of his essay. Nimmer's critique of the *Time* decision was that, since false-light invasions of privacy are not necessarily reputation damaging, it is inappropriate to use the same standards of judgment that apply to libel. He argues that false-light cases should be dealt with in the same way as Prosser's *fourth* category of invasions of privacy—the public exposure of embarrassing, though truthful, private facts—since the same interest, redress for injury to feelings, is involved.

Nimmer believes *Time v. Hill* to be an excellent illustration of his point. The Hill family had been held hostage in their home by three escaped convicts, and the incident was widely reported in the press at the time. A fictionalized account of their experience later became the story line for a book *The Desperate Hours*, followed with a Broadway play by the same . name and author. An article in *Life* magazine about the play, illustrated with photographs of some of the scenes taken at the former Hill home (from which the family had moved to escape continued publicity), indicated that the story had been "inspired by the family's experience." However, the book, play, and magazine photographs depicted the Hills as having been brutalized by the convicts and having resisted their attacks when, in reality, they had been treated courteously and there had been no violence. The Hills sued Time, Inc., owners of *Life* magazine, for invading their privacy, reviving a painful episode, and causing them severe emotional distress. It was in response to this suit that the Supreme Court ruled that the publisher could be held liable only if proven to have published the material knowing it to be false or with reckless disregard for its truth or falsity.

Nimmer comments:

> The Hill family was indeed depicted in a false light, and in such a manner that a trier of fact might well find it to be offensive to persons of "ordinary sensibilities." But surely nothing in such depiction was injurious to the reputation of any of the Hill family. A report of brutal treatment at the hand of criminals is hardly calculated to hold the victims up to public contempt, ridicule, and obloquy. It is submitted, then, that the Court in *Time* was wrong in applying to false light privacy cases in general, and to the particular case before it, a rule which can be justified only when the particular false light case contains defamatory elements.[27]

The facts of *Time v. Hill* do, indeed, lend support to Nimmer's argument. The circumstances of *Cantrell v. Forest City Publishing Company*, however, do not. In that case, the *Cleveland Plain Dealer* printed a story, with photographs, about the life situation of the Cantrell family five months after Mr. Cantrell had been killed in the collapse of a bridge over the Ohio River. The story, which portrayed the family as living in abject poverty and Mrs. Cantrell as unwilling to talk with a reporter about their conditions, contained a number of admitted inaccuracies and false statements, not the least of which was the fact that Mrs. Cantrell was not even at home when the reporter made his visit. The newspaper was sued for false-light invasion of privacy, making the Cantrells "the objects of pity and ridicule" and "causing them to suffer outrage, mental distress, shame, and humiliation."[28] The trial court, using the standard of "actual malice" called for by *Time v. Hill*, found in favor of the plaintiffs, and the U.S. Supreme Court affirmed that judgment.

Although the injury claimed by the Cantrells was to their own feelings, their discomfort was obviously based on the assumption that others would hold them in lower regard as a result of the *Plain Dealer* story. Thus, it is difficult to see how the case would be any different in principle if they had sued for libel. With respect to this kind of an example, it would seem that Nimmer's criticism of the Supreme Court for treating false-light privacy cases and libel cases alike is not well-founded.

What we seem to have in the false-light privacy area are two rather different sorts of problems. In those instances, like *Time v. Hill*, where placing people in a false light does not damage their reputation but nevertheless causes them psychological distress, I agree with Nimmer that whatever legal policy is adopted for the public exposure of embarrassing private *and truthful* facts should apply to such false-light cases as well. Otherwise, as Nimmer points out, the law may be in the "absurd" position of allowing punishment under Prosser's fourth branch of invasion of privacy for the publication of true statements, and not allowing punishment if statements on the same topic are false but actual malice cannot be proven.[29] Since embarrassment is what is at stake in both instances, it would not seem to matter whether that emotional state has been brought about by true or false communication.

On the other hand, in those false-light situations like *Cantrell*, where the emotional distress is clearly the result of damage to reputation, and the suit is for redress of that damage, it would appear that Nimmer is wrong and the Supreme Court right in wanting to treat false light in the same way as libel. Indeed, I see no need or justification for *any* privacy actions in such circumstances. Everything that has been said in the previous chapter about defamation should be applicable in these cases.

We come now to the fourth, and most difficult, of the Prosser categories—the public exposure of embarrassing, but truthful, private facts. The greatest problem with such cases is in finding guiding principles for distinguishing between information in which others have a legitimate interest and that which an individual should have a right to keep undisclosed. A second problem, assuming there are some kinds of subjects that ought not be discussed in public, is in determining what, if any, legal remedies for such invasions of privacy should be available. Unlike defamation cases, a right to reply would be of no use whatsoever, since whatever harm may be done occurs the moment exposure takes place. Even an award of damages after the fact may be small consolation to a person whose privacy has been invaded, although the availability of that kind of legal remedy may serve as a deterrent to would-be violators of other people's privacy. Finally, there is the possibility, in some instances, of injunctive relief against the public communication of private information where it becomes known in advance that such communication is about to take place or where the further circulation of material that has already been released may be stopped. Injunctions, of course, are fraught with more serious implications than civil damage actions, both because they involve the much-to-be-feared prior restraint of communication and because they invoke the criminal contempt powers of the courts.

As of this writing, the U.S. Supreme Court had not yet had occasion to confront this fourth category of cases, although a footnote to its *Time v. Hill* opinion suggests its approval of two standards that have been used in lower court decisions. One of these is that truthful accounts of *newsworthy* persons and events are protected by the First Amendment even though they may intrude on privacy. The other is that the First Amendment does *not* give license to revelations about people that "may be so intimate and so unwarranted in view of the victim's position as to outrage the community's notions of decency."[30]

Each of these standards raises as many questions as it answers. What is "newsworthy" and who decides? What is "outrageous" to a "community's notions of decency"? Lower courts have struggled with these issues in a variety of circumstances, and their responses have been less than consistent or definitive.

The most common cases in which these questions have arisen have been the publication of the names of rape victims in news stories about those events. There is no dispute as to the right and responsibility of the press to report the fact that a rape has occurred. But is the name of the victim a necessary or relevant part of such a news story? In the earlier part of this century, four state legislatures decided that it was not and adopted prohibitions against the publication of that information.[31] There have also been a number of common law invasion-of-privacy suits in state courts over the years for publication of a rape victim's name.

One of the factors that has complicated some of these cases is that the information communicated by the press was obtained from court records to which any citizen may have access. How can the news media be prevented from circulating that information, or punished for doing so, when it is already a matter of public record? In 1975 the U.S. Supreme Court said that they may not be thus restrained. The case involved a television news broadcast by a Georgia station which reported the name of a seventeen-year-old girl who had been raped and who died as a result of the attack. Her father sued the station for invasion of the family's privacy, and the Georgia courts rejected the broadcaster's claim that the communication was protected speech. The Supreme Court reversed that judgment, holding that "the First and Fourteenth Amendments command nothing less than that the States may not impose sanctions for the publication of truthful information contained in official court records open to public inspection."[32]

This decision in the Georgia case clearly, and I believe correctly, settled the issue of publicizing a rape victim's name, or any other information that might be viewed as an invasion of privacy, *if* it has been secured from open public records. It left unresolved by the Supreme Court the question of publicizing that kind of information when it has not been so obtained. Indeed, just three days prior to the Court's *Cox Broadcasting* decision, a District of Columbia judge reaffirmed a ruling he had made the previous year that the *Washington Post* did not have a constitutional right to print the name and address of a Maryland woman who had survived a rape and stabbing.[33] In this instance the name had not appeared on any publicly available police report or court document but had been secured from private sources. It was the judge's view that the plaintiff's identification was not newsworthy and that the public's interest in the story could have been satisfied adequately without the inclusion of her name and address.

A judgment that the victim's name is not a necessary element of a news story about a rape seems plausible on its face, yet it must be recognized as a proposition that depends on one's perspective and on the circumstances of particular cases. Marc Franklin, for example, has drawn a distinction between instances where "names add only a name" and those which he has labeled "name-crucial" situations.[34] An illustration of the latter which he describes is an incident in which a rape suspect, being held in jail pending trial, suffers severe injuries which his jailers claim to be the result of a fall down a flight of stairs. In such an instance it surely would be important for the public to know that the victim of the alleged rapist was the sheriff's daughter.

How can we be certain in almost any case that knowledge of the name of a rape victim might not be of critical value to somebody? That possibility must be weighed in the balance against the alleged values of nondisclosure. Franklin has noted some of these. He points out that a primary motive for suppression of rape victims' names is what he calls the "gallantry justification"—presumably resulting from an attitude in our culture that a woman who has been raped has been disgraced. He suggests it is no accident that the first three states in this country to adopt legislation prohibiting publication of the names of rape victims were all in the Deep South, where white women who had been raped by black men would be perceived as especially tainted.

The notion that it is a disgrace to have been raped provides the basis, also, for what Franklin calls the "law enforcement justification" for nondisclosure of rape victims' names. The theory here is that women who have been the victims of rape will not come forward to lodge a complaint with law enforcement officials unless they feel assured that their names will not be revealed publicly.

Neither the "gallantry justification" nor the "law enforcement justification" would carry any weight, of course, if our culture had a more enlightened attitude toward the victims of rape. We certainly do not regard it as shameful to be the target of any other kind of physical assault, and personally knowing people who have been attacked may produce a livelier concern about the problems of crime. It is also quite possible that the hush-hush sentiment which now prevails about the names of rape victims is itself a large contributor to the stigma attached to those victims, and that less secretive treatment of the topic would help to bring about a more understanding cultural norm.

What is more, a poll of newspaper editors taken by Marc Franklin suggests that prohibitions on the media against disclosure of the names of rape victims may be ineffective in accomplishing their purpose. If a community is small enough for most people who read the name in the paper or hear it on radio or television to know and have contact with the victim, it is likely that the information will spread by word of mouth anyhow. In a large community the name would be meaningless to most people who are exposed to it, unless it is that of a person or family of prominence, in which case we would be involved with what might fairly be considered a "name-crucial" situation.

Another context in which the issue of public exposure of embarrassing private facts has arisen, and in which the questions of newsworthiness and outrage to a community's notions of decency have been considered, is the situation in which an individual leading a respectable life in a community is suddenly exposed as having been involved in unsavory or illegal activities many years before. One of the early leading invasion-of-privacy cases, *Melvin v. Reid,*[35] was of this sort. It involved a former prostitute who had established a new life and was then confronted with a public exposure of her earlier activities. The California courts found in her favor when she sued for an invasion of her privacy.

Four decades after *Melvin v. Reid,* the California courts had another such case on their docket. This time a story in the *Reader's Digest* on the subject of truck hijacking related an incident that had occurred eleven years previously and mentioned the name of an individual who had been criminally involved. That person had since been rehabilitated, and his eleven-year-old daughter and a friend of hers learned for the first time about the father's past from this article. He claimed that he was "scorned and abandoned" as a result of the disclosure, and he brought an invasion of privacy suit against the magazine. Although conceding that the article dealt with a newsworthy topic, a unanimous California Supreme Court, relying heavily on the *Melvin v. Reid* precedent, found that the use of the man's name was of "minimum social value" and that a jury could properly find that particular item not to be newsworthy.[36] Invoking the community's-notion-of-decency concept, the court also commented that "revealing one's criminal past for all to see is grossly offensive to most people in America,"[37] and sent the case back to the trial court to determine whether the magazine had acted with "reckless disregard for the fact that reasonable men would find the invasion highly offensive."[38]

These two California decisions stand in sharp contrast to a 1940 United States Circuit Court of Appeals opinion in a case involving a *New Yorker* magazine article about a man who had been a widely publicized prodigy as a child. After having been the subject of national attention for his youthful genius, this individual chose to go into obscurity, where he led an exceptionally mundane life which was interrupted only by the *New Yorker*'s story of the child prodigy revisited. Despite the fact that the unwelcome publicity may have played a role in precipitating his early death, the court held that the subject matter of the magazine article was a matter of legitimate public interest and thus was not punishable as an invasion of privacy.[39]

Dean Prosser has written of this case that when it "is compared with *Melvin v. Reid* . . . what emerges is something in the nature of a 'mores' test, by which there will be liability only for publicity given to those things which the customs and ordinary views of the community will not tolerate."[40] Having wisely made that observation, Prosser appears to be undisturbed by the arbitrary nature of such a "mores" test. Explaining, and apparently defending, that kind of standard he writes:

> The ordinary reasonable man does not take offense at mention in a newspaper of the fact that he has returned from a visit, or gone camping in the woods, or that he has given a party at his house for his friends. . . . The law of privacy is not intended for any shrinking soul who is abnormally sensitive about such publicity. It is quite a different matter when the details of sexual relations are spread before the public gaze, or there is highly personal portrayal of his intimate characteristics or conduct.[41]

How Prosser makes the decision that it is all right for the world to know that we have gone camping in the woods but not that we have been sleeping around is as puzzling to me as it is for one court to decide that the *New Yorker* may deprive a man of his chosen obscurity because he was once a well-known child prodigy, but for another court to decide that the *Reader's Digest* may not identify a man who hijacked a truck eleven years earlier. Such are the vagaries of a community's notions of decency.

One last instance that well illustrates the difficulty—I would say the impossibility—of anyone fairly determining for everybody else what is or is not newsworthy, or what does or does not offend reasonable sensibilities, is the case of Oliver Sipple. Sipple is the ex-marine who knocked a gun out of the hands of a would-be assassin of then President Gerald Ford when he was on a visit to California. Shortly after the event, it was revealed in some of the news media that Sipple was an active member of the San Francisco gay community, a fact that had not been known to members of his family, who thereupon broke off communication with him. He then sued for invasion of his privacy.

Was Sipple's homosexuality a fact that was relevant to the news of his having possibly saved the life of the president of the United States? He obviously thought not, as did those who suggested that the news media would not have made a point of his being heterosexual if that had been the case. On the other hand, there were members of the gay community who found relevance and value in this news report, for it publicized the idea that a homosexual can be a hero just like anybody else. Reasonable people may differ over whether the journalists who first broke the story of Sipple's homosexuality used good judgment in so doing, but it does not seem to be an appropriate question for adjudication by our legal system. That view was apparently shared by San Francisco County Court Judge Ira Brown, who dismissed the case without opinion after it had been in litigation for five years.[42]

One answer which has been proposed for this problem unintentionally demonstrates for me its essential insolubility. In an article jointly authored by an assistant county attorney in Polk County, Iowa, and an assistant attorney general of the same state, it is suggested that "a community standard analogous to that applied by the courts in obscenity cases should be adopted.... under community standards determined by juries, publicity may be so offensive and indecent as to have no legitimate news, information, or entertainment value to the public."[43]

If the best we can do in finding a principle for the privacy area is to borrow from the hopeless morass of obscenity law its single most confusing standard, we are better off abandoning the effort altogether.[44]

Objection is sometimes made to this position because it seems passively to accept the proposition that the press can "convert something into a matter of public interest simply by writing about it."[45] A contrary view, expressed by Prosser in discussing the limited privacy rights of public figures, is that "public stature must already exist before there can be any [press] privilege arising out of it ... by directing attention to one who is obscure and unknown, [a publisher] cannot himself create a public figure."[46]

It seems to me to be both right and wrong, depending on the interpretation one puts on the statements, to say that the press can "convert something into a matter of public interest simply by writing about it" or can create a public figure "by directing attention to one who is obscure and unknown." It is right in the sense that events which might otherwise not receive attention from anyone, and would thus remain private, do enter the public domain simply by virtue of being reported in the media of communication. It is wrong if taken to mean that public *interest* necessarily follows from the mere reporting of an event. That will depend upon whether anybody who reads or hears the report finds it newsworthy. Although the public's appetite for gossip, as well as for significant news, may be large it is certainly not infinite, and there are surely times when journalists make bad guesses as to what will interest their readers and hearers. When that happens they will have failed to "convert something into a matter of public interest simply by writing about it" or to create a public figure by "directing attention to one who is obscure and unknown." If they succeed, it is because they have struck a responsive chord in at least a part of their audience, in which case it is not they alone who have made the information newsworthy. Newsworthiness is thus the product of an interaction between speaker and listener, writer and reader.[47] What is more, newsworthiness exists or does not exist regardless of whether a third-party judge of an event believes that it *merits* public interest. According to Emerson, Haber, and Dorsen, our judicial system has acknowledged this reality: "The courts today . . . tend to permit coverage of anything that is considered news. While definitions of news differ, the general tendency is to treat as news any matter that is of interest to the general public rather than merely what ought to be of interest."[48]

What I have argued thus far is that if restraints are to be imposed on the public exposure of embarrassing private facts it should not be done on the basis of the necessarily subjective opinion of a judge or jury that the revelation is not newsworthy or that it outrages a community's sense of decency. Are there, then, any other defensible grounds for restricting such communication? It was suggested earlier, in connection with the issue of "appropriation," that a helpful concept in drawing the line between permissible and prohibited activity is that of theft—taking and using symbols or information for personal gain. This notion of stolen goods may also provide a key to the resolution of many troublesome public-exposure-of-embarrassing-private-facts cases.

Many of the instances in which invasion-of-privacy suits have been brought are situations where the information that has been disclosed was obtained from the individual in question on the basis of an explicit pledge of confidentiality or a presumption that the subject's consent

would be required before any public communication took place. Since
the material would not have been provided in the first place had there
not been that kind of pledge or expectation of confidentiality, its exposure without consent, whether for monetary gain or not, is the same as
the taking and using of stolen goods. In such cases it seems to me that the
only problem for a court should be in deciding whether a confidence has
indeed been violated or whether private symbolic materials (e.g., photographs in nonpublic places) have, in fact, been taken without consent. If
they have, then legal redress is warranted. The opposite side of that coin
is that if consent *has* been given, no remedy should be available. The
latter is, indeed, the present state of the law as Prosser has described it:
"Chief among the available defenses [against an invasion-of-privacy
charge] is that of the plaintiff's consent to the invasion, which will bar his
recovery as in the case of any other tort."[49]

A few concrete cases will illustrate the difficulties that a court may have
in applying these principles.

In December 1974 a movie entitled *Hearts and Minds* was released by
its producers, Peter Davis and Bert Schneider. It was a documentary
about this country's involvement in the Vietnam War and included some
rather uncomplimentary segments of an interview with Walt Rostow,
who had been a top foreign policy advisor to the Kennedy and Johnson
administrations. In April 1974 Rostow was sent copies of the interview
clips that were to be a part of the film. He objected to some of them on
the ground that they misrepresented his views and contained remarks
that had been off the record. The filmmakers decided to include these
segments despite Rostow's objections, maintaining that they had not
agreed to give him veto power—a claim disputed by Rostow. Rostow
then sought a state court injunction against release of the movie, claiming an invasion of his privacy and a breach of the agreement he had
made with the filmmakers. Davis responded that their agreement had
not been breached and that the proper remedy for an invasion of privacy, if there was one, would be a suit for damages after release of the
film and not a prior restraint on freedom of speech.

An injunction was at first denied, then granted, then lifted again after
three weeks had passed. Rostow thereupon sued for invasion of privacy,
defamation, and breach of contract, and asked for another injunction
against further showing of the film. In May 1975 a California Superior
Court judge denied a motion by Davis to dismiss the suit, asserting that
"fairness demands that a person who submits himself to an interview for
a commercial venture as opposed to a news interview can dictate legitimate conditions to the use of such interview so he is not unfairly depicted" and that Rostow "had a right to express himself under conditions
or not to express himself" at all.[50] Attorneys for the two sides then

entered into negotiations which resulted in an out-of-court settlement. Although the terms of the agreement were confidential, the filmmakers said that no concessions on First Amendment issues had been made and that no limitations had been imposed on further distribution of the film.[51] One may infer that some kind of payment for damages was probably made.

The uncertainty as to whether there was an original understanding between Rostow and Davis concerning veto rights is, in my judgment, the only thing that makes this a difficult case. Whether Rostow had any legitimate rights in the matter hinges, I believe, on the resolution of that question. If Rostow granted the interview only on condition that he have the final say over what segments were to be used, *and if that condition was accepted by the interviewers,* what followed could be dealt with as a clear breach of contract, if not as an invasion of privacy. If no such condition was made, then the filmmakers had the right to use whatever they wished, and I do not believe it would have mattered whether the film was a "commercial venture," as the judge seemed to think, or a "news interview." Having seen *Hearts and Minds,* I would find it impossible to label it simply a "commercial venture" as distinguished from a series of "news" interviews and scenes. It was a powerful ideological statement about the Vietnam War, and whether making money was an additional motive of the producers seems to me, in this context, to be irrelevant for First Amendment purposes.

Let us postpone until after we have reviewed the next case the more difficult question of whether an injunction, as opposed to monetary damages, is an appropriate remedy when a confidence is violated. An instance in which that was a central issue was *Doe v. Roe,* involving publication of a book of psychiatric case histories that was enjoined from sale and distribution because a patient whose problems constituted a large portion of the volume claimed that the disguise of her identity was insufficient to prevent readers of the book who knew her from learning information of an intimate and embarrassing nature.[52]

Two undisputed premises underlie any consideration of this or like cases. The first is that the relationship between a patient and doctor, as between a client and lawyer, is confidential and privileged communication that may not be divulged without consent. The other is that psychiatric case histories are a vital part of scientific literature and that it is accepted practice to publish such data so long as the identity of patients is disguised. In *Doe v. Roe,* despite a factual finding of the New York trial court that the identity of the patient was sufficiently disguised to accord with the standards of the psychiatric profession in writing case histories, that court issued an order limiting distribution of the book solely to scientific channels. An appellate court then expanded the injunction to ban *all* distribution of the book. New York's highest court affirmed that decision, and the U.S. Supreme Court, after first granting review, ultimately decided that its writ of certiorari had been "improvidently granted" and dismissed the appeal.[53]

If, in fact, the patient's identity in this book was so disguised as to make her unrecognizable to people who knew her, there would appear to be no justification for the injunction that was issued or for any other kind of legal remedy. If, as she claimed, that was not the case, then I would regard the publication as a serious breach of patient-doctor confidentiality and would see no good reason to limit her remedies to after-the-fact damages when the harm would already have been done. Thus I would disagree with the position taken in the amicus brief of the American Civil Liberties Union in the case, expressed as follows:

> While privacy interests are critical, and indisputably in need of protection, prior restraint is not the appropriate vehicle. . . . Privacy rights should be vindicated by civil post-publication remedies appropriately limited by doctrines such as that in *New York Times Co. v. Sullivan* and *Time, Inc. v. Hill,* or by law suits designed directly to protect the right to privacy without unduly restricting the public flow of information. . . . Prior restraints are particularly odious and inappropriate in cases such as these, since they effectively create a criminal penalty where, in the absence of court interference, only a civil penalty is envisioned.[54]

One wonders if such unqualified language would have been written if the psychiatric case history in question had been headed with the actual name and address of the patient.

A third, and uncommonly complex case of this genre, was *Commonwealth v. Wiseman.*[55] Frederick Wiseman is a filmmaker who had produced a potent documentary entitled *Titicut Follies,* showing sordid conditions at the Bridgewater, Massachusetts, state hospital and prison for the criminally insane—conditions which were improved after the film received considerable attention, including first prize as the best documentary at the Mannheim Film Festival in 1967. State officials, professing concern for the privacy rights of recognizable inmates in "naked or embarrassing situations,"[56] but perhaps also concerned about protecting themselves from embarrassment, sought an injunction against further showing of the film. The trial court ordered that exhibitions of the film be limited to audiences consisting of "legislators, judges, lawyers, sociologists, social workers, doctors, psychiatrists, students in these or related fields, and organizations dealing with the social problems of custodial care and mental infirmity."[57] The supreme judicial court of Massachusetts added a requirement that when the film was shown even to those audiences it must include "a brief explanation that changes and improvements have taken place in the institution since 1966."[58] The U.S. Supreme Court refused to review the case, with Justices Douglas, Harlan, and Brennan dissenting from that decision.[59]

Key issues in the *Titicut Follies* litigation—properly so in view of the criteria suggested in this chapter—were whether mental hospital and prison inmates in a state facility have a right not to have their pictures taken for public display without their consent; whether they are competent to give that consent; and, if they are not, whether the state has a right to act on their behalf. In this particular instance, Wiseman had of course been permitted by Bridgewater officials to come into the institution in the first place, and he refrained from filming any inmate who communicated a protest. He also obtained releases in writing from *some* of the inmates who appeared in the film, and none of the others whose pictures were taken expressed any objection.

The state's supreme judicial court questioned the legitimacy of the written releases Wiseman had secured on the ground that they would be valid only if "the inmate ... had seen the film and fully understood how he was to be portrayed."[60] In the absence of a valid consent from *every* individual portrayed in the film, the court believed an injunction to be in order. Curiously, in view of that line of reasoning, the court also ruled that, since all or nearly all of Bridgewater's inmates were presumptively not mentally competent to sign valid releases, state officials, acting as *parens patriae*, would have to make those decisions for them. Thus the very officials who stood to lose politically by the revelations of the film were put in a position by the court of being able to prevent its exhibition by claiming an invasion of privacy on behalf of their inmates.

The case raises a number of very close questions. Clearly the public has a vital interest in knowing how its state correctional institutions are being managed, and Wiseman's film effectively served that end. It is not so clear to what extent the inmates of such an institution have a right to privacy and, more particularly, a right not to have their daily activities and living conditions filmed for public exhibition. If there is such a right at all, it is debatable whether it merits deference where the inmate is insufficiently in touch with reality to express an objection, if he has one, when he sees a camera aimed in his direction. A genuine concern by the institution's officials for the privacy rights of persons in their charge who are non compos mentis, and their attempts to protect those rights, should certainly be applauded and accorded a great measure of respect. Yet when, as here, their motivations seem less than altruistic, the claims they assert on behalf of the inmates should not go unquestioned. When the communicator has been as careful as Wiseman apparently was to respect the feelings and interests of those portrayed, insofar as that could be ascertained, and when all of the other factors we have discussed have been considered, the courts should have struck the delicate balance in favor of free circulation of *Titicut Follies.*

As difficult as the consent issue was in *Wiseman v. Massachusetts,* that is how relatively easy it was in three other invasion-of-privacy cases that have received attention from students of the subject.

In the first, a Ms. Barber had been hospitalized with an unusual malady—she was wasting away even though consuming large amounts of food. Understandably, and properly, in view of the newsworthiness of the event, a story of her problem appeared in the Medicine section of *Time* magazine. Not quite so understandably, and not nearly so properly, the story carried with it a picture of the patient in her hospital bed—a picture taken without permission by a news-service photographer while the reporter he was with tried, unsuccessfully, to persuade her to grant her consent. Judging the case by the principles proposed in this chapter, it would seem that the Missouri courts were correct in ruling in Ms. Barber's favor.[61] Her hospital room was not a public place, and to take her picture there and publish it without her consent was as clearly a case of "theft" of her privacy as one can imagine.

Similarly, in *York v. Story,* a woman who had gone to the police to report an assault was asked by one of the officers to undress so that a picture could be taken of her in the nude. She complied, presumably thinking that this was part of the law enforcement process involved in bringing her assailant to justice. When the policeman who took the picture and some of his fellow officers were found to have circulated the photograph around the station, suit was brought under the Federal Civil Rights Act. The courts had no trouble in seeing this as an invasion of the woman's right of privacy.[62] What she had "given" for one purpose, was "stolen" for another.

Finally, in *Neff v. Time,*[63] a federal district court was surely right in ruling *against* the plaintiff. In this instance, a photographer for *Sports Illustrated* magazine (owned by Time, Inc.) took thirty pictures of a group of fans at a Pittsburgh Steelers football game under conditions described as follows by the court:

> The photographer was on the field intending to take pictures of the Steelers players as they entered the field from the dugout. Neff and the others were jumping up and down . . . waving Steeler banners and drinking beer. . . . One of the group asked the photographer for whom he was working and was told Sports Illustrated, whereupon the group began . . . screaming and howling and imploring the photographer to take pictures. The more pictures taken of the group, the more they hammed it up.[64]

One of the pictures that was taken, showing the plaintiff, Neff, with his fly completely open (though nothing inside could be seen), was published in *Sports Illustrated* along with a story entitled, "A Strange Kind of Love." He sued for invasion of his privacy. Although the judge thought that the editor's deliberate decision to print the picture was in the utmost bad taste and would be likely to cause embarrassment to the subject, he concluded that

> a photograph taken at a public event which everyone present could see, with the knowledge and implied consent of the subject, is not a matter concerning a private fact. A factually accurate public disclosure is not tortious when connected with a newsworthy event even though offensive to ordinary sensibilities. . . . it is our opinion that the publication of Neff's photograph taken with his active encouragement and participation, and with knowledge that the photographer was connected with a publication, even though taken without his express consent, is protected by the Constitution.[65]

What if the group of which Neff was a part had not invited the cameraman over? Does one's presence in a public place by itself entitle a photographer to take and publish a picture of a man with an open fly? Prosser has said that an individual who is on a public street in a state of drunkenness is fair game for a photographer, but he has expressed uncertainty about a circumstance in which a cameraman with a telephoto lens focuses on a single individual in a crowd and then prints a picture portraying the person in an embarrassing pose.[66] I suspect the reason for Prosser's indecision about this circumstance is that not many of us have consciously thought about whether we expect any privacy, or have any right to expect it, when we are in the midst of a crowd in a public place. We usually do not assume that a camera somewhere is recording our every action, but there is also no reason to assume that this might not be happening. I would take the position that if we do not want others to see a particular behavior we ought not engage in it in public, even if we think we may be protected by the seeming anonymity of a crowd situation.[67]

In contrast, I believe that we *do* have a right to expect that cameras with telephoto lenses will not be aimed through the windows of our homes, that our telephones will not be tapped, our bedrooms bugged, our private conversations secretly recorded, or our letters opened by someone other than the addressee. The public exposure of material obtained in these ways should be prohibitable and punishable as an invasion of privacy.

What about the situation in which the *recipient* of a letter publishes its contents without authorization from the writer? Is that a matter of "theft" which should be the subject of legal restraint? If it is a Letter to the

Editor of a newspaper, authorization to publish is, of course, implicit, and there is no privacy problem. Otherwise, there are legal precedents going all the way back to the early part of the nineteenth century holding that letters may not be published by their recipient without the consent of the sender.[68] This is as it should be, for there is an implicit expectation of confidentiality in exchanges of private correspondence. If it were otherwise it would, in the words of Supreme Court Justice Joseph Story, "compel everyone in self defense to write, even to his dearest friends, with the cold and formal severity, with which he would write to his wariest opponents, or his most implacable enemies."[69]

Can consent once given to the public exposure of private facts be withdrawn at a later time? Prosser has stated as a general principle that "if the agreement is a matter of contract it is normally irrevocable."[70] In at least two cases that concept has been put to interesting tests.

In one, a movie entitled *Marlene* was produced portraying the true story of a sixteen-year-old girl in a Massachusetts juvenile home. Both she and her mother had given consent to the making of the film. When she reached the age of twenty-one the girl decided that she wanted to stop any further exhibitions of the movie, and she filed a privacy suit seeking to accomplish that end.[71] Much as one may sympathize with the girl's feelings in the matter, to allow post facto revocation of a valid consent, and thus to interfere with the communication of material that has already been in the public domain, would establish a hazardous principle. A Ronald Reagan might try to suppress all of his old movies because he found the behaviors of his more youthful years to be a current political liability. A scientist who has changed his or her views on some critical scientific question might attempt to purge the libraries of earlier and more naive writings on the subject. Even if rewriting history might save one some embarrassment, the law should not be an accomplice in such efforts.

A second case of this type grew out of an article published in *Sports Illustrated* in 1971 entitled, "The Closest Thing to Being Reborn." It was a story about devotees of the sport of body surfing, and it described in some detail the personality of one such buff, Michael Virgil, who was reputed to be the most daring surfer at California's most dangerous surfing site. In portraying the psychological characteristics that might shed light on his daredeviltry, the article reported such incidents of his youth as "putting out cigarettes in his mouth and diving off stairs to impress women, hurting himself in order to collect unemployment so as to have time for body surfing ... gang fights ... eating insects."[72] This information had been freely provided by Virgil in an extensive interview with the reporter, but when he later learned that the magazine story would not be confined to his activities as a surfer, he revoked his consent.

When the article was published despite his objections he sued for invasion of privacy.[73]

The question of whether a person has a right to revoke consent did not emerge as an issue in the court's disposition of the case. Rather, the matter was decided by the district court on the basis of a ruling by the U.S. Court of Appeals for the Ninth Circuit that the First Amendment right to publish newsworthy information is extremely broad. The circuit court had said, "A line is to be drawn when the publicity ceases to be the giving of information to which the public is entitled, and becomes a morbid and sensational prying into private lives for its own sake, with which a reasonable member of the public, with decent standards, would say that he had no concern."[74]

Applying that principle, Judge Thompson of the district court decided that Virgil's complaint did not satisfy the test: "Any reasonable person reading the Sports Illustrated article would have to conclude that the personal facts concerning Mike Virgil were included as a legitimate journalistic attempt to explain Virgil's extremely daring and dangerous style of body surfing. There is no possibility that a juror could conclude that the personal facts were included for any inherent morbid, sensational, or curiosity appeal they might have."[75]

Judge Thompson apparently assumed that, once the reporter had gotten the information, the question of whether he had a right to publish it was to be decided on grounds other than Virgil's claim of a right-to-revoke consent. Although the Virgil situation differs from the case of *Marlene* in that the material had not yet been made public when Virgil interposed his objections, it is similar in that an initial decision was freely made to expose private information. Like the proverbial "letting the cat out of the bag," once privacy has been waived can one reasonably expect to recapture it? I think not, unless, as I have said earlier, one has made a firm contract or entered into a clear understanding of confidentiality with provision for a veto power over disclosure. Such was not the case in *Virgil v. Time.*

There is one last complexity that must be addressed with respect to the public exposure of private facts. It concerns situations in which material that has been obtained through illegal intrusion or a guarantee of confidentiality is publicized by persons other than those who obtained it, either with or without the knowledge that they are trafficking in "stolen goods." Should communicators in such cases be subject to suit for invasion of privacy?

In the instance of publication without knowledge of the means by which the material was obtained, it seems clear that First Amendment protection is necessary and justified. Otherwise our legal system would be punishing communication by people who, without any awareness of wrongdoing, have simply engaged in the exercise of freedom of expression. That would be a serious erosion of First Amendment rights.

The question is quite different, however, when the would-be communicator knows how the material was gotten, either by virtue of having been told by the persons who transmitted it, or having conspired with them to get it, or because the target of the intrusion has learned of the impending publication and has sought to stop it. It seems to me that in the latter kind of situation injunctive relief should be available to a plaintiff and that where publication has already occurred damages for invasion of privacy should be possible.

There have been two significant court decisions in this matter, one which strongly supports the view that has just been expressed, and the other which takes a different direction. The first (which was acutally decided two years after the second) involved photographs that were published in 1963 with a *Life* magazine article entitled "Crackdown on Quackery." The plaintiff, Dietemann, had been under investigation for quackery and was ultimately arrested for practicing medicine without a license. The published photographs had been taken of him surreptitiously in his office, to which entry had been gained through a subterfuge planned by the reporters in cooperation with the district attorney.

The U.S. Court of Appeals for the Ninth Circuit took the following position, with which I fully agree:

> One who invites another to his home or office takes a risk that the visitor may not be what he seems, and that the visitor may repeat all he hears and observes when he leaves. But he does not and should not be required to take the risk that what is heard and seen will be transmitted by photograph or recording, or in our modern world, in full living color and hi-fi to the public at large or to any segment of it that the visitor may select.
>
> The First Amendment has never been construed to accord newsmen immunity from torts or crimes committed during the course of newsgathering. The First Amendment is not a license to trespass, to steal, or to intrude by electronic means into the precincts of another's home or office. It does not become such a license simply because the person subjected to the intrusion is reasonably suspected of commiting a crime.[76]

The other case was one in which columnist Drew Pearson published the content of papers removed overnight from the files of U.S. Senator Dodd of Connecticut by persons on his staff and photocopied for Pearson. The circumstances differed from *Dietemann v. Time, Inc.* only in that Pearson was not found to have "aided and abetted" the intrusion itself, though he admittedly knew he was publishing information derived from documents that had been taken without the senator's knowledge. In an opinion of troublesome logic, the U.S. Court of Appeals for the District of Columbia exonerated Pearson of invading Dodd's privacy.[77]

The court started from the premise that the persons who took the material from their employer's office may well have been guilty of intrusion. The opinion then observed that "injuries from intrusion and injuries from publication should be kept clearly separate,"[78] and that since Pearson did not aid and abet the intrusion he could not be held responsible for that particular act. The judges felt that "it would place too great a strain on human weakness to hold one liable in damage who merely succumbs to temptation and listens" to "an eavesdropper with an offer to share in the information gathered through eavesdropping."[79]

"Of course," the court went on to concede, "appellants did more than receive and peruse . . . they published."[80] But that act had to be judged independently of the intrusion, and the court found that since the publication consisted of information of "general public interest"—specifically alleged evidence of improper influence with the senator by lobbyists for foreign interests—it was "a paradigm example of published speech not subject to suit for invasion of privacy."[81]

In other words, the court of appeals placed the plaintiff in the "catch-22" position of not being able to sue Pearson for intrusion, because he did not participate in that act, and not being able to sue him for publishing the fruits of the intrusion, because the information obtained was considered to be of legitimate public concern. The loophole thus provided for Pearson to escape responsibility for the alleged invasion of privacy that resulted from this chain of events seems irreconcilable with the sensible principle enunciated by the ninth circuit in *Dietemann* that the First Amendment is not a license to steal personal information, even if it is done for the worthy goal of exposing wrongdoing.

Had Pearson not been aware of the means by which his information was secured, one could readily agree that providing a loophole for him was a First Amendment necessity. Such a precedent, though still leaving without any legal remedy some people who might be seriously damaged by invasions of privacy, can at least be justified by suggesting that such individuals must forego relief in order that greater damage not be done to our system of freedom of expression. But to ask them to make that kind of sacrifice for communicators who know they are dealing in stolen goods seems unjust. The fact that a communicator has not personally engaged in intrusion, and thus cannot be held liable for that wrong, should not free one knowingly to use the fruits of somebody else's intrusion by wrapping oneself in the cloak of the First Amendment.

There is, however, an arguably significant difference between the *Pearson* and *Dietemann* cases which might justify their disparate treatment. This line of argument would hold that the intrusion into Senator

Dodd's files does not fall into the invasion–of–personal–privacy category at all but is more akin to the unauthorized disclosure of information from a government agency, as occurred in the *Pentagon Papers* case, and thus is to be judged by standards appropriate to that area. The theft and/or unauthorized dissemination of information held by the *government*—for instance, by those who wish to blow the whistle on inefficiency or misuses of power—raises unique questions because true privacy rights of individuals are not at stake (unless the case involves the release of something like an income tax return) and because the information, unless falling into one of the classifications which may appropriately be kept secret (to be discussed in a later chapter), in a real sense "belongs" to the public and not to those officeholders who happen to have it in their possession. The question of whether a whistle blower can properly be punished for, or restrained from, the unauthorized disclosure of governmental information must depend, then, on whether that material has legitimately been kept secret. That would obviously not be the case where there have been abuses of authority or the improper withholding of data that the public has a right to know—which might plausibly be said of Senator Dodd's correspondence with lobbyists for foreign interests. What is more, in contrast to understandings and agreements voluntarily entered into by private parties, any attempt by public officials to impose on their employees a contractual obligation to keep secret everything they learn in the course of their employment, even if it is something the public is entitled to know and the government has no business keeping secret, should be legally unenforceable.[82]

One can accept this point of view with regard to government information, which I am inclined to do, and still wonder whether the senator's files and letters really fall into that category or should more properly be considered private documents whose unauthorized disclosure, even if possibly revealing an abuse of his office, deprives him not only of his privacy rights but also his rights to due process of law—more particularly the privilege against self-incrimination. In the latter event, one would have to conclude that Drew Pearson, knowing he was publishing stolen information, should have been found guilty of invasion of privacy. This is an exceptionally close case which could reasonably be decided either way.

To summarize the guiding principles proposed in this chapter, I have suggested that the concept of theft can provide the key in resolving the conflict between freedom of expression and privacy. When one's name, image, or works are appropriated by another for purely personal, monetary gain, legal redress should be available. "False-light" cases in which an individual's reputation is allegedly damaged should be treated no differently than alleged defamations. When it is not reputation, but mental distress, that is at stake, false light should be dealt with in the same way as the public exposure of embarrassing private, but truthful, facts. As for the latter category, I have urged that neither a court's judgment as to what is newsworthy nor a community's notions of decency should be determinative of what may be communicated without penalty. The question should be, How was the material obtained? If it has come from public records that are open to public inspection, is observable in public places, or has been revealed by the subject without any expectation of confidentiality or of veto rights, then there should be no barriers to its broader public exposure. Nor should it be possible to revoke consent that has once been given. Contrariwise, if the material has been taken from a private conversation, or from a private place, without consent, and perhaps even without the awareness of the person involved, anyone who publicizes it, knowing it to be "stolen property," should be liable not only for damages but subject to prior restraint as well.

I have acknowledged that the operation of these principles will sometimes work a hardship on particular individuals who will be paying more than their fair share of our society's costs for the maintenance of freedom of expression. Their lot is similar to those who are accidentally caught up in some event of public importance or who, indeed, are struck by any kind of serious accident. The United States Supreme Court put it well in *Time v. Hill:*

> One need only pick up any newspaper or magazine to comprehend the vast range of published matter which exposes persons to public view, both private citizens and public officials. Exposure of the self to others in varying degrees is a concomitant of life in a civilized community. The risk of this exposure is an essential incident of life in a society which places a primary value on freedom of speech and press.[83]

E. L. Godkin was right, in that very first essay on privacy in *Scribner's* in 1890, when he doubted that we could look to the law as the best solution for the problem of "mere wounds to feelings." No law that is sensitive to the First Amendment will ever be able to deal appropriately with the aggressive television reporter who aims his camera and sticks his microphone in the face of a sobbing mother who has just learned of the death of all of her children in a fire, and asks her how she feels. As in so many other areas of life, we must rely on the education of the tastes and the elevation of the sensitivities of our citizenry, and on their voluntary respect for the privacy of others, as the remedy most in keeping with the philosophy of a free society.

5 Stirring to Group Prejudice and Hatred

The last two chapters have dealt with the problems that arise when an individual is talked about in ways that may be hurtful. We turn our attention now to communication about *groups* of people that may have harmful consequences for the individuals who are members of those groups.

When we survey the recorded history of mankind we are struck by the fact that hostility between people on the basis of their group memberships—be it tribe, race, religion, or nation—seems to have been with us always. Often that hostility has spilled over into the brutalization or destruction of other human beings, whether Christians fed to the lions, Africans enslaved, Protestants and Roman Catholics engaged in a Thirty Years' War, or Jews put to death in Nazi concentration camps.

The current world scene is little different. Protestants and Catholics live in separate armed camps in Northern Ireland and vie bitterly for political power in the European lowlands. Arabs and Jews maintain an uneasy balance of power and terror in the Middle East. South Africa is but the worst manifestation of tension between blacks and whites that can also produce violence in London, England, or Chicago, Illinois. From the Untouchables of India to the Capitalist Roaders of China, people are categorized, labeled, and subjected to all of the abuses that the minds of others can conceive.

Segregation by group membership, discrimination on the basis of group membership, brutalization because of group membership, and perhaps ultimately genocide—these are the fruits of attitudes— prejudices and hatreds—that have been cultivated in one group toward another through processes of communication. In modern societies, books, movies, newspapers, radio, television, or ubiquitous wall posters are used in support of these ends. But the phenomenon existed long before there were any mass media of communication, and the mass media alone are insufficient. Ethnocentrism is ingrained in the child by communication from parents and peer groups. Adults are influenced by the communication of opinion leaders who are known personally to them. Only through these informal channels are the leaders of church, state, or political movements able indirectly to have an impact on these fundamental attitudes. Intergroup prejudices and hatreds begin, are ameliorated, are aggravated, and end in the communication networks of primary groups—family, household, gang or social clubs, neighborhood, work crew or business associates—with whom the individual spends most waking hours.

Faced with the horrors that group stereotypes and bigotry so often produce, sensitive and enlightened people have sought for ways to counter or prevent such attitudes. Persuasion, education, and exposure to individual members of other groups in favorable settings have all been tried, sometimes with great success and sometimes abysmal failure. Laws against overt acts of segregation and discrimination have been adopted, again with some victories and some defeats. When everything else has failed, and tensions have remained high, leaders of goodwill have been tempted to deal with the problem by making it illegal for anyone to engage in the public communication of racially or religiously defamatory material or to incite prejudice and hatred against others because of the groups to which they belong. Although it has been recognized that such laws cannot, as a practical matter, reach the informal talk that goes on in primary groups, and that the communication of hatred may simply be driven underground, it is felt that the imposition of a social penalty may reduce the dangers and is justified to protect the rights of those whose groups may be defamed. Every member of such a group, it is argued, may be victimized as a result of the slurs that are cast upon them collectively.

It is significant to note that never has it been proposed or attempted in democratic societies to use the law to restrain the purveying of group prejudice and hatred when packaged in subtle or sophisticated communication wrappings. Neither genteel jokes about the stupidity or depravity of particular ethnic or racial groups nor the promulgation of pseudoscientific theories about their genetic inferiority have ever been the target of legislative prohibitions. Stereotyped portrayals of blacks in television dramas or of women in school textbooks have been deplored and revised under the pressures of heightened consciousness, but never officially banned. Even the blunt attacks on world Jewry in Hitler's *Mein Kampf* have not been thought deserving of expurgation from the world's libraries, perhaps because they are expressed in the pages of a historic document.

It is only the crudest and most scurrilous diatribes addressed to large audiences through the cheapest media of communication—public speeches at open-air rallies, leaflets distributed or picket signs displayed on the public sidewalks, junk mail, and hate telephone calls—that have

been the subject of legal concern. And even here there have been striking differences in the responses of the democratic world and of various
jurisdictions within our own country.

The nations of Western Europe have assumed a much more restrictive
posture toward what is commonly referred to as "group libel" than has
the United States. The Consultative Assembly of the Council of Europe,
meeting in 1966, adopted model legislation that it recommended to its
member states which well represents the climate of legal thought in the
European democracies.[1] This model law provides that:

Article 1
A person shall be guilty of an offence:

(a) if he publicly calls for or incites to hatred, intolerance, discrimination, or violence against persons or groups of persons distinguished by colour, race, ethnic or national origin, or religion;

(b) if he insults persons or groups of persons, holds them up to
contempt or slanders them on account of their distinguishing par-
ticularities mentioned in paragraph (a).

Article 2
(a) A person shall be guilty of an offence if he publishes or distributes written matter which is aimed at achieving the effects referred
to in Article 1. . . .

Article 4
Organisations whose aims or activities fall within the scope of Articles 1 and 2 shall be prosecuted and/or prohibited.

Article 5
(a) A person shall be guilty of an offence if he publicly uses insignia
of organisations prohibited under Article 4.

(b) "Insignia" are, in particular, flags, badges, uniforms, slogans,
and forms of salute.

The two nations of Europe which we ordinarily think of as having the
greatest tolerance for freedom of expression, Denmark and England,
both place sharp limits on group libel. Section 140 of the Danish Criminal Code provides:

Any person who exposes to ridicule or insults the dogmas or worship
of any lawfully existing religious community in this country shall be
liable to simple detention, or in extenuating circumstances, to a fine.[2]

Section 266b further provides:

Any person who, by circulating false rumors or accusations persecutes
or incites hatred against any group of the Danish population because
of its creed, race, or nationality shall be liable to simple detention or, in
aggravating circumstances, imprisonment for any term not exceeding
one year.[3]

Group libel in Great Britain is dealt with in the Race Relations Act of 1965, Section 6(1) which reads:

A person shall be guilty of an offence under this section if, with intent to stir up hatred against any section of the public in Great Britain distinguished by colour, race, ethnic or national origins—
(a) he publishes or distributes written matter which is threatening, abusive or insulting; or
(b) he uses in any public place or at any public meeting words which are threatening, abusive or insulting, being matter or words likely to stir up hatred against that section on grounds of colour, race, or ethnic or national origins.[4]

The United States, in contrast, has taken a more liberal attitude toward such communication—perhaps because we are less sensitive to bigotry, perhaps because we are more sensitive to freedom of speech, but surely not because we have had fewer racists peddling their wares among us. Only four states—Connecticut, Indiana, Massachusetts, and West Virginia—have group libel laws on their books, and although the Judiciary Committee of the U.S. House of Representatives held hearings on proposed group libel legislation in 1963, no federal laws on the subject have ever been adopted. This in spite of the fact that in 1952 the U.S. Supreme Court upheld the constitutionality of an Illinois group libel law,[5] a law which that state's legislature saw fit to repeal in 1961.

The language of the Illinois statute that was sustained by the Supreme Court in *Beauharnais v. Illinois,* albeit by a slim 5–4 margin, merits attention, since it has served as the model for a few city councils here and there around the country that have chosen to adopt such legislation, and since its current constitutional status, in view of more recent Supreme Court decisions, is uncertain.

The law reads:

It shall be unlawful for any person, firm or corporation to manufacture, sell, or offer for sale, advertise or publish, present or exhibit in any public place in this state any lithograph, moving picture, play, drama or sketch, which publication or exhibition portrays depravity, criminality, unchastity, or lack of virtue of a class of citizens, of any race, color, creed or religion which said publication or exhibition exposes citizens of any race, color, creed or religion to contempt, derision or obloquy or which is productive of breach of peace or riots.[6]

In particular cities where racist groups, such as local Nazis, have become active and highly visible and the target populations correspondingly agitated, city councils have sometimes responded with the passage or attempted passage of group libel ordinances. For example, in the fall of 1975, following a summer of especially busy Nazi activity, the city attorney of Milwaukee, Wisconsin, proposed an ordinance (which was not adopted) that tracked almost verbatim the language of the Illinois law upheld in *Beauharnais*.[7] In the summer of 1977, confronted with a proposed march by Chicago-area Nazi leader Frank Collin, the Village of Skokie, Illinois, adopted an ordinance, among others that were designed to keep Collin out of town, that read in part:

> Sec. 28-23. The dissemination of any material within the Village of Skokie which promotes and incites hatred against persons by reason of their race, national origin, or religion, and is intended to do so, is hereby prohibited.
>
> Sec. 28-23.2. The phrase "dissemination of materials" includes but is not limited to publication or display or distribution of posters, signs, handbills, or writings, and public display of markings and clothing of symbolic significance.

The Skokie ordinances were challenged in federal court and were all found to be unconstitutional.[8] To reach that judgment with respect to the group libel law, it was necessary for the district court and circuit court of appeals to consider whether they were bound by the *Beauharnais* precedent, and both concluded that subsequent decisions had probably rendered *Beauharnais* obsolete. In so doing they subscribed to a position taken by several other courts[9] and to a line of reasoning akin to that which follows here.

The Supreme Court's majority opinion in *Beauharnais* rested explicitly on the presumption, enunciated ten years earlier in *Chaplinsky v. New Hampshire*, that certain "classes of speech" are outside the protection of the First Amendment. "These include the lewd and obscene, the profane, the libelous, and the insulting or fighting words—those which by their very utterance inflict injury or tend to incite an immediate breach of the peace."[10] The *Beauharnais* majority found *group* libel to be a logical offspring of *individual* libel and thus among those categories of expression that are not constitutionally protected.

Implicit in the Court's rationale was the notion that, in addition to being a legitimate offspring of individual libel, group defamation is also a first cousin to "fighting words." It was not only the damage to the reputation or psyches of the libeled group members about which the Court expressed its concern but also the violence and rioting that sometimes follow in the wake of racist agitation. Thus it would appear that group libel was brought into the family of the *Chaplinsky* unprotected categories because of its close kinship to both individual libel *and* fighting words.

To the extent that the premises which underlay the *Beauharnais* decision were modified by later Court rulings, the decision itself has also been unhinged. The first major post-*Beauharnais* event that had this effect was the Supreme Court's decision in *New York Times v. Sullivan* in 1964. As already noted, the *New York Times* opinion sharply curtailed the circumstances under which public officials might successfully sue for personal libel, and it affirmed a "profound national commitment to the principle that debate on public issues should be uninhibited, robust and wide open, and that it may well include vehement, caustic, and sometimes unpleasantly sharp attacks on government and public officials." But what is more relevant for our immediate concerns, *New York Times v. Sullivan* also explicitly turned away from the *Chaplinsky-Beauharnais* position that libelous utterances are *categorically* outside the ambit of possible First Amendment protection. Said Justice Brennan for a unanimous Court: "Like insurrection, contempt, advocacy of unlawful acts, obscenity, solicitation of legal business and the various other formulae for the repression of expression that have been challenged in this Court, libel can claim no talismanic immunity from constitutional limitations. It must be measured by standards that satisfy the First Amendment."[11]

Having thus undercut the unquestioned sanctity of libel laws—whether designed for use by individuals or groups—the Court next whittled away at the scope of the "fighting words" category. In *Cohen v. California* in 1971 the Supreme Court made clear that "fighting words" are only those that are "directed to the person of the hearer" in a "personally provocative fashion." In other words, the Court was saying that the "fighting words" concept had been developed to deal with individual, face-to-face encounters and was inapplicable to situations like that in *Cohen* where a message was being addressed to an audience-at-large and where anyone who found that message insulting or offensive "could effectively avoid further bombardment of their sensibilities simply by averting their eyes."[12] One can clearly infer, I think, that insulting statements about *groups* of people, addressed *to* groups of people, would not qualify as "fighting words" under the interpretation of that doctrine in *Cohen v. California*.

What is more, insofar as the viability of *Beauharnais* may have depended on a "fighting words" rationale, the Supreme Court's *Gooding v. Wilson* ruling in 1972 pulled out still another supporting leg. For in *Gooding* the Court held that "fighting words" may be punished solely where they "have a direct tendency to cause acts of violence by the person to whom, individually, the remark is addressed."[13] In other words, only when an immediate breach of the peace is threatened as a result of an abusive verbal attack by one individual upon another in a face-to-face encounter do we have a "fighting words" case. The utterance of words that are commonly thought to inflict *psychic* injury would, in the absence of the likelihood of an ensuing fight, not be punishable.

The city attorney of Milwaukee, Wisconsin, was apparently well aware of the impact that the *Gooding* decision had on *Beauharnais* when he drafted his own group libel ordinance for the City Council in 1975. For he changed one, and only one, small word in the language of the Illinois law that the Supreme Court had approved. Where Illinois had defined group libel as communication about races, colors, creeds, or religions that exposed them to "contempt, derision or obloquy *or* which is productive of breach of peace or riots" (italics mine), the proposed Milwaukee ordinance would have defined group libel as communication about races, colors, creeds, or religions that exposed them to "contempt, derision or obloquy *and* which is productive of breach of the peace or riots" (italics mine).

The effect of this kind of definition of group libel (substituting "and" for "or") is to make the offense indistinguishable from a multitude of other behaviors, symbolic or otherwise, that are punishable because they start fights in the streets. For such a purpose a group libel law is redundantly unnecessary since both common and statutory law already provide remedies generally for incitements to breaches of the peace or disorderly conduct. Indeed, there have been a number of cases in which such breach of peace or disorderly conduct convictions have been obtained against people who have engaged in group defamation. One instance that received considerable publicity occurred in Chicago in 1962 when three members of the White Youth Corps, an affiliate of the American Nazi Party, picketed in front of the State-Lake Theater, then showing a movie starring Sammy Davis, Jr. Their signs carried such messages as "How to be a Jew, lesson number 1 by Sammy the Kosher Coon." A crowd of onlookers gathered, some of them mumbling threats at the demonstrators. When the picketers ignored a police order to disperse, they were arrested and charged with disorderly conduct. Their conviction in the trial court was sustained on appeal.[14]

I am not suggesting that a disorderly conduct conviction of these particular demonstrators was appropriate, or that convictions of anyone for inciting a breach of the peace by uttering racist remarks are preferable to the use of group libel laws for the punishment of that behavior. We will return in a later chapter to the more generic First Amendment problems posed by speech *of any sort* that occurs in a hostile audience situation where a potential for reactive violence exists. What I wish to emphasize here is that if punishment for group libel is limited, either by statutes like the proposed Milwaukee ordinance or by the Supreme Court's *Gooding* decision, to contexts in which a breach of the peace is threatened, then the issues we face in evaluating the desirability of such limits are identical to those we will deal with later in discussing the broader topic of *any* offensive communication addressed to *any* hostile audience. Only insofar as punishment for group libel may be sought on the basis of alleged injuries that communication per se inflicts upon the psyches or reputations of others do we need to engage in a more particularistic evaluation of it. It is to that evaluation that we now turn.

An initial argument that is made in support of group libel legislation is identical to one offered earlier on behalf of laws against individual libel—that in the absence of officially sanctioned social controls those who are the targets of verbal abuse will resort to violent self-help measures which will rend the social fabric. As one writer, Hadley Arkes, has expressed it: " . . . the choice in the group libel problem is not between the restraint of free expression and the absence of restraint. It is rather a choice between two forms of restraint: one carried out by private groups operating outside the law, and another, of a more limited nature, carried out by legal authorities under the constraints of a formal statute."[15]

To establish social policy on the basis of this rationale would be to submit to vigilante blackmail. I have already presented a contrary, and I believe correct, response in our discussion of individual libel—that one of the presumptions of citizenship in a democracy must be the ability of people to learn to restrain themselves in the face of symbolic provocations by others and to fight offensive speech with more and better speech rather than with fists and clubs. If that is expecting too much of adult citizens in a free society, then we will need laws not only against individual and group libel but against every other kind of communication that might conceivably anger somebody else.

Arkes has further elaborated his view that the law is preferable to vigilantism as a control on group libel by arguing that legal restraints can be "of a more limited nature" and designed only "to reach the most odious cases."[16] It seems to me that in so arguing Arkes has exposed a basic flaw in his own case and in the case for group libel laws generally. If suppression is directed only at the crudest or most "odious" messages, it will be dealing with the most superficial aspects of the problem of group prejudice and hatred, for the most odious are likely to be the least effective in accomplishing their purposes. Such restrictions would do no more than provide false assurance that a serious problem was being dealt with. It is relevant to note here that England, with its strict Race Relations Act of 1965, has not been any freer of racial conflict in the streets than has the United States.

A second justification that is given for restraints on group defamation, again akin to the argument with respect to individual libel, is that such communication serves no useful function in the search for truth that is the purpose of a free marketplace of ideas. The assumption seems to be made that utterances which incite to group prejudice or hatred involve a falsification of reality that makes no contribution to the enlightened formation of public policy. There are a number of problems with that view.

The first is that most so-called defamatory utterances about large groups of people, identified by race, creed, or national origin, are not empirically verifiable or falsifiable. They tend most often to be statements of opinion, or more accurately the voicing of prejudices, rather than false statements of fact. How does one verify or disprove a reference to "dumb Poles," "crafty Jews," "lazy blacks," or "greasy Wops"? How many Poles have to be smart to give the lie to a generalization about their collective intelligence, and what is to be the measure of smartness or dumbness? What is meant by "crafty" or "lazy" or "greasy," and how does one find out how many there are of each in any group? When Joseph Beauharnais said, "If persuasion and the need to prevent the white race from becoming mongrelized by the negro will not unite us, then the aggression . . . rapes, robberies, knives, guns and marijuana of the negro, surely will," was he literally speaking lies or was he expressing a horrendously warped opinion? What of the White Youth Corps calling Sammy Davis, Jr., a "Kosher Coon"? Or Nazis carrying picket signs reading "White Power" and "Nigger Beware"? What of the hypothetical example offered by Arkes when he worriedly suggests that the slogan on a jacket like that of Paul Robert Cohen could read "Fuck the Jews" as easily as "Fuck the Draft."[17] Are these phrases measurable by any objective test of truth or falsehood?

Even when generalizations about groups of people are made that appear to assert facts, rather than opinions, falsifiability is still elusive, if not impossible. For example, if it is said, as George Lincoln Rockwell used to say to his college audiences, that the Jews control the mass media of communication in America, can such an assertion be definitively proven false? First, there would have to be agreement on what is meant by "control"—probably an insuperable task. Does it mean total ownership of all broadcasting stations and newspapers in the United States (which would be palpably false), or could it mean substantial influence (whatever that is) in the policymaking of the news divisions of the three major television networks (which would be extremely difficult to assess)? Also, who are Jews? Would that category include those whose parents were both practicing members of the faith but who had themselves left the religion, married non-Jews, and raised their children as Christians? Would persons be counted who had one grandparent that was Jewish, or who had been born Catholic and converted to Judaism? To subject these kinds of questions to legal adjudication would make as much sense as asking a jury to decide whether it is true or false that "the Jews killed Christ."

An alternative, of course, and the route that has been taken by the framers and supporters of group libel legislation, is to depart from the prevailing principle in individual libel law that truth is always a defense and to allow punishment for stirring others to group hatred even with statements that are not demonstrably false. Such a policy is then defended on the grounds that, although the speech may not be empirically false, it is socially worthless.

But this moves into dangerous territory. Who decides what is worthless and by what criteria? If the overarching purpose of the First Amendment is to guarantee a free exchange of views on all questions of public policy, are not the crudely expressed fears and hates of a Joseph Beauharnais with respect to relationships between blacks and whites as much a statement of his political and social views as they are a defamatory comment about several million of his fellow citizens, and should they not be taken into account as public policy is formulated?

I would go so far as to suggest that all allegedly defamatory comments about groups of people are necessarily also expressions of the communicator's political views. If a speaker says that "women's place is in the home," he is, at one and the same time, defaming 51 percent of our population and expressing a fundamental political position on a major question of public policy. Whether the communicator be an economic radical who advocates that all the "filthy capitalists" be stripped of their "ill-gotten gains" or a religious fanatic who preaches that those who do not follow "the true way" are sinners to be condemned and despised, attacks on impersonal, generic others have always been an integral part of public controversy. They cannot be separated out for punishment without doing violence to the First Amendment rights of those who are not sophisticated or skilled enough to conceal their prejudices in more palatable or more constructive modes of expression.

A third reason that is often given for the prohibition of group libel has to do with the emotional distress that such communication may cause to the members of the defamed groups. Two illustrations will serve to make the point. One is a scene in South Boston or Southwest Chicago in front of a public school to which black children are being bused for the first time. A crowd of angry white parents is on the sidewalk shouting racist slogans at the black youngsters as they walk toward the schoolhouse door. It can hardly be disputed that those children may bear emotional scars from such an experience.

The second scene could well have occurred in Skokie, Illinois. A group of Nazis marches in front of the Village Hall wearing brown uniforms and swastikas. Hundreds of residents of the community who are survivors of German concentration camps, and whose loved ones were starved and murdered there, have deeply painful memories aroused by the sight of the marchers. It can hardly be denied that such a demonstration would have been a frightful encounter for all concerned.

It is difficult not to seem callous in arguing that the anguish experienced by those exposed to such scenes is a price that must be paid for freedom of speech, but I must take that risk and so argue. Emotional distress can be caused for people by many kinds of communication in addition to group defamation, and that problem will be addressed more fully and in its more generic form in a later chapter. Suffice it to say here that I see no basis for distinguishing scurrilous communication about racial, religious, and ethnic groups from other kinds of utterances that may sting emotionally and that the position I will take generally with regard to such speech will provide no support for group libel legislation.

A last, and perhaps most seductive, argument in support of restraints on group libel is the thesis that communication which stirs up group prejudice and hatred leads ultimately to overt acts of segregation, discrimination, brutalization, even genocide—acts that a society should prohibit from the start. Repeatedly the point is pressed that Hitler's rise to political power in Germany might have been stopped if his early speeches and rallies had been suppressed. David Riesman has embellished this line of reasoning by proposing a psychological dimension:

> In the fascist tactic, defamation becomes a form of verbal sadism, to be used in the early stages of the conflict, before other forms of sadism are safe. The violence and daring of the verbal onslaughts exercise a great appeal over the imagination of lower middle-class folk who live insipid and anxious lives; the apparent daring of their leaders, moreover, is in sharp contrast to the balanced, and often timid, speaking and writing of the teachers, preachers, and politicians who, for them, have represented "democracy."[18]

What all this boils down to is the proposition that communication influences attitudes and attitudes shape action—a sweeping truism that no one could sensibly dispute. The difficulty with the argument is the same as that with all other arguments that advocate suppression of speech because of a presumed but remote, indirect, and unprovable link to particular illegal acts. When Hadley Arkes says of group libel and racist actions, "The lines of connection may be impossible to chart empirically, and yet reasonable men understand that the connections exist,"[19] he sounds remarkably like Chief Justice Warren Burger talking about laws against obscenity: "It is not for us to resolve empirical uncertainties underlying State legislation.... Although there is no conclusive proof of a connection between antisocial behavior and obscene material, the legislature of Georgia could quite reasonably determine that such a connection does or might exist.... From the beginning of civilized societies, legislators and judges have acted on various unprovable assumptions."[20]

Yet what Chief Justice Burger and four of his colleagues allowed in the obscenity area, and what Arkes would want with respect to group libel, the Supreme Court has firmly and wisely rejected for all other kinds of expression. It has said of "fighting words" that they cannot be punished in the absence of a "*direct* tendency to cause acts of violence"[21] (italics mine). It has said of personal libel that injury cannot be presumed, it must be proven.[22] And it has said of the advocacy of force or of illegal behavior generally that such advocacy cannot be proscribed unless it "is directed to inciting or producing *imminent* lawless action and is likely to incite or produce such action"[23] (italics mine).

Riesman may have been right in his suggestion that racist rhetoric has a powerful attraction to "lower middle-class folk who live insipid and anxious lives," but so do all other kinds of irrational appeals. By that logic we would have to outlaw the speech of all demagogues for fear that they will succeed in duping the "insipid" and the "anxious." (Incidentally, did Riesman here defame "lower middle-class folk"?)

Democracy places more faith in ordinary people. It operates on the premise that although demagogues may succeed now and then, here and there, as did Father Coughlin, Joe McCarthy, and Richard Nixon, in the long run they and their deceptions will be rejected. It also presumes that the suppression of potentially dangerous speech is a cure more deadly than the disease.

For example, in the case of group libel, one can be sure that if it is banned from the public arena it will go underground, there to fester and to take on the added appeal of forbidden fruit. Those who are responsive to such ideas will be sought out and found, while people of goodwill may be lulled into thinking that the battle against racisim has been won.

Another possible result of a restrictive approach is an increase in the deviousness and effectiveness of the purveyors of group hatred. One facet of the British experience, as described by Anthony Dickey, is instructive on this point:

> Regularly published papers, journals and magazines of racialist organisations immediately became more moderate in the presentation of their views as soon as the 1965 Act came into force. At least one leader of a racialist organisation has admitted that this has been to the advantage of his movement, for whereas the former virulently racialist language of his magazines had often alienated people who might otherwise have subscribed to his views on racial matters, more moderate language had increased the circulation of his publications.[24]

Finally, in the absence of any confrontations with group defamation, the ability of citizens to respond intelligently and effectively to racist

rhetoric would shrivel up from disuse. John Stuart Mill explained this
very well many years ago when he said that

> the only way in which a human being can make some approach to
> knowing the whole of a subject, is by hearing what can be said about it
> by persons of every variety of opinion, and studying all modes in
> which it can be looked at by every character of mind . . . not only the
> grounds of . . . opinion are forgotten in the absence of discussion, but
> too often the meaning of the opinion itself. . . . Instead of a vivid
> conception and a living belief, there remain only a few phrases re-
> tained by rote; or, if any part, the shell and husk only of the meaning is
> retained, the finer essence being lost. . . . The fatal tendency of man-
> kind to leave off thinking about a thing when it is no longer doubtful,
> is the cause of half their errors.[25]

Mill wisely warned us that it is only through a frequent reexamination
of our own beliefs and values, in the face of the most extreme—yes even
the most odious—challenges, that we are able to refresh and revitalize
our understanding of what we are all about. If we never hear the questions, we will soon forget the answers.

6   Prejudicing a Fair Trial

The Sixth Amendment to the United States Constitution provides, "In all criminal prosecutions the accused shall enjoy the right to a speedy and public trial, by an impartial jury. . . ." These simple words express a commitment to the most fundamental requirement of a free society's judicial system—the right of people who become involved with the law to a fair trial.

There are many ways in which persons can be deprived of a fair trial. Evidence may be suppressed. Witnesses may lie. Judges or jurors may be bribed or otherwise corrupted. But the circumstances that warrant our concern from a free speech point of view are those in which communication about persons who are on trial, or press commentary about their case, is claimed to so prejudice judges or jurors as to make an unbiased verdict impossible. As a result, it is suggested that First Amendment rights of free speech and press may sometimes have to be curbed in order to insure that the Sixth Amendment right to a fair trial is not abridged.

This problem has vexed our courts for most of the present century and has aroused the passions of press and bar alike. In one of the many cases in which our nation's highest tribunal was urged to choose sides in the conflict, the Supreme Court declared, "The authors of the Bill of Rights did not undertake to assign priorities as between First and Sixth Amendment rights, ranking one as superior to the other. . . . it is not for us to rewrite the Constitution by undertaking what they declined. It is unnecessary, after nearly two centuries, to establish a priority applicable in all circumstances."[1]

In the absence of any "priority applicable in all circumstances," the conflicts that have arisen have been dealt with on an ad hoc basis, leaving us with a checkerwork of somewhat unpredictable judge-made law on the subject. Let us examine that fabric and attempt to identify its possible flaws.

The earliest decisions involving a clash between unrestrained expression and a fair trial dealt with the most overt form of that conflict—cases in which mobs of people descended on courtrooms and, by their threatening presence and the communication of their angry feelings toward the defendant, so intimidated the judges and jurors as to make virtually impossible the rendering of an independent judgment. Often these cases occurred in the Old South, with blacks on trial for alleged offenses against whites; and although the procedures may have been an improvement over unadorned lynchings, where even the trappings of due process were dispensed with, the psychological climate could in fact be much the same.

The U.S. Supreme Court first took cognizance of this matter in 1915 with respect to a trial that had taken place in Atlanta, Georgia, two years earlier. Although a majority of the justices felt that in this instance the problem had been dealt with adequately through appellate review by the state courts, they did enunciate the broad principle that "if a trial is in fact dominated by a mob, so that the jury is intimidated and the trial judge yields, and so that there is an actual interference with the course of justice, there is, in that court, a departure from due process of law."[2]

Justice Oliver Wendell Holmes dissented from the Court's refusal to interfere with the judgment of the state courts and spoke even more vigorously about the injustices of mob rule. He said of the case:

> The trial... was carried on in a court packed with spectators and surrounded by a crowd outside, all strongly hostile to the petitioner.... when the Solicitor General entered the court, he was greeted with applause, stamping of feet and clapping of hands, and the judge... had a private conversation with the petitioner's counsel in which he expressed the opinion that there would be "probable danger of violence" if there should be an acquittal or a disagreement, and that it would be safer for not only the petitioner but his counsel to be absent from court when the verdict was brought in.... When the verdict was rendered, and before more than one of the jurymen had been polled there was such a roar of applause that the polling could not go on until order was restored. The noise outside was such that it was difficult for the judge to hear the answers of the jurors, although he was only ten feet from them....
>
> Mob law does not become due process of law by securing the assent of a terrorized jury.... It is our duty... to declare lynch law as little valid when practiced by a regularly drawn jury as when administered by one elected by a mob intent on death.[3]

Eight years later Justice Holmes was able to speak for a majority of the Supreme Court in finding another Southern trial, this time of five blacks in Arkansas, to have been unfairly dominated by mob influence.

> Shortly after the arrest of the petitioners a mob marched to the jail for the purpose of lynching them, but were prevented by the presence of

United States troops and the promise . . . that, if the mob would refrain . . . they would execute those found guilty in the form of law. . . . The court and the neighborhood were thronged with an adverse crowd that threatened the most dangerous consequences to anyone interfering with the desired result. . . . The trial lasted about three quarters of an hour, and in less than five minutes the jury brought in a verdict of guilty of murder in the first degree. According to the allegations and affidavits there never was a chance for the petitioners to be acquitted; no juryman could have voted for an acquittal and continued to live in Phillips county.[4]

Finally, in 1965, in upholding the constitutionality of a Louisiana statute that prohibited all picketing and parading "in or near a building housing a court" with intent to influence the administration of justice, the Supreme Court declared, "The constitutional safeguards relating to the integrity of the criminal process attend every stage of a criminal proceeding, starting with arrest and culminating in a trial. . . . There can be no doubt that they embrace the fundamental conception of a fair trial and that they exclude influence or domination by either a hostile or friendly mob. There is no room at any stage of judicial proceedings for such intervention; mob law is the very antithesis of due process."[5]

There are two subtle features of this last opinion that went significantly beyond the earlier decisions on mob rule and should not pass unnoticed and unquestioned. The first is the phrase "influence *or* domination" (italics mine), which suggests that it is not merely *intimidating* communication that can legitimately be restrained but that any kind of attempted extraneous persuasion may properly be barred from the environs of a courtroom. The second is the use of the phrase "hostile *or* friendly mob" (italics again mine), which introduces the notion that it is not only the defendant who has the right to a fair trial but that the prosecution, and the public it presumably represents, also have a right to secure a verdict from judges or jurors who have not been pushed into an acquittal by demonstrators friendly to the defendant. Since the Sixth Amendment speaks only of the right of an *accused* to a fair trial, the Supreme Court's action in thus appearing to extend the right of fair trial to the state is open to question.[6]

What I propose avoids having to resolve that question by taking a strong position against the Court's melding of the concepts of "influence" and "domination." If one accepts the argument, which is elaborated later in this book, that intimidating, threatening, or coercive speech can and should be distinguished from noncoercive influence or persuasion and, further, that intimidation can legitimately be restrained in a wide variety of settings, then one does not need a whole battery of special rules for courtrooms and trials that are grounded in the Sixth Amendment, and one does not need to decide whether the state, as well as the accused, has the right to a fair trial. I would maintain that *both* have a more generic right, as do people in many other circumstances, not to be the victims of intimidated decision making and that *neither* has a right to the total insulation of a trial from noncoercive and possibly innocuous influences. On the basis of these premises, I would argue, for example, that absolute bans on all demonstrations at courthouses are unjustifiably overbroad and that a distinction should be made between those that, in the particular circumstances, pose a real danger of intimidation and those that do not. Such a standard would provide adequate protection of the judicial system against mob rule and, at the same time, preserve the legitimate First Amendment interests that may be implicated in a courthouse demonstration.

But, it may be argued, courtrooms *are* different from all other settings in the extent to which they ought to be isolated even from possibly ineffective extraneous communication. As Justice Holmes said in still another early case involving published criticisms of the supreme court of Colorado, "The theory of our system is that the conclusions to be reached in a case will be induced only by evidence and argument in open court, and not by outside influence, whether of private talk or public print."[7] On the basis of that principle, it is regarded as out-of-bounds for anyone to communicate privately with a juror about a pending case or to lobby the sitting judge.

One can accept a few special rules of this sort, in recognition of the fact that a court is different from a legislative or administrative body where public opinion is a more appropriate concern, without going so far as to try to place the judiciary *entirely* outside the body politic (which it is not) or to insulate it totally from citizens expressing their views on litigation of social and political significance (which much of it is). Indeed, the Supreme Court itself, in a stream of decisions that departed sharply from the precedent of the Colorado case just alluded to, narrowly limited the extent to which published verbal attacks on judges and their rulings could be punished as contempts of court. Starting with *Bridges v. California* in 1941,[8] *Pennekamp v. Florida* in 1946,[9] *Craig v. Harney* in 1947,[10] and *Wood v. Georgia* in 1962,[11] the Supreme Court has consistently taken the position that public criticism of court proceedings can only be punished when it constitutes a clear and present danger to the administration of justice. Although the critical comments in each of these cases were vehement, the Court did not find that they had seriously interfered with the judicial process.

In recent years it has not been published potshots at judges, ex parte contacts with jurors, or angry mobs at courthouse doors that have created the most difficult free-speech-versus-fair-trial problems. Rather, it has been the influence on jurors' attitudes that is allegedly caused by prejudicial publicity which appears in the newspapers or on radio and television. The most problematic circumstances have been those in which defendants charged usually with sensational crimes appear to have been tried and convicted by the press before their official trial in the courtroom has ever gotten under way. The question that obviously arises is whether curbs must be imposed on press coverage of such cases in order to protect the defendant's right to a fair trial.

In 1959 the U.S. Supreme Court for the first time reversed a conviction because jurors had been exposed to news accounts of a defendant's prior criminal record—information which was thought to endanger their ability to render an impartial judgment.[12] Although the justices based this particular ruling on their supervisory power over procedures in the federal courts, rather than finding a violation of a constitutional right, they soon extended the principle in such a way as to root it in the Sixth Amendment and apply it to the states via the due process clause of the Fourteenth Amendment. That occurred two years later in *Irvin v. Dowd,* a case in which jurors had learned through pretrial press coverage that the defendant had confessed to twenty-four burglaries and six murders, and that he had unsuccessfully offered to plead guilty to the pending murder charge if the state would not demand the death penalty. Eight of the twelve jurors admitted to forming a pretrial opinion that the defendant was guilty, with "some going so far as to say it would take evidence to overcome their belief."[13] The Supreme Court had little difficulty in deciding that the accused's right to a fair trial had been prejudiced by these events.

Similarly, in *Rideau v. Louisiana* in 1963,[14] the Supreme Court felt compelled to reverse a conviction because of prejudicial pretrial publicity. In this instance a twenty-minute film showing the defendant confessing the commission of a murder to the police had been shown three times on a television station in the community where the trial was to take place. The Supreme Court said that the trial under these circumstances was "but a hollow formality," the real trial having taken place in the televised "kangaroo court . . . presided over by a sheriff, where there was no lawyer to advise Rideau of his right to stand mute."[15]

Finally, in the most celebrated of this series of decisions, the Supreme Court in 1966 held that Dr. Sam Sheppard, then serving a prison sentence in Ohio for the murder of his wife, had not had a fair trial, and he was ordered released from jail. The Court described the case as follows:

> For months the virulent publicity about Sheppard and the murder had made the case notorious. Charges and countercharges were aired in the news media besides those for which Sheppard was called to trial. In addition, only three months before the trial, Sheppard was

examined for more than five hours without counsel during a three-day inquest which ended in a public brawl. The inquest was televised live from a high school gymnasium seating hundreds of people.... bedlam reigned at the courthouse during the trial and newsmen took over practically the entire courtroom, hounding most of the participants in the trial, especially Sheppard.... Much of the material printed or broadcast during the trial was never heard from the witness stand, such as the charges that Sheppard had purposely impeded the murder investigation and must be guilty since he had hired a prominent criminal lawyer; that Sheppard was a perjurer; that he had sexual relations with numerous women.[16]

In each of these cases the justices of the Supreme Court assumed from the circumstances that jurors were likely to have been prejudiced by what they had seen or heard. But in 1975, in *Murphy v. Florida,*[17] they were unwilling to make that same assumption. Here, the defendant in an armed robbery case in Miami Beach, Florida, was described by the Supreme Court as follows: "... petitioner had been much in the news before. He had first made himself notorious for his part in the 1964 theft of the Star of India sapphire from a museum in New York. His flamboyant life style made him a continuing subject of press interest; he was generally referred to—at least in the media—as 'Murph the Surf.'"[18]

Acknowledging, "Some of the jurors had a vague recollection of the robbery with which petitioner was charged and each had some knowledge of petitioner's past crimes," the Court also noted that "none betrayed any belief in the relevance of petitioner's past to the present case. Indeed, four of the six jurors volunteered their views of its irrelevance, and one suggested that people who have been in trouble before are too often singled out for suspicion of each new crime—a predisposition that could only operate in petitioner's favor."[19]

In examining this situation the Supreme Court expressed the view that "juror exposure to information about a state defendant's prior convictions or to news accounts of the crime with which he is charged" does not by itself necessarily deprive a defendant of a fair trial. In order to be impartial, said the Court, jurors do not need to be "totally ignorant of the facts and issues involved." The opinion then quoted *Irvin v. Dowd* as follows: "To hold that the mere existence of any preconceived notion as to the guilt or innocence of an accused, without more, is sufficient to rebut the presumption of a prospective juror's impartiality would be to establish an impossible standard. It is sufficient if the juror can lay aside his impressions or opinion and render a verdict based on the evidence presented in court."[20]

The *Murphy* majority was willing to leave it "open to the defendant" to challenge and disprove the assurances given by jurors that their preconceptions could be laid aside, but it was not simply to be presumed that ultimate judgments automatically follow from preconceptions.

Justice Brennan, in his dissent, preferred to operate from an opposite premise. "It is of no moment," he said, "that several jurors ultimately testified that they would try to exclude from their deliberations their knowledge of petitioner's past misdeeds and his community reputation."[21] He, too, then turned for support to *Irvin v. Dowd:* "No doubt each juror was sincere when he said that he would be fair and impartial to petitioner, but the psychological impact requiring such a declaration before one's fellows is often its father. Where so many, so many times, admitted prejudice, such a statement of impartiality can be given little weight. As one of the jurors put it, 'You can't forget what you hear and see.'"[22]

Although it is obviously true that one may not *forget* what one hears and sees, the important question is what one *does* with that information. The procedure employed in our courts when a judge orders that something be "stricken from the record" assumes that those who heard it can and will ignore it, or at least will make a valiant effort to do so, when coming to a decision. The extent to which that is possible no doubt depends upon many variables, such as the sophistication of the hearer and the potency of the material itself. It is interesting that we usually worry more about juror than judge susceptibility to prejudicial communication, suggesting that we think it more likely that those with greater training or experience can more easily exclude extraneous considerations from their decision making. But even as to jurors, our system operates on the undoubtedly sometimes incorrect assumption that the average person is capable of resisting the often irrelevant (and thus prejudicial) emotional appeals of skillful trial lawyers.

The only reasonable conclusion one can draw from all of this is that sometimes some people (whether judges or jurors) are unduly influenced by irrelevant considerations and sometimes they are not; that prejudgment may, but does not necessarily, follow from exposure to prejudicial information or even from preconceptions if tentatively held. The Supreme Court may well have been correct in concluding that the juries in *Marshall, Irvin, Rideau,* and *Sheppard* had been rendered incapable of impartial judgment because of prejudicial publicity and that the jury in *Murphy* had not been so affected. It should be recognized, however, that those conclusions were based more on assumptions than on empirical data, just as was Justice Brennan's dissent in *Murphy*—a point that should be kept in mind as we proceed to explore other ramifications of the free-press-versus-fair-trial issue.

In all of the cases just reviewed here, the damage allegedly done by prejudicial communication was redressed by the Supreme Court's overturning of the defendant's conviction. Although the justices may have been distressed by the media's role, the remedy that was invoked did not directly affect the right of the press to behave as it had. It was not until 1976, in a sensational Nebraska mass murder case, that the Court confronted the question of a restraint, or so-called gag order, placed upon the press itself by a judge who hoped through this device to forestall the kind of prejudicial climate that might later cause appellate courts to invalidate the trial verdict. As it has consistently done with respect to other prior restraints upon the press, the Supreme Court held that the exceptional circumstances and heavy burden of proof that are required to justify such restraints were absent from the case.[23] Before even contemplating the subordination of the First Amendment rights of a free press to the Sixth Amendment rights of a criminal defendant, the Court insisted that the judiciary must first exhaust every other mechanism available to it for insuring fair trials. Three of the justices, with whom I would cast my lot, went so far as to suggest that Sixth Amendment rights can be protected adequately without *ever* resorting to the alternative of restraining the press.

What are the preferable mechanisms that the Court and others have suggested? How viable are they as solutions to the problem? To what extent do they really avoid interference with freedom of expression?

The first is removal of a trial from the community in which the crime has occurred to a location where press coverage may have been less intense. This might work well in some instances where the interest has been localized, but it is not likely to help matters in the most sensational cases where news coverage has been state or nationwide—and these are usually the ones posing the most serious problems of prejudicial publicity. As the Warren Commission complained in its report on the assassination of President John F. Kennedy, if Lee Harvey Oswald had not been killed by Jack Ruby it would have been difficult to find jurors for his trial anywhere in the United States who had not been saturated with prejudicial information about his alleged guilt.

A second method is postponement of the trial until the effects of press coverage of the crime may have diminished. This, of course, asks the defendant to trade off his constitutional right to a speedy trial in order to secure his right to a fair one. Aside from that shortcoming, there can be no assurance that impressions received from the press will fade with time or that commentary will not be revived when the trial is rescheduled. One of the justifications given by President Gerald Ford for his pardon of Richard Nixon was the belief that the climate of opinion would have made a fair trial for Nixon impossible for many, many months, if not forever.

A third mechanism is *voir dire,* the questioning and possible dismissal of prospective jurors who appear to have been prejudiced by pretrial publicity. As we have seen earlier, the best that can be expected from this process is the exclusion of those who are the most hopelessly biased and the acceptance of assurances from others that they are capable of laying aside the prejudicial information or preconceptions they may have. Whether they in fact do so is another matter.

The fourth procedure recommended by the Supreme Court is the use by trial judges of "emphatic and clear instructions on the sworn duty of each juror to decide the issues only on evidence presented in open court."[24] Like the striking of inadmissible evidence from the record after the jury has heard it, this method presumes a capacity for conscious, rational decision making that may not be in plentiful supply. Yet that presumption is not significantly different from the broader faith that underlies our entire system of freedom of expression and holds, with Justice Brandeis, that the best remedy for bad speech is a free market-place of ideas where decision makers are exposed to more and better speech.

Another recommended mechanism, where necessary, is sequestering the jury. This does not solve the problem of pretrial publicity but is designed to insulate jurors from any further extraneous communication once they have been impaneled and the trial is under way. It is an expensive process and works a hardship on jurors which may have a boomerang effect of causing them unconsciously to blame the defendant for the disruption of their lives. On the other hand, as the Supreme Court suggested in *Nebraska Press,* it may serve to emphasize the gravity of the juror's responsibility.[25]

None of the methods just reviewed impinges in any way on the rights of freedom of speech and press of those who wish to talk or write about a pending trial. Not so the procedures to which we now turn our attention, for, although they stop short of directly preventing the press from say-ing what it knows, a restrictive result is achieved indirectly by cutting off access to information that might be published if it were available.

Because the Sixth Amendment guarantees to a criminal defendant not only a speedy and fair trial but also a *public* one, moves to limit access to the courtroom or its records have been approached with caution. If the right to a public trial belongs *solely* to the accused, then of course there is the possibility that he or she may want to waive that right. But as with the question of a *fair* trial, it was never entirely clear what rights the public, or the press as its representatives, may have, independent of defendants and perhaps sometimes in conflict with defendants' perceived interests, to demand that judicial proceedings be open to their scrutiny. Despite a long-standing common-law tradition of public access to the judicial pro-cess,[26] despite the ubiquity of state constitutional provisions requiring openness in the courts,[27] and despite the fact that lower courts, both state and federal, had recognized either First or Sixth Amendment rights, or both, to public oversight of courtroom proceedings,[28] a narrow majority of the U.S. Supreme Court in 1979, while acknowledging "the general desirability of open judicial processes,"[29] flatly rejected the claim of a *Sixth* Amendment right to public trials for anyone other than criminal defendants[30] and took a pass temporarily on the invitation to find a First Amendment right to that same end.[31] Thus, the veil of secrecy which some courts had drawn over certain parts of the judicial process—in the instant case a pretrial hearing on suppression of evidence—was found to be an acceptable method of securing fair trials for defendants.

In addition to the closing of pretrial suppression hearings, trial court judges have often resorted to the impoundment or sealing of records to prevent material they believed to be potentially prejudicial to a fair trial or unnecessarily intrusive into personal privacy from being exposed to public view. Similarly, jury selection procedures, testimony by rape victims, and entire proceedings involving juveniles have sometimes been closed to the press and the public. A November 1977 review of these practices by the *New York Times* concluded that they increased in number following the Supreme Court's *Nebraska Press* decision of 1976. "One result of the decision," said the *Times* writer, "was that some judges tried to find ways other than gag orders to assure fair trials. Many judges simply began to hold evidentiary hearings in private or to clear courtrooms when particularly sensitive testimony was about to be given."[32]

First Amendment challenges to these practices met with mixed success. In Minnesota, the state supreme court was faced with press complaints in two murder cases where judges had sealed documents on the grounds that, if released prior to trial, they would make the securing of impartial juries difficult. One involved suppression of the formal criminal complaint filed by the state, and the other had to do with search warrants that had been issued during the investigation of the case. The Minnesota Supreme Court found that these secrecy orders had "the effect of either directly or indirectly interfering" with the press's "functions of collecting or disseminating the news," and they were ruled invalid.[33] The court said that the First Amendment does not allow for the sealing of records in a criminal proceeding unless there is proof that the information will pose a clear and present danger to a fair trial and there is no available alternative. The court also held that orders sealing court records are void unless prior notice has been given to the press and public along with an opportunity to appear in court to challenge their validity.

On the other hand, the U.S. Court of Appeals for the Fifth Circuit upheld a federal district court judge in Florida who had denied press access to transcripts of grand jury testimony and of bench conferences with lawyers, as well as to the names and addresses of the jurors and to some exhibits that had been identified in court but not received into evidence.[34] Although the court recognized that "such denials of access hamper newsgathering," it found that the particular documents sought by the press were not part of the public record in the case and that the press does not have a "First Amendment right of access to those matters not available to the public."[35]

In Arkansas, among other places, another related issue was adjudicated—namely, the exclusion of the press and public from jury selection processes. The trial judge in the case in question had closed *voir dire* proceedings at the request of a defendant's attorney who claimed that he wanted to avoid "adverse publicity" for his client. The Arkansas Supreme Court found that the judge had erred in closing the session:

> ...of all phases of a criminal trial, we can think of less reason to exclude the public, including the press, during the *voir dire* than at most any step taken during the course of litigation.... Cases have been reversed in this court because of answers given by prospective jurors on *voir dire* which subsequent investigation established were false, or at least incorrect, and which might have well disqualified the prospective juror. Particular spectators in a courtroom may know such facts and call them to the attention of interested parties.[36]

As for pretrial proceedings, the supreme court of New Hampshire supported a 1977 challenge by the Keene, New Hampshire, *Sentinel* to being excluded from a pretrial probable cause hearing of a person accused of sex-related offenses with minors. The newspaper had agreed not to publish the names of any juveniles that might be revealed during the hearings, and, in the circumstances of the particular case, the New Hampshire high court felt that the exclusion ran counter to its presumption in favor of open courtrooms.[37] The court made clear, however, that its decision did not mean that probable cause hearings could never be closed to the press.

A month later the highest court of New York ruled that trial judges in that state had broad authority to bar the press and public from pretrial hearings on the admissibility of evidence. The court indicated its belief that the right to a public trial is primarily that of the accused and that, although criminal trials are presumptively open to the public, neither the public nor the press has an absolute right to be present at all stages of such trials. The court went on: "To avoid becoming a link in the chain of prejudicial disclosures, trial courts have the power to exclude the public from pretrial suppression hearings.... At the point where press commentary on those hearings would threaten the impaneling of a constitutionally impartial jury in the county of venue, pretrial evidentiary hearings in this state are presumptively to be closed to the public."[38]

It was in its affirmation of this ruling that the U.S. Supreme Court announced its judgment that the Sixth Amendment provided no right of public access to the courtroom.[39] As to the possibility of a First Amendment right of public access to judicial proceedings, the Court's majority reserved judgment on that general proposition, finding that even if there were such a "putative right," it "was given all appropriate deference by the state . . . court in the present case."[40]

The four dissenters, also taking a pass on the First Amendment issue, sharply disagreed with the majority's understanding of the Sixth Amendment and recited an impressive array of documentation to support their view that the Sixth Amendment requires both trials and pretrial hearings to be open to the public, unless it is established that closure "is strictly and inescapably necessary in order to protect the fair trial guarantee."[41]

The dissent continued:

If, after considering the essential factors, the trial court determines that the accused has carried his burden of establishing that closure is necessary, the Sixth Amendment is no barrier to reasonable restrictions on public access designed to meet that need. Any restriction imposed, however, should extend no further than the circumstances reasonably require. Thus, it might well be possible to exclude the public from only those portions of the proceeding at which the prejudicial information would be disclosed, while admitting to other portions where the information the accused seeks to suppress would not be revealed. . . . Further, closure should be temporary in that the court should ensure that an accurate record is made of those proceedings held *in camera* and that the public is permitted proper access to the record as soon as the threat to the defendant's fair trial right has passed.[42]

Justices Powell and Rehnquist, who both concurred in the majority's stand on the Sixth Amendment and in the affirmance of the New York Court of Appeals judgment, were the only members of the Supreme Court who saw fit to address themselves to the First Amendment issue, and with diametrically opposed results. Justice Powell perceived a limited First Amendment right of access to courtroom proceedings, which could be overcome in the pretrial setting by a trial court's finding that "a fair trial for the defendant is likely to be jeopardized by publicity if members of the press and public are present and free to report prejudicial evidence that will not be presented to the jury."[43]

Justice Rehnquist, on the other hand, found that "there is no First

Amendment right of access in the public or the press to judicial or other governmental proceedings."[44] In his view, "lower courts . . . remain, in the best tradition of our federal system, free to determine for themselves the question whether to open or to close the proceeding."[45]

Only one year later the rest of the justices felt compelled to address this First Amendment issue head on, for the supreme court of Virginia had given its assent to the decision of a trial judge to close an entire criminal proceeding to the press and public solely on the basis of his own judgment that it was necessary, and without any consideration of less drastic alternatives—a course of action authorized by state statute. Except for Justice Rehnquist, there was unanimous agreement that the First Amendment does provide the press and public with a right of access to judicial proceedings—a right which had been violated in this case—although a majority could not coalesce around any particular phrasing of a supporting opinion.[46] Chief Justice Burger, joined by Justices White and Stevens in a plurality opinion, held that "the right to attend criminal trials is implicit in the guarantees of the First Amendment. . . . Absent an overriding interest articulated in findings, the trial of a criminal case must be open to the public."[47]

Justice Stewart wrote separately, apparently to emphasize his view that the right of access extends to civil as well as criminal trials—an issue which the Burger opinion had relegated to a somewhat ambiguous footnote—and to assert that where the courtroom is not large enough to accommodate everyone who may wish to attend, representatives of the press, as surrogates for the public, must be assured a place.[48]

Justice Blackmun reiterated his view of the previous year that it is in the Sixth Amendment, rather than the First, that the requirement of open judicial proceedings is properly to be found, and he expressed his concern about the uncertainty left by the Court's opinions as to where the limits are to be drawn on the First Amendment right of access that was being established.[49]

Justices Brennan and Marshall, although evidently pleased by the Court's recognition of the public's First Amendment right of access to government information, cautioned that "because 'the stretch of this protection is theoretically endless' . . . it must be invoked with discrimination and temperance. . . . An assertion of the prerogative to gather information must accordingly be assayed by considering the information sought and the opposing interests invaded."[50]

Because, in the case before them, the Virginia law and supreme court had authorized "trial closures at the unfettered discretion of the judge and parties,"[51] they were very clear that the First Amendment had been violated and that whatever "countervailing interests might be sufficiently compelling to reverse this presumption of openness need not concern us now."[52] Thus, for them as well as for the other justices, a working out of the balance between First Amendment rights and other competing interests in specific circumstances was left for another day.

A good example of the delicacy of that balancing process, as well as of the complexity of the competing claims, may be found in a case which had been adjudicated earlier by the U.S. Court of Appeals for the Seventh Circuit in 1977.[53] Four men had been convicted of rape at a trial in Saline County, Illinois, Circuit Court. They had exhausted their appeals in the state judicial system; they then sought habeas corpus relief from the federal courts claiming that they had been denied their Sixth Amendment right to a public trial. This claim was based on the fact that the trial judge had ordered the courtroom to be cleared of spectators when the prosecution called the alleged rape victim to testify. He had allowed the press to remain and had also given other spectators who wanted to stay in the courtroom the opportunity to state their names and reasons for wishing to be present. One such person, a minister, was permitted to remain "because of her position in the community and because of whom she represents," but the judge did not want anyone present "who has come out of curiosity only or who is concerned only with the progress of the case and desire to hear the testimony of this witness."[54]

In affirming the federal district court's denial of habeas corpus relief, the court of appeals weighed the competing interests on the scales and found in favor of the exclusion order.

It is well recognized that the interest of a defendant in having ordinary spectators present during trial is not an absolute right but must be balanced against other interests which might justify excluding them.... The ordeal of describing an unwanted sexual encounter before persons with no more than a prurient interest in it aggravates the original injury.... protection of the dignity of the complaining witness is a substantial justification for excluding spectators.[55]

The court further reasoned that "the action of the trial judge did not create any potential for secret abuse of the judicial power" since the press and others with a substantial interest were still on hand and the proceedings thus were not removed "from the forum of public opinion."[56]

This acknowledgment of the need for public scrutiny of court proceedings, though not to the extent claimed by the defendants as their right, is still somewhat in line with the broad rationale so well articulated by Justice Brennan in his concurring opinion in *Nebraska Press:*

Secrecy of judicial action can only breed ignorance and distrust of courts and suspicion concerning the competence and impartiality of judges; free and robust reporting, criticism, and debate can contribute to public understanding of the rule of law and to comprehension of the functioning of the entire criminal justice system, as well as improve the quality of that system by subjecting it to the cleansing effects of exposure and public accountability.[57]

Yet neither Justice Brennan nor, to my knowledge, any other justice of the Supreme Court has ever suggested that their own conferences should be transcribed and the records published. Like the secret deliberations of juries, discussions among appellate court judges have never been considered part of the "trial" which the Sixth Amendment requires to be public. The "cleansing effects of exposure and public accountability" can only be applied to the end product, not the internal processes, of such deliberations.

Before we can knowledgeably settle on general principles against which to assess the acceptability of the measures for protecting fair trials that have been reviewed thus far, we must expand the scope of our inquiry to some other practices that have been employed frequently. Of most significance are the restrictions that are commonly imposed on persons directly involved in pending litigation—law enforcement officials, government prosecutors, court personnel, defense attorneys, witnesses, plaintiffs, and defendants.

These restrictions take a variety of forms. Lawyers, whether for the prosecution or defense, are ethically bound by a provision of the American Bar Association Code of Professional Responsibility (also adopted by the Judicial Conference of the United States as a recommendation for rule making by federal district courts),[58] which states that it "is the duty of the lawyer not to release . . . information or opinion for dissemination by any means of public communication, in connection with pending or imminent criminal litigation . . . if there is a reasonable likelihood that such dissemination will interfere with a fair trial or otherwise prejudice the due administration of justice."[59]

The code goes on to specify that from the time of an arrest until the beginning of a trial attorneys are not to release any statements concerning:

> (1) the prior criminal record . . . , character or reputation of the accused . . . ; (2) . . . any confession, admission or statement given by the accused, or the refusal to make any statement; (3) the performance of . . . any examination or tests . . ; (4) the identity, testimony, or credibility of prospective witnesses . . . ; (5) the possibility of a plea of guilty . . . ; (6) any opinion as to the accused's guilt . . . or as to the merits of the evidence in the case.[60]

Once a trial has begun, lawyers are not to "give or authorize any extrajudicial statement ... relating to the trial or the parties or issues in the trial."[61]

Guidelines issued by the attorney general of the United States in 1965 govern the release of information to the news media by personnel of the U.S. Department of Justice. They provide that no statements should be made "for the purpose of influencing the outcome of a defendant's trial," and specifically identify the following:

(a) Observations about a defendant's character.
(b) Statements, admissions, confessions, or alibis attributable to a defendant.
(c) References to investigative procedures, such as fingerprints, polygraph examinations, ballistic tests, or laboratory tests.
(d) Statements concerning the identity, credibility, or testimony of prospective witnesses.
(e) Statements concerning evidence or argument in the case, whether or not it is anticipated that such evidence or argument will be used at a trial.[62]

Similar rules have been adopted or recommended for adoption by state and local governments for controlling the behavior of law enforcement officials working under their jurisdiction.

Finally, trial judges themselves have issued restrictive or "gag" orders on lawyers, witnesses, defendants, and other parties before the court, violations of which are punishable by contempt charges.[63]

Just as the media have fought against gag orders imposed upon them, so there have been numerous First Amendment challenges, in court and in the forum of public policy debate, to these restrictions on persons involved in litigation. Since different questions are raised with respect to government personnel, defense attorneys, and other parties, we shall look at each of these groups separately.

There is little serious argument maintaining a First Amendment right of police officers, sheriffs, prosecuting attorneys, federal investigators, court bailiffs, or other government officials to talk freely to the press or public about pending criminal cases. This does not mean that such persons never indulge in the practice but rather that the conduct is difficult to defend. The pretrial televised presentation of the defendant's confession to police in *Rideau* should not and would not have occurred under proper controls. Los Angeles Mayor Samuel Yorty caused deep distress to his own police department in 1968 when, shortly after the assassination of Robert Kennedy at the Ambassador Hotel, he made public the contents of two notebooks found in the possession of the alleged assassin, Sirhan Sirhan, including a statement about the "necessity" of assassinating Kennedy before June 5, 1968. Hesitant to criticize his boss in public, Police Chief Thomas Reddin nevertheless was quoted as saying circumspectly, "I feel that a release of material that would prejudice a trial would be extremely damaging."[64]

Restraints on government officials with respect to pending litigation are no different in principle than any curbs on the speech of employees that would undermine the appropriate performance of their duties. Mayor Yorty had no more business divulging evidence against Sirhan to the press than the janitor cleaning his office would have had in publishing the contents of his wastebasket.[65]

With reference to defense lawyers, however, the question is more difficult. Since all practicing attorneys are considered to be "officers of the court," defense counsel are usually regarded as appropriately subject to the same restrictions as prosecuting attorneys. The ABA Code of Professional Responsibility makes no distinction between the prosecution and defense, nor does the typical restrictive order issued by trial judges.

Yet there are good reasons for treating the two groups differently. The American Civil Liberties Union, in deciding to support the latter position, reasoned: (1) Public sentiment is generally sympathetic to the prosecution in criminal cases; the defense attorney often has an extra burden of overcoming community prejudice against his or her client. (2) Statements by prosecutors are more likely to be believed by the public than statements by defense attorneys, since the former persons are perceived as acting in the public interest and the latter as acting in the interest of their clients. (3) Most abuses regarding prejudicial publicity stem from prosecution and law enforcement officials; insofar as the right to a fair trial is primarily that of the accused, defense attorneys are not likely to be guilty of compromising that right.[66] Only if one assumes that lawyers for the defense have the capacity for prejudicing a fair trial does it make sense to place them under restrictions.

Restrictive orders directed to witnesses and parties in litigation are the most troublesome of all, for the government has no supervisory claim upon them other than through their involvement in the particular trial that is going on. Yet trial courts have not hesitated to impose such restraints, and most of them have withstood constitutional challenge.[67] Among the most widely publicized of such orders were those issued by Judge John Sirica in connection with the famous Watergate break-in trials. On October 4, 1972, at the request of defendant Howard Hunt, Judge Sirica silenced all other defendants, their lawyers, government officials, witnesses, potential witnesses, "alleged victims," and "all persons acting for or with them." He warned them against "making any extrajudicial statements to anyone, including the news media, concerning any aspects of this case which are likely to interfere with the rights of the accused, or the public, to a fair trial by an impartial jury."[68] Senator

George McGovern, who was campaigning for president of the United States at the time and making Watergate one of his major issues, immediately announced that he intended to pursue his First Amendment right of "informing the public about this act of political espionage,"[69] even though he conceivably could have been defined as an "alleged victim" of the break-in or as one "acting for or with them."

The following year Judge Sirica ordered James W. McCord, Jr., and Jeb Stuart Magruder, both of whom had already been found guilty, to stop making public speeches or granting interviews if they wished to remain free pending sentencing. The judge said their speaking could jeopardize a fair trial for others who might still be indicted in the case and that it was also a "disgrace" for Watergate conspirators to "profit from their wrongdoing" by earning large lecture fees.[70] The ACLU publicly protested the judge's order, claiming it to be a violation of the First Amendment.[71]

Not all appellate court decisions have sustained restrictions on trial participants and lawyers. One of the most significant opinions to the contrary was handed down by the U.S. Court of Appeals for the Seventh Circuit in *Chicago Council of Lawyers v. Bauer* in 1975,[72] the first federal appellate court ruling on the constitutionality of the standards governing extrajudicial statements by attorneys that had been recommended by the American Bar Association and the U.S. Judicial Conference in 1968 and thereupon adopted by most federal district courts.

The Seventh Circuit, in two earlier decisions, had indicated its view that court-ordered limits on public statements by lawyers and defendants should not be imposed unless the speech constituted a "serious and imminent threat" of interference with the fair administration of justice.[73] This criterion was a departure from the more easily met standard that had been employed by the U.S. Court of Appeals for the Tenth Circuit in 1969 and left standing by the U.S. Supreme Court, where restrictive orders were found to be acceptable whenever there was a "reasonable likelihood that prejudicial news prior to the trial would render more difficult the impaneling of a jury."[74]

In *Chicago Council of Lawyers* the Seventh Circuit took a more jaundiced view of limitations on the speech of trial participants, particularly of defendants and defense counsel, and concluded that the rules recommended by the ABA and Judicial Conference were far too broad. Noting that litigation may well involve matters of public concern and that lawyers "often are in a position to act as a check on government by exposing abuses or urging action," the court suggested that requiring them to withhold their comments until a trial is concluded may make it too late for any good to be done.[75]

The court's ruling provided that the particular circumstances of each case must be examined to determine whether the speech that is to be limited does, indeed, pose a serious and imminent threat to the fair administration of justice. It conceded that certain kinds of comments, in the absence of evidence to the contrary, might presumptively fall into that category—such as extrajudicial statements by prosecuting attorneys during the investigative stages of a case. On the other hand, it held that posttrial comments prior to sentencing "could never be deemed a serious and imminent threat" because judges have the discretion to take any relevant factors into account when deciding on a sentence.[76]

The Seventh Circuit also addressed the question of the validity of restrictive orders in civil litigation, since the ABA and Judicial Conference had proposed that the same standards be applicable to both criminal and civil proceedings. Because the discovery and appellate stages of civil litigation may last for years, because important social and political issues are often implicated in such cases, and because the impartiality of jurors may be less of a life-and-death matter, the court was unwilling to grant any presumption in favor of restrictions. The burden of demonstrating a serious and imminent threat would rest on those who wished to impose restraints.[77]

When, in 1976, the Subcommittee on Constitutional Rights of the U.S. Senate Judiciary Committee reviewed the problems of restrictive orders on trial participants and of closed judicial records and proceedings, their debt to the Court of Appeals for the Seventh Circuit was clear and explicit. The subcommittee recommended that Congress enact the "serious and imminent threat" standard into law but went even further to spell out limited conditions under which it might be applied:

I. A Restrictive Order Upon Trial Participants May Not Issue Unless:
  A. (Substantive Provisions)
    1. The prejudicial impact of the extrajudicial statement constitutes a serious and imminent threat to the fair administration of justice in that—
       (a) there is probable cause to believe that the extrajudicial statement will reach the jurors or potential jurors;
       (b) there is probable cause to believe that such statement upon reaching the jurors or potential jurors will create an impermissible level of prejudice; and
       (c) the prejudicial impact of the extrajudicial statement cannot be avoided or counteracted by alternative means less restrictive upon first amendment rights. . . .
  B. (Procedural Provisions)
    1. The court gives notice to interested parties of a hearing on any motion to issue the order;
    2. The judge states for the record his findings of fact justifying such an order; and

      3. There is available a procedure for an expedited, inter-
        locutory appeal concerning the merits of such an order;
        and, the appeal process is designed to produce a prompt
        judicial decision.
   C. (Standing Provision)
      1. Members of the press are accorded standing to litigate the
        propriety of such order.[78]

Similar provisions were recommended by the subcommittee for secrecy orders:

A Judge May Not Close Any Proceeding, Whether at the Pretrial Level
or during the Trial Itself, nor Seal Any Document Unless:
   A. (Substantive Provision)
      1. The failure to close the proceeding or to seal the document
        constitutes a serious and imminent threat to the fair adminis-
        tration of justice in that—
        (a) There is probable cause to believe that danger to the fair
           trial rights of the defendant, or other specified interests
           would result; and
        (b) There is probable cause to believe that the danger speci-
           fied in A (1) (a) cannot be avoided or counteracted by
           alternative means less restrictive upon first amendment
           rights. . . .
[B (Procedural Provisions) and C (Standing Provisions) are almost
identical to those quoted above in connection with restrictive orders
on trial participants][79]

The principles enunciated by the Subcommittee on Constitutional
Rights for dealing with court secrecy and with restrictive orders on trial
participants appear to me to strike as wise a balance as one can hope to
find in this complex field.[80] They are consistent in both letter and spirit
with the serious and imminent danger standard I have proposed for
dealing with courthouse demonstrations, with the U.S. Supreme Court's
clear-and-present-danger rulings on public criticism of judges, with the
criteria the Supreme Court claimed to be using in *Irvin, Rideau, Sheppard,*
and *Murphy,* and with the minimal requirements of all the justices in
Nebraska Press. Except for the job-related limitations on law enforcement
officials, court personnel, and public prosecutors described with approval earlier in this chapter, the principle of serious and imminent
threat to the fair administration of justice—buttressed by the requirements that there be probable cause to believe that "an impermissible level of prejudice" will actually be created and that all
alternatives to restrictions on speech have been exhausted—should
suffice to protect the vital rights that are guaranteed by the First and
Sixth Amendments.

There remain two other facets of the free speech–fair trial controversy which we have yet to address. I shall preface our discussion of them by indicating my belief that the principles just articulated also provide all the answer that we need for these problems.

The first is the issue of the televising, photographing, or tape recording of courtroom proceedings for circulation to the public by the news media. There has been a long history of opposition by the legal profession to these particular modes of communication about the judicial process, allegedly based on a concern for protecting that process from extraneous influences that are disruptive to the fair administration of justice.

In 1937 the American Bar Association adopted as Canon 35 of its code of ethics the following statement: "Proceedings in court should be conducted with fitting dignity and decorum. The taking of photographs in the courtroom, during sessions of the court or recesses between sessions, and the broadcasting of court proceedings are calculated to detract from the essential dignity of the proceedings, degrade the court and create misconceptions with respect thereto in the mind of the public and should not be permitted."

This was followed in 1946 by the adoption of Rule 53 of the Federal Rules of Criminal Procedure which provides that in federal courts, "The taking of photographs in the courtroom during the progress of judicial proceedings or radio broadcasting of judicial proceedings from the courtroom shall not be permitted by the court." When television came upon the scene, Canon 35 and Rule 53 were both amended to encompass that new medium of communication.

The language of Canon 35 suggests that its proponents may have been more concerned with matters of "dignity and decorum" than with substantive threats to the fair conduct of trials. To what extent that may also have been true of the U.S. Supreme Court in its first ruling on this question is not entirely clear. That decision came in 1965 in response to an appeal by Billie Sol Estes, who claimed that his conviction for fraud in a Texas court violated his Sixth Amendment right to a fair trial because of the coverage of the pretrial hearings by radio and television. The scene which led the majority to conclude that Estes had, indeed, been deprived of a fair trial was described in the Court's opinion as follows:

> ... initial hearings were carried live by both radio and television, and news photography was permitted throughout. The videotapes of these hearings clearly illustrate that the picture presented was not one of that judicial calm and serenity to which petitioner was entitled.... Indeed, at least 12 cameramen were engaged in the courtroom throughout the hearing taking motion and still pictures and televising the proceedings. Cables and wires snaked across the courtroom floor,

three microphones were on the judge's bench and others were beamed at the jury box and the counsel table. It is conceded that the activities of the television crews and news photographers led to considerable disruption of the hearings.[81]

Although the Court's sense of propriety was obviously offended by the commotion that had occurred during these proceedings, the support offered for its conclusion that an unfair trial had resulted sounds remarkably feeble:

> The State ... says that the use of television in the instant case was "without injustice to the person immediately concerned," basing its position on the fact that the petitioner has established no isolatable prejudice and that this must be shown in order to invalidate a conviction in these circumstances. The State paints too broadly in this contention, for this Court itself has found instances in which a showing of actual prejudice is not a prerequisite to reversal. This is such a case. It is true that in most cases involving claims of due process deprivations we require a showing of identifiable prejudice to the accused. Nevertheless, at times a procedure employed by the State involves such a *probability that prejudice will result* that it is deemed inherently lacking in due process. ... Television in its present state and by its very nature, reaches into a variety of areas in which it may cause prejudice to an accused. Still one cannot put his finger on its specific mischief and prove with particularity wherein he was prejudiced. This was found true in Murchison, Tumey, Rideau and Turner. Such untoward circumstances as were found in those cases are *inherently bad* and *prejudice to the accused was presumed.*[82] [All italics mine]

To limit particular forms of press coverage on the basis of *presumptions* and *probabilities* rather than proof of serious and imminent danger seems to me an unacceptable deviation from First Amendment principles. As Justice Stewart said for the four dissenters in *Estes v. Texas:*

> I think that the introduction of television into the courtroom is, at least in the present state of the art, an extremely unwise policy. It invites many constitutional risks, and it detracts from the inherent dignity of a courtroom. But I am unable to escalate this personal view into a per se constitutional rule. And I am unable to find, on the specific record of this case, that the circumstances attending the limited televising of the petitioner's trial resulted in the denial of any right guaranteed to him by the United States Constitution. ... Where there is no disruption of the "essential requirement of the fair and orderly administration of justice ... [f]reedom of discussion should be given the widest range." Pennekamp v. Florida ... Bridges v. California ... Cox v. Louisiana.[83]

Even Justice Harlan, who had joined with the majority's position in this particular case, felt compelled to write a separate concurring opinion expressing the view that the televising of court proceedings under other circumstances might be entirely compatible with the Sixth Amendment guarantee of a fair trial.

The "state of the art" of television, to which Justice Stewart referred and which he correctly anticipated might alter over time, did indeed change rapidly during the ensuing decade. Unobtrusive equipment, such as parabolic microphones and light-sensitive, noiseless cameras, became available, and with that development came a gradual softening of the opposition to their use. Texas and Colorado had been the first to permit some experimentation with TV coverage in their state courts, and in 1976 they were joined by Alabama, Florida, and Washington.[84] At the end of 1977, Georgia, Kentucky, and New Hampshire had also joined their ranks.[85] By February 1978 a special committee of the American Bar Association was ready to recommend that its code be changed to allow for unobtrusive television coverage of criminal trials, but after deferring action for a year the ABA's House of Delegates rejected that recommendation.[86]

Despite ABA inertia, approximately half of the states in the Union had begun to allow cameras in the courtroom under various conditions by the time the U.S. Supreme Court returned to the issue for a second time. In January 1981 a unanimous Court held that the accused in a Florida criminal case had failed to show that he had been deprived of a fair trial by television coverage and that state courts were free, if they wished, to allow cameras in the courtroom even over the objection of a defendant.[87] The court did not foreclose the possibility that in another case an appellant might be able to prove that the presence of cameras had prejudiced a fair trial, but the justices were unwilling, as in *Estes,* to assume the inevitability of that result. It should also be noted that the Court explicitly based its decision on the right of state judiciaries to govern their own procedures—within constitutional bounds, of course—and not on any First Amendment right of the press or public which required that photographic equipment be allowed in the courtroom.

In view of the fact that the basis for keeping cameras and tape recorders out of courtrooms is supposed to be the preservation of fair trials, it is ironic that change has occurred first in state *trial* courts and that appellate courts, more particularly those of the federal system, have adamantly resisted the trend. But, as the columnist Carl Rowan has argued:

> ...why should readers have to rely on my summary of what the opposing sides said in the Supreme Court about the right of women to receive abortion money under Medicaid? Or whether a special admis-

sions program for minorities at the University of California at Davis is an unconstitutional denial of the rights of Allan Bakke and other non-minority Americans?

When emotions run deep and the great mass of Americans feel that their lives hang in the balance, why shouldn't all people be able to see and hear for themselves how our ultimate interpreter of the law fashions a verdict that it calls justice?

Some federal judges are now saying openly . . . that if a handful of spectators (often friends, relatives and cronies of the justices and their staffs) can see and hear Supreme Court proceedings, so should all law students in America.[88]

And, I would add, why only law students?

A second issue related to free speech–fair trial that has received considerable attention in recent years concerns the extent to which lawyers and parties to litigation are free to express themselves in courtrooms in ways that are viewed by some as disruptive. Incidents that have come under scrutiny range from refusals to stand when a judge enters a courtroom, to cursing or shouting obscenities, to pounding on a table, to accusing a judge of having conducted "a star chamber proceeding" that "smacked of Stalinism, Hitlerism, Mussolinism, and all these isms."[89]

Since the behavior in question is most commonly engaged in by defendants and defense lawyers in anger and protest over what they have perceived as unfair treatment at the hands of the court, restrictions on such conduct can hardly be rationalized on the grounds that they are required to protect the *accused's* Sixth Amendment rights. What is truly at stake here is the right of the state to conduct its judicial business without interference—in other words, to maintain "order in the court." Insofar as disorder may, in fact, jeopardize a fair trial, that certainly has Sixth Amendment implications. But the larger concern is not so much for maintaining a *fair* trial as it is for avoiding a *chaotic* one.

The question is whether the degree of restriction currently practiced and found acceptable by our judicial system is appropriate, in a society governed by the First Amendment, to the ends it supposedly serves.

A *Chicago Sun-Times* reporter (and lawyer), Patrick R. Oster, has provided an interesting historical backdrop to this problem:

> The story goes that in the late 16th century an English barrister who was dissatisfied with a judge's ruling tossed a sheaf of papers at the judge to register his disgust.
>
> The papers fluttered toward the judge, and in the aftermath of this breach of decorum, it was decided that the barrister had to be disciplined to discourage him and others from further outbursts.
>
> The barrister was ordered to put his hand "on the bar"—the railing that separated the judge from the public—and the court bailiff was

told to cut it off, which he did, leaving the severed hand in place for
the salutary effect it might have on would-be upstarts.

Lawyers haven't been the same since.[90]

Oster's concluding allusion to the deference with which the majority
of attorneys approach their trial work is observably well taken. Most
lawyers are much more ready to fight in defense of freedom of speech
for citizens who exercise that right out on the streets than they are to do
battle for their own freedom of expression or for that of their clients
in the courtroom. Indeed, the notion that the First Amendment might
even apply to the latter domain has been amazingly late in arriving on
the legal scene.

The most venturesome and comprehensive study of that issue,
undertaken by lawyers themselves, was commissioned by the Association
of the Bar of the City of New York, and culminated in a report of its
Special Committee on Courtroom Conduct published in 1973.[91] A questionnaire was sent by the committee to every trial judge of general jurisdiction in the country and to lower criminal court judges in New York
and California. Of the 1,602 people who responded, only 107 (or less
than 7 percent) said they had experienced a total of 112 cases of trial
disruption in their entire judicial careers. With over 100 federal district
court judges replying, there were only five cases of disruption reported
by them.[92] The committee concluded: "By far the most startling revelation of the questionnaire returns was that there is no serious quantitative
problem of disruption in American courts. The Chicago and Black
Panther cases were not the tip of an iceberg, as feared by so many, but
the larger part."[93]

The committee proceeded to point out that, even to the extent that
disorder had occurred, it "should not be surprising in a proceeding
where the state is acting to deprive an individual of his freedom and
reputation; where there are stresses in the system, such as racism and the
pressures of due process; where there are occasional political prosecutions and overbearing judges; and where the proceeding is essentially
polemic and competitive, with emotion and temper never far from the
surface."[94]

Having made this gesture of human empathy and political insight,
the committee, like the good lawyers they were, could not forget that
severed hand on the British bar. Thus, they immediately went on: "Disorder is dangerous, nevertheless, because any interference with an or-
derly system of justice is threatening because some causes of disruption,
if not eliminated, could lead to more extensive interruption of trial proceedings, and a more serious deterioration in the legal process."[95]

And later, with respect to "disrespectful remarks" made by defense
attorneys: "We believe that the necessity for respect is inherent in the

very nature of the judicial process. A judge should be accorded every reasonable deference commensurate with his authority. He must be treated with respect to ensure that his decisions are based on reasoned principles instead of emotional reactions to insult. He must be treated with respect so that the legal process functions smoothly."[96]

What the committee had finally arrived at here was a sermon on etiquette not unlike the speech delivered by Chief Justice Warren Burger to the American Law Institute in 1971, which said in part:

> With passing time I am developing a deep conviction as to the necessity for civility if we are to keep the jungle from closing in on us and taking over all that the hand and brain of man has created in thousands of years, by way of rational discourse and in deliberative processes, including the trial of cases in our courts.... all too often, overzealous advocates seem to think the zeal and effectiveness of a lawyer depends on how thoroughly he can disrupt the proceedings or how loud he can shout or how close he can come to insulting all those he encounters—including the judges....
>
> At the drop of a hat—or less—we find adrenalin-fueled lawyers cry out that theirs is a "political trial." ...
>
> With all deference, I submit that lawyers who know how to think but have not learned how to behave are a menace and a liability, not an asset, to the administration of justice.[97]

Much as one may sympathize with the Chief Justice's impatience over the admittedly obnoxious behavior of a few ego-tripping advocates, and as strongly as one can agree on the desirability of a calm and reasoned approach to judicial decision making, it does not follow that good manners should be made compulsory or decorum mandated by law.

Yet that is essentially what happens in most American courts. And it happens with the blessing of our nation's highest court which, in giving its approval to everything from contempt citations to the binding and gagging of unruly defendants, declared as recently as 1970 that it was "essential to the proper administration of criminal justice that dignity, order and decorum be the hallmark of all court proceedings in our country."[98]

One can be forgiven for questioning whether binding and gagging the sole black defendant, Bobby Seale, at the Chicago Conspiracy Trial, did more to enhance or to undermine the dignity of that courtroom. It is of interest that, when Seale's conviction for contempt was reviewed by the U.S. Court of Appeals for the Seventh Circuit, that Court, consistent with the philosophy it had expressed in other related rulings, said:

> ... it has frequently been held, and considerable scholarly comment supports the view, that mere disrespect or affront to the judge's sense of dignity will not sustain a citation for contempt. The line between

insult and obstruction, however, is not clearly delineated, and at some point disrespect and insult become actual and material obstruction. . . .

"The fires which [the language] kindles must constitute an imminent, not merely a likely, threat to the administration of justice. The danger must not be remote or even probable; it must immediately imperil" [Craig v. Harney, 331 U.S. 367, 371 (1947)]. . . .

A showing of imminent prejudice to a fair and dispassionate proceeding is, therefore, necessary to support a contempt based upon mere disrespect or insult.[99]

I submit that once again the Seventh Circuit was closer, in this opinion, to the letter and spirit of the First Amendment than Chief Justice Burger has been. This view does require, of course, that judges learn to respond to occasional symbolic abuse with the equanimity we expect of other mortals in positions of authority, like legislators, bureaucrats, foremen, psychiatrists, and parents. What is called for is a demystification of the judicial process, perhaps at the expense of some of the forms, though not of the substance of "dignity, order and decorum."

Critical as I have been of our judiciary's stance with respect to ill-tempered comments in the courtroom, television coverage of judicial proceedings, restrictive orders on defendants and defense attorneys, and demonstrations on courthouse grounds, I feel impelled to conclude this chapter on a more positive note by returning once again to what is undoubtedly the most important aspect of the free press–fair trial controversy, and the one on which our system has by far the best record— the matter of gag orders on the press itself. One need only compare the Supreme Court's unanimous decision in *Nebraska Press Association v. Stuart* with the practices of the mother country of our legal system, England, to see how far the child has advanced beyond the parent.

English law provides for rigid controls, with contempt of court as punishment for transgressions, not only on all reporting of criminal proceedings but on press coverage of civil litigation as well.[100]

In contrast, *Nebraska Press* enunciated the doctrine that court-ordered prior restraints on press commentary about pending trials may be permitted only in the most exceptional circumstances, with three of the justices going so far as to declare that such restrictions are *entirely* prohibited by the First Amendment. The Court did not suggest that prejudicial publicity is not a problem; that voluntary self-restraint by the media, under such guidelines as many news organizations have developed, is not to be encouraged; or that steps short of gagging the press should not be taken to avoid the effects of communication that will clearly interfere with a fair trial. Quite the contrary. But the justices did recognize that muzzling the press deprives society of a vital check on its legal system. As the Court had observed earlier in *Sheppard v. Maxwell:*

A responsible press has always been regarded as the handmaiden of effective judicial administration, especially in the criminal field. Its function in this regard is documented by an impressive record of service over several centuries. The press does not simply publish information about trials but guards against the miscarriage of justice by subjecting the police, prosecutors, and the judicial process to extensive public scrutiny and criticism.[101]

Other commentators have elaborated on that record, noting in particular the instances when dangerous rumors have been scotched by accurate news reports about a crime, or when exculpatory evidence, alibis, or witnesses have been turned up as a result of investigations conducted or stories published by the press.[102]

Of course we pay some price for this freedom, as for all others. We run the risk that journalists may sometimes act in grossly irresponsible ways and that serious criminal offenses may go unpunished as a result. But these costs must be regarded as necessary and tolerable if we are to be serious about the First Amendment.

Part 3

Communication to Other People

7 Symbolic Battery

Part 2 of this book has dealt with possible harms to people that may result from unrestrained communication about them to others. Part 3 is concerned with modes of expression that are said to be injurious to those who are on the receiving end of the communication. It explores the kinds of harm that are thought to occur and assesses the justifications that are offered for restraints. The starting point will be with those categories of expression that might be characterized as symbolic battery—assaultive communicative behaviors that, according to Chafee, are "like acts because of their immediate consequences to the five senses,"[1] or as described by the U.S. Supreme Court, are "those which by their very utterance inflict injury."[2]

It is essential to the clarity of our analysis that we begin by making a distinction, too frequently obscured, between harms allegedly flowing from the *meaning* of a supposedly assaultive communicative act and those resulting from the *medium* through which the message is transmitted. Examples of assaultive media, regardless of the content of the communication, are the noise of a blaring portable radio on a bus or peaceful beach, high-intensity light from a rotating beam flashing intermittently across a bedroom window, the jangling of a telephone during a favorite TV show, or the ringing of a doorbell as one sits down to a long-awaited meal. Arguably assaultive messages, on the other hand, may range all the way from the proverbial and nonverbal "giving someone the finger" to a highly verbal cussing out.

A simple way of determining whether it is the medium or the message that is the alleged offender is to imagine the target person as a foreigner who does not understand either the language or the nonverbal symbols of our culture. If, in the absence of such meanings, the recipient might still feel attacked by a particular act of communication, it can be assumed it is the medium, rather than the message, that is responsible. To the extent that advocates of restrictions mix together their reactions to these separable elements, they tend to confuse our thinking with respect to the appropriateness of the limits they suggest. We shall, therefore, reserve consideration of the problem of assaultive media until the next chapter, and focus our attention here exclusively on those circumstances in which it is the meaning of the message that is claimed to be deserving of restraint.

There are four kinds of legal doctrine that have traditionally been invoked to deal with the variety of so-called speech-acts with which we are concerned here. The first is the concept of "fighting words," promulgated by the U.S. Supreme Court in *Chaplinsky v. New Hampshire* in 1942.[3] Second are the public nuisance laws that commonly appear on the books of local governments. Third is the notion of privacy rights for captive audiences—a right, as the Supreme Court described in 1970, "to be let alone."[4] Finally, there is the common-law tort of "intentional infliction of emotional distress"—a doctrine which allows for the recovery of damages against "one who by extreme and outrageous conduct intentionally or recklessly causes severe emotional distress to another."[5] Each of these concepts shall be examined and evaluated in turn.

Fighting Words

The "fighting words" doctrine has already been introduced in Chapter 2, where we noted that it has its roots in the debatable assumption that some communicative acts "are no essential part of any exposition of ideas, and are of such slight social value as a step to truth that any benefit that may be derived from them is clearly outweighed by the social interests in order and morality."[6]

Fighting words, as originally defined by the Supreme Court in *Chaplinsky,* have one or the other of two characteristics—they are "those which by their very utterance inflict injury *or* [italics mine] tend to incite an immediate breach of the peace."[7] What the Court had in mind here was the sort of communication it described two years earlier as "profane, indecent or abusive remarks directed to the person of the hearer." "Resort to epithets or personal abuse," the Court had then said, "is not in any proper sense communication of information or opinion safeguarded by the Constitution."[8] Whether the communication consisted of accusing a police officer of being a "damned Fascist" and a "God damned racketeer," as Chaplinsky had done, or calling the publicly assembled members of a school board "mother-fuckers," as occurred in a more recent case,[9] the premise has been that the ideational content of such communication is so minimal, and the potential for psychological injury to the listener or for a fight that is disruptive of social order so great, that legal restraints are justified.

Insofar as fighting words may be restricted because of their tendency to provoke reactive violence, rather than because of their impact on the psyches of their target, we shall postpone consideration of them until part 4 of this book when the full range of questions having to do with the maintenance of social order is addressed. Our interest in fighting words at this point is solely in their alleged capacity to inflict injury "by their very utterance"—what is sometimes referred to as the first branch of the two-pronged *Chaplinsky* standard.

My position on this matter has already been anticipated by comments that were made in Chapter 2. How it can seriously be argued that calling a policeman a "Fascist," or school board members "mother-fuckers," is without ideational content escapes me completely. Indeed I would suggest that it is precisely the ideational content that makes the listener so angry. Whether such epithets "are no essential part of any exposition of ideas" and are of "such slight social value as a step to the truth" as to strip them of constitutional protection are questions of somewhat greater seriousness deserving of a less terse response.

From one point of view there is probably nothing one can think of that is an *essential* part of the exposition of any idea; there are always alternatives that can be found, *if necessary*, for giving voice to one's feelings. This proposition has strongly influenced the First Amendment thinking of Supreme Court Justice John Paul Stevens, for example, who commented in a footnote to his opinion in *F.C.C. v. Pacifica Foundation,* "There are few, if any, thoughts that cannot be expressed by the use of less offensive language."[10] The problem with this view is that most people have a preferred way of expressing themselves in particular situations, and they may not be as articulate, effective, or as true to themselves in other modes. Despite Justice Stevens's assertion in the aforementioned footnote that a "requirement that indecent language be avoided will have its primary effect on the form, rather than the content, of serious communication," the First Amendment ought not to be regarded as giving our government the power to prescribe the style in which people communicate their beliefs. As the Supreme Court majority so well put it in *Cohen v. California,* the case of the young man who lettered "Fuck the Draft" on his jacket: " . . . words are often chosen as much for their emotive as their cognitive force. We cannot sanction the view that the Constitution, while solicitous of the cognitive content of individual speech, has little or no regard for that emotive function which, practically speaking, may often be the more important element of the overall message sought to be communicated."[11]

And, as Justice William Brennan added in his sharply worded retort to Justice Stevens in *F.C.C. v. Pacifica Foundation:* "The idea that the content of a message and its potential impact on any who might receive it can be divorced from the words that are the vehicle for its expression is transparently fallacious. A given word may have a unique capacity to capsule an idea, evoke an emotion, or conjure up an image."[12]

But in the limited case of personally abusive epithets, are there not countervailing interests that might justify the control of such communication in the public forum? This brings up the question of whether the "social value" of such communication "as a step to truth" is so slight as to warrant its subordination to the target person's interest in not being subjected to psychological attack.

How one quantifies the degree to which calling someone a foul name may be a "step to the truth," I confess I do not know, anymore than I would know how to measure the thickness of the target individual's psychological "skin." I am persuaded, however, that there was *some* significant social value, as a step to truth, in the "Telling It Like It Is" movement of the 1960s, personally abusive as that communication sometimes was. Calling Lyndon Johnson a murderer for his role in the Vietnam War ("Hey, Hey, LBJ, How Many Kids Have You Killed Today?"), or shouting four-letter words at "Honkies" as an expression of black frustration and rage, may have moved us faster toward perceiving the truth of those issues than all of the more refined dialogue of the intellectual elites. Many a dispute within families or between friends has been crystallized and clarified by the hurling of a choice epithet. This is not to deny that personalized emotional explosions frequently obscure the real issues between people and are often counterproductive. It is simply to assert that there is nothing intrinsically or inevitably non-truth-seeking about the rhetoric of personal abuse.

Given the possibility that epithets may sometimes be a useful commodity in the marketplace of ideas, we must place that consideration in the balance against the injury that is allegedly sustained by the targets of such communication. Recognizing that there is great variability in the degree to which people are bothered by being called unpleasant names, one must still question whether *any* psychic injury—more accurately it should be described as annoyance or anger—rises to a sufficient level of seriousness to warrant legal protection. When weighing that kind of interest against the claims of the First Amendment, I believe that the scales tip heavily in favor of freedom of expression.

It appears that this is the position that a majority of the U.S. Supreme Court has most recently adopted on the issue of fighting words. A series of opinions starting with *Gooding v. Wilson* in 1972,[13] and culminating with *Lewis v. New Orleans* in 1974,[14] has invalidated state and local laws that proscribe fighting words unless those statutes are limited to the punishment of utterances that "have a direct tendency to cause acts of violence by the person to whom, individually, the remark is addressed."[15] Without explicitly saying so, the Supreme Court seems to have chopped off the first branch of the *Chaplinsky* definition of fighting words.[16] If that is the case, I would regard it as a welcome advance.

Public Nuisances

Three years prior to *Gooding v. Wilson,* and thus without benefit of its guidance, the U.S. Circuit Court of Appeals for the District of Columbia was called upon to adjudicate a case in which Williams, a black laundromat manager who had been ordered by a policeman to move off the sidewalk in front of his place of business, told the officer that "no God damn policeman" and "no son of a bitch" was going to make him move.[17] The court found that the District of Columbia statute which Williams had been charged with violating was unconstitutionally overbroad unless construed to mean that punishment was possible only if something more than the mere utterance of profane language in public had occurred. That "something more," in the court's view, was "that the language be spoken in circumstances which threaten a breach of the peace."[18]

Having thus far anticipated the *Gooding* decision, the court of appeals then fell short of full clairvoyance. "For these purposes," the opinion went on, "a breach of the peace is threatened either because the language creates a substantial risk of provoking violence, or because it is, under 'contemporary community standards,' so grossly offensive to members of the public who actually overhear it as to amount to a nuisance."[19]

In other words, the court was saying that if communicators were not guilty of uttering words that had a tendency to cause violence by the individuals to whom their remarks were addressed, they might still be punished because of the impact of their utterances on bystanders. With that concept the court of appeals moved far beyond the realm of fighting words, which ever since *Chaplinsky* had been limited to face-to-face confrontations between two individuals, and invoked the doctrine of public nuisances, to which we now address ourselves.

Public nuisance laws are most commonly designed to restrict behavior that intrudes physically and offensively upon others, such as allowing one's dog to defecate on the sidewalks, spitting on buses or subways, smoking in theaters, or racing motorcycles through residential areas late at night. Insofar as these laws may impinge on acts of communication, it is usually the medium and not the message that is sought to be controlled—for example, noisy parties, blaring stereos, newspaper racks or literature tables that may block a sidewalk, glaring lights that could momentarily blind the driver of an automobile, or political stickers obscuring vital road signs. But the public nuisance concept also has been used to restrict conduct that offends solely because it cuts across the grain of prevailing social mores—like public drunkenness, public nudity, and public sex. Such restrictions sometimes catch in their net, in ways that raise serious First Amendment problems, behaviors that are purely acts of communication. Some illustrations will make the point.

The March 31, 1975, issue of *Newsweek* magazine displayed on its front cover a picture of a Vietnamese mother carrying a battle-scarred female child, the lower portion of whose body was unclothed. As a result, newsstand and bookstore owners in Dallas, Texas, ran afoul of a city ordinance which provided that pictures of the human genitals and buttocks could not be displayed where persons under seventeen might see them, unless completely or opaquely covered. To solve this "problem," white labels were pasted over the offending area of the magazine covers.[20]

In the summer of 1977, the chief deputy commissioner of motor vehicles for the State of Indiana announced that personalized automobile license plates would be available for 1978. Car owners could order any message they wanted of no fewer than two nor greater than six letters or numbers, provided that the particular combination was not already taken *and* provided that it would not say anything "too dirty or suggestive."[21] The commissioner said that the motor vehicle bureau would have a list of prohibited words in its master computer which would screen out unacceptable requests. The State Department of Motor Vehicles in California was less farsighted. Having already issued a set of plates reading "Hitler," the agency ordered their return after receiving complaints from the Anti-Defamation League of B'nai Brith.[22]

On March 13, 1972, Richard Erznoznik, the manager of a drive-in theater in Jacksonville, Florida, was charged with violating a city ordinance which read as follows:

> It shall be unlawful and is hereby declared a public nuisance for any . . . person connected with or employed in any drive-in theater in the City to exhibit or aid or assist in exhibiting, any motion picture, slide, or other exhibit in which the human male or female bare buttocks, human female bare breasts, or human pubic areas are shown, if such motion picture, slide, or other exhibit is visible from any public place.[23]

Erznoznik's conviction was overturned by the U.S. Supreme Court on the grounds that the ordinance in question "discriminated among movies solely on the basis of content,"[24] and that "the restriction is broader than permissible."[25] The Court majority noted that the law, as written, "would bar a film containing a picture of a baby's buttocks, the nude body of a war victim, or scenes from a culture in which nudity is indigenous."[26] As for the public nuisance justification, the opinion asserted: "Much that we encounter offends our esthetic, if not our political and moral sensibilities. Nevertheless, the Constitution does not permit the government to decide which types of otherwise protected speech are sufficiently offensive to require protection for the unwilling listener or viewer. Rather, . . . the burden falls upon the viewer 'to avoid further bombardment of [his] sensibilities by averting [his] eyes.'"[27]

If this principle enunciated by Justice Powell for a majority of the Supreme Court in *Erznoznik* were to be taken seriously, it would necessitate a change in all aspects of present public nuisance law affecting communication content—a departure from the status quo that seems required if the First Amendment is to become a fully effective shield against the imposition of majoritarian values on those who may wish to express themselves in nonconformist ways. But it would also require a fortitude which Justice Powell and a majority of his colleagues have not been able to sustain. Only three years after *Erznoznik,* the Court, with Justice Powell concurring, upheld the authority of the Federal Communications Commission to penalize the radio broadcast of so-called indecent language by the comedian George Carlin at a time of day when children were likely to be in the audience.[28] The Court conceded that its action permitted government control of communication content but justified that decision "on a nuisance rationale under which context is all-important. . . . As Justice Sutherland wrote, a 'nuisance may be merely a right thing in the wrong place—like a pig in the parlor instead of the barnyard.'"[29]

The Supreme Court, in this instance, claimed to be giving its approval only to a curb on what Justice Stevens and two of his colleagues identified as "patently offensive sexual and excretory speech."[30] But the rationale which the Court kept alive in the case, and which it described as an objection "not to this point of view, but to the way in which it is expressed,"[31] can be transferred easily to other categories of speech that do not "lie at the periphery of First Amendment concern,"[32] as Justice Stevens felt that Carlin's broadcast did. For example, note should be taken of a syndicated column by no less respected and ordinarily thoughtful a writer than Garry Wills, on the subject of the proposed Nazi march in Skokie, Illinois, in 1978.

"The relevant body of law in this case is not the First Amendment but nuisance statutes," wrote Wills.

People are not allowed to wander nude on downtown streets or to defecate there. "Flashers" are arrested outside girls' schools. . . . I know that all my parallels will be thrown aside as irrelevant because the Nazis scream their insults in words, and the First Amendment protects speech. Well, the woman tortured by obscene phone calls is afflicted by another person's speech. Is that speech protected by the

Constitution? . . . The Nazis . . . are, in effect, broadcasting an obscene phone call to a whole neighborhood instead of a single house.

I see no problem with police "suppressing" a march through Skokie.[33]

We will return to the particular question of obscene phone calls shortly, but I hope it is sufficient to point out here that the public expression of a political ideology, revolting as it may be, is a far cry from obscene phone calls or from human feces deposited on downtown streets. The flood of emotion that drowned the rationality of Garry Wills, as of so many others, in the Skokie tidal wave should remind us of the dangers to the First Amendment that lurk in the concept of public nuisances.

I would not want to leave the impression that full acceptance of the *Erznoznik* principle, from which the Supreme Court has chosen to shrink, is an easy course to take. As with so many other aspects of our system of free expression, there is a painful price that must be paid. This can best be illustrated by an incident that occurred in connection with the funeral of Eleanor Roosevelt at Hyde Park, New York, in 1962. Two men, who were arrested after telling a policeman they intended to picket that funeral carrying signs hostile to Mrs. Roosevelt, pled guilty and were sentenced to ninety days in jail for violation of a New York penal statute prohibiting any act that outrages public decency. Here was a situation where speech that would indisputably have been protected by the First Amendment at any other time or place was put outside the umbrella of that protection because the site chosen for the expression would have made it deeply offensive to the sensibilities of the mourners on the scene. No other harm was alleged. It was solely the content of the communication, interacting with the particular occasion, that placed it beyond the pale of our societal mores.

As tasteless and repulsive as the proposed picketing in that situation would have been to most of those present—and one recoils emotionally at the thought of it—we must ask ourselves whether ninety days in jail is the appropriate response for a free society to make. Can we not rely instead on the faith that the common sense of most people and the informal workings of social pressure will make such occurrences rare? And when they do happen, can we not wince and take them in our stride rather than using the law to shield our sensibilities from what we perceive as the world's ugliness? For what is ugly to one may not be ugly to another, and we run too great a risk of suppressing ideas and feelings of which we should be made aware when we allow conformist impulses to place certain kinds of communication "out of sight and out of mind."

Captive Audiences

The U.S. Supreme Court, in enunciating its *Erznoznik* doctrine, noted one exception to the general principle that, when confronted by offensive but constitutionally protected communication, the burden is upon viewers to avoid further bombardment of their sensibilities by averting their eyes.

> ...when the government, acting as censor, undertakes selectively to shield the public from some kinds of speech on the ground that they are more offensive than others, the First Amendment strictly limits its power.... Such selective restrictions have been upheld only when the speaker intrudes on the privacy of the home ...or the degree of captivity makes it impractical for the unwilling viewer or auditor to avoid exposure.... As Mr. Justice Harlan cautioned [in *Cohen v. California*]: "The ability of the government, consonant with the Constitution, to shut off discourse solely to protect others from hearing it is ...dependent upon a showing that substantial privacy interests are being invaded in an essentially intolerable manner."[34]

This, in simple terms, is the concept of the captive audience, another of the legal doctrines employed to justify restrictions on assaultive symbolic behavior. Most commonly it is "sexually-oriented material" that has been the subject of these controls, notable examples being the federal Anti-Pandering Act of 1967[35] and the Goldwater Amendment to the Postal Reorganization Act of 1970.[36] The first of these statutes authorizes individuals who have received mail which they believe to be "erotically arousing or sexually provocative" to compel the sender of that material to stop all future mailings to them. The second law requires mailers of "sexually-oriented advertisements" to purchase from the Post Office Department a list of persons who have indicated to the department that they do not wish to receive such material and to remove those names from their mailings.

In upholding the constitutionality of the Anti-Pandering Act, and, by extrapolation, of the later law as well, the U.S. Supreme Court asserted the broad principle that "the right of every person 'to be let alone' must be placed in the scales with the right of others to communicate."[37] After weighing the particular law in question on those scales the Court concluded:

> If this prohibition operates to impede the flow of even valid ideas, the answer is that no one has a right to press even "good" ideas on an unwilling recipient. That we are often "captives" outside the sanctuary of the home and subject to objectionable speech and other sound does not mean we must be captives everywhere.... The asserted right of the mailer, ... stops at the outer boundary of every person's domain.[38]

Because of the strong appeal that the right of privacy holds for those who have traditionally been among the most vigorous advocates of freedom of speech, the movement that has been underway in recent years to decriminalize the communication of obscene material to consenting adults has tended to be coupled with the advocacy of retention of controls over the so-called public thrusting of obscenity on nonconsenting audiences. When Denmark abolished its restrictions on the distribution and exhibition of pornographic literature and pictures in the late 1960s, it retained limitations on public displays of such material in shop windows. When the American Civil Liberties Union, in 1970, adopted a policy of absolute opposition to restrictions on obscenity, its Board of Directors made an exception for "statutes which prohibit the thrusting of hard-core pornography on unwilling audiences in public places"—a proviso which I persuaded the board to rescind three years later. When Justice Brennan, writing for a four-person minority of the Supreme Court in 1973, took the position for the first time that obscenity laws violate the First Amendment, he excluded from the purview of that opinion "distribution to juveniles or obtrusive exposure to unconsenting adults."[39] In this respect, the Brennan dissent followed precisely the recommendations of a prestigious national Commission on Obscenity and Pornography which had been established by Congress in 1967 and which submitted its report to the president and the public in 1970.

Although sexually oriented material (whether legally obscene or not) has been the prime concern of the defenders of supposedly captive audiences, it has not been their sole target. The picketing of private residences, sometimes in political protests directed to public officials but more often in disputes involving slum landlords, has been another arena in which the captive audience argument has been made, and many state and local governments have enacted laws prohibiting such activities.[40] The preamble to the Illinois statute on this subject typifies some of the thinking behind these prohibitions:

> The legislature finds and declares that men in a free society have the right to quiet enjoyment of their homes; that the stability of community and family life cannot be maintained unless the right to privacy and a sense of security and peace in the home are respected and encouraged; that residential picketing, however just the cause inspiring it, disrupts home, family and communal life; that residential picketing is inappropriate in our society, where the jealously guarded right of free speech and assembly have always been associated with respect for the rights of others. For these reasons the Legislature finds and declares this Article to be necessary.[41]

Although this particular Illinois law was struck down by the U.S. Supreme Court because its exemption for labor disputes was found to be in violation of the Equal Protection Clause of the Fourteenth Amendment, the Court made very clear that it saw no constitutional barrier to nondiscriminatory content-neutral regulation of residential picketing:

> Preserving the sanctity of the home, the one retreat to which men and women can repair to escape from the tribulations of their daily pursuits, is surely an important value. Our decisions reflect no lack of solicitude for the right of an individual "to be let alone" in the privacy of the home. . . . The State's interest in protecting the well-being, tranquility, and privacy of the home is certainly of the highest order in a free and civilized society.[42]

Another kind of allegedly assaultive communication that has run afoul of the captive-audience doctrine is political campaign advertising on public transit vehicles. A closely divided U.S. Supreme Court in 1974 upheld the right of a city transit system in Shaker Heights, Ohio, to refuse to sell car card space to candidates for public office while accepting other categories of advertising.[43] A majority of the justices regarded passengers on public transit vehicles as members of a captive audience who ought not to be subjected to political propaganda that they might find offensive.

On the other hand, a Court majority in 1980 found no captive-audience issue in a New York public utility company's use of its bill mailings to customers for the insertion of written material advocating the development of nuclear power. The state's Public Service Commission, with the approval of New York's highest court, had banned the inserts as intrusions on individual privacy, but the Supreme Court held that the state court had "erred in its assessment of the seriousness of the intrusion."[44] Invoking the precedent of *Cohen v. California*, Justice Powell said for the Court:

> Where a single speaker communicates to many listeners, the First Amendment does not permit the government to prohibit speech as intrusive unless the "captive" audience cannot avoid objectionable speech. . . . The customer of Consolidated Edison may escape exposure to the objectionable material simply by transferring the bill insert from envelope to wastebasket.[45]

Then there is the unwelcome telephone call, where commercial as well as lewd solicitations give rise to anger and resentment on the part of those holding the phone. So-called obscene calls (defined much more broadly than "obscene" literature) have long been subject to criminal penalties, and, with the advent of automated commercial solicitation devices, public sentiment has been building in support of restrictions on that mode of communication as well. Unlisted phone numbers provide some protection for those—estimated at about 14 percent of the population[46]—who are able and willing to pay an extra charge for the service, but random digit dialing by a caller (mechanical or human) can circumvent that barrier as well.

Finally, we have the Supreme Court decision in the George Carlin case, in which a majority relied both on the right "to be let alone" in one's home, and a societal interest in shielding children from offensive material, as grounds for government regulation of broadcast material.

The question to be addressed in all of these circumstances is: How truly captive is the allegedly captive audience? If we assume that the opposite of captivity is being free to escape, then one form of *non*captivity has already been identified by the Supreme Court in *Cohen v. California* and *Erznoznik v. Jacksonville*—situations where the audience is able to avert its eyes. When dealing solely with visual stimuli it is difficult to imagine many circumstances in which it is impossible to avert one's eyes after an initial encounter with offensive symbols. Thus it can be argued, and I would argue, that truly captive audiences are a rare phenomenon when only sight, and no sound, is involved.

But apparently the Supreme Court did not really intend to go that far with its averting-the-eyes concept, for the justices were unanimous in their holding that people have a right to ask the government to guard them from even an initial exposure to unwelcome sexually oriented material.[47] Averting their eyes while carrying the offensive item to a wastebasket, though apparently regarded as an adequate solution for nuclear power promotions from Consolidated Edison, is evidently not viewed by the Court as sufficient protection from the contamination of a sexually oriented advertisement.

This same Supreme Court opinion noted, with resignation, that, unlike the privacy to which we are entitled at home, "[w]e are often 'captives' outside the sanctuary of the home and subject to objectionable speech."[48] Despite that admission, a majority of the justices found themselves able to rule, just four years later, that averting one's eyes from a car card while riding the Shaker Heights rapid was not a sufficient escape route to keep the passengers from being considered a captive audience.[49] How the justices arrived at that conclusion is not revealed in their opinion, but there was one characteristic about the Shaker Heights situation that was not present in *Cohen* and *Erznoznik* and may have made the difference in their thinking. In the case of a public transit vehicle, a display ad is a kind of abiding presence so long as one is seated or standing somewhere in front of it. Cohen, on the other hand, was walking in his offensively lettered jacket through a corridor where others were also on the move, and Erznoznik's outdoor movie screen was only momentarily visible to passersby on the street (although it also could be seen from the stationary position of a nearby church parking lot).

The view of the courts as to what constitutes captivity vis-à-vis aural stimuli is more obscure, if that is possible, than it is with respect to visual communication. The response of the law to sound trucks and other kinds of loudspeakers in public places provides a good example. The U.S. Supreme Court has confronted that issue on three occasions—in 1948, 1949, and 1952—with confusing results.

In the first case, a Court majority recognized the necessity of public address equipment for the effective exercise of free speech rights, and struck down a city ordinance that allowed too much discretion to the police in granting or denying permits for the use of such equipment.[50] Justice Felix Frankfurter, in dissent, saw the decision as allowing speakers "to force unwilling people to listen."[51]

The following year, a five-man majority upheld, as a reasonable limitation, an ordinance that prohibited sound trucks from emitting "loud and raucous noises." The minority maintained that the practical effect of the restriction was to place a total ban on amplification systems and that this was incompatible with the First Amendment.[52]

Then, in 1952, the Court rejected a claim that radio broadcasts of music and commercials piped over loudspeakers on the city public transit vehicles were violations of a passenger's right not to listen.[53] The opinion suggested that had the broadcasts contained "objectionable propaganda" it might have been a different case, but that was not the issue before the Court. Justice Douglas's dissenting view was that passengers on city streetcars are a captive audience and that the case involved "a form of coercion to make people listen."[54]

Lower court rulings on this same subject, in the years that have ensued since these ambiguous Supreme Court decisions, have ranged all the way from upholding absolute prohibitions on the use of sound trucks in busy city streets or business districts[55] to overturning a requirement that such trucks must keep moving at a speed of at least ten miles an hour or shut off their sound.[56]

The ringing of doorbells by persons like Jehovah's Witnesses and political canvassers is another kind of aural communication that received relatively early attention from the U.S. Supreme Court. Here, despite the strong sentiment that one's home is one's castle, the Court was more sympathetic to competing First Amendment claims.[57] Perhaps this is because the way in which the issue was first posed in the Supreme Court involved city ordinances prohibiting all door-to-door solicitations whether everyone in the community wished to have that protection or not. It was apparently the Court's feeling that, since individuals who did not want to be solicited could post notices to that effect, a total ban enacted by the government was an unacceptable deviation from First Amendment principles, at least insofar as political and religious communication was concerned. With respect to a prohibition on the door-to-door selling of magazine subscriptions, however, the balance was struck in the opposite way[58]—a decision that might be different today in view of the Supreme Court's greater sensitivity to the First Amendment implications of some kinds of commercial speech.

Finally, there is radio and television broadcasting, the sounds of which "invade" the home whenever one's receiver is on. Because of the ease and freedom with which a listener can turn a set off, it is hard to see how the concept of a captive audience is at all applicable to this kind of communication—a view that *seemed* to have been acknowledged by the Supreme Court in *Rowan v. U.S. Post Office Department* when it said: "To hold less [than that a resident may post a notice against door-to-door solicitation] would tend to license a form of trespass and would hardly make more sense than to say that a radio or television viewer may not turn the dial to cut off an offensive or boring communication and thus bar its entering his home."[59]

Yet, in *F.C.C. v. Pacifica Foundation*, the Court's majority thoroughly garbled the captive-audience question by analogizing the impact of a fleeting communication (whose harm, if any, is purely psychic) to the possibly lasting effect of a physical attack. "To say that one may avoid further offense by turning off the radio when he hears indecent language," said the Court, "is like saying that the remedy for an assault is to run away after the first blow."[60]

It seems to me that it is possible to articulate clearer and more coherent standards for determining when "captivity" exists than have so far emerged from our legal system. I attempted to sketch out the broad contours of such criteria in a law review article published in 1972[61] and will reiterate and elaborate on those proposals here.

I would start with the basic proposition that the concept of captivity should be narrowly and literally understood to refer only to situations in which an audience is unable to get away from communication stimuli it finds offensive. This would exclude all circumstances where only the *initial* impact of communication is in question, and it would also exclude all settings in which the avoidance of *continued exposure* to the communication is physically possible by averting one's eyes.

In keeping with these principles, one would certainly agree with the U.S. Supreme Court that passersby in public places—such as in *Cohen* and *Erznoznik*—are *not* captive audiences whose "substantial privacy interests are being invaded in an essentially intolerable manner." One would have to disagree sharply, however, with the *Rowan* decision, since offensive mail can easily be thrown away immediately after an initial encounter with it. I believe that a federal district court in New York had a more accurate and more sensitive perception of captivity as it relates to the First Amendment when it addressed this question as follows: "The mail box, however noxious its advertising contents often seem to judges as well as other people, is hardly the kind of enclave that requires con-stitutional defense to protect 'the privacies of life.' The short, though regular journey from mail box to trash can . . . is an acceptable burden, at least so far as the Constitution is concerned."[62]

It follows also that we should firmly reject the position of the Supreme Court majority in *F.C.C. v. Pacifica Foundation* and heed, instead, the words of Justice Brennan's dissenting opinion, that

> unlike other intrusive modes of communication, such as sound trucks, "[t]he radio can be turned off" . . . with a minimum of effort. As Judge Bazelon aptly observed below, "having elected to receive public air waves, the scanner who stumbles onto an offensive program is in the same position as the unsuspecting passers-by in *Cohen* and *Erznoz-nik.* . . . he can avert his attention by changing channels or turning off the set." . . . Whatever the minimal discomfort suffered by a listener who inadvertently tunes into a program he finds offensive during the brief interval before he can simply extend his arm and switch stations or flick the "off" button, it is surely worth the candle to preserve the broadcaster's right to send, and the right of those interested to receive, a message entitled to full First Amendment protection. To reach a contrary balance, as does the Court, is clearly, to follow Mr. Justice Stevens' reliance on animal metaphors . . . "to burn the house to roast the pig." . . .
>
> The Court's balance . . . permits majoritarian tastes completely to preclude a protected message from entering the homes of a receptive, unoffended minority. No decision of this Court supports such a re-sult.[63]

Just as junk mail can be thrown in a trash can and a radio or television dial switched off, so can one close the door on an unwelcome solicitor and hang up the telephone on an unwanted call. In each instance there is no true captivity involved, since escape is immediately available. On the other hand, let us suppose that the solicitor on whom you have closed the door or the telephone caller on whom you have hung up continues to ring your doorbell or your phone after you have made it clear that you are not interested. That kind of persistent bombardment by aural stimuli from which you could escape only by leaving your home would certainly qualify as creating a captive-audience situation.

When we come to public transit vehicles, I believe that the distinction between visual and aural stimuli should be the central consideration. Those who are dependent on such transportation in order to get to work are as physically captive for the duration of the ride as people in their homes. Nothing forces them, however, to keep looking at a particular display ad they find offensive in the way they *are* forced to hear sound that may be piped over loudspeakers. I would argue, in accordance with the principles set forth above, that the latter is a state of captivity and the former is not. Indeed, I find it most revealing that the author of the Supreme Court's plurality opinion in *Lehman v. Shaker Heights,* Justice Blackmun, chose to describe the offensive display ads against which he was ruling as "the *blare* of political propaganda"[64] (italics mine)—a term normally used in connection with aural, not visual, stimuli.

The distinction between aural and visual communication may also be helpful in arriving at a logically consistent position with respect to residential picketing. Certainly the captive-audience doctrine should protect us, as we sit in our homes, from the continual din of singing, chanting, or yelling picketers on our front sidewalk. The question becomes more difficult, however, if the picketers march silently up and down. Here I would suggest that the presence or absence of captivity is dependent on how long the demonstrators remain. If they are there for an hour or so, it would be just as easy for residents of the home to avoid looking out the window or to pull their shades as it would be to throw away a piece of mail or hang up a telephone. If, on the other hand, the picketers keep coming back day after day, or remain for many hours, it becomes impossible for residents to leave their home and return to it without having to be exposed repeatedly to the offensive communication. It should be noted here that the state of captivity I am describing derives *not* from the philosophy that there is some special sanctity to the home but simply from the fact that it is a place in which one has to be located a good deal of the time, just as one may have to ride a public bus or train to get to work.

Furthermore, it should be pointed out that a state of captivity is possible not only when one is tied down to a particular location, as in a home or bus, but also when one is on the move and is pursued by others. This very circumstance occurred early in 1971 when members of the Jewish Defense League in New York City started following Soviet delegates to the United Nations around the streets and into grocery stores and lunch counters while addressing verbal protests to them.[65] So long as the JDL persisted, its targets were essentially being held captive to its communication. Had JDL members simply stood on a street corner and handed the Russians leaflets or yelled at them as they walked by, it would have been quite a different matter.

This last illustration may provide the clue to a resolution of the difficult problem of loudspeakers in public places, which are so often necessary for viable communication but are also so assaultive upon those who may not want to hear what is being said. If a stationary public address system is being used at a rally in a public stadium, a public park, or a public square, those who do not want to hear it can ordinarily move out of earshot and are thus not a captive audience. If, however, the people who do not want to listen live or work within the range of the sound being emitted, a balancing of First Amendment and privacy rights might justify the placing of reasonable time limits on such a rally (assuming those limits are administered evenhandedly for all gatherings and in an entirely content-neutral way).

With respect to sound trucks, so long as they keep moving no one is held captive to their communication beyond the initial impact. If they park in one place, however, and continue operating, they may indeed be forcing unwanted messages on unwilling listeners. Thus, I would not regard it as incompatible with the First Amendment to impose a regulation, such as that struck down by the California Supreme Court in *Wollam v. City of Palm Springs*,[66] which required sound trucks to keep moving or shut off their loudspeakers.

Automated commercial telephone solicitations, or "junk calls" as they are sometimes termed, raise new and rather difficult problems. However, I prefer to postpone that issue until the next chapter, on the premise that it is not really the content of these messages that makes them so offensive (they could be hawking political candidates as well as baby pictures) but rather the frequency with which one may be bombarded by the jangling of the telephone or interrupted from other pursuits to answer these uninvited and unwanted calls.

If the standards that I have proposed here for defining and dealing with the captive-audience problem seem somewhat skewed against privacy considerations in favor of freedom of expression, it is because that has been precisely my intent. I believe such weighting to be justified as a counterbalance to the natural forces that operate in favor of privacy. My thinking on this matter was expressed as well as I can articulate it in the 1972 law review article referred to earlier. I said that

> human beings have a significant ability mentally to reject many assaultive stimuli. The process known as "selective perception" enables us to generally choose what we wish to assimilate from the multitude of sensory bombardments surrounding us. We are able to hear without listening and to look without seeing, and we do so much of the time. . . . not only do our past experiences and present interests determine what we will perceive from our surroundings, but . . . we also have a strong tendency to screen out or to distort messages that are inconsistent with or contradictory to our current beliefs. We seek out reinforcement for what we already believe, and avoid as much as possible that which might create "cognitive dissonance."
>
> Given these tendencies, it may well be that the captive audience situation is not so serious an invasion of privacy as it has been thought to be. Indeed, one might argue that the possibilities of unwelcome messages penetrating the psychological armor of unwilling audiences

are so small that we ought to be worrying more about how to help unpopular communicators get through to reluctant listeners than how to give further protection from speech to those who already know too well how to isolate themselves from alien ideas.[67]

Intentional Infliction of Emotional Distress

The fourth, and last, of the legal doctrines that has sometimes been invoked as a shield against symbolic attacks is the tort of "intentional infliction of emotional distress." This concept is defined by the American Law Institute Restatement of Torts (1948), paragraph 46(1), as follows: "One who by extreme and outrageous conduct intentionally or recklessly causes severe emotional distress to another is subject to liability for such emotional distress, and if bodily harm to the other results from it, for such bodily harm."

Unlike most other legal doctrines affecting communication, where the long-term historical progression has been in the direction of greater latitude for expression and less opportunity for restriction, the notion that a person should be able to recover damages for emotional distress inflicted by words or other symbolic behavior has expanded over time. William Prosser, one of the leading authorities on the subject, said in 1939: "'Mental anguish' has been an orphan child. . . . the law has been reluctant, and very slow indeed, to accept the interest in peace of mind as entitled to independent legal protection. . . . The early cases . . . refused all remedy for mental suffering unless it could be brought within the scope of some already recognized tort."[68]

Writing on the same topic seventeen years later, Prosser was able to report that the doctrine had come into its own. He noted that, whereas the 1934 Restatement of Torts had rejected the infliction of emotional distress as an independent tort, that position was reversed in 1948, and in the ensuing years a growing number of state court decisions had given recognition to the concept.[69]

This is not to say that there were no successful suits for damages under the emotional distress doctrine prior to 1948, but they occurred in rather unusual circumstances. One of the early common-law precedents, for example, was an 1897 case in which a woman had a nervous breakdown after a practical joker had misled her into believing that her husband had been smashed up in an accident.[70] Wherever there has been that kind of physical consequence of emotional distress, the possibility of a court awarding damages has been enhanced. Indeed, a 1922 law review article observed, "It is then clear that fright as definitely affects the physical organism as does a blow with a club. . . . If the physical effect of strong emotional disturbance is a result that we can trace and see, it should be clear that the plaintiff's right to recovery for such disturbance should be recognized."[71] And Prosser, as late as 1956, still commented, "In the great majority of the cases allowing recovery the genuineness of the emotional distress has been evidenced by resulting physical illness of a serious character."[72]

Another exceptional kind of circumstance, recognized in 1917, had to do with a passenger on a train who was called a "lunatic" by the conductor and told that if the conductor were off duty he would be glad to give the passenger two black eyes. The supreme court of South Carolina sustained an award of damages against the railroad, holding that clients on a carrier ought not to be publicly humiliated by a company employee.[73] Similar decisions have been handed down with respect to employees of hotels, theaters, amusement parks, a circus, a telegraph office, and a dancing school.[74]

A more recent and bizarre case was that of a man in Indiana who made a series of telephone calls to women, posing as a doctor, telling them that their husbands were suffering from a contagious disease, and persuading more than a dozen of them to immediately shear or burn off their hair to prevent the parasite from spreading. Though he surely could have been sued by one of these women under the tort we are now discussing, he was in fact brought to trial by the state for practicing medicine without a license and for telephone harassment. A jury found him not guilty by reason of insanity.[75]

Although contemporary interpretations of the emotional distress tort by most state courts do not require that physical injury or illness must result in order for damages to be allowed, there are other ingredients that are either necessary or helpful if a plaintiff is to be successful in such a lawsuit.

One essential element is that the offending behavior be either deliberate or reckless—hence the label "*Intentional* Infliction of Emotional Distress." An early case in which this factor was missing was that of a woman in frail health who eventually died from the shock of seeing her child hit by a car. Recovery was denied in a suit against the driver of the car for the infliction of emotional distress on the woman, since it was clearly not his purpose to commit such an offense.[76]

The most common circumstances in which infliction of emotional distress suits are brought and sometimes succeed are those in which the act of communication has implicit or explicit in it a threat that is frightening to the target person.[77] This comes close to the kind of "assault" that is associated with "assault and battery," and which is defined in tort law as "the creation of an apprehension of" battery—that is, of actual physical touching.[78] The offending behavior in emotional distress cases, however, is one or more steps removed from the direct and explicit gestures toward immediate physical harm that are legally required for a finding of actual assault.

Many cases of this kind have involved debt collectors, who often engage in extremely aggressive and threatening conduct. A classic instance occurred in California where a trucker was threatened with having his truck wrecked if he did not pay his dues to the State Rubbish Collectors' Association. The supreme court of California concluded "that a cause of action is established when it is shown that one, in the absence of any privilege, intentionally subjects another to the mental suffering incident to serious threats to his well-being, whether or not the threats are made under such circumstances as to constitute a technical assault.[79] So widespread is the problem of bullying tactics by creditors that the U.S. Congress in 1977 adopted a Fair Debt Collection Practices Act that makes it illegal to call debtors at odd hours, threaten them or use abusive language.[80]

Another example of frightening communication was a case in Westchester County, New York, described by the court there as follows:

[The defendant had] dashed at plaintiff in a threatening manner in various public places, with "threatening gestures, grimaces, leers, distorted faces and malign looks"; driven his automobile behind that of plaintiff at a dangerously close distance; walked closely behind, or beside, or in front of the plaintiff on the public streets; and constantly telephoned the plaintiff at his home and place of business and either hung up or remained on the line in silence. It is alleged further that all of this has been done maliciously and for the purpose of causing physical and mental damage, and that the plaintiff has suffered severe mental and emotional distress, sleeplessness, and physical debilitation.

It seems probable that the complaint states a cause of action for assault . . . but the plaintiff does not urge the point. He claims to have stated a cause of action for the intentional infliction of emotional and physical harm.[81]

The court refused, as requested by the defendant, to dismiss the complaint and ordered that the plaintiff have an opportunity to prove his case at trial.

Similarly, an Illinois appellate court in 1977 refused to dismiss a complaint in a case involving an attorney's suit against a trucking company, one of whose drivers tailgated the lawyer's car along a stretch of tollway. The lawyer argued that being followed by a truck within two feet of his car, while they were traveling at seventy-five miles an hour, after he had signaled the truck to pass him, had inflicted "severe emotional distress" on his wife, his two teen-age daughters, and himself.[82]

Another consideration which may influence a court's judgment in emotional distress cases is whether the communicator knows that the target person is, in Prosser's words, "especially sensitive, susceptible and vulnerable to injury through mental distress at the particular conduct."[83] Prosser tells of one such case in which an eccentric old maid was conned into digging for a pot of gold that was said to be in her backyard, and of other instances where the communicator knew that the target individuals had heart conditions that might make them particularly vulnerable.[84] In contrast, the supreme court of Florida affirmed the dismissal of a suit against an employee of a grocery store who, when asked the price of an item by a customer, said to her, "If you want to know the price, you'll have to find out the best way you can . . . you stink to me." Although the customer claimed that this incident aggravated her preexisting heart disease and contributed to a heart attack that occurred thereafter, the court believed that, in the absence of knowledge about this on the part of the store employee, the behavior had to be evaluated in terms of its probable effect on a person of "ordinary sensibilities."[85]

Still another factor that may have a bearing on how seriously the courts will take a case of the alleged infliction of emotional distress is the presence of an authority relationship between the parties involved. Clearly the more power the communicator has over a target individual, the heavier is the impact of what is communicated. Thus, when officials in a Minnesota high school summoned a female student to the office, falsely accused her of unchastity, and threatened her with imprisonment, the emotional distress created for the girl was far greater than if the same things had been said to her by other students. The facts of the case were such that neither a charge of assault or of slander was supportable, but the court had no trouble in awarding damages for the intentional infliction of mental suffering.[86]

More recently the supreme court of the State of Washington reversed a lower court's dismissal of a suit for the tort of "outrage" (a synonym for emotional distress) in a case where a Mexican-American employee of the Crown Zellerbach Corporation claimed that "[d]uring the time of his employment he was subjected to continuous humiliation and embarrassment by reason of racial jokes, slurs and comments made in his presence by agents and employees of the defendant corporation on the job site and during working hours."[87] In addition to regarding the remarks in themselves as conduct that might justifiably lead a jury to award damages, the court noted, "When one in a position of authority, actual or apparent, over another has allegedly made racial slurs and jokes and comments, this abusive conduct gives added impetus to the claim of outrageous behavior."[88]

The decision of the Washington Supreme Court also discussed another feature of the tort of emotional distress that has generally been regarded as a necessary element of the offense, namely, that "the conduct be extreme and outrageous before liability will attach."[89] Quoting from an earlier opinion of its own,[90] the court wrote, "The prohibited conduct is conduct which in the eyes of decent men and women in a civilized community is considered outrageous and intolerable. Generally, the case is one in which the recitation of the facts to an average member of the community would arouse his resentment against the action and lead him to exclaim 'Outrageous!'"

Prosser said the same thing in slightly different language, describing the tort as extending only to behavior that is "so outrageous in character, and so extreme in degree, as to go beyond all possible bounds of decency and to be regarded as atrocious, and utterly intolerable in a civilized community."[91] As examples of what he meant by this, Prosser cited the early case we have already noted of the woman who had a nervous breakdown when told her husband had been in an accident, and a much later case in which a dead rat had been placed in a delivery of groceries.[92]

Having described the wide range of circumstances in which the intentional infliction of emotional distress has been charged, and having reviewed the considerations which may influence court reactions to such complaints, it is time to turn to a critical assessment of the concept.

When I first read the opinion of the Washington Supreme Court in the *Crown Zellerbach* case, I was particularly struck by the court's definition of emotional distress as being something that would lead an average member of the community to exclaim "Outrageous!" It reminded me that a cherished older friend of mine, a wise, witty and sensitive man, was constantly given to describing instances of injustice, duplicity, incompetence, or mere forgetfulness that he encountered as "Outrageous!" If all the behaviors to which he applied that adjective were subject to damage actions for the infliction of emotional distress, the doctrine would be limitless. I report my friend's idiosyncrasy only to suggest the boundless subjectivity that inheres in judgments like "outrageousness," and to point out that, as with the invasion-of-privacy cases discussed in Chapter 4, we are faced here with a "mores" test that is as variable as there are people and subcultures in any society. The Washington Supreme Court admitted as much in *Crown Zellerbach* when, after listing all the racial epithets (Wop, Kike, Spick, etc.) that it regarded as currently beyond the pale of decency, it justified that judgment by observing, "Changing sensitivity in society alters the acceptability of former terms."[93]

To subject people to punishment because they violate the "changing sensitivities" of a particular community at a particular time is to place freedom of expression on a precarious footing. It is to indulge in stereotyping like that of Prosser when he asserted categorically, "There is a difference between violent and vile profanity addressed to a lady, and the same language to a Butte miner and a United States marine."[94]

It is to invite radically unpredictable judicial decision making, such as that in an Ohio case where a seven-months-pregnant woman was accosted on the street by another who, in a loud voice, called her a "God damned son of a bitch," "a dirty crook," and similar epithets. She claimed that the remarks were designed to cause her emotional and physical injury, and that she did in fact suffer an illness requiring the attention of a doctor, though not affecting the birth of her child. The trial judge dismissed the case, an appellate court reversed the decision, and the state supreme court, by a 4–3 vote, reinstated the trial court's original judgment.[95]

The best illustration of the far-reaching First Amendment implications of the emotional distress doctrine is one of the several lawsuits that were filed in an attempt to stop a political demonstration by a group of self-styled Nazis in the heavily Jewish Village of Skokie, Illinois, in 1977–78. Sponsored by the Anti-Defamation League on behalf of a group of Skokie residents who were survivors of German concentration camps, the complaint sought an injunction against the march on the grounds that, if it took place, it would inflict irreparable emotional suffering on holocaust survivors who were exposed to it. The basic premise of the suit was summed up in a letter to the *New York Times* that was quoted in full by the plaintiff's unsuccessful petition to the Illinois Supreme Court for a rehearing of that court's order dismissing the complaint. Written by Dr. William Niederland, a clinical professor emeritus of psychiatry at the State University of New York's Downtown Medical Center, the letter argued:

> The discussion about the Illinois Supreme Court decision regarding the projected Nazi march in Skokie (editorial Jan. 31) ignores one important aspect: the precarious physical and emotional health of numerous concentration camp survivors, many of whom have suffered total family loss through Nazi persecution.
>
> In my clinical work with such survivors over the past 30 years, I have observed a series of lasting health disturbances which I have described in the professional literature as the survivor syndrome. Among other symptoms, this syndrome includes intense physical and emotional reactions to the sight of such symbols of persecution and murder as Nazi parades, swastikas and Nazi-like uniforms. These reactions manifest themselves not only in nightmares, anxiety dreams, increased tension states, fears of renewed persecution and other emotional disturbances but also in physical conditions of a potentially serious nature (hypertension, tachycardia, gastrointestinal disorders, etc.).
>
> Are the judges who decided in favor of the Nazi parade aware of the frequent and serious health damage which their decision is bound to inflict on many of the Skokie inhabitants? If they are unaware, I am

ready to provide them with the pertinent medical-psychiatric research and literature on the survivor syndrome.

In my considered opinion, the health risks in this case are potentially as great as those caused by shouting "fire" in a crowded theater.[96]

If one were to accept Dr. Niederland's reasoning, a number of consequences would seem necessarily to follow. First, those who display the symbols of nazism would have to be prohibited from appearing not only in front of the Skokie Village Hall but in any other public place where it might be expected that they would be seen by survivors of the holocaust. Second, a television documentary examining and vividly portraying neo-Nazi activity in the United States might have to be censored because of its impact on holocaust survivors. Such a portrayal could have even more of the effects described by Dr. Niederland than a single march by a small band of Nazis in Skokie because of the much greater magnitude of the threat depicted. If it is said that a television presentation is different because there is not the same intent on the part of the communicator to inflict emotional suffering, we then move into what I believe to be a constitutionally forbidden area of trying to read the minds and evaluate the motives of those—whether Nazis or television producers—who exhibit outrageous political symbols or bring hateful social messages to public attention.

Furthermore, there are no clear limits to the kind of communication that could be excluded from the public forum on the basis of this rationale. Deeply scarred as are the survivors of Hitler's madness, they are not alone. The sight of a Ku Klux Klan hood or cross burning might be just as traumatic for blacks who had lived through a KKK reign of terror. Indeed, it has been seriously suggested that such Klan behavior should also be prohibited for that very reason.[97] As for the display of a Confederate flag on a student's jacket in a racially tense Tennessee high school, it was not only proposed that the wearing of that symbol be banned, but school officials did, in fact, prohibit it and were upheld by a federal court decision.[98]

One final consideration: It cannot and should not be assumed that holocaust survivors, anymore than blacks, are monolithic in their responses to troubling symbolic stimuli. I will never forget the man who stood up at an ACLU meeting in the early 1960s and, in a thick German accent, identified himself as the only one in his entire family who had survived the concentration camps. He said he could not understand how there could be any doubt about defending the right of a group of Nazis to picket a movie in Chicago starring Sammy Davis, Jr., whom the Nazi picket signs described as a "Kosher Coon." The man's reasoning was simple. As he saw it, what made the essential difference between the

United States and Nazi Germany was that we had freedom of speech and they did not.

It was noted at the outset of this section that early legal thinking on the subject of emotional distress allowed much less latitude for restraint than contemporary doctrine, and that the 1934 version of the Restatement of Torts rejected entirely the infliction of emotional distress as an independent tort. An article appearing in the *Harvard Law Review* two years later explained the then-prevailing rationale: "Quite apart from the question of how far peace of mind is a good thing in itself, it would be quixotic for the law to attempt a general securing of it. Against a large part of the frictions and irritations and clashing of temperaments incident to participation in a community life, a certain toughening of the mental hide is a better protection than the law could ever be."[99]

If this philosophy were once again to be accepted, how would we deal with those bizarre circumstances in which common sense tells us there ought to be a remedy—the case of the woman who suffered a nervous breakdown when misled into believing her husband had been maimed in an accident, the Indiana telephone caller who caused women to set their hair on fire, the bullying debt collector, or the Westchester County man who "dashed at plaintiff in a threatening manner in various public places" and drove "his car behind that of plaintiff at a dangerously close distance"?

In some of these cases—the first two for example—there was physical as well as emotional injury. But beyond that, knowing falsehoods were communicated. The first woman's husband had not been in an accident. The other women's spouses did not have a contagious scalp disease. Indeed, in the first case, had the report of the husband's accident been true no one would seriously consider punishing the message bearer, even if the emotional and physical impact on the woman had been precisely the same and even if the messenger had wished her harm. This suggests that the core of the problem in such instances is the calculated falsehood, not the emotional response. We will return later in this book to a discussion of the general problem of lies and misrepresentations, whether their effect is emotional distress or not. The principles proposed there should suffice for the handling of the more particular kinds of cases we have been reviewing here.

As for the debt collectors and the Westchester County harasser, I would suggest, as the court itself did in the latter case, that the common law of assault may provide a sufficient basis for action. If that is inadequate, I would look to principles having to do with the more generic problem of intimidating and coercive speech, also to be dealt with later in this book, irrespective of whether emotional distress is one of the effects.

In short, I am proposing, in regard to the tort of intentional infliction of emotional distress, that we would be well-advised to return to one of the earliest precedents in the area and reaffirm the dictum enunciated by Lord Wensleydale more than a century ago: "Mental pain or anxiety the law cannot value and does not pretend to redress, when the unlawful act complained of causes that alone."[100]

8 Objectionable Sights and Sounds

At the outset of Chapter 7, a distinction was made between communication that is perceived by others to be assaultive because of the meanings it conveys (which was the subject matter of that chapter) and communication which is felt to be assaultive because of the medium employed. It was suggested that a way of differentiating assaultive media from offensive messages is to ask whether the stimuli in question would bother a foreigner who understood neither the language nor the nonverbal symbols of our culture. Examples cited were blaring loudspeakers and glaring lights. It shall be the purpose of this chapter to identify the free speech issues associated with restrictions that may be imposed on these objectionable sights and sounds and to propose criteria for dealing with the problem within the framework of the First Amendment.

As we found in our discussion of the captive-audience question in the last chapter, the intrusion on others created by sound, especially when it is amplified electronically, is far more troublesome than that created by visual stimuli, from which one's eyes can often be averted. Loudspeaker systems, whether stationary or mobile, in public places, impose themselves insistently on all within earshot, as do portable radios on public transit vehicles and public beaches. Hearers *may* be bothered by the kinds of words or music that are communicated, but more typically they are disturbed by the noise itself, irrespective of content. One scholar has pointed out, in discussing legal restraints on this kind of conduct, that "the values the state seeks to promote by such regulation, values of quiet and repose, would be threatened as much by meaningless moans and static . . . as by a 'political message.'"[1]

Quiet and repose are not the only interests that society seeks to preserve through restrictions on objectionable media of communication. Aesthetic values also are often invoked, and thus the boom is lowered on offensive sights as well as sounds. For instance, placards are usually not allowed to be affixed or messages painted on public buildings, and communities sometimes regulate the size, location, or electrical brightness of signs that are displayed on commercial properties or private homes—again regardless of content.

Perhaps the most unusual example of aesthetic concerns coming into conflict with freedom of expression was the case of the Stover family in Rye, New York. In 1956, and for several years thereafter, the Stovers had hung clotheslines across their front yard in protest against high local taxes. In 1961 an annoyed city enacted an ordinance prohibiting clotheslines in front or side yards abutting the public streets, with a waiver possibility provided for those who did not have backyards (which the Stovers did). When the Stovers persisted with their unusual communicative activity in defiance of the new ordinance, they were charged and convicted for its violation. Though conceding that the defendants were engaged in "a form of nonverbal expression" that had First Amendment characteristics, the New York Court of Appeals held that this interest was outweighed by the city's regulatory powers. "Aesthetics," said the court, "is a valid subject of legislative concern."[2]

It should be noted here that, unlike most of the other interests we will be dealing with in this chapter, aesthetic values are to some extent culture bound. Thus our suggested use of the "foreigner test" to determine whether offensiveness is due to a medium or a message may not be helpful in this area. A clothesline in a front yard, whether to communicate a protest against high taxes or because someone just wants to put it there, may be objectionable to the aesthetic sensibilities of Rye, New York, and not of some other culture, just as "a pig in the parlor" may seem a public nuisance to U.S. Supreme Court justices but not to a third-world peasant.

Beyond aesthetic considerations, or sometimes in combination with them, there are other societal interests which motivate restrictions on certain media of communication. Bans on highway billboards may be designed in part to preserve the beauty of the landscape, and in part to increase safety on the road by avoiding distractions or barriers to vision.[3] Newsstands or newspaper racks on public sidewalks may be forbidden because they are an obstruction to the easy flow of pedestrians. It is objectionable to attach political bumper stickers to road signs not only because they are unsightly but because they may obscure essential traffic warnings. Massive leafletting from an airplane creates huge litter pick-up costs for a municipality,[4] and, if soaked in a rain the leaflets might cause people walking over them to slip and fall.

The use of unique media of communication often provokes the assertion of unique countervailing interests. A case in point was the challenge brought in a U.S. District Court in New York to the federal statute which prohibits the deposit of any mailable matter in mailboxes without postage. A group of civic associations complained that this limitation on the hand delivery of nonpostaged newsletters and literature to the mailboxes of their constituents interfered with their First Amendment rights to distribute information and the rights of the would-be recipients to receive that information. The first time around, the district court judge found this complaint so lacking in merit that he dismissed the case. Noting that organizations were free to leave their messages on doorknobs, behind screen doors, and in other such alternative places, the judge accepted the government's arguments for keeping the material out of the mailboxes. One of the concerns expressed by the Postal Service was that "in many instances letter carriers have found it difficult to deposit mail in the overcrowded letter boxes, and in the larger cities this has worked considerable hardship on the carrier with resultant loss of time." Another was that the statute helps to prevent mail thefts by creating a situation in which the use of a mailbox by anyone other than a Postal Service employee will arouse suspicion.[5]

The U.S. Circuit Court of Appeals reversed the dismissal and remanded the case for trial.[6] In a concurring opinion, Judge Irving Kaufman advised the district court of the considerations that required a more thorough consideration of the issue:

> I do not question the power of Congress . . . to provide reasonable regulations for unobstructed access to delivery boxes. . . . But the postal power . . . may not be exercised in a manner that violates the fundamental freedoms guaranteed by the First Amendment. . . . the Postal Service must show that its asserted interest is substantial enough to outweigh the burden on free expression. . . . And in scrutinizing that balance, we must keep our thumb on the First Amendment side of the scales. . . .
>
> Given the fundamental right of house-to-house distribution, I believe a crucial consideration is whether the associations have any acceptable alternative to direct deposit in letterboxes. They allege that they do not. . . . that limited access and vagaries of climate together render alternative means of delivery, such as placement of the material behind screen doors or on driveways, inadequate. . . . none of the interests claimed by the Postal Service is so self-evident that mere assertion of it precludes the associations' claims.[7]

Judge Kaufman went on to note that the statute prohibits only the placing of *unstamped* material in mailboxes whereas the government's asserted interests in the restriction would be just as undermined by hand-delivered but *stamped* material.[8] Furthermore, he reminded the district court that there may be circumstances in which the U.S. mails would be too slow to get a particular message delivered whereas personal distribution could be much speedier.[9]

After hearing the case on remand, District Court Judge William Conner sharply changed his view and found the statute unconstitutional as applied to the plaintiffs and to similar noncommercial civic associations. He said:

> As the Second Circuit has emphasized, the activities of plaintiffs here ... fall squarely within the range of activities which the First Amendment was expressly designed to protect.... Plaintiffs have shown that these activities have been curtailed to a significant degree by observance of the statutory prohibition, that, in the areas in which they operate non-mailbox methods of delivery are much less satisfactory than mailbox delivery, and that the use of the mails to deliver their messages is both financially prohibitive for most civic associations and slow to a degree which significantly diminishes their effectiveness in alerting their constituents to local government meetings and other impending local government activity.
>
> The defendant, on the other hand, has not shown that failure to enforce the statute as to these groups would result in a substantial loss of revenue, or a significant reduction in the government's ability to protect the mails by investigation and prosecuting mail theft, mail fraud, or unauthorized private mail delivery service.[10]

Sometimes a medium of communication that is unobjectionable in one setting is offensive in another, again without regard to the particular message. Alexander Meiklejohn made the point long ago when he wrote, "No one, for example, may, without consent of nurse or doctor, rise up in a sickroom to argue for his principles or his candidate."[11] Nor, we should add, may anyone make an uninvited speech there on *any* topic, just as speech making of any sort is an unacceptable mode of behavior in a library reading room or in the galleries of Congress.

One can draw even finer distinctions on this particular matter. Speech making from the pews is appropriate at a Quaker worship service but "out of place" at a Roman Catholic mass. Interruptive shouting by the audience—whether friendly or hostile—may be an accepted norm at an outdoor political rally but entirely "beyond the pale" during the president's State of the Union Message to Congress.

In dealing with the issue of appropriateness of time and place, we need to be particularly careful not to confuse medium and content considerations, as it is easy to fall into that trap. The clearest way of avoiding the difficulty, whenever we are tempted to join in opposing the use of a particular medium of communication in a particular setting, is to ask ourselves if we would feel the same whether the message were friendly or unfriendly. In the case of the abortive picketing of Eleanor Roosevelt's funeral, for example, would we be shocked at the idea of *anybody* in a crowd outside the funeral of a prominent public figure carrying *any* signs, or would we not mind if messages such as "We Love You, Eleanor" and "We'll Miss, You, Eleanor" were displayed?

Similarly, is the objection to residential picketing an objection to *any-body* gathering with placards in front of a private home, or just to those who assemble to express some displeasure with the resident? To take an actual case, there was a significant difference in public reaction when Dick Gregory and his civil rights colleagues carried picket signs on the sidewalk in front of Mayor Richard J. Daley's Chicago home in 1965 and when an even larger group assembled in the same place in 1972, also carrying placards but this time welcoming the mayor back from his Michigan summer home where he had been recuperating from an extended illness.[12] Clearly, it must have been Gregory's message, not his medium, that was felt by many to be "out of place."

Finally, we should recognize the possibility that a medium of communication which is usually objectionable, whether conveying unfriendly or friendly messages, may become acceptable if the content is extraordinary. An example would be a telephone call in the middle of the night to a person who is ordinarily asleep at that time. Whether the call were from a stranger trying to sell pills for insomnia or from a friend wanting to chat about the late night TV movie that just went off the air, one's degree of annoyance would likely be quite great. However, if the message were that a member of the family had suddenly been taken critically ill or that the receiver of the call had just inherited a million dollars, it is probable that objection would not be made to having one's slumber interrupted.

Having reviewed a sample of the problems raised by allegedly objectionable sights and sounds, let us turn to a consideration of criteria that may be helpful in dealing with these matters.

The first and most critical standard required by the First Amendment in this area is implicit in much that has already been said. It is that any limitations imposed on supposedly offensive media of communication, if they are to be genuinely aimed at what they purport to control, must be absolutely content-neutral. Messages and symbols that most of our society approves must be subject to the same media restrictions as those that are disapproved. Media that may be used freely for acceptable messages must also be available for obnoxious ones. If there can be a St. Patrick's Day parade down State Street at high noon on a busy shopping day, the Gay Rights Coalition must have the same right. If major daily newspapers are allowed to be sold from newsstands on public sidewalks, so must the publications of the underground press. If the playing of electronically amplified music to advertise a political rally during the fall campaign is so offensive as to be banned from the sidewalks of a city's business district, then so must it be at Christmastime for Salvation Army Santa Clauses. If the local drive-in theater showing "sexually-oriented" films is required to build a fence high enough to block viewing of the screen from outside, that same requirement must be imposed on all drive-in theaters within the same jurisdiction. In short, if the government decides that pigs may not come into parlors, it should make no difference how cute a particular porker may be.

But content neutrality by itself is not enough to insure that First Amendment values are adequately safeguarded by restraints on offensive sights and sounds. For example, it might be decided that *all* uninvited telephone calls from strangers should be made illegal because of the unwelcome disturbance they so often create. Although the offenders sought to be curbed by such a prohibition would be mainly those who are in the business of selling products and services over the phone, it would also prevent activities like telephone campaigns to turn out voters and public opinion surveys—communications which, although perhaps objectionable to many, would be regarded by others as of sufficient social value to make them acceptable. What we are confronted with here is the necessity of taking a hard look at the competing interests involved to determine whether the First Amendment values in the use of a particular medium of communication are sufficiently great to counterbalance the annoyance it may cause. Such weighing of interests obviously entails some subjectivity in judgment, and the most we can ask is that reasonableness prevail.[13]

A rule of reason would tell us, I believe, that a ban on the relatively small number of uninvited telephone calls each of us receives from strangers is too harsh a reaction in view of the potential loss of socially significant communication that would result. On the other hand, we might reasonably decide that automated and prerecorded telephone calls from strangers are a different matter and ought to be made illegal. Here the scales could justifiably be tipped against such calls, in part because their potential frequency could much more easily rise to an intolerable level than calls which are manually dialed by human beings, and in part because the depersonalization of the message could reasonably be viewed as making it a less significant communication, or at least one that is more appropriately transmitted by mass media of communication.

Likewise, it would be patently unjustified, in view of the competing interests involved, for a city to take the position that all of its parks were to be used exclusively for recreational purposes and were unavailable for political rallies. Yet, it might be quite reasonable, at least as an abstract proposition, for a decision to be made that half of the city's parklands were to be so earmarked, with the other half open to First Amendment activities. I suggest that this is reasonable only as an abstract proposition because it would be necessary to examine the details of any particular plan before assenting to it. For instance, if the 50 percent of space made available for public meetings were all located in out-of-the-way places or were not distributed as fairly throughout the entire community as the recreational space, one would have to conclude that First Amendment interests had been given unacceptably short shrift when measured against the recreational needs of the community.

It is just this kind of particularistic analysis that has been employed by federal courts in adjudicating conflicts between the management of public airport and bus terminals and those, like anti-Vietnam War protesters or the Hare Krishna, who have sought to solicit for their causes in those locations. The courts have consistently, and I believe correctly, found that the distribution of literature in the large open areas of these facilities is insufficiently disruptive of the flow of traffic to justify restrictions, but that in more confined spaces, such as the "fingers" leading out to individual airline gates, prohibitions are warranted.[14]

Because of the inevitable subjectivity involved in this sort of decision making, and the fine lines that must often be drawn, there is always a danger that, unless we are vigilant, freedom of expression will not be given due weight. How much noise in public places is "too much" to be tolerated? How bright may lights be without causing "too much" discomfort? How much congestion on streets or sidewalks is "too much" to be allowed? How much audience participation at a meeting is "too much" of a disruption to the proceedings? These are all value judgments in which excessive deference to considerations of quiet, repose, convenience, or aesthetic sensibilities could play havoc with the First Amendment. To be sure, content neutrality will serve as something of a check on these interests getting out of hand, for if friend as well as foe is restricted, the public is not so likely to support unreasonable limitations. People may not want parades on the streets or rallies in the park to be prohibited if they realize that the fourth of July celebration would have to go with all the others. They may hesitate to ban the interruptive booing of public speakers if they know that at the same time they must eliminate interruptive applause.

But the public's level of tolerance for objectionable sights and sounds, even if somewhat heightened by the need to be content-neutral, cannot be the sole determiner of how much offensiveness is "too much" to be permitted. Although majoritarian sensibilities may be entitled to more respect in this than in other areas of First Amendment concern, because of the lesser likelihood of content-induced biases, there is still a need for the restraining hand of—hopefully—a more detached and analytical judiciary. Without that the Hare Krishna and all other solicitors would probably long since have been swept from our airport terminals, and perhaps all picketers banned from our city streets.

9   Debasing Attitudes and Values

If communication is so vital to the functioning of a free society as to warrant the extraordinary protections afforded to it by the First Amendment, it must have the power—we are often reminded—for harm as well as good. If speech can enlighten, it can also exploit. If literature can enrich our values, it can also debase them. If pictures can enhance our sensitivities, they can also dull them.

This premise, which can hardly be disputed by anyone who regards communication as a significant force in our lives, has led many to conclude that the regulatory powers of government should be invoked to shield the susceptible from some of these debasing influences. In contrast to the generally accepted principle, with respect to political discourse, that individuals can and should protect *themselves* from potentially injurious appeals, the view is taken that all or some of us need to be safeguarded *by the state* from certain other categories of expression.

Most commonly singled out for this kind of treatment is communication labeled as obscene or pornographic—that is, sexually oriented material, in either words or pictures, which is said to arouse lust in a reader or viewer, presumably creating "shameful" or "morbid" sexual attitudes. Closely akin to this category of expression is so-called indecent language—words, either printed or spoken, and often of four letters, that refer to sexual and excretory organs or processes.

A third kind of communication identified as a source of concern, particularly as it has become more prevalent in movie theaters and on television, is the pictorial portrayal of scenes of human violence. Though violence has for long been a subject of discussion in the print media, and played a role in classical drama as well, the detailed and vivid simulation of brutality made possible with film has indisputably posed new questions for consideration.

Finally, there has been increasing disquietude over the advertising of products that are potentially harmful to physical health—such as cigarettes, alcoholic beverages, and sugared foods. Again, concern over this kind of communication has grown as television has developed into the dominant influence that it has become in the lives of so many millions of people, particularly children.

Although it is occasionally claimed that some of the communication in these categories may have the *direct* effect of inducing people to engage in antisocial conduct and should be banned for that reason, this is not the most common rationale that is offered, nor is it the one we shall address in this chapter. Insofar as particular literature, movies, or television shows are alleged to trigger specific illegal acts, we shall deal with them under the heading of Incitement to Illegal Action in Chapter 12.

Nor shall we concern ourselves here with the peculiar problems raised by still or moving pictures that show the commission of presumptively illegal acts of violence or sexual abuse of children—so-called snuff films and child pornography. To the extent that the law seeks to prevent or punish any injurious and illegal *conduct* that is portrayed *in* these pictures, or that may be involved in their preparation, there is no First Amendment issue present. Once such material has been produced, however, and is being sold or distributed by persons who have not been party to its creation, restraints designed to interrupt its passage into the hands of consumers raise the same First Amendment questions as do restraints on pictures of simulated violence, of legally permissible sexual activity, or of gory news events.[1]

What we shall focus on in this chapter is the broad argument that the categories of expression described above should be regulated because of their *indirect* effect on reader or viewer conduct through the shaping of attitudes or, as some psychologists call them, behavioral predispositions. It is alleged that such expression is corrupting to public morality—that it creates a climate of social acceptance and encouragement for unhealthy behavior. The concern is not the maintenance of social order in any immediate sense but avoidance of the long-range, potentially harmful effects of deteriorating tastes and values. U.S. Supreme Court Chief Justice Warren Burger has described it as an "interest of the public in the quality of life and the total community environment."[2] For those who hold this view, there is a social responsibility to protect people from themselves as well as from each other.

It is with regard to the kinds of expression being discussed here, more than any others dealt with in this book, that a distinction is frequently drawn between adult and juvenile recipients of communication. For although there are some who would support prohibitions against the dissemination of this material regardless of whether it is directed to adults or children, and others who would bar obscenity from all irrespective of age but bar violence only from children, there are many more who would allow adults to see and hear whatever they wish but would restrain the dissemination to children of all sexually oriented material, of portrayals of extreme violence, of indecent language, and of the advertising of products harmful to their health. We will return later in this chapter to an analysis of the rationale underlying this distinction as well as to an evaluation of the other arguments made on behalf of restrictions, but we must first review the present posture of our legal system vis-à-vis these kinds of communication.

Only one of the several categories identified above—that of obscene material—is currently proscribed by law in the United States, whether communicated to adults or children. This is the case despite the fact that there were no statutory barriers to obscenity when the nation was founded and the First Amendment written, despite the fact that the Victorian attitudes which ushered in both state and federal restrictions on obscenity during the nineteenth century have long since given way to more permissive sexual mores, and despite the fact that in 1970 a national study commission, authorized by Congress and appointed by the president, recommended that all laws against the dissemination of sexually oriented material to consenting adults be eliminated.

But the U.S. Supreme Court, by a narrow 5–4 margin, is not yet convinced that the multitude of state and federal laws against obscenity are in violation of the First Amendment. To be sure, the Court has limited the coverage of such laws to "works which, taken as a whole, appeal to the prurient interest in sex, which portray sexual conduct in a patently offensive way, and which, taken as a whole, do not have serious literary, artistic, political, or scientific value."[3] On the other hand, it has given latitude to state and local communities to determine what constitutes patently offensive sexual conduct;[4] it has allowed obscenity convictions for the advertising of nonobscene material in a manner that "panders" to prurient interests;[5] and it has permitted stricter standards to be used in defining what is obscene for children than in defining obscenity directed to adults.[6]

Even the Court's minority, like the majority of the Commission on Obscenity and Pornography, while opposing restrictions on obscenity for consenting adults, supports them when they are aimed solely at dissemination to juveniles or when they are designed to prohibit the thrusting of obscene materials on unconsenting adults in public places.[7]

Although the Supreme Court has made clear its view that "sex and obscenity are not synonymous,"[8] it has nevertheless accepted some degree of government regulation even over the communication of sexually oriented material that does not fall within the boundaries of the obscene. In 1970, for example, it gave its unanimous approval to a statute enacted by Congress three years earlier which requires direct mail advertisers to refrain from sending any further material to any person who notifies the Postal Service that "the addressee in his sole discretion believes [the mail previously received from that mailer] to be erotically arousing or sexually provocative."[9] Encouraged by that decision, Congress shortly thereafter adopted another law which directs the Postal Service to maintain a list of all persons who indicate that they do not wish to receive *any* "sexually-oriented advertisements" in the mail and requires all mailers of such material to purchase that list from the Postal Service and purge those names from their mailings.[10]

Still another instance of Supreme Court approval of regulations imposed on nonobscene, but sexually oriented, material occurred in 1976 when a majority of the justices upheld the right of Detroit, Michigan, to use its zoning powers to limit the number of "adult" theaters and bookstores at particular locations.[11] Although there was in this case no prohibition throughout the city as a whole of "adult" materials, it did involve, in the words of Justice Stewart's dissenting opinion, "selective interference with protected speech whose content is thought to produce distasteful effects."[12] One of the justifications for that "selective interference" was articulated by Justice Stevens in a section of the Court's opinion which lost the support of Justice Powell and thus of the fifth vote necessary to give majority status to these particular words:

> ... even though we recognize that the First Amendment will not tolerate the total suppression of erotic materials that have some arguably artistic value, it is manifest that society's interest in protecting this type of expression is of a wholly different, and lesser, magnitude than the interest in untrammeled political debate.... few of us would march our sons and daughters off to war to preserve the citizen's right to see "Specified Sexual Activities" exhibited in the theaters of our choice.[13]

Another type of expression for which Justice Stevens is unwilling to "march our sons and daughters off to war" is indecent language—defined by the Federal Communications Commission and the Supreme Court as "patently offensive references to excretory and sexual organs and activities."[14] Again writing the opinion of the Court, and again losing a majority for this particular part of his rationale, Justice Stevens asserted, "While some of these references may be protected, they surely lie at the periphery of First Amendment concern."[15]

What held the Court's majority together in sustaining FCC disciplinary action against a radio station for broadcasting George Carlin's "Filthy Words" monologue, and in affirming the constitutionality of the federal statute on which that action was based, was the following set of propositions: (1) that, unlike other media of communication, broadcasting is licensed by government to operate in the public interest; (2) that it has "established a uniquely pervasive presence in the lives of all Americans," confronting the individual "not only in public, but in the privacy of the home"; (3) that it is "uniquely accessible to children, even those too young to read"; and (4) that the particular program in question was aired at a time of day when children were likely to be in the audience.[16] Given these conditions, the Supreme Court was willing to say that speech which would be protected by the First Amendment in other contexts can lose that immunity. As though it wished to emphasize the limited context of its ruling, but perhaps also to enliven its pages, the majority appended to its published opinion the full text of the Carlin monologue.

In sharp contrast to our legal system's long-standing preoccupation over the dissemination of sexually related communication, there has been an almost completely laissez faire attitude toward the portrayal of violence. The U.S. Supreme Court has had only two encounters with legislation aimed at depictions of violence, and in each instance the law was voided for vagueness. In 1948 the Supreme Court struck down a section of the New York state obscenity statute which imposed penalties on publications "principally made up of criminal news, police reports, or accounts of criminal deeds, or pictures, or stories of deeds of bloodshed, lust or crime."[17] Twenty years later, a Dallas, Texas, ordinance that sought to classify movies as "not suitable for young persons" if they were "likely to incite or encourage crime or delinquency" was also declared to be unconstitutionally vague.[18]

In recent years, public attention has increasingly focused on the problem of violence in the media, although most of the activity thus far has been directed to achieving greater self-restraint by the media managers rather than to imposing legal controls upon them. Campaigns by the PTA and the National Citizens Committee for Broadcasting have brought pressure on sponsors of television programs to cut down on the amount of violence they underwrite, and the FCC has also chosen to follow the persuasion route. In a Report on the Broadcast of Violent, Indecent and Obscene Material on February 19, 1975, the FCC advised Congress that "since government-imposed limitations raise sensitive First Amendment problems" the commission preferred to encourage self-regulation of violent programming by licensees themselves.

But even this course of FCC persuasion did not escape constitutional challenge. Late in 1976 a federal district court in California found that adoption by broadcasters of the Family Viewing Hour had occurred as the result of informal coercion by the FCC and that this constituted state action in violation of the First Amendment.[19] When that decision was appealed, however, the U.S. Court of Appeals found that the district court had erred in thrusting itself into the matter before the FCC itself had fully exercised its primary jurisdiction over the controversy through a formal administrative proceeding.[20]

No doubt less concerned about the First Amendment than either Judge Ferguson of the federal district court in California or the FCC, the City Council of Chicago, Illinois, adopted an ordinance in May of 1976 which could be the precursor of other such laws around the country, perhaps ultimately leading to more definitive litigation than we have yet had on the portrayal-of-violence issue.[21] The Chicago ordinance, requiring permits for the commercial exhibition of films to persons under eighteen years of age, authorizes the denial of such a permit to any motion picture whose "theme or plot is devoted primarily or substantially to patently offensive deeds or acts of brutality or violence, actual or simulated, such as but not limited to assaults, cuttings, stabbings, shootings, beatings, sluggings, floggings, eye gougings, brutal kicking, burnings, dismemberments and other reprehensible conduct to the persons of human beings or to animals and which, when taken as a whole, lacks serious literary, artistic, political, or scientific value."[22] The parallels between these specifications and the Supreme Court's criteria for obscenity cannot be accidental. Clearly the drafters of the ordinance intended for precedents from the obscenity area to be invoked whenever their handiwork is confronted with First Amendment challenges.

As has been the case with the portrayal of violence, substantial public concern about the advertising of products that may cause lung cancer, corrode one's liver, or rot one's teeth is of relatively recent vintage and has so far resulted in little government control. A major exception is the requirement that cigarette promotional material include a warning about the health hazards of the product, and an act of Congress in 1970, upheld by the Supreme Court in 1972,[23] prohibiting all advertising of cigarettes over radio or television.

In April 1978, however, the Federal Trade Commission announced a major rule-making procedure on the question of television advertising directed to children and invited public response to a series of proposals drawn up by the commission staff. These included a suggested prohibition on *all* television commercials when the viewing audience is "composed of a significant proportion of children who are too young to understand the selling purpose of or otherwise comprehend or evaluate the advertising"; a ban on "televised advertising for sugared food products directed to, or seen by audiences composed of a significant proportion of older children, the consumption of which products poses the most serious dental health risks"; and a requirement that all other advertising for sugared food products "be balanced by nutritional and/or health disclosures funded by advertisers."[24]

Although these particular FTC proposals have not survived public comment, advertiser opposition, and First Amendment scrutiny, they are symptomatic of a growing public dissatisfaction with at least some of the fruits of our free marketplace of ideas. Let us now turn to a consideration of the arguments that are made in behalf of more extensive government control over the kinds of communication that are felt to bear such unwanted fruit. What are the justifications that are offered for restraints on expression that may debase human wants and values, and how well do they hold up under critical examination?

One of the more esoteric and less frequent arguments that is put forth in this arena, but one that has far-reaching theoretical implications, is the contention that the freedom-of-speech clause of the Bill of Rights is meant to protect only expression that is addressed to our thought processes and not that which appeals to our senses. Based on a "faculties" psychology that prevailed in the early days of that discipline,[25] this view presumes that a clear distinction can be made between mind and feelings and that only messages aimed at the former are within the domain of the First Amendment.

This position is well illustrated by the comments of two scholars whose remarks speak for themselves. Ernest Van Den Haag, in discussing possible government controls over TV violence, has said:

> Perhaps the legal obstacles could be overcome, if as someday may happen, the courts finally interpret the First Amendment to refer to cognitive speech only—to information and descriptive communication of ideas or facts—and no longer to symbolic and pictorial expression, such as drama, poetry, or art, which are intended to address emotions, or to entertain, rather than purely to inform and address the intellect. The Founding Fathers were concerned with protecting political discussion and the communication of ideas and facts in general. It is doubtful that they meant the Bill of Rights to protect westerns, gangster movies, pornography, or soap operas, or to prevent the government from limiting the broadcasting of violence.[26]

And Harry Clor, dealing with motion pictures, has written:

> Some films "communicate ideas"—they address the mind (e.g. *Man's Fate* based on the novel by Andre Malraux). But there are very few of this type compared to the number of those whose effect upon attitudes and whose shaping of thought is only a by-product of their effect upon emotions and their appeal to senses or desires. Such films may influence men's thoughts, but they do not, in any significant degree, address the faculties of thought. They may alter the opinions of a community, but they do not espouse or discuss opinions. . . . such effect upon conduct as most films may have is the result of their influence upon inclinations or psychic dispositions. . . . It is one thing to have one's thought and conduct concerning sexual morality shaped by the reading of Bertrand Russell's arguments in a book like *Marriage and Morals* and quite another to have them shaped by the viewing of

films designed to present the most exciting scenes. In the former case the higher faculties are active; in the latter they are passive. In the former case one is invited to think about social or personal problems; in the latter, one is invited to experience sensations or desires.[27]

Besides the intellectual snobbery that permeates these passages, there is also an air about them of utter unreality. The Supreme Court said it well in *Winters v. New York*: "We do not accede to appellee's suggestion that the constitutional protection for a free press applies only to the exposition of ideas. The line between the informing and the entertaining is too elusive for the protection of that basic right. Everyone is familiar with instances or propaganda through fiction. What is one man's amusement, teaches another's doctrine."[28]

Although the Court, in the years since *Winters*, has not always held unswervingly to this insight, it has consistently rejected any all-encompassing invitation to write appeals to "baser" instincts out of the First Amendment. Were it to have done so, not only would television and movies have been cut by the censor's scissors, but many a political demagogue would have had to be muzzled as well. What baser instincts could one appeal to than those that have been exploited by the Joe McCarthys of our society? To allow the state to decide whether any particular communication is aimed at our "higher faculties" or at our "senses" and to forbid the latter would be to open the way for actions which could strike anywhere. If the citizens of a free society can be taught to ward off seductive logic, they should also be capable of learning to protect themselves from enticing sensations.

In contrast to the infrequency with which the previous line of argument is encountered, one can hardly read or hear a case for restrictions on debasing expression without being confronted with analogies drawn between allegedly harmful kinds of communication and a variety of physical evils. Richard Nixon said it when he rejected the recommendations of the Commission on Obscenity and Pornography: "The pollution of our culture, the pollution of our civilization with smut and filth is as serious a situation for the American people as the pollution of our once pure air and water."[29]

Irving Kristol said it when he argued that just as bearbaiting and cockfighting have been prohibited, because they debase and brutalize civilization, so should pornography be banned.[30]

And Warren Burger said it when he wrote for a Supreme Court majority in defense of obscenity laws:

> Totally unlimited play for free will . . . is not allowed in ours or any other society. . . . neither the First Amendment nor "free will" precludes states from having "blue sky" laws to regulate what sellers of

securities may write or publish about their wares. . . . Such laws are to protect the weak, the uninformed, the unsuspecting, and the gullible from the exercise of their own volition. Nor do modern societies leave disposal of garbage and sewage up to the individual "free will," but impose regulation to protect both public health and the appearance of public places. States are told by some that they must await a "laissez faire" market solution to the obscenity-pornography problem, paradoxically "by people who have never otherwise had a kind word to say for laissez-faire," particularly in solving urban, commercial, and environmental pollution problems.[31]

Additional behaviors that have been likened to debasing communication and cited as precedents to justify legal controls over it are gambling, prostitution, and drug traffic. These and other so-called victimless crimes (or, more accurately, counternormative behaviors involving willing participants) are, in fact, more similar to acts of communication than are chemical pollutants in the air and water, because one is free to accept or reject them. It is for that reason, indeed, that many people advocate the decriminalization of these essentially moral (or immoral) choices.

But we need not go so far as to adopt that position in order to oppose restrictions on allegedly harmful expression, for there remains a significant difference between arguably immoral *communication* and arguably immoral *conduct* that is as great as the gulf between verbal/pictorial pollutants of the psyche and physical pollutants of the environment. In both comparisons, communication is only *symbolic* behavior and thus, as we have argued in Chapter 2, deserving of analysis entirely distinct from that which is appropriate to physical acts. Such analysis might still conceivably lead to a conclusion that the communication of potentially harmful words and pictures should be banned, but *not* because they are comparable to the injection of heroin into our bloodstreams or kepone into our rivers.

A more powerful argument, by far, for restrictions upon obscenity, indecency, violence, and perhaps even blandishments to bad eating and smoking habits, is the claim that such communication strips human beings of their humanity and reduces them to a bundle of mere animal or physiological functions. Several writers, such as Irving Kristol,[32] Walter Berns,[33] and Harry Clor[34] have expressed this view, but none more extensively than Clor, who advocates expanding the definition of obscenity to include many of the other categories with which we are here concerned:

> These reflections suggest two preliminary definitions of obscenity: (1) obscenity consists in making public that which is private; it consists in an intrusion upon intimate physical processes and acts or physical-emotional states; and (2) it consists in a degradation of the human

dimensions of life to a sub-human or merely physical level. According to these definitions, obscenity is a certain way of treating or viewing the physical aspects of human existence and their relation to the rest of human existence. Thus, there can be an obscene view of sex; there can also be obscene views of death, of birth, of illness, and of acts such as that of eating or defecating. Obscenity makes a public exhibition of these phenomena and does so in such a way that their larger human context is lost or depreciated. . . .

In the broadest and most general terms, obscene literature is that literature which invites and stimulates the reader to adopt the obscene posture toward human existence—to engage in the reduction of man's values, functions, and ends to the animal or subhuman level.[35]

Closely akin to this view is the position of some feminists that pornography is a reflection of sexist male attitudes toward women—treating them as physical objects rather than as human beings. Though generally wary of limitations on free speech, one such writer has proposed that bans on this kind of material, "depicting the normal man as a sadist and the healthy woman as a willing victim," ought seriously to be considered.[36] Similarly, Irving Kristol has argued that the vituperative use of four-letter words directed at other individuals is a way of symbolically reducing them from persons to objects—again justifying legal restraints.[37]

I do not believe it can reasonably be denied that much of what passes for information, literature, and drama in our society is unadulterated trash and does, indeed, treat human beings as mere objects to be verbally abused, beaten bloody, raped, shot, or stuffed with excessive calories. My quarrel is not with this description of the problem but with censorship as a solution.

First I would suggest that we *are* members of the animal kingdom who have bodily needs and instincts and that something is awry if we try too desperately to hide or deny that fact. When Harry Clor says, "A man does not want outsiders looking at him while he is eating, because he does not want to be reduced in the eyes of others (and, hence, in his own eyes) to a collection of physical properties and reactions,"[38] I cannot help but wonder why he views that scene as a "reduction." Even the capacity for brutal violence, much as we may seek to curb it, is a fact of human experience that we are not likely to control successfully by pretending that it is not a part of our impulses. Many of us do treat each other as objects much of the time, and if that is reflected in the mirror held up to society by the mass media, the problem will not be solved by killing the messenger.

What is more, there is something contradictory about calling people to higher levels of humanity by limiting the range of experiences from which they may make their choices. If our problem is that we do not respect each other enough, that we exploit each others' gullibilities, that we resort to violence too easily, that we lust too much and love too little, I do not understand how improvement will be achieved by the censorship of communication, which is itself a coercive tool that treats us as objects to be manipulated by the censors rather than as human beings with the capacity to learn and choose for ourselves what is better and what is worse. I go back once again to Justice Brandeis and his recommendation, appropriate here as elsewhere, that "the remedy to be applied is more speech, not enforced silence."

I do not delude myself into believing that a greater offering of better quality fare in magazines, movies, and television will drive out all that is debasing. Fuller and richer lives would help more, and on that score animals may be better off than we, for as one writer has noted, "[N]o bull . . . will let its gaze be attracted by a photograph of a cow's rump."[39] There may also be a useful function, even in healthy lives, for pornography, scatology, and fantasized violence, as evidenced by the fact that so many authors of great literature have indulged in the production of such material on the side (e.g., Balzac's *Droll Stories*).

A jury of ordinary people in a federal obscenity trial in Cleveland, Ohio, in 1978, had what I think is the right idea in responding to Judge William Thomas's instruction, dictated by Supreme Court decisions on the subject, that an obscenity conviction must rest on a finding that the material in question would appeal to the prurient interest (i.e., a shameful or morbid interest in sex or excretion) *of an average person*. Said the jury in its message to the judge: "We are convinced that the average person has a normal, healthy response to sex. We don't believe the average person is capable of having a shameful or morbid interest in sex or excretions."[40]

Even if one accepts my view that "dehumanization" per se is not sufficient justification for placing restraints on movies or pictures, that still leaves unanswered the claim that such communication, by creating a climate of acceptance for unhealthy behavior, has the long-range effect of encouraging antisocial conduct and, for *that* reason, may be appropriately prohibited. Although our legal system is generally wary about dealing with matters that have only a tenuous and unproved connection to illegal acts, our courts have been less cautious in this regard on topics like obscenity. That issue was addressed as directly as it could be when the Supreme Court upheld the State of Georgia's obscenity law in 1973:

> But, it is argued, there is no scientific data which conclusively demonstrates that exposure to obscene materials affects men and women or their society. It is urged on behalf of the petitioner that, absent such a demonstration, any kind of state regulation is "impermissible." We reject this argument. It is not for us to resolve empirical uncertainties

underlying state legislation, save in the exceptional case where that legislation plainly impinges upon rights protected by the Constitution itself. . . . Although there is no conclusive proof of a connection between antisocial behavior and obscene material, the legislature of Georgia could quite reasonably determine that such a connection does or might exist. . . .

From the beginning of civilized societies, legislators and judges have acted on various unprovable assumptions. If we accept the unprovable assumption that a complete education requires certain books . . . and the well nigh universal belief that good books, plays, and art lift the spirit, improve the mind, enrich the human personality and develop character, can we then say that a state legislature may not act on the corollary assumption that commerce in obscene books, or public exhibitions focused on obscene conduct, have a tendency to exert a corrupting and debasing impact leading to antisocial behavior? "Many of these effects may be intangible and indistinct, but they are nonetheless real."[41]

Again, I am not inclined to quarrel so much with the premises of this argument as with the conclusion. Clearly a constant exposure to descriptions and portrayals of loveless sex *may* have an adverse effect on one's behavior. Research in this area provides considerable support for the proposition that those who have grown up on a steady diet of television violence may be more *prone* to engage in aggressive behavior than those who have not.[42] Who can deny that communication *may* have effects? That reading about a perfect crime may plant an idea in someone's head? That viewing a scene of torture may serve as a model to be imitated? The danger, however, lies in assuming without proof that these kinds of communication are the single or inevitable cause of particular illegal acts. The possibilities here, it has been pointed out, are endless:

Heinrich Pommerenke, who was a rapist, abuser, and mass slayer of women in Germany, was prompted to his series of ghastly deeds by Cecil B. DeMille's *The Ten Commandments*. During the scene of the Jewish women dancing about the Golden Calf, all the doubts of his life became clear: Women were the source of the world's troubles and it was his mission to both punish them for this and to execute them. Leaving the theater, he slew the first victim in a park nearby. John George Haigh, the British vampire who sucked his victims' blood through soda straws and dissolved their drained bodies in acid baths, first had his murder-inciting dreams and vampire longings from watching the "voluptuous" procedure of—an Anglican High Church Service.[43]

Suppression of communication that is presumed to have harmful long-term effects inevitably would prohibit much that is harmless for most people and would miss many other stimuli, like *The Ten Commandments* and Anglican church service, that might in fact touch off bizarre behavior. The trouble with legislators operating on the basis of Chief Justice Burger's "unprovable assumptions" is that it leaves them free to roam at will through fields in search of poisonous weeds with the likelihood that they will not know how to identify them and, meanwhile, will trample underfoot all of the wild flowers. I do not believe that the First Amendment was intended to be treated so carelessly.

There are other shortcomings to the censorship solution. It concedes to the communicators of debasing material a seductive power that we ought not be willing to grant. We should have more confidence in our ability to combat the effects of such communication without obliterating it. Nor should we give it the extra attraction of becoming forbidden fruit. As with group defamation, let us keep the wares out in the open, where we know what we are dealing with and can seek to offset their impact by offering and promoting better alternatives. This does not foreclose us from making known our dislike for what we may regard as unhealthy expression, nor from organizing voluntary associations to encourage a keener sense of responsibility and self-restraint on the part of those who manage the mass media. But to whatever extent human beings possess impulses in the direction of "higher" values—love, honor, respect, and healthful living—it ought to be possible through more and better communication to cultivate those tendencies and to demonstrate their superiority to "baser" instincts. If we cannot achieve that by persuasion and example, we certainly cannot do so by coercion.

The rationale that I have presented presumes that we are talking about human beings who have some capacity to make discriminating choices among the alternatives offered to them. The extent to which that presumption is valid is, of course, a matter of substantial dispute. At one extreme are those who believe that most people lack that ability, at least in the realm of moral decision making. We can turn once again to Harry Clor for a statement of that view:

> Why do we need to have public standards of decency? The issues which are the subject of such standards are highly perplexing and disturbing to the great majority of mankind. They concern the control and direction of powerful passions, the determination of the proper relation between the physical, social, and spiritual sides of life, and the moral judgments which are implicit in such terms as "higher" and "lower." No man (or very few) can resolve these problems alone, on the basis of his own private reasoning. Nor can he resolve them on the basis of a spontaneous "free exchange of ideas" with others. Therefore, we will always require some authoritative pronouncements on such subjects. . . . In matters so problematic, men rely upon guidance from the community in which they live. They need public standards.

But why should public moral standards require the support of law? Why can we not rely for their promulgation and maintenance upon society or the community?

Whatever may be the case in primitive communities, in civilized communities "society" is not an autonomous, self-regulating entity. Society does not resolve its problems autonomously without authoritative direction. In civilized times it is the political community which most effectively represents the common ends and interests of society and the political community characteristically acts by means of law.[44]

Considerably short of the Clor position, but still tending somewhat in that direction, are those who feel that the well-educated members of our society are capable of handling whatever debasing communication they may see or hear, but that the less educated populace is not. Thus, for example, most motion picture censorship laws have excepted from their purview films exhibited in educational or cultural institutions, and obscenity laws usually contain an exemption for those engaged in the scientific study of sexual mores and behavior. Theatrical performances have never been subjected to the kind of censorship aroused by movies, apparently because of their more limited and sophisticated (not to mention well-heeled) clientele. And Henry Miller's *Tropic of Cancer,* which had been available in hardcover at bookstores in this country for some time, did not become the target of police raids until 1961 when Grove Press came out with a paperback edition at ninety-five cents.

Finally, there are many who will concede that adults can be trusted to protect themselves from debasing expression but that children cannot be so trusted. Supreme Court Justice Lewis Powell spelled out this rationale in his concurring opinion in the George Carlin case:

The Court has recognized society's right "to adopt more stringent controls on communicative material available to youths than on those available to adults." . . . This recognition stems in large part from the fact that "a child . . . is not possessed of that full capacity for individual choice which is the presupposition of First Amendment guarantees." . . . Thus, children may not be able to protect themselves from speech which, although shocking to most adults, may be avoided by the unwilling through the exercise of choice. At the same time, such speech may have a deeper and more lasting negative effect on a child than an adult.[45]

Peggy Charran, president of Action for Children's Television, has put it this way:

We do not believe . . . that advertisers should be permitted to direct television commercials at the child audience. In our society, the law

has traditionally protected children from choices, as well as in-
strumentalities, which might prove harmful to them. This protected
status of children stems from a recognition that, in many areas, children lack the cognitive sophistication to evaluate possibilities, and
therefore deserve protection from choices which exploit their natural
vulnerabilities.[46]

One can hardly disagree with the proposition that people vary in their
discriminatory capacities and that, *as a general rule,* children may be less
discerning than adults. Yet we must immediately qualify that agreement
by noting that youth is not the only determinative factor. In addition to
those who are mentally retarded or senile, there are also other adults
with the tastes and acumen of the average ten-year-old, just as there are
many ten-year-olds who are unusually sophisticated. Native intelligence,
home environment, and educational opportunities all play important
roles. When Uganda's Minister of Education told a UNESCO conference
in New York in 1976 that a government-controlled press was necessary
in his nation because "Ugandans are not yet in a position to think and
decide on their own,"[47] he may have been underestimating his country-
men, but age was certainly not the causative factor he had in mind. Thus,
any scheme of state censorship based on age alone will fail in significant measure to meet the objective for which it has allegedly been
designed—the protection of all those, and only those, who are presumably incapable of taking care of themselves in the face of seductive communication. It is more likely, as the U.S. Supreme Court said in 1957 of a
Michigan effort in this direction, "to burn the house to roast the pig."[48]

Even assuming it were feasible—which I cannot imagine it to be—to
devise a system that would screen out of the audience only those incapable of making discriminating judgments, whether because of their age
or other reasons, would that then be a course we should take? I think
not.

First, we ought to be aware that for many of those we would be trying
to protect, our solicitude would be unnecessary. In order to be harmfully
influenced by some of the communication we are discussing, the message
must first be understood, and then there must be the capability of acting
on that understanding. With very young children, or persons with severe
mental retardation, both of those conditions may well be absent. Regarding sexually oriented material or "indecent" language, they may
neither comprehend it nor will they endow it with the heavy emotional
freight it might carry for a more aware adult. Justice Stevens, in trying to
rationalize the Supreme Court's contradictory rulings in its "Fuck the
Draft" decision and in the George Carlin case, said, "Although Cohen's
written message might have been incomprehensible to a first grader,

Pacifica's broadcast could have enlarged a child's vocabulary in an instant."[49] But Justice Stevens does not tell us what harm there is in an enlarged vocabulary for one who does not comprehend the words being uttered.

With regard to the advertising of unhealthful products directed to young children, even if understanding is achieved and wants are aroused, unless there are adults around who are willing to put up the money for the purchase of these items, harmful action cannot be taken. Youths who are mature enough to make their own money to buy candy and cigarettes also ought to be capable of learning the hazards involved.

Second, we must raise the question as to how people develop the capacity to discriminate and make better choices in their tastes, attitudes, and values. Are they suddenly and magically endowed with that ability at the age of ten, or twelve, or sixteen, or when they pass the STEP examination for high school freshmen? Does insulating them from debasing stimuli during their "tender" years help to achieve it? Or should they, on the contrary, be exposed to whatever they may encounter in the real world and given the guidance that will aid them in learning how to respond wisely and healthfully?

We are strangely selective in our society about the kinds of things from which we try to shield children and those to which we casually expose them. Sex and death are high on the list of realities we attempt to hide—probably because they were hidden from us—and as a result we do not handle them very well ourselves. On the other hand, we rather unashamedly parade our treatment of others as objects-to-be-manipulated rather than as people-to-be-respected, although all of our religious and ethical teachings exhort to the contrary. Be all that as it may, I would suggest that the "full capacity for individual choice which is the presupposition of First Amendment guarantees"[50] does not grow in a vacuum, but only out of the rich soil of the widest possible range of human experience.

A third and final difficulty with government censorship of communication to children is the thorny problems it creates in the delicate relationships between and among parents, children, and the state. Few would dispute the right of parents to do what they can, within the limits of their physical, economic, and psychological power, and within the confines of the law,[51] to control the communications environment of their minor offspring. They need not have radio or television sets in their homes, or they can try to regulate their use or even procure locking devises for them. They can, if they wish, bar the purchase with their money of toy guns, girlie magazines, or tickets to the movies. They may send their children to parochial or private schools[52] and, if they are like the Amish, may keep them out of high school altogether.[53] They may require them to attend church services or to listen to homemade sermons at the dinner table.

However, when parents demand that the government step in to help them control their children's communications environment, the appropriate response is not so clear. For one thing, it may be impossible for the state to assist one group of parents in exercising the kind of control they wish to exert over their children without simultaneously interfering with the rights of other parents who may want a broader exposure for their offspring. That is precisely the effect when a particular communication is cut off at its source by government censorship, such as the FCC action taken against the George Carlin broadcast, or when children are uniformly barred from the reception of certain categories of expression, such as is the case where city ordinances require movie theaters to turn them away from X-rated films, even if they are accompanied by their parents.

Justice Brennan's dissenting opinion in the Carlin case made this very point:

> As surprising as it may be to individual members of this Court, some parents may actually find Mr. Carlin's unabashed attitude towards the seven "dirty words" healthy, and deem it desirable to expose their children to the manner in which Mr. Carlin defuses the taboo surrounding the words. Such parents may constitute a minority of the American public, but the absence of great numbers willing to exercise the right to raise their children in this fashion does not alter the right's nature or its existence. Only the Court's regrettable decision does that.[54]

Even at a more individualized level, there is serious question as to what is an appropriate government response to parents who ask for aid in controlling their children. If, for example, a minor runs away from home to join a religious cult, should the parents be able to invoke the power of the state to return the child and force him or her to submit to a deprogramming experience? As a practical matter, of course, there is no way that parents can maintain continuing control over children who are determined to get away and who have the capacity to survive on their own. States, too, generally recognize their inability to be of much assistance to such parents and usually give up after a while. But this pragmatic resolution of the problem does not answer the theoretical question of whether a minor has any First Amendment protections against one's parents as one does against school officials.[55]

There is so little historical or legal precedent that would help us with this question in today's world that common sense may be our only useful guide. In that spirit I would propose what seems to me to be a fair trade: that in return for government noninterference in the exercise of parental control over the communications environment of their children—insofar as they can make that control stick with their own powers and without violating the law—the government will also refrain from using its powers to interfere, *at the behest of parents,* with First Amendment–related activities of children.

The positions asserted in this chapter may seem to some readers to reflect too great an optimism about human capabilities and too little a concern about the quality of our lives. I think that both perceptions would be inaccurate.

It is true that considerable emphasis has been given to the *capacity* of people, even of children, to protect themselves from presumptively harmful communicative stimuli. But that does not mean that this capacity is ordinarily as well developed or as fully utilized as it needs to be. Whatever optimism is reflected in the arguments that have been made here is based on future potential in this area rather than on past performance. Moreover, it is profoundly influenced by my conviction that there is no better alternative. For while reliance on government to act as the arbiter of tastes and values provides no assurance that the decisions it makes for us will be the best ones, it guarantees that whatever capacity people have to make healthy choices for themselves will remain underdeveloped.

As for the concern about the quality of our lives, it should be clear from what has been said throughout this chapter that my disagreement with critics of the debasing communication that bombards us is not with their lamentations about the problem but with the paternalistic solution some of them propose. Irving Kristol has suggested that there are essentially two views of democracy—one that sees it as a process of decision making above all, and the other that regards those processes only as means to the greater end of achieving a good life.[56] Or, to put it another way, the first sees human freedom as an end in itself and the second as a means to other ends. Kristol places himself in the latter camp, and I am in the former—not because I am uninterested in the good life but because I am more interested in how we go about the quest for it. I do not want somebody else deciding for me or my children what it is and handing it over to us. Unless we seek it for ourselves, it is not, in my view, worth finding.

10 Lies and Misrepresentations

In an earlier chapter we dealt with the issue of personal defamation and argued that, where time permits, the remedy most appropriate to a free society is more communication rather than legal limitation. The presumption was that people about whom falsehoods are spread, if they believe the utterances to be potentially harmful, will have the desire and should be provided with the channels of communication to set the record straight.

Different questions arise, however, when lies and misrepresentations about inanimate objects, past events, or the subjective intentions of the communicator may lead directly to audience action based upon that misinformation. Here there is no maligned third party with the motivation, capacity, and time to respond. Such falsehoods, if uncontradicted, deprive auditors of meaningful freedom of choice by polluting the stream of their decision-making processes. The options people have are sharply curtailed when they play with stacked decks of cards. One writer on the subject of lying, Sissela Bok, likens deceit to violence in that they are "the two forms of deliberate assault on human beings. Both can coerce people into acting against their will."[1]

There are at least three categories of communication, apart from defamation, in which the utterance of falsehoods has caused serious concern. The first is the all-too-common practice of distorting the truth in order to win votes in an election, gain converts to a religious cult, or develop public prejudices on issues of social concern. A second category embraces the wide range of circumstances in which people's money or property is taken under false pretenses—perhaps in the purchase of products deceptively advertised through the mass media, perhaps in response to the personal blandishments of an individual con artist, perhaps in the making of contributions to a misrepresented cause, or perhaps in the desperate search for a miracle cure to a physical ailment. Finally, and happily less frequent, are those instances in which physical harm is caused to people by the lies of others, such as the cases described in a previous chapter of the woman who had a nervous breakdown when a practical joker falsely reported to her that her husband had been in a serious accident, or the Indiana man who persuaded women to burn off their hair, allegedly to avoid a contagious infection. The classic hypothetical example of falsely shouting "Fire" in a crowded theater and causing a panic would also fall in this group.

Although there is little to distinguish these categories in terms of their moral repugnance, they have been viewed rather differently in the eyes of the law. By far the most extensive legal attention has been given to the second classification, involving deception in matters related to money, material goods, and contractual relationships. According to Prosser, in his description of the tort of "misrepresentation": "The action of deceit is of very ancient origin. There was an old writ of deceit as early as 1201, which lay only against a person who misused legal procedure for the purpose of swindling someone. . . . The typical case of deceit is one in which the plaintiff has parted with money, or property of value, in reliance upon the defendant's representations."[2]

Out of the early common law of deceit, later encompassed in the broader and, according to Prosser, vaguer term "fraud,"[3] there has grown a host of legal restrictions on misrepresentation in the realm of commerce. Not only may one individual sue another for having been cheated, but legislatures at both the state and national levels have adopted a variety of government regulations, prohibitions, and penalties to curtail deceptive trade practices.

The Federal Trade Commission, for example, has been empowered to monitor advertisements of goods and services in interstate commerce and take action against those found to be false and misleading. The commission may order the advertiser to "cease and desist"; it may impose fines; and it may even require, in some circumstances, that programs of corrective advertising be undertaken by offenders. Perhaps the most dramatic instance of the exercise of this power was an FTC ruling, in December 1975, requiring the manufacturer of Listerine to spend approximately $10 million—an amount equal to the average annual Listerine advertising budget during the decade from 1962 to 1972—to inform the public that "Listerine will not help prevent colds or sore throats or lessen their severity." A court challenge to this order was rejected by the U.S. Circuit Court of Appeals, and the U.S. Supreme Court declined to review that decision.[4]

The FTC is not alone among government agencies which police the truthfulness of communications. The Securities and Exchange Commission has responsibilities with respect to trade in securities, and the Food and Drug Administration oversees the labeling of products under its jurisdiction. Many agencies at the state level perform similar functions.

Laws have been adopted that require full disclosure of the financial obligations undertaken by borrowers—so-called truth-in-lending legislation. There is also on the books a federal statute that makes it illegal to use the U.S. mails or broadcast media "for obtaining money or property by means of false or fraudulent pretenses, representations or promises."[5]

In addition to these protections for the general public and to the common law of misrepresentation for individuals who have been swindled, there is another category of torts to which recourse may be had by persons who have suffered pecuniary loss as a result of false statements made by others about their business or property. Known variously as trade libel, unfair competition, or injurious falsehood, the tort appears similar to personal defamation but, according to Prosser, should not be confused with it.[6] Prosser says that "an aura of 'slander' has hung over it like a fog, obscuring its real character. . . . The plaintiff's title, or property, comes to be regarded as somehow personified, and so defined."[7] But, he goes on, the tort is really "one form of intentional interference with economic relations" and not a branch of defamation at all.[8]

Just as there has been a long tradition of legal recourse against falsehoods resulting in the loss of money or property, so the common law of deceit has also been available in those relatively infrequent instances, identified as our third category of problems, where the harm ensuing from a lie is to the body rather than to the belongings of the victim.[9] As noted in an early Minnesota case, "The injury to one's person by the fraud of another is quite as serious as an injury to one's pocketbook."[10]

In order for a common-law action of deceit to succeed, whether the injury is to person or to property, several requirements, described by Prosser, must be met.[11] Although they have been developed over a longer period of time than has contemporary First Amendment doctrine, and although little has been said explicitly relating the two areas, one cannot help but conclude from a review of these criteria that the thinking which has animated free speech theory has also served in a healthy way to limit the law of deceit. Our present-day understanding of the First Amendment would seem to call for no less protection of expression than these standards demand.

The first of the requirements is that the communication be a "false representation. . . . In the ordinary case . . . one of fact."[12] This excludes from restriction statements that are simply matters of opinion or cannot be subjected to an empirical test of their veracity. More will be said later about the difficulties that are sometimes encountered in distinguishing between statements of fact and opinion. For the moment it will suffice to have identified the principle that is involved and to hint at some of the complexities of the issue by reference to one form of advertising—known as "puffery"—that is *not* regarded as legally fraudulent even though the claims seem to be literally untrue.

A statement that a cigarette is made from the purest tobacco grown, that an automobile is the most economic car on the market, that a stock is the safest investment in the world, that a machine is 100 per cent efficient, that a household device is absolutely perfect, that a real estate investment will insure a handsome profit, that an article is the greatest bargain ever offered, and similar claims are intended and understood to be merely emphatic methods of urging a sale.... These things, then, the buyer must disregard in forming a sober judgment.[13]

Or, as one court has said, "[A] buyer has no right to rely on such statements."[14]

The second standard is: "Knowledge or belief on the part of the defendant that the representation is false—or what is regarded as equivalent, that he has not a sufficient basis of information to make it. This element often is given the technical name of 'scienter.'"[15]

This requirement reflects the same First Amendment philosophy as that expressed in the U.S. Supreme Court's landmark libel decision, *New York Times v. Sullivan*, that while innocent error may deserve protection, calculated falsehoods or reckless disregard of the truth do not. To be sure, an unintentional lie may be just as harmful to the person whose actions are affected by it as a calculated or reckless misrepresentation. But a communicator cannot be held responsible in a lawsuit for damages for the consequences of such an utterance.[16]

It is important to note here that this standard of scienter has not been required with respect to FTC regulations of advertising, presumably because sanctions other than punishment, such as cease-and-desist orders, may be invoked. According to Martin Redish, "[U]nder traditional FTC law, even the honest belief by one using the supposedly false information in advertising will not preclude Commission action."[17] Redish cites as an example a decision of the U.S. Court of Appeals for the Sixth Circuit which declared: "The fact that an advertiser made its representations in good or bad faith is not determinative of whether such statements are deceptive and misleading."[18] Similarly, the U.S. Supreme Court has held that the SEC need not prove scienter in injunction actions under Section 17(a)(2) of the Securities Act of 1933 which prohibits persons from obtaining money or property "by means of any untrue statement of a material fact or any omission to state a material fact," or under Section 17(a)(3) of the same act which forbids "any transaction, practice, or course of business which operates or would operate as a fraud or deceit."[19] The court reasoned that the language chosen by Congress in writing both of these provisions "quite plainly focuses upon the *effect* of particular conduct on members of the investing public, rather than upon the culpability of the person responsible."[20]

At the same time, however, the Supreme Court held that Section

17(a)(1) of the 1933 act which makes it illegal "to employ any device, scheme, or artifice to defraud," and Section 10(b) of the Securities Exchange Act of 1934 which also refers to "any manipulative or deceptive device or contrivance," do require a showing of scienter, even to obtain an injunction, since that appeared to the Court to be the congressional intent.[21] Many years earlier the Court had already decided that scienter must be proven under this provision of the 1934 act in cases where private parties brought after-the-fact damage suits.[22]

Although the scienter requirement involves our courts in the difficult task of probing the state of mind of communicators charged with fraud, it seems to be a necessary safeguard for innocent error, at least when punishment for misrepresentation is the consequence. The hazard in cutting loose from strict standards in this area is well illustrated by a 1978 proposal from the staff of the FTC to ban *all* advertising directed to very young children. The rationale offered was that such advertising is *inherently* deceptive because its audience is too young to understand that it has a sales purpose. In other words, regardless of whether the information contained in the ad is true or false, and regardless of whether the advertiser believes it to be true or false, it was argued that a lack of sophistication of the auditors makes any sales appeal to that audience misleading.[23] If deception is so broadly and loosely defined, the concept becomes meaningless. We should at least hold firm to the requirement that deceit in advertising has to do with statements that are empirically false, if not to the requirement that the deceiver know he is being dishonest. It is noteworthy in this regard that in May of 1980 Congress adopted legislation restricting the inquiry which the FTC had undertaken on this subject to a study of only advertising that is actually false.[24]

The third ingredient of a successful tort action for deceit is "[a]n intention to induce the plaintiff to act or refrain from action in reliance upon the misrepresentation."[25] Here, even more clearly than in the second standard, where it may also be implicit, intentionality is required. It is not enough that an utterance be false and be known to be false. The communicator must also want the audience to act on the basis of the falsehood. In the case of advertising it may be presumed that the speaker or writer wishes the audience to respond with a purchase, but the same cannot be assumed of every mode and instance of communication.

The fourth requirement for recovery is that there has been "[j]ustifiable reliance upon the representation on the part of the plaintiff, in taking action or refraining from it."[26] Thus, as in the case of puffing, an auditor may be expected to know better than to take some statements literally and to depend upon them.

Finally, there must be "[d]amage to the plaintiff, resulting from such reliance."[27] Again, unlike government regulation of false advertising where it is presumed that someone will act on the basis of the misleading information, success in tort action depends upon a showing that harm has in fact been done to the target of the communication.

The reader should be reminded at this point that, as with many of the other kinds of speech discussed in this book, misrepresentations can be communicated nonverbally as well as by spoken and written words. For example, a deceitful message is employed in the sale of a used car if the seller turns the odometer back to fewer miles than the vehicle has actually traveled. Injury to others can be caused by the driver of an automobile who flashes a misleading turn signal. On a much broader scale, a political movement might disguise its real purposes by adopting the symbols and trappings of a religious enterprise, or even of a competing political institution.

The previous illustration brings us back to the first category of deception mentioned at the outset of this chapter—that in which the truth is distorted to advance a political, social, or religious cause. Although the *ultimate* effect of such communication may sometimes be such tangible harms as the casting of ballots for an impeachable president or mass suicide in Jonestown, Guyana, the law has trod warily around the edges of this arena for fear of intruding on protected First Amendment rights. For what we are dealing with here is expression which is directed primarily to the inculcation of contestable beliefs rather than to immediate and clearly harmful action. Thus the philosophy of caveat emptor—let the buyer beware—has seemed more appropriate in this area, where the "buyer" is importuned ideologically, than where he or she is deceitfully solicited to part with money or property in exchange for deficient goods or services, or where the lie may immediately trigger something like a nervous breakdown.

It seems correct to me that the law should steer wide of intervention in this political-social-religious realm, even where calculated falsehoods are involved. There are at least three important reasons why this is sound First Amendment doctrine.

The first has to do with a problem alluded to earlier—that is, the difficulty encountered in distinguishing between statements of fact and opinion. Particularly in the realm of religion or of public and social policy, where empirical questions are almost inseparable from inference and interpretation, there is the danger that authoritative attempts to say what is or is not "true" would lead to the establishment of orthodoxies and heresies that have no place in a democratic society.

In the 1960 presidential election, for instance, one of the major themes of John F. Kennedy's campaign was the so-called missile gap between the Russians and ourselves, for which the incumbent Eisenhower-Nixon administration was blamed. Although it has since been suggested by Kennedy critics that there was no missile gap, and although this is a question that would *seem* to have been answerable at an empirical level, I have never heard it proposed that, in mid-campaign, some court, or some commission on fair election practices, should have had the authority to pronounce the "truth" of this matter, or to restrain Kennedy's use of the claim.

Similarly, during the last several months of the Nixon presidency, when Richard Nixon was busy explaining to the public that he was "not a crook" and that the contents of the White House tapes could not be divulged because to do so would endanger the "national security," one might have been tempted to wish for an authoritative national referee who could cry out "Foul" and eject this particular player from the game. Instead, we relied on the other players, in Congress, the press, and elsewhere, to expose the calculated falsehoods that ultimately brought down a president of the United States.

No so wisely, during the 1977 Christmas season a group of Hare Krishna solicitors, dressed in Santa Claus costumes, were arrested on the streets of downtown Chicago and told by the district police commander that they would have to stop collecting money "under false pretenses."[28] Presumably Santa Claus was regarded by the police to be a monopoly of Christianity, or of the Salvation Army, and thus it was perceived to be a nonverbal misrepresentation for the Hare Krishna sect to garb themselves in this manner. Again, the danger of government authorities asserting what is "true" or "false" in religious matters should be readily apparent.

A final illustration, which demonstrates how thin the line can be between fact and interpretation, occurred during the U.S. senatorial campaign of 1978 in Illinois between incumbent Charles Percy and challenger Alex Seith. A radio advertisement by the Seith campaign, aired over stations with predominantly black audiences, quoted Senator Percy as having expressed the wish that the former agriculture secretary Earl Butz was back in that office. Reminding the radio audience that Butz had been fired because he told a racist joke, the advertisement went on to suggest that with friends like Senator Percy who needed enemies? Percy, who had a good legislative record on civil rights, and who had in fact called for the firing of Butz at the time of his infamous joke, was indignant over this "misrepresentation" of his attitudes, although he had indeed uttered the quoted statement about Butz in a context where he was expressing his sympathy for Butz's agricultural policies.

Senator Percy's indignation over the allegedly deceitful radio advertisement was evidently shared by many thousands of voters, for the support which polls had previously shown running strongly in Seith's favor began to shift to Percy, who won an overwhelming victory on election day. The voters had adjudicated the dispute, apparently deciding that, whether the radio ad contained literally untrue statements or not, it was sufficiently objectionable in its implications to make the factual question relatively unimportant. That seems to me the most sensible disposition of such an issue and indicates that so long as public opinion rather than the law is the arbiter, as ought to be the case in the realm of public affairs, it may be unnecessary to distinguish fact from interpretation and opinion.

A second reason that the law can be kept out of such matters is that, as in the case of personal defamation, there are usually interested parties with the motivation and resources to expose and correct misrepresentations that may be promulgated by deceitful communicators. Politics, religion, and social action are disputatious enterprises in our society, with a wide range of advocates soliciting for their own causes and challenging the communication of their competitors. In addition, there is the watchdog role played by the press and the academy as well as by one's friends and relatives. Kennedy's missile gap and Nixon's national security claims did not go unquestioned, Seith's radio ad boomeranged severely, and I assume that had the police not arrested the Hare Krishna Santa Clauses, others would have found a way to let people know who they were.

To be sure, the same argument may be made and has been made about commercial advertising, and to the extent that there are, indeed, some kinds of solicitation for goods and services which are intensely competitive, it may be that consumers are more capable than has been assumed of protecting themselves from fraudulent appeals without assistance from the government. However, commercial competitors are usually more interested in promoting their own wares than in exposing the defects of others, private consumer protection associations do not have the resources to monitor more than a limited number of items nor the capacity to publicize their warnings to everyone who may be affected, and the press and academics only infrequently see their watchdog function as extending into the commercial realm. Thus we have cast the government, which does have the resources to investigate, and the presumed objectivity to evaluate, commercial claims, in a more paternalistic role vis-à-vis speech activities than would normally be acceptable.

The third and final argument for relying on the marketplace rather than the law to deal with political, social, and religious falsehoods is that, as with defamation, there is usually an opportunity between the utterance and responsive action for corrective speech to intervene. Ordinarily the solicitation is to *believe,* and not immediately to part with money or property. Thus the Brandeis admonition is once again appropriate— that "if there be time to expose through discussion the falsehood and fallacies . . . the remedy to be applied is more speech, not enforced silence."

It is easy, in theory, to assert that the category of deceitful communication we have just been discussing merits First Amendment protection while the other classifications described previously may not. It can be more difficult, in practice, to distinguish these categories, for the line between deception that influences religious, social, and political beliefs and that which steals money or causes physical injury may sometimes be extremely fuzzy.

The classic case that illustrates this problem is *United States v. Ballard,* decided by the United States Supreme Court in 1944.[29] The Ballards were the founders and leaders of the "I Am" movement, an ostensibly religious enterprise, who were charged with violation of the federal mail fraud statute for having collected large sums of money through solicitations which, according to the indictment, held out "false and fraudulent representations, pretenses and promises." Among other things, the Ballards claimed to have "attained a state of self immortality which enabled them to be free from ailments common to man," that they "could and would transmit that supernatural state to others willing to pay therefor," and that they had already healed hundreds of persons with medically incurable diseases. They urged that, because the world was coming to an end, there was no point in people saving money which might better be given to the movement. Their publications were allegedly the "result of divine visitations" from Jesus and Saint Germain, with whom they claimed to have shaken hands.[30]

When the case was tried in federal district court, the presiding judge decided that the freedom-of-religion clause of the First Amendment would not allow the jury to pass judgment on the truth or falsity of utterances involving religious experiences and doctrines. The only question that could properly be addressed, he thought, was whether the defendants believed what they said. He so instructed the jury, which found that the Ballards did not believe their own statements and were thus guilty of fraud in their solicitation of funds.

The U.S. Circuit Court of Appeals reversed the judgement of the lower court, holding that the question of the truth or falsity of the statements should not have been withheld from the jury and that there could not be a conviction unless at least some of the representations made were found to be false.[31] That ruling, in turn, was rejected by the U.S. Supreme Court, whose majority agreed with the position on that issue taken by the district court judge. Wrote Justice Douglas for the Court:

> Heresy trials are foreign to our Constitution. Men may believe what they cannot prove. They may not be put to the proof of their religious

doctrines or beliefs. Religious experiences which are as real as life to some may be incomprehensible to others. . . . The miracles of the New Testament, the Divinity of Christ, life after death, the power of prayer are deep in the religious convictions of many. If one could be sent to jail because a jury in a hostile environment found those teachings false, little indeed would be left of religious freedom. . . . The religious views espoused by respondents might seem incredible, if not pre-posterous, to most people. But if those doctrines are subject to trial before a jury charged with finding their truth or falsity, then the same can be done with the religious beliefs of any sect. When the triers of fact undertake that task, they enter a forbidden domain.[32]

The case was sent back to the court of appeals for consideration of other questions that had not been reached there, and on its second trip to the Supreme Court, two years later, the indictment was dismissed on the grounds that women had been excluded from the grand jury with which it originated.[33]

Justice Robert Jackson, dissenting from the original Supreme Court decision, argued that *neither* the truth of the statements *nor* the sincerity of the Ballards was any business of the law, and would have dismissed the indictment on that basis. With respect to the sincerity issue, he won-dered how people could be found to be dishonest without it being shown that what they said was not true. "How," he asked, "can the government prove these persons knew something to be false which it cannot prove to be false?"[34]

But he did not want the government to pass judgment on the question of truth or falsity either.

There appear to be persons—let us hope not many—who find re-freshment and courage in the teachings of the "I Am" cult. If the members of the sect get comfort from the celestial guidance of their "Saint Germain," however doubtful it seems to me, it is hard to say that they do not get what they pay for. Scores of sects flourish in this country by teaching what to me are queer notions. It is plain that there is wide variety in American religious taste. The Ballards are not alone in catering to it with a pretty dubious product.

The chief wrong which false prophets do to their following is not financial. The collections aggregate a tempting total, but individual payments are not ruinous. I doubt if the vigilance of the law is equal to making money stick by over-credulous people. But the real harm is on the mental and spiritual plane. There are those who hunger and thirst after higher values which they feel wanting in their humdrum lives. . . . When they are deluded and then disillusioned, cynicism and confusion follow. The wrong of these things, as I see it, is not in the money the victims part with half so much as in the mental and spiritual poison they get. But that is precisely the thing the Constitution put beyond the reach of the prosecutor, for the price of freedom of religion or of speech or of the press is that we must put up with, and even pay for, a good deal of rubbish.

Prosecutions of this character easily could degenerate into religious persecution. I do not doubt that religious leaders may be convicted of fraud for making false representations on matters other than faith or experience, or for example if one represents that funds are being used to construct a church when in fact they are being used for personal purposes. But that is not this case, which reaches into wholly dangerous ground.[35]

The other three dissenters, in an opinion written by Chief Justice Harlan Stone, were not only willing to accept and sustain the trial court judgment that the Ballards were guilty of fraud because they did not believe what was said, but they would also have allowed an examination of the truthfulness of the statements themselves. The chief justice explained:

I cannot say that freedom of thought and worship includes freedom to procure money by making knowingly false statements about one's religious experiences. To go no further, if it were shown that a defendant in this case had asserted as a part of the alleged fraudulent scheme, that he had physically shaken hands with St. Germain in San Francisco on a day named, or that, as the indictment here alleges, by the exertion of his spiritual power he "had in fact cured . . . hundreds of persons afflicted with diseases and ailments," I should not doubt that it would be open to the government to submit to the jury proof that he had never been in San Francisco and that no such cures had ever been effected.[36]

It appears to me that each of the positions set forth in this case—that of the court of appeals, that of the Supreme Court majority, that of Justice Jackson, and that of Chief Justice Stone—is partly right and partly wrong.

Both the Supreme Court majority and Justice Jackson agree that it is dangerous and constitutionally impermissible for courts to pass judgment on the truth or falsity of statements involving religious experiences and doctrines. In this I believe them to be correct, and the court of appeals and the chief justice to be wrong. My reasons are identical to those so well articulated in the Douglas and Jackson opinions quoted above and need no further elaboration.

In the disagreement between Justice Jackson and all the others as to whether legal judgments may properly be made about the sincerity of utterances concerning religious beliefs and experiences, I cast my lot with Justice Jackson's conclusion that such inquiries should be impermissible, though not with the reasoning that leads him there. His rhetorical question, asking how the government can prove that people know "something to be false which it cannot prove to be false," although seductively plausible at first glance, does not survive careful analysis. Whether one *believes* something to be false, and whether it *is* false, are different issues that can be dealt with quite separately. To be sure, it might be more difficult to prove that someone believes something to be false if it cannot also be shown that it is, in fact, false; but the latter is certainly not a precondition to the former. Conversely, if it can be shown that someone does not believe what he or she is saying, it raises some presumption that the utterance is false, but that does not necessarily follow either.

A better rationale for the Jackson position, it seems to me, is one which argues that, if the law is excluded by the First Amendment from passing judgment on the truth or falsity of statements concerning religious beliefs and experiences, it has just as little business passing judgment on the communicator's state of mind. As in the political realm we would no more have wanted a government agency or court to pronounce judgment on John F. Kennedy's *sincerity* about the missile gap than on the *validity* of the claim itself, so in the religious realm we should be as reluctant for the law to probe into whether people really believe they have shaken hands with Jesus as to inquire whether that has, in fact, happened.

Justice Jackson's objection to separating the question of truth or falsity from that of sincerity or insincerity is as applicable in areas where the law has a right to intervene against fraud as in those where it does not. To punish people for deceitful communication because they do not believe what they say, in the absence of any empirical finding that what they say is untrue, is to ignore the first requirement of the tort of deceit discussed earlier—namely, that the utterance must be false. It may well have been this principle which motivated the circuit court of appeals in the Ballard case to insist that a conviction required a finding by the jury that at least some of the statements made by the defendants were untrue. That court's mistake was not in demanding that more than insincerity was required in order to convict for fraud but rather in failing to distinguish between the kinds of subject matter that are appropriate in a trial for fraud and those that are not.

This brings us to the last, most central, and most difficult issue addressed but not definitively resolved in the Ballard opinions—the question as to what, if any, areas of "religious" communication may be subject to possible scrutiny by the law. Chief Justice Stone, and apparently the court of appeals, cast the net most broadly with their willingness to encompass "statements about one's religious experiences," *if* made in the context of soliciting money *and if* testable empirically (as, e.g., determining whether one was or was not in San Francisco on a given date). Justice Jackson took the narrowest stance, but even he would allow religious leaders to be convicted of fraud if they make "false representations on matters other than faith or experience," such as diverting contributions solicited for construction of a church building into their own pockets. The Supreme Court majority contributed only confusion by failing to make any distinctions among kinds of statements, by implying that *none* in the religious arena could be subjected to a test of truth or falsity, and by seeming to approve the district court posture that *all* might be submitted to a test of their sincerity.

Opening the door as wide as the court of appeals and Chief Justice Stone would have done invites intrusions on freedom of expression that, it seems to me, should not be risked. Whether or not one has shaken hands with "divine messengers" in San Francisco or on Mt. Everest is not something which the law should need to probe in order to determine if money or property have been misappropriated by religious leaders. Whether or not people should donate all of their possessions to the movement of their choice because the world is supposed to be coming to an end is not an empirical question at all. The promise that a medically "incurable" disease can be healed through faith is likewise not an empirically disprovable assertion, even though the underlying claim that hundreds have been so cured in the past may be demonstrably untrue. There is an essential difference, as we have repeatedly argued in this chapter, between selling *beliefs* that are supposed to be useful, and selling bottles of useless or harmful pills. It is a difference of which the Stone position fails to take cognizance.

As the view of the chief justice is too broad, so the Jackson position may be too narrow. To be sure, Justice Jackson is quite right when he notes that many persons may feel they have gotten what they paid for with their contributions in support of dubious doctrines and that the law is limited in its ability to make "money stick by over-credulous people." But he significantly underestimates the tangible harms that may result from pseudoreligious proselytizing. His assertion that the monies collected by religious charlatans may "aggregate a tempting total" but that "individual payments are not ruinous" is simply out of touch with reality. Several former members of the "Worldwide Church of God," for example, have charged that "church officials lived in mansions and drove expensive foreign sport cars while many of the 60,000 members had been reduced to poverty by the church's tithing policies, which made them contribute as much as 40 percent of their income."[37] It was also charged that "some members signed over their homes and stock portfolios to the church, which has an annual income of more than $60 million, because they believed the church's prophecy that the world would end in 1972."[38] I am not suggesting that a prosecution for fraud would have been an appropriate solution in this instance but only that Justice Jackson has not accurately described the dimensions of the problem.

In addition to the substantial money and property losses that are often associated with religious cultism, there can sometimes be incalculable physical harm, such as the mass suicides (or killings) of the People's Temple cult in Jonestown, Guyana, in 1978. Again, there may have been no constitutionally permissible basis for the government to have intervened in advance of that disaster, but the incident illustrates the shortcomings of Justice Jackson's assumption that the only "real harm [of false prophets] is on the mental and spiritual plane."

If Justice Jackson is correct, as all positions seem to agree, that religious leaders, like anyone else, should be liable for fraud if they divert funds collected for a church building to their own personal use, it should also be possible to charge them with fraud if, after the fact and in return for material considerations, they have not delivered on an explicit promise to heal a specific individual of a particular ailment, or if they have retained money given in anticipation of the end of the world long after the specified time for that cataclysm has passed without its occurrence. Otherwise any charlatan with any scheme for bilking gullible people of their material possessions could evade the law of deceit by donning the trappings of a "religion."

The principles I have suggested here may be difficult to apply in particular troublesome cases, but should ordinarily provide the guidance we need. Charges of fraud against Hare Krishna solicitors at the Los Angeles airport for allegedly telling a foreign visitor that American law required him to donate to their cause,[39] and for claiming they were collecting for a Roman Catholic mission and for the Muscular Dystrophy Foundation,[40] would seem permissible, because the money is given in direct response to an intentionally and palpably false utterance that has nothing to do with religious doctrine or experience.

On the other hand, the arrest in Chicago of a group of gypsy fortune-tellers, under a city ordinance making it illegal for persons to advertise that they have the ability to reveal future events or that they have other magical powers,[41] would seem to fall on the constitutionally impermissible side of the line. Surely people who call themselves religious leaders would be free to claim the ability to predict future events or to solve problems with hocus-pocus, so why should not the same hold good for individuals who happen to be gypsy fortune-tellers? The fact that some of these particular gypsies had, according to city investigators, been "preying on the elderly and persons who are desperately upset because of personal problems"[42] would not provide a basis for distinguishing them from pseudoreligious charlatans who do precisely the same thing. And going back once again to Justice Jackson, who can say that they do not get what they pay for?

There are other areas besides that of supernatural discourse in which difficulties have been encountered in drawing the line between constitutionally protected and unprotected categories of deceptive communication. One is the publication of books or pamphlets which, though not directly promoting the sale of a product, may have that effect. Another is the practice, sometimes employed in political campaigns, that is rather benignly called "dirty tricks." Let us address each in turn.

The first problem is illustrated through some cases discussed by Martin Redish in a thoughtful law review article examining the general topic of commercial speech and its relationship to the First Amendment.[43] Two of them, decided by the U.S. Circuit Courts of Appeal for the Third and Sixth Circuits, respectively, dealt with FTC actions in response to publications claiming that aluminum cookware was poisonous. In the Sixth Circuit case, the court upheld an FTC cease-and-desist order against the dissemination of this claim by a competitor of aluminum cookware.[44] But in the Third Circuit, a similar FTC order against the publisher of pamphlets making the very same contention was overturned.[45] The rationale of the latter decision was that, unlike the first case, the pamphlets did not constitute "advertising" because the communicator was "not materially interested in the cooking utensil trade."[46] Therefore, the publications were beyond the purview of the FTC's regulatory powers and were protected by the First Amendment.

Redish is sharply critical of the basis on which these cases were distinguished. He notes that

> if the degree of first amendment protection is to vary according to the presence of a direct personal interest in the acceptance by the public of the speaker's arguments, then a great deal of our political expression should logically receive less protection than it does. Candidates for public office, as well as political lobbyists and interest groups, obviously possess direct personal interest in the acceptance of their statements. The ultimate decision-makers, whether they be a jury, the voters, or the consumers, will most likely consider the personal interest of the speaker in evaluating his information and arguments. But that does not mean that the information conveyed by one with a personal interest should necessarily receive less first amendment protection than that disseminated by an objective observer.... the governmental interest in restricting false advertising does not really turn on whether the speaker himself has an interest in the product.... The concern is whether the dissemination of those theories will have the effect of

causing financial and/or physical harm to members of the purchasing public by inducing them to purchase and use products that simply do not accomplish what is claimed. . . . it is the general *effect* of encouraging or discouraging purchase, not the presence of a financial interest involved, that justifies governmental limitations of free speech. The harm which rightfully concerns the government may result even though the speaker had no financial interest.[47]

I strongly agree with the *first part* of the Redish critique. The presence of a material interest on the part of a communicator cannot be the sole criterion for deciding that utterances are without First Amendment protection, for the reasons Redish has indicated. The primary test, as he so well puts it in the third-last sentence quoted above, is whether the communication "will have the effect of causing financial and/or physical harm to members of the purchasing public by inducing them to purchase and use products that simply do not accomplish what is claimed."

But in the next quoted sentence Redish deviates from rigorous adherence to that standard by talking loosely about the "*general* effect of encouraging or discouraging purchase" (italics mine). To talk about *general* effects departs from the requirement of direct inducement to harmful *action* that we have been insisting upon for restrictions on deceptive communication and slips over into the area of inculcation of *beliefs*.

What is more, I think that Redish goes too far with the argument about financial interest when he suggests that limitations on deceptive speech may be permissible even in the absence of such an interest on the part of the communicator. It is one thing to *extend* First Amendment protection to communicators even though a financial interest is *present*, but it is quite another to *deny* them First Amendment protection in the *absence* of a material interest on their part. Material loss by an audience without corresponding material gain by a speaker would not, it seems to me, be a situation that satisfies the requirements of legally prohibitable deception.

Because his critique was concerned with the rationale, and not the results, of these decisions, Redish does not tell his readers whether he approves or disapproves of the outcomes. Our purposes here do not permit that luxury. It seems to me that the decisions were right, but for the wrong reasons. The salesmen for the competitor of aluminum cookware were using false claims to induce people to buy their own products, and thus the criteria we have identified as justifying legal restraints were fulfilled. The author of the pamphlets was propagating a false claim which may well have influenced the *beliefs* of some readers, but since he was not asking for, or collecting, their money nor directly urging them to any other kind of harmful action, I think the court was correct in finding his expression protected by the First Amendment.

A third case discussed by Redish involved the advertisement of certain drugs by a company called Koch Laboratories.[48] The FTC found that these ads were false and misleading and ordered a halt to their circulation. Koch appealed to the U.S. Court of Appeals for the Sixth Circuit, which upheld the FTC's ruling. However, the court declared that any attempt by the government to interfere with the distribution of a book that had been written by Koch, president of the company, which made the same claims for the therapeutic value of these drugs as did the ads, would violate the First Amendment.

Redish is again highly critical of the court's rationale in this case, finding it objectionable for First Amendment protection to turn on what he calls the "literary form" of the message—that is, whether it happens to appear in an advertisement or a book. He dismisses as untenable the court's effort to distinguish Koch's ads from his book on the grounds that the advertisements constituted false statements of "fact," whereas the book expressed the author's scientific theories:

> . . . the rather tenuous distinction between "fact" and "opinion" is a slender reed upon which to base a determination of first amendment protection. This is especially so in areas such as the sciences, where statements of opinion are really nothing more than the individual's views as to what the facts are. . . . Surely, in his book, Koch was not writing as an objective observer, but as an advocate for his medical theories. In any case, the fact that Koch's book contained numerous case histories, which presumably described the actual successes of his drug, certainly brings it within the realm of "fact."[49]

In a footnote to the passage just quoted, Redish adds the following observation, which seems to provide an insight worthy of more than an aside: "The court in *Koch* seemed more concerned with the fact that the advertising contained selling arguments and price lists while the book did not. 206 F.2d at 318–19. It is difficult to see how these facts are at all relevant to a distinction premised upon the difference between fact and opinion."[50]

Although Redish is no doubt correct in questioning the relevancy of selling arguments and price lists *to the fact-versus-opinion issue,* and also seems correct in rejecting "literary form" as a valid basis for determining the appropriateness of First Amendment protection, the court of appeals, by his own admission, apparently relied on neither of those premises as its central rationale. If, as he says, the court was "more concerned with the fact that the advertising contained selling arguments and price lists while the book did not," then I would suggest that the court was wiser than Redish thinks. It would have been basing its judgment of the applicability of First Amendment protection on whether the deceptive communication was a direct inducement to buy or was an inculcation of beliefs, and that is precisely the basis on which I think the decision should have been made. The literary form is really irrelevant, and the fact-versus-opinion issue would be germane only if it was crystal clear, as it evidently was not in this case, that one message was a false statement of fact and the other the proposing of dubious theories.

The U.S. Supreme Court contributed its share to the confusion on this issue in two attempts, in 1979 and 1980, to define the boundaries of First Amendment protection it had previously been extending to so-called commercial speech. Starting with *Bigelow v. Virginia* in 1975,[51] and proceeding through *Virginia State Board of Pharmacy v. Virginia Citizens Consumer Council*[52] and *Linmark Associates v. Township of Willingboro*[53] to *Bates v. State Bar of Arizona* in 1977,[54] the Court had abandoned an old doctrine, enunciated in 1942,[55] that commercial speech was entirely outside the realm of First Amendment concern. Instead, the Supreme Court had found that, because commercial speech often provides useful information to consumers and makes them aware of options that enhance their decision-making processes, First Amendment values are endangered when such communication is restricted. Thus, in turn, the advertising of abortion clinics, prescription drug prices, lawyers' fees for standard services, and homes for sale were all found protected by the First Amendment. At the same time, however, through this line of decisions the Court made it clear that it was not calling into question restraints on false and misleading commercial speech.

Therefore, it was not entirely inconsistent with these precedents for the Supreme Court, in its 1979 decision involving a Texas statute which prohibited the use of corporate trade names by optometrists, to overturn a lower court ruling that had found the law in violation of the First Amendment.[56] The Supreme Court majority's rationale was that the use of trade names by professionals provides numerous possibilities for deception of the public[57] and that, unlike the forms of commercial speech to which First Amendment protection had previously been extended, this particular mode of communication was not "self-contained and self-explanatory" and had "no intrinsic meaning."[58] In a footnote distinguishing this decision from its ruling of the previous year that a Boston bank could not be prohibited by state law from engaging in public debate on a pending referendum,[59] the Court described the speech in the Boston case as "categorically different from the mere solicitation of patronage implicit in a trade name."[60]

Part of the confusion created by the Court's ruling in this Texas case was identified by Justice Blackmun, writing a dissenting opinion for himself and Justice Thurgood Marshall, when he pointed out, correctly, I believe, that there is nothing "inherently" deceptive about the use of trade corporation names.

A trade name will deceive only if it is used in a misleading context. The hypotheticals posed by the Court . . . concern the use of optometric trade names in situations where the name of the practicing optometrist is kept concealed. The deception lies not in the use of the trade name, but in the failure simultaneously to disclose the name of the optometrist. . . . counsel for the State conceded at oral argument that §5.13(d) prohibits the use of a trade name even when the optometrist's name is also prominently displayed. It thus prohibits wholly truthful speech that is entirely removed from the justification on which the Court most heavily relies to support the statute.[61]

I would expand on Justice Blackmun's well-stated argument only by noting that the majority had once again relied on the naive premise, deplored earlier in this book and dating back as far as *Chaplinsky v. New Hampshire*, that words may have an "intrinsic meaning" apart from that which is in the eye of the beholder.

Furthermore, I believe the dissenters were right and in tune with the position advanced in this chapter, in arguing, in the particular case at hand, that ample information was available to the public to correct any false impressions that the use of trade corporation names might create, and that the "highly paternalistic" role assigned to the government by the state's law, and approved by the Supreme Court, was therefore incompatible with the principles of a free society.[62]

Finally, I think that confusion was compounded by the majority's resort to a seemingly unnecessary and irrelevant distinction between the Texas and Boston cases—unnecessary and irrelevant because there had been no issue of deception in the latter case. By describing the Boston bank's messages as "categorically different from the *mere* [italics mine] solicitation of patronage implicit in a trade name," because the bank was operating in the realm of public affairs, the Court appears to have injected a criterion into the argument that it had presumably abandoned when it brought commercial speech under the umbrella of First Amendment protection. Surely advertisers of the prices of prescription drugs and legal services are also engaged in the "solicitation of patronage," though perhaps the Court felt that this was not "mere" solicitation because it also enhanced public knowledge, whereas the use of trade names presumably did not. But if that is to be the basis on which the Court decides if commercial speech is to be protected by the First Amendment, it is a different basis from whether or not the communication is deceptive, and those issues ought to be kept more clearly separate. Otherwise we will have varying standards for determining deception, depending on whether the context is one of "mere" or "non-mere" solicitation of patronage. That will sink us into a hopeless morass. We will be on firmer ground, I believe, if we adhere to the principle suggested in connection with the *Koch* case which would keep the definition of deception constant but would deny or extend First Amendment protection depending on whether the deceptive communication was a direct inducement to buy or an inculcation of beliefs. Thus, the abortion clinic, pharmacist, lawyer, home seller, bank *and* optometrist would all be equally subject to restraint if they lied *in the course of selling their services* and would be equally free of restriction if they did not.

The Supreme Court's second contribution to a muddying of the commercial speech waters came in 1980 in an opinion striking down a ban issued by the Public Service Commission of New York against all promotional advertising for the use of electricity by the state's electric utility companies.[63] The commission had decided that such advertising was incompatible with the nation's commitment to the conservation of energy, and the state's courts upheld that order in the face of a free speech challenge by an electric utility company. The New York Court of Appeals found only limited First Amendment value to commercial advertising in "the non-competitive market in which electric corporations operate," and was therefore willing to accept the proposition that their right to engage in such speech could be subordinated to the government's interest in conservation.[64]

Although all of the members of the Supreme Court except Justice Rehnquist agreed with the majority's judgment that the commission's order violated the free speech clause of the First Amendment (a judgment which I endorse), only five of them joined in the prevailing analysis which, unfortunately from my point of view, was just enough to make it the law of the land. That opinion, written by Justice Powell, appears to proceed from two premises which I think have led the Court astray in its holding that the questions which determine whether commercial speech is or is not protected by the First Amendment, *in addition to* the matter of its truthfulness or falsity, are whether the government has a "substantial interest" which is advanced by restricting the speech, and does so in a way that "is not more extensive than is necessary to serve that interest."[65]

The first of these premises is that the "First Amendment's concern for commercial speech is based on the informational function of advertising."[66] Although it is true that the public's right to know about the availability of products and services and about various price options was the avowed basis for the Court's turning away, in *Bigelow v. Virginia* and the decisions which followed it, from the old doctrine that commercial speech is outside the bounds of First Amendment protection, I had hoped that there was also implicit in those rulings the recognition that there is sometimes a self-expression value for the communicator in commercial speech that goes beyond the interests of just the listener. As Redish has noted, for example, "Much advertising . . . represents the artistic creation of an individual, and as such deserves recognition as first amendment speech."[67] But more than that, and despite the justifiable cynicism we may have about the integrity of many advertising and sales-people, there are surely significant numbers of individuals in our society who sincerely, and sometimes passionately, believe in the value to others of their products and services and for whom the promotion of their wares is as important and as personally fulfilling as the preachings of any clergyman or politician.

I am aware that some critics totally reject this proposition, such as C. Edwin Baker who flatly asserts, "Commercial speech is not a mani-festation of individual freedom of choice,"[68] and says in explanation of this assertion "that the market dictates the content of commercial speech and, therefore, even if the speech happens to correspond to the speaker's values, the content is determined by the structure of the mar-ket and is not chosen by the speaker."[69] But I find Baker's rationale on this point both obscure and unpersuasive and regret that some justices of the Supreme Court may, consciously or unconsciously, share his point of view. For if they do it may explain, in part, their resistance to extending full First Amendment guarantees to nonmisleading commercial speech.

The second and more explicit premise animating those justices who hold to a double standard for commercial and noncommercial speech which goes beyond the question of truthfulness is:

> Our decisions have recognized "the 'common-sense' distinction be-tween speech proposing a commercial transaction, which occurs in an area traditionally subject to government regulation, and other vari-eties of speech." ... The Constitution *therefore* [italics mine] accords a lesser protection to commercial speech than to other constitutionally guaranteed expression.[70]

The trouble with this concept is that even in the context of "speech proposing a commercial transaction," so long as that speech is not false, coercive, or an integral part of otherwise illegal or prohibitable business activity, there is no justification for treating it differently from speech in any other context.

Justice Blackmun's concurring opinion in the electric utility advertis-ing case articulates what seems to me the logically correct position on this matter:

> I concur only in the Court's judgment ... because I believe the test now evolved and applied by the Court is not consistent with our prior cases and does not provide adequate protection for truthful, nonmis-leading, noncoercive commercial speech. ... I agree with the Court that this level of intermediate scrutiny is appropriate for a restraint on commercial speech designed to protect consumers from misleading or

coercive speech, or a regulation related to the time, place or manner of commercial speech. I do not agree, however, that the Court's . . . test is the proper one to be applied when a State seeks to suppress information about a product in order to manipulate a private economic decision that the State cannot or has not regulated or outlawed directly. . . . Mr. Justice Stevens appropriately notes: "The justification for the regulation is nothing more than the expressed fear that the audience may find the utility's message persuasive. Without the aid of any coercion, deception, or misinformation, truthful communication may persuade some citizens to consume more electricity than than they otherwise would." . . .

I seriously doubt whether suppression of information concerning the availability and price of a legally offered product is ever a permissible way for the State to "dampen" demand for or use of the product. Even though "commercial" speech is involved, such a regulatory measure strikes at the heart of the First Amendment. This is because it is a covert attempt by the State to manipulate the choices of its citizens, not by persuasion or direct regulation, but by depriving the public of the information needed to make a free choice. . . .

If the First Amendment guarantee means anything, it means that, absent clear and present danger, government has no power to restrict expression because of the effect its message is likely to have on the public. . . . Our cases indicate that this guarantee applies even to commercial speech.[71]

We come now to "dirty tricks" in the political arena, a phenomenon which poses great difficulties in drawing the line between constitutionally protected and unprotected deception. One of the most flagrant examples of this kind of behavior, at least among those that are publicly known, was the work of Donald Segretti on behalf of Richard Nixon in the 1972 Florida presidential primary election. The variety of activities in which Segretti and his cohorts engaged need to be looked at separately. What they all had in common was their goal—to aid and abet the defeat in the Democratic primary of Senator Edmund Muskie, who was perceived by the Nixon forces as the most formidable challenger to the incumbent president whom the Democrats might nominate. The Florida primary was seen as a place where the Muskie campaign for the Democratic nomination might well be derailed, and Segretti, by his own later admission, was assigned to do the dirty work.

One of his undertakings was the distribution of a letter written on stationery of the Citizens for Muskie organization, accusing Muskie primary opponents Hubert Humphrey and Henry Jackson of sexual misconduct—a communication apparently intended to create bad blood among these friendly rivals. Another was the printing and passing out of cards at a George Wallace rally which read, "If you like Hitler, you'll love

Wallace.... Vote for Muskie." A third was the distribution of posters which stated, "Help Muskie Support Busing Our Children Now." Still another was an ad run in a college newspaper reading, "Sane gentleman needs running mate. White preferred but natural sense of rhythm no obstacle. E. Muskie."

The first three of these activities became the basis of federal charges brought against Segretti in August 1973 for violation of Title 18, United States Code, Sections 612, 2, and 371, making it illegal to publish or conspire to publish statements in a federal election campaign which do not contain the names of the persons or groups responsible for them.[72] Segretti consented to a transfer of the case from Florida to the District of Columbia for the purpose of pleading guilty.[73]

Because the prosecution against Segretti was for failure to disclose the source of his material rather than for false statements, and because disclosure-versus-anonymity is an issue to be discussed at length later in this book, I will not deal here with the merits of the indictment or the law on which it was based. Rather I would like to use the Segretti example to raise questions about the possible applicability of the concept of fraud to his communications.

To begin with the easier incidents first, although none are open-and-shut matters, it seems to me that the Hitler/Wallace cards and the busing posters fail to meet the criteria we have been proposing as measures of punishable deceptions. Repulsive as these particular tactics were, they were no more susceptible to empirical verification or falsification than was Kennedy's missile gap; and their function was the influencing of *beliefs* about Muskie, not the stealing of money or property or the causing of physical injury. Sad as it may be, one can undoubtedly find many similar examples from American political life, ranging all the way from suggestions that an opponent is "soft on communisim" or "soft on crime" to grossly misleading information about the effects of a particular referendum on taxes.

The use of the Citizens for Muskie letterheads, and perhaps the ad in the college paper allegedly authored by "E. Muskie," are of a different order. It is one thing to publish material anonymously (which is the offense for which Segretti was convicted) and quite another to attach somebody *else*'s name to statements they never uttered. Just as the federal mail statute explicitly makes it illegal to use another person's name for purposes which are violative of that law,[74] so it would seem appropriate for legal action to be taken against the publication, broadcast, or circulation of *any* message—political or otherwise—where it is made to appear that the communication emanates from someone who is not responsible for it. Such behavior is little different in principle from the forgery of a signature or even outright theft, and it does not make sense to give it immunity because it occurs in a political context.

This is not to suggest that penalties should apply to erroneous *second-hand* reports of somebody else's words, such as when political candidates attribute to their opponents views they have never expressed. That is different from sending out a mailing over somebody else's name, or deliberately identifying a voice on radio as someone other than it is. Audiences should be expected to know and to be wary of the fact that communicators, in *repeating* the words of others, sometimes may distort or misrepresent the message, either deliberately or out of innocent error. Audiences cannot be expected, however, to doubt the authenticity of printed material bearing a supposed author's name or the announced identity of a voice being broadcast over the air.

The question as to what degree of suspended belief can reasonably be expected of an audience is also relevant to the matter of the "E. Muskie" college newspaper ad referred to above, and is the reason I have indicated that "perhaps" the ad was not in quite the same category as the appropriation of Muskie stationery. Given the context of a college paper, and the particular message involved, it seems arguable that the communication was so obviously a put-on that, as in the case of advertising puffery, readers could have been expected to know better than to take it seriously.

"Dirty tricks" are not confined to political campaigns, as a case in Philadelphia involving the socioreligious issue of abortion demonstrates. In April of 1977, a young woman placed a call to a number listed in the Philadelphia telephone directory under the boldface heading "ABORTION BIRTH CONTROL & PREGNANCY TESTING CLINIC," to make arrangements for an abortion. After giving her name and address, she asked that her parents, with whom she lived and who did not know about her pregnancy, not be told about the call. It turned out that the telephone number was actually that of an antiabortion organization known as Save Our Unborn Lives, Inc., which was engaged in a campaign to identify women seeking abortions and to try to stop them from that course of action. In this instance, the girl's parents were immediately visited by members of the group and informed of their daughter's condition, and one of the priests at the Catholic church which she attended was also told of her situation. One of the results of these revelations was a beating by the young woman's father, who refused to talk to her for at least a year thereafter. She sued Save Our Unborn Lives for fraud, invasion of privacy, breach of privileged communications, and assault.[75]

All of the requirements for the tort of deceit would seem to be met by the misleading telephone listing, despite its arguably falling within the realm of social or religious discourse. The telephone number was not that of an "Abortion Birth Control and Pregnancy Testing Clinic" and was thus a false statement of fact which those who placed the listing must have known to be deceptive. Surely, also, there was an intention to induce those consulting the directory to act in reliance on a misrepresentation, there was clearly justifiable reliance on the representation by this young woman who acted in direct response to it, and certainly there was damage to her resulting from that reliance. The question might be a closer one if there was indeed a clinic at the number listed which engaged in "pregnancy testing" and in "abortion birth control" counseling, because then it could be maintained that there was literally nothing false about the name. The invasion-of-privacy and breach-of-privileged-communications charges might still be viable, but a finding of deception would be difficult to sustain under those circumstances.

This leads us, however, to a consideration of whether communications which are not literally false in what they assert, but are deceptive because of information they omit or withhold, may properly be subject to legal restraints. Assuming that we are confining the discussion to statements which induce harmful actions rather than merely inculcating beliefs, I would cautiously support some restrictions in this area.

To begin with, if we are not talking about punishments, but simply orders to disclose information which a communicator has not been disclosing, I see no reason why a legislature should not be able, under the First Amendment, to adopt truth-in-lending statutes, or why a government agency should not be able to require cigarette manufacturers to include a health warning in their advertisements. In the absence of such knowledge, consumers may act in ways that cause them monetary or physical damage when they might not do so with more complete information. As Prosser has said, "[H]alf of the truth may obviously amount to a lie, if it is understood to be the whole."[76]

On the other hand, if we are talking about punishments through a tort action for damages, or a fine imposed by a government agency where there has been no previous cease-and-desist order or no legislative requirement of specific disclosure, then I have serious problems with the issue of omissions of information. Only if it can be proved—and this is extremely difficult—that the communicator knew full well that crucial information was being withheld, and that the omission was deliberately calculated to elicit a response that might not otherwise be secured, would it seem appropriate to allow for punitive legal intervention.

It bears repeating, as we conclude this chapter, that the arguments which have been presented in behalf of a narrowly limited role for the law with respect to deceptive communication do not spring from any feelings of moral acceptance toward calculated falsehoods nor from any innocence about the harm that they can do to other people. If uncontradicted and believed, they are a serious infringement on the freedom of choice of the listener, and it is that very freedom which the First

Amendment was designed to preserve. Yet, as we have seen, there are good reasons for moving cautiously in imposing legal restraints. We must not invest our government with the power to declare what is "true" and "false" in the realm of political, social, and religious *beliefs,* and we must diligently segregate the utterance of beliefs from empirically falsifiable statements of fact. Where there is "time to expose through discussion the falsehood and fallacies"—in other words, where there has been a call to think bad thoughts rather than a direct inducement to engage in financially or physically harmful acts—and where there are people with the motivation and channels of communication to respond, we should opt for that remedy rather than for reliance on the law.

Surely, for example, the federal courts were correct in striking down as unconstitutional an undoubtedly well-intentioned New York Election Law adopted in 1974 which prohibited persons involved in political campaigns in that state from engaging in "attacks based on racial, religious or ethnic background and deliberate misrepresentation of a candidate's qualifications, positions on a political issue, party affiliation or party endorsement."[77] Just as surely, the National Labor Relations Board has moved close to, if not over, the boundary of appropriate government regulation with a line of decisions handed down over the past two decades invalidating union representation elections because of misleading campaign communication, either by labor or management, about such matters as a company's wages or profits.[78] Except for a relatively short period of time in 1977–78, a majority of the board has adhered to a principle enunciated by the NLRB in 1962 that an "election should be set aside where there has been a misrepresentation or other similar campaign trickery, which involves a substantial departure from the truth, at a time which prevents the other party or parties from making an effective reply, so that the misrepresentation, whether deliberate or not, may reasonably be expected to have a significant impact on the election."[79]

A minority of the board, led by Commissioner John Penello and briefly achieving majority status in 1977–78, has taken a position much closer to that advocated in this book:

> Our fundamental disagreement with past Board regulation in this area lies in our unwillingness to embrace the completely unverified assumption that misleading campaign propaganda will interfere with employees' freedom of choice. Implicit in such an assumption is a view of employees as naive and unworldly whose decision on as critical an issue as union representation is easily altered by the self-serving campaign claims of the parties. . . . We believe that Board rules in this area must be based on a view of employees as mature individuals who are capable of recognizing campaign propaganda for what it is and discounting it.[80]

In an earlier opinion Commissioner Penello had suggested that "the Board should revert to its policy of setting elections aside only upon a showing of intentional deception rising to the level of fraud."[81]

Whether that standard of intentional deception will ever again be accepted by the National Labor Relations Board in its supervision of union representation elections, we should certainly hold firm to it in other areas where criminal or civil penalties are proposed for the utterance of falsehoods. Otherwise we not only run the risk of punishing unwitting error, but we lift from the shoulders of consumers of communication too much of the burden of healthy skepticism that ought always to be theirs.

11 Intimidation and Coercion

The justification we have accepted for the imposition of legal restraints on certain kinds of deceptive speech is that such communication deprives its auditors of genuine freedom of choice by undermining their decision-making processes. The same is true of speech which intimidates or coerces its audience, for they are likewise not free to decide and to act in accord with what their own unsubverted best judgment would otherwise dictate. As Yves Simon has phrased it, in drawing a distinction between persuasion and coercion: "To persuade a man is to awaken in him voluntary inclinations toward a certain course of action. Coercion conflicts with free choice; persuasion implies the operation of free choice."[1]

There are at least two significant differences, however, between deception and coercion—one that makes coercion potentially less resistible than deception and the other more so. With falsehoods there is always the possibility that exposure may occur through more speech and thus free the audience from its misconceptions before any action has been taken. With coercive communication, more speech provides no remedy, since ordinarily nothing has been hidden. But it is precisely this open nature of most intimidating expression that may make it more resistible than unexposed deception, for at least the target individual knows what is happening and makes a conscious, though not truly free, choice to accede.[2] Indeed, as we shall see shortly, there is a variety of possible reactions to coercive speech that is not available for those who have been misled.

What kinds of communication are commonly thought of as intimidating or coercive, and thus limiting of the free choice of those to whom they are addressed? The clearest examples are explicit threats to life or limb—warnings that death, physical injury, torture, or confinement will be administered if the listeners do not do what the speaker asks. Such messages may be delivered at gunpoint or tank point, or simply by people who are perceptibly bigger and stronger than those to whom they are speaking.

A second category of coercive communication is that which involves psychological duress of one sort or another. Included here would be such tactics as placing people under hypnosis for the purpose of inducing desired responses, using subliminal stimuli for the same end, blackmailing individuals by threatening to expose embarrassing personal information about them, and the whole range of social and interpersonal pressures that are frequently employed to win conformity to some end—ostracism, or the threat of ostracism, by peer groups, holding people up to shame and ridicule, or exploiting their guilts and fears. If these latter strategies are employed for what are regarded as good purposes—like passing the plate in church or using group pressure to keep former alcoholics from returning to the bottle—we tend not to think twice about the legitimacy of the methods. However, when they are used in aid of causes that are alien to us we call them "brainwashing," "thought reform," or "coercive persuasion."[3] If Yves Simon's definition is taken literally, the latter phrase would be a contradiction in terms, for to persuade is not to coerce and to coerce is not to persuade. But more of that shortly.

A third set of coercive tactics commonly employed in our society to elicit desired responses are those involving the use of economic pressure. Parents may threaten to cut off financial support to their children, employers may threaten to fire or demote employees, workers may threaten to withhold their labor or in fact initiate a strike, consumers may threaten to withhold their purchases or actually undertake a boycott, and business people may be threatened with lawsuits if they do not conform to particular demands.

Finally, there is the offer of rewards for compliance with a communicator's wishes—perhaps in the form of money, material goods, or selection for a desired position, perhaps in the granting of sexual favors, or perhaps even in the promise of entry to heaven. When harshly, or perhaps honestly, evaluated, these tactics are called bribery.

There are probably more conceptual and definitional difficulties in dealing with the problem of coercion than with any of the other topics discussed in this book. Let us begin our analysis by anticipating and attempting to clarify some of those issues.

The first is the matter of whether bribery even belongs under the heading of coercive communication. In a scholarly anthology of essays on the topic of coercion, for example, various of the authors included in the volume are in disagreement over that question.[4] On the one hand it can be argued that, since one is no worse off than before if one declines a bribe, there is nothing coercive about such an offer. Although the temptation may be strong, and although desirable advantages may be lost by turning down the opportunity, the fact that one suffers no punishment by declining is said to indicate an absence of coercion. One is entirely free to choose whether or not to accept the temptation that is presented.

The counterargument is that the offer of rewards, because it is a pressure extrinsic and irrelevant to the merits of the action proposed, weights the scales of the respondent's decision making in such a way that free will is not truly operating. Just as the fear of losing one's job or going to hell may lead to the making of choices one might not otherwise select, so the hope of improving one's lot may seriously distort the decision-making process. All of this, of course, depends on what we mean by "free will," and that is a complex question we need not try to settle at this point. It will be sufficient for our purposes here simply to recognize that offers of reward may be significantly different in kind from threats of punishment, but because both categories have in common the use of pressures extrinsic and irrelevant to the merits of the response they seek, it is convenient to consider them as related phenomena.

There is another characteristic that bribery shares with intimidation, which brings us to a consideration of one of the most difficult conceptual problems in this area. Like threats of punishment, offers of reward depend for their effectiveness on factors which vary greatly from communicator to communicator and from audience to audience. Unlike falsehoods which, if believed, invariably affect audience responses, threats and promises, even if taken at face value, may or may not be successful in achieving their goals. Whether they are is dependent, in the first place, on the power of the particular communicators to deliver on their words. Do they, in fact, have the strength, the resources, and the will to administer the threatened injury or produce the promised rewards? Even if they do, their capacity to make punishment credible still depends on the requisite degree of weakness and fear in the audience, just as their ability to make a reward enticing is dependent on the degree of the potential recipient's needs, wants, and willingness to be bought.

The working of these variables is well illustrated in Prosser's discussion of the common-law tort of assault. After defining assault as "any act of such a nature as to excite an apprehension of battery"—such as the shaking of a fist under someone's nose—Prosser goes on to note that "apprehension is not the same thing as fear, and the plaintiff is not deprived of his action merely because he is too courageous to be frightened or intimidated. . . . At the same time, the courts have been reluctant to protect extremely timid individuals from exaggerated forms of contact. . . . there must be an apparent ability and opportunity to carry out the threat immediately."[5]

Similarly the U.S. Supreme Court has recognized that some audiences are more easily coerced than others and that some communicators are more coercive than others. In upholding the disciplinary action that had been taken against an Ohio lawyer for violating professional rules against in-person solicitation of legal business (more popularly known as ambulance chasing), the Court noted that "the potential for overreaching [the Court's euphemism here for coercive communication] is significantly greater when a lawyer, a professional trained in the art of persuasion, personally solicits an unsophisticated, injured, or distressed lay person."[6]

In an ultimate sense, of course, even the most overwhelming imbalance of power between a communicator and audience can be countered by a target individual's fearlessness and willingness to endure pain or accept death—a "free choice" that is always available to everyone. Cassius said it well in Shakespeare's *Julius Caesar:*

> I know where I will wear this dagger then;
> Cassius from bondage will deliver Cassius;
> Therein, ye gods, you make the weak most strong;
> Therein, ye gods, you tyrants do defeat;
> ...life, being weary of these worldly bars,
> Never lacks power to dismiss itself.
> If I know this, know all the world besides,
> That part of tyranny that I do bear
> I can shake off at pleasure.[7]

It may seem like playing semantic games to assert that people always have "free will" in the face of coercive communication because of their ability to choose death, torture, or other injury over compliance. But it cannot be denied that these *are* alternative choices, albeit not very attractive and not providing much of a range of options. What this should remind us of is that freedom is really a matter of degrees, and that when we talk about coercion we are really talking about a sharply limited and unpleasant range of choices, whereas when we talk about persuasion we are talking about a much broader and happier range of choices, though never an infinite one. Thus it is that the phrase "coercive persuasion" may not be a contradiction in terms after all but rather a recognition that most situations in which human beings make choices are a mix of persuasive and coercive elements, and that sometimes the latter may predominate over the former, even though the former are not entirely absent.

One author, writing in a cynical vein about the persuasion process, has gone so far as to assert that "all expression that seeks a result is intended to 'coerce.'"[8] This, I think, is carrying a bona fide insight too far. Although it is true, as has just been suggested, that much persuasion contains some elements that have a coercive *effect,* it does not follow that all who engage in trying to influence others *intend* to achieve their ends regardless of the means. Certainly it is possible to wish for a response from others, but to wish for it only if it is freely given. To be sure, there are many situations in which communicators desire so strongly to achieve their goals that they do not care how coercively they are attained (perhaps foregoing only physical force). But clearly there are innumerable instances where respecting the autonomy and freedom of others is viewed by the communicator as a greater value than accomplishing a particular objective.

Another source of conceptual difficulty in dealing with acts of coercive communication is the fact that both symbolic and nonsymbolic behavior are commonly involved and are so closely intertwined that it is sometimes hard to know where one leaves off and the other begins. For example, a demand for money at gunpoint is a symbolic act—the words spoken are obviously symbols, and the gun, until it fires, also functions symbolically by stimulating images in the target's mind as to what will happen if he or she does not comply. A toy gun, if it appeared real, or an unloaded gun, if assumed to be loaded—both clearly symbols—would serve the same purpose. The firing of the gun, on the other hand, is about as nonsymbolic an act as can be imagined, and the chances of its occurrence may be so great if resistance is offered that the distinction between the symbolic and nonsymbolic elements of such an interaction is of larger theoretical than practical significance. The same can be said of the difference between a threat to fire people from their jobs and doing it, or a threat to cut off their funds and doing it.

To add further to the complexities, there are some kinds of coercive tactics—such as strikes and boycotts—which are simultaneously symbolic and nonsymbolic. To the extent that they function as nonverbal messages to their target—"If you comply with our wishes we will stop hurting you"—they are acts of communication; indeed, that is their overriding purpose. But to the extent that injury is being administered from the moment the strike or boycott begins, nonsymbolic effects are also operating. Sometimes they hurt the communicator as much, or nearly as much, as the target, but that does not make the punishment felt any less, and it is apparently a price the persuader is willing to pay to try to achieve the desired end.

Picketing is a particular kind of activity around which the confusion we are now discussing has often swirled. Insofar as picketing consists of people peacefully marching up and down with signs that call for their colleagues to withhold their labor, for prospective consumers to withhold their purchases, and for the picketed establishment to change its ways, it is purely symbolic behavior. The fact that the participants are walking instead of talking does not make it less so. If, however, picketers obstruct entryways, or jostle those who may try to cross their line, they are clearly beyond symbolism and into physical force. What has made picketing historically such a difficult free speech problem is that so frequently peaceful marching has spilled over into violent interaction (whether instigated by the picketers or their opponents), and even short of actual violence, the shouts, gestures, and sometimes mere presence of large numbers of picketers—all three being symbolic behavior—have been perceived by others to be as intimidating as if fists or rocks were flying. We will return to the question of what kinds of restrictions are appropriate in such circumstances. My concern here is only to illuminate the distinction between symbolic and nonsymbolic ingredients.

Two other activities, associated primarily with the Ku Klux Klan, should also be mentioned at this point. One is the wearing of hoods or masks; the other the burning of crosses. Both have been regarded as highly intimidating, and we will be addressing the question of legal restraints on such conduct shortly. Suffice it to note here that, although nonverbal, these are purely symbolic behaviors. Their significance is in the *meanings* they convey to the observer—meanings that are derived from the context in which the stimuli appear. There is nothing *intrinsically* intimidating about a mask or a bonfire, as the Mardi Gras parade or a college pep rally will attest. In contrast, the administration of drugs to other individuals in order to make them comply with verbal directions is clearly a nonsymbolic act of coercion.

Where in this particular scheme of things one would place influence through hypnosis or subliminal stimuli is a difficult question to answer. Direct physical contact is obviously absent, so in that sense the interaction might be considered only symbolic. On the other hand, without the mediation of the target's consciousness between stimulus and response, there is no generation of meaning in the usual sense of that word. Further compounding the problem, at least as concerns subliminal stimuli, is that it is not at all demonstrable that behavior can actually be controlled by that method. In any event, our decision as to how to deal legally with these particular phenomena will not be aided by attempting to distinguish symbolic from nonsymbolic elements.

A final conceptual problem we must address, related primarily to the issue of boycotts and their advocacy, is the question of whether the essential nature of that activity changes as the number of participants and their degree of organization grows. There is no doubt that with such growth the coercive potential of the boycotters increases substantially. One hundred people withholding their business from a merchant obviously differs quantitatively from the same act by an individual. But is there a qualitative distinction as well? Is there a significant difference in kind between a massive, but spontaneous, outpouring of consumer alienation from a product because that item is priced too high, and a carefully planned, well-organized boycott by a powerful labor union seeking better working conditions? What if the boycott is well planned and carefully organized but by a civic organization rather than a labor union?

One of the earliest U.S. Supreme Court decisions on the boycott issue, handed down in 1911 prior to the exemption of labor unions from the antitrust laws, took the view that numbers and organization do make more than a quantitative difference. This was the case described in Chapter 2 in which an AFL publication had identified the Bucks Stove and Range Company on its "Unfair" and "We don't patronize" lists. The Court, as indicated earlier, saw no violation of free speech rights in finding the union's action to be an illegal conspiracy in restraint of trade.

> In the case of an unlawful conspiracy, the agreement to act in concert when the signal is published, gives the words "Unfair," "We don't patronize," or similar expressions, a force not adhering in the words themselves, and therefore exceeding any possible right of free speech which a single individual might have. Under such circumstances they become what have been called "verbal acts," and as much subject to injunction as the use of any other force whereby property is unlawfully damaged.[9]

Aside from the Court's definitional magic whereby words are converted into verbal "acts" because of the circumstances in which they are uttered—a fallacy we have dealt with in Chapter 2—what is said here of more substance is that the nature of an act of persuasion is significantly altered when "a force not adhering in the words themselves" is added by virtue of "an agreement to act in concert." Such an agreement presumably means that people are participating in the boycott not only because they have been individually persuaded that it is right for them to withhold their business but because they have made a commitment to collective action to which they are unthinkingly, and perhaps even coercively, bound.

Archibald Cox attempted to clarify this issue by drawing a distinction between what he termed "signal" and "publicity" picketing.[10] Pursuing the line of thought sketched out by Cox, a more recent essay amplified his argument:

> Conceptually, all picketing can be divided into two broad categories on the basis of whether the support of the audience appealed to is sympathetically or coercively enlisted. The operative distinction in this analysis is whether the picketers are members of an organized and powerful combination by virtue of which they can impose economic sanctions, withhold economic benefits, and threaten social ostracism of a degree and magnitude which would enable them to coerce their audience into doing what they demand. The kind of apprehensions and fears created by this type of picketing rise far above minimal social

embarrassment sometimes associated with crossing picket lines. The merits of the dispute become irrelevant because the picketers' appeal is directed towards a coerced audience. . . .

Picketing by a union where the appeal for support is directed almost exclusively at other union members falls within this category. The union picket line under these circumstances operates as a "signal" to other union members to cease working for the picketed employer, and to stop transporting goods to and from his place of business. The refusal of the union member to cross a union picket line is motivated largely by his fear of economic sanctions or loss of his union membership. The success of this type of picketing is therefore a result of the economic leverage wielded against the hapless union member and not of the fact that he is in basic sympathy with the picketers' cause. . . .

However, not all picketing by unions can be classified as "signal picketing." This is particularly true where the audience appealed to is the public at large. However powerful a union may be, it has no control over members of the general public and can only enlist their support by persuading them of the merits of the picketers' position and the rightness of their cause. The audience appealed to is, therefore, an uncoerced one. Most non-union picketing is likewise directed at the general public and not at members of a group to which the picketers belong. Consumer, tenant, and civil rights groups, for instance, are generally small and loosely organized and therefore can neither exact blind loyalty in their audiences or invoke threats of economic sanctions. . . . This type of picketing is labeled "publicity picketing" by Professor Cox.[11]

Cox himself summarized his distinction by saying, "The critical inquiry is whether the employee's [i.e., picketers'] conduct involves an appeal to an uncoerced audience each individual in which is left free to choose his own course of conduct or invokes the power of an organized combination."[12] Still another author perhaps had in mind essentially the same contrast when he wrote of "boycotters who effect their purposes by inducing, rather than agreeing with, others not to patronize."[13]

Given this kind of analysis, it will come as no surprise that these writers see greater justification in First Amendment protection for "publicity" than for "signal" picketing, or for *urgings* to boycott than for *agreements* to boycott. But before we turn to the question of what our First Amendment posture ought to be with respect to this and the other categories we have identified, we must first review the present state of the law as it bears upon coercive communication.

Present Law

Threats of Physical Injury

There is little question where the law stands regarding explicit threats to life and limb. Restraints upon such speech have never been regarded as infringing upon the First Amendment. The common law of assault, as we have seen, provides a tort remedy for symbolic acts which place people in immediate apprehension of physical harm. Prosser elaborates as follows:

> There is no assault where the defendant is too far away to do any harm, or in mere preparation, as in bringing a gun along to an interview; it is when the defendant presents the weapon in such a condition or manner as to indicate that it may immediately be made ready for use, as where all that is necessary is to cock it, that the threat becomes sufficiently imminent to constitute an assault.
>
> It is probably upon the same basis that mere words, however violent, are held not to amount to an assault. Apparently the origin of this rule lay in nothing more than the fact that in the early days the King's Court had their hands full when they intervened at the first threatening gesture, or in other words, when the fight was about to start; and taking cognizance of all the belligerent language which the foul mouths of merrie England could dispense was simply beyond their capacity.[14]

If the common law of assault does not reach "mere" words, there is plenty of statutory law which does. Chapter 41 of the U.S. Criminal Code, entitled "Extortions and Threats," for example, makes it illegal to utter threats against the president of the United States and successors to the presidency,[15] to transmit in interstate commerce any threat to kidnap or injure another person,[16] and knowingly to deposit any threatening messages in the U.S. mails.[17] Chapter 13, entitled "Civil Rights," makes it a crime for two or more persons to "conspire to injure, oppress, threaten, or intimidate any citizens in the free exercise or enjoyment of any right or privilege secured to him by the Constitution," or to "go in disguise on the highway, or on the premises of another, with intent to prevent or hinder his free exercise or enjoyment."[18] There are also sections of the criminal code on the intimidation of voters,[19] on intimidation by public officials to secure political contributions,[20] and on obstructing justice by intimidating jurors, witnesses, or officers of the court.[21]

U.S. labor law makes it an unfair labor practice for an employer or a labor organization "to interfere with, restrict or coerce employees in the exercise of the rights" set forth in the act.[22] Finally, at the federal level, reference was made earlier to the Fair Debt Collection Practices Act, which provides that "[a] debt collector may not engage in any conduct the natural consequence of which is to harass, oppress, or abuse any person in connection with the collection of a debt."[23] Among the items listed as prohibited conduct is the "use or threat of use of violence."[24]

State law typically follows the same pattern as federal statutes in these matters. By way of illustration, the Illinois criminal code contains a section entitled "Intimidation," which reads in part as follows:

> A person commits intimidation when, with intent to cause another to perform or to omit the performance of any act, he communicates to another a threat to perform without lawful authority any of the following acts:
> (1) Inflict physical harm
> (2) Subject any person to physical confinement or restriction
> (3) Commit any criminal offense
> (4) Accuse any person of an offense
> (5) Expose any person to hatred, contempt or ridicule . . .[25]

There are also provisions in Illinois law regarding harassment of jurors[26] and conspiracy to prevent voting "by force, intimidation, threat, deception, forgery or bribery of any person."[27]

Psychological Duress

When we move to the realm of psychological duress we find that the law has been far less inclined to intervene. No one would dream of calling on the police to arrest a preacher threatening his congregation with hell and damnation for their sins, or a politician soliciting votes by attempting to frighten the electorate into believing that, if the opposition is elected, criminals will run rampant in the streets. So-called brainwashing by religious, political, fraternal, ethnic, communal, or corporate cults may be deplored but not prohibited. Yet some intrusions by government into this area have taken place.

We have just quoted, for example, from a section of the federal criminal code making it illegal to "go in disguise on the highway, or on the premises of another, with intent to prevent or hinder" the free exercise of civil rights. Many states and localities have similar laws on their books, apparently designed originally to cope with the intimidation and violence practiced by hooded goons of the Ku Klux Klan.[28] Although one purpose of such laws is to facilitate the recognition and apprehension of those who might engage in criminal conduct, another aim has been to prevent the psychological terror that can result from a confrontation with masked demonstrators.

But such legislation has also led to surely unintended consequences.

In January of 1974, for instance, a lawyer in Portland, Oregon, was arrested by a policeman on a downtown street as he was returning to his car, after a party, wearing a President Nixon mask. He was charged with violating a city ordinance that prohibited the wearing of disguises in public.[29] Of a more serious nature was a case in California where Iranian students, who regularly wore masks at their demonstrations against the Shah, in order to protect themselves from possible retribution by the Iranian secret police, were charged with violation of Section 650a of the State Penal Code, making it a crime to wear masks in public.[30] In a lawsuit filed on behalf of the students by the ACLU of Northern California, a state court of appeals struck down the statute as unconstitutionally vague and overbroad. Affirming the right of anonymous political protest, the court noted, "The state vigorously defends a statute which, if 205 years ago the Royal Colony of Massachusetts had had ... Samuel Adams and Paul Revere, with their band of colonials disguised as Indians, might never have reached Boston Harbor, the greatest Tea Party in our history would never have occurred, and there, unlike here, there was an intent to do a wrongful act."[31] It should be pointed out, however, that a separate provision of the California Penal Code, Section 185, which makes it illegal to wear masks in connection with criminal activity, was not challenged or affected by this lawsuit.[32]

Another area of government intervention against psychologically coercive expression was a Public Notice of January 24, 1974, from the Federal Communications Commission in response to complaints made during the 1973 Christmas season about television stations which had carried a particular product advertisement with the subliminal message, "Get It," flashed across the screen. Said the commission, "We believe that the use of subliminal persuasion is inconsistent with the obligations of a licensee, and therefore we take this occasion to make clear that broadcasts employing such techniques are contrary to the public interest. Whether effective or not, such broadcasts clearly are intended to be deceptive." The FCC noted that it had expressed concern about this problem in an earlier public statement in 1947, but that because the Television Code Board of the National Association of Broadcasters had voluntarily undertaken to encourage restraint, and because there seemed no immediate danger to the public from such communication, further action by the commission at that time seemed unnecessary.

It is interesting that the FCC chose to characterize subliminal stimuli as deceptive rather than coercive. Perhaps this was due to the fact that deception is a more familiar concept, with more precedents for its prohibition, than coercion; perhaps because a positive response to subliminal cues would be an *unwitting* response, and in that sense similar to the reactions triggered by false though consciously received statements;

perhaps because the *intent* of a subliminal communicator is indeed deceptive, even though the *effect* may be coercive; but perhaps also because our culture is not as sensitive as it might be to the issue of psychological domination. We tolerate so much in the way of coercive pressure in our everyday interpersonal and public communication that we may not even recognize it when we see it and can only comprehend it if it is described with the better understood, and in this case partially accurate, label of deception.

There is one kind of psychological pressure, however, which has attracted much public concern in recent years—and where the law has flirted with intervention—and that is the proselytizing by certain religious cults, particularly the Hare Krishna and the Unification Church of Sun Myung Moon (or "Moonies"). Beyond the plethora of articles and books discussing, exposing, or condemning the tactics of persuasion used by such groups, there also have been instances of the state throwing its weight against them. One form that this has taken has been for law enforcement officials to look the other way when the parents of converts to these cults have had their children, whether minors or not, kidnapped and forceably subjected to "deprogramming"—a technique that can best be described as fighting fire with fire. In instances where remedies have been sought in court by those subjected to these methods, deprogrammers have sometimes been found guilty of false imprisonment, but they have also been vindicated by judges whose sympathies were aroused, as one put it in a Rhode Island case, by "the solicitude which a mother holds for her daughter's health and well-being. Defendants, as agents for Mrs. Weiss, derived their motivation from this same maternal solicitude."[33]

Another way in which the power of the state has been invoked by parents seeking to deprogram children who have reached the age of majority is by their obtaining conservatorship or guardianship orders from friendly courts. This has been made possible by laws which were designed for another purpose—that is, to deal with the problem of adults who, because of senility, for instance, are mentally incompetent to handle their daily affairs.[34] Sometimes such orders have been issued without adversary hearings and with the mere fact of membership in a cult or a letter of "concern" from a physician or psychologist being accepted as proof of incompetency.[35]

Economic Pressure

Despite these few examples of government involvement in the area of psychological coercion, the more general stance of our legal system has been to avoid entanglement in these matters. Not so in the realm of economically coercive pressures, where there has been a long, though somewhat erratic, history of legal intervention to protect those subjected to such tactics. Particularly has this been true in the area of labor-management relationships, where a special body of law has developed whose principles may or may not always be applicable to other realms of interaction.

Picketing

Picketing has been one of the most litigated of these activities. According to one scholar of the subject, the earliest court decisions involving labor picketing simply assumed it to be a coercive and unlawful practice.[36] This writer describes many judges of that period as believing that "there could no more be 'peaceful picketing' than 'chaste vulgarity.'"[37] But in a 1940 decision in *Thornhill v. Alabama,* the U.S. Supreme Court recognized that peaceful labor picketing was entitled to First Amendment protection.[38] Justice Frank Murphy spoke for the Court:

In the circumstances of our times the dissemination of information concerning the facts of a labor dispute must be regarded as within that area of free discussion that is guaranteed by the Constitution. . . .

It may be that effective exercise of the means of advancing public knowledge may persuade some of those reached to refrain from entering into advantageous relations with the business establishment which is the scene of the dispute. Every expression of opinion on matters that are important has the potentiality of inducing action in the interests of one rather than another group in society. But the group in power at the moment may not impose penal sanctions on peaceful and truthful discussion of matters of public interest merely on a showing that others may thereby be persuaded to take action inconsistent with its interests.[39]

The *Thornhill* decision, described by Thomas Emerson as "cautious and inconclusive,"[40] was the beginning, rather than the end, of the Court's long struggle with the issue of picketing as a potentially protected form of expression. More often than not reasons were found for excluding the activity from First Amendment coverage. Just one year after *Thornhill,* for example, the Court upheld an injunction against the picketing of Meadowmoor Dairies because it was "enmeshed with contemporaneously violent conduct which is concededly outlawed."[41] And the following year, although the Court unanimously struck down an injunction against the picketing in question because it could "perceive no substantive evil of such magnitude as to mark a limit to the right of free speech,"[42] a concurring opinion by Justice Douglas provided still another possible rationale for placing picketing beyond First Amendment protection: "Picketing by an organized group is more than free speech, since it involves patrol of a particular locality and since the very presence of a picket line may induce action of one kind or another, quite irrespective of the nature of the ideas which are being disseminated. Hence those aspects of picketing make it the subject of restrictive regulation."[43]

The view suggested here by Justice Douglas was reiterated and elaborated in later decisions and is, of course, essentially the same as that put forth by Archibald Cox in discussing what he called "signal" in contrast to "publicity" picketing. Justice Black's contribution to this concept came in an opinion for the Court in *Giboney v. Empire Storage and Ice Company* in 1949, when he described the picketers in the case as "doing more than exercising a right of free speech or press. . . . They were exercising their economic power together with that of their allies to compel Empire to abide by union rather than by state regulation of trade."[44]

Justice Felix Frankfurter carried the same ball still further in two 1950 decisions. In one he said that "while picketing has an ingredient of communication it cannot be dogmatically equated with the constitutionally protected freedom of speech."[45] In the other, *Hughes v. Superior Court,* he provided a slightly more extensive explanation of the point:

> Publication in a newspaper, or by distribution of circulars, may convey the same information or make the same charge as do those patrolling a picket line. But the very purpose of a picket line is to exert influences, and it produces consequences, different from other modes of communication. The loyalties and responses evoked and exacted by picket lines are unlike those flowing from appeals by printed words.[46]

It should be noted that another feature of both the *Giboney* and *Hughes* cases, given as reason by the Supreme Court to deny First Amendment protection, was that the behavior sought by the picketers from the target employer would, in *Giboney,* have been in violation of state law and, in *Hughes,* contrary to public policy. Thus the Court concluded in *Giboney* that the First Amendment does not extend "its immunity to speech or writing used as an integral part of conduct in violation of a valid criminal statute,"[47] and, in *Hughes,* that picketing "is not beyond the control of the state if . . . the purpose which it seeks to effectuate gives ground for its disallowance."[48] We will return to a further consideration of this particular matter in the next chapter, which will deal generally with inducements to illegal action.

Finally in connection with these decisions, it should be pointed out that *Hughes* was not a case of picketing by a labor union but rather by a group called Progressive Citizens of America seeking an increase in the number of black employees in the target grocery store. Yet the Supreme Court's treatment of the matter did not differ from its handling of the labor picketing cases of that period.

Whatever doubt there may be concerning the status under the First Amendment of limitations on ordinary picketing, there is less uncertainty about restrictions on picketing directed at third parties in order to discourage them from doing business with a targeted establishment. According to one treatise on this subject, economic pressure on innocent third parties "was outlawed at common law long before it was attacked by statute."[49] The U.S. Supreme Court in 1942, ruling that picketers could be prohibited from demonstrating in front of Ritters Cafe to protest the use by the owner of nonunion workers *in the construction of his home,* declared that the state has the power to confine "the sphere of communication to that directly related" to the dispute.[50]

The *Ritter* decision foreshadowed passage by Congress in 1947 of an amendment to the National Labor Relations Act designed to outlaw so-called secondary boycotts and picketing related to them. Section 8(b)(4) of the act now makes it an unfair labor practice to "threaten, coerce or restrain any person" not party to a labor dispute for the purpose of "forcing or requiring [him or her] to cease using, selling, handling, transporting, or otherwise dealing in the products of any other producer ... or to cease doing business with any other person." A 1964 interpretation of that provision by the U.S. Supreme Court determined that it was to be carefully and narrowly construed. The case involved a strike by a Fruit and Vegetable Packers Union against apple picking and warehousing establishments in the State of Washington, and the advocacy of a consumer boycott against the purchase of Washington apples in Seattle grocery stores. Picketers had been positioned in front of a large number of stores of the Safeway chain urging customers not to buy apples. They did not otherwise interfere in any way with business at the stores, and their handbills clarified the fact that the protest was not aimed at Safeway itself. Under these conditions the Supreme Court felt that Section 8(b)(4) of the NLRA was inapplicable, arguing that "a broad ban against peaceful picketing might collide with the guarantees of the First Amendment."[51]

However, in 1980, a majority of the Court held that the statute *was* applicable in another Seattle situation where a labor dispute with the Safeco real estate title insurance company had led to the setting up of union pickets at five somewhat independent local title companies which dealt almost exclusively in the sale of Safeco insurance.[52] The Court's rationale was that, under the particular circumstances, the protest against a single product had the same effect as illegal secondary picketing. Justice Powell spoke for the Court:

> As long as secondary picketing only discourages consumption of a struck product, incidental injury to the neutral is a natural consequence of an effective primary boycott. ... But the Union's secondary

appeal against the central product sold by the title companies in this case is "reasonably calculated to induce customers not to patronize the neutrals at all." 226 N.L.R.B., at 757.... Product picketing that reasonably can be expected to threaten neutral parties with ruin or substantial loss simply does not square with the language or purpose of Sec. 8 (b) (4)...[53]

It is interesting to note that two of the six justices in the majority, Justices Blackmun and Stevens, withheld their support from the final paragraph of Justice Powell's opinion because of what they felt to be its too-easy acceptance of the general proposition that there are no First Amendment problems in the statutory prohibition against secondary picketing. They found it troubling that the distinction made by Congress between primary and secondary picketing is not a content-neutral regulation of the speech in question. They joined, nonetheless, in the Court's judgment because of the overriding government interest they saw in protecting neutral parties from, as Justice Blackmun put it, "coerced participation in industrial strife."[54]

It was noted earlier in this chapter that another provision of the NLRA makes it an unfair labor practice for an employer to coerce employees in the exercise of their rights under the act. A 1941 decision of the U.S. Supreme Court interpreted this aspect of the law to mean that pure speech could be considered part of such coercive behavior. Justice Murphy wrote for the Court:

> ...conduct, though evidenced in part by speech, may amount in connection with other circumstances to coercion within the meaning of the Act.... in determining whether a course of conduct amounts to restraint or coercion, pressure exerted vocally by the employer may no more be disregarded than pressure exerted in other ways.... The mere fact that language merges into a course of conduct does not put that whole course without the range of otherwise applicable administrative power. In determining whether the company actually interfered with, restrained, and coerced its employees the [National Labor Relations] Board has a right to look at what the company has said as well as what it has done.[55]

Still another section of the labor act prohibits so-called recognitional picketing—that is, picketing where "an object thereof is forcing or requiring an employer to recognize or bargain with a labor organization."[56] An interesting question arose as to whether the law applies to *threats* to picket for this purpose as well as to actual picketing. The U.S. Court of Appeals for the District of Columbia decided that it does:

> ...the manifest intent of Congress was to treat (1) picketing, (2) causing to be picketed, (3) threats to picket, and (4) causing (threats) to

picket as interchangeable. . . . that the Act specifically protects speech in some instances is irrelevant to the question of whether or not it was intended to regulate threats to picket. To maintain otherwise would would be no more convincing than to argue that as the Constitution protects some forms of speech, it must also protect threats and extortion. . . .

Whereas speech is oftentimes protected more than conduct because . . . it has less tangible results, it is not the case that threats to picket usually tend to be less deleterious to the interests of an employer than actual picketing. Indeed, depending on how the threat is made known, it may have virtually the same effect as an actual picket line. . . . There is, in fact, no rigid dichotomy possible between threatening to picket and picketing; threat is a significant aspect of the picketing itself, and a threat to picket may accomplish the same coercive objective as actual picketing.[57]

Threats of Legal Action

Threats to picket, or even threats to strike and boycott, are not the only kinds of purely verbal communication that carry economically coercive messages. Warnings of legal action against business people may also arouse fear for their bank accounts, and on occasion courts have come to their defense against that kind of intimidation. One such case, back in 1926, involved the Watch and Ward Society of Boston which, unhappy with the *American Mercury* magazine, threatened the publication with prosecution for obscenity. The publisher turned the tables, sued, and won a tort action against the society. Said the judge of the defendants:

They secure their influence, not by voluntary acquiescence in their opinions by the trade in question, but by coercion and intimidation of that trade, through the fear of prosecution if the defendant's views are disregarded. . . . The defendants have the right to express their views as to the propriety or legality of a publication. But the defendants have not the right to enforce their views by organized threats, either open or covert, to the distributing trade to prosecute persons who disagree with them.[58]

A more contemporary case, *Bantam Books v. Sullivan,* involved threats of prosecution against the distribution of allegedly objectionable material, where the threats came from a legislatively created agency, the Rhode Island Commission to Encourage Morality in Youth, rather than from a private organization. The U.S. Supreme Court approved an injunction against this kind of coercive pressure from a creature of the government.[59] Although the Court's expressed concern was about the state action in violation of the First Amendment rights of the plaintiffs, rather than about the danger to their economic interests, the decision did affirm the principle that coercive communication in the form of threats of prosecution can be restrained.

Strikes and Boycotts

When we leave the area of verbal threats which simply warn that financial harm may be inflicted in the future and move to strikes and boycotts where actual economic injury to the target *accompanies* verbal appeals for a change in behavior, we again find that legal remedies are available. But here other complexities come into play. Restrictions that are imposed on strikes and boycotts in the interest of preventing economic coercion involve a denial of the right of employees to withhold their labor— arguably a form of involuntary servitude—or of the right of consumers to decide what they are or are not going to buy. For these reasons the only legal restraints that have been countenanced are on *organized, collective* withholdings of labor or business dealings, and even then under limitations to be identified shortly. As one law review article on boycotts has put it: "So highly valued is freedom of contract . . . that the individual refusal to patronize, even though malicious, is never a tort. But because of the greater injuries which group action can inflict, the common law condemns concerted refusals to deal, as well as inducements of others not to deal."[60]

United States statutory law has reinforced the common law in this field. The basic document is the Sherman Anti-Trust Act of 1890 which prohibits any "contract, combination . . . or conspiracy, in restraint of trade or commerce among the several States or with foreign nations."[61] Early cases of boycotts by labor unions such as *Gompers v. Bucks Stove and Range Company* already described, all the way to more recent cases like Missouri's lawsuit against the National Organization of Women for its convention boycott of nonratified ERA states, have been tried under this law.

But the limitations on legal action against combinations in restraint of trade are as important, from a First Amendment point of view, as the prohibitions themselves. In establishing a special set of rules to govern labor-management interactions, through the National Labor Relations Act of 1935 and ensuing legislation, Congress has exempted labor unions from the antitrust laws. The common law, in defining tort remedies for "interference with reasonable business expectations," has developed the concept of "justification"—a notion which allows as a defense the claim that there was "just cause" or "legal excuse" on the part of those engaging in a boycott or other combination in restraint of trade.[62]

Thus, in an old common-law action against a Catholic bishop who had sent out a letter forbidding parishioners to read the plaintiff's newspaper, a court found justification for the clergyman's action in his desire to protect his religious faith.[63] On the other hand, in an equally old case brought under the Sherman Act, a U.S. Circuit Court of Appeals upheld an injunction against a boycott of Hearst publications organized by the Council of Defense in New Mexico, a state-sponsored agency established to support the country's war effort.[64] Presumably the court felt that the council's belief that our war effort required suppression of Hearst propaganda was insufficient justification for the economic coercion that had been exercised.

Two more recent cases illustrate the kind of balancing that is done on this issue. In 1955 a federal district court in Chicago had to decide whether to dismiss a complaint that sought an injunction against a motion picture projectionists' union which had refused to allow its members to show a film, entitled *Salt of the Earth,* that had been produced by another union with objectionably (to them) leftist political leanings. Since a contract between the projectionists' union and the theaters wishing to show the film forbade the use of nonunion operators, the union's withholding of its labor effectively made impossible the exhibition of the film. In refusing to dismiss the complaint the court ruled that unions are exempt from the Sherman Act only when carrying out bona fide union objectives or engaging in a labor dispute, and thus were not beyond its reach in this circumstance. As for the argument that men cannot be forced to work against their will, the court reasoned:

> Of course it is true that an injunction cannot order a man to work. What it can do is command that he refrain from engaging in unlawful activity. . . . The complaint asks not for an injunction ordering these defendants to work, but one restraining them from participating in an unlawful conspiracy. So long as they so refrain, whether these particular defendants work or do not work at particular jobs is a matter of indifference to the plaintiff.[65]

The other case is the one referred to a moment ago, *Missouri v. National Organization of Women,* in which a federal district court in Kansas City refused the state's request for an injunction against NOW's convention boycott of nonratified ERA states. The complaint had alleged that the boycott was a combination and conspiracy in restraint of trade in violation of the Sherman Act, as well as a "tortious infliction of economic harm without legal justification or excuse."[66] There was no dispute as to whether NOW was, indeed, engaged in a convention boycott of the state or over the fact that Missouri businesses had suffered economic injury as a result. The central issue was whether the Sherman Act applied to this kind of collective protest action. Judge Elmo Hunter found that it did not.

...the convention boycott complained of in this case takes place in what is essentially a political context. The parties have stipulated that the sole purpose of the boycott is ratification of an amendment of the Constitution. The participants are not moved by any anticompetitive purpose; they are not in a competitive relationship. The boycott can be characterized as "non-commercial," in that its participants are not business interests and its purpose is not increased profits. The boycott can also be termed "non-economic;" it was not undertaken to advance the economic self-interest of the participants....

Application of the Sherman Act to NOW's boycott campaign also would involve serious questions concerning the right of petition and the freedom of association protected by the first amendment.... For these reasons, this Court concludes that the Sherman Act does not apply to the actions of NOW in furtherance of its convention boycott campaign. "There are areas of our economic and political life in which the precepts of antitrust must yield to other social values." It is clear that this is such a case.[67]

In reaching this decision the district court gave extensive consideration to a 1961 U.S. Supreme Court case, *Eastern Railroad Presidents Conference v. Noerr Motor Freight Inc.*, in which an association of railroad companies had conducted a publicity campaign to urge stricter regulation of their competitors of the trucking industry.[68] In its ruling in that instance, the Supreme Court had said that "the Sherman Act does not prohibit two or more persons from associating together in an attempt to persuade the legislature or the executive to take particular action with respect to a law that would produce a restraint or a monopoly."[69] The fact that the motivation of the railroads was an anticompetitive one did not, in the Court's view, detract from their right to make their wishes known to representatives in Congress.

To hold...that the people cannot freely inform the government of their wishes would impute to the Sherman Act a purpose to regulate, not business activity, but political activity, a purpose which would have no basis whatever in the legislative history of the Act. Secondly, and of at least equal significance, such a construction of the Sherman Act would raise important constitutional questions. The right of petition is one of the freedoms protected by the Bill of Rights, and we cannot, of course, lightly impute to Congress an intent to invade these freedoms.[70]

This case differed significantly from the Missouri case, of course, in that the alleged violation of the Sherman Act was not an actual boycott in restraint of trade but the *advocacy* of *government* action *to* restrain trade. Nevertheless, the Supreme Court's comments about political activity in relationship to the Sherman Act seemed to Judge Hunter to be dispositive of the question before him as well.

Bribery

Our legal system's approach to bribery has paralleled its handling of threats to life and limb in that it has dealt with particulars rather than generalities. Chapter 11 of the U.S. Criminal Code, for example, has one section which outlaws bribery of public officials or witnesses by the offer or promise of "anything of value,"[71] another section which makes it illegal to offer appointment to a public office in return for a favor,[72] and still another addresses bribery in connection with sporting events.[73] Illinois statutes prohibit bribery with the intent to influence the performance of any public officer or employee,[74] vote buying,[75] and vote selling.[76] Florida law bans "attempts to influence or deceive any elector in giving his vote" through the use of "bribery, menace, threat or other corruption."[77] In Albany, Georgia, on November 20, 1978, the Reverend Clennon King, a black minister who had gained notoriety for his efforts to bring racial integration to President Jimmy Carter's church in Plains, was sentenced to a year's probation for attempting to buy votes. He had placed an ad in a local newspaper offering $100 to anyone who would vote for him in an upcoming election—provided that he won.[78]

Except for specified offenses of this sort, the law is generally unconcerned with persuasion that uses pledges of reward to win its objectives. Clergymen are free to promise heavenly glory, and parents to offer monetary incentives, for good behavior. Sexual favors may be offered with impunity in return for compliance with the wishes of the one proffering the inducement. Appointments, promotions, raises, or favorable public recognition may be dangled before those whose conformity to particular goals is sought. Were such persuasive strategies to be criminalized, a large portion of our population would be in jail.

Assessment of Present Law

Having reviewed the present legal status of various kinds of coercive communication, let us turn to the task of evaluating the legitimacy of restraints on such expression in the light of First Amendment values. In some instances the choice we should make seems clear, at least in principle; in others, as must be evident by now, the issues are immensely troublesome.

Threats of Physical Injury

Perhaps the least difficult category is that encompassing threats of death, physical injury, torture, or confinement. Here I think the law has been largely correct in its handling of the problem. For an audience to choose death or bodily harm instead of compliance, as it is theoretically "free" to do in the face of such "persuasion," is not genuinely much of an option. Since the First Amendment is premised on freedom of choice, it would seem to require that in these circumstances, at least, the listeners' rights should take priority over those of the speaker.

Furthermore, the problem of defining what constitutes a coercive threat of this sort is not insurmountable. To be sure, contextual variables must be taken into account, and that process can get complicated. But it is not unmanageable. Prosser provides us with one helpful insight in his discussion of the common law of assault:

> The only valid reason that mere words do not amount to an assault is that ordinarily they create no reasonable apprehension of immediate contact. But they may do so, and when they do, there should be no less of an assault than when the defendant shakes his fist. . . .
> Words may . . . give character to an act. . . . the words and the act together create an apprehension. . . . Likewise, the words may explain away the apparent intent to attack.[79]

Not only may words explain away an otherwise threatening gesture, or body language undercut otherwise threatening words, but the relative power of the parties to the interaction must also be fairly assessed. Although tort law, as described by Prosser, is surely right in holding that a plaintiff in an assault case should not be "deprived of his action because he is too courageous to be frightened or intimidated,"[80] the courts are also wise in being "reluctant to protect extremely timid individuals from exaggerated fears of contact."[81] Where there is no possibility of a communicator being capable of carrying out a threat, verbal or nonverbal, and where that fact is evident to the person or persons being addressed, the expression should not be defined as coercive.

Another question that must be dealt with in these matters is the seriousness of the message communicated. That has been an issue particularly in a number of cases involving alleged threats on the life of the president of the United States, although those cases differ from others in this general category in that the threat is often not addressed directly to the president but is announced to others. The only U.S. Supreme Court decision on the point, *Watts v. U.S.,* was an uncomfortably close, but I think correct, 5–4 ruling in which an eighteen-year-old black youth attending a rally in Washington, D.C., was overheard by a law enforcement officer telling a group of listeners that he was so opposed to the Vietnam War and the draft that "[i]f they ever make me carry a rifle the first man I want to get in my sights is L.B.J."[82] The majority found that "the kind of political hyperbole indulged in by the petitioner" did not qualify as a "true 'threat'" under the law but, taken in its context, was a "crude offensive method of stating a political opposition to the President."[83]

Left unresolved by this decision was a closely related issue that has divided the U.S. Circuit Courts of Appeal. It is whether, for a conviction to be obtained under the law threatening the life of the president, it is necessary to show that the person uttering the threat had a *subjective* "present intention to do injury to the President" (a requirement set down by an *en banc* ruling of the Court of Appeals for the Fourth Circuit in 1971),[84] or whether it is enough that the speaker merely comprehended the meaning of the words uttered and that those words, as heard *objectively* by others, might be viewed seriously enough so that, for instance, the Secret Service would take the precaution of investigating.[85] Despite the fact that the Supreme Court has denied review to several of the circuit court decisions taking the latter position, it seems to me that the subjective intent requirement of the Fourth Circuit is closer to the spirit of the *Watts* opinion than the other view and is the one that ordinarily ought to prevail. A "true" threat, in the sense discussed in *Watts,* is unlikely in the absence of a serious intent on the part of the communicator to carry it out if the opportunity becomes available.

There are, however, two other complicating subtleties that were explored in still another U.S. Circuit Court of Appeals decision, *U.S. v. Kelner,* in 1976.[86] This case involved an alleged violation, not of the law against threatening the life of the president but of the companion statute prohibiting the transmission in interstate commerce of "any threat to kidnap...or to injure."[87] In a televised interview the defendant, a spokesperson for the Jewish Defense League, referred to the visit to this country of Palestine Liberation Organization leader Yasir Arafat as follows: "We have people who have been trained and who are out now and who intend to make sure that Arafat and his lieutenants do not leave this country alive.... We are planning to assassinate Mr. Arafat.... Everything is planned in detail."[88]

Kelner was found guilty of violating the law; the court of appeals sustained his conviction; and the Supreme Court denied review. The trial judge, in his instructions to the jury, had made clear that "political hyperbole" does not constitute a true threat and that in order to convict the defendant they had to find that the statements were an expression of an intention to inflict injury "of such a nature as could reasonably induce fear."[89] In reviewing that jury charge, the court of appeals found that it did not require proof of "specific intent to carry out the threat" but that such proof is not necessary under the law. In other words, a fine line was drawn, and I think legitimately so, between an intent to actually execute a threat and an intent only to create the fear that it will be executed. The court of appeals phrased it this way: "So long as the threat on its face and in the circumstances in which it is made is so unequivocal, unconditional, immediate and specific as to the person threatened, as to convey a gravity of purpose and imminent prospect of execution, the statute may properly be applied."[90] Since the purpose of laws against this kind of communication is to protect as far as possible free and uncoerced behavior on the part of those who are addressed, the offense ought to be considered committed if fear is aroused that the threat will be executed, whether or not a real intention to execute it was actually present.

What is more doubtful about the appropriateness of Kelner's conviction than the issue of his intent is a second subtlety noted in a concurring opinion by Judge Meskill.[91] That is whether the law should apply to a television news broadcast such as that involved in this case. Although concurring in the affirmation of Kelner's conviction, because the provisions of the law appeared to have been met, Judge Meskill expressed doubt that Congress intended the ban to apply to the broadcast media. In any event, he described himself as "apprehensive about the implications of considering the broadcast media to be modes of communication in threat cases."[92]

The judge's concern seems well placed. In addition to the problems he identified, such as the fact that it is within the discretion of a television station to decide whether or not to broadcast a threat that has been taped (as it had been in *Kelner*), the case also raises the question as to whether a threat of physical harm which is announced to the world at large, rather than directed to the person being threatened, constitutes the sort of coercive communication from which people need to be protected. I would suggest that the answer should be "No," unless there is some evidence that the target of the message was aware of it and believed it to be a serious danger.

Moving from personal threats of physical harm directed at particular individuals to the more generalized kind of intimidation that may be presented, for example, to judges, jurors, and witnesses by a mob at a courthouse door, I would still be inclined to allow for legal restrictions, *provided,* again, that the threat, assessed in its *particular* context, is a serious one, and the balance of power is such that uncoerced behavior on the part of the participants in the trial is genuinely endangered. Thus, as indicated in an earlier chapter, I would oppose unqualified bans on protest gatherings in front of courthouses, for such assemblies ought generally to be regarded as protected by the First Amendment unless specifically and demonstrably coercive.

Psychological Duress

Just as the law, in my opinion, has been properly invoked to prohibit genuine threats against life and limb, so it has been appropriately wary of intervention when it comes to psychological pressures. Reprehensible as it may be from an ethical point of view for human beings to subject one another to the kind of emotional exploitation and social pressures that are so widespread in our society, there is simply no way to draw an unwavering line between legally acceptable and unacceptable "coercive persuasion." How would one distinguish between "brainwashing" by the Moonies or Hare Krishna and that engaged in by mainline religious sects, Alcoholics Anonymous, or even the constant bombardment of the values promoted on American television? How would one assess the rhetoric of a Joe McCarthy, a Franklin Roosevelt, a Richard Nixon, a Billy Graham, a Martin Luther King, or a Ronald Reagan? How could one separate "programming" from "deprogramming," aside from any physical compulsion, imprisonment, or starvation, of course? There are simply too many imponderables of the human psyche in the delicate balance between voluntary acceptance and involuntary compliance for the heavy hand of the law to be a useful instrument of adjudication. Better that these things be left to exposure, analysis, condemnation, counterpropaganda, psychotherapy, and education than to government censorship.

Where psychic pressure is combined with physical force, however, there should be no hesitancy for the state to interfere. Instead of supporting parents who kidnap their children or seek conservatorship orders to hold them prisoners to deprogramming, our courts should be guarding the victims against such tactics. Instead of laws that prohibit the wearing of all masks or disguises in public, or of hoods that allegedly intimidate, the provision of the California Penal Code which bans them only if worn in connection with what is otherwise criminal activity would seem to serve the necessities of adequate law enforcement without infringing on what ought to be protected nonverbal, but symbolic, behavior. Criminal statutes should not include provisions, such as that quoted earlier in the Illinois law against intimidation, which make it an offense to "expose any person to hatred, contempt, or ridicule," nor should symbolic events such as cross-burnings per se be made illegal. Fortunately, such prohibitions have, in practice, been dead letters.

Subliminal stimuli and hypnosis pose the closest questions in this category, for to the extent that they may be effective in controlling the behavior of unconsenting others they constitute forms of coercive communication which, although not physically intrusive upon the target person, are nevertheless impossible to resist. Under those circumstances, and relying on the same rationale as that presented in connection with threats of physical force, I would see no First Amendment barrier to outlawing such communication.

Economic Pressure

Picketing

The picketing of business establishments, with its implicit or explicit advocacy that workers should withhold their labor and consumers their purchases from the targeted enterprise, is undoubtedly an exercise of economic pressure. The question we must answer is whether the limitations it may impose on the freedom of choice of the picketed party are sufficient to justify restrictions on the right of the picketers to engage in what is essentially a symbolic act of communication which urges economic sanctions for noncompliance with its demands. The First Amendment, of course, is implicated on both sides of this equation.

As we have seen, the U.S. Supreme Court took the broad position in *Thornhill v. Alabama* that peaceful picketing *is* a constitutionally protected form of expression, but then proceeded to hedge that proposition with a variety of qualifiers. I believe that the Court's basic principle is correct for, as one writer has put it, "The application of economic pressure is a hallowed American tradition."[93] Urging workers to withhold their labor and consumers to withdraw their purchases, even if the exercise of those fundamental rights impinges on the rights of others to conduct their business as they please, is surely part of the public dialogue the First Amendment was designed to secure. I also believe that many of the Court's qualifying decisions in this area have been mistaken.

The first way in which I think the Court has been in error is its lack of sufficient care in distinguishing the peaceful aspects of picketing from violence and direct threats of violence. Admittedly, under the tense conditions of labor-management strife in the early years of this century, that was not always an easy thing to do. But it was apparently possible, for the dissenting justices were able to manage it. Contrast, for illustration, the majority and dissenting opinions in the Court's 1941 *Meadowmoor* decision, where an injunction was upheld because the picketing was "enmeshed with contemporaneously violent conduct." Justice Frankfurter spoke for the majority:

> No one will doubt that Illinois can protect its storekeepers from being coerced by fear of window-smashings or burnings or bombings. And acts which in isolation are peaceful may be part of a coercive thrust when entangled with acts of violence. The picketing in this case was set in a background of violence. In such a setting it could justifiably be concluded that the momentum of fear generated by past violence would survive even though future picketing might be wholly peaceful.[94]

Justice Black, joined by Justice Douglas in dissent, wrote with a finer pen:

... it is stipulated in the record that pickets "made no threats against any of these storekeepers, but peacefully picketed these stores...." There was no evidence to connect them with any kind or type of violence at any time or place.... There is no evidence and no finding that dissemination of information by pickets stimulated anyone else to commit any act of violence.

There was evidence that violence occurred.... Undoubtedly some of the members of the union participated in this violence.... It was eight months after this before any picketing occurred.... I fully recognize that the union members guilty of violence are subject to punishment in accordance with the principles of due process of law.... But it is going a long way to say that because of the acts of these few men, six thousand other members of their union can be denied the right to express their opinion to the extent accomplished by the sweeping injunction here sustained.[95]

And Justice Stanley Reed, in a separate dissent, said quite sensibly, "If the fear engendered by past misconduct coerces storekeepers during peaceful picketing, the remedy lies in the maintenance of order, not in denial of free speech."[96]

The Court came closer to what I would regard as the proper position on this matter in 1957 when it upheld an injunction against the picketing of the Rainfair Manufacturing Company in Wynne, Arkansas, but only insofar as the court order was directed to intimidation and acts of violence.[97] At the same time it invalidated the injunction to the extent that it covered the purely peaceful picketing part of the activity. Yet even here, in affirming the right general principle, the Court's opinion still reflected an inability to do the fine tuning necessary to separate intimidating from merely offensive communication. In responding to some of the symbolic behavior of the picketers, such as sticking out their tongues and holding their noses, deriding one of the "scab" workers for her pregnancy and another for her low-cut dress, Justice Harold Burton said for the Court:

> Several workers testified that the continuous name-calling and boisterous conduct of the strikers made them afraid, angry, ill or nervous and had an adverse effect on their ability to properly do their work.... The issue here is whether or not the conduct and language of the strikers were likely to cause physical violence. Petitioners urge that all of this abusive language was protected and that they could not, therefore, be enjoined from using it. We cannot agree. Words can readily be so coupled with conduct as to provoke violence.... if a sufficient number yell any word sufficiently loudly showing an intent to ridicule, insult, or annoy, no matter how innocuous the dictionary definition of the word, the effect may cease to be persuasion and become intimidation and incitement to violence.[98]

It is interesting that the Court had seemed more capable of drawing the appropriate distinctions sixteen years earlier when the offender was an employer rather than employees. Then, it will be recalled, the Court had instructed the NLRB to take another look at the question of whether the employees in the case had been subjected to coercion, and in so doing stated that it was permissible for the board to examine the employer's speech as well as his other conduct. At the same time, however, the Court made clear that pure speech may be deemed coercive only if it occurs as part of a larger pattern of conduct that is intimidating. "If the utterances are to be separated from the background," said the Court, "we find it difficult to sustain a finding of coercion with respect to them alone."[99]

A second quarrel that I have with the Supreme Court's handling of the picketing issue stems from its rulings in *Giboney* and *Hughes* that this mode of expression can be deemed an "integral part" of illegal conduct when the course of conduct being urged on the picketed establishment would, *if* adopted, be illegal or contrary to public policy. Even if we concede that picketing *can* sometimes be an "integral part" of illegal conduct, such as in a case where the marching and chanting are accompanied at frequent and regular intervals by rock throwing, I do not see how it becomes an integral part of illegal conduct by *advocating* illegal conduct. Rather it seems to me that such advocacy should be dealt with no differently than any other kind of advocacy of illegal action—whether by soapbox speeches, leaflets, radio broadcasts, *or* picketing—and that is a topic we will be treating in the next chapter.

My third problem is not only with the Court but also with the many law review articles which, in one way or another, have accepted as a determinative factor the distinction between "signal" and "publicity" picketing. That is not to say that I see no significant difference between picketing by a powerful labor union which "persuades" its members to stay away from work, and a picket line by a powerless civic group urging customers over whom it has no control to refrain from patronizing a grocery store. But the difference is one of degree and not of kind. A labor union could, in some instances, be just as weak and ineffectual as a powerless civic organization, and a consumer group, in particular circumstances, could be just as well-organized and effective as a powerful labor organization. A union's picket signs could be just as informative as those of a community group, and the latter's placards could be just as unenlightening as if they carried no signs at all.

One scholar who has agreed with this view that the distinction between "publicity" and "signal" picketing is unhelpful has suggested that it confounds two questions—first, the extent to which the target establishment is being coerced and, second, the extent to which those giving support to the picketers have been coerced.[100] But the two issues, though surely different, may be inseparable, since the degree of pressure experienced by the target is greater to the extent that the picketers also have coercive power over those to whom they are appealing for help.

I believe that the only relevant question for determining whether First Amendment guarantees should apply is whether the picketing is peaceful and devoid of threats of physical injury to the lives, limbs, or property of *either* the target *or* of potential workers and customers. The other criteria that have been suggested, or that have been used by the courts—such as the size of the picketing organization, its degree of organization, whether it is a labor, civil rights, consumer, or environmental group, or the extent to which it enjoys the loyalty of its members or of the community—have only to do with how successfully it can exercise its economic pressure, and that should not be a measure of its right to First Amendment protection any more than the success or failure of psychological pressure should be a determinant of its status under the law. Otherwise we would be saying that these kinds of extrarational persuasion are permitted only so long as they are ineffectual. I would say rather that they are permitted so long as they stop short of the threat or use of physical force.

Where does this bring us with respect to the special rules of federal labor law prohibiting the picketing of "innocent third parties" and banning "recognitional picketing" or the threat thereof? As to the first of these restrictions, I would begin by applauding the narrow definition of secondary picketing laid down by the Supreme Court in *N.L.R.B. v. Fruit and Vegetable Packers* and would join with the dissenters in the more recent Safeco insurance company case. I would then argue that, although limitations on secondary picketing by nonunion groups should be unacceptable, they may be justified within the limited confines of labor-management relations, where they may be viewed as the First Amendment price that has been paid for special picketing privileges that have been legislatively granted in return. For example, labor organizations have rights under Section 7 of the NLRA to picket in privately owned shopping centers where they and others would not have such a right, according to the Supreme Court, under the First Amendment.[101]

Similarly, it can be argued that the sacrifice of recognitional picketing is a fair price to have paid for federal guarantees of the right to collective bargaining and to government-supervised elections.

Threats of Legal Action

The threat of legal action against a business establishment, though it may indeed be a form of economic pressure to achieve the goals of the communicator, seems to me better handled, as the Supreme Court dealt with it in *Bantam Books v. Sullivan,* as state action in violation of the First Amendment (if the target is in the business of communications), or of other rights protected by the Constitution from government interference (if a different sort of business is involved). That is only possible, of course, where the threats have come from an agency of the state. If the threats emanate from a private group, as they did in *American Mercury v. Chase,* and if that group has only the power to complain but not to prosecute, it seems doubtful to me that the necessary ingredients are present to consider the communication truly coercive. It may well be that a court today would take the same position and that the *American Mercury* case is but a historical anachronism.

Strikes and Boycotts

Strikes and boycotts, as we have seen earlier in this chapter, combine symbolic and nonsymbolic behavior in the same course of conduct. The nonsymbolic ingredient, of course, is the withholding of labor or the withdrawal of purchases—both of which have immediate economic effects. But the larger purpose of a strike or boycott is to serve as a tool of persuasion, communicating to the business establishment a nonverbal message which says that punishment will cease if enough concessions are granted.

Unlike many other phenomena with a mixture of communicative and nonsymbolic elements, such as political assassinations or kidnappings for ransom, where the effects of the nonsymbolic action are morally and legally indefensible, strikes and boycotts can legitimately lay claim to legal protection for *both* ingredients. The symbolic portion is obviously a prime candidate for First Amendment coverage, and the nonsymbolic aspects are an implementation of basic human rights to work or not to work, and to buy or not to buy, as one chooses. The fact that the exercise of those rights may restrict the range of decision-making freedom for the target of a strike or boycott, introducing pressures that may be extrinsic and irrelevant to the merits of a dispute, is not sufficient justification to deny their use.

It is in recognition of this proposition that the right to strike has been given legislative sanction (though it is often denied to public employees, teachers, policemen, and firemen), that unions have been exempted from anti-trust laws, and that boycotts by other kinds of groups have been allowed where "justification" was found. But what of the exceptions to this principle and the qualifications of it that we have discovered in our review of present law?

To begin with, I would argue that certainly most government employees, including teachers, and in some circumstances even police and firemen, should have the right to exert their influence through the vehicle of a strike. The ACLU has enunciated what I think to be the proper standard, equally respectful of the individual and legitimate societal interests at stake:

> The right to strike may not be denied to public employees any more than to private employees, even if a strike should cause great inconvenience to the public. In those very few areas where even momentary interruption of service could lead to great catastrophe—as in a strike by municipal fire and police personnel, for example—limitations of the right to strike may be appropriate, but *only* when and if adequate machinery for handling employer-employee relations has been established. . . .
>
> It must be emphasized, however, that even partial curtailment of the right to strike can be justified only to prevent public disaster, not public discomfort.[102]

As for the special rules of labor law that prohibit such union activities as secondary boycotts, I believe that an acceptable rationale is the same as that presented for restrictions on picketing at secondary sites. We should also note that unions have received a special privilege in exemption from the antitrust laws, a necessary concomitant of the rights to strike and boycott, which are by definition "combinations in restraint of trade."

Having affirmed the general principle that unions should be exempt from antitrust actions, I hasten to add my belief that the complaint against the Chicago motion picture projectionists' union described earlier was properly decided by the court in that case. The judge was right, I think, in finding the union's exemption from antitrust law inapplicable in that instance, since the organization was not engaged in a labor dispute or otherwise acting on union-related matters. But more critical, I believe, was the court's recognition that, because of the union's contract with the theaters which forbade the use of nonunion projectionists, the union's refusal to allow its members to show *Salt of the Earth* constituted not merely economic *pressure* on the theaters to *win* conformity to some other end being sought by the union but a stranglehold that immediately *imposed* compliance, making the exhibition of the film an impossible choice, even though the theaters wanted to do it. This was not a case of union loyalties leading members to strike *in order to* pressure an employer into some concessions. It was a union ordering its members to refrain from work in circumstances where the withholding of their labor, per se, achieved a coerced result. Collective action of that sort should be prohibitable, whether the offending group is a labor union or any other kind of organization.

Turning to nonunion boycotts, I would first suggest that the government has no business becoming involved in such coercive persuasion, at least where the target is a communications enterprise. I believe the U.S. Court of Appeals was correct in 1920 in upholding an injunction against the boycott of Hearst publications by the New Mexico Council of Defense, although today its decision would no doubt be based on the First Amendment, as in *Bantam Books v. Sullivan,* rather than on the Sherman Anti-Trust Act. Similarly, when a Citizens Committee for Decent Publications became active in Evanston, Illinois, from 1959 to 1960, offering to bookstores and drugstores a "seal of approval" to display in their windows in return for removing "objectionable literature" (as defined by the committee) from their shelves, the ACLU objected on First Amendment grounds to the fact that, although the group claimed to be a private organization, the mayor had officially appointed the members of the committee, the city council had appropriated funds in support of its work, and the corporation counsel had conducted meetings of the group at the city hall.[103] When these and other ties to the city government were severed later in 1960, the ACLU withdrew its objections.

Groups which are entirely private in nature may sometimes be *tactically unwise* to pursue their goals through the boycott technique, but they should be *legally free* to do so if they wish. The Catholic church has had its Index of prohibited books and its campaigns against "objectionable" movies and theaters, and should certainly not have been accountable to the law for promoting its ideology in that way. Many Jews boycotted travel to Mexico when that nation voted in a way that displeased them at the United Nations; supporters of gay rights have refused to buy Florida oranges in protest against the Florida Citrus Commission's employment of Anita Bryant for their commercials; and the PTA and National Citizens' Committee for Broadcasting have urged economic pressure against the sponsors of violent television shows. Although none of these groups has been subjected to legal sanctions, and the National Organization of Women has won the lawsuit brought against it in Missouri for its convention boycott of unratified ERA states, the National Association for the Advancement of Colored People has had to battle a $1.2 million dollar damage judgment awarded by a Mississippi court for its 1966 civil rights boycott of white merchants in the town of Port Gibson.[104] Clearly that decision, too, should be reversed.

Despite the probability that each of the aforementioned boycotts would be found by a fair-minded court to have been undertaken with "just cause," and would also be considered "political activity" beyond the reach of the Sherman Act, I am troubled by both of those concepts. "Just cause" is a slippery criterion that almost invites abuse, and it puts our courts in the business of trying to distinguish between "good" and "bad" boycotts. It seems to me that, if we truly accept the principle that private collectivities have the right to withhold their business in order to influence a target establishment to change its ways, we cannot then make distinctions between the "good guys" and the "bad guys," anymore than we are permitted to do so in any other First Amendment area. On the other hand, if one believes that this particular mode of influence is unacceptably coercive, then it ought in all logic to be prohibited for "good" causes as well as "bad."

As for the distinction between "political" and "commercial" or "business" activity relied upon by the district court in *Missouri v. NOW* and by the U.S. Supreme Court in *Eastern Railroad Presidents v. Noerr* to exempt the parties in question from antitrust convictions, I am concerned that the same kind of confusion we encountered with respect to deceptive speech may infect this area as well. Making the right to join with others in restraint of trade depend on the absence of economic motives or financial gain could result in the prohibition, for example, of civil rights boycotts whose aims are to secure better jobs for blacks or to bring an end to red-lining practices by mortgage companies.

The dispositive question, in my view, should not be the presence or absence of an economic or financial interest but whether the collective action has a broader rhetorical goal—that is, to persuade its target to adopt a desired course, whereupon the boycott would end—or is an end in itself—that is, a restraint of trade which itself produces the result or advantage desired by its organizers.

Bribery

The final category of communication that has been addressed in this chapter is that of bribery—a matter which I believe to be quite satisfactorily governed by present law. Legal remedies are available to deal with specific abuses about which society has a legitimate concern, such as preventing the corruption of public officials or of our electoral and judicial processes. We have wisely left in the hands of each individual the responsibility for deciding how to respond to most other kinds of glittery inducements. If people are expected, without aid of the law, to protect themselves against a wide variety of extrarational economic and psychological pressures, as I have advocated in these pages that they should be, they can certainly be asked to handle offers of reward, whether in heaven or on earth. Surely those are the least coercive of all the modes of expression to which we have devoted our attention here.

Part 4   Communication and Social Order

12 Incitement to Illegal Action

All of the topics addressed thus far in this book have involved communication which is thought to be harmful to particular individuals or groups because of the way in which those persons are talked to or talked about. We move now to a consideration of expression which is believed to be dangerous to society at large because it may lead to the commission of criminal acts. A primary purpose of government, of course, is to preserve the peace—preventing, wherever possible, injury to life and property and, when prevention fails, punishing the transgressors. Because it is assumed that crimes may spring not only from the minds of those who commit them but from the inciting speech of others as well, the law has long regarded it to be within its province to restrain incitement to crime as well as criminal acts themselves.

Incitement under our legal system goes by many names—soliciting, inducing, procuring, and counseling, to mention but a few. In common law, solicitation has been an offense since at least 1801, when it was held to be a misdemeanor to solicit a servant to steal goods from his master.[1] Section 2 of the United States Criminal Code reads: "Whoever commits an offense against the United States or aids, abets, counsels, commands, induces, or procures its commission, is punishable as a principal."[2] Illinois law, defining solicitation as a crime, says, "A person commits solicitation when, with intent that an offense be committed, he commands, encourages or requests another to commit that offense." This statute goes on to prescribe penalties "not to exceed the maximum provided for the offense solicited.[3]

Before we can discuss the problem of incitement intelligently, two pervasive kinds of confusion about the topic must be addressed and cleared away. They are confusions affecting not only ordinary people who have occasion to think about the subject, but they have been shared and perpetuated by legal scholars and Supreme Court justices as well. The first is a confounding of speech which incites *to* illegal conduct with speech that is an integral part *of* illegal conduct. The second is a failure to distinguish between the problem of communicators who incite sympathetic listeners to commit crimes sought by the speaker against society and the very different question of communicators whose offensiveness to a hostile crowd "incites" that audience to violence against the speaker.

Speech That Is Integral to Illegal Action

In the previous chapter, critical reference was made to a 1949 decision of the U.S. Supreme Court in *Giboney v. Empire Storage and Ice Company*. Justice Black, writing the Court's opinion in that case, justified an injunction against picketing which he described as an "integral part" of illegal conduct because the course of action the picketers were urging upon the target business establishment would, *if undertaken*, have been in violation of state law. This is an example, par excellence, of the sort of confusion that has permeated this area. The speech, or picketing in that case, was in no way an integral part of illegal conduct. The picketers may, indeed, have been *advocating* that someone else *should* engage in illegal conduct but, if so, that would have been solicitation or incitement *to* illegal behavior, not a part *of* it. Although it may be argued that both are deplorable and that both should be punishable, they are nevertheless quite different phenomena. Solicitation *precedes* illegal behavior, which may or may not ever occur. Speech which is truly an integral part of illegal action cannot happen until a course of criminal conduct has actually been undertaken.

No one to my knowledge questions the legitimacy of punishing criminal acts even though speech may occur in the course of that conduct. There is room for serious dispute, however, over the extent to which incitement *to* illegal conduct should be prohibited. Thus it is essential to the clarity of our thinking to exclude from the latter discussion distracting illustrations of communication which, in fact, is an integral part of illegal action. We can best accomplish that by reviewing, and setting aside, the most frequent of such examples.

The first category consists of communication, whether verbal or nonverbal, which inevitably occurs during the actual execution of any crime that is committed by more than one person. A group of bank robbers must talk or signal to each other to coordinate their efforts, and the participants in a rioting mob cannot help but stimulate and reinforce one another by their shouts and gestures. Such expression is an integral part of the commission of a crime and, by virtue of that fact, cannot lay claim to First Amendment protection.

Perhaps a bit less obviously so, but still an integral part of illegal conduct, is communication that occurs among colleagues in crime during the incipient stages of their activity—first the agreement to undertake illegal action together, and then the plotting of the crime itself, including instructions in its execution. We will be returning in the next chapter to a consideration of some First Amendment problems that arise in connection with these early stages of criminal conduct—the so-called inchoate crimes of attempt and conspiracy. For our present purposes we need only take note of the fact that symbolic behavior which occurs in this context—be it voting to commit a crime, taking a vow or oath to do so, explaining to one another the layout of a bank to be robbed, instructing one another how to use the tools of the trade, where to place the dynamite, or when to light the match—all of this differs from incitement *to* illegal action in that the parties to the crime have already decided that they are going to act in violation of the law. Incitement, by definition, precedes such decision making.

One of the reasons it is easy to confound these issues is that there is sometimes a fine line, indeed, between incitement to illegal action that has not yet been decided upon and communication in implementation of crimes in which the participants have already determined to become involved. For instance, making a suggestion or a motion at a meeting that the group present *should* undertake a criminal course of conduct, speaking in support of that proposal, or offering a cash bounty to encourage participation in a crime, are all on the incitement side of the line. On the other hand, voting in support of such a motion, announcing the affirmative outcome of a vote, accepting a bounty and promising to act in return, or setting a time and a place for further planning of the agreed-upon action are all integral parts of the criminal plot that came into being the moment the individual participants had decided in their own minds to go forward.

Thomas Emerson, in his *System of Freedom of Expression,* has managed both to clarify and to obscure this particular problem, depending on which passages one reads. In distinguishing between what he regards as protected "expression" and unprotected "action," he asserts that

> conduct that amounts to "advice" or "persuasion" would be protected; conduct that moves into the area of "instruction" and "preparation" would not. The essential task would be to distinguish between simply conveying an idea to another person, which idea he may later act upon, and actually participating with him in the performance of an illegal act.[4]

And again:

> Clearly a historical account of the function of force and violence in society or an academic discussion of the necessity or propriety of its use would be classified as expression. Similarly, advocating in general terms the use of force or violence at some time in the future must be

considered expression.... As the communication approached the point of urging immediate and particular acts of violence, it would become closer to being classifiable as action. If such advocacy became merely an incidental part of a program of overt acts the total conduct would cross the boundary line. Instructions on techniques of sabotage, street fighting, or specific methods of violence are well into the area of action. A fortiori, training in para-military operations, including the wearing of uniforms, or organizing groups to engage in acts of violence fall within the action category. In essence, the line would be drawn between ideological preparation or indoctrination in the use of violence on the one hand, and participation in overt acts of preparation or actual use on the other.[5]

So far, so good. But then Emerson fumbles the ball.

Prediction or warning of violence in future contingencies, or justification of the use of violence under designated circumstances comes closer to the line. Yet so long as such utterances are general in character and relate to the future they would, in our view, remain within the area of "expression." ...On the other hand, the urging of immediate, specific acts of violence would, under circumstances where violence was possible and likely, fall within the category of "action." Such communication would be so interlocked with violent conduct as to constitute for all practical purposes part of the action; it would be in effect the beginning of action itself.[6]

Having thus fuzzed the line between communication that *precedes* a decision to act violently and that which comes *concurrently* or *subsequently,* it was inevitable that Emerson would muddy his analysis of the illustrative cases with which he follows this general statement. In the first of these, *State v. Schleifer,* Emerson quotes at some length from the words of a speaker who was charged, more appropriately than Emerson acknowledges, with *solicitation* to commit crimes. Said Schleifer to a group of his striking fellow workers:

You will never win the strike with soft methods. You young men *ought* to go out on the bridge. Don't use eggs; use coal or indelible ink. Break foremen's windows at their homes. Watch the scabs when they come from work, lay for them, especially on pay day. Take them in a dark alley and hit them with a lead pipe. That is the softest thing you can use. Reimburse yourselves for what we have sacrificed for five months. Don't forget to bump off a few now and then, so Mr. Pearson will know that you are not getting cold feet. You car men know how to take a brake shoe off. Take the brake shoe and put it under something that will put the cars off the irons. A little sand or emery in the journal boxes will help greatly.... Don't forget to tie them up with derailments. You boys *ought* to cut them all up.[7] [All italics mine]

Emerson comments on this incident as follows: "There was no allegation that any further illegal action had taken place. The decision did not deal with any constitutional issue of freedom of speech. In terms of First Amendment doctrine, however, one would readily conclude that verbal communication of this nature, in the context of a strike, constituted 'action' rather than 'expression.'"[8]

The next case Emerson discusses is *State v. Quinlan,* another instance of a worker talking to fellow strikers. This time the speaker said, "I make a motion that we go to the silk mills, parade through the streets, and club them out of the mills; no matter how we get them out, we got to get them out."[9]

Again sliding over the fact that this man was indicted for violating a statute making it illegal to "advocate, encourage, justify, praise, or incite," Emerson remarks that "the treatment of the communication as part of a course of action, whether or not it came to fruition, would seem entirely justified."[10]

In his third illustration, Emerson is more careful about the line between incitement and speech that is integral to illegal action. The case was that of an anarchist at a meeting in New York City denouncing the execution of fellow anarchists in Chicago the previous day. Said the speaker:

> The day of revolution will soon come. First of all will be Grinnell; then comes Judge Gary; then the Supreme Court of Illinois; then the highest murderers of the land, the Supreme Court of the United States. . . .
> I again urge you to arm yourself, as the day of revolution is not far off; and when it comes, see that you are ready to resist and kill those hirelings of capitalists. . . . They think they kill five of our brethren, but we will have a hundred or five hundred for every one they have murdered. I am an anarchist, and am willing to die for its cause.[11]

Although this communicator was convicted of violating a New York statute against unlawful assembly, Emerson disagrees with that decision: " . . . the communication would have to be classified as 'expression.' It was a general and indefinite call to revolution. The action urged was confined to the future, and directed against persons in Illinois and Washington, not in New York City. Under the circumstances, the language could scarcely be considered an integral part of any specific or immediate acts of violence."[12]

In a fourth example, however, Emerson is back once again to a blurring of the boundary between incitement and expression integral to illegal action. Commenting on the behavior of John Kasper, a racist who had gone to Clinton and Nashville, Tennessee, to stir up violent opposition to the desegregation of the public schools in those cities and was found guilty of *incitement* to riot for a number of inflammatory communications, Emerson writes, " . . . the result reached is probably correct. Kasper was urging immediate, specific acts of violence in a situation where violence was likely to occur. His speech was definitely an integral feature of a course of action on an extended scale to prevent integration of the schools by force and violence. The communication was thus properly treated as participation in the illegal action that shortly ensued."[13]

My point in this critique of Emerson's analysis is not that any or all of these speakers should have gone unpunished. That is a question to which we will return later in the chapter. It is simply to argue that all of these cases should be dealt with as problems in incitement *to* illegal action and not, as Emerson suggests for three of the four, in communication that is an integral part *of* illegal action.

Another category of communication which is so close to the line between incitement and speech that is integral to illegal action as to be a source of conceptual confusion is the advertising or soliciting for sale of products or services that are themselves illegal. Depending on particular state laws, this may include such things as marijuana, fireworks, and prostitution. Here we have to distinguish between two kinds of messages. First there could be advocacy of the *idea* of smoking marijuana, shooting off fireworks, or indulging in prostitution—communication which might or might not constitute a direct incitement *to* engage in those activities, depending on the circumstances, but which could never be considered an integral part of such conduct. Second would be advertisements or solicitations which announce the availability of, and actually offer for sale, particular goods or services that are illegal. Assuming the state has acted legitimately in determining that these products and practices are sufficiently harmful to justify their being banned, it follows that their sale may also appropriately be prohibited. But selling is an activity that includes not only the transfer of money but the offer of something for sale—and the latter is an act of communication. Such communication is an integral part of the selling process.[14] Therefore, if the sale is illegal, then any communication which is integral to that process is also illegal.

Whether the sale of certain products and services *should* be illegal is an entirely separate question and one that ought not to be confused with this discussion. The ACLU, for example, opposes prohibitions on solicitation by prostitutes, not because it regards such communication as First Amendment behavior that is separable from the "sale" that may be consummated but because it believes that prostitution itself is a victimless act that ought to be decriminalized, along with the solicitation accompanying it. Similarly one might argue that the prohibition of advertising of cigarettes over the electronic media is unjustified so long as the sale of cigarettes has not been outlawed. If it is society's judgment that smoking is sufficiently harmful to require a ban on the radio and television advertising of cigarettes, then sales should also be prohibited—along with the advertising that abounds in the print media. But if we are unwilling to make the sale of cigarettes illegal, I do not see how we can justify restraints on any truthful advertising that is a part of that selling process.[15]

Somewhat similar to the selling issue is a question that arose in a 1973 Supreme Court case, *Pittsburgh Press v. Pittsburgh Commission on Human Relations*.[16] The Pittsburgh newspaper, which had been running help-wanted advertisements in separate columns for males and females, was ordered by the city's Human Relations Commission to stop this practice because it was judged to be in violation of a city ordinance prohibiting sexual discrimination in employment. The publisher appealed to the courts on First Amendment grounds but lost the case at every level. A majority opinion of the U.S. Supreme Court found two bases for affirming the lower court rulings, both relevant to our present discussion.

The first rationale was that the newspaper's practice in this matter fell within the realm of "commercial speech," and for that reason was not entitled to the same degree of First Amendment protection as noncommercial expression. The Court noted that the prohibition was not directed against newspaper articles urging as a matter of social policy that sex discrimination in employment might be justified, nor criticizing the city's antidiscrimination ordinance, but rather against a "proposal of possible employment."[17] As for the newspaper's argument that, even if this were commercial speech, the commercial speech exception to the First Amendment should be abandoned, the Court fell back on a second line of defense:

> Whatever the merits of this contention may be in other contexts, it is unpersuasive in this case. Discrimination in employment is not only commercial activity, it is illegal commercial activity under the ordinance. We have no doubt that a newspaper constitutionally could be forbidden to publish a want-ad proposing a sale of narcotics or soliciting prostitutes. . . . Any First Amendment interest which might be served by advertising an ordinary commercial proposal . . . is altogether absent when the commercial activity itself is illegal and the restriction on advertising is incidental to a valid limitation on economic activity.[18]

The Supreme Court's handling of this particular case seems consistent with the distinction I have been urging here between incitement and expression that is integral to illegal action. A "Help Wanted—Male" or "Help Wanted—Female" ad is not a solicitation *to somebody else* to do something illegal; it is the first step *in* an illegal hiring practice *by an employer,* which has its inception the moment public notice is given that a job is available. The announcement of vacancies is an integral and necessary part of the hiring process.

A final example of the issue with which we are now dealing is the effort that has been made by many legislative bodies, at local, state, and federal levels, to attack the problem of real-estate "blockbusting" and "steering"—practices which aggravate the tendency of neighborhoods to become or remain racially segregated—by enacting prohibitions against what is essentially communicative activity. The federal Fair Housing Act of 1968, for instance, makes it unlawful "for profit to induce or attempt to induce any person to sell or rent any dwelling by representations regarding the entry or prospective entry into a neighborhood of a person or persons of a particular race, color, religion or national origin."[19] In addition to adopting similar laws at the local level to prevent the so-called panic selling of houses in anticipation of racial change in a neighborhood, some municipalities have also addressed the buying end of the real-estate transaction by prohibiting realtors from "steering" customers away from some neighborhoods and toward others through comments about the racial composition of the communities in question.

Not unsurprisingly, many people in the real estate business have complained, sometimes in court, that their First Amendment rights of free speech have been violated by these laws. Consistently, however, their challenges have failed. Although the explicit rationale usually used by the courts is that the expression in question is commercial speech outside the protection of the First Amendment, there is implicit in the decisions the additional assumption that the speech is an integral part of conduct which the state has legitimately made illegal.[20] In contrast, the U.S. Supreme Court has invalidated laws which, presumably passed with the same good intention of discouraging panic selling, prohibit individuals from posting "For Sale" signs on their property.[21] Since it is obviously not illegal and cannot be made illegal for people to sell their houses, a notice which offers such a sale—even though perhaps "commercial speech"— was viewed by the Court as communication protected by the First Amendment.

Speech to Hostile Audiences

A second widespread cause of confusion with respect to the law of incitement has been the failure of many judges and scholars to perceive that significantly different questions should be raised if a communicator's audience is antagonistic rather than supportive. The U.S. Supreme Court has had a mixed record on this matter, sometimes seeing and using the distinction to the benefit of communicators in the first category, and sometimes blurring the line to their detriment.

The Court's ambivalence was evident in its very first confrontation with the hostile audience problem in *Cantwell v. Connecticut,* a 1940 case which was finally resolved in favor of the Jehovah's Witnesses who had gone with their anti-Papist message into a neighborhood of New Haven, Connecticut, whose residents were approximately 95 percent Roman Catholic. On the one hand, the Court's opinion put into the same unprotected class the provocation of both supportive and hostile listeners to acts of violence:

> The offense known as breach of the peace embraces a great variety of conduct destroying or menacing public order and tranquility. . . . No one would have the hardihood to suggest that the principle of freedom of speech sanctions *incitement to riot* or that religious liberty connotes the privilege to *exhort others to physical attack* upon those belonging to another sect. When clear and present danger of riot, disorder, interference with traffic upon the public streets, or other immediate threat to public safety, peace, or order, appears, the power of the State to prevent or punish is obvious. . . . One may . . . be guilty of the offense if he commits acts or makes *statements likely to provoke violence* and disturbance of good order, *even though no such eventuality be intended.*[22] [All italics mine]

But then the decision separated out for protection the particular speech in the case before it:

> Cantwell's conduct . . . considered apart from the effect of his communication upon his hearers, did not amount to a breach of the peace. . . . We find in the instant case no assault or threatening of bodily harm, no truculent bearing, no intentional discourtesy, no personal abuse. . . .
>
> In the realm of religious faith, and in that of political belief, sharp differences arise. . . . To persuade others to his point of view, the pleader, as we know, at times, resorts to exaggeration, to vilification of men who have been, or are prominent in church or state, and even to false statement. But the people of this nation have ordained in the light of history, that, in spite of the probability of excesses and abuses, these liberties are, in the long view, essential to enlightened opinion and right conduct on the part of the citizens of a democracy.[23]

The Supreme Court was not so sympathetic two years later when it upheld the conviction for "fighting words" of Chaplinsky, another Jehovah's Witness. In *Chaplinsky,* as noted earlier, the Court defined "fighting words" as "those which by their very utterance inflict injury or tend to incite an immediate breach of the peace."[24] In the latter circumstances, where words are "likely to cause an average addressee to fight,"[25] the justices unanimously held that speech is unprotected by the First Amendment. After three more decades had passed, their position on this second branch of the *Chaplinsky* definition was essentially unchanged, and remains so to this day. For example, in 1971 a majority opinion described unprotected "fighting words" as "those personally abusive epithets which, when addressed to the ordinary citizen, are, as a matter of common knowledge, inherently likely to provoke violent reaction";[26] and, in 1972, as those which "have a direct tendency to cause acts of violence by the person to whom, individually, the remark is addressed" (quoting *Chaplinsky* which in turn was quoting the New Hampshire Supreme Court).[27]

But it is not only "fighting words" that have led the Supreme Court to uphold convictions of communicators addressing antagonistic listeners. In 1951 Irving Feiner, a soapbox speaker in Syracuse, New York, confronted with angry heckling from some members of a crowd of about eighty people, was arrested and convicted of disorderly conduct for refusing a police order to stop talking. Said the Court's majority:

> We are well aware that the ordinary murmurings and objections of a hostile audience cannot be allowed to silence a speaker, and are also mindful of the possible danger of giving overzealous police officials complete discretion to break up otherwise lawful public meetings. . . . But we are not faced here with such a situation. It is one thing to say that the police cannot be used as an instrument for suppression of unpopular views, and another to say that, when as here the speaker passes the bounds of argument and persuasion and undertakes incitement to riot, they are powerless to prevent a breach of the peace.[28]

Twenty years later a majority of the justices were still of the opinion that speakers could be punished for stirring hostile audiences to violence, but now they seemed to suggest, contrary to the view expressed by the Court in *Cantwell*, that the provocation had to be intentional. Said the Court, in exonerating Paul Robert Cohen of punishable speech: "Nor do we have here an instance of the State's police power to prevent a speaker from intentionally provoking a given group to hostile reaction. . . . There is . . . no showing that anyone who saw Cohen was in fact violently aroused or that appellant intended such a result."[29]

During the three decades between *Cantwell* and *Cohen*, the Supreme Court, in contrast to its foregoing opinions, also found several occasions on which to say that communicators could *not* be held responsible when hostile audiences gathered or threatened violence against them. In overturning a breach of peace conviction of Father Terminiello for a vitriolic racist speech delivered in a meeting hall in Chicago, the majority wrote in 1949 that "a function of free speech under our system of government is to invite dispute. It may indeed best serve its high purpose when it induces a condition of unrest, creates dissatisfaction with conditions as they are, or even stirs people to anger."[30]

Again, in 1963, reversing a breach of peace conviction of 200 black youths who had held a civil rights demonstration at the South Carolina state capitol building, the Court said, "The circumstances in this case reflect an exercise of ... basic constitutional rights in their most pristine and classic form. The petitioners ... were convicted upon evidence which showed no more than that the opinions which they were peaceably expressing were sufficiently opposed to the views of the majority of the community to attract a crowd and necessitate police protection."[31]

In 1969, the Court described an incident involving the picketing of Mayor Daley's home in Chicago by Dick Gregory and a group of about forty civil rights marchers, met by hundreds of angry neighbors, as "a simple case."[32] The opinion continued:

> Petitioners ... marched in a peaceful and orderly procession. ... the onlookers became unruly as the number of bystanders increased. Chicago police, to prevent what they regarded as an impending civil disorder, demanded that the demonstrators, upon pain of arrest, disperse. When this command was not obeyed, petitioners were arrested for disorderly conduct. ... There is no evidence in this record that petitioners' conduct was disorderly. ... The judgments are Reversed.[33]

And finally, in 1970, the Supreme Court overturned a disturbing peace conviction of an anti-Vietnam War group which had demonstrated in front of a U.S. Army recruiting station in Baltimore, Maryland.

> The marchers carried or wore signs bearing such legends as "Peasant Emancipation, Not Escalation," "Make Love not War," "Stop in the Name of Love," and "Why are We in Viet Nam?" ... A crowd of onlookers gathered nearby and across the street. ... The lieutenant in charge of the police detail testified that he "overheard" some of the marchers debate with members of the crowd about "the Viet Cong situation," and that a few in the crowd resented the protest. ... Clearly the wording of the placards was not within that small class of "fighting words" ... nor is there any evidence that the demonstrators' remarks to the crowd constituted "fighting words." Any shock effect caused by the placards, remarks, and peaceful marching must be attributed to the content of the ideas being expressed, or to the onlookers' dislike of demonstrations as a means of expressing dissent. But "[i]t is firmly settled that under our Constitution the public expression of ideas may not be prohibited merely because the ideas are themselves offensive to some of their hearers" ... or simply because bystanders object to peaceful and orderly demonstrations. Plainly nothing that occurred during this period could constitutionally be grounds for conviction.[34]

The net result of these rulings from our highest court leaves us in an uncertain situation where provocation of hostile audiences is sometimes treated as harshly as inflaming sympathetic listeners to violence and is sometimes viewed as "pristine and classic" First Amendment activity entitled to police protection from angry crowds. It appears that "fighting words" will consistently be punished if addressed to particular individuals who might respond violently; that speakers may not *intentionally* provoke hostile crowds to violence; but that entirely peaceful and polite communicators are likely to be regarded as within the law even if an audience disapproves so strongly of their ideas that it becomes disorderly. The legal fate is unpredictable of aggressive and persistent speakers expressing inflammatory messages in volatile situations where one cannot be certain about their true intentions or desires regarding possible violent reactions. Thus Terminiello's conviction was reversed, Feiner's was sustained, and review was denied to that of a soapbox orator in Chicago, Karl Meyer, who defied a police order to disperse when his audience became unruly. Left standing in this last case was a decision of the Illinois Supreme Court which said of the incident:

> Defendant admitted that the situation had become tense but he was willing to be attacked for the purpose of his cause. . . . The issue he raises is whether the police can prevent him from speaking simply because his audience might react with disorder or violence. This issue, in the context of a demonstration, was raised in *Gregory*. . . . The Supreme Court neither approved nor disapproved of our conclusion that the police may order the cessation of otherwise lawful conduct where they have made all reasonable efforts to maintain order, but the conduct is producing an imminent threat of uncontrollable violence or riot. We adhere to the view expressed in our *Gregory* opinion that they may make such an order and that the demonstrators or speakers may be arrested and prosecuted for failure to obey such an order. . . . Defendant was arrested when he wilfully refused to obey the order to disperse and attempted to continue the conduct which was producing the disorder. We hold that the defendant was properly convicted of interfering with the police in the discharge of their duty to maintain order.[35]

There appear to be two bases for the Supreme Court's view that speakers who provoke hostile audiences to violence may be held as accountable to the law as those who incite sympathetic crowds to illegal acts. The first seems to be a premise that some communicators deliberately seek out antagonistic audiences and intentionally stir them to violent reaction. Presumably they do this not because they want to commit suicide but in the hope that such an event will attract greater attention to their cause, will generate the sympathy that martyrs sometimes receive, or will expose to public view the ugly behavior of which their adversaries are capable.

A second, and alternative, possibility is that speakers who are not particularly seeking violent reactions may nevertheless understand full well that such behavior is a likely consequence of the kind of communication in which they are engaging. In such circumstances, as for example with the utterance of "fighting words," the Court seems to feel that "men must be held to have intended, and to be accountable for, the effects which their acts were likely to produce."[36] It is this sort of reasoning which could lead a police captain in the *Gregory* case to defend his arrest of the demonstrators by telling the press that, in a situation of that type, you arrest "the cause, not the mob."[37] It is little different from the Illinois Supreme Court's characterization of Karl Meyer's speech making it "the conduct which was producing the disorder " rather than viewing the emotional state of the audience as being the causative factor.

Even legal scholars with recognized commitments to the broadest possible interpretation of the First Amendment have accepted this second line of thought, at least insofar as it legitimizes the punishment of "fighting words." Professor Laurence Tribe, for one, says of "fighting words" that "[s]uch provocations are not part of human discourse but weapons hurled in anger to inflict injury or invite retaliation."[38] Professors Norman Dorsen and Joel Gora call such speech "the verbal equivalent of a slap in the face, and in common experience likely to beget violent reaction."[39] And Thomas Emerson, after vigorously rejecting the rationale as it might apply to all *other* hostile audience situations, embraces it with respect to "fighting words":

> It is frequently said that speech that is intentionally provocative and therefore invites physical retaliation, can be punished or suppressed. Yet plainly no such general proposition can be sustained. Quite the contrary, it is clear that expression which leads an opponent to violent counter-action nevertheless remains "expression" [and, thus, in Emerson's scheme, protected by the First Amendment], and that ensuing conduct of the opponent is separable "action." This rule applies even where the speaker is deliberately provocative. The provocative nature of the communication does not make it any the less "expression." Indeed, the whole theory of free expression contemplates that expression will in many circumstances be provocative and arouse hostility. The audience, just as the speaker, has the obligation to maintain physical restraint.
>
> Under the expression-action theory, the only point at which the communication could be classified as action is when the communicator in effect participates in an act of violence. This can be said to occur only when the provocation takes the form of a personal insult, delivered face to face. Such "fighting words" can be considered the equivalent of knocking a chip off the shoulder—the traditional symbolic act that puts the parties in the role of physical combatants. It is, in short,

the beginning of action. But the classification of provocative or insulting words as "action" is limited to direct encounters. Thus, if such
language is used in the course of a speech addressed generally to the
audience, even though the speaker refers to specific persons, organizations, or groups, the communication must still be considered "expression." Unless the speaker singles out specific members of his audience, and addresses insulting or fighting words to them personally, the
communication cannot be said to constitute part of action.[40]

It is unfortunate that what Emerson sees so clearly about the provocation of hostile audiences in general he, and others in the legal community, do not find applicable to "fighting words." For it is my contention
that in *all* of the circumstances in which antagonistic crowds or individuals respond or threaten to respond violently to communicators, the *audience* should be held responsible for its behavior, and not the speaker. I
believe that the provocation of hostile audiences is entirely different in
kind from the incitement of sympathetic listeners to illegal action, and
that it should be dealt with according to a distinctive set of principles.
The difference lies in the fact that violent *re*action, by definition, is born
in the psyche of the respondent. The idea to attack the communicator
is not implanted or urged by the speaker, as might an idea to commit
illegal acts be initiated and advocated by one who incites a supportive
audience. Violence is the listener's own idea, aroused perhaps by his or
her anger at the speaker's words or presence but not "incited" by the
speaker in the proper sense of that word.

What is more, if hostile audiences are not held responsible for their
own behavior, and are not restrained from indulging in reactive physical
violence, they will soon learn that they have the power to exercise a
"heckler's veto" over the speech of their antagonists. By threatening
violent responses listeners will be able to silence or have punished anyone whose words they find objectionable.

Although some readers may agree with me that people who are the
targets of "fighting words" or of provocative ideas have a choice of
whether or not to respond with violence, and should therefore be held
responsible for their own behavior, it may be wondered why the speaker
who *intentionally* inflames an audience to violent reaction should not at
least share responsibility for the consequences. The difficulty with that
notion is that unless such speakers openly admit that their purpose is to
create disorder—in which case the problem is conceptually no different
from incitement of a sympathetic crowd—one can only infer an intent
that may or may not actually be present. The residents of Skokie, Illinois,
in 1977–78, may have been convinced in their own minds that the only
purpose Frank Collin could have in planning a march in their community was to stir them to violence, but Collin never conceded that to be his

goal, nor would there be any way to prove that it was. There were just as many people in Chicago in the summer of 1966 who believed that the objective of Martin Luther King's marches on behalf of open housing into the most intolerant all-white neighborhoods of the city was to provoke reactive violence; and, indeed, there is reason to believe that Dr. King was not unhappy to see national television news coverage of angry mobs of counter demonstrators hurling rocks at him and his supporters. Yet to attribute to him the instigation of violence as his primary motive would be grossly speculative.

Does it follow from what has been argued here that the state is powerless to prevent riots and disorder that may result from hostile audience situations or to punish those who genuinely start the trouble? Not at all. Justice Black pointed the way in his dissent in *Feiner:*

> The police of course have the power to prevent breaches of the peace. But if, in the name of preserving order, they ever can interfere with a lawful public speaker, they first must make all reasonable efforts to protect him. Here the police did not even pretend to try to protect petitioner's right to talk, even to the extent of arresting the man who threatened to interfere. Instead, they shirked that duty and acted only to suppress the right to speak.[41]

An excellent 1976 article in the *Michigan Law Review* has spelled out in greater detail what I would regard as generally appropriate standards for police conduct in hostile audience situations:

A. Police may limit otherwise lawful conduct—
   (1) *only* if there is a clear and present danger of violence; and
   (2) *not* on the basis of (a) the character of the speech or (b) the intent of the speaker to arouse audience hostility
B. The police may order the speaker to depart *only*—
   (1) after the police have made all *reasonable* efforts (a) to control the spectator audience and (b) to order the audience to disperse
   (2) after the order to the speaker has been explained; and
   (3) safe escort has been offered to the speaker, with the permissible exception that time constraints may make the tendering of such offer impossible
C. Safe escort *must* be offered to a speaker ordered to depart
D. If the speaker departs within reasonable time he may *not* be charged with any offense incidental to the events of the otherwise lawful assembly
E. If the speaker *fails* to depart within a reasonable time, he may be—
   (1) subject to immediate removal by the police; and
      subject to sanctions for noncompliance with the order to depart[42]

I have only two problems with these guidelines. The first, with respect to B(1)(b), is the failure to make clear that only those in an audience who are unruly should be ordered to desist or disperse. Otherwise the police would be empowered to deprive speakers of their audiences—the functional equivalent of silencing them—as well as to deprive peaceful auditors of their right to hear what the speaker has to say.

My second problem is with the very last item, and it is one about which the article itself expresses some doubt. The essay suggests that criminal penalties for speakers who resist dispersal orders may not be justified and that some mechanism of "temporary protective custody" might be preferable.[43] On the other hand, punishments for violent behavior on the part of members of the crowd, or for their noncompliance with legitimate orders to disperse, seem to me to be entirely in order.

One further point made in the article, which I believe to be well taken, is that there is a need for more precise standards than we now have for determining what constitutes a "reasonable" police effort to control angry crowds and to protect unpopular speakers. After surveying a number of police departments in urban centers across the country, the authors concluded, "A major defect in police regulations is that they do not clarify the level of danger to public order needed to trigger dispersal or arrest of speakers or of members of the audience."[44] It is also suggested that "small police forces will be unable to cope with certain emergencies that would be within the capability of large cities."[45]

What is reasonable in a given situation, of course, is a matter of judgment that must take account of many variables in addition to the capacity of the police department. These would include the resources that may be available from the state to supplement the local police force, other contemporaneous demands upon the law enforcement establishment, the size of the crowd, the depth of its anger, its degree of homogeneity and organization, and the security characteristics of the physical environment in which the event occurs. Since the weighing of such considerations does not lend itself to mathematical computation, we must rely on the officials who are responsible for law enforcement, and on the courts which review their actions, to place higher priority on the preservation of First Amendment values than on excessive concern for public convenience and tranquility. They should also be sensitive to the fact that, if the police are consistently strong and uncompromising in their protection of the right of free speech in hostile audience situations, and if this is clearly known to the community, there will be less need in the long run for the use of police power than if the authorities equivocate in the face of threatened mob rule.

Genuine Incitement

We come at long last to a consideration of the issue with which this chapter was to be primarily concerned—that of speech which advocates, urges, or solicits illegal action from an audience which may be receptive to the speaker's inducements. This is a problem which has manifested itself in many different contexts over a long period of time and has received extensive consideration by our courts. The questions it raises, however, remain troublesome.

One sort of advocacy of illegal action which has occupied the attention of legislators, judges, and political theorists from the very birth of our nation—indeed, was responsible for that birth—is communication which urges its listeners to revolution. Revolution implies the attempted overthrow of government by force and violence, and that, of course, is illegal if one is operating within the framework of any established system. Although our country was founded in revolution, the Constitution and laws of the land prohibit revolution by others. Presumably this is justified because channels are available for peaceful change, which were not provided by King George III.

Article III, Section 3, of the U.S. Constitution, for example, establishes the crime of treason, defined as "levying war" against the United States or "adhering to their Enemies, giving them Aid and Comfort." The definition goes on to require the commission of some "overt act," and the Supreme Court has interpreted this to mean that "mere mental attitudes or expressions should not be treason."[46] Nevertheless, lower court convictions for treason have been left standing in which the defendant's "overt act" was the communicative behavior of making radio broadcasts for an enemy in wartime.[47] In one lower court decision of this genre, the following rationale was offered:

> While the crime [of treason] is not committed by mere expression of opinion or criticism, words spoken as part of a program of propaganda warfare, in the course of employment by the enemy in its conduct of war against the United States, to which the accused owes allegiance, may be an integral part of the crime. There is evidence in this case of a course of conduct on behalf of the enemy in the prosecution of its war against the United States. The use of speech to this end, as the evidence permitted the jury to believe, made acts of words.[48]

Supplementing the constitutional prohibition against treason, the U.S. Criminal Code contains a provision on "Rebellion and Insurrection" which sets down penalties for "[w]hoever incites, sets on foot, assists, or engages in any rebellion or insurrection against the authority of the United States or the laws thereof."[49] Beyond that, the Alien Registration

Act of 1940 (popularly known as the Smith Act, after its sponsor, Congressman Howard W. Smith) made it "unlawful for any person"

> (1) to knowingly or willfully advocate, abet, advise or teach the duty, necessity, desirability, or propriety of overthrowing or destroying the government of the United States by force or violence, or by the assassination of any officer of any such government;
> (2) with the intent to cause the overthrow or destruction of any government in the United States, to print, publish, edit, issue, circulate, sell, distribute, or publicly display any written or printed matter advocating, advising or teaching the duty, necessity, desirability, or propriety of overthrowing or destroying any government in the United States by force or violence;
> (3) to organize or help to organize any society, group, or assembly of persons who teach, advocate, or encourage the overthrow or destruction of any government in the United States by force or violence.[50]

We will return shortly to a discussion of the narrowing construction placed on this law by the U.S. Supreme Court. My purpose at this point is only to identify and describe the relevant statutes and cases.

In addition to federal law, most states have prohibitions of one kind or another on the advocacy of force and violence as a means of effecting political change. The earliest of these, New York's Criminal Anarchy Act, was adopted in 1902 by that state in the wake of the assassination of President William McKinley by an anarchist. California's comparable law, against "criminal syndicalism," has also figured prominently in major litigation.

Nearly as fearsome, from the point of view of national survival, as incitement to revolution has been communication which urges people to refuse service in the military forces. The Espionage Act of 1917 provided:

> Whoever, when the United States is at war, shall willfully cause or attempt to cause insubordination, disloyalty, mutiny or refusal of duty, in the military or naval forces of the United States . . . or shall willfully obstruct the recruiting or enlistment service of the United States . . . shall be punished by a fine of not more than $10,000 or imprisonment for not more than than twenty years, or both.[51]

The Smith Act carried the same offense over into peacetime with its provision that

> It shall be unlawful for any person, with intent to interfere with, impair, or influence the loyalty, morale, or discipline of the military or naval forces of the United States—
> (1) to advise, counsel, urge, or in any manner cause insubordination, disloyalty, mutiny, or refusal of duty by any member of the military or naval forces of the United States; or

(2) to distribute any written or printed matter which advises, counsels, or urges insubordination, disloyalty, mutiny, or refusal of duty.[52]

Finally, the Selective Service Act of 1948, the first peacetime conscription law in American history, provided punishment for anyone "who knowingly counsels, aids, or abets another to refuse or evade registration or service in the armed forces or any of the requirements of this title."[53] It was under this provision of the law that the dean of men of a small Mennonite College in Ohio was convicted for saying to a student, "Do not let them coerce you into registering";[54] and a pacifist physician in Kansas was found guilty of urging his stepson not to register for the draft and offering to finance him to go to Canada or Mexico.[55]

Another kind of incitement that has been a source of common social concern is that which stimulates the seizing or destruction of property, looting, arson, or rioting in the streets. Cases of this sort are legion, and convictions usually so noncontroversial that none has ever been looked at from a First Amendment point of view by the U.S. Supreme Court. We have already noted that the common law recognized solicitation to theft to be an offense as far back as 1801, and statutes prohibiting incitement to riot are ubiquitous at the state and local levels. Even the federal government felt it necessary to move into this field after the ghetto rioting which followed the assassination of Martin Luther King. Convinced that "outside agitators" were responsible for the trouble—a theory later discredited by the investigations and report of a National Commission on the Causes and Prevention of Violence—Congress adopted the so-called Rap Brown amendment to the Civil Rights Act of 1968 making it a crime to cross state lines to incite to riot.[56] It was dubbed the Rap Brown amendment because a major stimulus for the bill was an incident in Cambridge, Maryland, where black militant H. Rap Brown had come to town, delivered an inflammatory speech which was followed by the burning of a school, and then skipped out before they could arrest him. The famous Chicago Seven Conspiracy trial, growing out of disorders at the Democratic National Convention in the summer of 1968, was based on indictments for violation of this particular law, the constitutionality of which was affirmed by the U.S. Court of Appeals for the Seventh Circuit.[57]

We have earlier in this chapter made reference to the conviction for incitement to riot of John Kasper in Tennessee, where school buildings were dynamited and rioting occurred in protest against court-ordered school desegregation. Another well-publicized case, though involving no destruction, was that of Daniel Siegel, president of student government at the University of California, Berkeley, who urged 2,000 students gathered on Sproul Plaza on the campus to "go down there and take the park." Siegel was placed on disciplinary probation and deprived of his student government office by a university hearing board, and the federal district court to which he appealed that decision found his speech to be incitement to illegal action not protected by the First Amendment.[58]

More serious a matter than speech which might lead to the seizure or even destruction of property is that which may encourage violence against persons, including murder. Here again it is rarely suggested that such communication is an exercise of protected freedom of speech, but such claims are not entirely unheard of or necessarily lacking in any merit. In the Haymarket Riot of 1886 in Chicago, where police officers were killed by the explosion of a bomb, the authorities were never able to identify the bomb thrower. Those who were tried and convicted of murder, four of whom were hanged, had been found guilty of violating an Illinois "aiding and abetting" statute for speeches and publications which allegedly were responsible for the violence that occurred. In appealing their conviction to the U.S. Supreme Court, these defendants argued, unsuccessfully, that their constitutional rights had been violated by application to them of a statute which made an offense of "mere advice, not to do the particular crime charged, but advice to a general revolutionary movement."[59]

Of more recent vintage has been a series of incidents where bounties have been offered for killings urged by the communicator. In August of 1977 a temporary restraining order was issued by a county court against a taped telephone message sponsored by a Nazi group in Cicero, Illinois, which offered $200 "to the first white man or woman who will exercise his right to protect his life and property and blow one of these black criminals away."[60] A similar recorded telephone message from a Nazi organization in Houston, Texas, offering a $5,000 prize "for every nonwhite killed in an attack on a white person," was also temporarily enjoined; but a state appellate court overturned that decision on the grounds that the plaintiff had no standing to sue because he faced no personal threat from the communication.[61] Finally, in Los Angeles in 1979, a superior court judge dismissed a felony complaint against Irving Rubin, a leader of the Jewish Defense League, who had been charged with soliciting the murder of American Nazis at a press conference in which he said that "we are offering $500, that I have in my hand, to any member of the community . . . who kills, maims or seriously injures a member of the American Nazi Party . . . in the defense of the Jewish community." The judge accepted the argument of ACLU attorneys that Rubin's utterances were political hyperbole protected by the First Amendment.[62]

A state appellate court, however, by a 2–1 vote, overturned the lower court's ruling, finding from "the words and circumstances of Rubin's

offer" that "there was sufficient likelihood of his solicitation being interpreted as a call to arms, as a preparation of his group to violent action."[63]
The dissenting judge characterized Rubin's speech as "hyperbolized solicitation" designed "to attract attention to a sensitive and explosive national issue and to generate news on a national scale."[64]

A quite different order of problem is posed by the occasional allegation that a particular motion picture or television show has been responsible for stimulating individuals who have seen it to the commission
of acts of personal violence. The most serious such charge was an $11
million lawsuit filed in San Francisco against NBC and its local outlet for
a broadcast in 1974 of a two-hour drama called "Born Innocent," which
depicted a sexual assault on a teenage girl with a wooden rod by a group
of reformatory inmates. Following the airing of this program, four teen-
age girls, using an empty beverage bottle, imitated this scene in real life
and admitted to having gotten the idea from the television show. Suit
was brought on behalf of the victim, Olivia Niemi, against the broadcasters, seeking damages for their alleged negligence in airing this provocative scene. The judge in the case ultimately ruled that the network
and station could not be held liable unless it were proven that they
deliberately incited the crime, a burden of proof which the plaintiff's
lawyer admitted he could not sustain, leading to the dismissal of the
case.[65]

During the course of the trial, a *New York Times* story carried this
account of the proceedings:

> Miss Niemi believes that her youthful attackers were imitating a
> scene from the television show "Born Innocent." She contends that the
> network was negligent in broadcasting the violent scene at an early
> evening hour when, she says, NBC should have known that young
> people would watch it and be tempted to imitate it.
>
> NBC won an important procedural victory on Wednesday when
> Judge Dossee ruled that the trial was not to procede [*sic*] on this gen-
> eral claim of negligence, but instead must be limited to the narrow
> question of whether the broadcast actually "incited" the real-life
> attack.
>
> At the time, Judge Dossee resisted the efforts of Marvin E. Lewis,
> Miss Niemi's lawyer, to persuade him to define "incitement." Mr.
> Lewis contended that while he could show in a general sense that the
> broadcast stimulated and inspired the crime, he would have to drop
> his case if the judge required him to prove that NBC had deliberately
> advocated that members of the audience go out and imitate what they
> had seen on the television screen.
>
> But since Wednesday, Mr. Lewis apparently persuaded the judge to
> clarify the matter further. If Judge Dossee adopts the strictest defini-
> tion of "incitement"—a requirement that the jury find NBC to have

advocated imitation of the scene—a procedural tango will probably follow on Monday that would result in the trial's being aborted. . . .

If, on the other hand, Judge Dossee defines "incitement" in the broader sense of "stimulation," the trial will probably procede. . . .

The ambiguity stems from the fact that "incitement" is not defined in the Constitution or any statute book. It is a concept that has been created by the Supreme Court in a series of cases interpreting the First Amendment. It has come to be recognized, along with libel, slander, perjury, obscenity, and a few other kinds of speech, as an exception to the protections otherwise afforded by the the First Amendment to free speech and a free press.[66]

Another related matter arose in February 1979 with the release of a movie entitled *The Warriors,* a vivid and dramatic portrayal of teenage gang violence in New York City. A public furor over the film broke out when an eighteen-year-old youth was stabbed to death in a fight between rival gangs in the lobby of a theater showing the movie in Oxnard, California; another young man was shot and killed at a drive-in theater in Palm Springs, California; and a third boy was fatally stabbed in Boston by an acquaintance who had just seen the film. The distributor, Paramount Pictures, seriously considered removing the film from circulation and did, in fact, suspend print media advertising of it for nearly a week, but no further serious incidents occurred, and the film's run continued uninterrupted.[67]

In addition to the incitement of theft, draft resistance, and crimes of violence against persons, property, or the state, cases have also been litigated involving the advocacy of what might be termed moral offenses which our society has chosen to make illegal. Three such cases may be noted by way of illustration.

As far back as 1890 the U.S. Supreme Court upheld an Idaho territorial law which denied the right to vote or hold public office to anyone who "teaches, advises, counsels or encourages any person or persons to become a bigamist or polygamist." The Court said that if bigamy and polygamy are crimes, "then to teach, advise and counsel . . . are also criminal."[68]

Twenty-five years later the Supreme Court affirmed a conviction, under a statute of the State of Washington, making it illegal to print or circulate material that encourages the commission of crimes, for publication of an article entitled "The Nudes and the Prudes." The Court commented that "by indirection but unmistakably the article encourages and incites a persistence in what we assume would be a breach of state law against indecent exposure."[69]

And as recently as 1976 a federal district court upheld the authority of the University of Missouri to refuse recognition to a gay student group on the grounds that its presence and activities on campus would promote and incite violations of the state's law against sodomy.[70] Although this ruling was overturned by the court of appeals, which felt there was no showing that the students would be inciting immediate lawless action but would only be advocating greater understanding and acceptance of homosexuality, there was no suggestion by the court that direct incitement to violate state law would not have been prohibitable.[71] Indeed, in their dissent from the Supreme Court's refusal to review this case, Justices William Rehnquist and Harry Blackmun found the district court's position more persuasive than that of the court of appeals:

> . . . the issue posed in this case is the extent to which a self-governing democracy, having made certain acts criminal, may prevent or discourage individuals from engaging in speech or conduct which encourages others to violate those laws. . . . The University in this case did not ban the discussion in the classroom or out of it, of the wisdom of repealing sodomy statutes. The State did not proscribe membership in organizations devoted to advancing "gay liberation." The University merely refused to recognize an organization whose activities were found to be likely to incite a violation of a valid state criminal statute.[72]

Legal Principles Affecting Incitement

The difference of opinion among courts and judges exhibited in the *Gay Lib* case epitomizes the dilemma which has plagued the concept of incitement ever since people began thinking about it. Where is the line to be drawn between speech which discusses in general terms the undesirability of certain laws or established institutions and that which solicits their violation or destruction? Thomas Jefferson said in 1786 that "it is time enough for the rightful purposes of civil government, for its officers to interfere when principles break out into overt acts against peace and good order."[73] But without knowing for sure whether he would have categorized a direct incitement to illegal action as an expression of "principles" or an "overt act," his eloquence on the issue has not been particularly influential.

John Stuart Mill was more concrete and apparently closer to what has since become prevailing legal doctrine. He said in 1858 in his famous essay *On Liberty*, which was otherwise a vigorous and expansive defense of free speech:

> No one pretends that actions should be as free as opinions. On the contrary, even opinions lose their immunity when the circumstances in which they are expressed are such as to constitute their expression a positive instigation to some mischievous act. An opinion that corn-dealers are starvers of the poor, or that private property is robbery,

ought to be unmolested when simply circulated through the press, but may justly incur punishment when delivered orally to an excited mob assembled before the house of a corn-dealer, or when handed about among the same mob in the form of a placard.[74]

The distinction Mill drew was given its most succinct judicial formulation by Judge Learned Hand, then sitting on the federal district court bench in New York, when he wrote in *Masses Publishing Company v. Patten:*

> Words are not only the keys of persuasion, but the triggers of action, and those which have no purport but to counsel the violation of law cannot by any latitude of interpretation be a part of that public opinion which is the final source of government in a democratic state. . . .
> Political agitation, by the passions it arouses or the convictions it engenders, may in fact stimulate men to the violation of law. Detestation of existing policies is easily transformed into forcible resistance of the authority which puts them in execution, and it would be folly to disregard the causal relation between the two. Yet to assimilate agitation, legitimate as such, with direct incitement to violent resistance, is to disregard the tolerance of all methods of political agitation which in normal times is a safeguard of free government. The distinction is not a scholastic subterfuge, but a hard-bought acquisition in the fight for freedom.[75]

Judge Hand's selection of the "trigger" metaphor to illustrate his point was perhaps more apt than even he was aware, for, better than anything else which has been said on this subject in the many years since Hand wrote, it captures an idea which I believe can be our "key" to ultimately unraveling the incitement dilemma. It implies that, in response to some communication, human beings can be moved to action in the same way an inanimate object, like a gun, is triggered—that is, without the mediation of conscious choice or the exercise of free will. The only reason I suggest that Hand may not, in 1917, have been fully aware of the implications of his metaphor is the seemingly unqualified statement with which he follows it, to the effect that speech which has "no purport but to counsel the violation of law cannot *by any latitude of interpretation*" [italics mine] be considered eligible for First Amendment protection. But more on this point later.

Judge Hand did not have the last word in the *Masses* case. He was overruled by the U.S. Court of Appeals for the Second Circuit which seemed to take a considerably broader view of what constitutes illegal incitement. It was that court's contention that communication is punishable "if the natural and reasonable effect of what is said is to encourage resistance to the law, and the words are used in an endeavor to persuade to resistance."[76] Judge Hough, in a preliminary ruling of the court, had explained further: "It is at least arguable whether there can be any more direct incitement to action than to hold up to admiration those who do act.... The Beatitudes have for some centuries been considered highly hortatory, though they do not contain the injunction: 'Go thou and do likewise.'"[77]

Yet one scholar has suggested that Judge Hand and the court of appeals were not so far apart in their understanding of the issue. Zechariah Chafee wrote:

> It is possible that the upper court did not intend to lay down a very different principle from Judge Hand, but chiefly wished to insist that in determining whether there is incitement one must look not only at the words themselves but also at the surrounding circumstances which may have given the words a special meaning to their hearers. Judge Hand agreed with this, and regarded Mark Antony's funeral oration, for instance, as having counseled violence while it expressly discountenanced it.[78]

Whatever may have been the degree of agreement or disagreement between Learned Hand and the court of appeals as to the relevance of surrounding circumstances to a determination of incitement, the U.S. Supreme Court soon made it clear that it thought such considerations to be essential. In its landmark 1919 decision in *Schenck v. U.S.*, a unanimous Court, speaking through Justice Oliver Wendell Holmes, enunciated a famous doctrine which reechoed what John Stuart Mill had previously said:

> We admit that in many places and in ordinary times the defendants, in saying all that was said in the circular, would have been within their constitutional rights. But the character of every act depends upon the circumstances in which it is done.... The most stringent protection of free speech would not protect a man in falsely shouting fire in a theater and causing a panic.... The question in every case is whether the words used are used in such circumstances and are of such a nature as to create a clear and present danger that they will bring about the substantive evils that Congress has a right to prevent. It is a question of proximity and degree.[79]

Now a new metaphor had been introduced which was to become more ubiquitous than the "trigger" concept—that of fire. The Court was later to uphold convictions because a "single revolutionary spark may kindle a fire,"[80] and because of the "inflammable nature of world conditions."[81] And there must be hardly anyone who has not heard that one may not falsely shout fire in a crowded theater. Like a trigger, a lighted match sets off an inevitable and humanly uncontrollable chain of events for which the puller of the trigger or lighter of the match is held responsible.

Justice Holmes, having authored the clear-and-present-danger test, was soon to feel that a majority of his colleagues had stretched it beyond his recognition. Dissenting from a judgment that two radical leaflets published in protest against U.S. intervention in Russia would have the effect of undermining our World War I effort against Germany, Holmes said:

> I do not see how anyone can find the intent required by the statute in any of the defendants' words. . . . twenty years' imprisonment have been imposed for the publishing of two leaflets that I believe the defendants had as much right to publish as the government has to publish the Constitution of the United States now vainly invoked by them. Even if I am technically wrong and enough can be squeezed from these poor and puny anonymities to turn the color of legal litmus paper, I will add, even if what I think the necessary intent were shown; the most nominal punishment seems to me all that possibly could be inflicted. . . . I think that we should be eternally vigilant against attempts to check the expressions of opinions that we loathe and believe to be fraught with death, unless they so imminently threaten immediate interference with the lawful and pressing purposes of the law that an immediate check is required to save the country. . . . Only the emergency that makes it immediately dangerous to leave the correction of evil counsels to time warrants making any exception to the sweeping command, "Congress shall make no law . . . abridging the freedom of speech."[82]

But Holmes's position, joined by Justice Brandeis, was to continue as a minority one for half a century. It was immediately attacked by a prestigious law school dean as being blind to the dangers the country faced and reflecting an unnecessary bleeding-heart concern for a First Amendment which, in his view, was entirely secure. Said Dean John H. Wigmore, " . . . the *moral right of the majority to enter upon the war imports the moral right to secure success by suppressing public agitation against the completion of the struggle.*"[83]

In the Supreme Court's next major encounter with this issue, *Gitlow v. New York,* the majority, again over the protests of Holmes and Brandeis, adopted as their understanding of illegal incitement what Professor Chafee has described as the "bad-tendency test"—

> an English eighteenth-century doctrine, wholly at variance with any true freedom of discussion, because it permits the government to go outside its proper field of acts, present or probable, into the field of ideas, and condemn them by the judgment of a judge or jury, who, human nature being what it is, consider a doctrine they dislike to be so liable to cause harm some day that it had better be nipped in the bud.[84]

The bad-tendency doctrine, sometimes also described as "killing the serpent in the egg," was given detailed expression by the *Gitlow* majority as follows:

The statute does not penalize the utterance or publication of abstract "doctrine" or academic discussion having no quality of incitement to any concrete action. It is not aimed against mere historical or philosophical essays. It does not restrain the advocacy of changes in the form of government by constitutional and lawful means. What it prohibits is language advocating, advising, or teaching the overthrow of organized government by unlawful means. These words imply urging to action. . . .

The Manifesto, plainly, is neither the statement of abstract doctrine nor, as suggested by counsel, mere prediction that industrial disturbances and revolutionary mass strikes will result spontaneously in an inevitable process of evolution in the economic system. It advocates and urges in fervent language mass action which shall progressively foment industrial disturbances, and, through political mass strikes and revolutionary mass action, overthrow and destroy organized parliamentary government. It concludes with a call to action. . . . That utterances inciting to the overthrow of organized government by unlawful means present a sufficient danger of substantive evil to bring their punishment within the range of legislative discretion is clear. Such utterances, by their very nature, involve danger to the public peace and to the security of the state. They threaten breaches of the peace and ultimate revolution. And the immediate danger is none the less real because the effect of a given utterance cannot be accurately foreseen. The state cannot reasonably be required to measure the danger from every such utterance in the nice balance of a jeweler's scale. A single revolutionary spark may kindle a fire that, smoldering for a time, may burst into a sweeping and destructive conflagration. It cannot be said that the state is acting arbitrarily or unreasonably when, in the exercise of its judgment as to the measures necessary to protect the public peace and safety, it seeks to extinguish the spark without waiting until it has enkindled the flame or blazed into a conflagration. . . . it may, in the exercise of its judgment, suppress the threatened danger in its incipiency.[85]

Justice Holmes, speaking for himself and Justice Brandeis, had quite a different perception of both the communication in question in the case and the appropriate free speech principles to be applied:

. . . it is manifest that there was no present danger of an attempt to overthrow the government by force on the part of the admittedly small minority who shared this defendant's views. It is said that this Manifesto was more than a theory, that it was an incitement. Every idea is an incitement. It offers itself for belief, and if believed, it is acted on unless some other belief outweighs it, or some failure of energy stifles the movement at its birth. The only difference between an expression of opinion and an incitement in the narrower sense is the speaker's enthusiasm for the result. Eloquence may set fire to reason, but whatever may be thought of the redundant discourse before us, it had no chance of starting a present conflagration. If, in the long run, the beliefs expressed in proletarian dictatorship are destined to be accepted by the dominant forces of the community, the only meaning of free speech is that they should be given their chance and have their way.[86]

In this famous dissent, Holmes put his finger on what is really a core problem in the field we are now discussing—namely, that "every idea is an incitement" capable of setting "fire to reason," depending upon "the speaker's enthusiasm for the result." Any statute, such as the one that Gitlow was convicted of violating, which makes certain kinds of speech illegal regardless of the particular circumstances in which the words are uttered, despite the intent and potential effectiveness of the communicator, and without consideration of the capacity of the audience to make its own decision whether or not to act, necessarily runs afoul of the Holmes insight.[87]

Many years later, dissenting from a U.S. Supreme Court decision to return to the Utah Supreme Court for further consideration the conviction of a group of Mormons for conspiring to "advocate, counsel, advise and urge the practice of polygamy," Justice Wiley Rutledge exhibited a better-than-usual understanding of this issue when he wrote that

it is clear that some appellants urged certain particular individuals to practice polygamy. For present purposes I assume that such direct and personalized activity amounting to incitation to commit a crime may be proscribed by the state. However, the charge was not restricted to a claim that appellants had conspired to urge particular violations of law. Instead, the information as construed by the State Court broadly condemned the conspiracy to advocate and urge the practice of polygamy. This advocacy was at least in part conducted in religious meetings where, although pressure may also have been applied to individuals, considerable general discussion of the religious duty to enter into plural marriages was carried on.

Neither the statute, the information, nor the portions of the charge to the jury which are preserved in the printed record distinguish between the specific incitations and the more generalized discussions. . . . The Constitution requires that the statute be limited more narrowly. At the very least the line must be drawn between advocacy and incitement, and even the state's power to punish incitement may vary with the nature of the speech, whether persuasive or coercive, the nature of the wrong induced, whether violent or merely offensive to the mores, and the degree of probability that the substantive evil actually will result.[88]

But the most widely quoted statement of all in support of this position remains that penned by Justice Brandeis concurring in *Whitney v. California* in 1927:

Fear of serious injury cannot alone justify suppression of free speech and assembly. Men feared witches and burned women. It is the function of speech to free men from the bondage of irrational fears. To justify suppression of free speech there must be reasonable ground to fear that serious evil will result if free speech is practiced. There must be reasonable ground to believe that the danger apprehended is imminent. There must be reasonable ground to believe that the evil to be prevented is a serious one. Every denunciation of existing law tends in some measure to increase the probability that there will be a violation of it. Condonation of a breach enhances the probability. Expressions of approval add to the probability. Propagation of the criminal state of mind by teaching syndicalism increases it. Advocacy of law-breaking heightens it still further. But even advocacy of violation, however reprehensible morally, is not a justification for denying free speech where the advocacy falls short of incitement and there is nothing to indicate that the advocacy would be immediately acted on. The wide difference between advocacy and incitement, between preparation and attempt, between assembling and conspiring, must be borne in mind.

Those who won our independence by revolution were not cowards. They did not fear political change. They did not exalt order at the cost of liberty. To courageous, self-reliant men, with confidence in the power of free and fearless reasoning applied through the processes of popular government, no danger flowing from speech can be deemed clear and present, unless the incidence of the evil is so imminent that it may befall before there is opportunity for full discussion. If there be time to expose through discussion the falsehood and fallacies, to avert the evil by the processes of education, the remedy to be applied is more speech, not enforced silence. Only an emergency can justify repression. Such must be the rule if authority is to be reconciled with freedom. Such, in my opinion, is the command of the Constitution.[89]

The eloquent opinions of Justices Holmes and Brandeis, and the logic of their arguments, were apparently not sufficient to overcome the influence of the bad-tendency test when the Supreme Court was asked to respond to the alleged dangers of Communist subversion in the United States following World War II. In *Dennis v. U.S.* in 1951, the Court upheld convictions, under the Smith Act, of eleven leaders of the Communist Party, for conspiring to advocate the overthrow of our government by force and violence. Chief Justice Fred Vinson wrote for a plurality of the Court:

In this case we are squarely presented with the application of the "clear and present danger" test, and must decide what that phrase imports.... Obviously, the words cannot mean that before the Government may act, it must wait until the *putsch* is about to be executed, the plans have been laid and the signal is awaited.... Certainly an attempt to overthrow the Government by force, even though doomed from the outset because of inadequate numbers or power of the revolutionists, is a sufficient evil for Congress to prevent. The damage which such attempts create both physically and politically to a nation makes it impossible to measure the validity in terms of the probability of success, or the immediacy of a successful attempt.... We must therefore reject the criterion that success or probability of success is the criterion....

Chief Judge Learned Hand [at this time with the U.S. Court of Appeals for the Second Circuit] interpreted the phrase as follows: "In each case courts must ask whether the gravity of the 'evil,' discounted by its improbability, justifies such invasion of free speech as is necessary to avoid the danger." ... We adopt this statement of the rule.[90]

On the basis of this decision, a second group of Communist Party leaders were found guilty of violating the Smith Act and they, too, appealed to the Supreme Court. This time, however, the Supreme Court reversed the convictions. It found that the trial court judge had incorrectly instructed the jury regarding the Supreme Court's requirements for arriving at a guilty verdict under the Smith Act and attempted to clarify its construction of that Act:

In failing to distinguish between advocacy of forcible overthrow as an abstract doctrine and advocacy of action to that end, the District Court appears to have been led astray by the holding in *Dennis,* that advocacy of violent action to be taken at some future time was enough. It seems to have considered that, since "inciting" speech is usually thought of as calculated to induce immediate action, and since *Dennis* held advocacy of action for future overthrow sufficient, this meant that advocacy, irrespective of its tendency to generate action, is punishable, provided only that it is uttered with a specific intent to accomplish overthrow....

This misconceives the situation confronting the Court in *Dennis* and what was held there.... The essential distinction is that those to whom the advocacy is addressed must be urged to *do* something, now or in the future, rather than merely to *believe* in something....

We recognize that distinctions between advocacy or teaching of abstract doctrines, with evil intent, and that which is directed to stirring people to action, are often difficult and subtle to grasp.... But the very subtlety of these distinctions required the most clear and explicit instructions with reference to them, for they concerned an issue which went to the heart of the charges against these petitioners.[91]

Four years later the Court added: "We held in *Yates,* and we reiterate now, that the mere abstract teaching of the moral propriety or even moral necessity for a resort to force and violence is not the same as preparing a group for violent action and steeling it to such action. There must be some substantial direct or circumstantial evidence of a call to violence now or in the future."[92]

Thus the Supreme Court seemed to be saying that a line was to be drawn between urging people, on the one hand, to *believe* in the necessity of violent *action,* which is protected by the First Amendment even if the speaker's intention and hope is that the audience will ultimately act illegally, and urging people, on the other hand, to *take* illegal action, "now or in the future," which is not protected. The "subtlety of these distinctions" was not only "difficult to grasp," it was impossible; and the Supreme Court apparently recognized that fact by the time it arrived at its decision in *Brandenburg v. Ohio* in 1969. In a unanimous *per curiam* opinion, overturning the conviction of a Ku Klux Klansman for a speech demanding "revengance" against blacks, and striking down the Ohio Criminal Syndicalism Act on which the conviction was based, the Court enunciated a new First Amendment "principle that the constitutional guarantees of free speech and free press do not permit a state to forbid or proscribe advocacy of the use of force or of law violation except where such advocacy is directed to inciting or producing imminent lawless action and is likely to incite or produce such action."[93]

Gone from this opinion was any mention of the clear-and-present-danger test, which was thus deprived of a golden anniversary celebration. Gone was the possibility that a speaker could be punished for advocating illegal conduct *in the future,* for now, to be prohibited, the solicitation had to be to *imminent* lawless action. And gone was the killing of serpents in the egg, for now the action urged not only had to be imminent, but *likely* as well. The philosophy of Holmes and Brandeis had prevailed at last.

But even that victory was not enough for Justice Douglas. In a separate concurring opinion, he recalled Holmes's perception that "every idea is an incitement," and said of it, "We have never been faithful to that dissent."[94] After reviewing what he regarded as the unsavory history of the clear-and-present-danger test and the various perversions of it by the Court, he concluded:

> The line between what is permissible and not subject to control and what may be made impermissible and subject to regulation is the line between ideas and overt acts.
> The example usually given by those who would punish speech is the case of one who falsely shouts fire in a crowded theater.

This is, however, a classic case where speech is brigaded with action.... They are indeed inseparable and a prosecution can be launched for the overt acts actually caused. Apart from rare instances of that kind, speech is, I think, immune from prosecution.[95]

Unfortunately, this was not one of Justice Douglas's more lucid moments. He appears to embrace the strict Jeffersonian distinction between principles and overt acts, whatever it may have meant, but then immediately clouds the issue by describing the shout of fire in a crowded theater as "brigaded with action"—whatever that means. Confusion mounts when he says, "They are indeed inseparable and a prosecution can be launched for the overt acts actually caused." We are left uncertain whether the shout of fire is punishable, in his view, because it is an integral part of some unspecified and prohibitable act, or because it really is conceptually separable from overt acts but still punishable because of the action (presumably panic) it may *cause.*

Incidentally, neither Justice Douglas here, nor anyone else who has invoked the shouting-fire-in-a-theater illustration elsewhere, has ever explained how the analogy is relevant to the question of incitement *to illegal* action, or advocacy thereof. Nor have they proposed the only basis on which I can conceive of punishing such communication, and have so suggested in an earlier chapter—namely, that it causes physical injury to others by misrepresentation. *Truthfully* shouting fire in a crowded theater is presumably not only allowable but to be encouraged.

If what Justice Douglas meant to say in his *Brandenburg* concurring opinion, and what Thomas Jefferson intended in the Virginia Statute for Establishing Religious Freedom, is that speech which incites to illegal acts can *never* be punished, and that penalties may be placed only on overt acts themselves or on speech which is an integral part *of* those acts, they are a lonely minority indeed, and not even one that I would join. The closest our legal system has come to that, though it is still a good distance away, is the Supreme Court's *Brandenburg* formulation, which is the current law of the land.

An Evaluation and Proposed Set of Standards

If I had to choose between *Brandenburg* and its predecessors for a principle governing the law of incitement, I would clearly prefer the *Brandenburg* regime. It requires a contextual analysis of every situation where speech is to be punished; it requires that the danger of lawless action be immediate and likely; and, by its use of the phrase "directed to inciting," it implies a requirement of intent by the speaker to stimulate illegal action.

Its shortcomings, however, are grave. It omits the Brandeisian suggestion that the lawless action contemplated must be a "serious evil." It is not explicitly limited—though perhaps it is implicit—to situations where there is no "time to . . . avert the evil by . . . more speech." But most important, it fails, as Justice Douglas's opinion noted, to come to grips with the fact that "every idea is an incitement." Therefore, a way must still be found, after all the other criteria are satisfied, to clearly distinguish those "ideas" which should be punished for incitement from those which should not be.

As I hinted earlier, I believe the answer to that problem is to be found in Learned Hand's metaphor contrasting "triggers of action" and "keys of persuasion." If it is true, as I think it is, that there are some few and limited circumstances in which human beings, like inanimate objects, may be "triggered" rather than "persuaded" to illegal conduct, and if the person pulling the trigger knows that to be the case and deliberately exploits it, then and only then would I hold a communicator responsible for the results.

My central consideration in making this kind of determination would be the question of free choice on the part of listeners. Do they have the capacity to resist the communicator's inducements, or does the communication to which they are exposed set off an *inevitable* chain reaction over which they have no control? If the former, then it seems to me that they, and not communicators, should be held responsible for any crimes they may commit. If the latter, we must then ask if the communicators knew what they were doing and, if so, hold them accountable. If they have motivated their listeners to illegal action by deliberately deceiving them, they have deprived that audience of genuine choice in the matter and should take responsibility for the consequences. Similarly, if they have coerced their listeners to illegal action, under circumstances discussed in the previous chapter, they should be considered to have assumed responsibility for the results which may ensue.[96] Even where the listener has *some* capacity to resist, as in the case of bribery, communicators who employ such choice-limiting tactics of influence may legitimately be held to at least their share of the responsibility for what their efforts bring about. In short, to whatever extent speakers take control over the will of other persons, and make them their "tools" or their "guns," so to speak, they must be answerable for the action that results.

On the other hand, advocates or inciters of illegal action should *not* be held accountable for the behavior of listeners who are competent to reject their solicitations, even in highly emotional situations where reflective thought may *voluntarily* be abandoned by members of the audience. Unless deceived, coerced, or mentally deficient, human beings are *not* inanimate objects who are "triggered" by others; they are *not* piles of kindling waiting for a spark to ignite them.[97] They should *not* be relieved of responsibility for their own behavior by the buck being passed to someone else who may have planted an idea in their minds.

It is easier to assert this point of view as a general statement of principle than to defend it in the face of concrete illustrations which tempt deviation from it. But I cannot fairly shirk that task.

The first set of hard cases with which one espousing this position is likely to be confronted are the so-called How to Do It publications—those which describe in detail the techniques for committing antisocial acts. One such incident was the publication by an underground newspaper in Detroit in 1974 of an article describing the construction of "mute boxes"—instruments with which one can cheat the telephone company out of charges for long-distance calls. The Michigan Bell Telephone Company filed a complaint, and the paper was prosecuted for violation of the state's criminal fraud statutes. The state's attorney agreed to drop the charges when the newspaper indicated that it did not plan to republish the mute-box instructions.[98]

An instance which might seem to be of a more serious nature was that of a book entitled *How to Kill,* banned from importation into Canada in 1977. Written by an Ontario author, but published in the United States, it was described as listing ten ways to kill a person, with illustrations of decapitation and hatchet murders.[99]

Finally, in Orange County, California, during the 1969 Christmas season, an article appeared in an underground newspaper, under the by-line of "Robin Hood," suggesting that readers take care of their Christmas chores by shoplifting from major department stores. This issue of the paper was distributed free of charge to high school students in the area. Although those responsible for the article claimed it to be a tongue-in-cheek piece, the district attorney brought charges for solicitation to commit burglary and grand theft, later amended to a charge of contributing to the delinquency of minors.[100]

With all such incidents—and note that we are not discussing here instruction manuals or lectures prepared by and delivered to people who have already decided and agreed to engage in illegal conduct together—there is not only a question as to whether it was the serious intent of the author or publisher to encourage the commission of crimes. Even if that were the case, it would be difficult to demonstrate that the other criteria of the *Brandenburg* test had been met, let alone those of the narrower exception to First Amendment protection that I have proposed. How, for instance, could it be shown that a generally circulated newspaper, magazine, or book posed a threat of *imminent* lawless action where such action was *likely* to occur? Where, in these instances, is the absence of time for reflection on the part of the reader, or the lack of capacity to understand that what is described or proposed in the publication is illegal and to decide not to do it? Where is the deception, coercion, or control of will that could legitimately be characterized as a "trigger"? If restraints were to be allowed for such communication, we would have to purge our libraries of all mystery tales about the "perfect crime" and all technical treatises providing information on how to manufacture explosives or produce chemical poisons. Better that we rely on the people into whose hands such material falls to use it responsibly. If they do not, let them, not the publisher or writer, be punished.

Similarly once removed from imminent and likely action, and where the audience is likewise physically distant from, and fully capable of resisting, the inducements made, are those cases where speakers indulge in overheated rhetoric which is then reported to the public through the mass media or heard on a taped telephone message. When, in the wake of Martin Luther King's assassination, "Black Power" leader Stokely Carmichael held a news conference in which, according to Associated Press, he urged blacks "to arm themselves with guns and take to the streets in retaliation,"[101] no one even proposed that he be indicted for incitement. This despite the fact that:

> Carmichael told a news conference he wants America to "kill off the real enemy."
> He said that there would be executions in the streets. . . . declared that violence that erupted in city after city across the nation after King was shot in Memphis is "just light stuff" when compared with "what will happen."
> "We have to retaliate," he added.[102]

Yet, if Carmichael or any other speaker in that mode had direct access to time on television in a community where emotions were running high and anger was directed at a particular target, we can be sure that inciting communication under those circumstances would be a strong candidate for punishment. Conceivably the *Brandenburg* criteria could all be met. But even then I would have to ask, Where is the lack of capacity on the part of the listeners to decide not to act as the speaker urges? Where is the control of will that can be described as *triggering* an *inevitable* chain of events? And how can we distinguish this kind of communication from a broadcast like that of "Born Innocent," where it is assumed (no doubt correctly) that there was no *intent* to incite to personal violence but where that was nevertheless the effect? Are we to examine the motives of every communicator whose words, pictures, or other symbolic acts may lead someone, somewhere, to go out and commit a crime? Again I would suggest that we are better off to hold listeners responsible for their own behavior than to enter on such a course.

The dangers of doing otherwise are well illustrated by the California appellate court opinion in the case of Irving Rubin's Los Angeles press conference calling for the assassination of American Nazis in connection with the Skokie affair. Rather than seeing the media nature of that event as making it more doubtful that the *Brandenburg* criteria of imminence and likelihood of audience violence could be met, the court managed to turn logic upside down. On the issue of the likelihood of illegal action ensuing, the majority reasoned:

> In past years free speech cases have presented two contrasting images—one, the classroom professor lecturing his students on the need to resort to terrorism to overthrow an oppressive government . . . the other, the street demonstrator in the town square urging a mob to burn down city hall and lynch the chief of police. . . . But in these days of the global village and the big trumpet the line between advocacy and solicitation has become blurred; and when advocacy of crime is combined with the staging of a media event, the prototype images tend to merge. . . . When, as here, political assassination is urged upon a greatly enlarged audience, the incitement to crime may possess a far greater capacity for civil disruption than the oral harangue of a mob in the town square, for the unseen audience of unknown listeners may contain another Oswald, or Ruby, or Sirhan, or Ray, or Bremer, or Moore, or Fromm, who may respond literally to the invitation of the speaker, regardless of the speaker's true intent. . . . Here we are concerned with the practicality and feasibility of the solicitation—was it likely to incite or produce violence? We cannot, of course, answer this question with assurance, for the effect of emotional appeals for political violence on the actions of inherently unstable personalities remains obscure. But we think it a reasonable inference that serious reportage by respectable news media of a reward for murder tends in some degree to give respectability to what otherwise would remain an underground solicitation of limited credibility addressed to a limited audience, and thereby tends to increase the risk and likelihood of violence. Undoubtedly, the prosecution's case would be stronger if a specific Nazi Party member had been named as the target for assassination and if the demonstration had been one scheduled to take place in Los Angeles rather than in Skokie. Yet murder remains a crime, whether or not a specified victim is identified as the target.[103]

As to the question of imminence, the court was even more ingenious, if less lucid.

> Imminence, a function of time, refers to an event which threatens to happen momentarily, is about to happen, or is at the point of hap-

pening. But time is a relative dimension and imminence a relative term, and the imminence of an event is related to its nature. A total eclipse of the sun next year is said to be imminent. An April shower thirty minutes away is not. The event which concerns us here was the scheduled Nazi Party demonstration and march to be held in Skokie in five weeks, an event which had already attracted national attention. We think that in terms of political assassination the demonstration could be said to have been proximate and imminent, just as a Papal visit to Belfast, a Soviet chief of state's visit to Rome, a Presidential campaign trip to Dallas, and a Presidential inauguration in Washington, can each be said to be proximate and imminent, even though occurrence may be some weeks away. . . . Additionally, the seriousness of the threatened crime, i.e. the nature of the lawless action solicited, bears some relationship to its imminence. Generally speaking, the more serious the crime the greater its time span. Murder, the most serious crime of all, carries the longest time span of any crime, as shown by the lack of any time limitation on its prosecution. . . .

We think solicitation of murder in connection with a public event of this notoriety, even though five weeks away, can qualify as incitement to imminent lawless action.[104]

One must be forgiven, I think, for wondering if anything is left to the meaning of the word "imminent" if the foregoing passage is taken seriously.

Turning to the Tokyo Roses and Axis Sallys who broadcast messages to our troops in time of war, urging them to lay down their arms, surely the danger of desertion as a result of their blandishments is neither imminent nor likely. It is far more probable that their broadcasts will become the butt of widespread jokes, as they did in World War II. If people who engage in such communication are to be punished for their actions, let it not be based on an incitement rationale but rather because we have decided that working for an enemy in wartime is treasonous and, therefore, that speech which is an integral part of such conduct is just as punishable as producing weapons or designing battle plans.

Finally, what of the communicator who is in direct physical proximity to emotionally involved listeners and urges them to immediate violation of the law, where such action is a real possibility, thus meeting the *Brandenburg* tests. This is the famous John Stuart Mill illustration of the "excited mob before the house of a corn-dealer." It is the instance of a John Kasper stirring audiences to resist with violence the desegregation of schools in Tennessee; of a Rap Brown at the opposite end of the spectrum in Cambridge, Maryland; of the Schliefers and Quinlans urging fellow strikers to break people's heads; or of a draft counselor advising a young man to flee the country to avoid conscription. These are the hardest cases of all to defend, for common sense seems to cry out for punishment. Abraham Lincoln expressed what I am sure would be the popular sentiment in most such circumstances:

> Long experience has shown that armies can not be maintained unless desertion shall be punished by the severe penalty of death. . . . Must I shoot a simple-minded soldier boy who deserts, while I must not touch a hair of a wily agitator who induces him to desert? This is none the less injurious when effected by getting a father, or brother, or friend, into a public meeting, and there working upon his feelings, till he is persuaded to write the soldier boy, that he is fighting in a bad cause, for a wicked administration of a contemptible government, too weak to arrest and punish him if he shall desert. I think that in such a case, to silence the agitator, and save the boy, is not only constitutional, but withal, a great mercy.[105]

Yet even under conditions of intense emotional involvement, where illegal responses or attempts are a clear and immediate likelihood, public sentiment is not always favorable to punishment for inciting speech. When Frank Collin and his band of two dozen neo-Nazis decided to call off their scheduled march in Skokie and, instead, to hold a demonstration the preceding day at the Kluczynski Federal Building in Chicago's downtown area, they were greeted there by a crowd of some 3,000 angry counterdemonstrators restrained only by police barricades. Persons in that assemblage were heard shouting "Death to the Nazi Pigs," "Death, Death to the Nazis," "Smash the Nazis," and "Kill the Nazis."[106] But no arrests were made for incitement to murder, nor did anyone even suggest that they should have been made. Either we are more serious about protecting the security of corn dealers, strikebreakers, school buildings, and the draft than we are about the lives of American Nazis, or else we are enabled to think more clearly about the incitement issue when our minds are not clouded by feelings of sympathy for the would-be victims of inciting speech. I am inclined to think the latter is closer to the truth.

What the anti-Nazi counterdemonstration in Chicago on June 24, 1978, so beautifully illustrated is that a society which cherishes freedom of expression, as well as law and order, need not sacrifice the first to maintain the second. The police department decided that not only would it put forth maximum effort to protect Frank Collin's right to be symbolically provocative but that those who hated everything he represents could also give full symbolic expression to their feelings, even to the point of shouting for his blood. The job of police on the scene was to see to it that none in the crowd *acted* on such inducements, and they did that with professional skill and success.

This was not an audience—as most are not—that was composed of morons or of robots who had been duped or drugged to act with violence, as might be wished by agitators. It consisted of ordinary, though angry, human beings with the capacity to control their own behavior, who knew that they could and would be arrested if they engaged in violent conduct, and that nobody should be blamed for that eventuality but themselves. Similarly, Abraham Lincoln's clever juxtaposition of adjectives—pitting *wily* agitators against *simple-minded* boys—may have suited his rhetorical purposes at that time but surely overestimated the powers of wile possessed by most persuaders just as certainly as it disparagingly underestimated the capacity for self-determination of the normal American youth.

A democratic society simply cannot, in proper keeping with its philosophy, operate on the premise that its citizens are incapable of resisting seductive inducements to criminal behavior. No one in Tennessee needed to heed John Kasper's call to blow up school buildings or Rap Brown's urgings to burn them in Maryland. No one was obliged to act on the urgings of Schliefer in Connecticut or Quinlan in New Jersey to break heads, or the inducements of a college dean in Ohio or a stepfather in Kansas to resist the draft. Those who undertook such drastic measures—and not all did—must have had powerful motivations of their own to do so, without which the incitements to which they were exposed from others would surely have fallen on deaf ears. If what they did constituted being triggered like a gun, or kindled like a fire, then I do not know what the difference is between a human being and an inanimate object. I regret that so much of the law of incitement seems blind to that distinction.

13 Conspiracies and Attempts

In the previous chapter, reference was made to the concept of inchoate crimes—those which encompass the incipient or preexecution stages of criminal conduct. Writers on the law ordinarily include three kinds of behavior in this category—solicitations (or incitements) to crime, criminal conspiracies, and criminal attempts. Incitement has been divided from the other two for separate consideration in this book because it *precedes* any decision to act illegally, and thus poses questions different from those that should be addressed in situations where the determination to commit a crime has already been made. The latter is the case in both a conspiracy, which is the planning of a crime, and an attempt, which is a crime that is tried but not completed. It shall be our purpose in this chapter to review the doctrines of conspiracy and attempt and, since both may involve a substantial amount of communicative behavior, to assess the extent to which punishment for such conduct may be incompatible with the First Amendment.

Conspiracy Law Described

Conspiracy was defined in common law as an agreement among two or more people to perform an unlawful act, or a lawful act by unlawful means.[1] In the precedent-setting *Poulterer's* case in the English Court of Star Chamber in 1611, it was held that mere agreement to commit a crime, whether the crime is executed or not, is an offense.[2] But contemporary statutory law typically requires, in addition to an agreement, that some "overt act in furtherance of the conspiracy be proved."[3] This may be a "noncriminal and relatively minor act . . . if it is in furtherance of the conspiracy,"[4] and it need be performed by only one member of the group.[5] Indeed, the U.S. Supreme Court long ago made it clear that an "overt act of one partner may be the act of all without any new agreement specifically directed to that act."[6] "Having joined in an unlawful scheme," the Court later added, a conspirator is in no position to escape responsibility for what happens "until he does some act to disavow or defeat the purpose" of the conspiracy.[7] Otherwise, so long as the conspiracy is in process, "he is still offending and we think, consciously offending."[8]

The Supreme Court has described some circumstances, however, in which an individual might *not* be held responsible for illegal acts committed by coconspirators.

> A different case would arise if the substantive offense committed by one of the conspirators was not in fact done in furtherance of the conspiracy, did not fall within the scope of the unlawful project, or was merely a part of the ramification of the plan which could not be reasonably foreseen as a necessary or natural consequence of the unlawful agreement.[9]

Unlike the law of attempt which, as we shall see shortly, is applicable only in situations where the crime which is undertaken is not completed, punishment for conspiracy is possible whether the illegal objective is accomplished or not. As the Supreme Court has said: "The commission of the substantive offense and a conspiracy to commit it are separate and distinct offenses. . . . a conviction for the conspiracy may be had though the substantive offense was completed. . . . and the plea of double jeopardy is no defense to a conviction for both offenses."[10]

Thus, prosecuting officials may use conspiracy law as a vehicle to seek punishment where people have planned but have not actually executed a collaborative crime or have not done enough for it to be considered an attempt, where they have jointly planned *and* executed a crime but there is insufficient evidence to charge them with its commission, where prosecutors are not confident they can win their case on the charges they bring for committing the crime itself and wish to hedge their bet with an additional indictment for conspiracy that may be easier to prove, or where they have a strong case on both scores and want to impose the maximum possible punishment.

It will be important to our later assessment of conspiracy law to understand some of the premises on which it is based. The first and most obvious, at least with respect to those situations where a crime has not yet been executed, is to head off the evil before it occurs and to deter others from participating in criminal plots. Beyond that, it is believed that collaborative efforts to engage in illegal action pose greater dangers to society than individual enterprises and thus necessitate more versatile tools of law enforcement. It is said, for example, that the group involvement of a conspiracy "reduces the probability that the defendant can stop the wheels he has set in motion."[11] Indeed, the possibility that individuals will even *want* to stop those wheels may be diminished by their having made a commitment to the group's decision.[12] As another essay has put it: "Sharing lends fortitude to purpose. The actor knows, moreover, that the future is no longer governed by his will alone; others may complete what he has had a hand in starting, even if he has a change of heart."[13]

Additional considerations are that the moral support of coconspirators may provide a buffer against the social pressures of society which might otherwise serve as a deterrent, and the division of labor made possible by group effort may increase the efficiency with which the contemplated crime can be executed.[14] Furthermore, if conspiracies were not punishable, it is suggested that this would create a "pervasive anxiety in society,"[15] presumably because people would be apprehensive that secret plotting of crimes was taking place around them without anything being done about it. The clandestine character of the typical conspiracy not only arouses fears of the unknown. It has also been argued that communication which occurs in secret is, by virtue of that very fact, not a part of the open marketplace of ideas which the First Amendment was designed to protect.[16]

An excerpt from an old U.S. Supreme Court opinion expresses the kind of feeling that is generated by conspiracies:

> For two or more to confederate and combine together to commit or cause to be committed a breach of the criminal laws is an offense of the gravest character, sometimes quite outweighing, in injury to the public, the mere commission of the contemplated crime. It involves deliberate plotting to subvert the laws, educating and preparing the conspirators for further and habitual criminal practices. And it is characterized by secrecy, rendering it difficult of detection, requiring more time for its discovery, and adding to the importance of punishing it when discovered.[17]

A final point which needs to be emphasized about conspiracy law is that it deals with contemplated criminal conduct at an earlier stage than does the law of attempts. One scholar has reported that a major justification which is given for laws against conspiracies is that they provide a needed supplement to the narrower doctrine of attempts.[18] Another author, in contrasting conspiracy with the other inchoate crimes of incitement and attempt, has written, "Among the trio, conspiracy is the most distant from the completed harm."[19]

These distinctions are well illustrated in a passage from the U.S. Supreme Court's plurality opinion in *Dennis v. U.S.*, which involved an indictment for violating the conspiracy section of the Smith Act:

> The mere fact that from the period 1945 to 1948 petitioners' activities did not result in an attempt to overthrow the Government by force and violence is of course no answer to the fact that there was a group

that was ready to make the attempt. The formation by petitioners of such a highly organized conspiracy, with rigidly disciplined members subject to call when the leaders, these petitioners, felt that the time had come for action ... convince us that their convictions were justified on this score. And this analysis disposes of the contention that a conspiracy to advocate, as distinguished from the advocacy itself, cannot be constitutionally restrained, because it comprises only the preparation. It is the existence of the conspiracy which creates the danger.... If the ingredients of the reaction are present, we cannot bind the government to wait until the catalyst is added.[20]

Attempts Described

Having already, in the foregoing section, previewed the law of attempts, we come now to a brief description of that concept in its own right. Thomas Emerson has characterized it succinctly as follows:

> The crime of attempt punishes conduct that has not yet reached its final stage because of some intervening event, failure, or impossibility. The law has always, of course, recognized some limits on how far back in the chain of events the interrupted conduct can be punished. It is agreed, for instance, that mere thought cannot be made a crime.... There is, in other words, a constitutional requirement of an "overt act." ... The overt act would have to consist of substantial action, not just incidental or trivial.[21]

Illinois law, illustrative of what Emerson suggests, provides: "A person commits an attempt when, with intent to commit a specific offense, he does any act which constitutes a substantial step toward the commission of that offense."[22]

One law review writer has expressed the concern that a clear line is not always drawn between attempt and solicitation, and he offers some examples of the distinction.[23] "It is one thing," he says, "for A to solicit B to shoot C and another matter to have A shoot at C and miss him."[24] He then describes a 1902 British case, *Rex v. Krause,* in which a letter soliciting murder was sent to Johannesburg, South Africa, but never received. The writer was convicted of *attempt* to commit the crime of *solicitation.* The law review author regards that handling of the case as appropriately differentiating between attempt and solicitation. However, a second decision, this time in New York in 1843, did not, in the reviewer's judgment, properly distinguish between the two phenomena. The defendant, who had solicited another person to burn a barn and had provided a match with which to do it, was found guilty of *attempt.* The author argues that the charge should have been for solicitation, since attempt, which is a more serious offense, was not present in this case. He explains: "The solicitation is less likely than the attempt to result in the crime of arson as the solicitation involves the contingency of the solicitant being unwilling to become a party to the crime."[25]

Professor Emerson, after defining attempt, observes that "there has been very little effort to mesh the law of attempt with the law of the First Amendment."[26] The same has been said of conspiracy law, which developed long before the elaboration of contemporary First Amendment doctrine.[27] We must, therefore, take a careful and critical look at these inchoate crimes to assess their compatibility with a vigorous system of freedom of speech.

Conspiracy Law Evaluated

It will simplify our analysis and evaluation of conspiracy law if we deal separately with two distinct kinds of plots—those in which the objective is *action* which would clearly be illegal if executed, such as robbery, arson, or murder, and those where the objective is *communication* which might be punishable if consummated—so-called speech crimes such as defamation, obscenity, fraud, intimidation, or incitement to illegal conduct. It is this second branch of conspiracy law which has drawn the most fire from critical scholars. Since it is the more vulnerable of the two, we will address it first, and then move on to the greater First Amendment dilemma involved in conspiracies directed to indisputably unlawful action.

The central problem with prosecutions for conspiracies to commit speech crimes is that until the communication has actually been consummated it is usually impossible for either conspirators or law enforcement officials to know if the symbolic conduct is, in fact, going to be illegal. It is characteristic of most speech offenses, as we have seen repeatedly throughout this book, that they cannot be judged out of context. Ordinarily they become sufficiently harmful to be punished only when certain effects upon others are produced, and that is dependent on the particular circumstances in which the expression occurs and upon the dispositions of its recipients. This is one reason that prior restraints on speech are so frowned upon—and a prosecution for conspiracy to speak, at least in those instances where the objective of the conspiracy has not been achieved, is a form of prior restraint.

This problem is most clearly illustrated in cases where the objective of the group effort is the advocacy of illegal action, and it is in just such cases that we have had an abundance of American experience with conspiracy prosecutions. *Goldman v. U.S.*[28] was one of the early Supreme Court decisions of this genre, upholding a conviction for conspiracy to urge resistance to the draft in World War I. Other early landmark incitement cases—such as *Schenck v. U.S., Abrams v. U.S.,* and *Gitlow v. New*

York discussed in the previous chapter—were either exclusively or partially based on conspiracy-to-advocate-illegal-action charges, as were *Dennis v. U.S.* and *Yates v. U.S.* of the post–World War II era.

Of more recent vintage, at the lower court level, were two cases which attracted widespread national attention—*U.S. v. Spock*[29] and *U.S. v. Dellinger.*[30] In the former, charges were brought against a group of five persons, including the pediatrician Benjamin Spock and the Yale University chaplain William Sloan Coffin, for violating the section of the Selective Service Act which made it illegal to conspire to "counsel, aid and abet" resistance to the draft. It was solely a conspiracy trial. In *Dellinger,* the Federal Anti-Riot Act of 1968 was invoked for the first time, leading to the so-called Chicago Seven Conspiracy Trial, based on charges of crossing state lines to incite riots at the Democratic National Convention in 1968, *plus* charges of conspiracy to commit that same offense. Although all of the defendants in these two cases ultimately went unpunished, some on procedural grounds and others on evidentiary grounds, the court decisions did not question the constitutionality of the underlying conspiracy laws. The closest anyone came to that was a dissenting opinion in the court of appeals in the *Spock* case which offered the suggestion that conspiracy law is an unconstitutional weapon when directed against agreements where "(1) the effort was completely public; (2) the issues were all in the public domain; (3) the group was ill-defined . . . ; (4) the purposes in the 'agreement' are both legal and illegal; and (5) the need for additional evidence to inculpate . . . is recognized."[31]

One last example involving charges of a conspiracy to engage in communicative behavior is of interest because, unlike those already described, the speech "crime" which was the objective of the "plot" was not the incitement of others to illegal action but the distribution of an allegedly obscene movie, *Deep Throat.* Harry Reems, the film's star, along with eleven others who were involved in its production, distribution, and exhibition, were charged and found guilty in federal district court in Memphis, Tennessee, in 1976, of conspiring to violate a provision of federal law which prohibits the transport in interstate commerce of obscene material. The convictions were overturned on appeal because the trial court had employed erroneous standards for determining obscenity, but the basic validity of this kind of charge of conspiracy to commit a speech offense was not questioned.[32]

As noted earlier, critics of the use of conspiracy law when a group's objective is an alleged speech offense are not difficult to find, in part for reasons I have already indicated. One writer, for instance, has said:

> Respect for first amendment standards would seem to require that
> criminality turn on more than a bare prediction of both the nature and

probable consequences of words not yet uttered. . . . The justification for intervening through the criminal process in the case of unexecuted conspiracy to murder, for example, is that should the conspirators carry out their plans immediate and irreparable harm is likely to result to the victim. The case of conspiracy to commit a speech crime is hardly comparable.[33]

But even if illegal communication has been consummated, says another law review article, conspiracy is an inappropriate punishment for those who planned it: "Whenever the object is unlawful expression, the first amendment should bar the use of conspiracy law whether the objective has been accomplished or not."[34] This should be so, the article goes on, because without knowing the precise circumstances in which the ultimate communication will occur, "[a]t the agreement stage . . . an individual might be unaware that he is involving himself in a conspiracy and that the purpose of it is illegal."[35]

With respect to group efforts to engage in the particular speech "crime" of incitement, the critics find conspiracy law especially inappropriate. One essay argues that "to charge a speech conspiracy is to load one inchoate offense upon another."[36] A second maintains that "unlawful expression is itself an inchoate offense. The harm the legislature may act against, if there be any, lies not in the speech itself, but the actions which the expression may precipitate."[37]

What these criticisms add up to is a recognition that while all conspiracies, whether their goal be action or speech, are at least once removed from immediate harms which society has a right to prevent and punish, conspiracies *to speak* illegally are *twice* removed from such harms. Not only must the planned expression be consummated, which it may or may not be, but it then must have a harmful impact on others, which it may or may not have. Surely society's legitimate interest in restraining substantive evils can be met without resort to such a tool, which has so great a potential for the inhibition and punishment of innocent freedom of expression.

We come now to the more difficult question of whether conspiracies to commit crimes of action—like robbery, murder, or violent overthrow of the government—can legitimately lay any claim to First Amendment protection because so much that is involved in them is communicative behavior—from the making of the agreement itself, to the discussion of possible strategies and briefing of the participants, to the final giving of the "go ahead" signal. It would appear at first glance that this kind of symbolic conduct is no more entitled to First Amendment consideration than speech which is an integral part of already commenced illegal action, such as the communication between bank robbers during the course of a holdup. But there are some significant differences which should give us pause.

In the first place, as to cases where the objective of the conspiracy has not been consummated or has not even reached the stage of actual attempt, one has no sure way of knowing that the alleged conspirators were not simply indulging in fantasies and catharsis. Although it is true that most conspiracy statutes require, in addition to the communication of an agreement, the commission of some overt act in furtherance of the conspiracy, that requirement may be satisfied by still another act of communication, like making a phone call or sending a letter. Even what appears to be traditional First Amendment expression, such as a press conference in the *Spock* case, has been used to satisfy the overt act test. Despite Justice Holmes's statement that the purpose of the overt act criterion is to assure that "the conspiracy has passed beyond words and is on foot,"[38] the requirement "has tended to become a fiction or be disregarded in practice by the jury."[39]

Even when those who make an agreement to commit a crime are deadly serious in their intentions, they may be so lacking in the resources necessary to set it "on foot" that their communication about it might as well be sheer fantasy. Yet if one minor, and perhaps noncriminal, step is taken which the law might regard as an overt act in furtherance of their objective, they may find themselves tried and convicted of criminal conspiracy. Thus speech, divorced from any actual harm to society, would have been punished.

But what of those conspiracies which do reach the stage of a substantial attempt at consummation or are, in fact, consummated? The members of the group who actively participate in the attempt or in the commission of the substantive crime itself are, of course, liable to punishment for those offenses. What conspiracy law allows, besides *additional* punishment for the actual participants in the illegal conduct, is for sanctions to be applied against those who may have helped lay the plans and who lent their moral support but who were not involved in the ultimate stages nor directly enough linked to those acts to be found guilty as accessories to the crime. The danger here is that some of those individuals, like some persons who participate in an uncompleted conspiracy, may not have been serious about carrying the crime to its conclusion, or may have assumed that the group was incapable of its fulfillment but enjoyed sharing fantasies about it. Or, they may have intended to agree only to lawful objectives and lawful methods that were part of a mix of legal and illegal efforts. Their guilt, in that event, would be solely by association. As the court of appeals said of the circumstances in *U.S. v. Spock:*

...the means or intermediate objectives encompassed both legal and illegal activity, without any clear indication, initially, as to who intended what. This intertwining of legal and illegal aspects, the public setting of the agreement and its political purposes, and the loose confederation of possibly innocent and possibly guilty participants raise the most serious First Amendment problems.[40]

Spock also exposed another weakness in the rationale for punishing conspiracies—the assumption that the First Amendment is inapplicable because the communication which occurs in conspiracies is out of the public's view. But that was not the case in *Spock,* and it is not an invariant characteristic of all collaborative planning to engage in illegal behavior. Even when the goal of an alleged conspiracy is action rather than speech, such as an effort to forcibly disrupt the desegregation of a school or the construction of a nuclear power plant, the agreement and the discussion of its implementation may be entirely in the open.

What is more, the premise that conversations which take place in private are, by virtue of that fact, not a part of the marketplace of ideas which the First Amendment was designed to protect, is itself a dubious proposition. Everything that occurs outside the public view is not necessarily malevolent, nor does it take more than a small and intimate group of buyers and sellers to constitute a marketplace. This is not to say that plotting to assassinate a president is as benign as scheming to elect one. It is simply to suggest that the secrecy (or privacy) of communication is not per se a valid basis for denying it First Amendment consideration. This was clearly settled by the U.S. Supreme Court in 1979 when it invalidated the dismissal of a junior high school teacher in Mississippi for her private complaints to the building principal. Overturning a judgment of the U.S. Court of Appeals for the Fifth Circuit, the Supreme Court's unanimous opinion declared: "We are unable to agree that private expression of one's views is beyond constitutional protection."[41]

Some of the other assumptions underlying the law of conspiracy are also questionable. While it is no doubt true that "sharing lends fortitude to purpose," and that persons who commit themselves to a group effort may thereby experience a diminution in their incentive or ability to turn things around, it is also true that a group enterprise is more vulnerable to subversion than the plans of an individual. The larger the number of people involved, the greater is the possibility that someone may defect and expose the plot or that they may sow seeds of doubt within the group which could lead to reconsideration of the project.[42]

Also, it is not invariably true that the division of labor made possible by collective action poses greater dangers to society than do individuals acting alone. It is a well established finding of empirical research in group behavior that, while some tasks are performed more effectively by groups than by individuals, others are not. It depends entirely on the characteristics of the particular activity in question.[43] One law review article has noted, for example, that "in the case of conspiracies to commit minor criminal offenses, in which a lone wolf may operate as efficiently as a complex organization, the conspiracy concept seems inapplicable."[44]

Because of the doubts which have been raised about the assumptions on which conspiracy law is based, and because of the possible dangers it poses to innocent speech, the question that naturally follows is: "Who needs it?" Judge Learned Hand long ago described conspiracy law as the "darling of the modern prosecutor's nursery"[45]—so that is apparently one constituency. Another writer has suggested that conspiracies have great appeal to paranoia,[46] so that provides a second source of support. And a third critic contends, "Conspiracy gives the courts a means of deciding difficult questions without thinking about them."[47] Thus lazy judges might also mourn its passing.

But these are hardly good reasons for retaining what Phillip Johnson, a professor of law, has called "The Unnecessary Crime of Conspiracy."[48] Johnson does not advocate its abolition without offering what seem to be quite adequate alternatives. In view of the fact that most conspiracy charges are not brought about until after the criminal objective has been accomplished,[49] the law of complicity or accessorial liability would, according to Johnson, take care of a good part of the problem. The U.S. Criminal Code is clear that whoever "aids" or "abets" an offense is "punishable as a principal,"[50] and this would seem to suffice in cases where a crime has been consummated. As for those less frequent cases where conspiracy law is invoked against the *inchoate* crimes it was primarily designed to address, Johnson proposes that a rigorously defined and enforced law of attempt would be enough to protect society against those who actually participate in serious and substantial, but incomplete, steps toward the commission of illegal acts.

The Law of Attempt Evaluated

If the law of attempt is to serve in part as a substitute for that of conspiracy, it obviously cannot be assigned to the total oblivion proposed here for the latter offense. But before we grant it an entirely clean bill of health, we must recognize that, like conspiracies, attempts can be directed to the commission of so-called speech crimes as well as to crimes of action. One of the examples cited earlier in describing the law of attempt was just such a case—that of the abortive letter to South Africa soliciting a murder. Other hypotheticals can easily be conjured up—a libelous advertisement which one tries, without success, to place in a newspaper; an obscene book which one endeavors, but fails, to sell; or a fraudulent mail solicitation which is interrupted at the Post Office before distribution. We must rely on imaginary rather than real illustrations because the law of attempt has not, in practice, produced the abundance of prosecutions for inchoate speech offenses that the law of conspiracy has generated. Perhaps that is because the law of attempt is only applicable where an offense has not been consummated, and even in that realm it does not allow the tempting latitude to prosecutors provided by conspiracy law.

Be that as it may, I would argue that punishment should not be administered to attempted but aborted speech crimes, for the same reasons that conspiracies to commit speech offenses should not be punishable. Until an act of communication has been consummated, we do not ordinarily know its context or effects, and without that knowledge we cannot be confident it will be illegal. Punishment for an attempt to communicate is a prior restraint on speech which assumes not only that the speech, if uninterrupted, would have occurred precisely in the form attempted but that it would also have a harmful impact on others—assumptions which cannot usually be verified in advance. If speech is to be punished at all, under the narrow exceptions discussed in previous chapters of this book, let it be after the fact, not in anticipation of what may or may not happen.

In contrast to attempts to engage in what, if completed, might be considered speech crimes, substantial attempts to *act* illegally raise no bona fide First Amendment questions. The participants in such action pose a serious danger to society, even though talk may play some part, large or small, in their behavior. Just as expression which is an integral part of *ongoing* criminal conduct cannot lay claim to constitutional protection, so communication which is integral to a criminal attempt should similarly be punishable.

In sum, I propose that a healthy respect for the First Amendment would lead us to take the following steps:

1. Abolish conspiracy law entirely.
2. Abolish the law of attempts to commit speech offenses.
3. Maintain the law of attempts to commit crimes of action.
4. Maintain accessorial liability for those who are actual participants in attempts to commit crimes of action as well as for those who aid or abet the final consummation of criminal conduct.

Such a regime would, quite properly I believe, exempt from punishment those who conspire or attempt to commit speech offenses, and those who engage in plots to commit crimes of action but who do not themselves participate sufficiently in the implementation stages to be found guilty as accessories to the attempt or to the crime itself.

Part  Government Involvement in the Communication Marketplace

14

Facilitation of Citizen Expression

The focus of attention thus far in this book has been on the various kinds of communicative stimuli which are thought to be harmful to others and which may thus necessitate some measure of legal restraint upon the communicator. We shift now to a very different perspective. Our concern in these next four chapters will be with the impact on our society's communication processes of government policies and actions which are not designed for the primary purpose of restricting freedom of expression—indeed may in some instances have precisely the opposite intention—but may nevertheless be inhibitory of a free marketplace of ideas. We shall examine the needs and justifications for these policies and actions, the gains as well as losses to freedom of communication resulting from them, and possible alternatives which might provide a healthier environment for the nurturance of a freely functioning citizenry.

We shall look first at what may be characterized as "affirmative action programs" by government to facilitate and expand opportunities for the expression of a wide diversity of views. We shall then review governmental actions that compel communication from those who may not wish to speak, and governmental policies that withhold information without which it is difficult to speak. Finally we shall assess the impact on our system of freedom of expression of government itself as perhaps the single most influential communicator of all.

Providing and Regulating a Public Forum

Affirmative action by the government to enhance citizen expression begins, at the simplest level, with making available public sidewalks, streets, and parks for speeches or demonstrations, and providing police protection and traffic control for such events. This maintenance of a public forum in outdoor settings where people gather in the course of their daily affairs—even at the cost of some disruption in normal patterns of traffic—has long been recognized as a minimal contribution expected of the state to the facilitation of a marketplace of ideas. Justice Owen Roberts enunciated the principle in a 1939 U.S. Supreme Court decision:

> Wherever the title of streets and parks may rest, they have immemorially been held in trust for the use of the public and, time out of mind, have been used for purposes of assembly, communicating thoughts between citizens and discussing public questions. Such use of the streets and public places has, from ancient times, been a part of the privileges, immunities, rights, and liberties of citizens. The privilege of a citizen of the United States to use the streets and parks for the communication of views on national questions may be regulated in the interest of all; it is not absolute, but relative, and must be exercised in subordination to the general comfort and convenience, and in consonance with peace and good order; but it must not, in the guise of regulation, be abridged or denied.[1]

Although Justice Roberts was speaking for only a plurality of the Court when he uttered those words, the principle he expressed was reiterated by later majorities and has come to be accepted as the prevailing precedent in this field.[2]

If local governments wish to do so, they may take more than these minimal and ordinarily inexpensive steps to provide a public forum. They may erect platforms and bandshells in some of their parks, and even equip them with loudspeaker systems. They may build municipal auditoriums, convention halls, and stadiums and rent them out for public use. The governing boards of public libraries and public schools may also make their meeting rooms and auditoriums accessible to community groups when those facilities are not otherwise occupied.

Whether government is minimally or maximally involved in maintaining these kinds of public forums, there are a number of First Amendment questions which arise with respect to the way that it handles its management role. The first, and easiest to dispense with, is whether there can be any selectivity practiced on the basis of the ideas or points of view of groups seeking to use those facilities. Obviously the First Amendment, as well as the Equal Protection Clause of the Fourteenth Amendment, prohibits such discrimination by the state. The U.S. Supreme Court put the point succinctly in a 1972 decision:

> ...under the Equal Protection Clause, not to mention the First Amendment itself, government may not grant the use of a forum to people whose views it finds acceptable, but deny use to those wishing to express less favored or more controversial views. And it may not select which issues are worth discussing or debating in public facilities.... Once a forum is opened up to assembly or speaking by

some groups, government may not prohibit others from assembling or speaking on the basis of what they intend to say. Selective exclusions from a public forum may not be based on content alone, and may not be justified by reference to content alone.[3]

The question becomes more subtle, however, when the selectivity which government seeks to exercise is based not on the point of view of any particular group but rather on some general category of *kinds* of groups to which an excluded organization may belong. This has been a problem not so much with regard to outdoor gatherings, where government has generally avoided such discrimination, but with respect to the use of municipal meeting halls and stadiums, where governing boards have sometimes sought to distinguish between permissible uses—such as for cultural, sports, entertainment, and "noncontroversial" civic events—and impermissible uses—such as for political and religious assemblies.

The issue which must be faced in these circumstances is whether the categorization is reasonably related to some valid social interest or whether it invidiously discriminates on unjustifiable grounds. A Bill of Rights Committee of the American Bar Association once articulated the problem this way:

> An essential difference between a city and the private owner is that the latter can admit outsiders and exclude others on any whimsical basis he wishes. But surely a city has no such right. . . . A city may regulate reasonably but may not arbitrarily discriminate. This does not mean that the city is unable to make any choices. Thus it can keep adults out of children's playgrounds. But it cannot keep out red-headed children while admitting youthful blonds and brunettes, nor can it limit the park benches to members of one political party.[4]

In keeping with this principle, it would seem permissible, as has been indicated in an earlier chapter, for a municipality to set aside *some* of its parklands exclusively for recreational purposes, so long as ample and conveniently located park sites remain available for free speech activities. It would also seem justified, if demands for the space warranted it, to construct and earmark a stadium solely for sports events, an auditorium entirely for musical and dramatic performances, and a convention hall exclusively for commercial exhibitions. Needless to say, however, if one exception were made for a political gathering, the dike would be broken, and the exclusion of other such groups would no longer be constitutionally acceptable.

What of a public library or school which, desiring to maintain an image of nonpartisanship and serenity, decides to rent its auditorium only to "noncontroversial" groups whose meetings will not stir dispute in the community, and to exclude from eligibility all political, religious, or cause-oriented organizations? This is precisely what the library board of Evanston, Illinois, chose to do when it opened a new building, with a large meeting room on its second floor, in 1961. Aside from the curious set of values which would lead an educational institution to think that controversy is inimical to its purposes (unhappily not an uncommon view), and aside from what should be obvious to everyone, that renting out a public hall in no way carries with it government endorsement of ideas which may be expressed there by the users, there is the further difficulty of defining in any fair and reasonable way what constitutes a "noncontroversial" group. It was precisely this rock on which the Evanston library's policy foundered. Having on more than one occasion permitted its auditorium to be used for a presumably noncontroversial annual mock United Nations conference, sponsored by a number of local community organizations, the library board found itself with a suddenly controversial group on its hands when an anti-U.N. organization decided to protest against the meeting. After a first, timid inclination to solve the problem by withdrawing its meeting hall from use by the U.N. conference, the board thought better of the matter and changed its general rules instead. Wisely so, I believe, since noncontroversiality is hardly a category one can rely on for any stability. What is a noncontroversial group at one moment, or in some people's eyes—such as an environmental lobby or a wildlife protection society—may be highly controversial at another point in time, or in the eyes of different beholders.

Finally on this point, it has sometimes been argued that a public institution not only *may*, but *must*, exclude religious organizations from among those who are permitted to use its meeting facilities, on the grounds that to allow such usage would violate the First Amendment prohibition against the "establishment of religion."[5] Again, there is the flaw in this argument that renting an auditorium to a religious group on the same basis as it is rented to all other groups is in some way an endorsement or underwriting of that religion such as to constitute its "establishment." That might be a genuine problem were a school to allow a religious institution to use an auditorium at little or no cost for weekly services on a long-term basis, thus providing de facto, and constitutionally impermissible, financial support by relieving the organization of any need to build or otherwise find its own meeting place.[6] But for an occasional single meeting, or for a limited period of time while a group may be refurbishing its own quarters after a fire, it would seem an unduly harsh interpretation of the separation-of-church-and-state principle to single out religious organizations as unqualified to meet in public auditoriums.

What is more, to do so entangles the government in the same definitional problems as those attending the concept of noncontroversiality. What is a religious group and what is a religious meeting? Would a
nonsectarian play or concert that happened to be sponsored by a church
group be considered a religious activity ineligible to be performed on a
rented school stage? Is a session on Transcendental Meditation a religious assembly? And what of a community meeting that is cosponsored
by a combination of religious and secular organizations? Surely if
exemption of religious institutions from taxation is not a violation of the
Establishment Clause of the First Amendment—a far more dubious
proposition which has been overwhelmingly affirmed by the U.S. Supreme Court[7]—the lesser degree of subsidy afforded by the availability
of public meeting halls on terms that are identical to those for all other
groups hardly seems worthy of serious question.

Beyond the issue of selectivity in the kinds of groups that may make
use of a public forum, there is the question of the legitimacy of so-called
time, place, and manner regulations. Should the government, to draw
on an analogy suggested by Alexander Meiklejohn,[8] serve as a "moderator" to maintain a kind of Robert's Rules of Order for use of the
public forum, insuring that two or more people do not try to speak at the
same time or that two or more groups do not attempt to hold parades
simultaneously on the same street or in competition with rush-hour
traffic? Meiklejohn's answer was clearly "Yes," as has been that, consistently, of the U.S. Supreme Court.[9] Although I might quarrel with
attempted restrictions on "manner," as intrusions into the arena of
speech content,[10] and would suggest the amputation of that third finger
of the traditional "time, place and manner" trilogy, it is difficult to see
how reasonable regulations of time and place alone can be objectionable.
On the contrary, just as traffic rules increase everyone's overall freedom
of movement by imposing restraints on particular behaviors—such as
driving on the wrong side of the street or crashing red lights—so time
and place allocations in the public forum, assuming the impartiality of a
good "moderator," make it possible for all who wish to express themselves to get their fair chance.

Implicit in the foregoing, it should be recognized, is the right of government to require advance notification of, and perhaps reservations
for, the use of public places where there may be competing demands for
the space. Thus the courts have regularly upheld, as compatible with the
First Amendment, ordinances which require permits or licenses to hold
a parade in the streets or a rally in the park, so long as there is no
evidence of discriminatory treatment of applicants, and so long as the
criteria for the granting or denial of permission are clearly spelled out in
the law.[11]

But further complexities arise. How much advance notice is reasonable? If the required period is too long, spontaneity and timeliness of expression may be rendered impossible. If it is too short, the police may not be able to make the necessary traffic and safety arrangements. What may be a reasonable notice requirement for a parade down the main street or for the use of a heavily booked municipal auditorium may be quite unreasonable for a small gathering on an open plaza in front of a city hall. Each regulation has to be evaluated for reasonableness in its own particular context; the number of variables forecloses any other course.

What about a requirement, adopted in the interest of protecting the security of people in their homes, that door-to-door canvassers for political, social, and religious causes must register with the police, must obtain identification cards to carry with them or to display on their clothing, and perhaps must even check in at the police station each day on which they wish to canvass. The U.S. Supreme Court has struck down one such ordinance only because of its vagueness in describing who was required to register and how they were supposed to do it.[12] At the same time, the majority indicated its lack of objection to more clearly and narrowly defined regulations of this sort. Justices Brennan and Marshall concurred in finding the particular ordinance invalid, but had other problems with it in addition to its vagueness. They expressed concern that a registration or identification requirement for door-to-door canvassing makes anonymity impossible and may, by imposing undue burdens and obstacles, discourage such healthy First Amendment activities as the participation of volunteer canvassers in political campaigns.[13]

By standards of reasonableness, both majority and concurring opinions, though taking very different positions, might seem quite plausible. How, then, does one resolve such a dilemma, which apparently springs from the assignment of different priorities to the conflicting values involved. If one focuses primarily on the prevention of possible crimes and cares relatively less about maintaining an uninhibited public forum, it will seem sensible to establish a system of close surveillance over door-to-door canvassers. If, on the other hand, one values an unfettered marketplace of ideas more highly, one is likely to conclude, as I do, that the marginal gain in security provided by such surveillance is not worth its cost in terms of the chilling effect on expression which is likely to result.

Another matter which raises thorny First Amendment questions is the interposition of financial barriers to the securing of a permit for the use of public facilities. It is common practice, when public auditoriums are made available to private groups, for a rental fee to be charged which covers the costs of lighting, heating, and custodial services. No one, to

my knowledge, has ever challenged the constitutionality of such practices, nor would such a challenge seem at all justified. Likewise, it is not
unusual for fees to be charged for parade, rally, or sound truck permits,
and for such assessments to be upheld by reviewing courts so long as
they are reasonably related in amount to expenses "incident to the administration of the Act and to the maintenance of public order in the
matter licensed."[14]

Where the problem becomes difficult is when governmental bodies try
to shift to would-be communicators the financial burdens of large-scale
police protection, the cleanup of litter left by attending crowds, or insurance against physical injuries and property damage that may occur in
connection with a communication event—costs which are clearly beyond
the means of most private individuals and groups who seek to exercise
their First Amendment rights in the public forum. It should be seen as
one of the costs of operating local government that these services are
extended to the citizenry without charge, just as we send the fire department to homes or places of business which catch fire and do not
follow up the visit with a bill.

Not only would the cost of paying for such services be financially
prohibitive for most people who wish to communicate in public places,
but a requirement of liability insurance, in particular, has the practical
effect of excluding many extremist groups from the public forum, since
no insurance company will write a policy for them—either because their
views are anathema to the insurer or because a public demonstration in
the face of hostile crowds is simply too poor a financial risk. This was
precisely the issue that first gave rise to the proposed march into Skokie,
Illinois, by neo-Nazi leader Frank Collin. Collin had been blocked from
gathering in his home territory of Marquette Park by the Chicago Park
District's enforcement of an ordinance which conditioned the issuance of
permits for assemblies of more than 75 persons upon the obtaining of
$100,000/$300,000 in public liability insurance and $50,000 in property
damage insurance—policies which Collin was unable to secure even if he
could have afforded them. Looking for action elsewhere while his legal
challenge to this ordinance was pending in federal court, his attention
was drawn to Skokie by virtue of a nearly identical insurance rule governing the parks of that municipality. It was to protest against the Skokie
park insurance requirement that Collin announced his intention to
march up and down on the sidewalk in front of their village hall, and it
was in the wake of his later federal court victory over the Chicago Park
District insurance ordinance that he called off the march in Skokie.[15]

Although Federal District Court Judge George Leighton found that
Collin's First Amendment rights had been violated by the Chicago Park
District and ordered the issuance of a permit to him without the posting

of any insurance, the judge stopped short of declaring *all* insurance or indemnity requirements unconstitutional.[16] Just as a federal district court in Houston, Texas, several years earlier had struck down as discriminatory a particular insurance requirement without calling into question the concept of insurance requirements per se,[17] so Judge Leighton left to the creative imagination of municipal lawyers the possibility of devising an indemnification scheme, perhaps administered in a nondiscriminatory way by the city itself, which would hold communicators liable for injuries or damages resulting from their events. The door was left open—unfortunately, I believe—for the operation of a heckler's veto on speech via the indirect route of establishing prohibitively expensive costs for addressing hostile audiences in public places.

The relationship of money to the exercise of First Amendment rights has arisen as an issue not only where municipalities have attempted to put a price tag on rallies and parades but also where they have sought to circumscribe the ability of solicitors for political, religious, and charitable causes to raise funds while seeking supporters or converts. Perhaps the most ingenious of such regulations is that which was designed to dampen the activities of the Hare Krishna in airport terminal buildings. Having lost the constitutional battle to entirely exclude these unwelcome solicitors from terminal lobbies, a more limited remedy was devised which won court approval in at least one U.S. judicial circuit.[18] This was a rule which provided that money could be collected only at booths or tables set up for this purpose at designated locations, thus requiring solicitors who wished to raise funds to persuade the targets of their communication not only to listen to their pitch but to walk with them to a stand, which might be some distance away, to purchase literature or make a donation. The effectiveness of this device in achieving its goal was demonstrated at the O'Hare International Airport in Chicago where the Hare Krishna disappeared from the scene after an ordinance of this type was enacted by the city council late in 1979 and put into effect shortly thereafter.

A second similarly complex scheme to regulate the collection of money for social causes met with a less friendly reception in the courts, culminating in a U.S. Supreme Court opinion which implicitly cast a shadow over the airport regulations just described as well as explicitly striking down the ordinance at issue in the case.[19] The particular legislation in question was a requirement of the Village of Schaumburg in Illinois that charitable organizations must seek a permit to engage in the door-to-door solicitation of funds and that in order to obtain such a permit they would have to submit proof that at least 75 percent of the money they collected was used directly for charitable purposes other than administrative expenses, staff salaries, and salaries or commissions paid to the solicitors. Agreeing with the district court and the circuit court of appeals that the ordinance constituted an unacceptable burden on the exercise of First Amendment rights, the Supreme Court said:

> Soliciting financial support is undoubtedly subject to reasonable regulation but the latter must be undertaken with due regard for the reality that solicitation is characteristically intertwined with informative and perhaps persuasive speech seeking support for particular causes or for particular views on economic, political or social issues, and for the reality that without solicitation the flow of such information and advocacy would likely cease. Canvassers in such contexts are necessarily more than solicitors for money.[20]

The Supreme Court was certainly correct in perceiving that the ability to raise money for a cause is essential to its survival in our society and that to segregate fund raising from ideological advocacy in fact curtails the effectiveness of both. In response to the claim put forth by the Village of Schaumburg, as it has been with respect to Hare Krishna activity in airport terminals, that their restriction was needed to reduce the possibility of fraudulent solicitations, the Supreme Court wisely pointed out that penal remedies are available for fraud and that disclosure requirements are another available prophylactic measure less burdensome on First Amendment rights.

As for the argument which has been made in defense of the airport regulations that money transactions are more likely to interfere with the flow of traffic in a terminal lobby than mere conversations or the display of placards, it must be said that this is a dubious proposition and a rather simple empirical question for which an answer ought to be easily attainable by observational research. If it is indeed true that monetary transactions are slightly more space-and-time consuming than verbal interactions, the appropriate solution would seem to be to move *both* together to areas that are somewhat less congested than to impose radically more severe limitations on fund raising than on ideological advocacy. If the real motivation for segregating the collection of money from verbal blandishments is to give airport passengers a greater opportunity to resist the pressure to make an immediate and unreflective contribution, that is a paternalistic role which the First Amendment forbids the government from playing.

Another complex question which has arisen, this time in connection with the use of school auditoriums, is whether state action in violation of antidiscrimination provisions of the Fourteenth Amendment or of federal civil rights laws has occurred if a group using the assembly hall advocates racial, religious, or sexual discrimination; has a discriminatory membership policy; or excludes people from its meetings in the school auditorium on the basis of race, creed, or sex.

The first of these possibilities is the simplest to deal with. No one would suggest that the speech of a private citizen advocating discrimination, delivered from a soapbox, becomes state action because that soapbox happens to be located in a public park or on a public sidewalk. Moving the speech indoors and putting it on a rented school stage should not alter the principle. If there is any misunderstanding on the part of the public as to whether school officials endorse the speaker's views because they are expressed on school property, that can easily be clarified by a disclaimer notice. The solution is not to deny the speaker a platform to which he or she would otherwise be entitled.

The second circumstance, in which a group that seeks to hold a meeting in a public auditorium has a discriminatory membership policy, raises questions which are not essentially different from those in the first instance. Clearly such a group could not be denied access to public parks for the holding of rallies, to the streets for its parades, or to the steps of the capitol building for its speeches, and permitting those uses does not imply state approval of the organization's discriminatory membership policy. Moving their meetings inside to a rented public auditorium does not suddenly implicate the state in the group's membership practices anymore than occasional rentals by a religious society establishes a state church. There is at least one court decision to this effect, in an Arlington, Virginia, case involving the National Socialist White People's Party, where a U.S. circuit court of appeals rejected the argument that a discriminatory membership policy by the would-be user group is a valid basis for denying access to a public auditorium.[21]

Does the question become significantly different when a group which is using a public auditorium wishes to exclude people from attendance at its meeting because it does not like their sex, religion, or the color of their hair or skin? I think it does. Again resorting to the analogy of an outdoor assembly, when communicators decide to carry their messages to the streets and parks they cannot pick and choose who will be in their audience. Anyone who is on the street or in the park can stop to listen. It should be the same if their gathering is moved to an indoor public facility. If they want to have a meeting solely or secretly for whites or for blacks, for Jews or for Gentiles, for men or for women, for their own members or supporters, let them find a private meeting hall and not expect the taxpayers to facilitate their exclusionary gatherings. A federal district court in New York agreed essentially with this position in 1973 when it found that a meeting in a school auditorium of a black teachers' association which, with the knowledge of the building principal, had ejected white teachers from the hall, constituted state action in violation of the Civil Rights Act of 1964.[22]

Does acceptance of the foregoing proposition mean that a group which rents a public facility cannot charge admission to recoup the costs of its program or to raise funds for its cause, or that it cannot issue tickets as a way of insuring that its own members get seats before the doors are thrown open to the general public? I think not. So long as anyone, regardless of color, creed, or sex, who is willing to pay the price of admission is given a reasonable opportunity to do so, and so long as the doors of free meetings are open to the public—even if only after members have been seated—the group would have met its obligations for use of a public facility. To be sure, an organization which is able to fill the hall by giving or selling the first round of tickets to its own members and friends could thereby effectively exclude all others from the meeting, thus subverting the principle of open meetings in public places. But that is unlikely to be a common occurrence. If a group has that many supporters who wish to attend a meeting, it should be possible for those persons to have prior claim on the seats, since it is, after all, the sponsors who are paying the rent.

One last problem with respect to meetings which are held in public places, whether indoors or outdoors, is the extent to which the sponsors of such an assembly can expect to engage in communication uninterrupted by the audience, and whether they are entitled to call upon the police to enforce the degree of order which they would like to maintain. Here, by custom and by virtue of the difference between a free and a rented facility, legitimate distinctions can perhaps be drawn between outdoor and indoor gatherings. The soapbox orator on a busy street corner can hardly expect to be free of interruptions, whether from hecklers or the horns of passing automobiles. The sponsors of a rally in a reserved section of a park should not expect total immunity from sporadic heckling or be provided with police protection from it. But they ought to have a right, with the support of law enforcement officials, not to be drowned out by booing, chanting, or competing loudspeaker devices.

Inside a rented facility the problem becomes a bit trickier. Social mores would seem to dictate that the sponsors of such a meeting ought to be able to run it as they like, with or without audience participation; and most people are likely to respect that right. But what if they do not? Can the police be called to eject a talker from the audience? Does it make a difference whether time has been allowed for discussion or whether the sponsors have chosen to have no feedback whatsoever from the audience? These are difficult lines to draw, but I would suggest that, just as a group which chooses to make use of a public auditorium should not have carte blanche to maintain racial or religious "purity" in the composition of its audience, so it should not be able to call upon the police to silence all expressions of dissent. If it wants to run a meeting without any opportunity for audience participation, it should understand that some people in the audience may become restless under such a tight regime and occasionally attempt to break the bonds. The police should not be available to suppress such sporadic interruptions. On the other hand, if reasonable opportunity is provided for questions and discussion, and some in the audience do not think it enough, or if a member of the crowd makes it difficult or impossible for the planned program to proceed, then it would seem only fair that the sponsors have a right to call upon police to remove the source of the disruption.

Litigation on this issue is not uncommon, but the U.S. Supreme Court has yet to take a position, except by refusing to grant review to some unfortunate lower court rulings. In one of these, a man had been ejected from a George Wallace rally at a municipal stadium in Tallahassee, Florida, for carrying a sign reading, "Racism is Destroying My Country." He was told by the police that he could protest outside but that the Wallace organizers who had rented the stadium were entitled not to have people in their audience who might "create trouble." The Florida courts turned a deaf ear to his free speech claim, holding that "one's First Amendment rights end where the same rights of another begin."[23]

A second decision left standing by the U.S. Supreme Court involved a group of protesters attending a Billy Graham rally in a stadium in Knoxville, Tennessee, at which then President Richard Nixon was a guest speaker. Despite the fact that vendors were roaming through the generally noisy crowd of some 75,000 people selling their wares, the dissidents were found guilty of disturbing a meeting devoted to "religious worship" by chanting "Peace Now" and "Stop the War" during the President's address—a speech which was also interrupted frequently by cheers and applause.[24]

Unlike the U.S. Supreme Court, the supreme court of California has seen fit to take a vigorous freedom-of-expression stance with regard to heckling in public places—a position we can only hope may be emulated by other courts in the future. Reversing the convictions of four hecklers for disturbing an outdoor Fourth of July assembly in Coachella, California, at which congressional candidate John Tunney was speaking to the crowd, the California Supreme Court said:

> Audience activities, such as heckling, interrupting, harsh questioning, and booing, even though they may be impolite and discourteous, can nonetheless advance the goals of the First Amendment.... the Constitution does not require that the effective expression of ideas be restricted to rigid and predetermined patterns.... A cogent remark, even though rudely timed or phrased, may "contribute to the free interchange of ideas and the ascertainment of truth." ... The First Amendment contemplates a *debate* of important public issues.... its

protection can hardly be narrowed to the meeting at which the audience must passively listen to a single point of view. The First Amendment does not merely insure a marketplace of ideas in which there is but one seller. . . .

The public interest in an active and critical audience has long been recognized. The heckling and harassment of public officials and other speakers while making public speeches is as old as American and British politics; here, as in Great Britain, such protestant conduct has been thought to lie outside the realm of legal regulation except in the most egregious cases.[25]

Thus far in our discussion we have talked about the public forum only in terms of streets, sidewalks, parks, plazas, stadiums, and meeting halls. But there are many other kinds of public property where people may seek, and have sought, to express themselves. The question then arises as to which of these sites may be placed off limits by the government as inappropriate places for communication. This issue has been argued and litigated, for example, with respect to jail-house grounds,[26] the environs of the U.S. capitol building,[27] public libraries,[28] the waiting room of a government welfare office,[29] display ads on public transit vehicles,[30] and military bases.[31] Not disputed has been the right of government to prohibit speeches from the galleries of legislative bodies or uninvited discussion from nonmembers at any other meetings of public agencies.

Professor Geoffrey Stone, in an excellent analysis of this question,[32] has suggested that the problem was well solved by the U.S. Supreme Court's 1972 decision in *Grayned v. Rockford*, when a seven-man majority, speaking through Justice Marshall, said:

The nature of a place, the pattern of its normal activities, dictates the kind of regulations of time, place and manner that are reasonable. Although a silent vigil may not unduly interfere with a public library . . . making a speech in the reading room almost certainly would. That same speech should be perfectly appropriate in a park. The crucial question is whether the manner of expression is basically compatible with the normal activity of a particular place at a particular time.[33]

Stone asserts, "In this passage, the right to a public forum comes of age."[34] I would second that assessment. Although the guiding principle offered by the Court was easier to articulate in the abstract than it is to apply in concrete instances, fair judgments should be possible which give due respect to the normal activities of public facilities while at the same time protecting a healthy system of free expression. I would argue that, by these criteria, jail-house grounds, the environs of capitol buildings, spacious lobbies and waiting rooms of government offices, display ads on public transit systems, and military bases should rarely be placed off limits to First Amendment activity, but that hospitals, library reading rooms, galleries of legislative bodies, and courtrooms ordinarily should be out-of-bounds. Stone has proposed, correctly I believe, that not only should communicators be allowed to talk to people in a government waiting room, and to hand them leaflets, but that bulletin boards might well be provided there for the posting of notices, limited only by reasonable size regulations.[35]

The establishment of such a communication center is, of course, a discretionary matter for a public agency—and that is the case for any number of other facilities that might be created to enrich the marketplace of ideas. A city could, as some have done, build attractive kiosks, with bulletin boards for the posting of messages, on heavily trafficked sidewalks in the town center. A publically financed newsletter, such as those which have been sponsored by the League of Women Voters, could be mailed to all residents before an election, providing space for each candidate to place his or her credentials before the electorate. Government could, if it wished, operate a radio or television station which offered specified amounts of free time, on a first-come, first-served basis, to anyone who wished to communicate in that fashion with the public. All such facilities would, of course, have to be managed on a content-neutral basis.[36] For example, when the school board in Boston sent notices home to parents urging their support for a rally against forced busing, it was ordered by a federal court to make the same distribution system available to a pro-busing committee of parents who sought an equal opportunity.[37]

It may be precisely because of the need for neutrality, and the possible aggravations attendant upon maintaining such a stance in the face of popular pressures, that governments shy away from establishing forums that are not absolutely required of them. This is understandable, but it may be an abstinence a society like ours cannot afford. With the mass media of communication, particularly television, so dominant in our lives, and operated largely by private enterprises for whom profits have higher priority than the exposure of a variety of stimuli, it may be only through publicly operated alternative channels that the true diversity of our nation can be adequately expressed.

The operation of public broadcasting facilities on an open-to-all-comers or common-carrier basis would have historic precedent in the United States Postal Service—a common-carrier mode of facilitating citizen expression. A postal system was recognized by our Founding Fathers as vitally important to the functioning of a free society and became a part of the initial framework of government which they established. Lower rates, in the form of second- and third-class mailing privileges, have even been built into the system to ease the financial burden on those who distribute newspapers, magazines, books, and solicitations for the support of nonprofit causes. The postal service, in theory available to all who wish to use it for the transmission of their messages—the essence of the concept of a common carrier—regrettably has been in practice less than totally free from government interference with communication content.

For example, as noted earlier, Congress has adopted, and the Supreme Court upheld, restrictions on "sexually-oriented" mailings to those who do not wish to receive such material.[38] But those were not the first content-discriminatory controls over the use of the U.S. mails, nor are we likely to have seen the last of such measures. Writes historian William Preston:

> The notorious Alien and Sedition Acts of 1798 brought to a head the partisan political fury between Federalist and Republican papers and the Federalist Post Office favored its friends and delayed or suppressed the circulation of its opponents' press. . . .
>
> Slavery and abolition stimulated the first large scale censorship and warned America's newspapers that not every advocate was free to speak. Southern states and other hostile communities labeled abolition material incendiary and seditious. Andrew Jackson and his postmaster general, Amos Kendall, agreed to suppress the inflammatory matter. . . . Post Office policies during the Civil War proved that censorship had not been an administrative aberration. . . . historians have concluded that denial of the postal privilege was the "most effective" method of suppressing what public authorities considered to be "traitorous" and "seditious" publication.
>
> In the tumultous decades after the Civil War, the government developed additional codes of behavior that further narrowed the range of opinion suitable for mass circulation through the mails. . . . The Comstock Law and its later amendments made nonmailable any "lewd and lacivious" or "filthy" material or matter with an "indecent or immoral purpose." The definition was broad enough to exclude discussion of birth control, marriage counselling, and abortion for years. . . . But it was the World War I crisis that really unbalanced the press. With broad nonmailable categories, the government revoked the second-class privilege and denied the mails to some sixty Socialist newspapers during the war. . . .
>
> Totalitarian and radical propaganda revived fears of subversive infection in the late thirties and forties. Apart from seizing materials mailed from abroad, the Post Office once more revoked the second-class privilege of some 70 periodicals during World War II.[39]

These deviations from the content-neutrality which is supposed to characterize government management of a public forum underscore the trouble public officials have in resisting the temptation to use their power in behalf of their own policies or prejudices and to the disadvantage of those who may be out of favor. It is a temptation which only clear constitutional standards, enforced by vigilant adversaries and vigorous courts, can hold in check. To the extent that such checks and balances do not work, we fall short of attaining the kind of marketplace of ideas contemplated by the First Amendment.

Providing Resources, Tools, and Training for Participation in Public Discourse

The maintenance by government of content-neutral forums and common-carrier channels for citizen expression is of little value if potential users of those facilities do not have the capacity to take advantage of them. A minimum level of literacy is obviously essential, at least for the written media. Beyond that, the more information people have at their disposal, and the more skilled they are in talking, writing, listening, reading, and thinking, the more productive is the communication which flows between them. Thus the architects of democracy recognized the need for public schools and public libraries which provide the training and resources needed for competent participation in the marketplace of ideas. Indeed, in this country we have poured vast sums of money into public education and information services for the purpose, in part at least, of enhancing the quality of communication within the body politic.

If it has been difficult for government to remain impartial in operating a postal service or municipal auditoriums, it is well-nigh impossible in running schools and libraries. The opportunity, in fact the necessity, for making choices in the selection of teachers and administrators, of curricula and instructional materials, and in determining, with a finite budget, which books, magazines, newspapers, records, and films to buy, which guest speakers to invite, which exhibits to display—all of these decisions inevitably mean that tax-supported institutions continually put their thumbs on the scales in the shaping of public opinion.

Recognizing the impossibility of complete neutrality, our society has attempted to deal with this problem by developing processes, structures, checks, and balances to achieve as high a degree of fairness as we can. Teachers and librarians are presumably trained to make selections on the basis of professional criteria—not to promote their own views and prejudices but to employ standards of quality about which there is some relatively objective consensus and to respect the democratic principle of diversity. Good educators are not supposed to be propagandists. Their responsibility is to provide the stimulus and the resources for learning by others. The etymology of the verb "to educate" is "to lead out," not "to pour in."

To offset the biases which may infect the choices of individual teachers, most major decisions about textbooks and curricula, at least at the pre-college levels, are made by committees—of academic departments, of teachers plus administrators, of school boards, or even of state-wide commissions. These groups, of course, are not immune to the complaints, pressures, or more subtly implanted values of the citizens who elect them or pay their salaries. In theory a healthy exercise of democracy, this process has, in practice, too often degenerated to ugly vigilantism, where a minority, or even a majority, in a community has imposed know-nothing restrictions on schools or teachers who were trying to do a professional, and perhaps unacceptably exciting, job of educating their students. Sometimes even state legislators have gotten into the act, whether to ban the teaching of evolution or to require the recital of prayers, and the U.S. Supreme Court has had to intervene to declare such measures unconstitutional.[40]

Given the facts that it is the taxpayers who foot the bills for public schools and libraries, that the personnel who govern and staff them are supposed to be servants, not masters, of the citizenry, and that ultimate authority in a democracy rests with the voters, how can we object if a teacher is dismissed by the proper authorities for expressing unacceptable political ideas in a classroom,[41] if textbooks are ordered by the school board to be dropped from the curriculum because they are "un-American,"[42] if a drama club performance of "Inherit the Wind" is canceled by a school principal because it is "pro-evolution,"[43] or if books are removed from the library shelves because of parental complaints about their "filthy" language?[44] And why are objections only heard about teacher *dismissals,* play and speaker *cancellations,* or book *expungements* and not about the applicants for teaching jobs who are not hired in the first place, the plays that are never selected for performance, the speakers who are never invited to appear, or the hundreds and thousands of books that might have been chosen for the curriculum or purchased for the library and were not?

Clearly discriminations among people and materials are, and must be, made all the time when government gets into the information and education business. The question is how and by whom these judgments should be made in a society where the majority is supposed to rule, but not to overrule the rights guaranteed to its minorities by the Constitution. The answer must lie in a careful balancing process where all of the competing interests are given due weight, with none in unrestrained control and none completely neglected.

Thus a school board must have the right, assuming due process, to dismiss a teacher or order a change in the curriculum, but not in total disregard of community, student, or faculty sentiment (whether expressed by a majority or minority—and it is often difficult to tell which it is), and not in defiance of the First Amendment, which forbids state action based solely on disapproval of points of view that have been propounded.[45] Textbooks and instructional materials should be selected and changed by people who are experts in the particular subject matter area—but, again, not with total disregard for the opinions of students, of the community, and of nonexperts who may have valuable insights which have escaped the notice of a possibly too-parochial outlook by professionals in the field. Librarians must decide what books to order and what periodical subscriptions to place, renew, or cancel, based on the needs of the clientele they serve and on their own profession's training and guidance. Popular demand may well be a consideration for including something that might not otherwise have been purchased, but it should not be a factor in excluding an item which has already been secured and shelved.[46]

Plays should be selected, speakers invited, and school newspapers written by individuals or groups who have been duly chosen for those functions because they are regarded as qualified for the task. Having been delegated this responsibility, they should be free to exercise it according to their own best judgment.[47] To be sure, they should be responsive to the feelings of others and sensitive to complaints from students, faculty, administrators, school board, or community. But the ultimate decisions, along with the responsibility of living with the consequences, should be theirs. This does not mean that others who may be held legally responsible for what is done—such as a school board being sued for libel—should not be able to exercise control insofar as that is necessary to protect themselves from those particular sanctions—but it should be only "insofar as that is necessary." Nor does it mean that persons who repeatedly demonstrate in their performance that they are incapable of responsibly handling this kind of public trust cannot, by due process, be removed from the assignment, anymore than a science teacher who does nothing but talk politics in class or a librarian who spends an entire year's budget on comic books cannot be fired. It does mean that *singular* mistakes of judgment may have to go uncorrected—perhaps even be defended—and their consequences lived with by all those associated with the enterprise, in the interest of preserving a broader freedom for everyone to learn and to grow.

In sum, what is being proposed here is wide latitude for those who make the initial selections of personnel and materials, on the assumption that they will act with the sensitivity and fairness which trustees of public funds and power should exhibit, and that a diversity of decision makers will tend naturally to produce a diversity of judgments. They should be encouraged, perhaps even bound by required procedures, to consider as broad a spectrum of advice as possible from all interested parties before making their final decisions. Once those conclusions have been reached, however—the teacher or librarian hired, the textbook, film, or play selected, the guest speaker invited, the newspaper editor chosen, the journal subscription ordered, the exhibit put in place—unless something illegal or unauthorized is taking place, the First Amendment should protect that choice from dismissal, cancellation, or expungement because others disapprove or are offended. If, over time, it becomes apparent that a person making these choices is not acting with the degree of sensitivity, balance, and professionalism required of one who holds a public trust, then separation from that responsibility is an appropriate solution. The censorship of particular communication is not.

Difficult as it may be for government to operate a public school or public library without offending either the First Amendment or some segment of community opinion, at least its responsibilities for fairness and its accountability to the electorate are reasonably clear. Not so when the state appropriates money to help support educational, informational, cultural, or research activities which are undertaken, and may also be partially funded, by private individuals and quasi-private associations. Whether they be art, history, or science museums, opera, symphony, or theater companies, individual artists and scholars, private universities, so-called public television stations (which, under the present U.S. system, are not truly public), or political campaigns, the relationships are complex and the free speech considerations accordingly somewhat obscured.

The problem is intensified by the fact that, unlike most European nations, we have had relatively little historic experience in our country with this sort of enterprise, but in recent years have become rather suddenly and heavily involved. Since World War II the budgets of major private universities in the United States have grown enormously dependent on government grants and research contracts, to the point where these institutions could not survive in anything like their present form were public funds to dry up. National Endowments for the Humanities and for the Arts, which make federal grants in those two areas of activity, were not established by Congress until 1965, at a funding level of $2.5 million each. By 1979 the budgets for both had increased to nearly $150 million, a sixtyfold growth during a fourteen-year period.[48] Every state in the nation now has a state arts council, the largest of which, the New York State Council on the Arts, distributed $27 million in 1977 to over 1,000 dance companies, orchestras, historical societies, filmmakers, museums, playwrights, etc.[49]

In 1967 the Public Broadcasting Act was adopted by Congress, establishing a Corporation for Public Broadcasting to infuse tax dollars into the support of programming for a Public Broadcasting System and to help sustain the locally governed educational stations which were to become a part of that network. Allocations of federal money for this purpose have steadily increased in the ensuing years.

Finally, in 1974, with a series of amendments to the Federal Election Campaign Act of 1971, Congress established a system of public financing for presidential campaigns in the form of matching grants to candidates in primaries who qualify by raising at least $5,000 in each of twenty states, and for nominating conventions and the general election providing total funding up to a maximum specified differentially for major and minor parties. Proposals have since been made to extend public financing to campaigns for Congress but have thus far not met with success.

The First Amendment issues raised by the use of public funds for these methods of facilitating citizen expression are troublesome. They are extensions, in more complicated form, of the questions we have already discussed with regard to public schools and public libraries— questions of selection, of maintaining diversity and balance among competing values, and of after-the-fact censorship of particular activities. Furthermore, there are questions of allocation of resources as between those who are already established and those who are not, and between those who are more or are less worthy of support, which are not faced in quite the same way by public schools and libraries. Some examples of the difficulties follow.

In May of 1979 a citizens' organization called the Center for Science in the Public Interest announced the results of a survey of science museums in the United States which raised concerns about the influence of corporate gifts on the nature of museum exhibits. Singled out for particular notice was the Museum of Science and Industry in Chicago, and more especially an exhibit there on nuclear energy sponsored by the Commonwealth Edison Company of Illinois.[50] The organization's executive director was quoted in the Chicago press as saying of the museum that "most of the new exhibits are sponsored by industry and are really flashy commercial displays and it's really propaganda. As long as the museum receives public funds (from the Chicago Park District) it should be a responsible institution."[51]

According to the newspaper account of the Commonwealth Edison matter:

> The group characterized the multimedia display as "little more than an unrestrained advocacy of the suggested virtues of nuclear power," by fully praising the wonders of nuclear power, while downplaying or being deliberately deceitful about its drawbacks.[52]

The museum's director, Victor J. Danilow, responded as follows:

He conceded that corporations probably wouldn't give big donations to the museum unless they were assured some control over the exhib-it's contents, but he said the museum retains veto power.

And he added that not only is the museum not obligated to present opposing views, but that it's impossible to do so. "We are not an ency-clopedia, and we're not a newspaper. . . . We're a museum with limited space, limited resources. So it's necessary to make choices as to what you present." . . .

Asked about the exhibit, Danilow said it "gives the museum's posi-tion. We are pronuclear. We feel there is a place for nuclear energy."

And he accused the center for Science in the Public Interest of attacking corporate-sponsored exhibits "because some of the exhibits do not necessarily support their viewpoints, which may be anti-establishment in nature or anticorporate in nature."[53]

In these comments, Mr. Danilow revealed some understanding and some insensitivity concerning the First Amendment issues which are our concern here. Clearly he was right in asserting that, with limited space and resources, a museum has to make choices in what it exhibits. His museum's policy of retaining veto power over the content of displays proposed by private corporations is certainly necessary to the exercise of its responsibilities as a quasi-public institution which receives city funds. But one is left by his statements with the uneasy feeling that he does not know when or how to exercise that veto power. One can fairly infer from his remarks that the museum's relationship with the large corporations to which it is beholden may be cozier than it should be or than it is with the larger community to which it should also be accountable. Surely it is not the business of a musuem heavily subsidized by public funds to have a "position" that is "pronuclear," anymore than it should be antinuclear or partisan on any issues of current political controversy.

As for Mr. Danilow's comments about the absence of a museum's obligation, in contrast to that of an encyclopedia or newspaper, to pre-sent opposing views, he appears to turn upside down what is required of those institutions. Encyclopedias and newspapers, being entirely private press enterprises, have no obligation other than their own sense of pro-fessionalism to present opposing points of view. A museum which is partially funded with the taxpayer's money, on the other hand, has a serious obligation, if not to be a public forum where political issues are debated, at least not to let itself become a billboard for just one side of an important public argument. Insofar as the exhibits in such a museum do promote values which are in controversy, there indeed ought to be some presentation, appropriate in format to the particular institution, of "opposing views."

The issues raised by the museum example are not as different as one might at first think from those posed with respect to "public" television stations. Here, again, are entities funded in part by government money, in part by membership subscriptions and other individual contributions, and in part by corporate grants. Like museums, they are governed by quasi-public boards of directors and serve an entirely public information, education, and cultural function. They have limited space (i.e., air time) and resources and must, therefore, be selective in their programming. In their treatment of controversial subject matter they have an obligation to present a diversity of views—in fact, are required to do so by the Public Broadcasting Act of 1967.[54] Unlike privately owned stations, they are prohibited from promulgating, through editorials, the views of their management.[55] Corporate grants are supposed to be made with no ideological strings attached, although they can be earmarked for support of particular programming.

Just as a museum seeks to offer exhibits of the highest quality, and thus might be said to be discriminating against that which is of less value, so a public broadcasting station exercises, and must exercise, discretion in what it considers worth airing. Such qualitative judgments are a central characteristic of all governmentally supported cultural enterprises, and therein lies a problem of sizable magnitude.

For instance, when Jimmy Carter became president of the United States in 1977 he appointed new chairmen for the National Endowments for the Arts and the Humanities—Livingston L. Biddle, Jr., and Joseph D. Duffey, respectively—both of whom came to office with the purpose of shifting the emphasis of those agencies to the support of a less "elite" clientele.[56] In May of 1979 the *New York Times* reported on the matter as follows:

> Now that Mr. Duffey and Mr. Biddle have been in office for 17 months, is there any hard evidence that such a shift has been taking place? . . . After several months of investigating the two agencies . . . it is possible to say that there is now a discernible and growing trend toward the politically popular policy of assisting newer, more regionally dispersed "populist" groups rather than traditional "elitist" cultural institutions. . . . For example, in 1973 about 33 percent of direct grant funds at the Humanities went to support projects to make the Humanities comprehensible and useful to the public. By fiscal 1978, 52 percent was targeted for public outreach; and by fiscal 1980, approximately 55 percent will be used for that purpose. . . . In fiscal 1977, total grants to groups located in New York were about 23 percent of all obligated agency grant funds. By fiscal 1978, the amount had decreased to about 19 percent. . . .
>
> Last year before the House Appropriations Interior Subcommittee, Mr. Duffey reported: "We support organizations which are close to the work places of Americans—labor unions, farmers' groups, business and professional associations—as forums for debate on political and philosophical issues. . . . By making the encouragement of curiosity in the humanities a part of the work of local civic, ethnic, and

cultural organizations, we helped diversify the meaning of the humanities in American life." . . .

Testifying before Congress last year, Mr. Biddle said: "When I was the congressional liaison for the endowment several years ago, there was a concentration of grants and monies in New York, California, and Massachusetts. . . . I think if we were to compare those years with today, however, we would see a shifting. It would be my wish to see a greater shifting as time goes on so that the arts indeed become available to all our people. . . .

The Arts Endowment's five-year plan, the first ever officially completed by the agency, emphasizes support for individuals as well as for emerging rather than established institutions.[57]

Critics of these new directions have been vocal. Nancy Hanks, a previous chairperson of the Arts Endowment, told the *New York Times:*

"You put the money in the arts where it will do some good and that usually ends up to be the quality institutions." She gave an example of a $600,000 opera grant. "If the money had gone, say, to the Norfolk Symphony Orchestra instead of the Metropolitan Opera, Norfolk couldn't have created opera as great as the Met's. The Met sets the goals; goals are set by institutions that are able to put on productions that give people vision."[58]

And Ms. Hanks's former deputy, Michael Straight, charged, "'Jimmy Carter's concept of the endowments is political. . . . Under the populist ethic of this Administration, the needs of the large organizations won't be met.'"[59]

But the most vitriolic attack came early in the new administration in a *New York Times* article by Hilton Kramer:

It is well-known that these appointments have been made in response to the campaign waged by Senator Claiborne Pell (Democrat, R.I.) against the "elitist" biases of N.E.H. under its former chairman, Ronald S. Berman. As one of the original sponsors of the legislation that brought the endowments into being, Senator Pell enjoys great power and prestige in this particular realm of government policy. . . . Senator Pell's campaign against "elitism"—not always distinguishable from an outright attack on mind—was quite in keeping with the President's "populist" ideology. . . . Are we really prepared to endorse Senator Pell's philistine notions of culture, and President Carter's apparent politicization of it, as official national policy?

The truth is, the whole concept of "elitism," as it is now applied to public discussions of cultural policy, is disgracefully evasive, euphemistic and demagogic. It is used to signify snobbism and special privilege, and thus something anti-democratic and more or less threatening to the common good. It suggests conspiracy and unearned advantage, something restrictive and forbidden and vaguely villainous. So potent has this word become in political parlance that it has been emptied of its intellectual content and made to serve the purposes of an ideological myth.

For in the real world of culture and the arts, it stands for nothing more or less than the influence of acknowledged achievement of a high order. According to the latest dictionary to reach my desk . . . an elitist is the "best and choicest part, as of society or a profession," and elitism is the "belief in the leadership of an elite." It is against this "leadership" of the "best" that we are now being invited by the government to seek redress. And in the name of what? Supposedly some grass-roots concept of culture that in actuality is likely to be little more than the old political pork-barrel dressed up to look like a quaint horn of plenty.[60]

Despite these criticisms, and despite the shift in emphasis which did occur under the Carter administration, the fact remains that institutions like the Metropolitan Opera, New York Philharmonic, Metropolitan Museum of Art, and American Council of Learned Societies continued to receive the largest single chunks of money, albeit a lesser proportion of their budgets than formerly.[61] This is not to say that the issue joined by Hilton Kramer, Michael Straight, and Nancy Hanks, on the one hand, and Joseph Duffey and Livingston Biddle, on the other, is not one that merits serious consideration, but to suggest that it may be of a different nature than Messrs. Kramer and Straight would have us believe. It is not, I think, a question of President Carter's appointees politicizing what had previously been nonpolitical judgments based purely on quality, but rather a matter of expanding the criteria of selection to include such values as geographical and ethnic dispersion and the development of promising but not-yet-accomplished talent. To the extent that this diverts support from established cultural centers to the untried and the unpolished it may be characterized as anti-elite; but that is hardly the same as a "philistine attack on the mind." Instead, it can be viewed as an effort to offset to a small degree the tremendous advantages in access to resources enjoyed by established institutions and locales and to correct for the subtle cultural—yes, even political—biases which may be brought to the selection process by the panels of establishment judges who dispense these governmentally funded awards. To open up that process to a broader diversity of participants strikes me not only as a healthy trend but one that is required by the First Amendment. If quality gets lost in the shuffle it will not be because Norfolk and the Navajos have gotten a bit more of the action and New York City less, but because those who have the responsibility for allocating funds have failed to do their jobs with sufficient care. Just as in the operation of a public school, the arrangement of a museum, or the management of a public television station, so in the selection of recipients for arts and humanities grants it should be possible to create a procedure for the making of qualitative judgments that minimizes, if it cannot totally eliminate, the personal, social, and political prejudices of individual decision makers. Perhaps merely being sensitive to the dangers of these possible distortions is a long first step toward their control.

The same tension between the new and the established which exists in the educational and cultural realms is present as well in our current system of public financing of presidential campaigns, where money is dispensed to parties and candidates in proportion to the size of the vote they receive and to the private matching funds they are able to raise. Thus, as with the Metropolitan Opera, the Republicans and Democrats get more, and the Socialists, who may need the money the most, get less. But how could it be otherwise if the taxpayer is footing the bill? Fly-by-night candidates who attract only a handful of supporters are hardly entitled to lay claim on public moneys to promote what may be an entirely bizarre cause. It can only be hoped that, as with a new theory which the scientific establishment regards as crazy but which eventually proves sound, or a new artistic endeavor which the cultural establishment views as bizarre but which ultimately wins appreciation, so a new political movement which is perceived as unhinged but may be speaking the truth will find nongovernmental sources of financing that enable it to survive and gain converts. One can expect a democratic society to be tolerant, perhaps even appreciative of the value of political deviants, but one cannot expect it to pay their campaign bills.

Because the public financing of political campaigns must, in order to make sense to taxpayers, discriminate among parties and candidates on the basis of their popular support, this is one form of government facilitation of citizen expression which I believe must be forsaken if we are to remain true to First Amendment principles. At least with respect to the discriminatory selections that are made by public schools, libraries, museums, broadcasters, and endowments for the arts and humanities, there is the promise that judgments can and will be based on viewpoint-neutral criteria of quality. By contrast, the differential allocation of public funds among political candidates can have nothing to do with their merit or with any criteria other than their proximity to society's mainstream. That is not an acceptable standard under the First Amendment for appropriating money from the public treasury.

The problem of after-the-fact censorship by museums, public broadcasters, or dispensers of government grants for the arts, humanities, and sciences is not essentially different from that which we have already discussed in connection with public schools.and libraries. Once a selection has been made of a particular museum, exhibit, theater company, play, speaker, writer, artist, or scholar, support should not be cut off or the communication suppressed because some are offended by it. If the recipients of government support demonstrate over a period of time a consistently poor quality of performance in whatever enterprise they are engaged, that is certainly justification for not providing *additional* funding, just as a public school or library need not continue the employment of an incompetent member of the staff. But the censorship of communicative activity which has already been commissioned is inappropriate.

Thus, when the governor of New Hampshire, in May of 1974, withdrew a $750 grant which had been made by the state's Commission on the Arts to *Granite Magazine* because he believed a poem it had published was obscene, his action should not have been allowed to stand. Unfortunately, the federal courts to which an appeal was taken dismissed the case for want of a substantial federal question, even though it was federal money which was being dispensed through the state's arts council.[62]

Even a foreign nation with more experience in this field, and with a reputation for liberality considerably greater than that of the former governor of New Hampshire, is not without fault in its management of the problem. To be specific, the following story appeared in the news in 1978:

> Jens Joergen Thorsen, the Danish film director who wants to make a film on the sex life of Jesus, is suing the Danish government for withdrawing financial support from the production two years ago. Denmark funds Danish productions and initially had offered $170,000 for making the film, but support was withdrawn after an international uproar from Christians who considered the subject matter blasphemous.[63]

Because of the danger of this kind of censorship whenever the public's money is being used, it is sometimes suggested that we would be better off if the state stayed entirely out of the business of supporting private and quasi-private informational and cultural activities and let them fend for themselves. As one commentator has described government funding of the arts, "It is, after all, a European invention of questionable roots in the court life of Europe—hardly a suitable precedent for a democracy in the latter half of the 20th century."[64]

To be sure, there is something unseemly about a democratic government playing the role of grand patron of the arts, culture, scholarship, and entertainment in the manner of pre–twentieth century kings and queens. But the alternative is even more unseemly, with artists, scholars, and boards of governors of educational and cultural institutions scrambling to cater to the whims of wealthy donors and foundations

whose criteria for selection and censorious impulses are far more quixotic than even a rather bungling government agency is likely to be. If
we accept as a fact of contemporary life in America that there will be
no museums, no opera, no symphonies, no public broadcasters, no
private universities, no teams of scholars doing research on complex
questions without more money to support them than can be provided from ticket sales, membership subscriptions, tuition charges,
and a willingness to work for a certain amount of psychic income, then
we must face the choice of obtaining the necessary funds from private
philanthropists or the public treasury. The solution we have come to in
this country of relying on both sources seems a reasonable way of avoiding the worst evils of depending exclusively on one or the other.

Requiring Access to Privately Owned Forums and Media

If government in the United States limits its facilitation of citizen expression to providing a public forum, public schools, public libraries, and
public aid to quasi-private informational and cultural enterprises, there
will still remain significant barriers to the optimum flow of communication in our society. That is so because vital forums and media for expression in America are privately owned and operated, and if they are accessible only to those who find favor with the management's gatekeepers
many points of view will fail to reach large segments of the population.
If, however, the state intervenes, through law and court interpretations
of the First Amendment, to compel some degree of public access to these
forums and media, would-be communicators will have greater assurance
that audiences they need to reach in order to be effective will be exposed
to their messages. Whether, or to what extent, the power of government
should be used in this way is the question to which we now turn our
attention.

This issue arose in its earliest form in a case decided by the U.S.
Supreme Court in 1946, *Marsh v. Alabama*.[65] The setting was a company
town by the name of Chickasaw, and the dispute came about when a
Jehovah's Witness sought to distribute her literature on the streets of
that town in defiance of a prohibition against such activity promulgated
by the corporation which owned the property. In overturning her conviction for criminal trespass, the Supreme Court said:

> Ownership does not always mean absolute dominion. The more an
> owner, for his advantage, opens up his property for use by the public
> in general, the more do his rights become circumscribed by the statu-
> tory and constitutional rights of those who use it. . . . Whether a corpo-
> ration or a municipality owns or possesses the town the public in either

case has an identical interest in the functioning of the community in such a manner that the channels of communication remain free. . . .

When we balance the Constitutional rights of owners of property against those of the people to enjoy freedom of press and religion, as we must here, we remain mindful of the fact that the latter occupy a preferred position.[66]

Having established the precedent that property ownership does not carry with it a right to exclude unwanted communication from an entire town, the Supreme Court was confronted two decades later with the question of that decision's applicability to privately-owned-and-operated shopping centers, which mushroomed across the country after World War II. The Court's first response was to find the two settings analogous. Holding that a labor union could not be prohibited from picketing a store in the Logan Valley Mall near Altoona, Pennsylvania, the majority reasoned that a shopping center is the "functional equivalent" of the business district of a company town—a place generally open to the public, where large numbers of people gather who ought to be accessible to those who wish to communicate with them.[67]

Justice Black, dissenting from that decision, wrote:

But *Marsh* was never intended to apply to this kind of situation. *Marsh* dealt with the very special situation of a company-owned town, complete with streets, alleys, stores, residences, and everything else that goes to make a town. . . . I can find very little resemblance between the shopping center involved in this case and Chickasaw, Alabama. There are no homes, there is no sewage disposal plant, there is not even a post office. . . . All I can say is that this sounds like a very strange "town" to me.[68]

It was Justice Black's view, rather than that of the *Logan Valley* majority, which ultimately prevailed. Four years later, in a case from Portland, Oregon, a five-man majority ruled that antiwar leafletters could be barred from a shopping center mall, since there were nearby public streets and sidewalks where they could communicate their message, and since that message, unlike the one in *Logan Valley,* was not directly relevant to the activities of the shopping center.[69] The four dissenters charged that the majority opinion, despite its qualified language, was, in fact, a repudiation of the *Logan Valley* decision. In just four more years they were proved correct. Responding to a case from North DeKalb, Georgia, a six-man majority explicitly overruled the *Logan Valley* precedent and held that *Marsh v. Alabama* and the First Amendment do not apply to privately owned shopping centers.[70]

If the prevailing justices thought that they had thus put the shopping center matter finally to rest they failed to reckon with the resiliency of the issue or the creativity of lower court jurists. In 1979 the California Supreme Court ruled that, even if the First Amendment to the federal constitution did not protect the right to peacefully solicit signatures on a petition and to distribute pamphlets in a privately owned shopping center, the state's own constitution did.[71] Now it was the shopping center owner who went to the U.S. Supreme Court claiming a violation of the Bill of Rights. More particularly, he argued that the state supreme court's interpretation of the California constitution constituted a "taking" of private property in violation of the Due Process Clauses of the Fifth and Fourteenth Amendments as well as a violation of his First Amendment right not to have to use his property to sponsor the messages of others.

The U.S. Supreme Court, without dissent, rejected both claims, holding that its own interpretation of the free speech clause of the First Amendment did not "limit the authority of the State to exercise its police power or its sovereign right to adopt in its own Constitution individual liberties more expansive than those conferred by the Federal Constitution."[72] The Court found that since the speech activities in question would not "unreasonably impair the value or use" of the shopping center,[73] there was no "taking" of property without due process of law. As for the owner's First Amendment claims, the Court responded that (1) since he had already opened up his property to members of the public, the views they might express there would not likely be identified as his own; (2) the state was not dictating the display of any particular message or requiring of him the affirmation of any belief; and (3) he was free to disavow or disclaim sponsorship of any ideas he did not like.

Apparently to insure that the Court would not be viewed as having backed off in any significant way from the rationale of its own view that federally guaranteed freedom of expression does not extend to private shopping centers, and to warn of possible limits to the Court's tolerance for states inclined to grant "individual liberties more expansive than those conferred by the Federal Constitution" (i.e., by the Supreme Court?), Justices Powell and White wrote separate concurring opinions which contained a litany of qualifications to the majority opinion. It did not necessarily apply, they wrote, to *all* shopping centers, for there might be some situations in which free speech activities would be so annoying to customers as to constitute a deprivation of the owner's property rights. It certainly did not apply, they felt, to individual "freestanding stores," hotels, or the lobbies of private buildings where "customers might well conclude that the messages reflect the view of the proprietor."[74] And it might well not apply, they said, perhaps more in hope than certitude, to a state-required right of access to private property for the expression of views which the owner finds morally repugnant.

Justice Marshall, on the other hand, who had authored the Court's *Logan Valley* opinion originally opening shopping centers to First Amendment activities, and who had opined its passing in the rulings that followed, wrote separately to "applaud" the California Supreme Court's decision and to reiterate his belief that a majority of his own colleagues held "an overly formalistic view of the relationship between the institution of private ownership of property and the First Amendment's guarantees of freedom of speech."[75]

If judges can differ over the question of whether, for free speech purposes, a shopping center is more like a company town than not, it is to be expected that they will differ over the status of migrant worker camps. That is precisely what has happened. In one such case, the U.S. Court of Appeals for the Fifth Circuit ruled that labor organizers could not be excluded from a camp owned by the Talisman Sugar Company because its characteristics were such as to bring it under the company-town precedent.[76] But in a second case, involving another camp operated by the Campbell Soup Company, the U.S. Court of Appeals for the Seventh Circuit found the property sufficiently different from that of a company town to allow the corporate owner to bar a migrant service organization from the premises.[77]

I believe that the central question in all of these cases should not be the extent to which a particular locale resembles an entire town but whether it is a large and open area where people gather in sizable numbers and, if so, whether the proposed communicative behavior is "basically compatible with the normal activity" of the site—the same test that has been applied to comparable public places. By these criteria, the owners of large shopping centers, migrant worker camps, and exposition grounds, like those of company towns, would, as the Supreme Court put it in *Marsh v. Alabama,* have to forego "absolute dominion" over their property because of the "preferred position" of First Amendment rights. It is but a small intrusion on their property rights to ask such property owners to accommodate nondisruptive, albeit unwelcome, communication as the price of their doing business on such a grand scale with so many members of the public. Their property is "private" in only the most technical of senses, and they ought not be entitled to invoke the privacy concept when they wish to be restrictive, while abandoning it for the purpose of reaching the widest possible public for their enterprise.

Of far more importance to the would-be communicator in our modern, technological society than the kinds of forums just discussed are the privately-owned-and-operated mass media of communication—radio, television, and large-circulation newspapers. Without access to these media, one's communication efforts are severely limited in the numbers of people one can reach and, thereby, in the impact one can have on the mass culture in which we live. Indeed, it might be said that in today's America a point of view which fails to catch the attention of one of the national television networks is a point of view that for all practical purposes has little chance of surviving in any significant way.

Because the electronic and print media in the United States are privately owned and managed, a similar problem to that of company towns and shopping centers is encountered if those who are in control of these properties are not willing to allow their use for the communication of certain kinds of messages. A critical difference, however, is that owners of newspapers and broadcasting stations are themselves in the business of communication; indeed, their property is solely a channel of communication, and the audience that can be reached through it is one which they have cultivated by offering material that people wish to see, hear, and read. If access to their facilities by others is sought in the name of freedom of speech, we are confronted with two competing First Amendment claims rather than with a clash between the First Amendment on the one hand and ordinary property rights on the other, as is the case when outside communicators seek access to company towns and shopping centers. The question then becomes whether laws constitutionally can be adopted or the First Amendment interpreted to require those who own newspapers or broadcasting facilities to provide space or time in their media for the communication of messages which might not otherwise be promulgated there. The answer which has been given to that question by our courts is in the form of a double standard—namely, that the first Amendment prohibits *any* such requirements from being placed on the print media but that broadcasters may be imposed upon to some degree. Let us examine the details of this regime and make an assessment of its merits.

Qualifications on the First Amendment right of broadcasters had their origins in the Radio Act of 1927 when Congress decided that, because of the limited amount of air space available, radio stations would have to be licensed by the government. Since choices would be made among competing applicants, and the winners would thus enjoy a special privilege bestowed by the state to use the "public's airwaves," they would have an obligation, in return, to operate their facilities for the "public interest, convenience, and necessity"—a phrase borrowed from laws governing public utilities. Congress, if it had so chosen, could have taken an entirely different route of requiring licensees to be common carriers for the messages of others, like a telegraph company. That option was rejected in favor of the freedom of broadcasters to control the content of their programs, subject only to the public interest standard. This scheme was carried forward by the Communications Act of 1934, which still governs radio and television in the United States.

It was on the basis of the public interest standard that the Federal Communications Commission, which was established to implement the act, enunciated the Fairness Doctrine, requiring broadcasters, when dealing with controversial public issues, to present a diversity of views.[78] Although this doctrine did not demand the granting of direct access to the air for those whose positions may have been inadequately represented but left to the discretion of broadcasters the particular manner of achieving fairness, it nevertheless did say to broadcasters that they were not entirely free to do what they pleased with their programming.

Beyond the general Fairness Doctrine, however, there have been a few specific obligations laid upon broadcasters for direct access to their facilities. Section 315 of the Communications Act provided that if a station gave or sold time to any candidates for public office to promote their campaigns, it was required to provide equal opportunities to all other candidates for the same office. Furthermore, in 1967 the FCC promulgated rules governing personal attacks and political editorials.[79] The first provided that if any individual or group is attacked during the discussion of controversial issues of public importance, notification and a transcript of the comments must be given to the person or group attacked, and an opportunity to respond must be offered. The second required that if a station broadcasts an editorial which takes a position for or against any candidate for political office, the opponent or the candidate, as the case might be, must be notified and granted time to reply.

It was inevitable that at least some of these limitations on the freedom of broadcasters to do as they pleased with their stations would be challenged as violations of their First Amendment rights, and that issue was faced and definitively resolved by a unanimous Supreme Court in 1969.[80] In an opinion which dealt simultaneously with a challenge to the Fairness Doctrine in general brought by the Red Lion Broadcasting Company, and a challenge to the personal attack rule in particular brought by the Radio and Television News Directors Association, the Supreme Court found no constitutional infirmity in either. As to the contention that these regulations infringed upon the freedom of speech of broadcasters, the Court said that

> as far as the First Amendment is concerned those who are licensed stand no better than those to whom licenses are refused. A license permits broadcasting, but the licensee has no constitutional right to be the one who holds the license or to monopolize a radio frequency to the exclusion of his fellow citizens. There is nothing in the First

Amendment which prevents the Government from requiring a licensee to share his frequency with others and to conduct himself as a proxy or fiduciary with obligations to present those views and voices which are representative of his community and which would otherwise, by necessity, be barred from the airwaves.... It is the right of the viewers and listeners, not the right of broadcasters, which is paramount.... It is the purpose of the First Amendment to preserve an uninhibited marketplace of ideas in which truth will ultimately prevail, rather than to countenance monopolization of that market.[81]

If this opinion seemed to indicate that the Court was inclined to give short shrift to both the property and First Amendment rights of radio and television station owners, that impression was sharply corrected four years later. Then, in *Columbia Broadcasting System v. Democratic National Committee,*[82] the issue was whether a claimed First Amendment right of members of the public to purchase time for editorial advertisements on issues of current controversy should take priority over the claimed First Amendment right of broadcasters to have a policy of not selling time for such ads. In adjudicating between those conflicting claims, a majority of the Supreme Court came down on the side of the broadcasters. The Court began its argument by looking back to the legislative history of the Radio Act of 1927 and the Communications Act of 1934 and noting that Congress had explicitly rejected the common carrier concept. The opinion continued:

> ...it seems clear that Congress intended to permit private broadcasting to develop with the widest journalistic freedom consistent with its public obligations.... The broadcaster ... is allowed significant journalistic discretion in deciding how best to fulfill its Fairness Doctrine obligations.... The basic principle underlying that responsibility is "the right of the public to be informed, rather than any right on the part of government, any broadcast licensee or any individual member of the public to broadcast his own particular views on any matter...." Consistent with that philosophy, the Commission on several occasions has ruled that no private individual or group has a right to command the use of broadcast facilities.[83]

Justice Douglas concurred in the disposition of the case but for very different reasons. For him the *Red Lion* decision, in which he had not participated because of illness, had been a mistake, because even the Fairness Doctrine was, in his view, an unacceptable invasion of the free speech rights of broadcasters. He would have nothing to do with the double standard that had been accepted by Congress and the Court for the electronic and print media. "My conclusion," he said, "is that the TV and radio stand in the same protected position under the First Amendment as do newspapers and magazines."[84]

The dissenting opinion of Justices Brennan and Marshall urged the striking of a different balance between the competing claims of broadcasters and the public from that reached by the majority:

> ...the Court's reliance on the Fairness Doctrine as the *sole* means of informing the public seriously misconstrues and underestimates the public's interest in receiving ideas and information directly from the advocates of those ideas without the interposition of journalistic middlemen....
>
> Our legal system reflects a belief that truth is best illuminated by a collision of genuine advocates. Under the Fairness Doctrine, however, accompanied by an absolute ban on editorial advertising, the public is compelled to rely *exclusively* on the "journalistic discretion" of broadcasters who serve in theory as surrogate spokesmen for all sides of all issues. This separation of the advocate from the expression of his views can serve only to diminish the effectiveness of that expression.... if the public is to be honestly and forthrightly apprised of opposing views on controversial issues, it is imperative that citizens be permitted at least *some* opportunity to speak directly for themselves as genuine advocates on issues that concern them....
>
> Moreover, a proper balancing of the competing First Amendment interests at stake in this controversy must consider, not only the interests of broadcasters and of the listening and viewing public, but also the independent First Amendment interest of groups and individuals in effective self-expression.... the right to speak can flourish only if it is allowed to operate in an effective forum—whether it be a public park, a schoolroom, a town meeting hall, or a radio and television frequency. For in the absence of an effective means of communication, the right to speak would ring hollow indeed.... any policy that *absolutely* denies citizens access to the airwaves necessarily renders even the concept of "full and free discussion" practically meaningless.
>
> Regrettably, it is precisely such a policy that the Court upholds today.[85]

Having lost the constitutional struggle for a right of direct entry to over-the-air radio and television channels, advocates of public access looked with hope to the growth of cable television as a promising alternative medium through which individuals and groups might be able to reach a mass audience. The Federal Communications Commission intensified those hopes in 1972 when it promulgated rules which required that cable operators in the top 100 television markets of the country must design their systems to have at least twenty channels, four of which were to be earmarked for public, educational, and governmental access, with the public access channels to be available on a first-come first-served nondiscriminatory basis. In 1976 the FCC extended this requirement to all cable television systems serving more than 3,500 subscribers.[86] In 1979, however, the U.S. Supreme Court found it beyond the jurisdiction of the FCC to impose this common-carrier obligation on cable operators.[87] If anyone was going to do that, said the justices, it would have to be the Congress.[88]

Thus the Supreme Court, though bringing a halt to the FCC requirement that cable systems provide public access channels, saw no constitutional barrier to federal *legislation* which would accomplish the same goal. Depending upon whether Congress chose to exercise its authority in that way would depend the right of access to cable television. Presumably, in the eyes of the Supreme Court, the First Amendment is neither a barrier nor a requirement to that end. In view of the almost unimaginable potential of cable television for expanding and diversifying the marketplace of ideas, it is to be hoped that the Congress will seize the opportunity left open to it by the Court.

Turning now to the print media, it can be said quite simply at the outset that, insofar as any possible legal right of public access to newspapers and magazines is concerned, those institutions have been treated as First Amendment sacred cows. This has occurred despite a strong effort to persuade the courts that the ever-increasing centralization of ownership of mass circulation newspapers in fewer and fewer hands necessitates at least as much government intervention to guarantee the presentation of a diversity of views as has been required with respect to radio and television stations, which have grown in numbers and variety at the same time that the newspaper world has been contracting. The intellectual leadership for this effort was provided by Professor Jerome Barron in a widely discussed article which appeared in the *Harvard Law Review* in 1967, overoptimistically entitled, "Access to the Press—a New First Amendment Right."[89] After noting the decreased diversity of newspaper ownership in the United States, and the growing number of one-newspaper towns, Barron argued that our First Amendment thinking has been dominated by a romantic myth of a free marketplace of ideas which does not in fact exist. His proposed remedy was a legally enforceable right of access to the press, to be achieved either by judicial decree or by statutory enactments. But neither of those avenues has led to any success.

To be more specific, a number of different legal theories were tried, both before and after the Barron article, to win court orders against newspapers which had refused to accept paid advertisements proffered to them. In one set of cases it was contended that newspapers had a common-law obligation to publish advertisements.[90] Another claim was that rejection of particular advertising copy constituted state action forbidden by the First Amendment, because of the monopoly position enjoyed by the newspaper.[91] In addition to that contention, it has also been argued, in a suit brought by the Amalgamated Clothing Workers Union against the four major Chicago daily newspapers who had all rejected an ad the union wished to place, that government entanglement with the press through the granting of such privileges as exemption from jury service for its employees, press passes issued by the police, pressrooms maintained in government buildings, and certain tax exemptions not enjoyed by other entities, justifies a finding of state action sufficient to bring the First Amendment into play against a newspaper's rejection of an ad.[92] All of these arguments have been rejected by judges who seem mesmerized by the First Amendment interests of publishers and relatively unconcerned about the interests of those seeking access to the media.

Attempted statutory remedies for this problem have tended to focus on unpaid access to the news and editorial pages of a paper rather than paid access to its advertising columns, and these efforts have met with a similar lack of enthusiastic response. For example, in 1974 a bill was introduced in the New Jersey State Senate which would have given any persons subjected to criticism by a newspaper editorial a legally enforceable right to respond. The proposal was killed in the Senate's Democratic Conference and thus never brought to the floor.[93] And in 1976 a bill was offered in the Ohio State Senate which would have required newspapers to print retractions and rebuttals for any alleged errors at the request of anyone named in a presumptively false story. This measure was buried in committee.[94]

But the most significant and notable case in this area involved a Florida right-to-reply statute, already on the books, which provided that any newspaper which published an attack on the personal character or official record of any candidate for public office was obligated to print, free of charge, and in space of equal length and prominence, any reply the candidate wished to make. The *Miami Herald* contended that the law was a violation of the freedom-of-press clause of the First Amendment and won on that argument in a Florida circuit court. The supreme court of Florida, however, overturned that decision, finding that the First Amendment was enhanced, rather than abridged, by the statute, because of the "broad societal interest in the free flow of information to the public."[95] The newspaper appealed to the U.S. Supreme Court, where Jerome Barron unsuccessfully argued in defense of the law. In 1974, in *Miami Herald Publishing Company v. Tornillo,* the Supreme Court unanimously and unequivocally reversed the judgment of the Florida Supreme Court:

> . . . advocates of an enforceable right of access to the press vigorously argue that Government has an obligation to ensure that a wide variety of views reach the public. . . . It is urged that the claim of newspapers

to be "surrogates for the public" carries with it a concomitant fiduciary obligation to account for that stewardship. . . .

However much validity may be found in these arguments, at each point the implementation of a remedy such as an enforceable right of access necessarily calls for some mechanism, governmental or consensual. If it is governmental coercion, this at once brings about a confrontation with the express provisions of the First Amendment. . . . A responsible press is an undoubtedly desirable goal, but press responsibility is not mandated by the Constitution and like many other virtues it cannot be legislated. . . . The Florida statute fails to clear the barriers of the First Amendment because of its intrusion into the function of editors.[96]

What should be our evaluation of these positions taken by our legal system with respect to access to the mass media? Influenced as I have been to a considerable extent by Professor Barron's logic,[97] I start from the premise that the double standard we have established for the electronic and print media rests on foundations which are not sufficiently solid to support it any longer.[98]

The argument that broadcasters have greater obligations to society than the print media because they use the "public's airwaves" overlooks the fact that newspapers and magazines are distributed over the "public's streets" or are sent through the "public's mail" at taxpayer-subsidized postage rates. The justification for regulating broadcast programming because of the *physically* finite amount of air space allocated to a limited number of "privileged" licensees, in contrast to an allegedly unlimited number of potential printing presses, founders on the *economic* facts of life which have produced a far greater diversity of radio and television stations than of mass circulation newspapers, with no indication that this trend will do anything but continue in the same direction in the future. The claim that broadcasting has a more powerful influence on its audience than the print media, and thus must be kept under greater control to protect the public interest, suffers from two serious flaws. First as to radio, I am aware of no evidence that it is, in fact, a more influential channel of communication than newspapers, magazines, or books. But even if it were, as television clearly seems to be, there is nothing in the history or philosophy of the First Amendment to suggest that its protections were intended to vary according to the potency of the particular speech or press in question.

If we abandon this double standard, as I think we must for the reasons just enumerated, what kind of single standard shall we put in its place? Shall we have *no* legally enforceable right of access to *any* of the privately operated mass media of communication? Shall there be *some* rights of access to *all* of them, and if so, what rights? Shall there be some rights of

access to *some* of them, and if so, what shall be the distinguishing criterion among media if it is not to be whether they happen to fall in the
print or electronic category?

I would propose that we answer the first of these questions in the
negative, and opt for *some* legally enforceable rights of access to privately
operated mass media. Rather than looking to the First Amendment as
requiring such rights—a course which is clearly doomed to failure in the
light of *Columbia Broadcasting System v. Democratic National Committee* and
Miami Herald Publishing Company v. Tornillo—I would propose instead to
go the statutory route, hoping against the odds that a way can be found
to persuade the Supreme Court that the First Amendment, in spirit as
well as in letter, *permits* that kind of affirmative action by the legislative
branch of government to facilitate citizen expression and expand the
marketplace of ideas.

I would suggest a positive answer to the second question, arguing only
insofar as *paid* advertisements are concerned, that *all* media which are
in the business of selling space or time to others should be prohibited by
law from discriminating among potential clients on the basis of the content of the ads they wish to place. I would take as the model for such
legislation our public accommodation laws, which prohibit restaurants
and hotels that open their doors to the public's business from discriminating among customers on the grounds of their race. The theory
behind such legislation is that once a private facility "goes public" to the
extent of soliciting business on the open market, rather than functioning
as a private club, it must forego the right to pick and choose its customers
on the basis of personal prejudice. Deriving the profits which it does
from doing business with the public, it has commensurate obligations to
serve that public fairly.

Similarly, I see no reason why the owners of a communication channel
who choose to go into the business of selling a certain portion of their
space or time to the public in order to help finance their operation
should be permitted to reject or to censor particular ads because they
disapprove of the views expressed or their manner of expression. The
advertising columns of a newspaper, or commercials on the air, are
purely and simply business enterprises. To regard them as a wing of the
owner's rights of free speech or free press is to endow them with a status
which they do not merit. As Justice Brennan so insightfully put it in his
C.B.S. v. D.N.C. dissent:

> . . . it must be emphasized that this case deals *only* with the allocation
> of *advertising* time—airtime that broadcasters regularly relinquish to
> others without the retention of significant editorial control. Thus we
> are concerned here not with the speech of broadcasters themselves
> but, rather, with their "right" to decide which *other* individuals will

be given an opportunity to speak in a forum that has already been opened to the public.[99]

If there is a valid social interest, arising out of principles of racial justice, in preventing hotels and restaurants that serve the public from refusing to accommodate blacks or any other identifiable racial group among their customers, there is a social interest of comparable weight, springing from the philosophy of the First Amendment, in prohibiting those who control channels of public communication from excluding messages they do not like from their advertising arena.

Such a prohibition would not interfere in any way with the right of media owners to determine the total amount of time or space they wish to devote to advertising, anymore than public accommodation laws tell restaurants or hotels how many seats or rooms they must have. It is only within the boundaries which they themselves have established that they must take customers on a first come–first served basis, and without charging higher prices for categories of clients whose business they might want to discourage.

If there were such a statutory access requirement, with powers of censorship denied to media gatekeepers, then owners and managers would have to be relieved of any possible legal liability for what is said by others in the advertisements which are transmitted. And audiences would have to be brought to understand that what is communicated in advertisements does not represent the views of the medium itself, just as audiences are expected to know that political candidates who now buy time for spot announcements on radio or television are not speaking for the management of those stations. These are surely not insurmountable difficulties.

But what of a situation where, in advance of publication or broadcast, media managers have reason to believe that the message of a proposed advertisement would, if communicated, constitute illegal behavior? If ads cannot be rejected by media gatekeepers on the grounds of their content, can they be stopped in any other way, so that the media do not find themselves in the position of facilitating offenses, even though they have been relieved of legal liability? One permissible means, of course, would be for media managers to try to persuade such would-be advertisers to change their message in order to avoid running afoul of the law. Failing that, they might ask law enforcement officials to seek an injunction against the proposed advertisement, leaving it to the judiciary to decide whether there are, indeed, legal grounds for imposing a prior restraint. That is the kind of question which properly belongs in the courts anyhow.

Moving from a claimed right of paid to unpaid access to privately operated media, we encounter significantly more persuasive reasons for resistance to such claims. Required public access to the nonadvertising space in newspapers or time on the air invades an area that is otherwise used for communication authored or selected by the management and, since there is no charge, the likelihood is great that, unless severe limits are drawn, the demands for space and time will exceed any reasonable possibility of their being accommodated.

Yet I am not prepared, for these reasons, to abandon all thought of endorsing legislation which requires some narrowly defined rights of unpaid access to the most pervasive of the mass media. I shall first suggest the circumstances under which such rights of access might be justified, and then identify the particular kinds of access rights which might be reasonable.

I would begin the analysis by asking whether, in a particular community, or the nation as a whole, there is, in fact rather than theory, a sufficient diversity and competition among sources in each mass medium—radio, television, newspapers, and magazines—that a wide range of stimuli reach large numbers of people through the natural processes of a free and open marketplace. Or, to put the question the other way around, is there such a concentration or monopoly of ownership of channels in a particular medium as to create a situation in which the bulk of the audience for that medium is exposed to a rather monolithic view of the world? In the latter circumstances it seems inevitable that those who enjoy such a monopoly will have derived so many benefits from the public as to justify the imposition on them of a modest set of public access obligations.

More concretely, I believe that many of the arguments made to the court in the Amalgamated Clothing Workers case deserve more serious consideration than they have received. Newspapers do receive many special privileges from our society and the state—the right to sell their product from newsstands and news racks on public sidewalks; press passes, press conferences, press galleries, and pressrooms; significantly reduced postage rates; to mention but a few. I am not for a moment suggesting that these privileges are undesirable, but only that it is not unreasonable to require something to be given in return. Similarly, our three major television networks, CBS, NBC, and ABC, and the local stations affiliated with them have achieved their position of dominance over the television sets of the nation, as well as their ample profits, not only through a government licensing process, which is a privilege that has been extended to others as well, but through fortuitous historic and economic forces for which they owe some debt to the public.

If it is agreed that those media which I have characterized as the most pervasive and concentrated can justifiably be asked to pay access "dues" to the society from which they benefit so richly, there is still the problem of determining where on the continuum from total monopoly to wide diversity the line should be drawn between those who are required to participate and those who are not. This will have to be a somewhat arbitrary legislative judgment, based primarily on quantitative considerations, and little more can be done here than to suggest some general guidelines. Clearly, the three national television networks, the leading daily or weekly newspapers in one- or two-paper towns, and local television stations in towns where there are only two or three would fall on the near-monopoly side of the line. Just as certainly, there is at present such a variety of magazines on the national market, and of radio stations in large urban centers, that those channels should be free of unpaid public access obligations. The difficult judgments would come at the center of the continuum, and would have to depend on the best statistics available regarding the number of viewers or readers who rely predominantly on a particular source in relationship to the size of the total audience for that medium in whatever is defined as the relevant community. For example, a formula might be established such that if three or fewer channels together have a nearly exclusive monopoly on two-thirds or more of the estimated total audience for that medium, then public access requirements would apply to those particular channels. Thus, for the television medium, even if new networks were to come onto the national scene, so long as the Big Three still held a combined position of dominance over at least two-thirds of the total television audience, unpaid public access obligations would still apply to them. The same kind of formula could also be employed with respect to newspapers or television stations in a local community.

The second question which must be answered, beyond determining to whom unpaid public access obligations should apply, is what the nature of those requirements should be. I would preface that discussion by urging the abolition of the Fairness Doctrine for broadcasting and the avoidance of any comparable scheme which might be conceived for the print media. Unlike a requirement that members of the public be allowed direct access to a channel of communication to present their own views, the Fairness Doctrine puts the government in the business of evaluating material which is originated or selected by the media themselves and judging whether it passes according to what has proved to be a rather elusive set of standards. Even though broad discretion is left to broadcasters in fulfilling their fairness obligations, there is always the threat that the FCC, looking over their shoulders, may decide, as it not infrequently has done in the past, that a complainant is correct in asserting that the doctrine has been violated and that the situation must be remedied. If the Supreme Court is to be consistently concerned, as it claimed it was concerned in the *Miami Herald* case, about government "intrusion into the function of editors," then surely it should have more doubts than it seems to have about enforcement of the Fairness Doctrine.

In contrast to demanding fairness of the messages originated and selected by media management, requirements for public access merely stipulate certain conditions under which free space or time must be relinquished to others, thus avoiding the necessity for a government arbiter to pass judgment on the content of anyone's communication. Let us turn now to a consideration of what those conditions should be.

I would propose two sets of unpaid public access requirements. The first would be a right of reply, in space or time of equal length and visibility, to editorial attacks on any individual or group, whether involved in a political campaign or not, and to editorial endorsements of, or opposition to, any candidate for public office. The right would not apply to the so-called neutral reportage of news events or of other people's comments, although it could be invoked if the medium provided a free platform directly to someone other than its own editors to engage in attacks on individuals or groups or to support or oppose a political candidate. Thus, Section 315 of the Communications Act would be retained, and the present FCC personal-attack and political editorial rules would be extended to a wider spectrum of occasions than they now cover. The Supreme Court would have to be convinced to reverse its *Miami Herald* decision, allowing even a broader range for compelled replies to newspaper editorials than was provided by the Florida statute, which was limited to editorial criticisms of political candidates.

There is, of course, a danger that these kinds of right-to-reply requirements can have an inhibiting effect on the willingness of the media to engage in the sort of robust discussion and criticism which is necessary to a truly free marketplace of ideas. Were that to be demonstrably the case, I would regard it as too high a price to pay for public access and would back away from the proposal. But I believe that it need not be the inevitable consequence of such a regime, and self-fulfilling prophecies should be viewed with suspicion. Media owners and managers ought to be able to accept the fact that giving over a certain amount of space or time to others to reply to attacks which are made upon them is simply a normal cost of doing business in their field, and that it may even enliven and improve their product as well as substantially increase its audience and its social value. Rather than avoiding controversial material which might trigger replies, they could conceivably learn to welcome that possibility.

The second set of public access requirements that I would suggest, unlike the first, would not be triggered by something the medium itself had said but would be a standing obligation to allocate at least a certain percentage of its space or time, on a regular basis, for unexpurgated letters to the editor or taped messages, or for solicited and unsolicited guest editorials and columns. The amount to be so allocated would have to be a matter of legislative judgment, but, to be reasonable, should not exceed more than perhaps 5 percent of a medium's total space or time. Since there would likely be more communicators wishing to avail themselves of these opportunities than could be accommodated, and the right would not belong to any particular persons who had been attacked, some selection of messages would have to be made. Rather than requiring a first come–first served procedure, which would provide no assurance of the quality that a medium might justifiably wish to maintain in the interest of not boring its audience, this is a point at which media gatekeepers might well be allowed to exercise their own discretion. They could be exhorted to base their judgments on quality rather than viewpoints, but it would have to be recognized that content-based prejudices might well play some part in the process. In view of the fact that the media have made a large investment in cultivating their audiences, and have a large stake in maintaining them, it is probably only fair to allow them that degree of latitude in fulfilling their unpaid public access obligations.

It should be recognized that many media owners and managers, on a voluntary basis, have already taken some of the steps that have been suggested here as legal obligations. Guest editorials and columns, substantial amounts of space for letters to the editor, and invitations to readers to send in corrections of factual errors they may discover, have become standard fare in significant numbers of newspapers. Most radio and television stations regularly offer equal time to responsible individuals and groups for replies to the editorials which are broadcast, and some have entered into agreements to present over the air a certain number of so-called Free Speech Messages prepared by various community organizations.

This is all to the good, and to the extent that the tendency may grow, there will be less need for government intervention. But until such time as there is more assurance than our system now provides that the mass media will expose their audiences to the kind of diversity which lies out there in the real world, the legal imposition of access requirements on the giant communicators of our nation and our communities seems a small price for them to pay in the interest of the facilitation of citizen expression. The U.S. Supreme Court put it well in *Red Lion* when it said: "It is the purpose of the First Amendment to preserve an uninhibited marketplace of ideas in which truth will ultimately prevail, rather than to countenance monopolization of that market."[100]

15

Compulsions to Communicate

When the history of religious thought in twentieth-century America is written, it is not likely that the Jehovah's Witnesses will be said to have had a major influence. An honest account, however, of the development of First Amendment doctrine would have to recognize that this zealous sect had played a significant role. Their part in testing and defining the outer limits of government control over use of the public forum and communication to hostile audiences has been noted in previous chapters. But of no less importance to the ripening of free speech theory was the refusal of the Witnesses to allow their children to be compelled by the state to participate in school conducted flag-salute and pledge-of-allegiance rituals. After losing the first round of that battle in the U.S. Supreme Court in 1940,[1] their persistence was rewarded only three years later when the Court reversed itself and handed them a victory of grand proportions, establishing a right of silence under the First Amendment.[2] Said Justice Jackson for the Court: "To sustain the compulsory flag salute we are required to say that a Bill of Rights which guards the individual's right to speak his own mind, left it open to public authorities to compel him to utter what is not in his mind."[3]

As with all First Amendment rights which it has acknowledged, the Supreme Court qualified its endorsement of the right to silence by noting that there was in the flag ritual case no clear and present danger which would justify the state in compelling this sort of symbolic conformity.[4] Thus, while establishing with one hand the proposition that people may refuse to talk when the government insists that they do so, the Court, with its other hand, suggested that countervailing interests may sometimes limit that prerogative. It shall be the purpose of this chapter to review the circumstances in which government compulsions to communicate have been attempted, to identify those which have been sustained and those invalidated by the courts, and to offer an evaluation of these restrictions on the right of silence.

Oaths and Affidavits

The first category of compulsory speech we shall examine is that of oaths and affidavits—requirements, for example, that people swear their loyalty to the state, affirm their intention "to uphold the Constitution and the laws of the land," or promise to give testimony which is "the truth, the whole truth, and nothing but the truth," so help them God.

Compulsory oath taking has an ancient history in the affairs of both church and state, which suggests a powerful social impulse, if not legitimacy, for this particular form of mandatory communication. One can only speculate about the forces underlying this tradition, but such conjecture may be helpful in our assessment of the merit of these requirements.

It is likely that one of the most important of these forces has been a sheer need on the part of those in authority to make a display of their power. To be able to compel expressions of obeisance not only reminds those who are so compelled of their subordination to something greater than themselves but serves as an example to others that the enforcing agents are powerful enough to demand deference from them as well. Conversely, an inability to extract verbal affirmations of allegiance may be perceived by some as weakness in an institution, thus undermining its effective authority.

The stock which people so often place in being able to pressure even their friends and associates into saying what they want to hear—be it a compliment on one's work or appearance, an apology for a wrong committed, or an avowal of undying love, even in circumstances where both parties know full well they are engaged in a verbal charade which masks their true feelings—suggests a widespread belief in a kind of word magic that can reshape reality merely by saying it is so. Faith in this magic, so common at the interpersonal level among peers, is even more pervasive where power between the parties is unequal and the ability to extract involuntary communication thus all the greater. Given the frequency with which parents, teachers, and bosses resort to this process to reinforce their feelings of authority, it is not surprising to find leaders of church and state having recourse to the same technique.

Lest it appear that these comments pay too little respect to the conventional wisdom of the ages, let me hasten to concede that this historical tradition may have some support in modern psychological theory and research. What I have labeled word magic, some psychologists might describe as a process of reducing cognitive dissonance—a postulated phenomenon for which there is considerable empirical evidence.[5] According to the theory of cognitive dissonance, people have a need to think themselves consistent in beliefs and actions and to eliminate discrepancies of which they are aware by changing either their behavior or their attitudes in the direction of congruence. According to this theory, it should be possible to modify people's behavior by inducing them to avow belief in the state of affairs desired by the persuader. It has been thought that the so-called brainwashing technique relies, in part, on this strategy.

On the other hand, experimental research on cognitive dissonance has also revealed that subjects who behave in dissonant ways because of substantial rewards or punishments—characterized by researchers as "forced compliance"—or who can find some other justification for their dissonant acts are less likely to change their attitudes to bring them into conformity with the behavior than subjects for whom the rewards, punishments, or justifications are of a smaller order.[6] The explanation offered for these findings is that those who have been coerced into dissonant actions can rationalize the discrepancy between what they do and what they believe by placing responsibility on the external coercive agent, thus not experiencing it so much as internal dissonance.[7] It would follow that the reverse should also be true—that is, people who are coerced into avowing dissonant beliefs would be less likely to bring their behavior into conformity with those beliefs than persons uttering them voluntarily.

If the foregoing analysis is viewed as too psychological an explanation for society's oath-taking tradition, one can find practical and legalistic reasons for it as well. If an oath is compelled, and the person in question is then found to have violated that oath, punishment can be administered with a clearer conscience than if there has been more ambiguity as to what constituted expected behavior. To put it another way, if one promises to do something and then does not do it, the offense is felt to be greater than if there has been no explicit statement of intentions made. Thus a reason for the swearing in of witnesses is to put them on plain notice that they are not only expected to tell the truth but that failure to do so constitutes perjury, for which they can be punished. Similarly, the taking of an oath of office upon assuming public responsibilities may be viewed not only as creating some pressure beyond the individual's own sense of commitment to perform in accordance with the promises made, but also as providing a standard against which conduct can be measured, and a legitimate basis for discipline or ouster if that standard is not met. To say that one has violated his or her oath of office seems stronger than to say that there has been a failure to perform one's duties.

On the other hand, it can be argued that it is not only an unnecessary but an insulting ritual to ask honest and responsible individuals to give verbal assurances that they will do what they know full well they are supposed to do. What is more, for those who have no intention of performing as expected, promises roll so easily off their lips as to make them meaningless. Again the question seems to be whether words themselves may have some power to transform reality.

Be that as it may, our political system has relied on sworn statements for many purposes, and for the most part these requirements have gone unquestioned as possible violations of a First Amendment right to silence. That has been entirely true of oaths of office and the swearing in of witnesses, but only partially true, as we shall now see, of pledges of allegiance to the state.

In addition to the flag-salute ritual successfully overturned by Jehovah's Witnesses, another challenged effort by government in the United States to produce conforming behavior through compulsory communication has been the so-called loyalty oath or affidavit, which became particularly popular during the Cold War period following World War II. At the federal level, for instance, Section 9(h) of the Taft-Hartley Act of 1947 required that officers of labor unions seeking the benefits of the National Labor Relations Act had to file an affidavit disclaiming membership in, or affiliation with, the Communist Party, or belief in the overthrow of the United States government by force or any illegal means. Although a First Amendment attack on this legislation failed in 1950 to win agreement from a majority of the Supreme Court,[8] the provision was repealed by Congress in 1959.[9]

At state and local levels, many bills were adopted during the same era requiring a wide variety of loyalty oaths as a condition, in some cases for employment as teachers in the public schools, in some cases for any employment in the public sector, and in some instances for obtaining a place on the state's election ballot. The first challenges to this kind of legislation in the U.S. Supreme Court were turned back in 1951,[10] but a decade later they began meeting with success.

In 1961 the Supreme Court found a Florida statute requiring all state employees to swear that they did not lend "aid, support, advice, counsel or influence to the Communist Party" unconstitutionally void for vagueness.[11] In 1964 the same standard was used to strike down two State of Washington loyalty oaths for teachers.[12] Two years later an Arizona loyalty oath for employees of that state fell under the axe, this time primarily because the Supreme Court's majority found it to be unacceptable guilt by association for the state legislature to have concluded that anyone who belonged to any organizations whose purposes were the forcible overthrow of government was incapable of honestly swearing to uphold the constitution and to faithfully discharge his or her duties of office.[13] That ruling was followed, in 1967, by one declaring invalid a New York loyalty program for teachers, also because of the guilt by association on which it was premised, and because it conditioned public employment on the surrender of a constitutional right which, in the Court's view, could not have been abridged by direct government action.[14] Finally, that same year, the very Maryland law whose oath requirement for access to the ballot the Court had sustained in 1951 was now found wanting as applied to a university teacher, in light of the Washington, Arizona, and New York decisions which had been handed down in the meanwhile.[15]

Following this string of defeats for state loyalty oaths, the worm turned once again, but only part way around. In a group of cases decided between 1968 and 1972, the Supreme Court affirmed lower court rulings which had upheld oath requirements for teachers in New York and Colorado.[16] The essential difference between the oaths required in these cases and those which had been struck down in the earlier set of decisions was that these were what are known as "positive" or "affirmative" oaths, in contrast to the so-called test oaths or disclaimers which had previously been found constitutionally defective. A positive oath is one in which people are asked to *affirm,* in *general* terms, their support of the Constitution, their willingness to faithfully discharge their duties, or their belief in democratic principles, leaving to their own understanding and interpretation the obligations they have thus sworn to undertake. A test oath or disclaimer, on the other hand, is one which asks people to *disavow* adherence to *specific* beliefs, activities, or organizational memberships—attitudes and behaviors which in their own minds may be entirely compatible with good citizenship.

The Supreme Court majority's understanding of this distinction between affirmative and test oaths and its method of applying the concept to specific instances was explained in its opinion in *Cole v. Richardson* in 1972.[17] The case involved a Massachusetts oath requiring public employees to swear, first, to "uphold and defend the Constitution," and, second, to "oppose the overthrow of the Government by force, violence or by any illegal or unconstitutional method." Chief Justice Burger, writing for the Court, began by summarizing the kinds of test oaths which had been found unacceptable in the past:

> We have made clear that neither federal nor state governments may condition employment on taking oaths which impinge rights guaranteed by the First and Fourteenth Amendments respectively, as for example those relating to political beliefs. . . . Nor may employment be conditioned on an oath that one has not engaged, or will not engage, in protected speech activities such as the following: criticizing institutions of government; discussing political doctrine that approves the overthrow of certain forms of government; and supporting candidates for public office. . . . Employment may not be conditioned on an oath denying past, or abjuring future, associational activities within

constitutional protections; such protected activities include memberships in organizations having illegal purposes unless one knows of the
purpose and shares a specific intent to promote the illegal purpose.[18]

He then turned to a description of the more acceptable positive oaths:

> Several cases recently decided by the Court stand out among our
> oath cases because they have upheld the constitutionality of oaths,
> addressed to the future, promising constitutional support in broad
> terms. These cases have begun with a recognition that the Constitution
> itself prescribes comparable oaths in two articles. Article II . . . pro-
> vides that the President shall swear that he will "faithfully execute the
> office . . ." Article VI . . . provides that all state and federal officers
> shall be bound by an oath "to support this Constitution." . . .
> The Court has further made clear that an oath need not parrot
> the exact language of the constitutional oaths to be constitutionally
> proper.[19]

Finally, the Court's opinion applied these criteria to the Massachusetts
oath under immediate consideration:

> The District Court in the instant case properly recognized that the
> first clause of the Massachusetts oath, in which the individual swears to
> "uphold and defend" the constitutions of the United States and the
> Commonwealth, is indistinguishable from the oaths this Court has
> recently approved. Yet the District Court applied a highly literalistic
> approach to the second clause to strike it down. We view the second
> clause of the oath as essentially the same as the first. . . . such a literal
> approach to the second clause is inconsistent with the Court's ap-
> proach to the "support" oaths. . . . We have rejected such rigidly literal
> notions and recognized that the purpose leading legislatures to enact
> such oaths . . . was not to create specific responsibilities but to assure
> that those in positions of public trust were willing to commit them-
> selves to live by the constitutional processes of our system. . . . Just as
> the connotatively active word "support" has been interpreted to mean
> simply a commitment to abide by our constitutional system, the second
> clause of this oath is merely oriented to the negative implications of
> this notion; it is a commitment not to use illegal and constitutionally
> unprotected force to change the constitutional system. The second
> clause does not expand the obligation of the first; it simply makes clear
> the application of the first clause to a particular issue. Such repetition,
> whether for emphasis or cadence, seems to be wont with authors of
> oaths. That the second clause may be redundant is not ground to
> strike it down; we are not charged with correcting grammar but en-
> forcing a constitution.[20]

The dissenting justices not only had difficulty with the majority's determination that the second clause was not of the disclaimer variety but

expressed doubts, as well, about *all* loyalty oaths. Justice Douglas felt that the second phrase required "that appellee 'oppose' that which she has an indisputable right to advocate."[21] Justice Marshall, joined by Justice Brennan, described the second phrase as unconstitutionally vague and overbroad, and then went on to make the following observation about the entire issue:

> The Court's prior decisions represent a judgment that simple affirmative oaths of support are less suspect and less evil than negative oaths requiring a disaffirmance of political ties, group affiliations, or beliefs. . . .
>
> Yet I think it is plain that affirmative oaths of loyalty, no less than negative ones, have odious connotations. . . . We have tolerated support oaths as applied to all government employees only because we view these affirmations as an expression of "minimal loyalty to the Government." . . .
>
> It is precisely because these oaths are minimal . . . that they have been sustained. That they are minimal intrusions into the freedom of government officials and employees to think, speak, and act makes them constitutional; it does not mean that greater intrusions will be tolerated. . . . Within the limits of the Constitution it is, of course, for the legislators to weigh the utility of the oaths and their potential dangers and to strike a balance. But, as a people, we should always keep in mind the words of Mr. Justice Black . . . "I am certain that loyalty to the United States can never be secured by the endless proliferation of 'loyalty' oaths; loyalty must arise spontaneously from the hearts of people who love their country and respect their government."[22]

The dissenters' objections in *Cole v. Richardson* may not have been in vain, for two years later the Court struck down an Indiana requirement that candidates seeking access to the ballot in that state had to file an affidavit swearing they did not advocate the overthrow of government by force or violence.[23] Appearing to follow the reasoning of Justice Douglas's *Cole* dissent, a majority of the Court found that, since the theoretical advocacy of revolution is protected by the First Amendment, one cannot be required to disavow such advocacy as a condition to being placed on the ballot. If we attempt to reconcile this decision with that of the majority in *Cole* we will either have to give up in failure or conclude that the line the Court has drawn between acceptable affirmations and unacceptable disclaimers is too fine to be perceived with the naked eye.

What is even more puzzling about these loyalty oath opinions of the Supreme Court than the haziness of the border between positive and test oaths is the utter absence of any reference to the right of silence which had been enunciated in the Jehovah's Witnesses' flag ritual case in 1943. When loyalty oaths were struck down in the 1960s it was on the grounds of vagueness, guilt by association, or discriminatory conditions of public employment. Not until 1977, when another Jehovah's Witness was in the Supreme Court complaining about New Hampshire's refusal to let him put tape over the motto embossed on his state automobile license plate reading "Live Free or Die," did the right-to-silence precedent suddenly and surprisingly reappear.[24] Then, in seemingly unequivocal language, the Court said:

> We begin with the proposition that the right of freedom of thought protected by the First Amendment against state action includes both the right to speak freely and the right to refrain from speaking at all.... The right to speak and the right to refrain from speaking are complementary components of the broader concept of "individual freedom of mind." ... Compelling the affirmative act of a flag salute involved a more serious infringement upon personal liberties than the passive act of carrying the state motto on a license plate, but the difference is essentially one of degree. Here, as in *Barnette*, we are faced with a state measure which forces an individual, as part of his daily life ... to be an instrument for fostering public adherence to an ideological point of view he finds unacceptable.... The First Amendment protects the right of individuals to hold a point of view different from the majority and to refuse to foster, in the way New Hampshire commands, an idea they find morally reprehensible.[25]

Unless one accepts the unlikely proposition that the Supreme Court regards Jehovah's Witnesses as having greater First Amendment rights than anybody else, one can only infer from the foregoing cases that the Court must perceive some unarticulated difference between communication compelled from ordinary citizens going about their daily affairs and that required of persons seeking public employment, public services, a place on the ballot, or even the right to cast a ballot.[26] Another possibility, of course, is that the Court is simply not sufficiently aware of this particular dissonance in its free speech doctrine to feel a need to eliminate it.

It should come as no surprise to the reader, after the preceding discussion, that I have grave doubts about the compatibility of the oath-taking process with a robust interpretation of the First Amendment. It seems to me that the Supreme Court was indisputably correct, in its flag-salute and license-plate opinions, in finding a right of silence implicit in the right to speak, and that the Court has seriously erred in shelving that insight when dealing with the issue of oaths and affidavits. It is understandable that the justices, accountable to the entire U.S. Constitution, would not feel free to reject as violations of the First Amendment oaths of office plainly required by Articles II and VI, or others identical to them. But those of us not burdened with the Court's responsibilities can perhaps be allowed the luxury of suggesting that Articles II and VI are archaic in their oath requirements, reflective of an era in which there was considerably more ritual and deference to authority than today, and a less expansive understanding of freedom of expression.

I would not go so far as to propose that Articles II and VI be amended to delete these requirements, but am rather inclined to agree with Justices Marshall and Brennan that such affirmative oaths of office are "minimal intrusions into the freedom of government officials" which can be accepted so long as we do not tolerate "greater intrusions." It is akin to our looking the other way, as regards the separation of church and state, when government functions are opened and closed with prayers by clergymen. Furthermore, it seems to me that the values to be gained from the swearing in of public officials, as well as of witnesses, in the form of clear notice of social expectations and fair warning of behavior that is punishable, are sufficient to justify these particular kinds of "minimal intrusion."

However, when we move to anything that is arguably a disclaimer, or even to positive oaths which may be required to register to vote, to obtain a passport, or to secure a place on the ballot, it is difficult to see any valid social purpose which is sufficient to offset the insult to dignity and the restraint on freedom which such compulsory utterances entail. Unthinking tradition is certainly not enough of a reason to perpetuate the practice, let alone to pretend it is compatible with the First Amendment.

Government Investigations

A second arena in which compulsions to communicate have clashed with the desire of people to remain silent is that of government demands for information in connection with putative efforts to prevent subversion or to investigate alleged criminal activity. This battle has been waged in a number of sectors, with the state emerging as the victor at least as often as not.

The most celebrated of these struggles occurred during the late 1940s, 1950s, and early 1960s between legislative committees looking into so-called un-American activities and persons subpoenaed to testify about their alleged knowledge of, or involvement in, such behavior. The Committee on Un-American Activities of the U.S. House of Representatives, more popularly known as HUAC, was the most publicized in this field, but a subcommittee of the U.S. Senate headed by Joseph R. McCarthy, and comparable bodies established by legislatures at the state level, were also busily at work. The procedures which they followed often left much to be desired from a due process point of view, and the lives and reputations of many innocent persons were seriously damaged as a result.

It was not until 1957, after a decade of largely unrestrained activity by these legislative committees and other agencies of government engaged in the same pursuit, that the Supreme Court imposed its first limitations on this kind of compelled communication. Overturning a contempt of Congress conviction of a labor union official who had refused to answer questions put to him by HUAC, the Court held that the committee was obligated to make clear to its witnesses what the purpose of its inquiry was and the relevance to that purpose of the specific questions being asked.[27] On the same day, the Court also set aside the contempt conviction of a man who had declined to respond to questions put to him by the attorney general of New Hampshire about a lecture on socialism he had delivered at the state university.[28] Although the Court ultimately rested these decisions on due process rather than First Amendment grounds, its opinion noted the dangers to freedom of expression in these sorts of investigations. Said Chief Justice Earl Warren for the Court in the HUAC case:

> The Bill of Rights is applicable to investigations as to all forms of governmental action. Witnesses cannot be compelled to give evidence against themselves. They cannot be subjected to unreasonable search and seizure. Nor can the First Amendment freedoms of speech, press, religion, or political belief and association be abridged. . . .
>
> Abuses of the investigative process may imperceptibly lead to abridgment of protected freedoms. The mere summoning of a witness and compelling him to testify, against his will, about his beliefs, expressions or associations is a measure of governmental interference. And when those forced revelations concern matters that are unorthodox, unpopular, or even hateful to the general public, the reaction in the life of the witness may be disastrous. This effect is even more harsh when it is past beliefs, expressions or associations that are disclosed and judged by current standards rather than those contemporary with the matters exposed.[29]

Despite its recognition of the First Amendment values at stake, the Supreme Court was soon to determine that the competing government interest in gathering information deemed necessary to protect itself against subversion could be sufficient to outweigh an individual's right not to speak. Applying this "balancing doctrine" in a pair of 1959 decisions, again involving challenged inquiries made by HUAC and the attorney general of New Hampshire, a five-man majority of the Court found in favor of the state and upheld the contempt convictions.[30] Writing for the majority in the HUAC case, Justice Harlan said:

> . . . the protections of the First Amendment . . . do not afford a witness

the right to resist inquiry in all circumstances. Where First Amendment rights are asserted to bar governmental interrogation resolution
of the issue always involves a balancing by the courts of the competing
private and public interests at stake in the particular circumstances. . . .
We conclude that the balance between the individual and the governmental interests here at stake must be struck in favor of the latter, and
that therefore the provisions of the First Amendment have not been
offended.[31]

Justice Black, in dissent, countered, "Such a balance . . . completely
leaves out the real interest in Barenblatt's silence, the interest of the
people as a whole in being able to join organizations, advocate causes and
make political 'mistakes' without later being subjected to governmental
penalties for having dared to think for themselves."[32]

The balance arrived at by the majority was struck again in 1961 when
two more contempt convictions for refusing to answer HUAC's questions about membership in the Communist Party were upheld,[33] and
when approval was given to the State of California's denial of admission
to the bar of an applicant who had also refused to answer such questions.[34]

The Court felt quite differently, however, about state demands that an
organization turn over its entire membership list to the government.
Despite an old 1928 precedent in which the authority of the State of New
York to compel the Ku Klux Klan to disclose its membership had been
affirmed,[35] the justices in 1958 and again in 1960 unanimously held that
chapters of the National Association for the Advancement of Colored
People in Alabama and Arkansas could not be required to turn over
their membership lists to the state.[36] In other closely related but more
narrowly decided rulings, a bare majority struck down an Arkansas statute which required public school teachers to file annual affidavits listing
all of the organizations of which they had been members or contributors
during the previous five years,[37] and overturned the contempt conviction of an NAACP officer who had refused to produce his group's membership records for a committee of the Florida legislature investigating
alleged Communist infiltration of the organization.[38]

The close division within the Supreme Court over how to weigh the
government's claimed needs for information to preserve its security
against the right of individuals and groups to remain silent about their
political beliefs and associations has reappeared in the Court's striking of
a balance between the needs of our system of justice to secure all relevant
material about criminal conduct and the right of investigative reporters
to refuse to divulge confidentially obtained information. A five-man
majority of the court, in *Branzburg v. Hayes,* held, in 1972, that reporters,
like all other citizens, have an obligation to respond to grand jury sub-

poenas and to answer the questions put to them in the course of a criminal investigation.[39] One of the dissenters, Justice Douglas, argued that "unless the reporter himself is implicated in a crime . . . a newsman has an absolute right not to appear before a grand jury."[40] The other three dissenters, Justices Stewart, Brennan and Marshall, while conceding that reporters might legitimately be required to reveal confidences if a compelling need for their information were demonstrated and there were no alternative means of obtaining it, felt that the majority's less qualified position represented a "crabbed view of the First Amendment" reflecting "a disturbing insensitivity to the critical role of an independent press in our society."[41]

Questions which divide the Supreme Court so closely and consistently over a substantial period of time are not likely to be ones for which there are easy answers, and that is particularly true of government demands on its citizens for involuntarily provided information. We could, if we wished, add still further examples to the catalogue of circumstances where this issue can arise—questions by census-takers about religious affiliations, inquiries from departments of revenue about earnings and real property, or interrogations by the police of witnesses at the scene of a crime. Clearly our posture must vary in accordance with the circumstances, and only flexible guidelines or principles will be of much help. Unfortunately, with flexibility there is always the possibility of abuse.

Our first principle, I believe, ought to be that the right of silence is always to be seriously reckoned with, even if ultimately subordinated to overriding concerns. It should never be taken for granted that a government demand for information is so reasonable and legitimate that no right-thinking person would want to reject it. Maintaining silence about one's religion, one's earnings, one's associations, or even one's knowledge about illegal conduct by others may also be perfectly reasonable and legitimate interests which should not be lightly infringed. The mere fact that a person wishes not to speak about a matter should create an initial presumption against compelled utterances on that subject.

Conversely, as a second principle, there are certain kinds of information which are so obviously needed by the government to perform its most basic functions that the right of silence must clearly give way. Knowledge of earnings and property in order to assess taxes would surely fall in that category. Knowledge of criminal conduct would come very close, although the law has seen fit, for a variety of good reasons, to allow exceptions for spouses, doctors, lawyers, clergymen, and, in some states under some circumstances even reporters.

A third principle I would offer is that rarely, if ever, can justification be found for compelling the communication of information as to a person's *beliefs and associations*—religious, social, or political. The antisocial

action of individuals is the only proper concern of the state, and that
cannot legitimately be inferred from their beliefs or associations. The
fundamental flaw in what was done for so many years by HUAC was not
its frequently careless procedures or its indulgence in exposure for exposure's sake, but the basic mandate of the legislation through which it
was established—to investigate un-American activities *"and propaganda."*
For government to investigate propaganda is to move into the realm of
beliefs and associations and thus inevitably to intrude on protected First
Amendment freedoms. Had the Supreme Court followed this third
principle throughout the 1950s and 1960s it would have found its
balancing task much easier, and would have had to come out the other
way in all of the cases reviewed above where government inquiries with
respect to suspected subversion were upheld.

Fourth, and last, with respect to the issue of compelling reporters, or
for that matter scholars and free-lance writers, to provide to the criminal
justice system information secured by them on a promise of confidentiality, it seems to me that the principle supported by Justices
Stewart, Brennan, and Marshall in their *Branzburg* dissent was a
Solomon-wise compromise between the extremes of the majority and
Justice Douglas. It gives substantial deference to the right not to speak in
these circumstances, placing on the government a heavy burden to find
other ways to secure the information that is wanted. It recognizes, however, that such alternatives sometimes may not be available, and that the
need for the information may be so compelling as to justify a subordination of the interests in silence that are present. That seems a more
genuine act of balancing than to put all the weight on one side.

Disclosure Requirements

The third and last category we shall examine, where government demands for communication may conflict with desires to remain silent, is
that of disclosure requirements—rules which impose upon speakers and
writers an obligation to identify themselves in certain ways, to divulge
information as to the sources of their financial support, or to tell more
than they may wish about a product or service they are offering for sale.
The primary purpose of such requirements is to help the public to
evaluate the messages being presented to them by providing information
about possible motivations and biases of the communicators and about
details of their propositions which might not otherwise be available. The
resistance to such demands springs not only from the possibility that
there is something shady which communicators wish to hide, but the
more legitimate concerns that the information sought is nobody else's

business; that its disclosure might hamper, rather than aid, an objective evaluation of the message by the audience; and that in some circumstances one cannot speak freely or honestly unless protected from possible retribution by a shield of anonymity.

Our experience with disclosure in the United States has covered a variety of requirements. Those which have been challenged in the courts on either First Amendment or other grounds have more often than not been sustained. One of the earliest U.S. Supreme Court decisions upholding a requirement of this sort dealt with a Post Office regulation which provides that publications seeking second-class mailing privileges must file and make public information concerning their ownership.[42] Two decades later, the Court sustained the Federal Corrupt Practices Act of 1925, which required the filing of information concerning receipts and expenditures of money by political organizations involved in presidential elections.[43] In neither of these cases was the First Amendment issue directly addressed, but that was to change as time went on and similar matters came before the courts.

In 1938 Congress adopted the Foreign Agents Registration Act requiring that persons who engage in lobbying or propaganda activities in this country on behalf of a foreign power must register and file copies of their literature with the government as well as provide information about their receipts and expenditures of funds.[44] When the Supreme Court upheld this legislation in 1943,[45] though rejecting its applicability to a citizen who was not found to have been acting on behalf of a foreign principal, Justice Black made these remarks about the law's relationship to the First Amendment:

> Resting on the fundamental constitutional principle that our people, adequately informed, may be trusted to distinguish between the true and the false, the bill is intended to label information of foreign origin so that hearers and readers may not be deceived by the belief that the information comes from a disinterested source. Such legislation implements rather than detracts from the prize freedoms guaranteed by the First Amendment.[46]

There followed passage, in 1946, of the Federal Regulation of Lobbying Act,[47] imitated widely at the state level, which required registration and public accounting of receipts and expenditures by persons who seek to influence the passage or defeat of legislation. Challenged on free speech grounds, the statute was upheld by the Supreme Court, but only after being construed to apply narrowly to paid lobbyists in direct communication with members of Congress and not to amateur or grass-roots persuasion such as writing letters to one's representative.[48] Chief Justice Warren explained the Court's rationale:

Present-day legislative complexities are such that individual members of Congress cannot be expected to explore the myriad pressures to which they are regularly subjected. Yet full realization of the American ideal of government by elected representatives depends to no small extent on their ability to properly evaluate such pressures. . . .

Toward that end, Congress has not sought to prohibit these pressures. It has merely provided for a modicum of information from those who for hire attempt to influence legislation or who collect or spend funds for that purpose. It wants only to know who is being hired, who is putting up the money, and how much. . . .

Under these circumstances, we believe that Congress . . . is not constitutionally forbidden to require the disclosure of lobbying activities.[49]

Prior to this decision Congress had also adopted the Internal Security Act (or McCarran Act) of 1950, among other things calling for registration with the attorney general of so-called Communist-action and Communist-front organizations, including the names and addresses of their officers and an accounting of all moneys received and expended. This information was to be open for public inspection, and any communication mailed or broadcast to the public by these groups was to be labeled as coming from "a Communist organization."[50] A Subversive Activities Control Board was created to determine whether particular groups were Communist-action or Communist-front organizations and, if so, to order them to register.

The crucial test of these provisions came as a result of the government's attempts to enforce a 1953 decision of the SACB finding that the Communist Party of the United States was obligated to register under the act. Litigation over the matter occupied the attention of federal courts for more than a decade until, finally, the Communist Party, through a series of largely technical legal victories, defeated the government's efforts.[51] This happened despite a finding of the U.S. Supreme Court, midway through the battle, that the registration requirement of the McCarran Act did not violate either the First Amendment or any other provision of the Constitution.[52] That ruling was of no more help to the government in its efforts to enforce SACB orders against other groups than it was against the Communist Party. As a result of these failures, and with concern over Communist subversion in America having considerably abated, the SACB was allowed to die in 1973 for lack of funding, and the registration provision of the McCarran Act became, for all practical purposes, a dead letter.[53]

A rather different approach to disclosure, taken at both federal and local levels, has been legislation requiring that political campaign literature be identified as to its source. A federal statute to this effect governs elections for the presidency and Congress,[54] and some thirty-six states have also adopted laws prohibiting anonymous campaign communication.[55]

These statutes have met a mixed fate. The federal law was challenged in a North Dakota senatorial race in 1960 and was sustained by a U.S. District Court there.[56] State courts in California and Ohio have also approved of bans on anonymous campaign literature.[57] On the other hand, state or federal courts have struck down such restrictions in Massachusetts, New York, and Texas.[58]

The U.S. District Court in New York relied in its decision on a precedent established by the Supreme Court in *Talley v. California* in 1960, a ruling which had struck down a Los Angeles city ordinance prohibiting the distribution of any handbill "which does not have printed on the cover, or the face thereof, the name and address of . . . (a) The person who printed, wrote, compiled or manufactured the same. (b) The person who caused the same to be distributed. . . ."[59] The majority opinion in that case, written by the same Justice Black who had praised the Foreign Agents Registration Act for helping "hearers and readers . . . not be deceived by the belief that the information comes from a disinterested source," set forth an eloquent rationale in support of anonymity:

> Anonymous pamphlets, leaflets, brochures and even books have played an important role in the progress of mankind. Persecuted groups and sects from time to time throughout history have been able to criticize oppressive practices and laws either anonymously or not at all. The obnoxious press licensing law in England, which was also enforced on the Colonies was due in part to the knowledge that exposure of the names of printers, writers and distributors would lessen the circulation of literature critical of the government. . . . Before the Revolutionary War colonial patriots frequently had to conceal their authorship of distribution of literature that easily could have brought down on them prosecutions by English-controlled courts. Along about that time the Letters of Junius were written and the identity of their author is unknown to this day. Even the Federalist papers, written in favor of the adoption of our Constitution, were published under fictitious names. It is plain that anonymity has sometimes been assumed for the most constructive purposes.[60]

The dissenters responded trenchantly: "The Constitution says nothing about freedom of anonymous speech."[61]

The concern for full disclosure in the particular context of political campaigns—a narrower target than that at which the blunderbuss Los Angeles ordinance had been aimed—provided the motivation for one of several far-reaching amendments to the Federal Election Campaign Act which were adopted by Congress in 1974. The disclosure provisions required all candidates and political committees in federal election campaigns to record and report the names, addresses, and occupations of all persons making contributions of $100 or more within a calendar year as well as the recipient and purpose of every expenditure over $100. Furthermore, any individual or group, other than candidates and political committees, who independently spent more than $100 in a given year in support of a candidate was also required to record and report those expenditures.

In 1976 the U.S. Supreme Court passed judgment on the constitutionality of these and the other amendments to the federal election law.[62] The majority began its discussion of the disclosure issue by setting forth the standard of judgment it would employ:

> We have long recognized that significant encroachments on First Amendment rights of the sort that compelled disclosure imposes cannot be justified by a mere showing of some legitimate government interest. . . . We have required that the subordinating interests of the state must survive exacting scrutiny. We have also insisted that there be a "relevant correlation" or "substantial relation" between the governmental interest and the information required to be disclosed.[63]

The opinion then proceeded to identify the government interests involved in the disclosure requirements at hand:

> First, disclosure provides the electorate with information "as to where political campaign money comes from and how it is spent by the candidate" in order to aid the voters in evaluating those who seek federal office. It allows voters to place each candidate in the political spectrum more precisely than is often possible solely on the basis of party labels and campaign speeches. The sources of a candidate's financial support also alert the voter to the interests to which a candidate is most likely to be responsive and thus facilitates predictions of future performance in office.
>
> Second, disclosure requirements deter actual corruption and avoid the appearance of corruption by exposing large contributions and expenditures to the light of publicity. . . . A public armed with information about a candidate's most generous supporters is better able to detect any post-election special favors that may be given in return.[64]

But the Court was also aware of the First Amendment values at stake:

> It is undoubtedly true that public disclosure of contributions to candidates and political parties will deter some individuals who might otherwise contribute. In some instances, disclosure may even expose contributors to embarrassment or retaliation. These are not insignificant burdens on individual rights, and they must be weighed carefully against the interests which Congress has sought to promote by this legislation.[65]

Against this backdrop the Supreme Court upheld all of the disclosure requirements, with two relatively small qualifications. The first was that an exemption should be allowed for any minor party which could show "a reasonable probability that the compelled disclosure of a party's contributors' names will subject them to threats, harassment or reprisals from either government officials or private parties."[66] The second was that persons other than candidates or political committees who spend money independently to support a candidate need to disclose "only funds used for communications that expressly advocate the election or defeat of a clearly identified candidate."[67]

Chief Justice Burger was the sole member of the Court to dissent from the ruling on disclosure, and then only because it applied to contributions as small as $10 or $100. Said the chief justice:

> The public right to know ought not be absolute when its exercise reveals private political contributions. Secrecy, like privacy, is not *per se* criminal. On the contrary, secrecy and privacy as to political preferences and convictions are fundamental in a free society. For example, one of the great political reforms was the advent of the secret ballot.... The balancing test used by the Court requires that fair recognition be given to competing interests. With respect, I suggest the Court has failed to give the traditional standing to some of the First Amendment values at stake here.... To argue that a 1976 contribution of $10 or $100 entails a risk of corruption or its appearance is simply too extravagant to be maintained. No public right to know justifies the compelled disclosure of such contributions, at the risk of discouraging them. There is, in short, no relation whatever between the means used and the legitimate goal of ventilating possible undue influence. Congress has used a shotgun to kill wrens as well as hawks.[68]

Just as the Los Angeles ordinance struck down in *Talley* had fared less well against constitutional challenge than had narrower demands for identification on election campaign literature and campaign contributions, so efforts by the telephone company to require sponsors of taped phone messages to identify themselves have fallen afoul of the First Amendment. In two cases, one in California and another in New York, both involving a group called "Let Freedom Ring," whose taped and unidentified right-wing messages could be heard by dialing a particular number, state courts found the disclosure requirement invalid.[69] The California Supreme Court said of the matter, "In this context, anonymity may be an indispensable prerequisite to speech."[70]

One further kind of disclosure rule which has not even made it as far as the courts was contained in bills proposed to the Ohio and South Dakota legislatures in 1976. The statutes would have required newspapers and magazines published in those states to identify the authors of all articles (the South Dakota version) or of all editorials (the Ohio version) contained in their publications.[71] Both proposals died in committee.[72]

Moving briefly from the political to the commercial realm, we have already noted in an earlier chapter the variety of disclosure requirements imposed by the government with the goal of attempting to protect people from being induced under false pretenses to part with their money. These range from the labeling requirements of the Pure Food and Drug Act,[73] to the federal Truth-in-Lending law requiring disclosure of the full cost of taking out a loan,[74] to orders for corrective advertising such as the one imposed by the Federal Trade Commission on the maker of Listerine. This is a distinct kind of disclosure requirement, serving a quite different purpose from the others we have been describing, and will warrant separate evaluation.

It is now time to turn to that process of evaluation for all of the disclosure requirements which have been reviewed here. In the course of that review we have encountered most of the supporting and opposing arguments that can be offered on the subject. By summarizing those arguments we will have a starting point for our assessment of their merit.

The most compelling reason advanced in behalf of disclosure requirements is that audiences need to know the sources of messages to which they are exposed in order adequately to evaluate them. There is little doubt that people *do* rely, sometimes quite heavily, on their knowledge of a speaker's or writer's credentials in arriving at judgments about what is said. Indeed, in one of the earliest and most famous of treatises on the communication process, Aristotle said of the speaker, "We might almost affirm that his character [ethos] is the most potent of all the means to persuasion."[75]

Whether audiences *should* depend as much as they do on the credentials of communicators to help them decide on the value of what is communicated is another question, but certainly some of that information is useful. On matters involving complex problems of science, engineering, medicine, law, taxes, or military weaponry, knowledge about the training and experience of those advising us what to do is surely important. On issues having to do with social and moral values, the ideological commitments or biases of the communicator may be illuminating. And with respect to political or economic decision making, the financial interest of those seeking to influence our thinking is certainly worth knowing. As one commentator has observed, "Once we know the axes that are being ground, we are able to make the discount for self-interest that every judge and lawyer...recognizes as essential."[76]

Beyond the information which disclosure provides for an audience, the second major value urged by supporters is its deterrent effect on

irresponsible communication. That deterrent may be a fear of social
ostracism or deprivation of a job or of customers because other people
are offended by the recklessness of the communication, or it may be a
concern that legal action, such as suits for libel, will be brought against
the communicator. If such sanctions are to be effective in preventing
harmful speech, it is obviously necessary for the source of the message to
be known. The primary justification, for example, offered by the City of
Los Angeles on behalf of the disclosure ordinance struck down in *Talley*
was to identify those who might be responsible for fraud, false advertising, obscenity, and libel. As one advocate of disclosure has written:
" . . . such laws can be of extreme value because the most vicious type of
propagandist is usually the one who is most eager to conceal his connections, his income and expenditures, and who will not take responsibility for what he advocates."[77]

Opposition to disclosure is based heavily on a turning inside out of the
two arguments put forth by its supporters. With regard to the role of the
communicator's credentials in evaluating a message, it is pointed out that
such information can be irrelevant, misleading, or unjustifiably prejudicial. "An idea should stand or fall on its own merits," says one writer on
the subject.[78] And the publishers of *Manas,* a periodical for intellectuals,
declare on their editorial page in every issue: "Manas is a journal of
independent inquiry. . . . Editorial articles are unsigned since Manas
wishes to present ideas and viewpoints, not personalities."

What is more, the kinds of disclosure required may not be at all en-
lightening for the purpose of better informed evaluations of the material. As a critic of the Los Angeles ordinance pointed out: " . . . in most
situations more than just the identity of the source will be necessary for
there to be any substantial informative effect. . . . [Is it] clear that the
name 'Manuel Talley' would convey more to the recipient than would
the name 'National Consumers Mobilization?'"[79]

As to the deterrence rationale, disclosure opponents respond, "That's
just the point!" Fear of retribution may indeed inhibit communication,
but not only the irresponsible kind which most people might want to see
deterred. Justice Black's opinion for the Supreme Court in *Talley* makes
this argument about as eloquently as it can be stated, but many others
have urged the same point. The North Dakota violator of the federal law
requiring identification of political campaign literature claimed a fear of
retribution as the basis of his argument that the statute violates the First
Amendment. A note in the *Yale Law Journal* reports that from "1789–
1809 no fewer than six presidents, fifteen cabinet members, twenty
senators, and thirty-four congressmen published political writings either
unsigned or under pen names."[80] And Arthur Garfield Hays once wrote
that "all men are not heroes . . . [a man] may well refrain from joining a

movement . . . if his connection with it might cause him personal injury. . . . If the Abolitionists in the early days had been obliged to come out in the open, their cause might not have progressed very far."[81]

The *Yale Law Journal* article also comments that not only may disclosure be a deterrent to valuable communication but that it is a "selective deterrent" against the most unpopular views. "Yet," the commentary goes on, "it is the rebel and the heretic for whom, to a large degree, the first amendment protections were forged."[82]

Opponents of disclosure requirements, besides calling attention to these reverse sides of the supporters' coins, also rest their case on the First Amendment right to silence and the concomitant belief that communicators ought to be free to say as much or as little as they choose in presenting themselves and their causes to the public. Just as the secret ballot not only protects voters from possible retribution for their votes but also allows them, as a matter of principle, to keep their political preferences a private matter if they wish, so the right to engage in anonymous communication provides an opportunity, if people desire to avail themselves of it, to make known their views without being identified with them.

In assessing these positions one cannot help but agree with an insight offered by the *Yale Law Journal* essay just referred to when it says, "Both arguments—that disclosure tends to promote truth and that anonymity tends to promote truth—have merit."[83] The dilemma is in deciding to which consideration one should give the greatest weight. In striking that balance we confront a different problem from that presented by oaths and investigations, where the competing forces are an alleged *government* interest in the compelled communication, on the one hand, and an asserted First Amendment right of silence, on the other. Here the First Amendment claim of a right to silence is opposed by another First Amendment value—the public's right to know. Disclosure is required by the government not for its own needs but on behalf of the public which is the audience for the communication. That makes it much harder for an exponent of the First Amendment to choose sides.

Difficult as that choice may be, I come down on the side of anonymity in all but the most limited circumstances. In only two areas would I defer to the interests in disclosure. The first is that in which the purpose is to prevent deception in the taking of people's money. The second is in the giving of *large* sums of money to promote the election of candidates for political office.

I believe that the first exception is justified—and have so indicated in the chapter on "Lies and Misrepresentations"—for the same reason that restrictions are acceptable on statements which are factually false and are made in the selling of goods and services. The rationale for such restrictions, it may be recalled, is that deception which may directly induce behavior that is financially or physically harmful is appropriately the target of legal remedies. If what *is* said may be restrained to avoid that kind of harm, then it follows that what is *not* said, but clearly needs to be said in order to avoid the same harm, may also be subject to government regulation.

The other exception is justified, I believe, for the second of the reasons given by the Supreme Court in upholding the disclosure-of-campaign-contributions requirement of the 1974 election law—that is, to "deter actual corruption and avoid the appearance of corruption by exposing large contributions and expenditures to the light of publicity. . . . A public armed with information about a candidate's *most generous supporters* [italics mine] is better able to detect any post-election special favors that may be given in return."[84]

This is a distinctly different interest from the first reason given by the court—"to aid the voters in evaluating those who seek federal office"—and does not suffer from the same infirmities because, in the reality of present-day politics, it, unlike the other, is rooted in an unquestionably compelling and overriding need. Yet, as Chief Justice Burger so aptly noted in his dissent, the danger of corruption stems only from large contributions, and it is therefore only those to which required disclosure ought to apply, thus preserving the right of contributors to express their political preferences with anonymity so long as they do so in sums which are not potentially corrupting.[85] The Court's majority opinion also conceded that not all contributions have an equal potential for corruption, and therefore the same need of being disclosed, when it suggested that "the governmental interest in disclosure is diminished when the contribution in question is made to a minor party with little chance of winning an election."[86] Even large contributions to candidates with no chance of winning fail to pose the danger of a corrupting influence on public officials, and that may be one of the reasons the Supreme Court was so willing to allow exemptions from the disclosure of all contributors for minor parties which could show that revelation of their patrons might lead to their harassment.

Having discussed the exceptions to a right of anonymity which I would allow, let me now turn to a situation-by-situation elaboration of the more general proposition that compelled disclosure is a practice which ordinarily ought to be forsaken in the interest of the most vigorous possible system of freedom of expression. I shall begin with the circumstance in which there seems the widest agreement that disclosure is an inappropriate requirement—that of the authorship of newspaper and magazine editorials—and shall conclude with the registration of foreign agents, where I assume the least sympathy is to be found for unidentified communication.

It is instructive to speculate about the probable causes of the uniformly negative reaction to the idea of requiring newspapers and magazines to identify the authors of particular articles. Part of it, no doubt, springs from the sacred-cow status of the press in our vision of what a free society is supposed to be. But beyond that I suspect there is a recognition that providing an author's name in that context is not likely to be relevant or helpful to an appraisal of the material presented and may be a serious deterrent to frank expression. That the same awareness has not extended to compelled identification of handbills or of taped telephone messages is probably due to the fact that such communication is so often used by nonconformists of one type or another whom the majority of people would just as soon see deterred, not because their messages are illegal but because they are unpopular. Yet that is the very kind of communication whose sources most need the protections of anonymity and whose content is most likely to be dismissed without a fair hearing on account of its authorship. It is not expecting too much of citizens in a democracy, I think, to exercise their critical capacities and learn to deal with this kind of material on the basis of its intrinsic merit in the absence of knowledge about its source. This is not to suggest that such information is always irrelevant or unhelpful, or that it is not to be desired if voluntarily supplied, but simply to assert that the chilling effect of *compelled* disclosure is too great a price to pay for it.

The registration and disclosure provisions of the McCarran Act, imposed on Communist organizations, have been discredited by the passage of time, if not by our courts. It was an insult to the common sense of the American public to believe that it had to be warned against Communist propaganda through labels, or to fancy that labels of that kind would in any way be useful to a thoughtful evaluation of the ideas expounded. On the contrary, it could only have encouraged stereotyped reactions. We are indebted to the groups which successfully refused to comply, whatever may have been their motives, for saving us from the embarrassment of having enforced upon the nation such an anti-intellectual regime.

The disclosure requirements for obtaining second-class mailing privileges also seem a useless burden on communication. It should be sufficient for securing such permits to show that the material to be mailed is in a format which qualifies for the privilege.

As for statutes which demand identification on political campaign literature, some of which have been upheld by the courts and others struck down on the basis of the *Talley* precedent, I find it impossible to distinguish them in principle from the Los Angeles handbill ordinance or to exclude them from the rationale which led to that law's downfall. Admittedly, the latter regulation swept more broadly, and the Supreme Court's opinion in the case suggested that a narrowly drawn law, aimed more specifically at the evils, such as fraud, which were supposedly its target, might have passed constitutional muster. But to require the identification of *all* campaign literature is just as much a dragnet technique for inhibiting, or finding those responsible for, fraud and last-minute libels as the method employed in Los Angeles. Indeed, it is difficult to conceive of any disclosure requirement designed to deal with the problem of deceit and defamation which does not at the same time have a chilling effect on other communication.

Surely we can find more sensitive tools for combating harmful campaign communication. If what is said is illegal, by criteria previously discussed in this book, searching out and finding the perpetrator is no different or more difficult a task from that confronted by law enforcement officials with respect to any other offense, for which those responsible do not usually oblige us by announcing their names and addresses. If the communication falls short of constituting a violation of the law but is still unethical, hopefully voters can and will learn to be suspicious of such messages, particularly when circulated on the eve of an election. Unidentified communicators do pay a price in credibility with audiences in return for the privilege of maintaining their anonymity, and that is only fair. Thoughtful readers and listeners will want to know everything which is relevant to the making of intelligent decisions and may well count it against communicators if they hide their identity. But that is a natural consequence of a free marketplace of ideas; it is not a penalty imposed by the government. To compel disclosure is to deprive communicators of the right to take their chances with the public, attempting to persuade them that their message is more important than its source. The public is capable of deciding for itself whether it wants to buy from salespersons who do not make known their credentials.

The registration and compelled disclosure of the financial supporters of paid lobbyists poses a closer question, and is a policy that has understandably withstood constitutional challenge in the courts. It seems eminently reasonable, at first glance, that legislators and the public should be made aware of the sources of support of those who, for hire, bring pressure to bear on the legislative process.

But that analysis overlooks a number of important considerations. The first is a question as to why individuals who participate in lobbying activities as paid professionals should have less of a right to the exercise of discretion in revealing their identity than those who are unpaid. Public relations officials of corporations, labor unions, and community organizations are also paid communicators, as are political officeholders, but that does not necessarily mean they believe any less in their causes than supportive volunteers. It may be interesting for an audience to know if those who address them are being paid for their labors, but that does not, by itself, tell very much. It may be more revealing to know *who* is paying the bills, and that is certainly another of the purposes of lobbying disclosure requirements. But therein lie still further problems.

To begin with, if the lobbyist is representing a cause organization and disclosure of the sources of its funding is required, as it now is under federal law for all contributions of $500 or more, a back door is opened to the compelled disclosure of membership and patron lists which are otherwise protected by the right of anonymity in political associations. It does not make sense that one should be able to spend as much money as one pleases in unidentified persuasion addressed to the public but not be allowed to join together with others in anonymous communication directed to legislators through a paid messenger. Nor does it make sense that we require registration and disclosure of legislative lobbyists but not of those whose lobbying is directed to the executive branch of government.

There are also serious difficulties in defining the groups and individuals to be covered by a lobbying disclosure law. Should it only apply to persons and organizations for whom lobbying is a principal activity, as the present federal law has been interpreted to apply? If so, where does one draw the line and how does one justify different rules for those who fall on the compelled disclosure side of it? Should people who spend their own money on lobbying activities be subject to the same requirement to disclose their expenditures as those who hire others to lobby for them? They are not now required to do so, and that disparity seems difficult to justify. Furthermore, how can we rationalize the distinction between direct communication with legislators, for which registration and disclosure is required, and indirect persuasion by creating a climate of opinion in the media or exerting pressure through the legislator's constituents and large contributors which may ultimately be more effective than face-to-face lobbying activities?

Finally, one must doubt if legislators, constantly barraged with a multitude of messages, have the time to check the files to learn the sponsorship of those who accost them in the halls. Lawmakers who have not learned to evaluate the significance and merit of the persuasion directed to them without reliance on such information are going to be in trouble with or without disclosure requirements.[87]

We now come to the last and least-often-questioned form of disclosure—that of the registration of foreign agents. As is the case with the regulation of domestic lobbyists, we encounter at the outset of any discussion of this topic some baffling definitional problems. The Foreign Agents Registration Act of 1938, as amended in 1942 and 1966, defines a foreign agent as anyone who engages in political activities in the United States on behalf of a foreign principal, and who acts "either directly or indirectly" under the "direction or control" of that foreign principal.[88] Exemptions are provided for diplomats and consular officials and their staffs so long as they remain within the arena of their official duties; for persons engaging "in private and nonpolitical activities in furtherance of the bonafide trade and commerce of such foreign principal"; for solicitors of charitable contributions to relieve human suffering; for those involved in religious, academic, and scientific pursuits; and for lawyers representing their foreign clients in judicial or administrative proceedings.[89] Exemption is *not* available for persons otherwise covered by the law simply because they happen to be American citizens or because they are not paid for their efforts. Thus a domestic organization which is in sympathy with particular goals of a foreign state, and works for their advancement, can be required to register if it is acting directly or indirectly "under the control" of that state.[90] The difference between acting "under the control" of a foreign nation and acting independently in support of its goals thus becomes critical and can sometimes be an almost impossible distinction to draw.

According to a 1977 report prepared for the U.S. Senate Foreign Relations Committee on the operation of the FARA:

The effective monitoring and enforcement of the registration requirements has been a problem since the inception of the Act in 1938. . . . Agents who qualify under one of the exemptions are not required to register. However, no formal claim of exemption is required to be made; persons deeming themselves exempt under the terms of the Act simply do not register as foreign agents. Thus potential registrants often make a determination of their status on their own. . . . If their activities are never made known to the Department [of Justice], their failure to register and the legitimacy of their claimed exemption will never come to light.[91]

Not only is it assumed that there are significant numbers of people who ought to be registered under the act and are not, but it also seems to be true that many are registered who need not be. Again, according to the Foreign Relations Committee study:

Under the commercial exemption . . . agents of foreign principals are not required to register if they are only engaged in "private and nonpolitical activities in furtherance of bonafide trade or commerce of such foreign principal." . . . By longstanding practice, the Department of Justice has required tourist promotion groups or other similar entities which are encompassed within the statutory ambit to register. Such groups do not arrange tours, book flights or perform other services usually associated with a commercial tourist agency. Rather, in most instances they are concerned with the encouragement of tourism in the country involved through media campaigns. . . .

Although the material gathered is for the most part routine and noncontroversial, the Department strongly favors continued registration.... it is said that affirmatively requiring registration provides an opportunity to monitor promotional matter which on occasion goes beyond mere tourist promotion and actually concerns itself with encouraging investment or political statements....

It would appear that at the heart of the Justice Department's justification for continuing the tourist promotion registration requirement is its presumption that the political and economic objectives of a foreign government are inextricably related....

However, some question may be raised whether the man-hours expended on monitoring and reviewing the considerable volume of materials generated by the tourist promotion groups in fact produces commensurate informational benefit.[92]

It is a fact of history that the FARA was adopted by Congress as a result of an investigation by a committee of the House of Representatives into Nazi efforts to influence public opinion in the United States just prior to World War II.[93] The Senate report observes what has happened in the years since:

...the 1966 amendments...were intended to shift the focus away from subversion and to spotlight foreign interest lobbying.... Today, the foreign agent is principally a promoter of a nation's legitimate economic interests.... However, the association of the Act, in the eyes of many, with earlier efforts to curtail foreign intelligence activities has stigmatized the registration process. It is that association which is in large part responsible for the difficulty encountered by those administering the Act in obtaining voluntary compliance by those required to register.[94]

One cannot help but wonder why the advocacy of legitimate foreign interests, be they economic or political, needs to have its sponsorship identified when it comes from persons taking their direction from a foreign power and not when it comes from others who spontaneously promote the very same goals. If the rationale is that foreign governments are advantaged competitors in the marketplace of ideas because of the financial resources they have at their disposal, then disclosure should not be required of those who are *unpaid* agents of foreign interests and it *should* be required of the many wealthy proponents of domestic causes. If the rationale is that the First Amendment does not apply to foreign participation in American public discourse, then why have we not prohibited it altogether rather than merely requiring its disclosure?

The answer to this last question, I presume, is that we have confidence in the ability of our citizens to evaluate the communication to which they may be exposed by foreign powers, just as they must pass judgment on the merits of domestic persuasion. If that is so, it seems a contradictory lack of trust to insist upon the imposition of a special label which tells them to beware of advocacy which is inspired from abroad.

It does not matter that foreign states may have no First Amendment right to anonymity when they join in our political dialogue. What matters is that *we* not change the rules of *our* game for some of the participants. We do not need to impose such a handicap on them. It establishes a bad precedent, and it softens our own First Amendment muscles.

16   Government Secrecy

The previous chapter has dealt with the circumstances under which the government may be justified in compelling its citizens to speak when they prefer to remain silent. Here we shall be concerned with the claims of government itself to a right of silence when citizens may wish it to speak.

Freedom of expression as a means for the exercise of popular sovereignty is an empty vessel without access to the information necessary for intelligent decision making. As James Madison once said: "A popular government without popular information, or the means of acquiring it, is but a Prologue to a Farce or a Tragedy; or, perhaps both. Knowledge will forever govern ignorance: And a people who mean to be their own Governors, must arm themselves with the power which knowledge gives."[1]

And as Justice Brennan has said more recently:

> ... the First Amendment embodies more than a commitment to free expression and communicative interchange for their own sakes; it has a *structural* role to play in securing and fostering our republican system of self-government.... Implicit in this structural role is not only "the principle that debate on public issues should be uninhibited, robust, and wide open" ... but the antecedent assumption that valuable public debate—as well as other civic behavior—must be informed. The structural model links the First Amendment to that process of communication necessary for a democracy to survive, and thus entails solicitude not only for communication itself, but for the indispensable conditions of meaningful communication.[2]

Yet much essential knowledge is in the hands of agencies and officials of government who can thwart the democratic process by keeping relevant material secret. That is why the public's right to know is a vital element of the First Amendment, and why the burden of proof for justifying the withholding of information should always be on the shoulders of the would-be withholder.

Not only does the public *need* information to exercise its responsibilities of citizenship, but, in a most fundamental sense, data in the hands of government *belongs* to the public, having been collected through use of taxpayers' money and by the exercise of authority derived from the people as a whole. For government officials to hold back material from those to whom it belongs, without exceptionally good reason, is the height of presumptuousness. It is amazing, for instance, that until as recently as 1978 the papers of the presidents of the United States were regarded as *their* property, to be disposed of at *their* discretion.[3] Yet these were papers written by or to them as a result of their holding an office to which the public had elected them and for which the public paid the bills. The presumption that *any* information gathered by officers of government in the course of their official duties is their property rather than that of the people seems explainable only as a holdover from the days when public officials were masters, rather than servants, of the people.

Having said all this, it becomes immediately apparent upon closer analysis that *some* information collected by agencies of government and *some* knowledge about deliberative processes engaged in by government officials must be withheld from the public for good and sufficient reasons. It shall be our task in the pages which follow to review the areas in which it has been claimed that governmentally held data must remain secret and to ask whether the reasons offered are indeed good and sufficient. These claims may be classified into four general categories, each of which shall be explored and assessed in turn[4]: (1) the need to protect the privacy and other legitimate personal interests of those about whom information is gathered, (2) the need to insure candid deliberative processes, (3) the need to safeguard the public's economic interests, and (4) the need to preserve the physical safety of society and its institutions. No attempt will be made to examine every one of the innumerable particulars within these broad categories, for such an exhaustive discussion is unnecessary for our purposes. Illustrations will suffice to provide us with a basis for evaluating the principles which have governed and should govern in each arena.

Protecting Privacy and Other Legitimate Personal Interests of Those about Whom Information Is Gathered

There are several kinds of information collected by government which so obviously warrant confidential treatment that no one would seriously question the denial of public access to them. Certainly this is true of the income and expenditure data filed by individuals on their tax returns. It applies as well to financial information and trade secrets that must be submitted to the government by business entities which could be of advantage to their competitors if made publicly available. The material about particular individuals contained in personnel and medical files held by public institutions—whether of employees and job applicants, of students and candidates for admission to schools, or of hospital patients and agency clients—is clearly not the business of persons other than those who must see it in order to perform whatever functions the information is intended to serve. The names of persons killed or injured in military service should surely not be publicized until after the next of kin have been notified.

These commonsense exceptions to the public's right to know were well recognized when Congress first committed itself, in federal legislation, to the more general proposition that information possessed by the government should ordinarily be available to the people. The Freedom of Information Act of 1966, which made that commitment, also provided for nine categories of exemptions from disclosure.[5] One was for "trade secrets and commercial or financial information obtained from a person and privileged or confidential."[6] Another was for "personnel and medical files and similar files the disclosure of which would constitute a clearly unwarranted invasion of personal privacy."[7] The first of these exemptions was to some extent a redundancy, since earlier statutes establishing regulatory agencies such as the Securities and Exchange Commission and the Federal Trade Commission had already made provision to protect, where necessary, the confidentiality of material submitted to them. The second of these exemptions was considered important enough to warrant further reinforcement by adoption of the Privacy Act of 1974, operationalizing the right of "an individual to prevent records pertaining to him obtained . . . for a particular purpose from being used or made available for another purpose without his consent."[8]

There are hazards in relying too heavily on commonsense perceptions of the obvious, for a number of traditional assumptions concerning information thought to require confidentiality have been called into question in recent years. Reconsideration, if not change, is certainly merited on these issues.

One of the most interesting of these problems has to do with adoption records, which historically have been kept secret from those to whom they pertain. According to a 1979 study of the matter:

> As stated by an English judge 23 years ago, the law draws a "veil" between the past and present lives of adopted persons and makes it "as opaque and impenetrable as possible, like the veil which God has placed between the living and the dead." . . . the laws of almost all states (and most foreign countries) require that the original birth certificate of the adopted child be sealed and that a new birth certificate be issued, bearing the names of the adoptive parents. Simi-

larly, records of court proceedings which made the adoption legal are also put under seal and, in some states, the records of the adoption agency are placed out of reach as well.

The exact number of states which currently permit an adoptee to obtain copies of court records or original birth certificates . . . is certainly less than a handful . . . this writer found only three: Alabama, South Dakota, and Virginia. In these states an adoptee may gain access to relevant records only when he reaches the age of majority.[9]

The rationale for secrecy in this area has consisted of several considerations. One is the interest of birth parents in putting and keeping the past behind them, for whatever reasons they may have, such as the desire of an unwed mother to enter a new relationship without revealing her earlier sexual history. Another is the interest of adoptive parents in preventing possible disruption of their relationship with an adopted child by the appearance in their lives of the birth parents. Finally, it has sometimes been thought that it may be in the best interest of children for the very fact of their adoption, or of their illegitimacy, if that be the case, to be kept secret from them.

With the development in the 1970s of the "Search for Roots"[10] by large numbers of adoptees, and the consequent challenges in courts and elsewhere to the veil of secrecy maintained by government over these records, traditionally accepted premises have been called into question. A 1978 research project involving thirty-eight parents who had placed their children for adoption found that, of the 75 percent who subsequently remarried, 86 percent had told their spouses about the matter, and only 14 percent had not. If the child wanted it, 82 percent expressed interest in a reunion with the adoptee, and only 5 percent expressed a desire entirely to forget the past.[11]

Another study by the same investigators conducted in 1974, and based on fifty adoptees who had found and had reunions with their birth parents, produced the following results:

> Ninety percent of the adoptees were satisfied with the outcome of the reunion, most of them reporting a sense of personal fulfillment, resolution of genealogical concerns, and diminished identity conflicts. Eighty-two percent of the encountered birth parents were positive and accepting, and only 10 percent reacted adversely. . . . In contrast, many of the adoptive parents had difficulty adjusting initially to the experience. Thirty-six percent of the adoptive parents were cooperative and understanding, 20 percent were mildly upset, and 10 percent were quite hurt. . . . permanent damage to the adoptive family relationship resulted rarely.[12]

What can be concluded from this research is that, while secrecy of adoption records may suit the desires of some of those affected, an intensely significant right to know is cut off for a great many more. Further, it should be observed that making such information available to those adoptees who wish to have it (and that is all the reformers have seriously advocated) does not in any way prevent adoptive parents who choose to do so from keeping unquestioning children from knowing they have been adopted, or from discouraging those who do know from seeking out their original parents. The information would be made available only to those who ask the government for it and, if the right of privacy of birth parents is felt to be as important as the right of adoptees to know their origins, disclosure could be made contingent on the consent of the former. But the state paternalism involved in a blanket policy of secrecy for all adoption records seems, in the light of new insights and newly asserted needs, to be unjustified.

An earlier chapter has dealt with questions that have been raised about bans on publication of the names of rape victims, but only in contexts where disclosure is made by journalists after they have obtained the information from open public records or through their own devices. It is a different matter to ask whether police and court officials should attempt to keep such names secret in the first place. For as the Supreme Court has said in connection with another subject, "The right to speak and publish does not carry with it the unrestrained right to gather information."[13]

The doubts expressed in Chapter 4 about the legitimacy of restraints on press publication of rape victims' names have little or no applicability to the initial government withholding of this kind of knowledge. That is because the government has come into possession of the information, not because it is in the communications business but to carry out law enforcement and criminal justice functions with respect to the particular incident. As with tax returns and job applications, there seems to be no justification for government release of such information which is sufficient to outweigh the privacy interests of the individual who is directly affected. If the knowledge is obtained and communicated by others without the complicity of government, that is a different matter whose legitimacy will turn primarily on the manner in which the information was procured.

The question of withholding the names of juveniles involved in criminal acts is somewhat more difficult to deal with. As in the rape-victim matter, the U.S. Supreme Court has definitively settled the issue, insofar as press publication of the names of juvenile offenders is concerned, with its 1979 ruling that the First Amendment prohibits the punishment of those who, having legally obtained the knowledge, choose to make it public.[14] But, again, that is not the question here. Rather it is whether state laws and court practices which commonly bar release in the first instance of this information by government officials are based on sound premises.

The interest thought to be served by secrecy in this matter is to avoid a stigmatizing of the reputations of youthful offenders, whose rehabilitation as good citizens is presumed to be made more difficult by such notoriety. It is also taken for granted, of course, that there is more hope of rehabilitation for juvenile delinquents than for adult offenders, whose names are not handled with the same circumspection. Finally, it is assumed that the public's need or right to know the names of youngsters who engage in antisocial conduct is sufficiently insubstantial to be outweighed by the greater social concern for rehabilitation.

There are a number of difficulties in this analysis. First, it is no longer as clear as it was once presumed to be that there is a consistently significant difference between the rehabilitative prospects for juvenile and adult offenders. But even if we suppose that there is, it is not at all certain that the paternalistic shielding of individuals by the state from the social consequences of the adverse publicity associated with criminal acts is more helpful to their rehabilitation than their having to deal head-on with the experience of being identified as persons who have run afoul of the law. Finally, at least with respect to the most serious offenses, there is cause to doubt that the public's interest in knowing the identity of the offender is any less when it is a youngster than when it is an adult. For all of these reasons, there has not only been a recent increase in press reporting of the names of juvenile offenders in instances where journalists have discovered their names, but questions have also been raised more frequently, and I believe justifiably so, about the merit of the state's withholding that information from the start.

A final, and somewhat macabre, example of the questioning of old assumptions concerning government secrecy occurred in the federal courts in Texas in 1977 when a Dallas television station challenged the refusal of the state's Department of Corrections to allow it to film the first execution that was scheduled to take place under a new Texas capital punishment law. Although members of the press have been allowed to witness and report verbally, or through artists' sketches, on executions in the United States, and were ultimately given permission to do so in this instance, the idea of a television broadcast of an execution in living—or, more accurately, dying—color was apparently too novel a method of public enlightenment for the U.S. court of appeals, which rejected the television station's First Amendment claim.[15]

Unfortunately, the issue in this case was posed and resolved by the court in terms of whether a broadcaster has a right of access to government information which is greater than that available to the public at large. Thus the question of a possible First Amendment right of the people themselves to watch their public servants putting someone to death was not addressed. As to that issue, I would contend that, bizarre as it may be, the importance of the fullest possible understanding by the people of a social policy they have authorized, and which is carried out on their behalf, outweighs whatever interests there may be in providing a measure of privacy to persons being executed or in sparing the sensibilities of potential viewers. Indeed, it is ironic that a practice which historically was carried out with great public display, presumably as a deterrent to others, has in our society been placed so far out of sight. One cannot help but wonder if it is because the advocates of capital punishment are not so sure it is a practice they can defend with confidence and comfort.

In the reexamination of assumptions underlying government secrecy for the protection of privacy, not all of the pressures have been in the direction of seeking greater openness. In at least one instance, just the opposite was the case. The matter arose in Minnesota in connection with records maintained by the Department of Public Welfare on abortions performed with Medicaid assistance. The name of the patient, the name of the physician, and the fee charged for the operation were among the items of information in the department's files. The Catholic Bulletin Publishing Company sought to obtain, presumably for publication in its *Bulletin,* the names of all the doctors who performed abortions in 1976–77, how many they performed, and the total amount of money they were paid for these services. The state medical association went to court in an attempt to prevent disclosure of the information but was told that the Minnesota public records statute required its release.[16] When the medical society appealed to the state supreme court, the Minnesota Civil Liberties Union joined its effort:

> In its friend-of-the-court brief, the Minnesota Civil Liberties Union argued that publication of abortion information will endanger the doctors' and patients' privacy rights. It contended that processing may lead to an inadvertent slip in the disclosure of the data about the patient's identity. Also, women may be inhibited from exercising their constitutional rights to have an abortion if they fear the next request will be for the release of their names.[17]

These arguments sound plausible, and the information in question would seem at first glance to fall in the general category of medical data, which is none of the public's business. On the other hand, assuming steps were taken to guarantee that the names of the patients were kept confidential, it is at least arguable that the public was entitled to the knowledge sought about the physicians. Whatever privacy rights the doctors might have concerning their work, and the tax moneys spent in connection with it, is conceivably of lesser weight than the public's right of access to what may be relevant information on a subject of intense political controversy. Yet, because the relevancy of the particular data to that discussion is not entirely clear, except for purposes of harassment, this is at best an extremely close question. It is one, I believe, that could be decided either way legitimately.

Insuring Candid Deliberative Processes

Just as it has long been taken for granted that an individual's income tax returns and government-held medical records should not be open for public inspection, so it has always been assumed that certain kinds of deliberations and correspondence in the conduct of government business are appropriately kept confidential. This has been true for all three branches of government.

For the judiciary, the secrecy of jury discussions and of judges' conferences has been regarded as nothing short of sacred. Only under such conditions is it believed that the participants will be able to speak their minds honestly, be flexible and open to persuasion by others, and be free to cast their votes without fear or favor. There would have to be powerful evidence to the contrary—not likely to be found—before the presumption against openness in this setting can or should be overcome.

For legislators it has likewise been commonly assumed that they have a need and a right to conduct some of their business in "executive session" (closed to the press and public), both for the reasons of candor just cited in connection with the judiciary and because they may be talking about matters which fall into one of our other categories of legitimately secret information. One writer has described the need for legislative committee executive sessions in this way:

> Behind closed doors nobody can talk to the galleries or the newspaper reporters. Buncombe is not worthwhile. Only sincerity counts. Men drop their masks. They argue to, not through each other. That is one reason why it would be a calamity if the demand for pitiless publicity of committee deliberations should ever prevail.
> ...publicity would lessen the chance for the concessions, the compromises, without which wise legislation cannot in practice be secured. Men are averse to changing their positions or yielding anything when many eyes are watching. It is in the conference room that agreements are reached, results accomplished.[18]

Without questioning these advantages of closed meetings, it is not apparent that, by themselves, the gains are sufficient to outweigh the costs to the public's right to know. The shaping of public policy is a process to which the citizenry presumably ought to be privy, even if some inhibitions on candor and flexibility result. As Chief Justice Burger so aptly put it in his 1980 opinion discussing the newly recognized right of public access to criminal trials: "People in an open society do not demand infallibility from their institutions, but it is difficult for them to accept what they are prohibited from observing."[19]

It is ironic that the chief justice thus unwittingly made a point which might be applied just as well to the conferences of Supreme Court justices as to trial proceedings and the meetings of legislative and administrative agencies.

Public access to the deliberations of government bodies generally is an idea whose time has recently come in many places. In the decade between 1967 and 1977, open meeting laws of one kind or another were adopted by thirty-seven states, with another eleven having been passed in the years just prior to that period.[20] These statutes cover everything from meetings of boards of education and zoning commissions to city councils and committees of the state legislature. Typically exemptions are provided for discussions of such matters as the hiring, firing, and discipline of personnel, collective bargaining, litigation in which the governmental unit is or may be involved, and prospective real estate purchases or sales, but the free-wheeling use of closed meetings that characterizes our federal government is sharply curbed.

Passing these laws has been easier than implementing them, and a sizable amount of enforcement litigation has ensued. One of the common problems and remedies is described as follows:

> Under such statutes legislative debate, compromise, and decision frequently occur in private sessions and the decision is then routinely ratified at a public meeting....
>
> Having become aware that an informal conference permits the crystallization of secret decisions to a point just short of ceremonial acceptance, courts have been willing to find, when the statutes permit, that meetings which might deal with matters on which forseeable action might be later taken must be open.[21]

This, of course, is no solution for tête-à-têtes which may occur over cocktails, on the golf course, or by telephone. Where there is a will on the part of public officials to subvert the public's right to know, legal mechanisms are not a highly effective safeguard. Unless and until officers of government can be brought to appreciate not only the right but the positive value of public participation in the governing process, they are not likely to be its faithful servants.

The need for confidentiality in the deliberations and memoranda of the executive branch of government has been both assumed and disputed from almost the beginning of our nation's history. President George Washington balked when Congress asked for documents pertaining to General St. Clair's expedition against the Indians and to negotiations surrounding the Jay treaty, and Thomas Jefferson rejected a congressional request for letters in his possession about the Aaron Burr conspiracy.[22] Furthermore:

Since Jefferson's day, hardly a decade has gone by when presidents have not refused congressional requests for information. . . . President Truman alone was involved in 15 major incidents of this kind between 1948 and 1952. . . . Even Presidents like William Howard Taft and Calvin Coolidge, notorious for the restrained view they took of presidential power, refused to concede that it lies within the authority of the legislature to compel the disclosure of information the executive feels it necessary to conceal.[23]

Disagreement over this issue has intensified with the passage of time. It has been estimated that prior to 1940 there were a total of eighteen incidents when presidents refused to turn requested information over to the Congress,[24] whereas approximately 130 such refusals were reported between 1964 and 1973.[25] The term "executive privilege" came into popular use in the 1950s following the Eisenhower administration's efforts to ward off the probings of Senator Joseph McCarthy,[26] and, despite the concept's being described as a "constitutional myth" in a 1974 book by a leading scholar of the subject,[27] it was also given its first explicit constitutional recognition by the U.S. Supreme Court in that same year.[28] Although the Supreme Court concluded, in the particular case before it, that executive privilege did not extend to Richard Nixon's withholding of taped conversations being sought as evidence in the Watergate cover-up criminal trial, the justices unanimously found a basis for the privilege, as claimed by the president, in Article II of the Constitution. The Court explained:

In support of his claim of absolute privilege, the President's counsel urges two grounds. . . . The first ground is the valid need for protection of communications between high government officials and those who advise and assist them in the performance of their manifold duties; the importance of this confidentiality is too plain to require further discussion. Human experience teaches that those who expect public dissemination of their remarks may well temper candor with a concern for appearances and for their own interests to the detriment of the decision-making process. Whatever the nature of the privilege of confidentiality of presidential communications in the exercise of Art. II powers the privilege can be said to derive from the supremacy of each branch within its own assigned area of constitutional duties. Certain powers and privileges flow from the nature of enumerated powers; the protection of confidentiality of presidential communications has similar constitutional underpinnings.[29]

Although an official blessing from the Supreme Court for the particular doctrine of executive privilege was thus rather late in coming, the
notion that information in the hands of the executive branch of government may be withheld from public scrutiny had long been recognized in
legislation passed by Congress. The Housekeeping Act of 1789 first gave
to the heads of executive departments the power to withhold material
which was in their hands.[30] According to Francis Rourke: "This housekeeping act has been at the center of the struggle over executive secrecy
for many years. It has figured in countless legal tests in which the courts
have upheld the right of the head of an executive agency to forbid his
subordinates to disclose information coming to them in their official
capacity."[31]

In 1946 the Administrative Procedure Act was adopted, whose purposes and consequences are also described by Rourke:

> A principal objective . . . was to force executive agencies to disclose
> data bearing on such matters as their internal organization and dis-
> tribution of authority. . . .
>   However, the . . . Act, while generally requiring the publication by
> executive agencies of information relating to their organization, pow-
> ers, and procedures, also identifies certain specific circumstances in
> which an agency may withhold information from public disclosure.
> According to the act, administrative secrecy is permissible where
> "there is involved (1) any function of the United States requiring se-
> crecy in the public interest or (2) any matter relating solely to the
> internal management of an agency." To the extent that the protection
> thus afforded secrecy is found insufficient, administrative agencies
> may resort to the further provision of the statute which states that
> information should "be made available to persons properly and di-
> rectly concerned except information held confidential for good cause
> found." . . . Since the law identifies several circumstances in which the
> publicity requirement does not apply, executive agencies were quick to
> rely on it as a general sanction for withholding rather than disclosing
> information.[32]

By 1958 a heightened sensitivity in Congress to the problem of executive secrecy resulted in passage of an amendment to the Housekeeping
Act of 1789 revoking its grant of authority to withhold information from
the public. Nevertheless, the bill's sponsor, Congressman John Moss,
"was obliged to assure his congressional colleagues that passage of his
amendment would not endanger the secrecy of military and diplomatic
records, income tax returns, trade secrets received by the government in
confidence, Federal Bureau of Investigation reports, or information that
could be withheld legitimately under other laws enacted by Congress."[33]

As to those other laws, a 1960 report of the House Subcommittee on

Government Information found there were "172 statutes which permit government information to be withheld from the public, as compared with 75 statutes which specifically require the dissemination of official data."[34]

The most significant step taken by Congress to reverse presumptions of secrecy in the executive branch of government was, as indicated earlier, the Freedom of Information Act of 1966. But, as we have also seen, the exceptions swallowed up substantial parts of the rule. Two of those exceptions might apply to the protection of candor in executive deliberations. Exemption no. 2 refers to matters "related solely to the internal personnel rules and practices of an agency," and exemption no. 5 to "inter-agency or intra-agency memorandums or letters which would not be available by law to a party other than an agency in litigation with the agency." Beyond that, exemption no. 3 is a catch-all category of matters "specifically exempt from disclosure by statute."

The Freedom of Information Act was followed in 1972 by the Federal Advisory Committee Act, which established the rule that advisory committees and study panels of the federal government should hold open meetings.[35] Four years later Congress adopted the Government in the Sunshine Act which provides that any federal agency "headed by a collegial body composed of two or more individual members, a majority of whom are appointed . . . by the President with the advice and consent of the Senate" shall open its meetings to public observation "where such deliberations determine or could result in the joint conduct or disposition of official agency business."[36] This latter statute lists ten categories of exemptions, many of which are the same as or similar to those contained in the Freedom of Information Act.

It is clear from this history of tension between secrecy and disclosure with respect to the deliberations of executive agencies of government that there are powerful and legitimate forces working in both directions. Candor in the giving and seeking of advice, creativity in exploring new ideas, and sharp criticism in evaluating people, organizations, and policies would surely be muted in a regime of total openness. On the other hand, secrecy may breed irresponsibility and even deliberate plotting in high places against the public interest, as we learned to our sorrow in the Watergate affair. Woodrow Wilson once said, though perhaps in a bit of overstatement: "I, for one, have the conviction that government ought to be all outside and no inside. I, for my part, believe that there ought to be no place where anything can be done that everybody does not know about. . . . Everybody knows that corruption thrives in secret places, and avoids public places, and we believe it a fair presumption that secrecy means impropriety."[37]

What is more, there seems to be a natural tendency in bureaucracies, perhaps out of a drive for survival but perhaps only out of laziness, to hide more of their deliberations from outside scrutiny than is truly necessary for the protection of candor.[38] As one commentator has said, " . . . no one likes to conduct his or her business in a fish bowl. The first instinct is one of caution. There is risk to disclosure with no apparent prospect of offsetting benefits."[39]

But, as another has suggested with some skepticism: "Fear of displeasing *superiors* [italics mine] in the government hierarchy is probably the major inhibiting factor in 'speaking out' within the bureaucracy. If anything, the possibility of disclosure might have a correcting influence. Subordinates could speak more honestly if they knew that the public stood in judgment of their superiors as well as themselves."[40]

What seems needed in this area is a delicate balancing of competing interests, some of which are legitimate and some not. Policy no. 7 of the American Civil Liberties Union, in what it labels the "advice privilege" (to avoid the unfortunate connotations of "executive privilege"), is as careful a statement of this balance as we are likely to find:

> The advice privilege may be claimed on behalf of a witness summoned by a congressional committee only at the direction of the President personally.
>
> The advice privilege may be asserted only with respect to questions concerning recommendations, advice, and suggestions passed on for consideration in the formulation of governmental policy.
>
> The advice privilege may not be asserted with respect to questions concerning what has been done, as distinct from what has been advised.
>
> The advice privilege may not be asserted with respect to questions concerning facts acquired by the witness while acting in an official capacity.
>
> The separation of "fact" from "advice," while sometimes difficult, is not impossible. . . . Without the separation, an advice privilege invites abuse.
>
> Congress may require answers to questions about actions or advice by government officials which it has probable cause to believe constitute criminal wrongdoing. In such situations, of course, individuals summoned before a congressional committee are entitled to exercise their constitutional rights, including, for example, the privilege against self-incrimination.
>
> The above guidelines apply to the assertion of the advice privilege to withhold documents as well as personal testimony. . . . The privilege extends not to entire documents, but only to those portions of documents which meet the criteria set out above to justify the advice privilege.[41]

Safeguarding the Public's Economic Interests

We have already seen that a common exception written into state open-meeting statutes is for the discussion of pending litigation or real estate transactions in which the governmental unit is or may be involved. Exemption no. 8 of the federal Freedom of Information Act refers to matters "contained in or related to examination, operating, or condition reports prepared by, on behalf of, or for the use of an agency responsible for the regulation and supervision of financial institutions." And the U.S. Supreme Court has interpreted exemption no. 5 of the FOIA, dealing with interagency or intraagency memoranda, as covering the Domestic Policy Directives of the Federal Open Market Committee of the Federal Reserve System, which are monthly statements described by the Court in this way:

> The Directive summarizes the economic and monetary background of the FOMC's deliberations and indicates in general terms whether the Committee wishes to follow an expansionary, deflationary, or unchanged monetary policy in the period ahead. The Committee also attempts to agree on specific tolerance ranges for the growth in the money supply and for the federal funds rate. . . .
>
> The day-to-day operations of the Account Manager are guided by the Domestic Policy Directive. . . .
>
> The Federal Reserve Board is required by statute to keep a record of all policy actions taken by the FOMC with respect to open market operations. . . . This document is called the Record of Policy Actions. . . . The Record of Policy Actions is published in the Federal Register almost as soon as it is drafted and approved in final form by the Committee. The Domestic Policy Directive, however, exists as a document for approximately one month before it makes its first public appearance as part of the Record of Policy Actions. Moreover, by the time the Domestic Policy Directive is released as part of the Record of Policy Actions, it has been supplanted by a new Directive and is no longer the current and effective policy of the FOMC.[42]

The Supreme Court concluded, with respect to these documents, as follows: " . . . we think that if the Domestic Directives contain sensitive information not otherwise available, and if immediate release of these directives would specifically harm the government's monetary functions or commercial interests, then a slight delay . . . would be permitted under Exemption 5."[43]

Although a dissenting opinion in this case questioned the applicability of exemption no. 5 to these specific documents, and also raised some doubts about the presumption that their immediate availability would harm the government's economic interests,[44] it is unlikely that anyone would take issue with the general proposition that there are some kinds of information in the hands of government officials whose premature disclosure might create, if not economic havoc, at least windfall profits for those in a position to take financial advantage of the knowledge. This could be true of certain court decisions as well as the actions of administrative agencies and legislative bodies.

The only serious question in this area is to determine what kinds of disclosure may have these damaging effects on the public treasury or the nation's economy. That requires a series of judgments about a wide variety of particulars which is beyond both our purpose here and the author's competence.

Preserving the Physical Safety of Society and Its Institutions

Public access to certain classes of information may undermine the ability of law enforcement agencies to prevent the commission of crime or to apprehend its perpetrators. It may endanger the lives of individuals, the physical safety of institutions, and the security of society as a whole. These are interests which cannot be ignored in our pursuit of open government. Neither can they be given unquestioning deference.

Exemption no. 7 of the Freedom of Information Act acknowledges the first of these interests when it excludes from the general requirement of disclosure "investigatory files compiled for law enforcement purposes except to the extent available by law to a party other than an agency." Not only must data about persons actively under investigation be kept confidential, but revelations about investigative techniques and the identity of information sources may also need to be avoided in the interest of continued law enforcement effectiveness and the safety of individuals who are involved.

Yet even so obviously legitimate a concern as protecting the lives of informers cannot always take precedence over competing needs for information. In the context of litigation, for example, the U.S. Supreme Court has held that the so-called informer's privilege is not absolute:

> Where the disclosure of an informer's identity . . . is relevant and helpful to the defense of an accused, or is essential to a fair determination of a cause, the privilege must give way. . . . The problem is one that calls for balancing the public interest in protecting the flow of information against the individual's right to prepare his defense. Whether a proper balance renders nondisclosure erroneous must depend on the particular circumstances of each case, taking into consideration the crime charged, the possible defenses, the possible significance of the informer's testimony, and other relevant factors.[45]

Another context in which the Supreme Court has intervened to adjudicate between the competing claims of public disclosure and the government's obligation to maintain the physical safety of people and institutions has been that of press and citizen access to state and federal prisons to interview inmates or otherwise inspect those facilities. There has been no dispute over the claim that the public has a legitimate interest in knowing what goes on in our prisons. Rather the issue has been posed as one of the nature and extent of the openness required by the Constitution. In other words, what may prison officials properly do to limit and control the conditions of access? Obviously security considerations would preclude members of the public wandering into and around a prison whenever, wherever, and in whatever numbers they choose. Just as obviously, it would seem that a total ban on access is indefensible.

In the Supreme Court's first confrontation with this problem, a majority agreed with a lower court ruling that the California prison system's regulation prohibiting news-media interviews with specified inmates did not violate the First Amendment. Although the issue was raised and resolved, as in the Texas execution coverage case, in terms of *press* freedom rather than *public* access, the Court's comments had plain implications for the latter as well:

> We note at the outset that this regulation is not part of an attempt by the State to conceal the conditions in its prisons or to frustrate the press' investigation and reporting of those conditions. Indeed, the record demonstrates that, under current corrections policy, both the press and the general public are accorded full opportunities to observe prison conditions. The Department of Corrections regularly conducts public tours through the prisons for the benefit of interested citizens. In addition, newsmen are permitted to visit both the maximum and minimum security sections of the institutions and to stop and speak about any subject to any inmates whom they might encounter. If security considerations permit, corrections personnel will step aside to permit such interviews to be confidential. Apart from general access to all parts of the institutions, newsmen are also permitted to enter the prisons to interview inmates selected at random by the corrections officials. . . .
> The sole limitation on newsgathering in the California prisons is the prohibition in §415.071 of interviews with individual inmates specifically designated by representatives of the press. This restriction is of recent vintage. . . . it was found that the policy in effect prior to the promulgation of §415.071 had resulted in press attention being concentrated on a small number of inmates who, as a result, became virtual "public figures" within the prison society and gained a disproportionate degree of notoriety and influence among their fellow

inmates. Because of this notoriety and influence these inmates often became the source of severe disciplinary problems.[46]

The Court concluded that, since the new and more restrictive rule "merely eliminated a special privilege formerly given to representatives of the press vis-à-vis members of the public generally,"[47] that privilege could also be withdrawn: "The First and Fourteenth Amendments bar government from interfering in any way with a free press. The Constitution does not, however, require government to afford the press special access to information not shared by members of the public generally."[48]

This decision was handed down in tandem with a similar one involving an almost identical rule of the federal Bureau of Prisons. Justice Powell's dissenting opinion in this second case, joined by Justices Brennan and Marshall, spoke directly to the matter of the *public's* right to know, and it spelled out the way in which that right was unjustifiably restricted by the regulation on the press in question:

> What is at stake here is the societal function of the First Amendment in preserving free public discussion of government affairs.... public debate must not only be unfettered; it must also be informed. For that reason this Court has repeatedly stated that First Amendment concerns encompass the receipt of information and ideas as well as the right of free expression....
>
> In my view this reasoning also underlies our recognition in *Branzburg* that "news gathering is not without its First Amendment protections."... An informed public depends on accurate and effective reporting by the news media. No individual can obtain for himself the information needed for the intelligent discharge of his political responsibilities. For most citizens the prospect of personal familiarity with newsworthy events is hopelessly unrealistic. In seeking out the news the press therefore acts as an agent of the public at large. It is the means by which the people secure that free flow of information and ideas essential to intelligent self-government. By enabling the public to assert meaningful control over the political process, the press performs a crucial function in effecting the societal purpose of the First Amendment....
>
> Because I believe that the ban against prisoner-press interviews significantly impinges on First Amendment freedoms, I must consider whether the Government has met its heavy burden of justification for that policy....
>
> The District Court ... found ... that the "big wheel" theory does not justify the Bureau's categorical prohibition of all press interviews, and the Court of Appeals endorsed this conclusion.... the Bureau has not shown that it is unable to identify disruptive "big wheels" and to take

precautions specifically designed to prevent the adverse effects of media attention to such inmates. In short, the remedy of no interview of any inmate is broader than is necessary to avoid the concededly real problems of the "big wheel" phenomenon.[49]

Justice Powell concluded his opinion with an eminently reasonable and eloquent appeal for a greater degree of sensitivity by the Court when balancing limitations on newsgathering against the public's right to know:

> The Court's resolution of this case has the virtue of simplicity. Because the Bureau's interview ban does not restrict speech nor prohibit publication nor impose on the press any special disability, it is not susceptible to constitutional attack. This analysis delineates the outer boundaries of First Amendment concerns with unambiguous clarity. It obviates any need to enter the thicket of a particular factual context in order to determine the effect on First Amendment values of a nondiscriminatory restraint on press access to information. As attractive as this approach may appear, I cannot join it. I believe that we must look behind the bright-line generalities, however sound they may seem in the abstract, and seek the meaning of First Amendment guarantees in light of the underlying realities of a particular environment. Indeed, if we are to preserve First Amendment values amid the complexities of a changing society, we can do no less.[50]

It may be a commentary on the wisdom of the Supreme Court's majority in this matter that the U.S. Bureau of Prisons, having won from the Court the right to maintain an absolute ban on press interviews with specified inmates, soon adopted the more qualified approach urged by the dissenters. In May of 1976, only two years after the Supreme Court's decision on the matter, the director of the Bureau of Prisons announced a new experimental policy permitting news-media interviews with inmates in most federal prisons.[51]

Yet this was not to be the end of the issue as far as the Supreme Court was concerned. In 1978 the Court ruled on an appeal from a U.S. district court order which had enjoined the sheriff of Alameda County, California, from denying television station KQED a right of access to a portion of the county jail, known as Little Greystone, where a prisoner had committed suicide and where conditions were alleged to be responsible for deep prisoner discontent.[52] After KQED had filed its complaint in federal court, the sheriff began a program of monthly tours of county jail facilities for both the press and public, but the tours did not include the section where the suicide had occurred, nor were cameras, tape recorders, or interviews with inmates allowed.

The district court's order, affirmed by the U.S. Court of Appeals for the Ninth Circuit, enjoined the sheriff from denying news-media access to the jail, including the Little Greystone facility, and from prohibiting their use of cameras, tape recorders, or inmate interviews. With Justices Marshall and Blackmun not participating in consideration of the case, the Supreme Court, by a 4–3 vote, reversed the judgment of the lower courts. However, only three of the four justices who constituted the majority agreed with the lead opinion written by Chief Justice Burger. That opinion once again reiterated the earlier expressed view that the press has "no constitutional right of access to prisons or their inmates beyond that offered to the general public,"[53] but then went on to assert a much broader proposition affecting the public as well as the press:

> The public importance of conditions in prison facilities and the media's role of providing information afford no basis for reading into the Constitution a right of the public or the media to enter these institutions, with camera equipment, and take moving and still pictures for broadcast purposes. This Court has never intimated a First Amendment guarantee of a right of access to all sources of information within government control. . . . Whether the government should open penal institutions in the manner sought by respondents is a question of policy which a legislative body might appropriately resolve one way or the other.
>
> A number of alternatives are available to prevent problems in penal facilities from escaping public attention. . . . Citizen task forces and prison visitation committees . . . grand juries . . . a prosecutor or a judge. . . . We must not confuse what is "good," "desirable," or "expedient" with what is constitutionally commanded by the First Amendment. . . .
>
> "The Constitution is neither a Freedom of Information Act nor an Official Secrets Act." . . . Stewart, "Or of the Press," 26 Hast. L.J. 631, 636 (1975).[54]

Justice Stewart, who provided the fourth vote for reversal of the lower court rulings, may not have entirely appreciated being quoted in support of the plurality's view. At least he saw fit to withhold his support from that opinion, writing instead a concurring opinion which took the position that, although the broad district court order at issue was unwarranted, "KQED was entitled to injunctive relief of more limited scope."[55] He agreed with the chief justice's opinion that "[t]he First and Fourteenth Amendments do not guarantee the public a right of access to information generated or controlled by government, nor do they guarantee the press any basic right of access superior to that of the public generally. The Constitution does no more than assure the public and the press equal access once government has opened its doors."[56] But, he went on:

> We part company . . . in applying these abstractions to the facts of

this case. Whereas he appears to view "equal access" as meaning access that is identical in all respects, I believe that the concept of equal access must be accorded more flexibility in order to accommodate the practical distinctions between the press and the general public.

When on assignment, a journalist does not tour a jail simply for his own edification. He is there to gather information to be passed on to others, and his mission is protected by the Constitution for very specific reasons. "Enlightened choice by an informed citizenry is the basic ideal upon which an open society is premised." . . . Our society depends heavily on the press for that enlightenment. . . .

That the First Amendment speaks separately of freedom of speech and freedom of the press is no constitutional accident, but an acknowledgement of the critical role played by the press in American society. The Constitution requires sensitivity to that role, and to the special needs of the press in performing it effectively. . . . if a television reporter is to convey the jail's sights and sounds to those who cannot personally visit the place, he must use cameras and sound equipment. In short, terms of access that are reasonably imposed on individual members of the public may, if they impede effective reporting without sufficient justification, be unreasonable as applied to journalists who are there to convey to the general public what the visitors see.[57]

The three dissenters were unwilling to subscribe to the majority's unqualified position that there is no constitutionally protected right of access for either press or public to governmentally controlled information:

The preservation of a full and free flow of information to the general public has long been recognized as a core objective of the First Amendment. . . . It is not sufficient . . . that the channels of communication be free of governmental restraints. Without some protection for the acquisition of information about the operation of public institutions such as prisons by the public at large, the process of self-governance contemplated by the Framers would be stripped of its substance.

For that reason information gathering is entitled to some measure of constitutional protection.[58]

In approving of the district court's injunction, which had given access to the media but not to the general public, the dissenting opinion said:

If a litigant can prove that he has suffered specific harm from the application of an unconstitutional policy, it is entirely proper for a court to grant relief tailored to his needs without attempting to redress all the mischief that the policy may have worked on others. Though the public and the press have an equal right to receive information and ideas, different methods of remedying a violation of that right may sometimes be needed to accommodate the special concerns of the one or the other.[59]

It seems to me that dismissing the Constitution as neither a Freedom of Information Act or an Official Secrets Act depreciates the vital role that access to information plays in the functioning of a free society. The alternative need not be to allow anyone who pleases to tramp through the nation's jails or rifle through government files at will. The First Amendment can weigh in on the side of Freedom of Information and against Official Secrets without producing such results. The dissenting opinions in the Supreme Court's prison-access cases have sensibly pointed the way in that direction, and we can be grateful that the federal Bureau of Prisons, at least, has chosen to follow their course rather than the one marked out by the majority.

The last arena of government secrecy we shall examine—that concerning national defense and foreign relations—is by far the most significant and troublesome of all, both from the point of view of the public's right to know and the state's obligation to protect the physical safety of the country. It is an area in which the need for concealment of certain data, such as military weaponry and operational plans, is as apparent as any need for secrecy can be. But it is also a field in which the public's right to know what the government is doing about matters involving its very survival can be, and has been, grossly abused.

Long before there were any legislative mandates or executive orders in this area, the judiciary had recognized a common-law privilege against the disclosure of military and diplomatic secrets.[60] The classification of documents into various categories of secrecy by administrative agencies was begun on a systematic basis during World War I,[61] and executive orders governing the classification of material have been promulgated regularly by presidents of the United States ever since the administration of Franklin D. Roosevelt.[62]

Whereas Roosevelt's executive order dealt only with military matters, Harry Truman broadened the field of classified data in 1951 to include other national security and diplomatic matters.[63] The next proclamation in the series, no. 10501 issued by Dwight Eisenhower in 1953, is described by Francis Rourke:

> This new rule was ostensibly designed to widen the flow of official information to the public. As stated in the press release accompanying Eisenhower's action, "the order will make it possible for our citizens to know more of what their government is doing. . . . the danger of misuse of the order to hamper freedom of information, so vital to the preservation of our form of government, is minimized." The features of the new order that were designed to achieve this result included a reduction in the number of agencies entitled to classify information, the elimination of the category of "restricted" information (the new system provides for only three categories of classified information: top

secret, secret, and confidential), and the establishment of procedures for declassifying documents that no longer need to be kept secret.

However, in spite of its intent, this order, like all previous efforts to control the dissemination of official information, has come under heavy attack. This criticism rests partly on the charge that the Eisenhower order, like the Truman directive which preceded it, tends to keep a great deal more information secret than common sense or the national security require.[64]

Presidents subsequent to Eisenhower have issued their own orders on the classification and declassification of documents, each proclaimed by its author to be a further step in the reduction of government secrecy. Richard Nixon's executive order no. 11652, for example, promulgated in 1972, made substantial cuts in the number of people authorized to classify information[65] and in the length of time required before automatic declassification or mandatory review would take place.[66] It also established an Interagency Classification Review Committee to monitor the classification and declassification process.[67] But this order, too, was criticized for its defects by the staff of the House Subcommittee on Government Information.[68] Among other things, the staff noted that the order provided no specific penalties for overclassification or misclassification of information; it permitted the government to conceal the identity of the classifiers of particular documents; and it confused the meaning of the term "national defense" with "national security," and the term "foreign relations" with "foreign policy."[69]

Against this historical background it was hardly necessary for Congress to add its authority to support administrative withholding of security information. Nevertheless, in adopting the Freedom of Information Act of 1966, the very first exception to disclosure that was listed was for matters "specifically required by Executive Order to be kept secret in the interest of the national defense or foreign policy." What is more, prior to a 1974 amendment to the Freedom of Information Act, the validity of a claim by an executive agency that particular material was exempt from disclosure was not even reviewable by judicial inspection, *in camera,* of disputed documents. The 1974 amendment providing for such a check on executive discretion was adopted only over the veto of President Gerald Ford.

There has probably been no time in United States history when public attention has been more sharply riveted on abuses of government secrecy committed in the name of national security than during the years immediately preceding and following Richard Nixon's resignation from the presidency. It began with the administration's unsuccessful attempt in 1971 to stop publication by the *New York Times* and *Washington Post* of the so-called Pentagon Papers, a classified history of American involvement in Vietnam which had been photocopied and leaked to the press. There followed the trial of Daniel Ellsberg and Anthony Russo as the ones allegedly responsible for that disclosure, and the ensuing revelation that members of a White House "plumbers' unit" had broken into the office of Daniel Ellsberg's psychiatrist seeking information from his personal records. The effort by President Nixon and his aides to conceal this event on the grounds of national security, as well as the cover-up of the far broader range of illegal behavior surrounding the break-in at the Watergate headquarters of the Democratic National Committee, became major concerns of hearings before the Senate committee investigating the Watergate affair in 1973 and the House Judiciary Committee impeachment proceedings in 1974.

Fast on the heels of the Nixon resignation, three major inquiries were undertaken into secret and improper activities of the entire U.S. intelligence community over the preceding two decades. One was by a commission appointed by President Ford and chaired by Vice-President Nelson Rockefeller, another was by a committee of the U.S. Senate headed by Senator Frank Church, and the third was by a House Select Committee on Intelligence led by Congressman Otis Pike. Among the most outrageous of the "national security" secrets disclosed through these investigations were plots by the Central Intelligence Agency to assassinate certain disfavored foreign leaders, and the FBI's COINTELPRO (Counter-Intelligence Program) which had attempted to disrupt civil rights and radical political organizations and had even tried to turn the Mafia against the Communist Party.

The Pike committee's tribulations in trying to examine and expose questionable conduct by the intelligence agencies were themselves a sobering study of the problem of government secrecy. Part of that narrative has been related, from one person's perspective, by Gregory S. Rushford:

> As a staff member of the House Select Committee on Intelligence, I was charged with investigating how well the intelligence agencies had been doing their job. It was a simple and reasonable question, but in trying to get an answer, I encountered the bureaucratic obstacles that hide the truth about government performance.
>
> The story of those obstacles, and our attempts to surmount them, sheds light on the present balance of power between the executive and legislative branches. Despite recent press stories that Congress is reasserting itself, the CIA—exceptional in many ways but in this one quite typical—used every executive branch tactic to frustrate our investigation. . . .
>
> We started off with a series of hearings on the intelligence budget. . . . We saw the same budget books they present to the appropriations committees and learned how vague they were. After repeated telephone calls, we managed to get a few documents delivered right

to our offices, but when we looked at them, we found entire pages missing—only the "Top Secret" stamp remained. Staff investigators who asked for further details could not get them. . . . The National Security Agency (which monitors foreign communications) would not give us even the basic document which controls its operations. . . .

The testimony of Colby [director of the CIA] and Gen. Lew Allen of the National Security Agency illustrated one other way the intelligence agencies have traditionally thwarted congressional oversight. Over the years both the CIA and the NSA have answered hundreds of questions from congressional committees by providing *summaries* of internal documents, almost always self-serving, and not the documents themselves. What is the difference? Colby had said, in one of our closed sessions, that "certain differences had arisen between a certain ambassador and the CIA personnel" over the wisdom of one covert operation. We finally got hold of the original document, which put the matter in somewhat different terms. The ambassador had actually said to the CIA station chief, "To hell with your headquarters. If you don't go along with this, I will instruct the Marine guards to take you and place you on the airplane and ship you out of here."

. . . The Mideast hearing was designed to explore why the intelligence agencies had failed at the job they were supposed to carry out—namely, to provide accurate information on international developments.

Just one day after we held that hearing, President Ford announced that we would be denied any further classified information. He asked us to return our files and later compared us to common criminals. What the committee had done the previous afternoon was to vote in closed session to publish a portion of an official CIA post-mortem of the Mideast failure.

. . . In public session the CIA had read us two of the seven paragraphs of the post-mortem, both moderately favorable to the agency. But it had refused to declassify the other five. That afternoon the committee spent hours on those five paragraphs and realized the CIA had no reasonable grounds for keeping them secret. They did not reveal any intelligence sources and methods—the two items the CIA might legitimately want to protect—but they did demonstrate just how badly U.S. intelligence had performed prior to the Middle East war. There was no "national security" at stake, only bureaucratic self-protection.[70]

The House Committee completed its work at the beginning of 1976. The immediately ensuing events are described in detail by an editor of the *Washington Monthly:*

The committee staff drafted its final report in January, and it reflected the streetfighter style. Written in non-bureaucratic prose (one person who read the first draft called it "anecdotal, one-sided, over-dramatized and childishly written"), the report chronicled every devious move of the present Secretary of State, and every intelligence-gathering failure of the CIA. Here were all the embarrassing moments: Tet, Czechoslovakia, Portugal, Iraq, Cyprus, Italy; and a record of Kissinger's attempts to suppress the truth about them. In mid-January the first draft was submitted to the executive branch; or more precisely, to Mitch Rogovin, an Arnold and Porter lawyer who had been retained by the CIA and was acting as chief contact between the agency and the committee. Rogovin parceled out the draft to the State Department and the CIA for comment, collected the comments, and passed them back to the committee.

In its second draft, the committee made some of the requested changes. Unlike the first, however, this one was not sent out for executive branch comments. Instead, it was given to the committee members for final approval. For the staff, it was the culmination of months of exhausting work. During the final drafting process, staff members had been up late most nights, typing in the office or at home, catching a few hours sleep when they could. On Friday, January 23, the committee voted 9 to 4 to approve the report for publication.[71]

That weekend the CBS news correspondent Daniel Schorr somehow managed to obtain a copy of the study and, in his Sunday night broadcast, prior to official release of the report, disclosed some of its most newsworthy highlights to the listening public. The following morning the *New York Times* carried a story of the report's highlights, written by John Crewsdon, who had also seen a copy of the document over the weekend. The Ford administration, which had been attempting during the previous week to secure deletions and changes in various portions of the committee's report, now shifted its attention to the full House of Representatives, where it sought to have the committee's decision to publish the report overturned.[72] On January 30, the House voted 246–124 to withhold the report until it had been censored to the satisfaction of the executive branch of the government.[73]

Newsman Schorr was now in the awkward position of having in his possession an uncensored copy of a report which his government had decided to suppress, even though the heart of its contents had already been revealed over CBS and in the *New York Times*. His decision, as a journalist, to release the full report for publication in the *Village Voice* brought the wrath of both the administration and the Congress down on his head, leading to intensive, albeit unsuccessful, efforts to discover who among the government employees with access to the document had, without proper authority, made a copy available to Schorr during that January weekend. That the nation's security suffered no harm from publication of this report, as it had earlier suffered no harm from publication of the Pentagon Papers, says more about the illegitimacy of much government secrecy in this area, and does so more effectively, than all the studies and treatises on the subject have been able to say.

If we accept the premise to which I believe we are driven by logic and experience—that there are some state secrets which legitimately must be kept secret to protect the nation's security, but many more which constitute unjustified abuses of the public's right to know, it then becomes our task to attempt to clarify the boundary line between the two. The words of Justice Stewart in his Pentagon Papers concurring opinion provide a useful overall philosophy for that endeavor:

> When everything is classified, then nothing is classified, and the system becomes one to be disregarded by the cynical or the careless, and to be manipulated by those intent on self-protection or self-promotion. I should suppose, in short, that the hallmark of a truly effective internal security system would be the maximum possible disclosure, recognizing that secrecy can best be preserved only when credibility is truly maintained.[74]

To become more specific, we must turn for help to those with some experience in the national security field who share a commitment to "maximum possible disclosure" consistent with legitimate safety needs. One such person is Morton Halperin, who served as a top-level staff member of the National Security Council, headed by Henry Kissinger when the latter was national security advisor to President Nixon. After Halperin had resigned his post in disagreement with administration policies, he was the target of a twenty-one-month wiretap on his home telephone which was later found by a federal court to be in violation of the Fourth Amendment guarantee against unreasonable searches and seizures.[75]

Halperin was the senior author, with Daniel N. Hoffman, of a 1977 book entitled *Top Secret: National Security and the Right to Know,* in which a thoughtful and responsible set of proposals is put forth for reform of the government's secrecy system. In contrast to the traditional approach to security secrets, which considers only the possible dangers to national defense and foreign policy in deciding whether information should be withheld from the public, the Halperin-Hoffman system invokes a balancing test which places on the other side of the scales the positive First Amendment values of public knowledge and debate about matters affecting the nation's physical safety. "Our proposals," say the authors, "would reverse the presumption that public debate is a dangerous and inappropriate process."[76]

Halperin and Hoffman would have their classification system "established by legislation rather than by Executive order" because "it is unrealistic to expect any President to carry out truly effective reform since it would mean the restriction of his own freedom of action. . . . It is very clear that uncontrolled executive discretion is central to the disease, and the curtailment of that discretion must be part of any cure."[77]

They suggest three broad classifications of information: (1) that which should be automatically released; (2) that which should be presumptively secret; and (3) that which does not clearly fall in either of the first two categories, thus requiring the exercise of discretion on a case-by-case basis.

The principle governing the category of material to be automatically released is stated in general terms as follows: "Information necessary to congressional exercise of its constitutional powers to declare war, to raise armies, to regulate the armed forces, to ratify treaties, and to approve official appointments must be made available not only to Congress but to the public."[78]

An itemization of more specific classes of information is then proposed for this category, with a supporting rationale for each:

(a) *Americans engaged in combat or in imminent prospect of combat.* Congress's powers to declare war, to raise funds for and to regulate the armed forces are of little practical significance if the President can order armed forces into combat without even informing Congress. . . . Congress has already legislated a narrow requirement for public disclosure in the War Powers Bill.

We see little risk to national security from our proposal to strengthen this requirement; certainly an enemy or potential enemy will ordinarily be aware that American forces are engaged in combat against them or are in a combat zone. In any case, we believe that the implications of combat activity create a paramount public interest in disclosure. . . .

Only the fact of combat or introduction of forces would have to be made public. Details of combat plans and operations could be kept secret.

(b) *American forces abroad.* Congress's power to declare war and the public's right to debate questions of war and peace can also be vitiated by the peacetime stationing of American forces on the front line, where they will inevitably be drawn into combat if a war should start. The only reason for taking such measures in secret would be to avoid domestic criticism; obviously the arrival of American forces will not long remain secret in the area where they are stationed. . . .

(c) *Nuclear weapons abroad.* . . . we propose that the President be required to report publicly the countries in which the United States stores nuclear weapons.

Nuclear weapons are qualitatively different from other armaments. Their use anywhere would injure humanity in profound and lasting ways. The presence of nuclear weapons in a particular country not only implies that they might be used in its defense; it also creates a risk of their unauthorized use by the host government, or of their seizure by domestic dissidents or invading forces. . . .

Since the United States keeps nuclear weapons in special storage facilities, their presence in a foreign country is seldom, if ever, secret from Soviet satellite reconnaissance. Secrecy on this question seems designed to avoid public debate in the host country as well as the United States. . . .

(d) *Financing of foreign combat operations or foreign military forces.* . . . Military assistance can be a prelude to the use of American forces. For this reason alone, a requirement of public release seems appropriate. Moreover, it is difficult to see how such disclosure would harm national security. The ability of recipient governments to keep the secret is often quite limited, and potential enemies are likely to be well aware of American involvement. . . .

(e) *Commitments to do any of the above; commencement of negotiations contemplating such commitments.* . . .

If public debate is to be meaningful, it must be timely. Before the United States undertakes a combat commitment, an agreement to station troops abroad, or to supply military aid, the prospect of the agreement should be made public. . . .

(f) *Intelligence organizations: existence, budgets and function.* . . . Our proposal would require that enough information be made public to permit Congress and the public to decide whether the organizations should exist, what functions they should perform, and how much they should spend. . . .

National security does not appear to require that the overall budgets of these agencies be kept secret. . . .

(g) *Weapons systems: concepts and costs.* Once a weapons system has been developed and is ready for production, it may be too late to decide not to deploy it. Often billions have already been spent, and enormous bureaucratic and industrial momentum has built up behind the program. Effective congressional and public control requires discussion of *proposed* new programs. . . .

Public disclosure would involve the general outline of the proposed development and the estimated cost of the system—not its technical detail. Such limited disclosure, it is true, might have the effect of alerting a potential enemy to our new system, allowing him to copy or neutralize it sooner than might otherwise have occurred. Yet disclosure may be equally conducive to mutual agreements not to develop the proposed system. . . .

(h) *Actions in violation of law.* It is of course unrealistic to ask the President to supply Congress with a list of illegal actions he is undertaking. However, it would not be inappropriate to place an obligation upon any official of the executive branch who learns of unlawful activities to make the information public. . . .[79]

The classes of information to be regarded as presumptively secret in the Halperin-Hoffman scheme are introduced with this general proposition: "For a few narrow categories of information, mostly technical, public disclosure does not appear useful for policy debate. It could, however, be expected to give substantial assistance to potential adversaries. Such information, though it should be available to Congress on a secret basis, is entitled to a heavy presumption against public disclosure."[80]

The particular items in the presumptively secret classification, with their respective rationales, are presented as follows:

(a) *Weapons systems: details of advanced weapons systems design and operational characteristics.* . . . Secrecy makes it harder for other countries to manufacture these weapons, to counteract them, or to exploit their vulnerabilities. Such secrecy need not interfere with the necessary public debate on appropriations measures, provided that enough information is disclosed to establish the cost and the benefits of the system. Likewise, secrecy need not and should not interfere with appropriate public participation in the effort to institute arms control agreements. . . .

(b) *Details of plans for military operations.* Our scheme would require the United States to reveal that it was engaging, or about to engage, in military operations against another country. But the public and Congress need not know the precise operational details in order to debate the wisdom of planned or current operations. . . .

(c) *Ongoing diplomatic negotiations.* Diplomatic negotiations cannot, in many cases, be carried on successfully if one or both countries continuously make public the negotiating positions of both sides. Public negotiations very quickly turn into propaganda sessions; the real negotiations, if they survive, occur quietly behind the facade of the formal ones. . . . While the fact of negotiations should be announced, the positions put forward in the negotiations may properly be kept secret during the period when the negotiations are under way. . . .

(d) *Intelligence methods: codes, technology, and spies.* Specific details of American information gathering activities should be kept secret. . . . There is no need for the public or Congress to know the precise operational details of such programs as satellite reconnaissance or foreign governmental communications interception. . . .

The identity of particular spies, or other information compromising to ongoing lawful operations, would of course be appropriate matter for secrecy as well.[81]

The third and last broad category of the Halperin-Hoffman system consists of national security information which does not fit clearly into either of the first two classifications. This material is to be judged on a case-by-case basis.

In such cases, the balancing of the value of disclosure to the public, as against the possible harm to the defense or foreign policy of the

United States, is left initially to the classifying official. Weighing these factors should proceed on the principle that release is required unless one can reasonably judge that the probable costs to national security clearly outweigh the value of the information for public debate.[82]

These judgments would be subject to independent review, as would all classification decisions, by a Classification Review Board, which also

would be responsible for the release of information more than three years old, though the head of the classifying agency would be able to apply to the Review Board for extension of the period of secrecy. . . .

The Board should also be empowered to seek release of information less than three years old. . . .

Another function of the classification board would involve the deletion of properly classified information from certain current documents, particularly studies produced by the intelligence community, and their public release. The Central Intelligence Agency, the Bureau of Intelligence and Research in the State Department, and, to a lesser extent, the intelligence agencies in the Department of Defense produce many analyses of the world events that would be of great value to Congress and the public. These documents are often classified merely because they contain a relatively small amount of information obtained from clandestine sources. In many cases, an unclassified version of these documents could be produced with a very small amount of effort.[83]

Halperin and Hoffman also address the problem of enforcing any system of government secrecy, concluding that "administrative and political sanctions are a more credible and appropriate approach than criminal penalties. . . ."[84] Since we have not generally concerned ourselves in this book with the particular enforcement mechanisms which limit freedom of expression, we will not do so here with respect to the advantages and disadvantages of the various possible types of post facto punishment available for breaches of secrecy. We must, however, depart from our previous pattern in order to deal with one of the most difficult and dangerous unresolved issues on our national First Amendment agenda—that of *prior restraints* to prevent the general publication of legitimately classified, but nonetheless somehow disclosed, national security secrets.

It has been noted in our earlier chapters on defamation and on privacy that prior restraints on communication have always been viewed by our legal system with far greater suspicion than post facto penalties. That is primarily because they not only threaten to punish communicators solely for proceeding to disseminate their messages regardless of whether post facto penalties for the same behavior could withstand a First Amendment challenge, but they also deprive members of the potential audience of ever having a chance to hear and evaluate those messages for themselves. Furthermore, in the case of court injunctions, which are the most typical kind of prior restraint,[85] a probable conviction for contempt of court hangs over the heads of would-be communicators for expression which, if it were only to be punished after the fact, could well evoke lesser penalties. Finally, where timeliness of communication is critical to its effectiveness, the delay that prior review imposes, even if only a temporary restraint results, may for all practical purposes be tantamount to suppression of the message.

Although there are those who have suggested that the First Amendment was designed to prohibit *all* previous restraints on speech and press, allowing only after-the-fact punishments for unprotected expression,[86] that has not been the view of the U.S. Supreme Court for the past half-century. In a landmark decision in 1931, involving an injunction in Minnesota against allegedly libelous material, the Court enunciated a general principle of First Amendment law that "the protection even as to prior restraints is not absolutely unlimited. But the limitation has been recognized only in exceptional cases."[87] Slightly more than three decades later, in a book and magazine censorship case from Rhode Island, the Court added, "Any system of prior restraints of expression comes to this Court bearing a heavy presumption against its constitutional validity."[88] And in May of 1971, striking down an injunction against leafleting and picketing in a residential community in Illinois, the Court held that the government "carries a heavy burden of justification for the enforcement of such a restraint."[89]

It was not until the Pentagon Papers cases, however, that the Supreme Court was faced with the necessity of applying these principles to a circumstance where the communication in question allegedly posed a danger to national security. Although two members of the Court, Justices Black and Douglas, were willing to say that the First Amendment prohibits *all* prior restraints,[90] the other four who joined with them in rejecting the government's request for an injunction took a less absolutist view of the matter. Justice Brennan's position was that, although exceptions to the rule against prior restraints may be allowed, they must be truly rare.

> The entire thrust of the Government's claim throughout these cases has been that publication of the material sought to be enjoined "could," or "might," or "may" prejudice the national interest in various ways. But the First Amendment tolerates absolutely no prior judicial restraints of the press predicated upon surmise or conjecture that untoward consequences may result. . . . only governmental allegation and proof that publication must inevitably, directly and immediately cause the occurrence of an event kindred to imperiling the safety of a

transport already at sea can support even the issuance of an interim restraining order.[91]

Justices Stewart and Byron White suggested that they might have taken a different view of the situation had Congress specifically granted to the executive and judicial branches of government the power to restrain the kind of communication at issue. In the absence of such a legislative mandate they felt that the First Amendment forbade an injunction unless it were shown that disclosure of the information "will surely result in direct, immediate, and irreparable damage to our nation or its people."[92] They did not believe the government had met that test.

Justice Marshall found the absence of congressional authorization for prior restraints, such as the one sought, to be critical to his determination of the judgment to be rendered, and joined with the majority primarily for that reason.[93] Presumably he, like Justices Stewart and White, might have supported the government's effort to suppress publication of the Pentagon Papers had Congress, in spite of the First Amendment, seen fit to authorize such prior restraints.

It was precisely this latter question which moved to the fore on the next occasion that the U.S. government sought to stop a publication on the grounds of national security, in *U.S. v. The Progressive*—a case having the dubious distinction of being the first in our entire history in which a court enjoined an act of communication on the basis of a national security claim.[94]

The case arose when the *Progressive* magazine, headquartered in Madison, Wisconsin, decided to publish an article in its April 1979 issue entitled, "The H-Bomb Secret: How We Got It, Why We're Telling It." The author of the article, a free-lance writer named Howard Morland, with a background of a few college science courses, had set out to learn as much as he could about the design of nuclear weapons from reading material on the subject in unclassified government publications, encyclopedia references, physics textbooks, and magazine articles, from visits to nuclear production facilities, and from interviews with personnel of the Department of Energy.[95] The resulting article was intended to explode the myth that nuclear weapon technology is any longer a secret. The *Progressive*'s editor explained:

> It was our feeling, last summer, that the Government had invoked secrecy for thirty years to keep Americans from questioning the nuclear arms race. How much justification was there for the secrecy, we wondered, and what kind of information was being withheld that might help people formulate informed judgments on such vital questions as environmental risks, occupational health and safety threats, nuclear proliferation and the continuing arms race, and the astronomical costs of the nuclear weapons program?

In a letter to the *Progressive* last July 7, Howard Morland summarized his assignment, as he understood it after two conversations
with Sam Day [managing editor]:
"We agreed," Morland wrote, "that nuclear weapons production has
prospered too long in an atmosphere of freedom from public scrutiny.
The *Progressive* should raise the visibility of the nuclear warhead assembly line, which stretches in a great arc across America from
Tampa, Florida, to Amarillo, Texas. Corporate connections should be
explained. The Bomb should be described in sufficient detail to allow
readers to see nuclear warheads as pieces of hardware rather than as
score-points in a contest. . . .
"By the end of August," Morland continued, "I hope to know as
much as it is legal to know—and possible for a layman to
understand—about thermonuclear warhead design. . . ."[96]

When a rough draft of the Morland article came into the *Progressive*
office in January 1979, copies were sent to several nuclear experts to
check it for accuracy. Without the magazine's knowledge or consent, one
of those copies was passed along to the Department of Energy, triggering a chain of events which was to culminate in a warning from the
department's general counsel that unless the *Progressive* agreed not to
publish the article, the government would initiate legal action to stop it.[97]

The government took the position that the article contained "Restricted Data," defined by the Atomic Energy Act of 1954 as "all data
concerning (1) design, manufacture, or utilization of atomic weapons;
(2) the production of special nuclear material; or (3) the use of special
nuclear material in the production of energy, but shall not include data
declassified or removed from the Restricted Data category."[98]

According to the provisions of the Atomic Energy Act it is illegal to
communicate, transmit, or disclose restricted data "with reason to believe
such data will be utilized to injure the United States or to secure an
advantage to any foreign nation."[99] Furthermore, the law explicitly authorizes the attorney general to "make application to the appropriate
court for an order enjoining such acts or practices."[100]

The government's answer to the admitted fact that Morland had
written his article without the aid of any classified or illegally obtained
information was that the restricted data category is not limited to government material but may include information created by private citizens. Such information, claimed the government, is "data restricted at
birth" and, by the terms of the Atomic Energy Act, remains restricted
unless and until it has been removed from that category by the proper
authorities.[101]

This sweeping power to enjoin even the dissemination of ideas born in
the minds of private individuals was defended by the government, and

granted by the district court, on the grounds that publication of information in the Morland article would constitute a danger to national security. Secretary of State Cyrus Vance had submitted an affidavit asserting that publication "would substantially increase the risk that thermonuclear weapons would become available or available at an earlier date to those who do not now have them" and that "[i]f this should occur, it would undermine our nonproliferation policy, irreparably impair the national security of the United States, and pose a grave threat to the peace and security of the world."[102] Secretary of Defense Harold Brown and Energy Secretary James Schlesinger said essentially the same thing.[103]

Affidavits were also filed with the district court by a number of nuclear scientists, but they were sharply divided into two camps. There were those like Roger Batzel, Robert Thorn, and Hans Bethe who contended that the Morland article contained information which was not already publicly available and would thus substantially hasten the development of thermonuclear weapons by countries seeking a nuclear capability.[104] But there were others, such as Theodore Postol, who maintained that "the article by Morland contains no information or ideas that are not already common knowledge among scientists, including those who do not have access to classified information,"[105] and Hugh DeWitt who said:

> This "secret" has been regarded for over twenty-five years as highly classified. Yet there is by now enough information in open publications that a capable physicist could deduce the basic idea for himself without access to classified literature. An intelligent and resourceful reporter could probably do the same thing. . . .
>
> If this article by Morland is not published, I expect that it will be only a short time before another reporter working independently for a different publication will uncover the same information and write a very similar article. In short, after more than twenty-five years the H-bomb is not so secret anymore.[106]

The American Civil Liberties Union, representing the *Progressive*'s editor and managing editor on appeal, in a brief submitted jointly with Howard Morland's attorneys to the U.S. Court of Appeals for the Seventh Circuit, presented the following line of argument:

> The article written by Howard Morland, to be published by *The Progressive,* discusses the important political issues of proliferation of nuclear weapons and the dangers of government secrecy. The article is not a blueprint for the manufacture of a hydrogen bomb. Rather, it is political speech designed to foster and encourage public debate about important public issues. As such, it is precisely the kind of speech protected by the First Amendment. . . .

Despite repeated Supreme Court decisions imposing a "heavy presumption against the constitutionality of any prior restraint," the district court stopped the defendants from publishing an article of political commentary on the basis of conclusory, speculative, and untested governmental affidavits which, even if true, fail to meet the required standard. Under controlling Supreme Court decisions, the government is required to prove that publication will "surely or inevitably" result "directly and immediately" in "grave and irreparable harm." But the government in this case has shown, at most, that publication "could possibly" cause "serious" harm at some indefinite point in the not-immediate future. And even that speculative and tentative showing was not permitted to be tested by cross-examination. . . .

. . . in proving certainty of harm, the government must present evidence, not speculation or conclusory allegations. . . . Proof that publication "could" or "might" or "may" cause the requisite harm is not enough. . . .

The government's affidavits in this case, even if true, do not prove or even allege that publication will lead to "virtually certain," "sure" or "inevitable" harm. . . . Indeed, although the district court misunderstood the standard, and misquoted Justice Stewart by substituting "likelihood" for "surely" . . . the court did not in its memorandum opinion find even that the harm would be likely, let alone virtually certain, sure or inevitable:

[T]he article could possibly provide sufficient information to allow a medium size nation to move faster in developing a hydrogen weapon. It could provide a ticket to by-pass blind alleys. [It] could accelerate the membership of a candidate nation in the thermonuclear club. . . .

These conditional and equivocal findings, on their face, fail to meet the certainty standard established in *New York Times*. . . .

Harm must be not only certain, but "imminent." Here again, that requirement emerged from a careful and deliberate rejection of a much lower standard urged by the government in the Pentagon Papers case. . . .

The independent requirement that the harm flow "directly and immediately" from publication reflects the considered judgment of the Supreme Court that proof of imminent harm is necessary to avoid the imposition of a prior restraint based on speculation and conjecture. Imminence is also necessary to ensure that prior restraint is the last resort, that there is not time to pursue "less drastic alternatives" to avert or minimize the threatened harm. . . . Thus, the "imminence" requirement reflects the common-sense judgment that as the threatened harm becomes more remote in time, it becomes less certain that it will occur at all. Proof of "direct and immediate" harm is therefore essential to establish a constitutionally sufficient causal relationship between publication and injury. . . . The government's affidavits suggest only that harm might eventually occur at some unspecified time in the future.... They do not claim, let alone prove, that publication will "directly" and "immediately" result in the actual use of fusion weapons or even in their production or acquisition....

Harm must be not only certain and imminent, but "grave" and "irreparable."...

Even if true, the most the government's affidavits demonstrate in this case is that publication of the Morland article would increase the risk of the proliferation of nuclear weapons *capability*, not the actual proliferation of nuclear weapons or the increased risk of their use against the United States, its allies, or any other country.... the harm claimed by the government here is not that publication of the Morland article will lead to death or destruction.... Rather, it points only to an increased risk of unspecified dimension in the indefinite future that a few technologically sophisticated nations may have a greater capability, if they choose to develop it, to construct thermonuclear weapons sooner than they would otherwise be able to do. This harm is insufficiently grave to meet the Pentagon Papers standard....

Finally ... this Court must measure the harm that would be caused by publication not in the abstract, but as an increment to the real dangers that will continue to exist despite the prior restraint on these defendants. Although the district court apparently believed prior restraint would prevent the nuclear destruction of "human life" on "an awesome scale" ... it would not. The nations that give this country the greatest concern already have the H-bomb. And the government concedes that the Morland article would be of use to nations only if they already have or can readily acquire atomic bombs, which are necessary to ignite H-bombs. Although use of thermonuclear weapons could cause an incrementally greater harm than fission weapons, fission weapons already provide an enormous capacity for massive nuclear destruction. Prior restraint here would not prevent the risk of nuclear destruction. That risk already exists.

In summary, the extraordinarily strict three-part standard established by the Supreme Court in the Pentagon Papers case, and reaffirmed in *Nebraska Press*, constitutes an "almost insuperable presumption against the constitutionality of prior restraints even under a recognized exception." ... The government's affidavits in this case, even if true, do not meet a single element of that standard, let alone all three. For that reason, the injunction should be set aside.[107]

As it turned out, there was no need for the court of appeals to decide whether the injunction should be set aside. Oral arguments were heard in the case in Chicago on Thursday, September 13, 1979, but on Sunday, September 16, just three days later, a small Wisconsin newspaper, the *Madison Press Connection*, published a letter written by a California computer programmer, Charles Hansen, which contained essentially the same information as the *Progressive* article. Hansen had sent his letter to Senator Charles Percy, with copies to several newspapers, including the *Daily Californian*, which also intended to print it but was prevented from doing so by a temporary restraining order issued in a federal district court in San Francisco on Saturday night. On Monday morning, with 8,000 copies of the *Madison Press Connection* already in circulation, the government announced that it would ask the courts in both San Francisco and Chicago to dismiss its cases against the *Daily Californian* and the *Progressive* magazine.[108] A justice department spokesman indicated that, although a preliminary investigation would be undertaken to determine if prosecutions might be brought for violations of the criminal provisions of the Atomic Energy Act, the prior restraints which the government had obtained had been rendered useless by the Sunday publication of Charles Hansen's letter in Madison, Wisconsin.[109]

One can argue narrowly, as the ACLU did in the *Progressive* case, that censorship of the Morland article was invalid simply on the basis of the *New York Times v. U.S.* principle that it would not "surely result in direct, immediate, and irreparable damage," and thus avoid the necessity of defending an absolutist view that all injunctions against communication under all possible circumstances are unconstitutional. Yet that is a position which has substantial attractions and strong advocates.

Its first great advantage, of course, is that it allows the public to hear whatever anyone may have to say. If there is any conceivable value in a message it will not go unheard. Furthermore, by confining the controls on unprotected expression to after-the-fact punishment, the particular context and actual effects of an act of communication can be assessed. Thus restraints imposed on the basis of speculative harms or abstract definitions are avoided. Also avoided are penalties for defiance of authority per se—for instance, contempt of court—as contrasted with those which are responsive to the offense itself. Last, but by no means least, the possibility is eliminated that, where time is of the essence, an act of communication may be tied up in prolonged court proceedings and cloaked in secrecy—a process which actually occurred in the *Progressive* case.

Despite these powerful arguments against prior restraints, there are instances where common sense seems to dictate that, if clearly and immediately harmful communication can be prevented from spreading any further than it already has, legal steps should be taken to try to stop it. Examples are not hard to come by. Reference was made in an earlier chapter to the possibility of a book being written by a psychiatrist in which confidences revealed by a clearly identifiable patient are published for all the world to know. A similar invasion of privacy, equally deserving of efforts to stop it, would be the attempted publication by an employee or ex-employee of the Internal Revenue Service of information gleaned from people's tax returns. In our chapter on "Lies and Mis-representations," note was taken, without objection, of the Federal Trade Commission's use of cease-and-desist orders, the administrative equivalent of injunctions, against false advertising. Similarly legitimate, it seems to me, is the federal statute which authorizes the use of in-junctions to prevent violations of the copyright law.[110] Furthermore, Justice Brennan, in his Pentagon Papers opinion, wrote of information "imperiling the safety of a transport already at sea" as the kind which could appropriately be restrained in advance. This was an interesting modification of the classic example so often used in this connection, but which, in an earlier form, referred to newspaper publication of the "sailing dates of transports."[111] Presuming this to have been a conscious alteration of the hypothetical example by Justice Brennan, he may have been motivated by the realization that the sailing date of a troop trans-port could be changed if word about it had leaked out, whereas a ship already at sea would inevitably be endangered. Another illustration of communication with the same sort of immediately hazardous effects would be the exposure of the identity and location of an intelligence-gathering agent serving in a hostile foreign country.

If we open the door to prior restraints on national security or other equally compelling grounds for the kinds of information just described, is there any way that abuses of the process, such as in the Pentagon Papers and *Progressive* cases, can be avoided? I believe that there is. The answer, I think, is to be found in the undoing of a 5–4 decision of the U.S. Supreme Court handed down in 1967, *Walker v. Birmingham,* in which the conviction of a group of civil rights demonstrators for march-ing in violation of a state court injunction was sustained.[112] The march-ers had attempted in good faith to secure permits from Birmingham, Alabama, officials for parades on Good Friday and Easter Sunday, 1963, but were rebuffed by the city's Public Safety Commissioner, Eugene "Bull" Connor. When they decided to go ahead with their plans to march anyhow, city officials went to court and obtained an injunction against their holding any demonstrations without a permit. Believing the court's order to be as unconstitutional a violation of their First Amendment rights as the city's refusal to grant them a permit in the first place, they defied both and, predictably, were found in contempt of court. In sus-taining that conviction the U.S. Supreme Court's majority conceded the possibility that the Birmingham permit ordinance may have been unconstitutionally vague and overbroad, that the city may have been administering it in a discriminatory manner, and that the injunction requiring compliance with that order may have been of questionable propriety. Nevertheless, said the majority, the place to present those challenges was through the appellate processes of the courts and not by marching first and seeking vindication later:

This Court cannot hold that the petitioners were constitutionally free to ignore all the procedures of the law and carry their battle to the streets. One may sympathize with the petitioners' impatient commitment to their cause. But respect for the judicial process is a small price to pay for the civilizing hand of law, which alone can give abiding meaning to constitutional freedom.[113]

The irony of this decision was that, just two years later, another case came before the Supreme Court involving the same set of events in Birmingham and one of the same persons who had been found guilty in *Walker* of contempt of court, but this time the issue was a conviction for violation of the permit ordinance itself rather than of the court injunction. Now the U.S. Supreme Court was unanimous in finding the ordinance unconstitutionally discretionary, and the conviction for its violation therefore invalid.[114] In other words, as a result of these two decisions, the Supreme Court has said that persons may later be vindicated if they exercise their First Amendment rights in defiance of an unconstitutional law, but that defiance of a court injunction, whether it is valid or not, is unforgivable. Laws which offend the First Amendment can be challenged in the streets, but injunctions can be challenged only in court.[115]

The four dissenters in *Walker v. Birmingham* would not have allowed for this strange state of affairs, and in their position lies what I think to be the correct solution to the problem of prior restraints on expression. Chief Justice Warren, Justice Douglas, and Justice Brennan each put it his own way, in opinions in which the others, including Justice Abe Fortas, all joined.

Chief Justice Warren spoke first:

Petitioners were served with copies of the injunction at various times on Thursday and on Good Friday. Unable to believe that such a blatant and broadly-drawn prior restraint on their First Amendment rights could be valid, they announced their intention to defy it and went ahead with the planned peaceful demonstrations on Easter weekend. On the following Monday, when they promptly filed a motion to dissolve the injunction, the court found them in contempt, holding that they had waived their First Amendment rights by disobeying the court order.

These facts lend no support to the court's charges that petitioners were presuming to act as judges in their own case, or that they had a disregard for the judicial process. They did not flee the jurisdiction or refuse to appear in the Alabama courts. Having violated the injunction, they promptly submitted themselves to the courts to test the constitutionality of the injunction and the ordinance it parroted. They were in essentially the same position as persons who challenge the constitutionality of a statute by violating it, and then defend the ensuing criminal prosecution on constitutional grounds. It has never been thought that violation of a statute indicated such a disrespect for the legislature that the violator always must be punished even if the statute was unconstitutional. On the contrary, some cases have required that persons seeking to challenge the constitutionality of a statute first violate it to establish their standing to sue. Indeed, it shows no disrespect for law to violate a statute on the ground that it is unconstitutional and then to submit one's case to the courts with the willingness to accept the penalty if the statute is held to be valid.

. . . the city had no need of an injunction to impose a criminal penalty for demonstrating on the streets without a permit. The ordinance already accomplished that. In point of fact, there is only one apparent reason why the city sought this injunction and why the court issued it: to make it possible to punish petitioners for contempt rather than for violating the ordinance, and thus to immunize the unconstitutional statute and its unconstitutional application from any attack. I regret that this strategy has been so successful.[116]

Justice Douglas added:

An ordinance—unconstitutional on its face or patently unconstitutional as applied—is not made sacred by an unconstitutional injunction that enforces it. It can and should be flouted in the manner of the ordinance itself. Courts as well as citizens are not free "to ignore the procedure of the law," to use the Court's language. The "constitutional freedom" of which the Court speaks can be won only if judges honor the Constitution.[117]

And Justice Brennan concluded:

. . . the Court empties the Supremacy Clause of its primacy by elevating a state rule of judicial administration above the right of free expression guaranteed by the Federal Constitution. And the Court does so by letting loose a devastatingly destructive weapon for suppression of cherished freedoms heretofore believed indispensable to maintenance of our free society. I cannot believe that this distortion in the hierarchy of values upon which our society has been and must be ordered can have any significance beyond its function as a vehicle to affirm these contempt convictions. . . .

The vitality of First Amendment protections has . . . been deemed to rest in large measure upon the ability of the individual to take his chances and express himself in the face of such restraints, armed with the ability to challenge those restraints if the State seeks to penalize that expression. The most striking examples of the right to speak first and challenge later, and of peculiar moment for the present case, are the cases concerning the ability of an individual to challenge a permit or licensing statute giving broad discretion to an individual or group, such as the Birmingham permit ordinance, despite the fact that he did not attempt to obtain a permit or license. . . .

Yet by some inscrutable legerdemain these constitutionally secured rights to challenge prior restraints invalid on their face are lost if the State takes the precaution to have some judge append his signature to an *ex parte* order which recites the words of the invalid statute. . . . The *ex parte* order of the judicial officer is glorified above the presumably carefully considered, even if hopelessly invalid, mandates of the legislative branch.

. . . The ability to exercise protected protest at a time when such exercise would be effective must be as protected as the beliefs themselves. . . . It is a flagrant denial of constitutional guarantees to balance away this principle in the name of "respect for the judicial process." To preach "respect" in this context is to deny the right to speak at all.

. . . Constitutional restrictions against abridgments of First Amendment freedoms limit judicial equally with legislative and executive power. Convictions for contempt of court orders which invalidly abridge First Amendment freedoms must be condemned equally with convictions for violation of statutes which do the same thing. I respectfully dissent.[118]

The net effect of adopting the position of the *Walker* dissenters just quoted, as I propose that we do,[119] would be to allow the government to seek and perhaps to obtain injunctions against expression in the narrowly limited kinds of circumstances such as that envisioned by the *New York Times v. U.S.* test or the unauthorized publication of personal confidences. But such injunctions would be largely early warning systems only. Those against whom they were directed could, if they believed the restraints to be unconstitutional, immediately violate them with the same impunity, and at the same risk of being found wrong, as if they were transgressing an arguably invalid statute or engaging in potentially tortious conduct.

To be sure, they might have more difficulty in defending themselves with a claim of no intent to do harm, or lack of knowledge of harmful effects, than in the absence of an injunction, and they might also suffer greater penalties if ultimately found guilty. But those strike me as reasonable prices to pay for the right to defy the judgment of a court and still go unpunished if later found to have engaged in behavior protected by the First Amendment. Whether, under such a regime, the officers of the *New York Times* would have gone ahead and printed the Pentagon Papers, or those at the *Progressive* magazine would have published the Morland article in the issue for which it was originally planned, we cannot be sure. But at least their decisions would have depended on the courage of their convictions about the First Amendment legitimacy of the messages they wished to communicate rather than upon their unwillingness, right or wrong, to go to jail simply for defying the sacrosanct order of a court.

17   The Government as Communicator

Although profound problems are created for a democratic society when its public officials do not communicate enough, there are also troublesome issues raised by a government which talks too much. It is to those matters that we now turn our attention.

The circumstances in which government officials *must* communicate with the public in order to do their jobs effectively are too numerous to be itemized here. Examples will suffice for our purposes. The president, governors, mayors, and their top aides need to keep the people informed of actions taken by the government on their behalf, of policies and problems requiring their cooperation, and of crises that must be dealt with. Government agencies must make known the services they offer to the public, many of which are themselves of an informational nature, such as instruction and advice on health, education, farming, commerce, or energy. The armed services and many other departments of government need to advertise to recruit qualified personnel to fill their ranks and must engage in public information activities to maintain a satisfactory working relationship with those whom they serve and upon whose confidence their effectiveness depends. Legislators have an obligation to make known to their constituents their views and their votes on current issues and are even provided with free mailing privileges to facilitate that process.

Communication from government officials becomes problematic, however, when they use the time and resources made available to them by the taxpayers' money to promote their partisan political goals, to enhance their personal careers, or to diminish the reputations of other people. These problems grow increasingly serious as the mass media of communication become more centralized and government officials acquire the ability to have access to those media far in excess of any competitors. The extreme case, of course, is the totalitarian regime which floods a country with its propaganda to the total exclusion of all other points of view.

What makes this a complicated question for a democratic society is that

410

a certain amount of partisan and self-serving communication by public officials is not only inevitable but is a necessary by-product of the governing process. The mere occupancy of an office like president or vice-president of the United States, secretary of state, governor, mayor, or U.S. senator provides experience, authority, and visibility which give an advantage to whatever the officeholder says and enhance that individual's chances of continuing to have influence in the future. What is more, political leaders are supposed to have convictions on controversial issues and are expected to express their views and to seek support for carrying them into action. Although we require that, during the course of a campaign for reelection, incumbent officeholders pay for what clearly can be defined as campaign expenses out of separate moneys raised for that purpose, there is no way they can be prevented from taking indirect advantage of their incumbency, and the tax dollars which support it, to advance their own causes. Every speech which they make or press conference they hold, every trip they take, every letter they write and phone call they answer, every service they perform, every program they implement, every vote they cast or veto they exercise can be helpful to their reelection.

It is also immensely difficult to separate the necessary functions of keeping the citizenry adequately informed about the workings of its departments of government from a bombardment of the public with communication designed primarily to justify an agency's questionably useful existence, to help it to build a bigger empire, to satisfy the vanity of its leaders, or to distract attention from its waste and incompetence. According to a *New York Times* report in 1978:

> The Federal Government is spending at least $1 billion a year to inform and sell the American people on its programs.
>
> Nearly 20,000 public information and public affairs workers, moviemakers and broadcasters, writers, editors and advertising specialists work for the government. Their salaries range up to $50,000 for top press officers, some of whom hold the rank of Assistant Secretary in the Cabinet....
>
> While few would maintain that none of the public information efforts fill a legitimate governmental need, literally hundreds of press releases are issued daily to promote statements and speeches by agency officials. Exhibits in Federal office buildings display larger-than-life pictures of department and agency heads. Agencies provide taped news broadcasts to radio stations around the country.
>
> Virtually no Government agency, no matter how tiny, is without a public relations program....
>
> The Defense Department has one of the Government's largest public information and public relations forces. It costs more than $25 million a year, excluding advertising for recruitment. The Pentagon

has a press and public affairs staff of 316 persons, and more than 1,200 military and civilian public relations workers are scattered among the military services and other Defense Department agencies. . . .

An official of the Office of Management and Budget said, "When you look at the functions of each department and what needs to be communicated, and then see what is being put out, there is clearly more being done than is absolutely necessary."

But public information chiefs, such as Ernest Lotito at the Commerce Department, staunchly defend their efforts. "We're here to get information out to the public," Mr. Lotito said. "The news media couldn't survive without us."[1]

This tension between what is an appropriate and inappropriate use of government resources for communication by public officials runs through almost every conceivable field of their activities. Presidents from the beginning of the nation's history have sought to persuade both the public and the Congress to support and vote for their policies, just as opposition legislative leaders have long decried what they have characterized as excessive pressure and propaganda from the executive branch of government.[2] With the advent of radio and television, the ability of chief executives to go "over the heads" of legislators and appeal directly to the people was enormously facilitated, to the point where thoughtful critics have cautioned that the balance of power in our political system has been seriously endangered.[3] Franklin D. Roosevelt, with his remarkable facility for the use of radio, was the first to exploit this new technology to its fullest in support of his legislative programs. Richard Nixon utilized to a greater extent than any of his predecessors the presidential technique of preempting prime television time on all three networks simultaneously, thus leaving the bulk of the national audience with no viewing alternative.[4]

In more recent times we have witnessed concerted public campaigns by Jimmy Carter's administration to win approval—first for the Panama Canal treaty, and then for the Strategic Arms Limitation Treaty with the Soviet Union. According to a General Accounting Office study made in 1979 at the request of a treaty opponent, Senator Barry Goldwater, the administration had spent approximately $600,000 in the preceding year on public information activities in support of the ratification of SALT II, which included "supplying speakers, arranging conferences, preparing and distributing publications and providing interviews and press releases."[5] Although Senator Goldwater no doubt hoped to embarrass the administration by publicizing this information, no one seriously contended that such expenditures were either illegal or improper.

That was not the case, however, with respect to an incident which occurred as a result of the Carter administration's lobbying efforts to secure ratification by the states of the Equal Rights Amendment to the Constitution. With an uphill fight pending for ratification in the Nevada legislature early in 1979, an apparently overeager director of the Interior Department's Bureau of Reclamation in the Lower Colorado Regional Office sent a directive to subordinates which read as follows:

> ...the President emphasizes that every resource of the federal government is to be applied in eliminating discrimination and inequality based on sex. He directs the head of each department and agency to (1) make the most of public appearance opportunities to demonstrate the administration's commitment to the Equal Rights Amendment; and (2) include in public speeches, where appropriate, language emphasizing the importance of ERA.
>
> Accordingly, I am asking each supervisor in this region to comply with the above directives regardless of personal preferences or political opinions. This is not to be considered a partisan issue, but one which federal employees are now obliged to support.[6]

When officials in Washington learned of this order, a second memorandum from the same author soon followed: "...Bureau of Reclamation Commissioner Keith Higginson has directed me to retract the communication, as my message was inappropriate and contrary to department policy."[7] Presumably it was considered legitimate for government officials to be asked to speak out in support of their administration's policies but not if it meant they had to lie about their own convictions.

What about officials, however, who lie voluntarily on behalf of the government when they think that to do so will serve the best interests of some policy or program which is being pursued, perhaps in dealing with a hostile foreign power, or with a domestic crisis which seems to require that the public temporarily be misled. The history of such episodes in our country has not been a happy one and suggests that deception of the public, for whatever motives, usually boomerangs in ways that are more harmful than if the truth had been told in the first instance.

A classic illustration was the U-2 episode of the Eisenhower administration, when an American reconnaissance plane was shot down over the Soviet Union. Our government's first response to Premier Khrushchev's announcement on May 1, 1960, that the plane had been brought down was to claim that it was merely on a weather observation flight and had accidentally strayed over the Soviet border from Turkey. The National Aeronautics and Space Administration even issued a detailed description of the meteorological studies of which this flight was a part.[8] Not until the Russians disclosed that the captured pilot of the plane had confessed to being on a CIA mission to photograph Soviet military installations did President Eisenhower acknowledge that our government's original story was a false "covering statement" to protect the secrecy of our intelligence-gathering activities.[9]

The doubts raised by this incident about the credibility of our government were incalculably intensified by the Nixon administration's deceptions concerning the bombing of Cambodia during the Vietnam War, not to mention the false assurances given by the government in the early 1950s about the safety of atomic bomb tests in Nevada and Utah to residents of the area, who have since been the victims of a disproportionately high percentage of cancer cases.

While there are few who can be found to defend these particular falsehoods, it is not uncommon for public officials to argue in justification of less blatant forms of prevarication. Former President Carter's press secretary, Jody Powell, was one such person, and his attitude has been shared by other holders of his office:

> Powell's philosophy as chief spokesman for President Carter was discussed in a recent interview with RKO General Broadcasting. A transcript was released Monday.
>
> "I have not always told the press corps everything I know, and in some cases I have attempted to avoid answering a question," Powell said. "But I have not intentionally given the press corps false or wrong information."
>
> When asked whether he had ever knowingly misled reporters, Powell replied, "I think there is a legitimate area in which it is permissible for me or any other press secretary to attempt to steer people away from a story that you would just as soon not see done that day, if you can do so without saying things that are not true."[10]

Apart from the issue of government speech which is misleading, there is the question of communication by public officials and agencies which is outside the proper sphere of their activities. A case in point was a resolution adopted by the Denver school board to use district facilities and funds to work for the defeat of a proposed amendment to the state constitution which would have altered the authority of all levels of state government to spend tax dollars. The school board had decided that its action was authorized by a state law which allowed political subdivisions to "make contributions . . . in campaigns involving only issues in which they have an official concern."[11]

A federal district court in Colorado thought otherwise:

> The characterization of a campaign issue as being of official concern is not a judgment which can be made solely by the board of education. Such an interpretation would give unlimited discretion to the school

board to use school funds and school facilities whenever it suited the personal preference of the majority of the members.

What is of "official concern" to a school district board of education is to be determined by reference to the official powers and duties delegated by the general assembly in the school laws. A special election for the sole purpose of voting on a school bond issue is a convenient illustration of a campaign involving "only issues in which they have an official concern." A proposed amendment to the state constitution on a general election ballot is not such a matter.

. . . It is the duty of this court to protect the political freedom of the people of Colorado. The freedom of speech and the right of the people to petition the government for a redress of grievances are fundamental components of guaranteed liberty in the United States.

A use of the power of publicly owned resources to propagandize against a proposal made and supported by a significant number of those who were taxed to pay for such resources is an abridgement of those fundamental freedoms.[12]

Overstepping the appropriate bounds of their job definitions is a problem with regard to individual public officeholders as well as boards, commissions, or agencies as a whole. Is it proper, for instance, for U.S. cabinet officers with nonpartisan responsibilities, such as those of the attorney general, secretary of state, or secretary of defense, to participate in a campaign for reelection of the president they serve? Or, at an entirely different level but with similar implications, should members of the office staff of a congressman or senator, who are paid out of tax money to do the government's business, devote any of their on-the-job time, effort, or resources to their employer's efforts to win reelection?

One of the main purposes of the establishment of a civil service system, of course, and of legislation like the federal Hatch Act[13] and similar laws in all of our states which prohibit partisan political activity on the part of government employees,[14] was to prevent such persons from unfairly tipping the balance of the political scales in favor of incumbents, as well as to protect public job holders from being drafted into partisan activity by their superiors. That has not settled the issue for many government employees, however, since the Hatch Act applies only to those working in the *executive* branch of the federal government and even there exempts officials in policymaking positions, just as state laws typically cover only those in classified civil service jobs and leave patronage workers untouched. What is more, there have been repeated, though unsuccessful, legal challenges to the constitutionality of these statutes by covered employees who have argued that the prohibitions are a violation of their free speech rights.[15] Objection has been made particularly to the vagueness of the definitions of prohibited behavior and to the broad reach of the legislation—affecting, as it usually does, both off-the-job and on-the-job conduct, and persons like custodial employees or letter carriers who are not in positions where they are likely to be able to influence the political process unduly. The classic example of these defects is the instance noted by Justice Douglas of a nurse in a Veterans Administration hospital who was found in violation of the Hatch Act for having placed an advertisement in a local newspaper urging her friends in the community to vote for her father for the Democratic nomination for county sheriff.[16]

As for the traditional patronage system under which people have been hired for public employment as a reward for political activities on behalf of those in power and replaced when their patrons were turned out of office, our courts have begun to find that practice constitutionally defective. A 1976 U.S. Supreme Court opinion held that the First Amendment forbade the firing of persons from non-policymaking, non-confidential government jobs solely because of their political beliefs and associations, and a 1980 decision modified that ruling to make the determinative criterion for the permissibility of a political dismissal the question of whether party affiliation is necessary or relevant to the effective performance of a particular job.[17] On the basis of the first of those Supreme Court rulings a federal district court in Chicago found, in 1979, that what the Constitution forbids in the way of politically motivated *dismissals* from public employment should logically extend as well to *hirings* and *promotions* on a patronage basis.[18] The judge reasoned that the use of government jobs as an incentive for political work on behalf of incumbents constituted official discrimination against political expression, association, and equal participation in the electoral process by independent candidates and voters.[19]

Another, and rather different, set of questions about the government as communicator has to do with the use of public office as a "bully pulpit" to pressure, cajole, or embarrass private citizens or associations into conforming with a standard of behavior which government may be powerless to compel by law, or which it prefers to achieve, if it can, without legal action. In his excellent book on *Secrecy and Publicity,* Francis E. Rourke has identified and discussed several kinds of government action of this sort.

One category is the threat or use of adverse publicity by the executive branch of government, most commonly by its regulatory agencies, to influence or control the decisions and practices of private businesses. A noteworthy example was the so-called jaw-boning of the steel industry by the administration of John F. Kennedy that achieved the recision of a round of steel price increases which, in the president's view, threatened the health of the economy. Less effective, but in the same vein, were the efforts of the Carter administration to secure compliance with its voluntary wage and price increase guidelines.

As to regulatory agencies, Rourke notes their success "in using the mere threat of adverse public attention to bring about the settlement of complaints without the necessity of formal hearings."[20] He elaborates:

> Much has been made, for example, of the value of threatened publicity in effecting the conspicuously successful record of the Securities and Exchange Commission in controlling the investment field without the necessity of formal litigation. Only rarely has the SEC found it necessary to hold a public hearing in connection with its regulation of the marketing of securities. Fear of the adverse publicity connected with the public airing of a complaint has been sufficient pressure to bring about compliance with SEC suggestions for alterations in the language of a prospectus. This is so, of course, largely because successful flotation of an issue of stock demands absolute confidence in the integrity of the product offered for purchase by investors. . . .
>
> One of the most famous of all attempts to use the publicity sanction in national administrative regulation came with the establishment of the National Recovery Administration in 1934. The NRA relied almost entirely on its blue eagle symbol as a means of imposing codes of fair competition upon broad segments of American Industry. It withheld the right to display this symbol from firms which refused to cooperate in renouncing the practices of cut-throat competition which NRA officials regarded as being primarily responsible for demoralizing the economy. For a time at least, the NRA succeeded in making the blue eagle a virtual symbol of national patriotism. . . .
>
> In state regulation, also, the threat of adverse publicity has come to play an important role in the informal enforcement of administrative law. One of the areas of state administration in which its effectiveness has been most recently proved is in the operation of newly enacted state fair-employment practice acts. In this case the effectiveness of the publicity sanction has been vital to the success of the legislation concerned, since the assumption upon which FEP laws were enacted was that the law could be administered with a minimum of resort to formal litigation. This conciliation philosophy . . . is rooted in the consideration that excessive reliance upon legal coercion would be in ill accord with a basic purpose of fair employment legislation—the improvement of group relations. . . . the publicity connected with . . . a hearing is in itself punishment, whatever the verdict of a hearing tribunal may be. From the point of view of a business firm it becomes a vital necessity to avoid such a hearing, since public relations considerations may be given precedence over whatever estimate the firm may make of its legal position in the case.[21]

A second category of extralegal control via government publicity is that of the legislative investigating committee which, for the ostensible purpose of considering remedial legislation, holds hearings to expose wrongdoing on the part of those suspected of some sort of antisocial conduct. Focusing the glare of publicity on their behavior, whether or not it is technically illegal, may subject them to public opprobrium and deter others from similar actions.

Setting aside for the moment the legitimacy of this *means* of social control, the history of the past few decades has clearly demonstrated that it can serve both worthy and unworthy *ends*. Congressional investigations into organized crime and the rigging of television quiz shows alerted the public to serious problems in need of attention, as did the Watergate hearings, chaired by Senator Sam Ervin, which were of unparalleled value in exposing the details of that affair to public scrutiny. On the other hand, the damage to innocent people and their reputations done by the investigations into allegedly subversive activities by the House Committee on Un-American Activities and the Senate subcommittee on government operations chaired by Joseph R. McCarthy are too well known to require elaboration.

Rourke has proposed what I think to be the key to determining when the adverse publicity generated by legislative inquiries is or is not a legitimate tool of social control:

> ...it is extremely important to maintain a distinction between the exposure of activities and the indictment of individuals. In the congressional inquiry into the rigging of television quiz programs, for example, the task before Congress was that of publicizing an unsavory state of affairs in an industry subject to regulation by an agency that was then under congressional scrutiny. It was not the legislature's function to pass on the guilt of every individual who had appeared as a contestant on these shows.... There is a difference between the exposure of an individual that is incidental to the investigation of a problem and an investigation that is carried on for no other purpose than that of holding isolated individuals up to public scorn.... "Exposure for exposure's sake," as long as it is aimed at activities rather than individuals has historically always been, and must necessarily continue to be, a proper function of congressional investigations. It only becomes improper when a legislative committee arrogates to itself a judicial function, and deliberately sets itself up to determine the guilt or innocence of particular individuals.[22]

To assert that communication emanating from legislative committee hearings may sometimes constitute an improper exercise of government power is not to suggest that it can or should be legally restrained. On the contrary, insofar as statements made by congressmen and senators are concerned, the Constitution explicitly provides that "for any Speech or Debate in either House, they shall not be questioned in any other place."[23] This congressional immunity was created to insure that government policymakers could engage in frank and uninhibited discussion of the public's business. But, like any privilege, it can be abused. What is needed, in the interest of fairness, is self-restraint on the part of legislators when what they say may inflict injury on the target of their remarks.

If it is inappropriate for the legislature to play judge and jury with respect to individual citizens, what about statements of *executive* officers of government which invite public scorn to be directed at persons thought guilty of misdeeds? In order to act boldly in the public interest, should administrators also be immune from retribution when, in the course of their official duties, they focus the spotlight of adverse publicity on people they feel it necessary to expose? As far back as 1896 the U.S. Supreme Court held that immunity from libel suits was necessary for the effective functioning of members of the president's cabinet,[24] and in 1959 that principle was extended to lower level officials as well.[25]

But, again, as with legislators, great harm can be done if this privilege is exercised with insufficient restraint. Individuals who are the object of attack may be found guilty in the court of public opinion for behavior which is not only entirely within the law but which, if given a fair hearing, might be judged ethically defensible as well. On the other hand, the conduct may indeed be reprehensible and deserving of the condemnation it receives.

Two incidents well illustrate the tensions involved in matters of this kind. The first occurred in Illinois in 1974 when the then governor of the state, Dan Walker, issued a press release describing two Chicago attorneys and real-estate speculators as "unscrupulous men" whose actions were "unconscionable" and "a simple case of greed." What they had done was to purchase, for $59.81, a home worth $25,000, which was auctioned off by the county for unpaid back taxes. They then sought to evict a poor widow living in the house who claimed that her taxes had fallen into arrears by mistake.[26] Although the lawyers had apparently done nothing illegal, their action attracted the attention of the press, and the governor gave official expression to the moral outrage felt by many people in the community. A $6 million libel suit filed against Governor Walker for having "cast a strong stigma" on the reputation of the two lawyers was dismissed by the state supreme court on the grounds that the governor had absolute immunity from libel suits when making statements in connection with his official responsibilities.[27] The court, however, was apparently uneasy about some of the implications of the case:

> We emphasize that today's decision is not an endorsement of either the tenor or the content of the defendant's statements concerning the

plaintiffs. The Governor's position could undoubtedly have been expressed to the people with language less calculated to injure the plaintiffs' personal and professional reputation. While it is unfortunate that
the application of executive immunity may occasionally deny relief to a
deserving individual, the sacrifice is justified by the public's need for
free and unfettered action by its representatives.[28]

The other incident took place in New York City in the fall of 1979 and
concerned a program inaugurated by Mayor Ed Koch to have the city-
owned radio and television stations broadcast the names of men found
guilty of patronizing prostitutes. According to the initial *New York Times*
report of the matter, the mayor:

> said that the practice and the threat of public scorn would be a de-
> terrent to the patronizing of prostitutes. And he said it would right the
> imbalance in what he characterized as the tendency of the legal system
> to punish prostitutes, but not their customers.
> Mr. Koch said that although the State Legislature had seen the
> "unfairness" of that approach and had passed a law increasing the
> penalties for customers of prostitutes, some judges had not been
> carrying out the law in this area. . . .
> The Mayor said broadcasting the names would be similar to the
> early American practice of putting lawbreakers in stocks. . . .
> "That was a deterrent because who wants to be in stocks?" said Mr.
> Koch. "But we're not allowed to put people in stocks anymore, so
> instead, what I'm going to do is to focus public attention by putting
> their names in stocks, meaning reporting them on the radio, and
> hopefully the newspapers will put their names in stocks by putting
> them in print."[29]

The first broadcast of this so-called John Hour occurred on the city's
stations on October 23, 1979, and listed the names and addresses of nine
individuals who had been convicted of patronizing prostitutes since the
mayor's warning announcement of October 9.[30] A spokesperson for the
New York Civil Liberties Union complained that the mayor had "over-
stepped his bounds and has usurped the judicial functions of government by imposing additional penalties beyond those handed out by the
courts."[31] The director of the municipal broadcast system replied, "The
ACLU might not like it, but there is nothing they can do about it. This is
freedom of the press and it's all public record."[32]

Both of these parties to the dispute were, of course, correct. The
mayor's scheme was transparently an extralegal use of state power to impose social sanctions on persons who had engaged in what was deemed
to be insufficiently punished behavior. Yet, in this instance, unlike
Governor Walker's explicit pronouncement of moral judgment, the
executive was "merely" giving wider circulation to information that was

already publicly available. It was, nonetheless, a narrow path which Mayor Koch had walked.

Indeed, it should be evident from our review of all the arenas in which government acts as a communicator that close questions of propriety are a common occurrence. What is needed is a principle which provides some guidance in determining whether particular kinds of government communication fall on the appropriate or inappropriate side of the line, always recognizing that such judgments are likely to be as debatable as are the acts themselves which are being assessed.

I would suggest that any guiding philosophy adopted in this area must accept the following premises: (1) that many officers of government must, and will, engage in substantial communication with the public in order to do their jobs; (2) that the authority, experience, resources, visibility, and access to the media provided by their offices will inevitably endow their speech with competitive advantages in the marketplace of ideas; (3) that it is unrealistic to expect government officeholders to be privately uncommitted in their political and social beliefs or to be capable of complete objectivity and nonpartisanship in their presentation of themselves to the public; and (4) that, at least with respect to elected policymaking officials, it is not even desirable for them to keep their views under wraps.

On the other hand, it seems to me that a democratic society must meet the requirement that the taxpayers' money not be used to dominate the marketplace of ideas with the voice of government and, conversely, that those who disagree with government policies, who are critical of government officeholders, or have been accused of wrongdoing by government officials have ample opportunity to make their feelings known to the public. The critical issue, I believe, is not so much whether the government speaks but whether others are able to talk back, and to do so with a fighting chance of prevailing. The stronger and more articulate the citizenry, and the more open the media to its voices, the less we need worry about the government as communicator.

This point of view is consistent with the solution offered, for example, by Minow, Martin, and Mitchell in their critique of *Presidential Television:*

> Few would have the president communicate less. . . . The problem, however, is that television is also something that the opposition political party and the Congress were "supposed to do" if they are to perform their institutional roles of checking presidential power. The president's preeminent television presence is of concern when it threatens to become a practical monopoly.[33]

The adoption of this philosophy, which puts the primary burden of keeping government communication in line on the checks and balances provided by the separation of powers within government itself, and by the critical functioning of press and public, does not mean that government officials should have no obligations of self-restraint. It does not follow that, because we immunize them from *legal* retribution for what they say, we should not exhort and educate them to ethically responsible communication. Surely they should be warned against the hazards and immorality of deceiving the public or of using the public's money for purposes of self-aggrandizement. They should be reminded of the boundaries of their authority and, where applicable, of the necessity of nonpartisanship for the effective performance of their particular duties. Finally, they should be made sensitive to the power to injure others which they may hold in their tongues and their pens, and of the obligation to use that power cautiously and sparingly, if at all.

Part  Conclusion

18   The Boisterous Sea of Liberty

The central purpose of this book has been to seek a coherent set of guiding principles for the resolution of conflicts between freedom of expression and the competing interests with which it may clash—principles rooted in a keener understanding of the communication process and a more vigorous commitment to the values of a free society than have characterized the adjudication of these issues in the past. It was not expected that a perfect philosophy could be found which would provide ready answers to the closest questions that might arise. It was hoped, however, that a careful review and critical analysis of each of the areas in which serious controversy has occurred would uncover common threads that might be woven into a sturdier fabric of First Amendment doctrine than has yet been fashioned by our legal system. What follows is a summary of that quest.

We began with the proposition that one must look at the particular context in which acts of communication occur in order to assess the appropriateness of limitations on expression, thus rejecting the view that there are certain categories of speech which, by definition, are always out of bounds. We also assumed that the First Amendment applies to a broad range of symbolic conduct, whether oral or written, rational or emotive, verbal or nonverbal. Even behaviors which are not normally engaged in for communicative purposes were nominated as potential candidates for First Amendment protection when functioning symbolically.

Four basic principles have emerged from this study:

I. Unless the harm done by an act of communication is direct, immediate, irreparable, and of a serious material nature, the remedy in a free society should be more speech. The law is an inappropriate tool for dealing with expression which produces mental distress or whose targets are the beliefs and values of an audience.

II. Unless deprived of free choice by deception, physical coercion, or an impairment of normal capacities, individuals in a free society are responsible for their own behavior. They are not objects which can be *triggered* into action by symbolic stimuli but human beings who *decide* how they will respond to the communication they see and hear.

III. So long as there is a free marketplace of ideas, where the widest possible range of information and alternatives is available, individuals will be the best judges of their own interests. The law is properly used to enrich and expand that communications marketplace and to insure that it remains an open system.

IV. Government in a free society is the servant of the people and its powers should not be used to inhibit, distort, or dominate public discourse. There must be compelling justification whenever the government requires unwilling communication of its people or withholds information in its possession from them.

I

The first principle, as we have seen, necessitates abandonment of the law of defamation except for those circumstances in which a communicator of allegedly defamatory material refuses to disseminate a reply or, in those rare instances, like the eve of an election, where calculated falsehoods about a candidate may do damage before there is time to refute them. Otherwise we should operate on the assumption that the right to reply to alleged defamations will be a sufficient remedy in a society whose members have learned to listen critically and with suspended judgment to personal attacks.

Unlike defamatory falsehoods, which can be undermined by refutation, the public exposure of truthful but private information may cause immediate and irreparable embarrassment. Nonetheless, if the information has not been obtained by theft or the promise that it will be kept confidential, legal remedies are inappropriate. Once a cat has been let out of its bag, the owner cannot expect to retrieve it by declaring the feline unnewsworthy or an outrage to the community's sense of decency.

Similarly, the psychological distress, revulsion, or anger that may result from the ethnic diatribes of bigots, the epithets of personal antagonists, or the tastelessness of exploiters of the media must be accepted as the price we pay for living in a free and sometimes licentious society. We should have a right not to be held captive to the continuing bombardment of unwanted communication, but must not expect to be insulated from that which is momentary or transient and which we have the capacity to tune out. Children as well as adults must develop the ability to detect and reject dehumanizing values and false prophets, looking to the law to protect them only from those charlatans whose blandishments can lead directly and immediately to material loss or physical injury.

Communication which poses a serious and imminent threat to the fair administration of justice may also be curtailed. Law enforcement officials may be prohibited from making prejudicial pretrial statements, hearings and records may be closed to the press and public when essential, intimidating and disruptive behavior may be barred from the courtroom, and trial participants may be placed under restrictive orders. The press and public, however, should be free to say whatever they know, since their speech can be offset, and fair trials secured, by measures short of the suppression of their communication.

II

The second principle calls for a substantial departure from our current understandings of the respective responsibilities of communicators and their audiences. It holds only the members of an audience liable for any violence or other illegal behavior to which they may be provoked or solicited, except in those circumstances where the inciting communicator coerces or deceives them into taking the action in question. In such cases, the speaker, having presumed to take control over the lives of others, must accept the responsibility which goes with that power.

The law should be available to protect individuals from being driven into *any* behavior, legal or illegal, by believable threats of physical force or by calculated and credible deception. Psychological and economic pressures, however, if unaccompanied by physical coercion, are an exercise of the freedom of expression of communicators which the normal audience, with sufficient will and without the aid of the law, can resist. Persons who are mentally incompetent by virtue of infancy, retardation, illness, or senility pose a special problem. Communicators who knowingly "persuade" such individuals to act in particular ways assume some measure of responsibility for the ensuing behavior because their audience is not fully capable of making free choices.

III

In a modern mass media–oriented society such as ours there are powerful tendencies in the direction of a homogenization of the marketplace of ideas and the presentation of a monochromatic view of the world. In order for there to be the diversity of communication which is necessary for people to make free and informed choices, the third principle contemplates affirmative action to counterbalance these pressures toward uniformity.

To begin with, the law must be uncompromising in its protection of the right of nonconformists, as well as others, to disseminate their views in public places so long as the primary function of those places is not substantially impaired. Inconvenience, annoyance, or offense to aesthetic sensibilities should not be sufficient justifications to prohibit expression in the public forum. What appear to be plausibly reasonable regulations of time and place should be subjected to the most critical scrutiny as to their intent and their effect upon our system of freedom of expression and must, in any case, be scrupulously content-neutral. Even private property which is quasi-public in character should be open to communication activities which are compatible with its functions.

Diversity must be a guiding principle for the operation of public schools and public libraries as well as for the allocation of public moneys to the support of quasi-private cultural, informational, and scholarly enterprises. Privately owned and operated media of communication which choose to sell advertising space or time to the public should not be allowed to reject proffered ads on the grounds of their content. And those private enterprises which enjoy a virtual monopoly over a particular medium market should be obligated to allow replies to their editorial attacks and to donate a portion of their time or space, on a first come–first served basis, for public access purposes.

IV

The fourth principle recognizes that the government of a large and technologically advanced nation, although perhaps originally designed to facilitate the self-fulfillment of its citizens, develops inclinations to subvert the free marketplace of communication which is essential to that purpose. The "servant of the people" acquires an appetite for power which, if unchecked, transforms the servant into master.

Among the manifestations of this arrogation of authority are unnecessary demands that people speak when they wish to remain silent. Whether it be in the form of compulsory oaths of loyalty, official inquiries into the beliefs of individuals, compelled disclosure of confidences about associates, or involuntary identification of the sponsorship of communication, the presumption of a right to impose these requirements must constantly be challenged.

Even more pervasive and more subversive of democratic values than these kinds of compelled communication are the tendencies of public officials to treat the information which comes into their hands as if it were their own private property. That there are valid reasons for maintaining the confidentiality and secrecy of some of the material gathered or produced by agencies of government cannot be denied— considerations of personal privacy, candid advice, economic equity, and physical security. But these should be infrequent exceptions, supported by obvious and overwhelming evidence of their indispensability, rather than the commonplace practices they have so often become.

The voice of government, when it enters the marketplace of public discourse, must not be so loud as to drown out its competitors. If members of the society are sufficiently fearless and articulate, and have adequate access to the mass media of communication, public servants can be vocal without endangering the system of checks and balances. Self-restraint on the part of government officials is necessary, however, when the resources at their disposal lend so much weight to their participation that no other views have any chance of prevailing.

All of these principles require a strong and vigilant citizenry for their faithful implementation. The regime which they envision is not one for the squeamish or apathetic. It is not for those who lack the courage of their convictions. It is not for those, described long ago by Thomas Jefferson, as "timid men who prefer the calm of despotism to the boisterous sea of liberty."[1]

Notes

Chapter 1

1. See, for example, Zechariah Chafee, *Free Speech in the United States* (Cambridge: Harvard University Press, 1948); Thomas Emerson, *The System of Freedom of Expression* (New York: Random House, 1970); and Leonard Levy, *Legacy of Suppression: Freedom of Speech and Press in Early American History* (Cambridge: Harvard University Press, Belknap Press, 1960).

2. The American Civil Liberties Union, for example, supports the recovery of compensatory damages for libel (ACLU Policy no. 6) and accepts limitations on the expression of opinion that creates a "clear and present danger" of immediate unlawful action (Policy no. 90).

3. See, for example, Edmond Cahn, "Justice Black and First Amendment Absolutes—a Public Interview," *New York University Law Quarterly* 37 (1962): 549.

4. Justice Black sat on the U.S. Supreme Court bench from 1937 to 1971. His record of devotion to the First Amendment was closely paralleled by that of Justice William O. Douglas, who was on the bench from 1939 to 1975, the longest tenure in the Court's history.

5. For example, his dissents in *Cohen v. California,* 403 U.S. 15 (1971), and in *Tinker v. Community School District,* 393 U.S. 503 (1969), and his opinions for the Court majority in *Giboney v. Empire Storage and Ice Company,* 336 U.S. 490 (1949), and *Adderley v. Florida,* 385 U.S. 39 (1966).

6. Ever since its unanimous decision in *Chaplinsky v. New Hampshire,* 315 U.S. 568 (1942), the Supreme Court has made it clear that legislative restrictions on "certain well-defined and narrowly limited classes of speech" such as the obscene and the libelous are not, in the Court's view, in conflict with the First Amendment.

7. In *Stromberg v. California,* 283 U.S. 359 (1931), the Supreme Court struck down a California law which prohibited the political display of red flags. There were similar laws on the books of thirty-one other states. In *Yates v. United States,* 354 U.S. 298 (1957) at 324–25, the Court limited the applicability of the federal Smith Act and other antisubversive legislation to situations in which "those to whom the advocacy [of revolution] is addressed must be urged to *do* something, now or in the future, rather than merely to *believe* in something." And in *Brandenburg v. Ohio,* 395 U.S. 444 (1969), a still more restrictive rule was laid down by the Court. Now the First Amendment protects the advocacy of revolution "ex-

cept where such advocacy is directed to inciting or producing imminent lawless action and is likely to incite or produce such action." 395 U.S. at 447.

8. 268 U.S. 652 (1925) at 666.

9. 299 U.S. 353 (1937) at 364.

10. *West Virginia Board of Education v. Barnette*, 319 U.S. 624 (1943) at 637–38.

11. *Legacy of Suppression*, p. 174.

12. "Introduction—Is Freedom of the Press a Redundancy: What Does It Add to Freedom of Speech," *Hastings Law Journal* 26 (1975): 640–41.

13. U.S. Supreme Court Chief Justice Warren Burger believes that "historical evidence does not strongly support this explanation." He suggests as an alternative possibility that the terms were written into the First Amendment as a mere "stylistic change" when the original language proposed by James Madison was shortened in committee. Footnote no. 3 in concurring opinion in *First National Bank of Boston v. Bellotti*, 435 U.S. 765 (1978) at 798.

14. It is noteworthy in this connection that the most authoritative recent book dealing with First Amendment issues, that by Professor Thomas Emerson, is entitled *The System of Freedom of Expression*.

15. Justice Stewart's speech is reprinted under the title "Or of the Press" in the *Hastings Law Journal* 26 (1975): 631. The quoted excerpt is at 633–34.

16. "Introduction," p. 641.

17. "A Preferred Position for Journalism?" *Hofstra Law Review* 7 (1979): 600.

18. *Ibid.*, p. 601.

19. *Ibid.*

20. *First National Bank of Boston v. Bellotti* at 798.

21. *Ibid.* at 801 quoting *Branzburg v. Hayes,* 408 U.S. 665 (1972) at 704–5 quoting *Lovell v. Griffin*, 303 U.S. 444 (1938) at 450.

22. *Ibid.* at 802.

23. "Introduction," p. 658.

24. "Or of the Press," p. 635.

25. "Introduction," pp. 646–47.

26. "Or of the Press," p. 635.

27. "The Constitution, the Press, and the Rest of Us," *Washington Monthly* (November 1978), pp. 51–52.

28. "Defamatory Non-Media Speech and First Amendment Methodology," *University of Southern California Law Review* 25 (1978): 923.

29. "The Press *Is* Different: Reflections on Justice Stewart and the Autonomous Press," *Hofstra Law Review* 7 (1979): 580.

30. *Ibid.*

31. *Ibid.*, p. 583.

32. *Ibid.*, pp. 581–82.

33. Brief for Respondents, In the Supreme Court of the United States in *Herbert v. Lando*, October Term, 1978, pp. 55–56.

34. "A Preferred Position," p. 607.

Chapter 2

1. 403 U.S. at 18.
2. *The First Amendment and the Future of American Democracy* (New York: Basic, 1976), pp. 186–205.
3. 403 U.S. at 25–26.
4. Franklyn Haiman, "Speech v. Privacy: Is There a Right Not to Be Spoken To?" *Northwestern University Law Review* 67 (1972): 189.
5. *Political Freedom* (New York: Harper & Bros., 1948).
6. Meiklejohn's grounding of freedom of speech in the necessities of the process of self-government has had profound influence on First Amendment theory and practice, since the acceptance of his premise sharply circumscribes the arena in which First Amendment protections operate. Put in its simplest terms by Meiklejohn, *Political Freedom*, p. 26: "The First Amendment . . . is not the guardian of unregulated talkativeness. It does not require that, on every occasion, every citizen shall take part in public debate. . . . What is essential is not that everyone shall speak, but that everything worth saying shall be said." Following this thesis, legal scholars such as Lillian R. BeVier, "The First Amendment and Political Speech: An Inquiry into the Substance and Limits of Principle," *Stanford Law Review* 30 (1978): 299, and Robert Bork, "Neutral Principles and Some First Amendment Problems," *Indiana Law Journal* 47 (1971): 1, have urged that the constitutional guarantees of freedom of speech and press be interpreted as encompassing only political speech. Similarly, Supreme Court justices like John Paul Stevens have assigned a lower order of value to categories of expression such as sexually oriented communication than to political dialogue. See discussion in Chapter 9 of Justice Stevens's opinion in *Young v. American Mini Theatres*, 427 U.S. 50 (1976). In contrast to the Meiklejohnian view, writers such as C. Edwin Baker, "Scope of the First Amendment Freedom of Speech," *UCLA Law Review* 25 (1978): 964, have looked to concepts of individual autonomy, integrity, creativity, and self-expression as root values underlying the First Amendment, leading Baker, for example, to propose a "liberty model" of the First Amendment in contradistinction to the self-government model.

One need not adopt either of these views to the exclusion of the other. Thomas Emerson, for instance, lists individual self-fulfillment *plus* participation in decision making, the search for truth, and the maintenance of stability as underpinnings for his "full protection" theory of freedom of expression. *The System of Freedom of Expression*, pp. 6–7. And Vincent Blasi, in proposing still another basic function of the First Amendment—the "checking value" on possible government excesses and corruption—makes clear that he views his theory as complementary to, rather than a substitute for, other free speech values. See *The Checking Value in First Amendment Theory*, Samuel Pool Weaver Constitutional Law Series no. 3 (Chicago: American Bar Foundation, 1977), p. 528. It is similarly my position that none of the values of free expression which have been identified here or elsewhere need be, or should be, excluded as foundation stones of our First Amendment edifice.

7. Book review of Alexander Meiklejohn's *Political Freedom*, *Harvard Law Review* 62 (1949): 891.

8. *Political Freedom*, p. 54.

9. Dissenting opinion in *Gertz v. Welch*, 418 U.S. 323 (1974) at 358–59.

10. *Free Speech*, pp. 149–50.

11. *Chaplinsky v. New Hampshire* at 571–72.

12. *Ibid.* at 572.

13. "Verbal Acts and Ideas—The Common Sense of Free Speech," *University of Chicago Law Review* 16 (1949): 328. This note concludes that the First Amendment protects only words of "an idea-conveying nature" and not "verbal acts."

14. *Free Speech*, pp. 151–52.

15. *The System of Freedom of Expression.*

16. *Ibid.*, p. 3.

17. *Ibid.*, p. 60.

18. *Gillars v. United States*, 182 F.2d 962 (D.C.Cir. 1950) at 971.

19. *The System of Freedom of Expression*, p. 61.

20. *Ibid.*, pp. 337–38.

21. *Ibid.*, p. 338.

22. *Ibid.*

23. *Gompers v. Bucks Stove and Range Co.*, 221 U.S. 418 (1911) at 439.

24. *The System of Freedom of Expression*, p. 445.

25. Edward T. Hall's *The Silent Language* (Garden City, N.Y.: Doubleday, 1959) was the forerunner of a flood of books and journal articles dealing with the nonverbal communication process. See, for notable examples, Ray Birdwhistell, *Kinesics and Context* (Philadelphia: University of Pennsylvania Press, 1970); Mark Knapp, *Nonverbal Communication in Human Interaction* (New York: Holt, Rinehart & Winston, 1972); and Albert Mehrabian, *Silent Messages* (Belmont, Calif.: Wadsworth, 1971).

26. The legal community should not be criticized too severely for its inertia in this respect in view of the fact that the professional association of scholars and teachers of speech did not change its name from Speech Association of America to Speech Communication Association until 1970 and has rejected proposals to go an additional step to calling itself the American Communication Association.

27. *Tinker v. Community School District.*

28. *West Virginia Board of Education v. Barnette.*

29. *U.S. v. O'Brien*, 391 U.S. 367 (1968).

30. *Smith v. Goguen*, 415 U.S. 566 (1974); *Spence v. Washington*, 418 U.S. 405 (1974); *Cahn v. Long Island Vietnam Moratorium Committee*, 418 U.S. 906 (1974); *Sutherland v. Illinois*, 418 U.S. 907 (1974); *Farrell v. Iowa*, 418 U.S. 907 (1974), 421 U.S. 1007 (1975).

31. *Stromberg v. California.*

32. *West Virginia Board of Education v. Barnette* at 632.

33. *U.S. v. O'Brien* at 376.

34. "Symbolic Conduct," *Columbia Law Review* 68 (1968): 1102.

35. *Ibid.*, pp. 1109–10.

36. *Ibid.*, pp. 1113–16.

37. Brief of Appellant, In the Supreme Court of the United States in *Street v. New York*, October Term, 1968, p. 22.

38. *The System of Freedom of Expression*, p. 80.

39. *Ibid.*, p. 81.
40. *Ibid.*
41. *Ibid.*, p. 84.
42. *Ibid.*, p. 86.
43. *Ibid.*, p. 89.
44. Paul Watzlawick, Janet Beavin, and Don Jackson, *The Pragmatics of Human Communication* (New York: Norton, 1967), p. 49.
45. From the Virginia Statute Establishing Religious Freedom.
46. Melville Nimmer relies on this same concept when he distinguishes, for First Amendment purposes, between the "meaning" and "non-meaning" effects of an act. "The Meaning of Symbolic Speech under the First Amendment," *University of California at Los Angeles Law Review* 21 (1973): 36.
47. Thomas Emerson approaches this same distinction in discussing the obscenity issue when he talks about "whether a person is trying to *tell* something or *do* something, whether his conduct is representation or actuality," in *The System of Freedom of Expression,* p. 495.
48. *People v. Stover,* 191 N.E.2d 272 (N.Y. 1963).
49. *Rider v. Board of Education of Independent School District,* 414 U.S. 1097 (1973).
50. The *Chicago Sun-Times* (April 17, 1975) shows a picture of striking garbage collectors dumping a load of manure on the steps of the city hall in Berwyn, Illinois, as a protest addressed to the mayor.
51. See n. 46, *supra.*
52. See, for example, *U.S. v. Malinowski,* 472 F.2d 850 (3d Cir. 1973).
53. The *New York Times* (October 29, 1976) describes the dropping of 125,000 leaflets on the Government Center area of Boston by the Mystic Valley Gun Club in opposition to a referendum proposing to ban the private ownership of handguns.
54. "The Meaning of Symbolic Speech," pp. 44–45.
55. *Schenck v. U.S.,* 249 U.S. 47 (1919) at 52.
56. *Chaplinsky v. New Hampshire* at 571–72.
57. *Beauharnais v. Illinois,* 343 U.S. 250 (1952) at 266.
58. *Giboney v. Empire Storage and Ice Co.* at 498.
59. *Barenblatt v. U.S.,* 360 U.S. 109 (1959) at 126.
60. *Cox v. Louisiana,* 379 U.S. 536 (1965) at 554.
61. *Brandenburg v. Ohio* at 447.

Chapter 3

1. L. Green, "Relational Interests," *Illinois Law Review* 31 (1936): 35.
2. "'Actions for Slaunder'—Defamation in English Law, Language, and History," *Quarterly Journal of Speech* 57 (1971): 281.
3. *Ibid.*, p. 282.
4. *Ibid.*, p. 276.
5. 376 U.S. 254 (1964).
6. 418 U.S. 323 (1974).
7. *Garrison v. Louisiana,* 379 U.S. 64 (1964); *Rosenblatt v. Baer,* 383 U.S. 75

(1966); *Curtis Publishing Co. v. Butts,* 388 U.S. 130 (1967); and *Rosenbloom v. Metromedia,* 403 U.S. 29 (1971).

8. 376 U.S. at 270.

9. *Ibid.* at 279.

10. *Ibid.* at 300.

11. *Ibid.*

12. *Ibid.* at 301.

13. *Ibid.* at 297.

14. See, for example, his opinion in *Curtis Publishing Co. v. Butts.* See, also, Cahn, "Justice Black and First Amendment Absolutes."

15. *Garrison v. Louisiana.*

16. *Rosenblatt v. Baer.*

17. *Curtis Publishing Co. v. Butts.*

18. *Rosenbloom v. Metromedia.*

19. 418 U.S. at 345.

20. *Ibid.* at 344.

21. *Ibid.* at 350.

22. *Ibid.*

23. *Garrison v. Louisiana* at 75.

24. *Whitney v. California,* 274 U.S. 357 (1927) at 377.

25. See Richard C. Donnelly, "The Right to Reply: An Alternative to an Action for Libel," *Virginia Law Review* 34 (1948): 867.

26. *Ibid.,* p. 886. At the time of publication of the Donnelly article in 1948 the author identified Austria, Finland, Greece, Hungary, Japan, Norway, and Yugoslavia as having German-type laws, and Belgium, Egypt, Haiti, Rumania, and Syria as having French-type laws.

27. *Miami Herald Publishing Co. v. Tornillo,* 418 U.S. 241 (1974).

28. *Ibid.* at 258.

29. One writer on this subject notes that it is quite commonly the case that the libel remedy is "not attended with much publicity, if any, and, if resisted by the defendant, occurs long after the libel has spread its poison." John J. Fleming, "Retraction and Reply: Alternative Remedies for Defamation," *University of British Columbia Law Review* 15 (1978): 15.

30. "Right of Reply Statutes: Unconstitutional Abridgment of the Freedom of the Printed Press," *Northwestern University Law Review* 69 (1974): 143.

31. David M. Hunsacker, "Freedom and Responsibility in First Amendment Theory: Defamation Law and Media Credibility," *Quarterly Journal of Speech* 65 (1979): 25.

32. For example, a bill designed to undercut the *New York Times v. Sullivan* decision and make it easier for public officials to sue for libel was proposed in Congress in June 1976 as Senate Bill 3600, the Federal Anti-Defamation Act. Its chief sponsor was Senator William Scott (R.-Va.). Its list of cosponsors, with one or two exceptions, read like a roster of the Senate's extreme right wing—James Allen (D.-Ala.), James Eastland (D.-Miss.), Roman Hruska (R.-Neb.), Paul Laxalt (R.-Nev.), Jesse Helms (R.-N.C.), and Strom Thurmond (R.-S.C.).

33. For example, in his opinion in *Young v. American Mini Theatres,* 427 U.S. 50 (1976) at 70, Justice John Paul Stevens asserted that "even though we recognize

that the First Amendment will not tolerate the total suppression of erotic materials that have some arguably artistic value, it is manifest that society's interest in protecting this type of expression is of a wholly different, and lesser, magnitude than the interest inspired by Voltaire's immortal comment ["I disapprove of what you say, but I will defend to the death your right to say it"]. Whether political oratory or philosophical discussion moves us to applaud or to despise what is said, every schoolchild can understand why our duty to defend the right to speak remains the same. But few of us would march our sons and daughters off to war to preserve the citizen's right to see 'Specified Sexual Activities' exhibited in the theater of our choice."

Justice Potter Stewart's response to the Stevens opinion was to describe it as standing Voltaire's comment on its head. "For if the guarantees of the First Amendment were reserved for expression that more than a 'few of us' would take up arms to defend, then the right of free expression would be defined and circumscribed by current popular opinion. . . . The fact that the 'offensive' speech here may not address 'important topics'—'ideas of social and political significance' . . . does not mean that it is less worthy of constitutional protection." 427 U.S. at 86.

34. For example, in 1974 the mayor of Macon, Georgia, sued a local radio station, WBML, for a comment made by an unidentified woman during a call-in talk show. In response to the mayor's public condemnation of the streaking fad, the woman said that the mayor seemed to have forgotten that he had been seen standing nude in his own yard. The Georgia courts refused to grant summary judgment to the station, holding that if the station wished to avoid going to trial on the question of "actual malice" (a public official being involved) it would have to assume the burden of establishing the *non*existence of actual malice in its motion for summary judgment. Rather than undertaking that expense, WBML settled the case with a nominal payment to the mayor.

In 1975, the *Texas Observer,* a liberal fortnightly journal with a circulation of about 10,000 and a virtually nonprofit budget, had to defend itself against a five-million dollar libel suit for a two-article expose of child-care facilities in the Lone Star State. The legal costs of the case, even if won, could drive such a publication out of business. Shortly after this litigation had begun, the editor of the *Observer* reported that he had rejected another story on some allegedly illegal business dealings in Dallas because he could not afford to get sued again.

35. *Branzburg v. Hayes.*

36. The principle that libel plaintiffs are entitled to know the source of an allegedly defamatory remark was established in *Garland v. Torre,* 259 F.2d 545 (2d Cir. 1958), cert. denied 358 U.S. 910 (1958), affirming a contempt conviction of a reporter who refused to divulge the source of an alleged defamation published about film actress Judy Garland. Many later cases have relied on the *Garland* precedent. The right of a libel plaintiff to explore editorial decision-making processes in an effort to prove actual malice was enunciated by the U.S. Supreme Court in *Herbert v. Lando,* 441 U.S. 153 (1979).

37. *Bindrim v. Mitchell,* App., 155 Calif. Rptr. 29 (1979), cert. denied as *Mitchell v. Bindrim,* 444 U.S. 984 (1979).

38. 155 Calif. Rptr. at 37.

39. *Ibid.* at 38.
40. *Ibid.* at 39.
41. *Ibid.*
42. *Mazzacone v. Willing,* 369 A.2d 829 (Pa. 1976) at 833.
43. *Willing v. Mazzacone,* 393 A.2d 1155 (Pa. 1978).
44. 283 U.S. 697 (1931).
45. 379 U.S. at 75.
46. *Buckley v. Littell,* 394 F.Supp. 918 (S.D.N.Y. 1975).
47. *Buckley v. Littell,* 539 F.2d 882 (2d Cir. 1976) at 896.
48. *Littell v. Buckley,* 429 U.S. 1062 (1977).

Chapter 4

1. This distinction is made by both Leon R. Yankwich, "Recent Developments in the Law of Creation, Expression, and Communication of Ideas," *Northwestern University Law Review* 48 (1953): 543; and by Melville Nimmer, "The Right to Speak from Times to Time: First Amendment Theory Applied to Libel and Misapplied to Privacy," *California Law Review* 56 (1968): 935.

2. It is apparently for this reason that some scholars of the subject have viewed invasion of privacy and defamation as both rooted in the same interest, that is, the protection of reputation. See, for example, William L. Prosser, "Privacy," *California Law Review* 48 (1960): 398; and Harry Kalven, Jr., "Privacy in Tort Law—Were Warren and Brandeis Wrong?" *Law and Contemporary Problems* 31 (1966): 340.

3. *Privacy and Freedom* (New York: Atheneum, 1967), p. 14.

4. "Privacy and a Free Press: A Contemporary Conflict in Values," *New York Law Forum* 20 (1975): 510.

5. E. L. Godkin, "The Rights of the Citizen—IV: To His Reputation," *Scribner's* 8 (1890): 58.

6. "The Right to Privacy," *Harvard Law Review* 4 (1890): 193.

7. *Rights of Privacy* (Skokie, Ill.: National Textbook, 1977), p. 145.

8. *Privacy and Freedom,* p. 346.

9. "Privacy."

10. *Ibid.,* p. 389.

11. *Ibid.,* p. 392.

12. *Roberson v. Rochester Folding Box Co.,* 64 N.E.2d 442 (N.Y. 1902).

13. *Pavesich v. New England Life Insurance Co.,* 50 S.E. 68 (Ga. 1905).

14. "Privacy," p. 406.

15. Or, as the Georgia Supreme Court explained it in the *Pavesich* case: "The form and features of the plaintiff are his own. The defendant insurance company and its agents had no more authority to display them in public for the purpose of advertising the business in which they were engaged than they would have had to compel the plaintiff to place himself upon exhibition for this purpose." 50 S.E. at 217.

16. A reliance on theft as the key concept in adjudicating invasion-of-privacy claims seems compatible with the point of view advanced by Law Professor Richard A. Posner, who has written extensively on privacy as a question of

economics. See, for example, "The Right of Privacy," *Georgia Law Review* 12 (1978): 393; and "Privacy, Secrecy, and Reputation," *Buffalo Law Review* 28 (1979): 1. Although Posner's analysis has been described by another legal scholar of the privacy issue, Edward J. Bloustein, as "pretentious and immodest," Bloustein concedes that it may not be "wrong." See "Privacy Is Dear at Any Price: A Response to Professor Posner's Economic Theory," *Georgia Law Review* 12 (1978): 452.

17. The law was challenged by the American Civil Liberties Union in Rhode Island Superior Court, *Garabedian v. Michaelson* (C.A. 76-3674).

18. *Spahn v. Julian Messner, Inc.,* 221 N.E.2d 543 (N.Y. 1966), vacated and remanded for consideration in light of *Time v. Hill,* 387 U.S. 239 (1967); affirmed on remand, 233 N.E.2d 840 (N.Y. 1967). Appeal dismissed by agreement of parties, 393 U.S. 1046 (1969).

19. For example, since the adoption of the New York privacy statute in 1903 there has been a steady stream of litigation in that state testing and clarifying the parameters of the law. In an early group of cases involving documentary films, the principle was established that photographic reports of news events are not subject to the provisions of the statute. In *Colyer v. Richard K. Fox Publishing Co.,* 162 App. Div. 297 (N.Y. 1914), Justice Walter Smith wrote that "the statute does not apply to the publication of a newspaper in a single issue, but also the statute does not apply to the publication of a picture or a name in a single set of films of actual events, issued at one time for distribution . . . as a matter of current news." In *Sarat Lahiri v. Daily Mirror,* 295 N.Y.S. 382 (1937), the court granted protection to the publication of a picture of an individual that was run in conjunction with a feature story on a matter of public interest. The opinion suggested that, if the connection between the story and the picture had been more tenuous than it was in this instance and if it had been clearer that the picture was used by the newspaper for its own promotional purposes, recovery for appropriation might have been possible. In 1952 the New York courts ruled that the televised coverage of entertainment that occurred during halftime at a football game did not constitute prohibited appropriation of an act just because the broadcast of the game was commercially sponsored. The court said that there is no use for advertising purposes, as required by the law, unless someone's name or picture is used in a commercial itself or in direct connection with the product being sold. *Gautier v. Pro-Football, Inc.,* 304 N.Y. 354 (1952).

On the other hand, courts have often been unwilling to grant protection to the use without consent of a person's name or likeness in a work of fiction or in an embellished story of someone's experience that is more fantasy than fact. Such was the outcome, for instance, in a Florida case, *Cason v. Baskin,* 159 Fla. 31 (1947); in a New York case, *Sutton v. Hearst Publishing Co.,* 277 App. Div. 155 (1950); and in a federal case, *Garner v. Triangle Publications,* 97 F.Supp. 546 (S.D.N.Y. 1951).

20. *Zacchini v. Scripps-Howard Broadcasting Co.,* 351 N.E.2d 454 (Ohio 1976).

21. *Zacchini v. Scripps-Howard Broadcasting Co.,* 433 U.S. 562 (1977) at 574–75.

22. *Ibid.* at 580–81.

23. *Ibid.* at 575, n. 12.

24. As was pointed out in n. 2, *supra,* Dean Prosser and Professor Kalven

regarded *both* defamation and privacy actions as designed to protect one's reputation. Given that premise, false-light privacy cases become indistinguishable from suits for libel and slander. On the other hand, Professor Nimmer (n. 1, *supra*) regards the distinction between injury in the eyes of others and injury to one's own feelings as significant and believes that Prosser, Kalven, and the U.S. Supreme Court have been led astray in ignoring it.

25. *Time v. Hill* and *Cantrell v. Forest City Publishing Co.*, 419 U.S. 245 (1974).

26. "The Right to Speak," pp. 962–66.

27. *Ibid.*, pp. 965–66.

28. 419 U.S. at 248.

29. "The Right to Speak," p. 963.

30. This phrase, quoted in the *Time v. Hill* footnote, originally appeared in a U.S. circuit court of appeals opinion in *Sidis v. F-R Publishing Co.*, 113 F.2d 806 (2d Cir. 1940) at 809.

31. South Carolina in 1909, Florida and Georgia in 1911, and Wisconsin in 1925. See Marc A. Franklin, "A Constitutional Problem in Privacy Protection: Legal Inhibitions on Reporting of Fact," *Stanford Law Review* 16 (1963): 128.

32. *Cox Broadcasting Corp. v. Cohn*, 420 U.S. 469 (1975) at 495.

33. *Hunter v. Washington Post*, 43 U.S. Law Week 2059 (D.C.Super.Ct. 1974).

34. "A Constitutional Problem," pp. 128, 134.

35. 397 Pac. 91 (Calif. 1931).

36. *Briscoe v. Reader's Digest Association*, 483 P.2d 34 (Calif. 1971).

37. *Ibid.* at 43. This comment of the California Supreme Court seems inconsistent with an opinion expressed by the U.S. Supreme Court in a libel action brought by a candidate for public office which said that "a charge of criminal conduct, no matter how remote in time or place, can never be irrelevant to an official's or a candidate's fitness." *Monitor Patriot v. Roy*, 401 U.S. 265 (1971) at 277.

38. *Ibid.* at 44. It should be noted that even if there had been no *Reader's Digest* article, the daughter might still some day have stumbled across the information about her father, perhaps in an old newspaper. One such case actually occurred when a newspaper published an anniversary reproduction of an old front page, and a reader learned for the first time about the sordid circumstances of his parents' death.

39. *Sidis v. F-R Publishing Co.*

40. "Privacy," p. 398.

41. *Ibid.*, p. 397.

42. *Sipple v. San Francisco Chronicle*, 48 U.S.Law Week 2726 (1980).

43. Linda N. Woito and Patrick McNulty, "The Privacy Disclosure Tort and the First Amendment: Should the Community Decide Newsworthiness?" *Iowa Law Review* 64 (1979): 187.

44. Another proposal which seems just as fraught with hazards is the adoption of some kind of "public benefit" or "social utility" test, with the specific guidelines to be developed by legislation. Ernest D. Giglio, "Unwanted Publicity, the News Media, and the Constitution: Where Privacy Rights Compete with the First Amendment," *Akron Law Review* 12 (1978): 257. The author of this article attributes the inspiration for this proposal to the study and recommendations of a

British commission which argues that everything which is "of public interest" is not "in the public interest." Younger Committee, *Report of the Committee on Privacy,* 1972.

45. Beytagh, "Privacy and a Free Press," p. 467.

46. "Privacy," p. 411.

47. Richard Posner's economic analysis of the privacy issue also lends support to this argument. He comments, for example, "The expression 'idle curiosity' is misleading. People are not given to random, undifferentiated curiosity. . . . The economist does not believe . . . that supply creates demand." See "The Right of Privacy," p. 396.

48. Thomas Emerson, David Haber, and Norman Dorsen, *Political and Civil Rights in the United States,* 3d ed. (Boston: Little Brown, 1967), 1:1258.

49. "Privacy," p. 419.

50. *Press Censorship Newsletter* (April–May 1976), p. 81.

51. *Ibid.*

52. 307 N.E.2d 823 (N.Y. 1973), opinion amended 310 N.E.2d 539 (N.Y. 1973).

53. *Roe v. Doe,* cert. granted 417 U.S. 907 (1974), cert. dismissed as improvidently granted, 420 U.S. 307 (1975).

54. American Civil Liberties Union amicus curiae brief, In the Supreme Court of the United States in *Roe v. Doe,* October Term, 1974.

55. 249 N.E.2d 610 (Mass. 1969).

56. *Ibid.* at 617.

57. *Commonwealth v. Wiseman,* Mass. Superior Court of Equity, No. 87538, decree dated and entered July 9, 1969.

58. 249 N.E.2d at 619. Wiseman found this requirement unacceptable and chose to refrain from showing the film under such conditions.

59. *Wiseman v. Massachusetts,* 398 U.S. 960 (1970).

60. 249 N.E.2d at 617, n. 9.

61. *Barber v. Time,* 159 S.W.2d 291 (Mo. 1942).

62. 324 F.2d 450 (9th Cir. 1963), cert. denied 376 U.S. 939 (1964).

63. 406 F.Supp. 858 (W.D.Pa. 1976).

64. *Ibid.* at 859.

65. *Ibid.* at 861–62.

66. "Privacy."

67. This was precisely the view expressed by the California Supreme Court in *Gill v. Hearst Publishing Co.,* 253 P.2d 441 (Calif. 1953), involving a picture taken of an affectionate couple sitting together at an ice-cream counter in a Los Angeles farmers' market.

68. Westin, *Privacy and Freedom,* pp. 336–37.

69. *Ibid.*

70. "Privacy," p. 420.

71. *Koloski v. Hall,* Mass. Superior Court (CA-75-2338A).

72. *New York Times,* January 4, 1977.

73. *Virgil v. Time,* 424 F.Supp. 1286 (S.D.Calif. 1976).

74. *Virgil v. Time,* 527 F.2d 1122 (9th Cir. 1975).

75. 424 F.Supp. at 1289.

76. *Dietemann v. Time, Inc.*, 449 F.2d 245 (9th Cir. 1971) at 249.

77. *Pearson v. Dodd*, 410 F.2d 701 (D.C.Cir. 1969).

78. *Ibid.* at 705.

79. *Ibid.*

80. *Ibid.*

81. *Ibid.* at 703.

82. It should be noted that this position is in direct conflict with that taken by the U.S. Supreme Court in *Snepp v. U.S.*, 444 U.S. 507 (1980), a decision regarded by many critics, including this author, as a grave mistake.

83. 385 U.S. at 388.

Chapter 5

1. Natan Lerner, "International Definitions of Incitement to Racial Hatred," *New York Law Forum* 14 (1968): 52.

2. *Danish Criminal Code,* adopted April 15, 1930. English translation (Copenhagen: G.E.C. Gad, 1958).

3. *Ibid.*

4. Anthony Dickey, "English Law and Race Defamation," *New York Law Forum* 14 (1968): 16–17.

5. *Beauharnais v. Illinois.*

6. *Illinois Revised Statutes,* chap. 38, sec. 471.

7. Ruth McGaffey, "Group Libel Revisited," *Quarterly Journal of Speech* 65 (1979): 157.

8. *Collin v. Smith,* 578 F.2d 1197 (7th Cir. 1978), cert. denied 439 U.S. 916 (1978).

9. *Cincinnati v. Black,* 220 N.E.2d 821 (Ohio 1966) at 828; *Tollett v. U.S.,* 485 F.2d 1087 (8th Cir. 1973) at 1094, n. 14; and Judge Skelly Wright concurring in *Anti-Defamation League v. F.C.C.,* 403 F.2d 169 (D.C.Cir. 1968) at 174, n. 5.

10. 315 U.S. at 571—72.

11. 376 U.S. at 269.

12. 403 U.S. at 21.

13. 405 U.S. 518 (1972) at 524.

14. *Lambert v. Chicago,* 197 N.E.2d 448 (Ill. 1964).

15. "Civility and the Restriction of Speech: Rediscovering the Defamation of Groups," *The Supreme Court Review,* ed. Philip B. Kurland (Chicago: University of Chicago Press, 1974), p. 327.

16. *Ibid.,* p. 331.

17. *Ibid.,* pp. 314–15.

18. "Democracy and Defamation: Fair Game and Fair Comment. I," *Columbia Law Review* 42 (1942): 1086. Professor Riesman may have modified his views on group libel since writing this article in 1942. In a letter dated September 1, 1978, to Norman Dorsen, chairman of the American Civil Liberties Union, he indicated his intention to rejoin the organization as an expression of support for its "courageous course of action" in defending the right of the American Nazi group to march in Skokie.

19. "Civility and the Restriction of Speech," p. 292.

20. *Paris Adult Theatre I. v. Slaton*, 413 U.S. 49 (1973) at 60–61.
21. *Gooding v. Wilson* at 524.
22. *Gertz v. Welch.*
23. *Brandenburg v. Ohio* at 447.
24. "English Law and Race Defamation," p. 24.
25. "On Liberty," in *The Harvard Classics*, ed. Charles W. Eliot (New York: P. F. Collier & Son, 1909), 25:223, 242, 246.

Chapter 6

1. *Nebraska Press Association v. Stuart*, 427 U.S. 539 (1976) at 561.
2. *Frank v. Mangum*, 237 U.S. 309 (1915) at 335.
3. *Ibid.* at 345–50.
4. *Moore v. Dempsey*, 261 U.S. 86 (1923) at 88–89.
5. *Cox v. Louisiana* at 562.
6. Mob influence on a trial is not the only context in which the Supreme Court has suggested that the state, as well as a criminal defendant, has the right to a fair hearing. For example, in *Singer v. U.S.*, 380 U.S. 24 (1965), the Court upheld the constitutionality of rule 23(a) of the Federal Rules of Criminal Procedure which provides that a defendant may not waive the right to a jury trial without the consent of the government. In so doing, the Court said, "The Constitution recognizes an adversary system as the proper method of determining guilt, and the Government, as a litigant, has a legitimate interest in seeing that cases in which it believes a conviction is warranted are tried before the tribunal which the Constitution regards as most likely to produce a fair result. This recognition of the Government's interest as a litigant has an analogy in rule 24(b) of the federal rules, which permits the Government to challenge jurors peremptorily." *Ibid.* at 36.
7. *Patterson v. Colorado*, 205 U.S. 454 (1907) at 462.
8. 314 U.S. 252 (1941).
9. 328 U.S. 331 (1946).
10. 331 U.S. 367 (1947).
11. 370 U.S. 375 (1962).
12. *Marshall v. U.S.*, 360 U.S. 310 (1959).
13. 366 U.S. 717 (1961) at 728.
14. 373 U.S. 723 (1963).
15. *Ibid.* at 726–27.
16. *Sheppard v. Maxwell*, 384 U.S. 333 (1966) at 354–57.
17. 421 U.S. 794 (1975).
18. *Ibid.* at 795.
19. *Ibid.* at 800–801.
20. 366 U.S. at 723.
21. *Murphy v. Florida* at 807.
22. 366 U.S. at 728.
23. *Nebraska Press Association v. Stuart.*
24. *Ibid.* at 564.
25. *Ibid.*

26. "Trial Secrecy and the First Amendment Right of Access to Judicial Proceedings," *Harvard Law Review* 91 (1978): 1900–1901. See, also, both the majority and dissenting opinions in *Gannett v. DePasquale,* 443 U.S. 368 (1979), which agree on this point.

27. See n. 3 of Justice Blackmun's dissenting opinion in *Gannett v. DePasquale* at 414–15.

28. In *Gannett v. DePasquale,* 372 N.E.2d 544 (N.Y. 1977), the New York courts acknowledged the presence of First Amendment interests in access to judicial proceedings on the part of the press and public but found them outweighed by the dangers of prejudicial pretrial publicity. In *U.S. v. Cianfrani,* 573 F.2d 835 (3d Cir. 1978), a U.S. court of appeals found that the Sixth Amendment right to a public trial belonged to the public as well as the defendant.

29. *Gannett v. DePasquale,* 443 U.S. at 393.

30. *Ibid.* at 379–81, 387.

31. *Ibid.* at 391–92.

32. *New York Times,* November 26, 1977.

33. *Northwest Publications v. Anderson,* 259 N.W.2d 254 (Minn. 1977).

34. *Miami Herald Publishing Co. v. Krentzman,* 558 F.2d 1202 (5th Cir. 1977), cert. denied 435 U.S. 968 (1978).

35. *Ibid.* at 1209.

36. *Commercial Printing Co. v. Lee,* 553 S.W.2d 270 (Ark. 1977) at 273.

37. *Keene Publishing Co. v. Keene District Court,* 380 A.2d 261 (N.H. 1977).

38. *Gannett v. DePasquale,* 372 N.E.2d at 550.

39. *Gannett v. DePasquale,* 443 U.S. 368 (1979).

40. *Ibid.* at 392.

41. *Ibid.* at 440.

42. *Ibid.* at 444–45.

43. *Ibid.* at 400.

44. *Ibid.* at 404.

45. *Ibid.* at 405.

46. *Richmond Newspapers Inc. v. Virginia,* 100 S.Ct. 2814 (1980).

47. *Ibid.* at 2829–30.

48. *Ibid.* at 2840.

49. *Ibid.* at 2842.

50. *Ibid.* at 2834.

51. *Ibid.* at 2839.

52. *Ibid.*

53. *U.S. ex.rel. Latimore v. Sielaff,* 561 F.2d 691 (7th Cir. 1977).

54. *Ibid.* at 693.

55. *Ibid.* at 694–95.

56. *Ibid.* at 694.

57. 427 U.S. at 587.

58. *New York Times* (September 30, 1968).

59. Paul C. Reardon, "The Fair Trial—Free Press Standards," *American Bar Association Journal* 54 (1968): 343, recommendation 1.1.

60. *Ibid.*

61. *Ibid.*

62. "Statement of Policy Concerning the Release of Information by Personnel of the Department of Justice Relating to Criminal Proceedings," Office of the Attorney General, Washington, D.C., April 16, 1965.

63. An attempt was made in 1965 to write into federal law the provision: "It shall constitute a contempt of court for any employee of the United States, or for any defendant or his attorney . . . to furnish or make available for publication information not already properly filed with the court which might affect the outcome of any pending criminal litigation, except evidence that has already been admitted at the trial." The bill, known as S.290, sponsored by Senator Wayne Morse, provided the basis for extensive congressional hearings on the free press–fair trial issue on August 17–20, 1965, but it did not receive favorable action. U.S., Congress, Senate, Subcommittee on Constitutional Rights and Subcommittee on Improvements in Judicial Machinery of Committee on the Judiciary, *Free Press and Free Trial*, 89th Cong., 1st sess., 1965.

64. *Chicago Daily News* (June 6, 1968).

65. A more complicated problem presents itself when congressional investigators, who are also government employees, conduct public hearings on matters which may later go to court and where the rights of those who ultimately will be criminal defendants may be seriously compromised by the exposures that occur at these committee hearings. This was a difficulty that constantly plagued the Senate Watergate Committee chaired by Senator Sam Ervin, although great pains were taken by the senators and their aides to tread carefully in these areas. In fact, all of the principals except Richard Nixon were eventually tried in court, and under what were generally regarded as fair conditions. Sometimes, however, it may happen that the public interest is best served by the kind of timely exposure that a public congressional probe may provide, even if that means that individual criminal acts may have to go unpunished because of the impossibility of providing a fair trial for those who have been accused of wrongdoing.

66. ACLU Policy no. 221, *1976 Policy Guide of the American Civil Liberties Union*, pp. 188–90. See, also, "Fair Trial/Free Press: Committee Recommendations and Complete Background of ACLU Consideration," unpublished memorandum to board of directors from Due Process Committee, January 28, 1971.

67. See, for example, *Central South Carolina Chapter, Society of Professional Journalists v. Martin*, 556 F.2d 706 (4th Cir. 1977), cert. denied 434 U.S. 1022 (1978); and *Leach v. Sawicki*, 77-368 (Ohio, 1977), cert. denied 434 U.S. 1014 (1978).

68. *New York Times* (October 5, 1972).

69. *Ibid.*

70. *Chicago Daily News* (September 5, 1973); *New York Times* (September 6, 1973).

71. *Chicago Sun-Times* (September 14, 1973).

72. 522 F.2d 242 (1975).

73. *Chase v. Robson*, 435 F.2d 1059 (7th Cir. 1970); and *In Re Oliver*, 452 F.2d 111 (7th Cir. 1971).

74. *U.S. v. Tijerina*, 412 F.2d 661 (10th Cir. 1969) at 663, cert. denied 396 U.S. 990 (1969).

75. 522 F.2d at 250.

76. *Ibid.* at 257.

77. *Ibid.* at 258.
78. U.S., Congress, Senate, Committee on the Judiciary, *Staff Report on Free Press–Fair Trial,* 94th Cong., 2d sess., October 1976, p. 8.
79. *Ibid.,* pp. 21–22.
80. Essentially the same principles appear to have been given approval by the American Bar Association in a series of amendments to its free press–fair trial standards adopted by the ABA House of Delegates in September 1978. The only apparent difference was that the ABA used the language of "clear and present danger to a fair trial" rather than "serious and imminent threat to the fair administration of justice" as its test for the acceptability of bans on extrajudicial statements by criminal case lawyers, and for the sealing of court records or the exclusion of the public from pretrial proceedings. *American Bar Association Journal* 64 (1978): 1335.
81. *Estes v. Texas,* 381 U.S. 532 (1965) at 536.
82. *Ibid.* at 542–44.
83. *Ibid.* at 601–2, 615.
84. "TV in Court: Seven States Approve," *News Media and the Law* (December 1977), pp. 25–26.
85. *Ibid.,* p. 26.
86. *Chicago Sun-Times* (February 12, 1978), *New York Times* (February 13, 1979).
87. *Chandler v. Florida,* 101 S.Ct. 802 (1981).
88. *Chicago Daily News* (November 29, 1977).
89. A contempt of court conviction for this last comment was sustained in *U.S. v. Schiffer,* 351 F.2d 91 (6th Cir. 1965).
90. *Chicago Sun-Times* (January 10, 1974).
91. Norman Dorsen and Leon Friedman, *Disorder in the Court* (New York: Pantheon, 1973).
92. *Ibid.,* p. 6.
93. *Ibid.* The reference here is to the so-called Chicago 7 Conspiracy trial in the courtroom of Judge Julius Hoffman in 1969–70 and the Black Panther trial of 1970–71 before Judge John Murtagh in New York City.
94. *Ibid.,* p. 9.
95. *Ibid.*
96. *Ibid.,* p. 149.
97. *New York Times* (May 19, 1971).
98. *Illinois v. Allen,* 397 U.S. 337 (1970) at 343.
99. *U.S. v. Seale,* 461 F.2d 345 (7th Cir. 1972) at 369–70.
100. Arthur L. Goodhart, "Newspapers and Contempt of Court in English Law," *Harvard Law Review* 48 (1935): 885; James L. McGuigan, "Crime Reporting: The British and American Approaches," *American Bar Association Journal* 50 (1964): 442.
101. 384 U.S. at 350.
102. See, for example, Howard Felsher, *The Press in the Jury Box* (New York: Macmillan, 1966).

Chapter 7

1. *Free Speech,* p. 150.
2. *Chaplinsky v. New Hampshire* at 572.
3. *Ibid.*
4. *Rowan v. U.S. Post Office Department,* 397 U.S. 728 (1970) at 736.
5. *American Law Institute Restatement of Torts,* sec. 46-1 (1948).
6. *Chaplinsky v. New Hampshire* at 572.
7. *Ibid.*
8. *Cantwell v. Connecticut,* 310 U.S. 296 (1940) at 309–10.
9. *Rosenfield v. New Jersey,* 408 U.S. 901 (1972).
10. 438 U.S. 726 (1978) at 743.
11. 403 U.S. at 25–26.
12. 438 U.S. at 773.
13. 405 U.S. 518 (1972).
14. 415 U.S. 130 (1974).
15. *Gooding v. Wilson* at 524.
16. One analyst of these decisions believes there to be no doubt that the protection of a listener's sensibilities provided by *Chaplinsky v. New Hampshire* is a dead letter as a result of *Gooding v. Wilson.* Mark C. Rutzick, "Offensive Language and the Evolution of First Amendment Protection," *Harvard Civil Rights–Civil Liberties Law Review* 9 (1974): 1.
17. *Williams v. District of Columbia,* 419 F.2d 638 (1969).
18. *Ibid.* at 646.
19. *Ibid.*
20. *Chicago Sun-Times* (March 13, 1975).
21. *Chicago Sun-Times* (June 12, 1977).
22. *New York Times* (June 3, 1979).
23. *Erznoznik v. Jacksonville,* 422 U.S. 205 (1975).
24. *Ibid.* at 211.
25. *Ibid.* at 213.
26. *Ibid.*
27. *Ibid.* at 210–11.
28. *F.C.C. v. Pacifica Foundation.*
29. *Ibid.* at 750.
30. *Ibid.* at 743.
31. *Ibid.* at 746.
32. *Ibid.* at 743.
33. *Chicago Sun-Times* (February 27, 1978).
34. *Erznoznik v. Jacksonville* at 209–10.
35. 39 U.S.C. sec. 3008.
36. 39 U.S.C. sec. 3010–11; 18 U.S.C. sec. 1735–37.
37. *Rowan v. U.S. Post Office Department* at 736.
38. *Ibid.* at 738.
39. *Paris Adult Theatre I v. Slaton* at 114.
40. For a review of state laws and lower court rulings on this subject prior to 1966 see Alfred Kamin, "Residential Picketing and the First Amendment," *Northwestern University Law Review* 61 (1966): 177. See, also, "Picketing the Homes of

Public Officials," *University of Chicago Law Review* 34 (1966): 106. A later treatment of the topic is found in "Comment, Picketers at the Doorstep," *Harvard Civil Rights–Civil Liberties Law Review* 95 (1974): 101. Three lower court rulings on residential picketing laws are of particular relevance here. In Rhode Island a federal district court upheld a municipal antiresidential picketing ordinance on the ground that such activity was a "serious invasion of the right of privacy," *People Acting through Community Effort v. Doorley*, 338 F.Supp. 574 (D.R.I. 1972), but the U.S. court of appeals overturned that decision because it found that an exception made for picketing in connection with a labor dispute (a common caveat in such laws) constituted a violation of the equal protection clause of the Fourteenth Amendment. 468 F.2d 1143 (1st Cir. 1972). In contrast, the Wisconsin Supreme Court, in *Wauwatosa v. King*, 182 N.W.2d 530 (Wisc. 1971), upheld an antiresidential picketing ordinance, despite the exemption of labor disputes from its coverage. More generally, the supreme court of Pennsylvania overturned an injunction against the picketing of a slum landlord at his home, holding the location in question to be a "reasonable situs" for the demonstration, since the target could not be found anywhere else. *Hibbs v. Neighborhood Organization*, 252 A.2d 622 (Pa. 1967).

41. *Illinois Revised Statutes*, chap. 38, sec. 211-1.
42. *Carey v. Brown*, 100 S.Ct. 2286 (1980) at 2295–96.
43. *Lehman v. Shaker Heights*, 418 U.S. 298 (1974).
44. *Consolidated Edison Co. of New York v. Public Service Commission of New York*, 100 S.Ct. 2326 (1980) at 2335.
45. *Ibid.* at 2335–36. The two dissenters, while not taking issue with the Court's captive audience analysis, objected to its decision on the grounds that a public utility, as a state-created monopoly, does not have the privilege to require, in effect, that its ratepayers subsidize its political messages. Let the company, they suggested, use its shareholders' resources, if they wish, to underwrite separate mailings or to engage in other forms of communication. *Ibid.* at 2342–43.
46. *New York Times* (September 14, 1977).
47. *Rowan v. U.S. Post Office Department.*
48. *Ibid.* at 738.
49. *Lehman v. Shaker Heights.*
50. *Saia v. New York*, 334 U.S. 558 (1948).
51. *Ibid.* at 563.
52. *Kovacs v. Cooper*, 336 U.S. 77 (1949).
53. *Public Utilities Commission v. Pollak*, 343 U.S. 451 (1952).
54. *Ibid.* at 463–65.
55. *State ex. rel. Nicholas v. Headley*, 48 So.2d 80 (Fla. 1950); *Brinkman v. Gainesville*, 64 S.E.2d 344 (Ga. 1951); *Commonwealth v. Geuss*, 76 A.2d 500 (1950), affirmed 81 A.2d 553 (1951), appeal dismissed 342 U.S. 912 (1952).
56. *Wollam v. Palm Springs*, 379 P.2d 481 (Calif. 1963).
57. See, for example, *Martin v. Struthers*, 319 U.S. 141 (1943).
58. *Breard v. Alexandria*, 341 U.S. 622 (1951).
59. 397 U.S. at 737.
60. 438 U.S. at 748–49.
61. Franklyn S. Haiman, "Speech v. Privacy: Is There a Right Not to Be

Spoken To?" *Northwestern University Law Review* 67 (1972): 153.
62. *Lamont v. Commissioner of Motor Vehicles.*
63. 438 U.S. at 765–66.
64. 418 U.S. at 305.
65. *New York Times* (January 13, 1971).
66. 379 P.2d 481 (Calif. 1963).
67. Haiman, "Speech v. Privacy," p. 184.
68. William L. Prosser, "Intentional Infliction of Mental Suffering: A New Tort," *Michigan Law Review* 37 (1939): 879.
69. William L. Prosser, "Insult and Outrage," *California Law Review* 44 (1956): 40.
70. *Wilkinson v. Downton,* 2 Q.B. 57 (1897).
71. Herbert F. Goodrich, "Emotional Disturbance as Legal Damage," *Michigan Law Review* 20 (1922): 503.
72. Prosser, "Insult and Outrage," p. 53.
73. *Lipman v. Atlantic Coast Line Railroad Co.,* 93 S.E. 714 (1917).
74. Prosser, "Intentional Infliction of Mental Suffering," pp. 882–83.
75. *Chicago Sun-Times* (March 4, 1978).
76. *Waube v. Warrington,* 258 N.W. 497 (1935).
77. For a further discussion of this particular problem, see Leon Green, "'Fright' Cases," *Illinois Law Review* 27 (1933): 761.
78. John W. Wade, "Tort Liability for Abusive and Insulting Language," *Vanderbilt Law Review* 4 (1950): 64.
79. *State Rubbish Collectors Association v. Siliznoff,* 240 P.2d 282 (Calif. 1952).
80. 15 U.S.C. sec. 1692.
81. *Flamm v. Van Nierop,* 291 N.Y.S.2d 189 (1968).
82. *Chicago Sun-Times* (December 16, 1977).
83. Prosser, "Insult and Outrage," p. 50.
84. *Ibid.*
85. *Slocum v. Food Fair Stores of Florida,* 100 So.2d 396 (Fla. 1958).
86. *Johnson v. Sampson,* 208 N.W. 814 (Minn. 1926).
87. *Contreras v. Crown Zellerbach Corp.,* 565 P.2d 1173 (Wash. 1977) at 1174.
88. *Ibid.* at 1176.
89. *Ibid.* at 1175.
90. *Browning v. Slenderella Systems,* 341 P.2d 859 (Wash. 1959) at 864.
91. Prosser, "Insult and Outrage," p. 44.
92. *Great A & P Co. v. Roch,* 153 Atl.22 (Md.1930).
93. 565 P.2d at 1177.
94. Prosser, "Intentional Infliction of Emotional Distress," p. 887.
95. *Barstow v. Smith,* 78 N.E.2d 735 (1948).
96. *New York Times* (February 7, 1978).
97. Public statement by then U.S. Congressman Abner J. Mikva, *Skokie Life* (March 30, 1978).
98. *Melton v. Young,* 465 F.2d 1332 (6th Cir. 1972).
99. Calvert Magruder, "Mental and Emotional Disturbance in the Law of Torts," *Harvard Law Review* 49 (1936): 1035.
100. *Lynch v. Knight,* 9 H.L.C. 577 (1861) at 598.

Chapter 8

1. John Hart Ely, "Flag Desecration: A Case Study in the Roles of Categorization and Balancing in First Amendment Analysis," *Harvard Law Review* 88 (1975): 1499.

2. *People v. Stover* at 272. For an extended treatment of aesthetic regulations and the First Amendment, see also Stephen F. Williams, "Subjectivity, Expression, and Privacy: Problems of Aesthetic Regulation," *Minnesota Law Review* 62 (1977): 1.

3. For example, a statute prohibiting all off-premises, outdoor billboard advertising in the State of Maine was upheld as a valid exercise of government policy by a federal district court in *John Donnelly and Sons v. Mallar*, 453 F.Supp. 1272 (D.Maine 1978). Similar laws at the local level were upheld by the New York Court of Appeals in *Suffolk Outdoor Advertising v. Hulse*, 373 N.E.2d 263 (N.Y. 1977); and by the California Supreme Court in *Metromedia v. San Diego*, 592 P.2d 728 (Calif. 1979). The latter decision was being reviewed by the U.S. Supreme Court as this book went to press.

4. *New York Times* (October 29, 1976).

5. *Council of Greenburgh Civic Associations v. U.S. Postal Service*, 448 F.Supp. 159 (S.D.N.Y. 1978).

6. *Council of Greenburgh Civic Associations v. U.S. Postal Service*, 586 F.2d 935 (2d Cir. 1978).

7. *Ibid.* at 937–38.

8. *Ibid.* at 938.

9. *Ibid.* at 939.

10. *Council of Greenburgh Civic Associations v. U.S. Postal Service*, 490 F.Supp. 157 (S.D.N.Y. 1980) at 162–63. In January 1981 the U.S. Supreme Court noted probable jurisdiction on an appeal from this decision. *U.S. Postal Service v. Council of Greenburgh Civic Associations*, 49 *U.S. Law Week* 3492 (1981).

11. *Political Freedom*, p. 25.

12. *Chicago Daily News* (July 17, 1972).

13. Stephen Williams, in his discussion of this general subject, distinguishes between "equal access" (content-neutrality) and "minimum access" (which he believes is required if alternative channels of communication are inadequate). Thus he finds a total ban on billboards acceptable—since in his judgment billboards are not a necessary mode of expression—whereas a prohibition of political signs in the windows of private homes would be unacceptable. "Subjectivity, Expression, and Privacy," pp. 40–46.

14. See, for example, *Wolin v. Port of New York Authority*, 392 F.2d 83 (2d Cir. 1968), cert. denied 393 U.S. 940 (1968), and *Chicago v. Chicago Area Military Project*, 508 F.2d 921 (7th Cir. 1975), cert. denied 421 U.S. 992 (1975).

Chapter 9

1. A characteristic of some of the legislation that has been passed in recent years to address the child pornography problem has been a failure to distinguish between the production and the distribution of such material and thus to recognize the differing First Amendment implications of the two processes. See, for

example, *St. Martin's Press v. Carey,* 410 F.Supp. 1196 (S.D.N.Y. 1977), 605 F.2d 41 (2d Cir. 1979).

2. *Paris Adult Theatre I v. Slaton* at 58.
3. *Miller v. California,* 413 U.S. 15 (1973) at 24.
4. *Ibid.* at 30–34.
5. *Ginzburg v. U.S.,* 383 U.S. 463 (1966).
6. *Ginsberg v. New York,* 390 U.S. 629 (1968).
7. The Supreme Court's minority view was articulated by Justice Brennan's dissenting opinion in *Paris Adult Theatre I v. Slaton* at 73.
8. *Roth v. U.S.,* 354 U.S. 476 (1957) at 487.
9. *Rowan v. U.S. Post Office Department* at 728.
10. 39 U.S.C. sec. 3010.
11. *Young v. American Mini Theatres.*
12. *Ibid.* at 85.
13. *Ibid.* at 70.
14. *F.C.C. v. Pacifica Foundation* at 743. The words in question in this particular case were fuck, shit, piss, cunt, cocksucker, motherfucker, and tits.
15. *Ibid.*
16. *Ibid.* at 748–51.
17. *Winters v. New York,* 333 U.S. 507 (1948).
18. *Interstate Circuit v. Dallas,* 390 U.S. 676 (1968).
19. *Writers Guild v. F.C.C.,* 423 F.Supp. 1064 (C.D.Calif. 1976).
20. *Writers Guild v. American Broadcasting Co.,* 609 F.2d 355 (9th Cir. 1979), cert. denied 101 S.Ct. 85 (1980).
21. *Chicago Sun-Times* (May 27, 1976).
22. *City of Chicago Municipal Code,* sec. 155-5.
23. *Capitol Broadcasting Co. v. Mitchell,* 333 F.Supp. 582 (D.D.C. 1971), affirmed 405 U.S. 1000 (1972).
24. *Federal Register* (April 27, 1978), p. 17967.
25. See Philip Harriman, *New Dictionary of Psychology* (New York: Philosophic Library, 1947), pp. 134–35.
26. "What to Do about TV Violence," *The Alternate: An American Spectator* (August/September 1976), pp. 7–8.
27. *Obscenity and Public Morality* (Chicago: University of Chicago Press, 1969), pp. 52–53.
28. 333 U.S. at 510.
29. *New York Times* (October 25, 1970).
30. "Pornography, Obscenity and the Case for Censorship," *New York Times Magazine* (March 28, 1971), p. 24.
31. *Paris Adult Theatre I v. Slaton* at 64.
32. "Pornography, Obscenity and the Case for Censorship."
33. *The First Amendment and the Future of American Democracy* (New York: Basic, 1976), pp. 212–15.
34. *Obscenity.*
35. *Ibid.,* pp. 225, 230.
36. Robin Morgan, "Check It Out: Porn, No. But Free Speech, Yes," *New York Times* (March 24, 1978).

37. "Pornography, Obscenity and the Case for Censorship."
38. *Obscenity*, p. 226.
39. Allaine Robbe-Grillet, "For a Voluptuous Tomorrow," trans. Richard Howard, *Saturday Review* (May 20, 1972), p. 46.
40. *New York Times* (July 26, 1978).
41. *Paris Adult Theatre I v. Slaton* at 60–63.
42. For an extensive summary of the scientific literature on this question, see Dennis L. DeLeon and Robert L. Naon, "The Regulation of Televised Violence," *Stanford Law Review* 26 (1974): 1292–1303. But see, also, Thomas G. Krattenmaker and L. A. Powe, Jr., "Televised Violence: First Amendment Principles and Social Science Theory," *Virginia Law Review* 64 (1978): 1123, who offer a critical analysis of the social science literature and conclude that the case has not been adequately made for the theory of a causal relationship between the viewing of televised violence and ensuing violent behavior.
43. Earl F. Murphy, "The Value of Pornography," *Wayne Law Review* 10 (1964): 655.
44. *Obscenity*, p. 190.
45. *F.C.C. v. Pacifica Foundation* at 757.
46. Letter to the Communications Media Committee of the American Civil Liberties Union, April 3, 1978.
47. *Chicago Sun-Times* (November 6, 1976).
48. *Butler v. Michigan*, 352 U.S. 380 (1957) at 383.
49. *F.C.C. v. Pacifica Foundation* at 749.
50. See Justice Powell quotation, n. 45, *supra*.
51. That is to say, short of gross neglect or extreme physical abuse.
52. *Pierce v. Society of Sisters*, 268 U.S. 510 (1925).
53. *Wisconsin v. Yoder*, 406 U.S. 205 (1972).
54. *F.C.C. v. Pacifica Foundation* at 770.
55. *Tinker v. Community School District*.
56. "Pornography, Obscenity and the Case for Censorship."

Chapter 10

1. Sissela Bok, *Lying* (New York: Pantheon, 1978), p. 18.
2. William Prosser, *Handbook of the Law of Torts*, 3d ed. (St. Paul, Minn.: West Publishing, 1964), pp. 698–99.
3. *Ibid.*, p. 702.
4. *Warner-Lambert Co. v. F.T.C.*, 562 F.2d 749 (D.C.Cir. 1977), cert. denied 436 U.S. 950 (1978). The FTC's original order in this case had specified that the corrective ads must read, "Contrary to prior advertising, Listerine will not help prevent colds or sore throats or lessen their severity." The court of appeals deleted the phrase "Contrary to prior advertising," regarding it as unnecessarily punitive.
5. 18 U.S.C. sec. 1341, 1343.
6. William Prosser, "Injurious Falsehood: The Basis of Liability," *Columbia Law Review* 59 (1959): 425.
7. *Ibid.*, p. 427.

8. *Ibid.*, p. 428.

9. Prosser, *Handbook*, p. 698.

10. *Flaherty v. Till*, 137 N.W. 815 (Minn. 1912).

11. *Handbook*, pp. 699–700.

12. *Ibid.*, p. 699.

13. Fowler V. Harper and Mary Coate McNeeling, "A Synthesis of the Law of Misrepresentation," *Minnesota Law Review* 22 (1938): 1004.

14. *Kimball v. Bangs*, 11 N.E. 113 (Mass. 1887).

15. Prosser, *Handbook*, p. 699.

16. Even when considering false statements from a moral, rather than a legal, point of view, Sissila Bok points out, "The moral question of whether you are lying or not is not *settled* by establishing the truth or falsity of what you say. In order to settle this question, we must know whether you *intend your statement to mislead.*" *Lying*, p. 6.

17. "The First Amendment in the Marketplace: Commercial Speech and the Values of Free Expression," *George Washington Law Review* 39 (1971): 461. Another author, however, has made the following observation about section 14(a) of the act establishing the Federal Trade Commission, which makes the dissemination of false advertising a misdemeanor: "The section does not require that advertising be intentionally or negligently misleading. This provision conflicts with the Supreme Court's holding that the First Amendment requires that criminal statutes prohibiting dissemination of unprotected speech make scienter an element of the crime. Because the FTC has not yet invoked the criminal sanction, the constitutionality of 14(a) has remained untested." Rosemarie Sbaratta, "Notes: First Amendment and Misleading Advertising," *Boston University Law Review* 57 (1977): 859.

18. *Dougherty, Clifford, Steers and Shenfield, Inc. v. F.T.C.*, 392 F.2d 921 (6th Cir. 1968) at 925.

19. *Aaron v. S.E.C.*, 446 U.S. 680 (1980).

20. *Ibid.* at 697.

21. Three Justices dissented from this part of the Court's decision because they were not so sure that the majority was right about what Congress intended and because of their understanding of a historical difference in the requirements for damage actions for fraud and injunctive relief in courts of equity. They argued that "common-law courts consistently have held that in an action for recision or other equitable relief the fact of material misrepresentation is sufficient, and the knowledge or purpose of the wrongdoer need not be shown." *Ibid.* at 710.

22. *Ernst and Ernst v. Hochfelder*, 425 U.S. 185 (1946).

23. Federal Trade Commission, Staff Report on Television Advertising to Children, February 1978.

24. *New York Times* (May 1, 1980). The fact that this was part of a broader corporate and congressional vendetta against the more aggressive regulatory role which the FTC had been playing generally in the Carter administration does not, in my opinion, detract from the correctness of the reaction to the FTC staff proposal on this particular matter.

25. Prosser, *Handbook*, pp. 699–700.

26. *Ibid.*
27. *Ibid.*
28. *Chicago Sun-Times* (December 16, 1977).
29. 322 U.S. 78 (1944).
30. *U.S. v. Ballard,* 138 F.2d 540 (9th Cir. 1943) at 542–43.
31. *Ibid.*
32. 322 U.S. at 86–87.
33. *Ballard v. U.S.,* 329 U.S. 187 (1946).
34. 322 U.S. at 93.
35. *Ibid.* at 94–95.
36. *Ibid.* at 89.
37. *New York Times* (November 6, 1977).
38. *Ibid.*
39. *Chicago Sun-Times* (January 27, 1979).
40. *New York Times* (January 28, 1979).
41. *Chicago Sun-Times* (September 29, 1977).
42. *Ibid.*
43. "The First Amendment."
44. *Perma-Maid Co. v. F.T.C.,* 121 F.2d 282 (6th Cir. 1941).
45. *Scientific Manufacturing Co. v. F.T.C.,* 124 F.2d 640 (3d Cir. 1941).
46. *Ibid.* at 644.
47. "The First Amendment," pp. 461–62. This argument is reinforced by Justice Stevens's concurring opinion in *Central Hudson Gas and Electric Corp. v. Public Service Commission of New York* at 2358 when he says, "Neither a labor leader's exhortation to strike, nor an economist's dissertation on the money supply, should receive any lesser protection because the subject matter concerns only the economic interests of the audience. Nor should the economic motivation of a speaker qualify his constitutional protection; even Shakespeare may have been motivated by the prospect of pecuniary reward."
48. *Koch v. F.T.C.,* 206 F.2d 311 (6th Cir. 1953).
49. "The First Amendment," p. 463.
50. *Ibid.*
51. 421 U.S. 809 (1975).
52. 425 U.S. 748 (1976).
53. 431 U.S. 85 (1977).
54. 433 U.S. 350 (1977).
55. *Valentine v. Chrestensen,* 316 U.S. 52 (1942).
56. *Friedman v. Rogers,* 440 U.S. 1 (1979).
57. Examples given were that the "trade name of an optometrical practice can remain unchanged despite changes in the staff of optometrists upon whose skill and care the public depends when it patronizes the practice. Thus, the public may be attracted by a trade name that reflects the reputation of an optometrist no longer associated with the practice. A trade name frees an optometrist from dependence on his personal reputation to attract clients, and even allows him to assume a new trade name if negligence or misconduct casts a shadow over the old one. By using different trade names at shops under common ownership, an

optometrist can give the public a false impression of competition among the shops." *Ibid.* at 13.

58. *Ibid.* at 12.

59. *First National Bank of Boston v. Bellotti.*

60. 440 U.S. at 11–12.

61. *Ibid.* at 24–25.

62. *Ibid.* at 27.

63. *Central Hudson Gas and Electric Corp. v. Public Service Commission of New York,* 100 S.Ct. 2343 (1980).

64. *Ibid.* at 2348.

65. *Ibid.* at 2351. In this particular case the majority found that the Public Service Commission's ban did not meet these tests.

66. *Ibid.* at 2350.

67. "The First Amendment," pp. 446–47.

68. "Commercial Speech: A Problem in the Theory of Freedom," *Iowa Law Review* 62 (1976): 3.

69. "Scope of the First Amendment," p. 996, n. 102.

70. 100 S.Ct. at 2349–50.

71. *Ibid.* at 2355–56.

72. *U.S. v. Segretti,* case no. 73-153-CR-T-K (M.D.Fla.), Grand Jury Charges, August 24, 1973.

73. U.S., Department of Justice, Watergate Special Prosecution Force, Press Release, September 17, 1973.

74. 18 U.S.C. sec. 1342.

75. *Bonacci v. Save Our Unborn Lives, Inc.,* Common Pleas Ct. (Phila.Co. Pa. 1978).

76. *Handbook,* p. 711.

77. *Vanasco v. Schwartz,* 401 F.Supp. 87 (E.D.N.Y. 1975), summarily affirmed 423 U.S. 1041 (1976).

78. See, for example, *Hollywood Ceramics Co., Inc.,* 140 N.L.R.B. 221 (1962), reaffirmed more recently in *General Knit of California, Inc.,* 239 N.L.R.B. 101 (1978).

79. *Hollywood Ceramics Co. Inc.* at 224.

80. *Shopping Kart Food Market, Inc.,* 228 N.L.R.B. 1311 (1977) at 1313.

81. *Medical Ancillary Services, Inc.,* 212 N.L.R.B. 582 (1974) at 584.

Chapter 11

1. *Philosophy of Democratic Government* (Chicago: University of Chicago Press, 1951), p. 109. C. Edwin Baker makes this same point when he excludes from his "liberty model" of the First Amendment speech which is coercive. Says Baker, "Presumably, a major reason for a preferred status for freedom of speech is that speech behavior is normally noncoercive; instead, it depends for its power on increasing the speaker's own awareness or on the voluntary acceptance of listeners. . . . Both the concept of coercion and the rationale for protecting freedom of speech draw from the same ethical requirement that the integrity and autonomy

456 Notes to Pages 209–17

of the individual moral agent must be respected." See "Scope of the First Amendment," pp. 998–1001.

2. As Sissila Bok puts it, " . . . deceit controls more subtly for it works on belief as well as action." *Lying,* p. 18. Thus, she concludes that there are some situations, such as parents attempting to keep a small child from falling into a pond, where force would be preferable to lying. *Ibid.,* p. 210.

3. Examples of entire books devoted to the description and analysis of these processes are Edward Hunter, *Brainwashing in Red China* (New York: Vanguard, 1951); Robert Jay Lifton, *Thought Reform and the Psychology of Totalism* (New York: Norton, 1961); Edgar H. Schein, Inge Schneier, and Curtis Barker, *Coercive Persuasion* (New York: Norton, 1961).

4. J. Ronald Pennock and John W. Chapman, eds., *Coercion* (Chicago: Aldine-Atherton, 1972).

5. *Handbook,* pp. 38–39.

6. *Ohralik v. Ohio State Bar Association,* 436 U.S. 447 (1978) at 464–65.

7. Act 1, sc. 3.

8. Manuela Albuquerque Scott, "The Invisible Hand and the Clenched Fist: Is There a Safe Way to Picket under the First Amendment?" *Hastings Law Journal* 26 (1974): 180.

9. *Gompers v. Bucks Stove and Range Co.* at 439.

10. "Strikes, Picketing and the Constitution," *Vanderbilt Law Review* 4 (1951): 574.

11. Scott, "The Invisible Hand," pp. 177–78.

12. "Strikes," p. 602.

13. Harold W. Horowitz, "Legal Aspects of 'Political Black Listing' in the Entertainment Industry," *Southern California Law Review* 29 (1956): 263. This is also the position of a law review note, "Political Boycott Activity and the First Amendment," *Harvard Law Review* 91 (1978): 659, which argues that exhorting or inducing others to participate in a boycott should never be prohibited but that "concerted refusals to deal" should be subject to the law of conspiracy, even if engaged in for political purposes.

14. *Handbook,* p. 39.

15. 18 U.S.C. sec. 871.

16. 18 U.S.C. sec. 875(b).

17. 18 U.S.C. sec. 876.

18. 18 U.S.C. sec. 241.

19. 18 U.S.C. sec. 594 provides penalties for "Whoever intimidates, threatens, coerces, or attempts to intimidate, threaten, or coerce, any person for the purpose of interfering with the right of such person to vote or not to vote as he may choose, or of causing such other person to vote for, or not to vote for, any candidate for the office of President, Vice-President, presidential elector, member of the Senate . . ."

20. 18 U.S.C. sec. 606.

21. 18 U.S.C. sec. 1502 provides penalties for "Whoever corruptly, or by threats of force, or by any threatening letter or communication, endeavors to influence, intimidate or impede any witness . . . or any grand or petit juror, or officer in or of any court. . . ."

22. 29 U.S.C. sec. 158.

23. 15 U.S.C. sec. 1692(d).

24. *Ibid.*, subsec. (1).

25. *Illinois Revised Statues*, chap. 38, sec. 12-6.

26. *Ibid.*, chap. 38, sec. 32-4.

27. *Ibid.*, chap. 46, sec. 29-18.

28. See Jack Swertfeger, "Comment: Anti-Mask and Anti-Klan Laws," *Journal of Public Law* 1 (1952): 182. The author finds that thirteen states have strong laws on the subject and another eight have weak laws. Also, fifty cities and towns in seven southern states have such laws. He notes with approval that "none of these laws requires proof of specific intent as part of the definition of the crime" because of the "difficulty of proving to a jury that the person accused of violating the law had worn a mask with the intention of intimidating or harming another person" (p. 189).

He also notes, with regret, that prior to the passage of these laws, "authorities could not arrest the hooded Klansmen the *moment* they appeared in their regalia in public" (p. 184).

29. *Chicago Sun-Times* (January 24, 1974).

30. *Open Forum* (February 1979), p. 1.

31. *Ghafari v. Municipal Court*, 150 Calif. Rptr. 813 (1978).

32. *Open Forum* (February 1979), p. 1.

33. *Weiss v. Patrick*, 453 F.Supp. 717 (D.R.I. 1978) at 724.

34. Greta Spendlove, "Legal Issues in the Use of Guardianship Procedures to Remove Members of Cults," *Arizona Law Review* 18 (1976): 1095.

35. American Civil Liberties Union, *Deprogramming: Documenting the Issue.*

36. Edgar A. Jones, Jr., "Picketing and Coercion: A Jurisprudence of Epithets," *Virginia Law Review* 39 (1953): 1023.

37. *Ibid.*, p. 1024.

38. 310 U.S. 88 (1940).

39. *Ibid.* at 102, 104.

40. *The System of Freedom of Expression*, p. 438.

41. *Milk Wagon Drivers Local 753 v. Meadowmoor Dairies, Inc.*, 312 U.S. 287 (1941) at 292.

42. *Bakery and Pastry Drivers v. Wohl*, 315 U.S. 769 (1942) at 775.

43. *Ibid.* at 776–77.

44. 336 U.S. at 503.

45. *Teamsters Union v. Hanke*, 339 U.S. 470 (1950) at 474.

46. 339 U.S. 460 (1950) at 465.

47. 336 U.S. at 498.

48. 339 U.S. at 465–66.

49. "The Common Law and Constitutional Status of Antidiscrimination Boycotts," *Yale Law Journal* 66 (1957): 400.

50. *Carpenters and Joiners Local 313 v. Ritters Cafe*, 315 U.S. 722 (1942) at 727.

51. *N.L.R.B. v. Fruit and Vegetable Packers*, 377 U.S. 58 (1964) at 63.

52. *N.L.R.B. v. Retail Store Employees Union Local 1001*, 100 S.Ct. 2372 (1980).

53. *Ibid.* at 2377.

54. *Ibid.* at 2379.

55. *N.L.R.B. v. Virginia Electric and Power Co.*, 314 U.S. 469 (1941) at 477–78.

56. Sec. 8(b) (7) (c).

57. *General Service Employees Union Local 73 v. N.L.R.B.*, 578 F.2d 361 (D.C.Cir. 1978) at 367, 369.

58. *American Mercury v. Chase*, 13 F.2d 224 (D.Mass. 1926) at 225.

59. 372 U.S. 58 (1963).

60. "The Common Law and Constitutional Status," p. 398.

61. 15 U.S.C. sec. 1.

62. "Legal Responsibility for Extra-Legal Pressure," *Columbia Law Review* 62 (1962): 475.

63. *Kuryer Publishing Co. v. Messmer*, 156 N.W. 948 (Wisc. 1916).

64. *Council of Defense v. International Magazine Co.*, 267 F. 390 (8th Cir. 1920).

65. *I.P.C. Distributors v. Chicago Moving Picture Machine Operators*, 132 F.Supp. 294 (N.D.Ill. 1955) at 299–300.

66. 467 F.Supp. 289 (W.D.Mo. 1979). Judge Hunter's rationale was accepted, and his decision sustained, by the U.S. circuit court of appeals, 620 F.2d 1301 (8th Cir. 1980), cert. denied 101 S.Ct. 122 (1980).

67. *Ibid.* at 304–5.

68. *Eastern Railroad Presidents Conference v. Noerr Motor Freight, Inc.*, 365 U.S. 127 (1961).

69. *Ibid.* at 136.

70. *Ibid.* at 137–38.

71. 18 U.S.C. sec. 201.

72. 18 U.S.C. sec. 210.

73. 18 U.S.C. sec. 224.

74. *Illinois Revised Statutes*, chap. 38, sec. 33-1.

75. *Ibid.*, chap. 46, sec. 29-1.

76. *Ibid.*, chap. 46, sec. 29-3.

77. *Florida Statutes*, sec. 104.061.

78. *Chicago Sun-Times* (November 30, 1978).

79. *Handbook*, p. 40.

80. *Ibid.*, p. 38.

81. *Ibid.*, p. 39.

82. 394 U.S. 705 (1969) at 706.

83. *Ibid.* at 708.

84. *U.S. v. Patillo*, 438 F.2d 13 (4th Cir. 1971) at 15.

85. This standard has been accepted, and the subjective intent requirement rejected, by the Second Circuit in *U.S. v. Compton*, 428 F.2d 18 (1970), cert. denied 401 U.S. 1014 (1971); the Fifth Circuit in *Rogers v. U.S.*, 488 F.2d 512 (1974), reversed on procedural grounds, 422 U.S. 35 (1975); the Sixth Circuit in *U.S. v. Lincoln*, 462 F.2d 1368 (1972), cert. denied 409 U.S. 952 (1972); the Seventh Circuit in *Ragansky v. U.S.*, 253 F. 643 (1919); the Ninth Circuit in *Roy v. U.S.*, 416 F.2d 874 (1969); and the Tenth Circuit in *U.S. v. Hart*, 457 F.2d 1087 (1972), cert. denied 409 U.S. 861 (1972). The underlying law, 18 U.S.C. sec. 871(a), says merely that the threat must be "knowingly and willfully" made.

86. 534 F.2d 1020 (2d Cir. 1976), cert. denied 429 U.S. 1022 (1976).

87. 18 U.S.C. 875(c).

88. 534 F.2d at 1021
89. *Ibid.* at 1025.
90. *Ibid.* at 1027.
91. *Ibid.* at 1029–30.
92. *Ibid.* at 1030. Further criticisms of the court of appeals decision in this case are found in "United States v. Kelner: Threats and the First Amendment," *University of Pennsylvania Law Review* 125 (1977): 919.
93. Scott, "The Invisible Hand," p. 181.
94. 312 U.S. at 294
95. *Ibid.* at 313–16.
96. *Ibid.* at 319.
97. *Youngdahl v. Rainfair,* 355 U.S. 131 (1957).
98. *Ibid.* at 135, 138.
99. *N.L.R.B. v. Virginia Electric and Power Co.* at 479.
100. Charles O. Gregory, "Constitutional Limitations on the Regulation of Union and Employer Conduct," *Michigan Law Review* 49 (1950): 191.
101. See *Hudgens v. N.L.R.B.,* 424 U.S. 507 (1976), and the ensuing decision by the N.L.R.B., 230 N.L.R.B. 73 (1977).
102. ACLU Policy no. 54, *1976 Policy Guide of the American Civil Liberties Union,* pp. 86–87.
103. *Evanston Review* (January 7, 1960).
104. *Clairborne Hardware Inc. v. N.A.A.C.P.,* no. 78,353 (Miss. Ch. Ct. August 9, 1976). The judgment against the NAACP was upheld by the Mississippi Supreme Court, but the amount of damages was deemed excessive and the case was returned to the lower court for a new determination of damages. *New York Times* (December 11, 1980).

Chapter 12

1. John W. Curran, "Solicitation: A Substantive Crime," *Minnesota Law Review* 17 (1933): 499.
2. 18 U.S.C. sec. 2.
3. *Illinois Revised Statutes,* chap. 38, sec. 211-1.
4. Emerson, *The System of Freedom of Expression,* p. 75.
5. *Ibid.,* p. 125.
6. *Ibid.,* pp. 328–29.
7. *State v. Schleifer,* 121 A. 805 (Conn. 1923).
8. *The System of Freedom of Expression,* p. 330.
9. *State v. Quinlan,* 91 A. 111 (N.J. 1914).
10. *The System of Freedom of Expression,* p. 330.
11. *People v. Most,* 27 N.E. 970 (N.Y. 1891) at 971.
12. *The System of Freedom of Expression,* p. 331.
13. *Ibid.,* p. 333.
14. One interesting federal court decision has quite clearly made what I believe to be the correct distinction between, on the one hand, a sales transaction which is conduct that is subject to reasonable economic regulation by the state even though speech is a part of that process, and, on the other hand, commercial

advertising which is divorced in time and place from actual sales and is therefore protected by the First Amendment unless it is a false inducement to buy or invites participation in an illegal transaction. The case arose as the result of a prohibition by Pennsylvania State University against business enterprises coming into residence halls on the campus to conduct sales demonstrations and ensuing sales to groups of students if they had not been invited in by the group or had been invited in by only one person to do business with that individual (which they were permitted to do). American Future Systems, Inc., challenged the rule, claiming interference by the state university with their free speech rights. The district court, later affirmed by the U.S. circuit court of appeals, rejected that claim and wrote: "It is beyond dispute that American Future System has a right under the First Amendment to disseminate certain information with respect to the product it sells. . . . The Court is not convinced that American Future Systems has a constitutionally protected right to sell its merchandise to college students in the manner it has selected. . . . a business transaction in which speech is an essential but subordinate component. . . . Penn State has attempted to separate business transactions from the speech which accompanies them. . . . does not restrict the ability . . . to advertise in student newspapers or on student radio stations or to provide consumer information to students either through use of the telephones or the United States mails . . . only from appearing on campus without an invitation in an attempt to transact business or from appearing on campus with an invitation in an attempt to transact business with more than one student." *American Future Systems, Inc. v. Pennsylvania State University*, 464 F.Supp. 1252 (M.D.Pa. 1979) at 1261–62, affirmed 618 F.2d 252 (3d Cir. 1980).

15. In further support of this point, see Justice Blackmun's concurring opinion in *Central Hudson Gas and Electric Corporation v. Public Service Commission of New York* discussed in Chapter 10.

16. 413 U.S. 376 (1973).

17. *Ibid.* at 385.

18. *Ibid.* at 388–89.

19. 42 U.S.C. sec. 3604(e).

20. See, for example, *U.S. v. Hunter*, 459 F.2d 205 (4th Cir. 1972), cert. denied 409 U.S. 934 (1972); and *U.S. v. Bob Lawrence Realty*, 474 F.2d 115 (5th Cir. 1973), cert. denied 414 U.S. 826 (1973).

21. *Linmark Associates v. Township of Willingboro*.

22. 310 U.S. at 308–9.

23. *Ibid.* at 309–10.

24. 315 U.S. at 572.

25. *Ibid.* at 573.

26. *Cohen v. California* at 20.

27. *Gooding v. Wilson* at 524.

28. *Feiner v. New York*, 340 U.S. 315 (1951) at 320–21.

29. *Cohen v. California* at 20.

30. *Terminiello v. Chicago*, 337 U.S. 1 (1949) at 4.

31. *Edwards v. South Carolina*, 372 U.S. 229 (1963) at 235.

32. *Gregory v. Chicago*.

33. *Ibid.* at 111–13.

34. *Bachellar v. Maryland*, 397 U.S. 564 (1970) at 566–67.

35. *Meyer v. Chicago*, 253 N.E.2d 400 (Ill. 1969), cert. denied 397 U.S. 1024 (1970).

36. *Abrams v. U.S.*, 250 U.S. 616 (1919) at 621.

37. *Chicago Sun-Times* (August 5, 1965).

38. *American Constitutional Law* (Mineola, N.Y.: Foundation Press, 1978), p. 605.

39. "The Burger Court and Free Expression: Property Interests or Maximum Protection" (Thomas M. Cooley Lectures, 1979).

40. *The System of Freedom of Expression*, pp. 337–38.

41. 340 U.S. at 326–27.

42. "Note, Hostile-Audience Confrontations: Police Conduct and First Amendment Rights," *Michigan Law Review* 75 (1976): 181–82.

43. *Ibid.*, p. 200.

44. *Ibid.*, p. 187.

45. *Ibid.*, p. 191.

46. *Cramer v. U.S.*, 325 U.S. 1 (1945) at 28.

47. *Chandler v. U.S.*, 171 F.2d 921 (lst Cir. 1948), cert. denied 336 U.S. 918 (1949); *Best v. U.S.*, 184 F.2d 131 (lst Cir. 1950), cert. denied 340 U.S. 939 (1951); *D'Aguino v. U.S.*, 192 F.2d 338 (9th Cir. 1951), cert. denied 343 U.S. 935 (1952).

48. *Gillars v. U.S.* at 971.

49. 18 U.S.C. sec. 2383.

50. 18 U.S.C. sec. 2387, 2(a).

51. 18 U.S.C. sec. 2388(a).

52. 18 U.S.C. sec. 2387, 1(a).

53. Later incorporated into the Selective Service Act of 1967, 50 U.S.C. App. Sec. 462(a).

54. *Gara v. U.S.*, 178 F.2d 38 (6th Cir. 1949), affirmed by an equally divided court, 340 U.S. 857 (1950).

55. *Warren v. U.S.*, 177 F.2d 596 (10th Cir. 1949), cert. denied 338 U.S. 947 (1950).

56. 18 U.S.C. sec. 2101–2.

57. *U.S. v. Dellinger*, 472 F.2d 340 (7th Cir. 1972), cert. denied 410 U.S. 970 (1973).

58. *Siegel v. Board of Regents*, 308 F.Supp. 832 (N.D.Cal. 1970).

59. *Spies v. People*, 122 Ill. 1 (1887); *Spies v. Illinois*, 123 U.S. 131 (1887); as described by Emerson, Haber, and Dorsen, *Political and Civil Rights*, 1:52–53.

60. *Chicago Tribune* (August 13, 1977).

61. *New York Times* (January 19, 1978).

62. *Open Forum* (March 1971), p. 1.

63. *People v. Rubin*, App., 158 Calif. Rptr. 488 (1979) at 494, cert. denied 101 S.Ct. 80 (1980).

64. *Ibid.* at 495.

65. *Olivia Niemi v. N.B.C.*, as reported in *Chicago Sun-Times* (August 9, 1978).

66. *New York Times* (August 5, 1978).

67. *New York Times* (February 23, 1979).

68. *Davis v. Beason*, 133 U.S. 333 (1890) at 342.

69. *Fox v. Washington*, 236 U.S. 273 (1915) at 277.
70. *Gay Lib v. University of Missouri*, 416 F.Supp. 1350 (W.D.Mo. 1976).
71. *Gay Lib v. University of Missouri*, 558 F.2d 848 (8th Cir. 1977).
72. *Ratchford v. Gay Lib*, 434 U.S. 1080 (1978) at 1082–83.
73. *Virginia Statute for Establishing Religious Freedom.*
74. *The Harvard Classics*, 25:260.
75. 244 F. 535 (S.D.N.Y. 1917) at 540.
76. *Masses Publishing Co. v. Patten*, 246 F. 24 (2d Cir. 1917) at 38.
77. *Masses Publishing Co. v. Patten*, 245 F. 105 (2d Cir. 1917) at 106.
78. *Free Speech*, pp. 49–50.
79. 249 U.S. at 52.
80. *Gitlow v. New York*, 268 U.S. 652 (1925) at 669.
81. *Dennis v. U.S.*, 341 U.S. 494 (1951) at 511.
82. *Abrams v. U.S.* at 628–31.
83. "Abrams v. U.S.: Freedom of Speech and Freedom of Thuggery in War-Time and Peace-Time," *Illinois Law Review* 14 (1920): 554.
84. *Free Speech*, p. 322.
85. 268 U.S. at 664–69.
86. *Ibid.* at 673.
87. See, also, on this point Hans A. Linde, "'Clear and Present Danger' Reexamined: Dissonance in the *Brandenburg* Concerto," *Stanford Law Review* 22 (1970): 1163. Linde says at p. 1183: "The first amendment invalidates any law directed in terms against some communicative content of speech or of the press, irrespective of extrinsic circumstances either at the time of enactment or the time of enforcement, if the proscribed content is of a kind which falls under any circumstances within the meaning of the first amendment."
88. *Musser v. Utah*, 333 U.S. 95 (1948) at 99–100.
89. 274 U.S. at 376–77.
90. 341 U.S. at 508–10.
91. *Yates v. U.S.* at 320–27.
92. *Noto v. U.S.*, 367 U.S. 290 (1961) at 297–98.
93. 395 U.S. at 447.
94. *Ibid.* at 452.
95. *Ibid.* at 456–57.
96. See in this connection G. F. Schueler, "The Notion of 'Incitement,'" *Philosophy and Rhetoric* 7 (1974): 89. Although he discusses this issue from a moral rather than a legal point of view, Schueler arrives at the same conclusion regarding the responsibility for incitement.
97. See on this point Thomas Scanlon, "A Theory of Freedom of Expression," *Philosophy and Public Affairs* 1 (1972): 204. He says at p. 212: "A person who acts on reasons he has acquired from another's act of expression acts on what *he* has come to believe and has judged to be a sufficient basis for action. The contribution to the genesis of his action made by the act of expression is, so to speak, superseded by the agent's own judgment." For a further and more recent discussion of the Scanlon point of view, see Harry H. Wellington, "On Freedom of Expression," *Yale Law Journal* 88 (1979): 1105.

98. *Press Censorship Newsletter* (September–October 1976), p. 78. In a similar case in the State of Washington, the State Supreme Court upheld a judgment against a newspaper for publishing an article which told readers how to create false telephone credit card numbers and thus make free calls. The conviction had been obtained under a state law which made it illegal to publish such information "with the intent that it be used, or with knowledge or reason to believe that it will be used, to avoid the payment of any lawful charge." *State v. Northwest Passage*, 585 P.2d 794 (Wash. 1978).

99. *Chicago Tribune* (September 11, 1977).

100. *Open Forum* (June 1970), p. 1.

101. *Chicago Daily News* (April 5, 1968).

102. *Ibid.*

103. 158 Calif. Rptr. at 490–91, 493.

104. *Ibid.* at 492–93.

105. Roy P. Basler, ed., *Collected Works of Abraham Lincoln* (New Brunswick, N.J.: Rutgers University Press, 1953–55), 6:266–67.

106. *Chicago Tribune* (June 25, 1978); *Chicago Sun-Times* (June 25, 1978).

Chapter 13

1. "Notes—Conspiracy and the First Amendment," *Yale Law Journal* 79 (1970): 872.

2. Albert J. Harno, "Intent in Criminal Conspiracy," *University of Pennsylvania Law Review* 89 (1941): 624.

3. "Developments in the Law—Criminal Conspiracy," *Harvard Law Review* 72 (1959): 945. The general federal conspiracy statute is 18 U.S.C. sec. 371, which provides, "If two or more persons conspire either to commit any offenses against the United States, or to defraud the United States, or any agency thereof in any manner or for any purpose, and one or more of such persons do any act to effect the object of the conspiracy, each shall be fined . . . or imprisoned . . . or both."

The Illinois criminal code, as an example of state law, defines conspiracy as follows: "A person commits conspiracy when, with intent that an offense be committed, he agrees with another to the commission of that offense. No person may be convicted of conspiracy to commit an offense unless an act in furtherance of such agreement is alleged and proved to have been committed by him or by a co-conspirator." *Illinois Revised Statutes*, chap. 38, sec. 8–2.

4. "Developments in the Law," p. 945.

5. *Ibid.*

6. *U.S. v. Kissel*, 218 U.S. 601 (1911) at 608.

7. *Hyde v. U.S.*, 225 U.S. 347 (1912) at 369.

8. *Ibid.*

9. *Pinkerton v. U.S.*, 328 U.S. 640 (1946) at 647–48.

10. *Ibid.* at 643.

11. "Developments in the Law," p. 924.

12. *Ibid.*

13. Herbert Wechsler, William Kenneth Jones, and Harold L. Korn, "The

Treatment of Inchoate Crimes in the Model Penal Code of the American Law Institute: Attempt, Solicitation, and Conspiracy," *Columbia Law Review* 61 (1961): 958–59.

14. "Developments in the Law," p. 924.

15. "Notes—Conspiracy," p. 876.

16. Wallace Mendelson, "Clandestine Speech and the First Amendment—A Reappraisal of the Dennis Case," *Michigan Law Review* 51 (1953): 553. See, also, Morris L. Ernst and Arthur Joel Katz, "Speech: Public and Private," *Columbia Law Review* 53 (1953): 620.

17. *U.S. v. Rabinowich*, 238 U.S. 78 (1915) at 88.

18. Phillip E. Johnson, "The Unnecessary Crime of Conspiracy," *California Law Review* 61 (1973): 1137.

19. David Filvaroff, "Conspiracy and the First Amendment," *University of Pennsylvania Law Review* 121 (1972): 195.

20. 341 U.S. at 510–11.

21. *The System of Freedom of Expression*, pp. 407–8.

22. *Illinois Revised Statutes*, chap. 38, sec. 8-4.

23. Curran, "Solicitation."

24. *Ibid.*, p. 504.

25. *Ibid.*, p. 578.

26. *The System of Freedom of Expression*, p. 407.

27. Filvaroff, "Conspiracy."

28. 245 U.S. 474 (1918).

29. 416 F.2d 165 (1st Cir. 1969).

30. 472 F.2d 340 (7th Cir. 1972), cert. denied 410 U.S. 970 (1973).

31. 416 F.2d at 186.

32. *U.S. v. Peraino*, no. CR-75-91 (W.D.Tenn. May 6, 1976), no. 78-5100 (6th Cir. August 4, 1978).

33. Filvaroff, "Conspiracy," pp. 200, 234–35.

34. "Notes—Conspiracy," p. 884.

35. *Ibid.*, p. 885.

36. Filvaroff, "Conspiracy," p. 235.

37. "Notes—Conspiracy," p. 880.

38. *Hyde v. U.S.* at 388.

39. Emerson, *The System of Freedom of Expression*, p. 407.

40. 416 F.2d at 169.

41. *Givhan v. Western Line Consolidated School District*, 439 U.S. 410 (1979) at 413.

42. This point is suggested by Filvaroff, "Conspiracy."

43. See Marvin Shaw, *Group Dynamics*, 2d ed. (New York: McGraw-Hill, 1976), pp. 58–65. See, also, Barry Collins and Harold Guetzkow, *A Social Psychology of Group Processes for Decision-Making* (New York: Wiley, 1964), pp. 13–55.

44. "The Conspiracy Dilemma: Prosecution of Group Crime or Prosecution of Individual Defendants," *Harvard Law Review* 62 (1948): 285.

45. *Harrison v. U.S.*, 7 F.2d 259 (2d Cir. 1925) at 263.

46. Al Katz, "A Psycho-Analytic Peek at Conspiracy," *Buffalo Law Review* 20 (1970): 239.

47. Johnson, "The Unnecessary Crime," p. 1188.

48. *Ibid.*
49. Filvaroff, "Conspiracy."
50. 18 U.S.C. sec. 2.

Chapter 14

1. *Hague v. C.I.O.,* 307 U.S. 498 (1939) at 515.
2. See Harry Kalven, Jr., "The Concept of the Public Forum: Cox v. Louisiana," in *The Supreme Court Review,* ed. Philip B. Kurland (Chicago: University of Chicago Press, 1965), pp. 12–21.
3. *Chicago Police Department v. Mosely,* 408 U.S. 92 (1972) at 96.
4. Amicus curiae brief submitted to the U.S. Supreme Court in *Hague v. C.I.O.,* as quoted in Chafee, *Free Speech,* p. 419.
5. Just such an argument was made, and accepted by a federal district court, in a case involving a state university regulation prohibiting the use of its buildings for religious worship. *Chess v. Widmar,* 480 F.Supp. 907 (W.D.Mo. 1979). However, the contention was rejected, and the district court's decision was overturned, by the U.S. Court of Appeals for the Eighth Circuit, 635 F.2d 1310 (8th Cir. 1980). That decision was awaiting review by the U.S. Supreme Court as this book went to press (*Widmar v. Vincent,* no. 80-689).
6. In the state university case to which reference was made in the previous note the district court judge alluded to the fact that the religious group in question sought to use the facilities on a regular basis. *Ibid.* at 915.
7. *Walz v. Tax Commission of New York,* 397 U.S. 664 (1970).
8. *Political Freedom,* p. 49.
9. This principle was recognized in the passage quoted earlier from *Hague v. C.I.O.,* and was reiterated in *Schneider v. State,* 308 U.S. 147 (1939), and in *Cox v. New Hampshire,* 312 U.S. 569 (1941), as well as in many other decisions since that time.
10. I borrow here from the modern insight of Marshall McLuhan that "the medium is the message." This concept has received some implicit recognition by the Supreme Court, most particularly in the majority opinion of Justice Harlan in *Cohen v. California.*
11. See, for example, *Cox v. New Hampshire.* Also see *Poulos v. New Hampshire,* 345 U.S. 15 (1971).
12. *Hynes v. Oradell,* 425 U.S. 610 (1976).
13. *Ibid.* at 623–28.
14. *Cox v. New Hampshire* at 577. The *Cox* decision upheld a parade permit ordinance under which a fee of $300 was charged.
15. *New York Times* (June 23, 1978).
16. *Collin v. O'Malley,* no. 76C2024 (N.D.Ill. June 22, 1978).
17. *Houston Peace Council v. Houston City Council,* 310 F.Supp. 457 (S.D. Texas 1970).
18. *International Society of Krishna Consciousness v. Eaves,* 601 F.2d 809 (5th Cir. 1979).
19. *Village of Schaumburg v. Citizens for a Better Environment,* 444 U.S. 620 (1980).
20. *Ibid.* at 632.

21. *National Socialist White Peoples Party v. Ringers,* 473 F.2d 1010 (4th Cir. 1973).

22. *Auerbach v. African American Teachers Association,* 356 F.Supp. 1046 (E.D.N.Y. 1973).

23. *Carlson v. City of Tallahassee,* 249 So.2d 866 (Fla. 1970), cert. denied 403 U.S. 910 (1971).

24. *Reynolds v. Tennessee,* 414 U.S. 1163 (1974).

25. *In Re Kay,* 464 P.2d 142 (Calif. 1970) at 147–48.

26. In *Adderley v. Florida* the U.S. Supreme Court, by a 5–4 margin, upheld a trespass conviction of a group of civil rights demonstrators who had disobeyed the sheriff's order to leave the grounds of a Tallahassee jail house.

27. In *Capitol Police Chief v. Jeanette Rankin Brigade,* 409 U.S. 972 (1972), the U.S. Supreme Court summarily affirmed a lower court ruling that a federal statute limiting parades and assemblies on the Capitol grounds was incompatible with the First Amendment.

28. In *Brown v. Louisiana,* 383 U.S. 131 (1966), the U.S. Supreme Court held that the silent presence in a public library of a group of blacks protesting the library's refusal to serve them because of their race was protected by the First Amendment.

29. In *Albany Welfare Rights Organization v. Wyman,* 493 F.2d 1319 (2d Cir. 1974), the right to talk with people and pass out leaflets in the waiting room of a welfare office was affirmed.

30. In *Lehman v. Shaker Heights,* discussed at greater length in Chapter 7 of this book, the U.S. Supreme Court ruled that a public transit agency could refuse to accept political advertisements for display in its vehicles even though it allowed commercial advertisements.

31. In *Greer v. Spock,* 424 U.S. 828 (1976), the U.S. Supreme Court held that military installations need not, and perhaps should not, be regarded as public forums available for use by partisan political speakers.

32. "Fora Americana: Speech in Public Places," in *The Supreme Court Review,* ed. Philip B. Kurland (Chicago: University of Chicago Press, 1974), pp. 233–80.

33. 408 U.S. 104 (1972) at 116.

34. "Fora Americana," p. 251.

35. *Ibid.,* pp. 258–61.

36. Geoffrey R. Stone, "Restrictions of Speech Because of its Content: The Peculiar Case of Subject-Matter Restrictions," *University of Chicago Law Review* 46 (1978), p. 81, has raised the question as to whether discrimination based on subject matter rather than viewpoint, such as that between political and commercial advertisements approved in *Lehman v. Shaker Heights,* that between sexually oriented and other kinds of advertising approved in *Rowan v. U.S. Post Office Department,* or that between partisan political speakers and other persons addressing public issues approved in *Greer v. Spock* can properly be viewed as content-neutral. He argues, and I agree, that it should not be so viewed.

37. *Bonner-Lyons v. School Committee of City of Boston,* 480 F.2d 442 (1st Cir. 1973).

38. See the discussion in Chapter 7 of the Federal Anti-Pandering Act of 1967, the Goldwater Amendment to the Postal Reorganization Act of 1970, and *Rowan v. U.S. Post Office Department.*

39. "Balanced News: A View from the Post Office," *Civil Liberties Review* (January–February 1979), pp. 71–74. For a more detailed treatment of this subject, see Dorothy Ganfield Fowler, *Unavailable: Congress and the Post Office* (Athens: University of Georgia Press, 1977).

40. In *Epperson v. Arkansas*, 393 U.S. 97 (1968), Arkansas' prohibition against the teaching of evolution in public schools and state universities was struck down as a violation of the separation of church and state. In *Engel v. Vitale*, 370 U.S. 421 (1962), state-sponsored prayers in the public schools of the State of New York were invalidated on the same grounds.

41. A case in point was that of Ronald Kunkle, fired by the school board of Eugene, Oregon, on December 18, 1967, allegedly for voicing "anti-Vietnam War opinions to his fifth grade class." *National Observer* (January 25, 1967).

42. This was the final outcome of a bitter dispute that raged in Kanawha County, West Virginia, for over four years. *New York Times* (December 3, 1978).

43. In the spring of 1963 the principle of Harlem High School in a suburb of Rockford, Illinois, prohibited performances of "Inherit the Wind" as a junior class play. *Chicago Tribune* (March 31, 1963). The drama teacher in charge of the production, Ruth Ann Johnston, was later fired from her job after proceeding with the show at another theater in the community. *Chicago Daily News* (June 8, 1963).

44. Such an incident gave rise to litigation in Chelsea, Massachusetts, where a federal district court found the school board in violation of the First Amendment for removal of a book from the school library. *Right to Read Defense Committee of Chelsea v. School Committee of Chelsea*, 454 F.Supp. 703 (D.Mass. 1978).

45. For example, the U.S. Supreme Court, in *Pickering v. Board of Education*, 391 U.S. 563 (1963), invalidated the dismissal of a Lockport, Illinois, school-teacher because he had written a letter to the local newspaper which was critical of the school's handling of its finances.

46. A U.S. circuit court of appeals, in *Minarcini v. Strongsville School District*, 541 F.2d 577 (6th Cir. 1976), held that a school board had no right to remove from the school library a book which had been duly acquired, but an opposite conclusion on the same issue was reached in another circuit in *Presidents Council District 25 v. Community School Board No. 25*, 457 F.2d 289 (2d Cir. 1972).

47. For example, it has been held that a student newspaper had a First Amendment right to publish an article on birth control which school officials had sought to prohibit. *Gambino v. Fairfax City School Board*, 564 F.2d 157 (4th Cir. 1977).

48. *New York Times* (May 13, 1979).

49. *New York Times* (October 16, 1977).

50. *Chicago Sun-Times* (May 28, 1979).

51. *Ibid.*

52. *Ibid.*

53. *Ibid.*

54. Sec. 396.

55. Sec. 399(g) (1) (a).

56. *New York Times*, (May 13, 1979).

57. *Ibid.*

58. *Ibid.*

59. *Ibid.*

60. *New York Times* (October 16, 1977).

61. The Metropolitan Opera, for example, received grants from the National Endowment for the Arts totaling $550,000, or about 2.2 percent of its total expenditures in 1974, whereas in 1979 it received $700,000, or about 1.8 percent of its costs. The American Council of Learned Societies, representing forty-three national scholarly groups which have traditionally been the principal recipients of humanities endowment grants, received $2 million in 1978 as against $2.7 million in 1976. *New York Times* (May 13, 1979).

62. *Advocates for the Arts v. Thomson,* 532 F.2d 792 (1st Cir. 1976), cert. denied 429 U.S. 894 (1976).

63. *Chicago Tribune* (November 25, 1978).

64. Anne Prichard, "Government Funding of the Arts," unpublished memorandum to the Free Speech/Association Committee and Communications Media Committee of the American Civil Liberties Union, January 11, 1977, p. 1.

65. 326 U.S. 501 (1946).

66. *Ibid.* at 506–7.

67. *Amalgamated Food Employees v. Logan Valley Plaza,* 391 U.S. 308 (1968).

68. *Ibid.* at 330–31.

69. *Lloyd Corp. v. Tanner,* 407 U.S. 551 (1972).

70. *Hudgens v. N.L.R.B.*

71. *Robins v. Pruneyard Shopping Center,* 592 P.2d 341 (Calif. 1979).

72. *Pruneyard Shopping Center v. Robins,* 100 S.Ct. 2035 (1980) at 2040.

73. *Ibid.* at 2042.

74. *Ibid.* at 2050.

75. *Ibid.* at 2045–46 quoting from his own dissent in *Hudgens v. N.L.R.B.* at 542.

76. *Petersen v. Talisman Sugar Corp.,* 478 F.2d 73 (5th Cir. 1973).

77. *Illinois Migrant Council v. Campbell Soup Co.,* 574 F.2d 374 (7th Cir. 1978).

78. As early as 1929, in its third annual report, the Federal Radio Commission, predecessor agency of the FCC, had indicated its view that broadcasters had a moral obligation to be fair in their handling of public issues. That moral obligation was converted to a legal requirement by the FCC in a 1941 decision *In the Matter of the Mayflower Broadcasting Co.,* 8 F.C.C. 333 (1941).

79. 47 C.F.R. sec. 73.123 (1973).

80. *Red Lion Broadcasting Co. v. F.C.C.,* 395 U.S. 367 (1969).

81. *Ibid.* at 389–90.

82. 412 U.S. 94 (1973).

83. *Ibid.* at 110–13.

84. *Ibid.* at 148.

85. *Ibid.* at 188–96.

86. 59 F.C.C.2d 294 (1976).

87. *F.C.C. v. Midwest Video Corp.,* 440 U.S. 689 (1979).

88. *Ibid.* at 709.

89. *Harvard Law Review* 80 (1967): 1641.

90. *Ibid.,* p. 1667.

91. *Associates and Aldrich Co. v. Times Mirror Co.,* 440 F.2d 133 (9th Cir. 1971).

92. *Amalgamated Clothing Workers v. Chicago Tribune*, 435 F.2d 470 (7th Cir. 1970), cert. denied 402 U.S. 973 (1971).

93. *New York Times* (May 11, 1974).

94. *Press Censorship Newsletter* (September–October 1976), p. 122.

95. *Tornillo v. Miami Herald Publishing Co.*, 287 So.2d 78 (Fla. 1973) at 82.

96. 418 U.S. at 247–58.

97. In addition to the *Harvard Law Review* article already cited, Barron has developed his position further in "An Emerging Right of Access to the Media," *George Washington Law Review* 37 (1969): 487; and in a book entitled *Freedom of the Press for Whom?* (Bloomington: University of Indiana Press, 1973).

98. This contrasts with a position taken by Lee C. Bollinger, Jr., "Freedom of the Press and Public Access: Toward a Theory of Partial Regulation of the Mass Media," *Michigan Law Review* 75 (1976): 1, in which he urges that, although the rationale which has been offered for the differential treatment of the electronic and print media is seriously flawed, we should nonetheless retain this scheme of "partial regulation," because it provides a balance in which the regulated and unregulated sectors serve as checks on one another.

99. 412 U.S. at 199–200.

100. 395 U.S. at 390.

Chapter 15

1. *Minersville School District v. Gobitis*, 310 U.S. 586 (1940).

2. *West Virginia Board of Education v. Barnette*.

3. *Ibid.* at 634.

4. *Ibid.*

5. For a summary of this research, see Chester Inko, *Theories of Attitude Change* (New York: Appleton-Century-Crofts, 1967), chap. 10, pp. 206–84.

6. *Ibid.*, pp. 223–52.

7. *Ibid.*

8. *American Communications Association v. Douds*, 339 U.S. 382 (1950).

9. 73 Stat. 525 (1959).

10. In *Gerende v. Board of Supervisors of Elections of Baltimore*, 341 U.S. 56 (1951), the Supreme Court upheld a provision of Maryland's Ober law which required candidates for public office to swear that they were not subversive persons in order to secure a place on the ballot. In *Garner v. Board of Public Works of Los Angeles*, 341 U.S. 716 (1951), an ordinance was affirmed requiring all city employees to sign affidavits stating whether they were or ever had been members of the Communist Party and to take an oath that they did not advocate the violent overthrow of the government or belong to any organization which did.

11. *Cramp v. Board of Public Instruction*, 368 U.S. 278 (1961).

12. *Baggett v. Bullitt*, 377 U.S. 360 (1964).

13. *Elfbrandt v. Russell*, 384 U.S. 11 (1966).

14. *Keyeshian v. Board of Regents of the University of the State of New York*, 385 U.S. 589 (1967).

15. *Whitehill v. Elkins*, 389 U.S. 54 (1967).

16. *Knight v. Board of Regents*, 269 F.Supp. 399 (S.D.N.Y. 1967), affirmed 390 U.S. 36 (1968); *Hosack v. Smiley*, 276 F.Supp. 876 (D.Colo. 1967), affirmed 390

U.S. 74 (1968); *Ohlson v. Phillips,* 304 F.Supp. 1152 (D.Colo. 1969), affirmed 397 U.S. 317 (1970); and *Biklen v. Board of Education,* 333 F.Supp. 902 (S.D.N.Y. 1971), affirmed 406 U.S. 95 (1972).

17. 405 U.S. 676 (1972).

18. *Ibid.* at 680.

19. *Ibid.* at 681–82.

20. *Ibid.* at 683–84.

21. *Ibid.* at 689.

22. *Ibid.* at 696–98.

23. *Communist Party of Indiana v. Whitcomb,* 414 U.S. 441 (1974).

24. Surprisingly, because the plaintiff in the case and the federal district court which granted the injunction he sought against the state had taken the position that placing the tape over the slogan was an act of nonverbal communication protected by the First Amendment. The Supreme Court bypassed that line of argument and based its decision, instead, on the right-to-silence premise. *Wooley v. Maynard,* 430 .U.S. 705 (1977).

25. *Ibid.* at 714–15.

26. This last phrase is a reference to the Supreme Court's dismissal of an appeal from a decision of the Florida Supreme Court upholding an affirmative oath as a prerequisite of registering to vote. *Fields v. Askew,* 279 So.2d 822 (Fla. 1973), appeal dismissed 414 U.S. 1148 (1974).

27. *Watkins v. U.S.,* 354 U.S. 178 (1957).

28. *Sweezy v. New Hampshire,* 354 U.S. 234 (1957).

29. *Watkins v. U.S.* at 188–97.

30. *Barenblatt v. U.S.; Uphaus v. Wyman,* 369 U.S. 72 (1959).

31. *Barenblatt v. U.S.* at 126–34.

32. *Ibid.* at 144.

33. *Wilkinson v. U.S.,* 365 U.S. 399 (1961); *Braden v. U.S.,* 365 U.S. 431 (1961).

34. *Konigsberg v. California,* 366 U.S. 36 (1961).

35. *New York ex. rel. Bryant v. Zimmerman,* 278 U.S. 63 (1928).

36. *N.A.A.C.P. v. Alabama,* 357 U.S. 449 (1958); *Bates v. Little Rock,* 361 U.S. 516 (1960).

37. *Shelton v. Tucker,* 364 U.S. 479 (1961).

38. *Gibson v. Florida Legislative Investigating Committee,* 372 U.S. 539 (1963).

39. 408 U.S. 665 (1974).

40. *Ibid.* at 712.

41. *Ibid.* at 725.

42. *Lewis Publishing Co. v. Morgan,* 229 U.S. 288 (1913), upholding 39 U.S.C. sec. 4369.

43. *Burroughs and Cannon v. U.S.,* 290 U.S. 534 (1934).

44. 22 U.S.C. sec. 611–621.

45. *Viereck v. U.S.,* 318 U.S. 236 (1943).

46. *Ibid.* at 251.

47. 2 U.S.C. sec. 267.

48. *U.S. v. Harriss,* 347 U.S. 612 (1954).

49. *Ibid.* at 625–26.

50. 50 U.S.C. sec. 781.

51. *Communist Party v. U.S.*, 331 F.2d 807 (D.C.Cir. 1963), cert. denied 377 U.S. 968 (1964); *Albertson v. S.A.C.B.*, 382 U.S. 70 (1965); *Communist Party v. U.S.*, 384 F.2d 957 (D.C.Cir. 1967).
52. *Communist Party v. S.A.C.B.*, 367 U.S. 1 (1961).
53. See Emerson, *The System of Freedom of Expression*, pp. 141–42.
54. Originally 18 U.S.C. sec. 612, this statute was repealed by Congress in May 1976 and replaced simultaneously by an amendment to the Federal Election Campaign Act of 1971 which incorporated essentially the same requirement. 2 U.S.C. 441(d).
55. See *Talley v. California*, 362 U.S. 60 (1960) at 70, n. 2.
56. *U.S. v. Scott*, 195 F.Supp. 440 (D.N.D. 1961).
57. *Cannon v. Justice Court*, 393 P.2d 428 (Calif. 1964); *State v. Babst*, 135 N.E. 525 (Ohio 1922).
58. *People v. Duryea*, 351 N.Y.S.2d 978 (N.Y. 1974), affirmed 354 N.Y.S.2d 129 (N.Y. 1974); *Commonwealth v. Dennis*, 329 N.E.2d 706 (Mass. 1975); *Hill v. Printing Industries*, 382 F.Supp. 801 (S.D.Tex. 1974).
59. 362 U.S. at 60.
60. *Ibid.* at 64–65.
61. *Ibid.* at 70.
62. *Buckley v. Valeo*, 424 U.S. 1 (1976).
63. *Ibid.* at 64.
64. *Ibid.* at 66–67.
65. *Ibid.* at 68.
66. *Ibid.* at 74. The Socialist Workers Party filed suit in 1974 to gain an exemption of this kind. After extended litigation, the U.S. District Court for the District of Columbia in 1979 approved a consent decree, agreed to by the defendants (the Federal Election Commission and Common Cause), exempting the party from disclosure at least through the 1984 election. *New York Times* (January 11, 1979).
67. 424 U.S. at 80.
68. *Ibid.* at 237. Chief Justice Burger's reference to $10 contributions had to do with a provision of the law requiring candidates and political committees to keep records of the names and addresses of all persons donating $10 and over, even though only those over $100 had to be reported and disclosed.
69. *Huntley v. Public Utility Commission*, 442 P.2d 685 (Calif. 1968); *Matter of Figari v. New York Telephone Co.*, 303 N.Y.S.2d 245 (N.Y. 1969).
70. 442 P.2d at 689.
71. *Press Censorship Newsletter* (September–October 1976), p. 122.
72. *Ibid.*
73. 21 U.S.C. sec. 301.
74. 15 U.S.C. sec. 1601.
75. *The Rhetoric*, trans. Lane Cooper (New York and London: Appleton-Century, 1932), p. 9.
76. James L. Fly, "Full Disclosure: Public Safeguard," *Nation* (January 29, 1949), p. 122.
77. Bruce L. Smith, "Democratic Control of Propaganda through Registration and Disclosure," *Public Opinion Quarterly* 6 (1942): 27.

78. Arthur Garfield Hays, "Full Disclosure: Dangerous Precedent," *Nation* (January 29, 1949), p. 122.

79. "Disclosure as a Legislative Device," *Harvard Law Review* 76 (1963): 1275.

80. "The Constitutional Right to Anonymity: Free Speech, Disclosure and the Devil," *Yale Law Journal* 70 (1961): 1085.

81. "Full Disclosure," pp. 121–22.

82. "The Constitutional Right to Anonymity," p. 1109.

83. *Ibid.*, p. 1112.

84. *Buckley v. Valeo* at 67.

85. *Ibid.* at 236–39.

86. *Ibid.* at 70.

87. As one law review writer has succinctly put it, "If Congress succumbs to vigorous lobbying, that is not the fault of the lobbyist." David E. Landau, "Public Disclosure of Lobbying: Congress and Associational Privacy after *Buckley v. Valeo*," *Howard Law Journal* 22 (1979): 52.

88. 22 U.S.C. sec. 611.

89. 22 U.S.C. sec. 613.

90. Furthermore, it should be noted that a domestic organization which supports the goals of a foreign political party that is not in power, such as the Irish Republican Army, and which sends money *to* that party rather than receiving money *from* it, is not only required to register as a foreign agent if it works under the direction or control of the foreign principal but can also be required to disclose the names of its American members and contributors. *Attorney General v. Northern Ireland Aid Committee,* 346 F.Supp. 1384 (S.D.N.Y. 1972), affirmed without opinion, 465 F.2d 1405 (2d Cir. 1972).

91. U.S. Congress, Senate, Committee on Foreign Relations, *The Foreign Agents Registration Act.* Committee print S382-29 prepared by the Congressional Research Service, August 1977, p. 17.

92. *Ibid.*, p. 28.

93. *Ibid.*, p. 5.

94. *Ibid.*, p. 13.

Chapter 16

1. Gaillard Hunt, ed., *Writings of James Madison* (New York: Putnam's, 1900–10), 9:103, letter to W. T. Barry, August 4, 1822.

2. *Richmond Newspapers v. Virginia* at 2833.

3. The presumption was changed by Congress as a result of the country's experience with the Nixon presidency. The first step was taken in 1974 with passage of the Presidential Recordings and Materials Preservation Act, PL 93-526, designed to insure that all tape recordings of conversations involving Nixon and his aides in the White House or the President's Office in the Executive Office Building, as well as other papers and documents, would be preserved under the control of the archivist of the United States. This was followed by the passage of broader legislation applying to all presidents—the Presidential Records Act of 1978, PL 95-591, which flatly states, "The United States shall reserve and retain complete ownership, possession and control of presidential records." 44 U.S.C.

sec. 2202. The act further provides, "The Archivist shall have the affirmative duty to make such records available to the public as rapidly and completely as possible consistent with the provisions of this Act." 44 U.S.C. sec. 2203(f) (1). Vice-presidential records were made subject to the same rules as those of presidents. 44 U.S.C. sec. 2207.

4. Not included here is the secrecy that may sometimes be necessary to protect a fair trial, since that poses unique problems already discussed in Chapter 6.

5. 5 U.S.C. sec. 552.

6. 5 U.S.C. sec. 552(b) (4).

7. 5 U.S.C. sec. 552(b) (6).

8. 5 U.S.C. sec. 552(a).

9. Alan Sussman, "Sealed Adoption Records v. the Adoptee's Right to Know the Identity of His Birth Parents," *Children's Rights Report*, Juvenile Rights Project, American Civil Liberties Union Foundation (February 1979), p. 2.

10. This was the headline for a story on this subject appearing in the *Washington Post* (July 16, 1972). Similar stories appeared in the *New York Daily News* (July 28, 1975: "The Adopted: They Fight for the Right to Find Their True Parents"), and in the *New York Times* (March 1, 1975: "Yearning").

11. Reuben Panor, Annette Baran, and Arthur Sorosky, "Birth Parents Who Relinquish Babies for Adoption Revisited," *Family Process* 17 (1978): 329.

12. Arthur Sorosky, Annette Baran, and Reuben Panor, *The Adoption Triangle* (Garden City, N.Y.: Anchor, 1978), pp. 195–96.

13. *Zemel v. Rusk*, 381 U.S. 1 (1965) at 17.

14. *Smith v. Daily Mail Publishing Co.*, 443 U.S. 97 (1979). The same conclusion was reached by the Court in a case involving disclosure by a Virginia newspaper of the name of the judge under investigation by a state judicial review commission whose proceedings were, by law, supposed to be confidential. The Court held that the First Amendment prohibits the criminal punishment of persons who are not parties to the commission proceedings for disclosing truthful and legally obtained information. The Court, however, made clear that it was not addressing the possible punishment of persons who divulge information that has been secured by illegal means or who have an obligation, by virtue of their participation in the proceedings or their employment by the commission, to maintain secrecy. *Landmark Communications v. Virginia*, 435 U.S. 829 (1978).

15. *Garrett v. Estelle*, 556 F.2d 1274 (5th Cir. 1977), cert. denied 438 U.S. 914 (1978).

16. *Minnesota Medical Association v. Minnesota*, no. 423466 (Minn. Dist.Ct., Ramsey Co., December 11, 1977).

17. *News Media and the Law* (July 1978), p. 32.

18. Robert Luce, *Congress: An Explanation* (Cambridge: Harvard University Press, 1926), pp. 12–13.

19. *Richmond Newspapers v. Virginia* at 2825.

20. Susan T. Stephanson, "Government in the Sunshine Act: Opening Federal Agency Meetings," *American University Law Review* 26 (1976): 154, n. 3.

21. Norman Dorsen, Paul Bender, and Burt Neuborne, *Emerson, Haber and Dorsen's Political and Civil Rights in the United States*, 4th ed. (Boston: Little, Brown, 1976), 1:388–89.

22. Francis E. Rourke, *Secrecy and Publicity* (Baltimore: Johns Hopkins Press, 1966), p. 65.

23. *Ibid.*, pp. 66–68.

24. *Ibid.*, p. 66.

25. Stephen Gard, "Executive Privilege: A Rhyme without a Reason," *Georgia Law Review* 8 (1974): 811.

26. Raoul Berger, *Executive Privilege: A Constitutional Myth* (Cambridge: Harvard University Press, 1974), pp. vii, 1–2.

27. *Ibid.*

28. *U.S. v. Nixon*, 418 U.S. 683 (1974).

29. *Ibid.* at 705–6.

30. "National Security and the Public's Right to Know: A New Role for the Courts under the Freedom of Information Act," *University of Pennsylvania Law Review* 123 (1975): 1441.

31. *Secrecy*, p. 59.

32. *Ibid.*, pp. 57–58.

33. *Ibid.*, p. 60.

34. *Ibid.*, p. 57.

35. PL 92-463, 86 Stat. 770.

36. PL 94-409, 90 Stat. 1241, 5 U.S.C. sec. 552(b).

37. *The New Freedom* (New York and Garden City, N.Y.: Doubleday Page, 1913), p. 76.

38. See, for example, Rourke's discussion of this issue in *Secrecy*, pp. 21–22, and his reference to Max Weber's studies of the matter.

39. Elias Clark, "Holding Government Accountable: The Amended FOIA," *Yale Law Journal* 84 (1975): 747.

40. L. Michael Hager, "The Constitution, the Courts and the Cover-Up: Reflections on *U.S. v. Nixon*," *Oklahoma Law Review* 29 (1976): 606.

41. *1976 Policy Guide of the American Civil Liberties Union*, p. 22.

42. *Federal Open Market Committee of the Federal Reserve System v. Merrill*, 443 U.S. 340 (1979) at 344–47.

43. *Ibid.* at 363.

44. *Ibid.* at 364–67.

45. *Rovairo v. U.S.*, 353 U.S. 53 (1957) at 60–61.

46. *Pell v. Procunier*, 417 U.S. 817 (1974) at 830–32.

47. *Ibid.* at 831.

48. *Ibid.* at 834.

49. *Saxbe v. Washington Post*, 417 U.S. 843 (1974) at 862–68.

50. *Ibid.* at 875.

51. *Press Censorship Newsletter* (September–October 1976), p. 92.

52. *Houchins v. KQED*, 438 U.S. 1 (1978).

53. *Ibid.* at 11.

54. *Ibid.* at 9–15.

55. *Ibid.* at 16.

56. *Ibid.*

57. *Ibid.* at 16–17.

58. *Ibid.* at 30–32.

59. *Ibid.* at 39.

60. Rourke, *Secrecy,* pp. 63, 88. According to Rourke, the leading Supreme Court case on the subject is *Totten v. U.S.,* 92 U.S. 105 (1876). He also refers to *U.S. v. Haugen,* 58 F.Supp. 436 (1944), which held, at 438, "The right of the army to refuse to disclose confidential information, the secrecy of which it deems necessary to national defense, is indisputable."

61. Dorsen, Bender, and Neuborne, *Political and Civil Rights,* 1:345.

62. Executive order no. 8381, 3 C.F.R. 634 (1940).

63. Executive order no. 10290, 3 C.F.R. 789 (1951).

64. *Secrecy,* pp. 75–76.

65. A 1971 survey by the House Subcommittee on Government Information had estimated that some 55,000 persons were authorized to classify material under the Eisenhower directive. See Dorsen, Bender, and Neuborne, *Political and Civil Rights,* 1:346.

66. *Ibid.*

67. *Ibid.,* p. 347.

68. *Ibid.*

69. *Ibid.*

70. "Making Enemies: The Pike Committee's Struggle to Get the Facts," *Washington Monthly* (July–August 1976), pp. 42–47.

71. David Ignatius, "Dan Schorr: The Secret Sharer," *Washington Monthly* (April 1976), p. 9.

72. *Ibid.,* pp. 9–11.

73. *New York Times* (January 30, 1976).

74. *New York Times v. U.S.,* 403 U.S. 713 (1971) at 729.

75. *Halperin v. Kissinger,* 434 F.Supp. 1193 (D.D.C. 1977).

76. Morton Halperin and Daniel N. Hoffman, *Top Secret: National Security and the Right to Know* (Washington, D.C.: New Republic Books, 1977), p. 73.

77. *Ibid.,* p. 55.

78. *Ibid.,* p. 57.

79. *Ibid.,* pp. 58–65.

80. *Ibid.,* p. 58.

81. *Ibid.,* pp. 66–67.

82. *Ibid.,* p. 68.

83. *Ibid.,* pp. 75–76.

84. *Ibid.,* p. 85.

85. Some legal scholars have argued that it is a mistake for discussions of the prior-restraint issue to focus, as they so often do, on court injunctions, and to ignore the fact that other kinds of government actions—such as indiscriminate post facto prosecutions of speech activities—can have chilling effects that are, for all practical purposes, akin to prior restraints. One writer would define a prior restraint as "[a]ny governmental action that significantly curtails the dissemination of information and ideas prior to an adequate determination that the materials are unprotected by the First Amendment." Thomas R. Litwack, "The Doctrine of Prior Restraint," *Harvard Civil Rights-Civil Liberties Law Review* 12 (1977): 522. Two other authors, writing in the same vein, have suggested that to properly understand the prior-restraint problem one must look not at the *form* of

the restraint—that is, whether it occurs before or after the communication takes place—but at its *substance*—that is, whether it, in fact, operates to chill or inhibit speech activities. See Stephen R. Barnett, "The Puzzle of Prior Restraint," *Stanford Law Review* 29 (1977): 539; and William P. Murphy, "The Prior Restraint Doctrine and the Supreme Court: A Reevaluation," *Notre Dame Lawyer* 51 (1976): 898.

86. This absolutist view regarding prior restraints has looked to a statement from Blackstone for its original authority. In his *Commentaries* (William Carey Jones, ed. [San Francisco: Bancroft-Whitney, 1915–16], 6:151), Blackstone had written in 1769 that "the liberty of the press . . . consists in laying no previous restraints upon publication, and not in freedom from censure for criminal matters when published." The U.S. Supreme Court, in a 1907 opinion, had seemed to be sharing the Blackstone position when it said of the provisions of the First Amendment that "the main purpose of such constitutional provisions is 'to prevent all such *previous restraints* upon publications as had been practiced by other governments,' and they do not prevent the subsequent punishment of such as may be deemed contrary to the public welfare." *Patterson v. Colorado* at 462.

87. *Near v. Minnesota* at 716.

88. *Bantam Books v. Sullivan* at 70.

89. *Organization for a Better Austin v. Keefe*, 402 U.S. 415 (1971) at 419.

90. *New York Times v. U.S.* at 714–24.

91. *Ibid.* at 725–27.

92. *Ibid.* at 730.

93. *Ibid.* at 740–48.

94. Federal District Court Judge Robert Warren issued a preliminary injunction in Milwaukee, Wisconsin, on March 26, 1979, against publication of an article which the *Progressive* magazine had planned to include in its May 1979 issue. *U.S. v. The Progressive*, 467 F.Supp. 990 (W.D.Wisc. 1979). Six months later, while an appeal of this decision was pending in the U.S. Court of Appeals for the Seventh Circuit the government dropped the case. This timetable contrasts sharply with *New York Times v. U.S.*, where a federal district court judge in New York, having first issued a temporary restraining order which was in effect for four days, then rejected the government's request for an injunction. He agreed, however, to a stay of his decision pending appeal. The U.S. Court of Appeals, in reversing the district court decision and remanding the case for further consideration, continued the stay. That restraint remained in effect until the U.S. Supreme Court's reversal of the appellate court ruling. From the very beginning to the very end of these proceedings, a total of only fifteen days, from June 15 to June 30, 1971, had transpired.

95. Erwin Knoll, "Born Secret," *Progressive* (May 1979), pp. 12–14.

96. *Ibid.*, pp. 13–14.

97. *Ibid.*, pp. 14–16.

98. 42 U.S.C. sec. 2014(y).

99. 42 U.S.C. sec. 2274.

100. 42 U.S.C. sec. 2280.

101. Knoll, "Born Secret," pp. 15–16.

102. "United States v. The Progressive," *Progressive* (May 1979), p. 36.

103. *Ibid.*, pp. 36–38.

477 Notes to Pages 401–12

104. *Ibid.*, pp. 38–40.
105. *Ibid.*, pp. 36–37.
106. *Ibid.*, pp. 38–39.
107. Joint Brief of Appellants Knoll, Day, and Morland in *U.S. v. The Progressive*, no. 79-1429, U.S. Court of Appeals for the Seventh Circuit, pp. 13, 15, 23–25, 26–28, 29–34.
108. *New York Times* (September 18, 1979). Two weeks later the U.S. Court of Appeals for the Seventh Circuit did dismiss the case against the *Progressive*, and the Morland article was published in the November issue of the magazine. 610 F.2d 819 (7th Cir. 1979).
109. *New York Times* (September 18, 1979).
110. 17 U.S.C. sec. 101(a).
111. Chafee, *Free Speech*, p. 10.
112. 388 U.S. 307 (1967).
113. *Ibid.* at 321.
114. *Shuttlesworth v. Birmingham*, 394 U.S. 147 (1969).
115. The principle that persons who violate an injunction may not defend themselves against a contempt conviction by a collateral attack on the constitutional validity of the court's order is known as the "collateral bar rule." Historically this rule was invoked quite frequently in both federal and state courts to uphold contempt convictions for the violation of antistrike and antidemonstration injunctions, although used less commonly in cases where the press had defied judicial gag orders. See Richard Harris, "Gag Orders on the Press: A Due Process Defense to Contempt Citations," *Hastings Constitutional Law Quarterly* 4 (1977): 187, who also notes, "The function of the collateral bar rule is to discourage disobedience" (p. 203). See, also, Richard F. Watt, "The Divine Right of Government by Judiciary," *University of Chicago Law Review* 14 (1947): 409, for a discussion of the collateral bar rule as it was used (or misused, according to Watt) in a famous contempt conviction for a strike called by John L. Lewis and the United Mine Workers Union.
116. 388 U.S. at 327, 334.
117. *Ibid.* at 338.
118. *Ibid.* at 338, 345, 346, 349.
119. It should be noted here that a "number of states reject the [collateral bar] rule in free speech cases." Douglas Rendelman, "Free Press and Fair Trial: Review of Silence Orders," *North Carolina Law Review* 52 (1973): 148–55. The California Supreme Court, for example, discarded the rule for that state over a decade ago in *In re Berry*, 436 P.2d 273 (Calif. 1968) at 280.

Chapter 17

1. *New York Times* (August 6, 1978).
2. Rourke, *Secrecy*, pp. 9, 183–87; James L. McCamy, *Government Publicity* (Chicago: University of Chicago Press, 1939), pp. 6–15.
3. Newton Minow, John Bartlow Martin, and Lee M. Mitchell, *Presidential Television* (New York: Basic, 1973).
4. *Ibid.*, pp. 31, 63.
5. *New York Times* (April 19, 1979).

6. *Chicago Sun-Times* (January 28, 1979).

7. *Ibid.*

8. Rourke, *Secrecy*, p. 5.

9. *Ibid.*, pp. 5–6. Also, for a full discussion of this episode and many other instances of government deception, see David Wise, *The Politics of Lying* (New York: Random House, 1973).

10. *Chicago Tribune* (December 5, 1978).

11. *Mountain States Legal Foundation v. Denver School District*, 459 F.Supp. 357 (D. Colo. 1978).

12. *Ibid.* at 359–61.

13. 5 U.S.C. sec. 7324(a) (2).

14. See *Broadrick v. Oklahoma*, 413 U.S. 601 (1973).

15. *United Public Workers v. Mitchell*, 330 U.S. 75 (1947); *U.S. Civil Service Commission v. National Association of Letter Carriers*, 413 U.S. 548 (1973); *Broadrick v. Oklahoma*.

16. *U.S. Civil Service Commission v. National Association of Letter Carriers* at 600.

17. *Elrod v. Burns*, 427 U.S. 347 (1976); *Branti v. Finkel* 445 U.S. 507 (1980).

18. *Shakman v. Democratic Organization of Cook County*, 481 F.Supp. 1315 (N.D.Ill. 1979).

19. *Ibid.*

20. *Secrecy*, p. 130.

21. *Ibid.*, pp. 130–34.

22. *Ibid.*, pp. 173–74.

23. Article I, section 6. The U.S. Supreme Court, in *Hutchinson v. Proxmire*, 443 U.S. 111 (1979) has said that the "Speech and Debate" Clause applies only to activities which are integral to the deliberative processes of Congress itself (such as committee hearings and floor debates) and not to newsletters, press releases, or the republication of speeches originally delivered on the floor.

24. *Spalding v. Vilas*, 161 U.S. 483 (1896).

25. *Barr v. Matteo*, 360 U.S. 564 (1959). The Court, in this decision at 571, offered the rationale that "officials of government should be free to exercise their duties unembarrassed by the fear of damage suits . . . suits which would consume time and energies which would otherwise be devoted to governmental service and the threat of which might appreciably inhibit the fearless, vigorous, and effective administration of policies of government."

26. *Chicago Daily News* (May 28, 1976).

27. *Blair v. Walker*, 349 N.E.2d 385 (Ill. 1976).

28. *Ibid.* at 389.

29. *New York Times* (October 10, 1979).

30. *Chicago Tribune* (October 24, 1979).

31. *Ibid.*

32. *Ibid.*

33. *Presidential Television*, p. 160.

Chapter 18

1. J. G. de Roulhac Hamilton, ed., *The Best Letters of Thomas Jefferson* (Boston: Houghton Mifflin, 1926), p. 85, letter to Philip Mazzei, April 24, 1796.

Addendum

As indicated in the Foreword, new court decisions will sometimes require the modification of comments that have been made in this book. Three such rulings were handed down by the U.S. Supreme Court at the end of its 1980–81 term, after the preceding pages were already in press but while there was still time to add this postscript.

In the first of these, *Heffron v. International Society of Krishna Consciousness,* the Court upheld the authority of state fair officials to confine the distribution and sale of literature and the solicitation of funds by the Hare Krishna and all others to designated booths, rather than allowing free rein of the entire fair grounds for these purposes. The Court was unanimous in finding the restriction on monetary transactions in such crowded areas to be a reasonable time and place regulation of First Amendment activity, so long as it applied equally to everyone, as it did in this instance. Four of the justices, however, dissented as to the restriction on the distribution of *free* literature, believing that such conduct posed no greater problem to the flow of pedestrian traffic than oral exchanges, which were, of course, allowed to anyone walking through the fair grounds.

The rationale of this decision would seem to apply to the comparable limitations that have been imposed in airport terminal buildings, contrary to the suggestion on page 304 that a shadow may have been cast over such regulations by *Village of Schaumburg v. Citizens for a Better Environment* in 1980, where the majority opinion noted that the solicitation of financial support is an integral part of the promotion of any cause. Although continuing to acknowledge that a group's fund raising is as much a First Amendment activity as its speech making, the Court has apparently answered to its own satisfaction what I described as the empirical question of whether money transactions interfere with the flow of pedestrians in confined areas more than verbal exchanges. It has concluded that they do, thus warranting a greater degree of regulation when the state so chooses. If the Court is right in this, then the four partial dissenters have offered a more vigorous, and hence preferable,

First Amendment solution to this problem than the one I had proposed of confining both monetary and nonmonetary solicitations to less congested locations. They would restrict only the fund-raising activities and leave all freely offered oral and written advocacy unrestrained.

The second decision, in *U.S. Postal Service v. Council of Greenburgh Civic Associations,* overturned the lower court finding discussed on pages 158–60, that the federal statute prohibiting the deposit of unstamped material in individual mailboxes is an impermissible burden on the exercise of First Amendment rights. The Supreme Court's majority was more sympathetic to District Court Judge Conner's initial dismissal of the case than to the revision of his views which had been prompted by the U.S. Circuit Court of Appeals. Seven of the justices, not all of them for the same reasons, found the justifications offered in defense of the law more persuasive than had Circuit Judge Kaufman or Judge Conner after trial. Only Justices Marshall and Stevens were unwilling to subordinate the First Amendment interests at stake in the matter to what Justice Stevens aptly described as a "middle-aged" statute that "must have been violated literally millions of times" by a citizenry which is "at best only dimly aware of the law." This in itself was sufficient for him, as it is for me, to conclude "that the statute is indeed much broader than is necessary to serve its limited purpose."

The third and final ruling, announced on the very last day of the Court's term, provides a fitting note on which to close this book, for it reminds us of the often unpredictable variety of responses and the lack of finality of resolution that the recurring tensions between speech and law in a free society are capable of producing. In *Metromedia, Inc. v. City of San Diego* the Court struck down an ordinance which had banned off-premise billboards in San Diego, California, but the justices were unable to muster a majority in support of a single rationale for their decision. Indeed, four of the six justices voting to strike down the law would have sustained it if it had prohibited only billboards carrying commercial messages, while the other two would have objected to that very kind of discrimination. Their reason for voting to invalidate the ordinance was because it constituted a total ban on an entire medium of communication without sufficient justification by the city.

The dissenting justices were persuaded that an absolute ban on this particular mode of communication, whether limited to commercial advertising or extending to all messages, was well within the legitimate authority of local governments. But each of them felt impelled to write a separate opinion, their differences appearing to be more in style than in substance but apparently sufficient to make all three of them unwilling to join in one another's statements. Justice Rehnquist's dissent, while accepting his own share of the blame, declared it "a genuine misfortune to have the Court's treatment of this subject be a virtual Tower of Babel, from which no definitive principles can be clearly drawn."

A clearer, although not necessarily easier, disposition of the case might have been achieved had it been addressed as a straightforward competition between the First Amendment values of this particular medium of communication and a state's interests in traffic safety and aesthetics. But that got confounded by the four-person plurality's injection into the picture of commercial versus noncommercial speech—an issue whose terms have still to be adequately defined and which raises more questions than the Court has yet answered satisfactorily. For although most of the justices have assented to the proposition that truthful commercial communication comes under the umbrella of the First Amendment, they have not been willing to bring it all the way in out of the rain. So long as it, or any other entire category of discourse, continues per se to be relegated to second-class citizenship in the free speech community, we can expect that the confusion of *Metromedia, Inc. v. City of San Diego* will be perpetuated.

Index of Cases

483

Subject Index

Abortion records, 374–75
Abrams, Floyd, 15
Access to mass media, 48–49, 326–39, 427–28
Accessorial liability, 293–94
Action for Children's Television, 177
Actual malice test, 44–47, 57–60, 66–68
Administrative Procedure Act of 1946, 378
Adoption records, 370–72
Adult bookstores, 167
Adult theaters, 167
Advertising: editorial on radio and television, 329–30, 428; false and misleading, 182–87, 196–201; in the print media, 331–32, 334–35, 428; of illegal products and services, 250–51; televised to children, 169
Advocacy: of abstract doctrine, 267–75; of illegal action, 222, 236, 246–50, 261–83; of revolution, 4, 261–62, 268–76
Aesthetics as justification for restrictions, 157–58
Affidavits. *See* Oaths
Affirmative action to facilitate expression, 297–339, 427–28
Affirmative oaths. *See* Positive oaths
Airport terminal buildings, 304–5, 479
Alien and Sedition Act of 1798, 311
Alien Registration Act of 1940, 261–63, 273–74, 286
American Bar Association: Bill of Rights Committee, 299; Canon 35, 120; Code of Professional Responsibility, 114, 116–17

American Civil Liberties Union, 77, 116–17, 140, 154, 239, 240, 250, 264, 380, 401, 404
American Civil Liberties Union of Northern California, 219
American Law Institute, 125, 148
Anonymity, 354–67
Anti-Defamation League, 136
Anti-Pandering Act of 1967, 139, 166–67, 311 n. 38
Antitrust action, 226–28, 238–40
Appropriation, 63–66, 85
Aristotle, 358
Arkes, Hadley, 94–95, 97–98
Armbands, 11, 26
Assassinations, 33–35
Assault, 149–50, 217, 230
Assembly, right to peaceable, 9–10
Association, freedom of, 9–10, 343, 348–50, 351–52
Atomic Energy Act of 1954, 400, 404
Attempt, 247, 284–85, 287–88, 293–94
Attorney General guidelines for release of information, 115

Bad tendency doctrine, 270–71, 273
Baker, C. Edwin, 202
Balancing doctrine, 38–40, 119, 349–50, 380, 393
Ballots, access to, 346–47
Bar association admissions, 350
Barron, Jerome, 331–33
Batzel, Roger, 401
Beauharnais, Joseph, 95–96
Berns, Walter, 16–17, 172
Berrigan, Phillip, 33
Bethe, Hans, 401